# Occupational Crime

## The International Library of Criminology, Criminal Justice and Penology
### Series Editors: Gerald Mars and David Nelken

**Titles in the Series:**

# Occupational Crime

*Edited by*

# Gerald Mars

*Universities of North London and Northumbria Business Schools*

## Ashgate

DARTMOUTH

Aldershot • Burlington USA • Singapore • Sydney

Published by
Dartmouth Publishing Company
Ashgate Publishing Limited
Gower House
Croft Road
Aldershot
Hants GU11 3HR
England

Ashgate Publishing Company
131 Main Street
Burlington, VT 05401-5600 USA

Ashgate website: http://www.ashgate.com

**British Library Cataloguing in Publication Data**
Mars, Gerald
    Occupational crime. – (The international library of
    criminology, criminal justice and penology)
    1. Employee crimes  2. White collar crimes
    I. Title
    364.1'68

**Library of Congress Control Number**: 2001091912

ISBN 1 85521 382 6

Printed in Great Britain by The Cromwell Press, Trowbridge, Wiltshire

# Contents

## PART III　　　MANAGERIAL RESPONSES

# Acknowledgements

The editor and publishers wish to thank the following for permission to use copyright material.

American Psychological Association for the essays: Jerald Greenberg (1990), 'Employee Theft as a Reaction to Underpayment Inequity: The Hidden Cost of Pay Cuts', *Journal of Applied Psychology*, **75**, pp. 561–68. Copyright © 1990 American Psychological Association; Joyce Hogan and Robert Hogan (1989), 'How to Measure Employee Reliability', *Journal of Applied Psychology*, **74**, pp. 273–79. Copyright © 1989 American Psychological Association.

Cambridge University Press for the essay: Stuart Henry and Gerald Mars (1978), 'Crime at Work: The Social Construction of Amateur Property Theft', *Sociology*, **12**, pp. 245–63.

Egypt Exploration for the essay: T. Eric Peet (1924), 'A Historical Document of Ramesside Age', *Journal of Egyptian Archaeology*, **10**, pp. 116–27.

International Thomson Publishing for the essay: Gerald Mars (1996), 'Employee Deviance', *International Encyclopaedia of Business & Management*, pp. 1161–67. Copyright © 1996 Thomson Business Press.

John Wiley and Sons, Inc. for the essay: Melville Dalton (1959), 'The Interlocking of Official and Unofficial Reward', in Melville Dalton (ed.), *Men Who Manage*, New York: John Wiley and Sons, Inc., pp. 194–217.

Kluwer Academic Publishers for the essay: Jason Ditton (1977), 'Perks, Pilferage, and the Fiddle', *Theory and Society*, **4**, pp. 39–71. With kind permission from Academic Publishers.

Oxford University Press for the essay: Edward W. Sieh (1987), 'Garment Workers: Perceptions of Inequity and Employee Theft', *British Journal of Criminology*, **27**, pp. 174–90.

Perpetuity Press Limited for the essay: Joshua Bamfield and Richard C. Hollinger (1996), 'Managing Losses in the Retail Store: A Comparison of Loss Prevention Activity in the United States and Great Britain', *Security Journal*, 7, pp. 61–70. Copyright © 1996 Perpetuity Press Limited. Perpetuity Press publish the *Security Journal*, and can be contacted at PO Box 376, Leicester, LE2 1UP, email info@perpetuitypress.co.uk, phone 0116 221 7778.

Psychology Today for the essay: Lawrence R. Zeitlin (1971), 'Stimulus/Response: A Little Larceny Can Do a Lot for Employee Morale', *Psychology Today*, **5**, pp. 22, 24, 26, 64. Copyright © 1971 Sussex Publishers, Inc. Reprinted with permission from Psychology Today Magazine.

Sage Publications, Inc. for the essays: Steven L. Sampson (1987), 'The Second Economy of

# Series Preface

The International Library of Criminology, Criminal Justice and Penology, represents an important publishing initiative to bring together the most significant journal essays in contemporary criminology, criminal justice and penology. The series makes available to researchers, teachers and students an extensive range of essays which are indispensable for obtaining an overview of the latest theories and findings in this fast changing subject.

This series consists of volumes dealing with criminological schools and theories as well as with approaches to particular areas of crime, criminal justice and penology. Each volume is edited by a recognised authority who has selected twenty or so of the best journal articles in the field of their special competence and provided an informative introduction giving a summary of the field and the relevance of the articles chosen. The original pagination is retained for ease of reference.

The difficulties of keeping on top of the steadily growing literature in criminology are complicated by the many disciplines from which its theories and findings are drawn (sociology, law, sociology of law, psychology, psychiatry, philosophy and economics are the most obvious). The development of new specialisms with their own journals (policing, victimology, mediation) as well as the debates between rival schools of thought (feminist criminology, left realism, critical criminology, abolitionism etc.) make necessary overviews that offer syntheses of the state of the art. These problems are addressed by the INTERNATIONAL LIBRARY in making available for research and teaching the key essays from specialist journals.

GERALD MARS
*Professor in Applied Anthropology, Universities of North London*
*and Northumbria Business Schools*

DAVID NELKEN
*Distinguished Research Professor, Cardiff Law Schoool,*
*University of Wales, Cardiff*

# Introduction

**Theories, Motives and Meanings**

Everyone has a tale to tell about occupational crime. When discussed, it encourages a 'beat this one' exchange, with each example more outrageous than the last. Newspapers frequently carry accounts of work-based scams. Alongside those of muggings and funerals, they are a part of everyone's, everyday, common experience. This is so even if they are not always recognized for what they are – even if their existence is denied in a particular case or in a particular occupation.

There are wide variations in estimates of the money and goods that are calculated as being 'creamed off' from particular workplaces or occupations as well as in the percentages of workers believed to participate. There are even wider variations in the assessments of total figures for a whole economy. Many of the essays in this volume attempt such calculations, with, as we shall see, sometimes very different outcomes.

Occupational crime – the 'built-in' crime of ordinary people in ordinary jobs – is treated by most practitioners as integral to their normal work. It is found in the whole range of occupations, at all levels and in all professions, although details become less available and definitions vary as we move up the social ladder. Yet despite the fact that these activities are widespread and well known, and that cases continuously recur in historical accounts, it is an area blurred by contradictory perceptions, denials and arguments over definition. Definitions inevitably involve an element of arbitrary choice and the exclusion of areas that some would regard as integral. To consider all possible aspects of occupational crime, for instance, would involve too extensive a treatment for a single volume. This collection thus excludes material on computer crime and on workplace sabotage which each have their own volumes in this series – see Hollinger, 1997 and Mars, 2001.

Further dilemmas of definition also occur because many activities that are considered criminal, or which are tolerated (with or without managerial collusion) at lower levels, are accommodated as entitlements or perks at higher ones. These variations will have to be discussed and assessed before we can understand how differing standpoints not only influence understanding but lead to differing prescriptions, justifications and moralities.

A problem with occupational crime as a category is that it falls across a number of established areas in criminology as well as straddling other similarly 'conglomerate' disciplines such as management with its interest in organizational studies, human resource management and industrial relations. All of these varying approaches impose a different vision of the area. Some occupational crime can justifiably be considered as fraud (Levi, 1999); some as corporate crime, particularly where there is collusion between management and labour to rip off customers (Croall, 1989). Both fraud and corporate crime are often treated as aspects of white-collar crime, and Nelken has charted and discussed the implications of the contested nature of this area (Nelken, 1994a and 1994b). Especially relevant here is the distinction that has emerged between the treatment of organizations as victims of crime and organizations as the perpetrators of crime. The managerial implications of occupational crime are discussed in Part III of this Introduction. A useful rule of thumb definition that acknowledges the varying strands impacting on occupational crime and its wide ranging and varied elements is:

> The movement of resources to individual private use that do not appear in official accounts – or that appear in official accounts under different [and often intentionally misleading] headings and which are acquired by individuals through their relationship to a job. These resources may derive directly from the job itself or be allocated from an outside source that relates to the job. (Mars, 1994: p. 10)

Further causes of confusion and disagreement arise from the intrusion of moral views into this area. Morality, and therefore condemnation, certainly have a place, even a central one, in man's affairs. But morality must be suspended – although not necessarily negated – if understanding is to proceed. Condemnation may be satisfying, but it does not help explanation. Not only must we suspend morality and rein in condemnation, we must also attempt to understand the morality and standpoints of others who are parties to occupational crime, whether as practitioners, employers and controllers or the preyed-upon public.

As we shall see, confusion also arises because of the prevalence of different kinds of explanation. We have useful explanations for levels of incidence that emphasize the dominance of a single factor – for example, the presence of marginal workers (Tucker, Chapter 4, this volume) or the size of a company's plant (Smigel, 1956). We also have explanations that reflect particular interests such as those of management and the security industries, which are concerned with control and tend to favour psychological explanations based on personality assessment as discussed in Part III. Finally, we find wide variations in method that range from the detailed ethnographic case study, usually much concerned with context, to the often context-free, number-crunching, statistically-based survey. We therefore find competing and complementary explanations for varying incidences, all having some validity but none offering total explanation.

Jason Ditton, (Chapter 1), offers a perceptive account of different definitions that apply to similar behaviours by which 'invisible wages' supplement the formal pay people receive in return for their labour. By recourse to detailed historical references, he shows how invisible wages adapt and change as the historical context changes. Differing and shifting definitions in the common usage of terms such as 'the fiddle', theft', 'perks' and 'pilferage', when contextualized, are shown to reflect the relative power positions of employer and employee. Such invisible wages, as he observes, are 'crucial to the persistence and growth of modern capitalism because of their solution to those disciplinary problems not soluble in money alone' (p. 21). This is not, however, to assert – nor to be fair does Ditton – that variations of invisible wages are not also crucial to other kinds of socio-political systems.

Ditton, primarily concerned with historical shifts, therefore shows how definitions were, and still are, blurred and adapted to serve the interests of the powerful. Usually these are employers, although they can also be employees. His examples are primarily rurally derived and reflect shifts in the working conditions of agricultural workers from traditional *Gemeinschaft* communities. By contrast, Henry and Mars in Chapter 2 are more concerned with modern and urban industrial society. They argue that what they call 'normal crime' is essentially different from 'amateur property theft' – that is, the pilfering and fiddling by ordinary people who earn their basic incomes from full-time legitimate employment. Such theft is primarily characterized by wheeling and dealing rather than obtaining pecuniary advantage, implying that its dominant function is social rather than material. Yet the criminal justice system defines it in material terms and, to do so, it has to employ a specific form of language – the language of market or pecuniary exchange which deals, for instance, in prices and cost values when these rarely enter into social exchange. Not only is such language inappropriate but because it obscures the underlying differences between pecuniary activity and the sphere of social exchange, it is accordingly less than fully effective as a means of understanding, legislating or controlling these activities. (For alternative control methods, see Henry, 1985 and for comparative analyses of spheres of economic exchange see Polanyi, 1944 and Bohannan, 1963, ch. 15.)

Chapter 3 starts with the criminologist's distinction between deviance and crime – crime being simply behaviour that is against the law and deviance referring to the wider range of illicit behaviours. The fact that this volume is entitled *Occupational Crime*, even though it also covers deviance, acknowledges a more popular usage.

Demonstrating the use of Cultural Theory, Mars (Chapter 3) adapts a model derived from anthropology (Douglas, 1970, 1978; Thompson, Ellis and Wildavsky, 1990). He examines how the different ways in which all jobs at all levels are structured (that is, 'organized') serve to facilitate or inhibit particular types of occupational deviance. He offers four archetypal ways of organizing work with four associated sets or 'families' of behaviours. These are justified by four linked sets of values and attitudes. Since he shows that it is the way in which jobs are structured that defines their characteristic behaviours, including deviance, we not only have a new typology of occupational deviance and crime but a new typology of occupations.

Mars also identifies a number of 'fiddle prone factors' which, when found together, facilitate deviance. These are the equivalent, in occupational crime studies, of the concept of crimogenesis in the wider field of criminology. This essay shows that occupational deviance is rarely anarchic or 'wild', but is invariably subject to socially set rules, moral codes and limits. It negates personality explanations of occupational deviance ('rotten apple theories') and firmly sets this kind of behaviour and its associated and justifying values within a comparative sociological context. A fuller account of Cultural Theory applied to occupational crime can be found in Mars (1994).

We now consider a range of explanations that concentrate on the importance of particular factors in facilitating occupational crime. First, we consider the view of inequity theorists, following Adams (1965). They argue that workers, considering themselves short-changed on 'the wage/effort bargain', would tend to remedy their perceived inequity by other means, including theft. James Tucker (Chapter 4) offers a useful review of this field and concludes that occupational crime by employees is often a response to perceived deviance by an employer. It is best treated, he argues, not as an aspect of the criminal justice system but of social control – or rather, perhaps, as an outcome of competing visions of appropriate control.

Building on the seminal work of Hollinger and Clark (1983, pp. 69–78), Tucker finds that the tendency towards theft is more common among marginal employees such as 'cosmopolitan' and mobile technicians who lack control over their work when compared to, say, 'localized' managers who do not (Gouldner, 1957–8). This, he states, helps explain why the young and 'engineers and computer specialists employed in manufacturing firms [are] more significantly theft prone than other high status employees' (p. 71). It is also an indication, given that marginality in employment is increasing, why managers will become less able to reduce its levels.

Edward Sieh (Chapter 5) is also concerned with workers' perceptions of unfairness (or 'inequity') and its influence on the incidence of occupational theft. Despite the findings of a range of authors, however, Sieh found no correlation among the garment workers he studied. Since unfairness is a common justification for theft, this is an area worthy of inquiry. Sieh attributes his finding – or rather negative finding – to effective union organization and the presence of strong work groups. The union was able to institutionalize effective grievance procedures, whilst work groups exerted group controls. Both minimized perceptions of inequity and therefore reduced incidence. (See also Sieh, 1993 for a more general view of equity theory applied to occupational crime.)

Greenberg, (Chapter 6), in assessing the effects of perceptions of inequity, found that when workers pay was temporarily reduced by 15 per cent, their theft rates rose in comparison with workers suffering no reduction. However, when management explained their reasons for the cut (reduced sales, avoiding possible closure), their theft rates fell. There were no indications of the presence of unions, or of strong work groups, or of whether lower theft levels were maintained over time.

In a classic essay, Donald N. M. Horning (Chapter 7) considers the ways in which occupational thieves avoid self-definition as criminals – a process which facilitates this activity. His study, based on semi-structured interviewing in a Midwest electronics plant, found that workers identified three classes of property: personal, corporate and of uncertain ownership. Pilfering of this last category was not considered theft, nor did its perpetrators or their workmates consider themselves as thieves if the items taken were small, inexpensive, plentiful, not readily accountable and for personal use. Horning also comments on the significance of work group presence as limiting theft, noting that groups acted to protect members who stole, but only if they operated within accepted limits – a point also discussed by Mars in Chapter 11. Positive self-definition in relation to occupational crime is an area elaborated upon by Cressey (1953), Hollinger (1991) and in particular detail by Ditton (1977). For an introduction to the wider debate within criminology on what is there termed 'neutralization', see the work of Sykes and Matza (1957) who coined the concept.

One of the earliest pioneers in the field of occupational crime is Melville Dalton whose study of managerial deviance, *Men Who Manage* published in 1959, is a classic with few rivals. In Chapter 8, taken from that work, he unpicks 'The Interlocking of Official and Unofficial Reward', showing that formal rewards do not have the flexibility needed to reward extra effort and 'out of role' contributions by managers, especially in crises. Because formal rewards tend to be 'boxed in' and relatively inflexible, administrations have to informally supplement them. The problem, of course, is that such supplements tend to become subject to personal comparisons, be extended to those less worthy, be abused and become institutionalized. This links to Ditton's discussion of the evolution of perks, discussed in Chapter 1.

Dalton is at pains to note that such 'interlocking of reward' is 'an inherent, not a diabolical shortcoming' (p. 146) and arises because of the inherent fluidity of the manager's role and its occupational context. It is worth noting that flexible reward for effort beyond the normal course of duty is a feature of many occupations that demand quick, fluid adjustments and where talents and flair vary widely. Salaried journalists, for instance, are allowed flexibility of expenses on the accepted basis that 'a good story deserves good expenses', (Mars, 1994, p. 47). Trouble arises, of course, when such a system of institutionalized, adaptive reward is misunderstood and redefined as theft by, say, a manager or accountant new to a workplace, who adopts a universalist and often inappropriate system of rules.

It is relatively easy to acknowledge the links between informal, 'off the books' activity discussed above and the formal economy of the workplace: easy but rarely addressed. In the final essay of Part I (Chapter 9), Stuart Henry, however, extends the discussion and sets occupational crime – the hidden economy of pilfering and fiddling – within the wider, macro context of the informal and formal economies. He demonstrates their essential symbiosis to show how they mutually support and complement each other, live off each other and mutually adapt and amend each other.

## Cases and Comparative Contexts

Detailed ethnographic accounts of work have a chequered reputation in social science research, particularly in the Unites States which, paradoxically, pioneered ethnographic study in Western societies. They are currently liable to be too readily dismissed as anecdotal 'one-offs'. Now the fashion seems to be for massive, number-crunching and statistically-based questionnaire surveys which are seen as easier to carry out, quicker to perform, cheaper, surer in their outcomes and as having the imprimatur of an alleged scientific provenance. They can also allow input from involved parties, such as commissioning managers, who thus have some control over what might prove, to them, to be dangerous outcomes.

Surveys are certainly useful for identifying and highlighting correlations and for testing pre-existing hypotheses. But detailed ethnographies are unrivalled at developing hypotheses in the first place. It is vital that we have both – surveys *and* careful, imaginative and detailed ethnographic case studies – if we are to have effective understanding. Using the techniques of the anthropologist, 'participant observer' accounts have frequently proved to be the seed corn of the social sciences. Through them we can create and explore new concepts and develop hypotheses as well as appreciate the importance of contextual setting.

Donald Roy, a participant observing sociologist, provides just such a study (Chapter 10). An early enthusiast of occupational ethnography, Roy here gives an account of output restriction and 'goldbricking' (the building of cash credits), in a machine shop paying workers by the piece – forms of incentive and production now in decline with the growth of new technologies. But Roy's overall insights are still of relevance. He reveals the central role of the work group in setting and maintaining levels and standards, the ingenuity involved in rebalancing the power between management and labour, the optimizing of effort and reward. These are carefully assessed and delineated as only a participant observer can. We have here a neat account of a system formally established by management to satisfy its ends but effectively subverted by its group-based workforce to achieve theirs.

In Chapter 11, Mars, an anthropologist, analyses the normal working of the traditional dock worker's basic labour unit, the gang, and shows how its normal work roles articulate to form a cohesive social grouping designed to effectively unload cargo. He then demonstrates how the gang's normal organization and its roles for normal work are each subverted to facilitate theft. Two facilities are required for theft: having access to cargo or/and being able to offer support to others who have access. Most work roles involve possession of one facility; possession of both defines the gang's highest status, possession of neither, its lowest. It follows, since prestige on the dock defines prestige in the outside community, that theft from the dock is firmly institutionalized as an aspect of everyday life and that non-participants have little standing not only on the dock but also in the community.

To facilitate the illegitimate task of thieving from the dock, the gang, in effect, redesigns a system designed by management. The difficulty for management lies in designing a process to permit the one whilst eradicating the other. There are parallels here with Roy's case in Chapter 10 and with the situation in many organizations.

Such integrated work groups invariably develop their own controls and morality and define the levels and categories of deviance collectively considered appropriate. In the Newfoundland docks, a formula, 'working the value of the boat', allowed dispersed gang members to act in unison and coordinate and maintain levels of pilferage with relative security. Understood levels of pilferage were those accepted by gang members and tolerated by management. Such integrated groups are well set to protect their members who work within collectively agreed categories and levels and to impose sanctions against members who transgress them. They are also effective in mobilizing collective strategies against managerial proposals for change.

Colquhoun, (Chapter 12) a magistrate (judge), in London's East End during the 1790s, offers an account of massive thefts from London's docks based on cases he had judged. Again, we find collaborative cooperation within and between working teams able to subvert a legitimate system for unloading boats. He, too, notes the conflict in views and definitions between the 'takers' who talk of 'perks' and the 'taken' who refer to 'theft'. A similar distinction between perks and theft is recorded by Gilding (1971) when referring to pilferage by coopers – the makers and repairers of barrels – in the Port of London in the 1950s. Their perk was to siphon alcohol from barrels by boring a fine hole, inserting a straw and sucking out the contents. This practice was called 'tapping the Admiral', a phrase dating from 1805 when Lord Nelson's body was shipped home from Trafalgar. The body was placed in a rum barrel to preserve it, but when the barrel was opened it was found to be dry. Chaucer also noted this practice in the fourteenth century (Chaucer, 1951, p. 500). It has since been eradicated with the introduction of metal barrels.

When I discussed Colquhoun's data in the mid-1960s with a magistrate from London's East End, he confirmed that the then current methods of stealing cargo in London matched those recorded by Colquhoun, 250 years earlier. They were also, in essence, identical with those I had recorded in Newfoundland in the early 1960s (Chapter 11).

Since the design of cargo boats (and of barrels) in the centuries, prior to containerization in the 1960s, had hardly altered, the technical underpinning common to all these contexts was similar. Similar technologies facilitate similar illicit, cooperative and parallel work organizations based on combinations of access and support.

Since a port's throughput of cargo has a degree of continuity, the groups involved are also able to operate with continuity or, at least, regularity. Regularity has further implications. Neighbourhood and kinship become active and integral, not only in ensuring a continuity of reliable and, in effect, pre-trained recruits but also a continuity of institutionalized networks to arrange illicit distribution. These factors contribute to the historically attested crimogenic nature of dockland communities worldwide (see Hobbs 1998 for an account of London's East End criminality). As Dalton puts it, these are factors having nothing to do with 'diabolical shortcoming' in the psyches of the people involved. They are a product of the way in which work is designed and structured (as outlined in Chapter 3), of how it can be redesigned and restructured by cohesive work groups, and how this is consolidated and its gains distributed via kinship and community organization. It is not deviant to pilfer in the circumstances described; rather, it is deviant to be straight.

An intriguing case of warehouse theft is recorded by Peet in Chapter 13. He shows how fabrics and grain were being spirited from a store, again through collusion between levels, inside/outside collaboration and access and support alliances. The cooperative structure he describes directly parallels the similar organization to which I was party in a military store some 50 years ago. Thirty years later I found pilferage being similarly effected in an East End London food store. The principal difference in these cases is that Peet's data refers to theft from a royal store of Ramesses V, a Pharaoh living in ancient Egypt over 3000 years ago. The cultural contexts may vary, even the technologies may change but collaborative – that is, social – principles and controls remain remarkably unaltered.

Hollinger and his colleagues, in Chapter 14, give account of their exemplary survey questionnaire study of deviance in an anonymous national sample of staffs in fast food restaurants. They show what can be achieved with a careful and imaginatively constructed questionnaire, sophisticated sampling and a sound integration of pre-existing knowledge. Whereas researchers had previously considered workplace deviance as unidimensional, Hollinger and his colleagues distinguish (at least in this kind of milieu), three types of coexisting deviance: personal property, altruistic and production deviance, together with their very different social correlates. In so doing, they thus raise interesting questions about the social correlates of marginality, equity and the social sphere of exchange as discussed in Chapters 2, 4, 5 and 6.

The restaurant industry, though by no means homogeneous, does appear extensively fiddle prone since most restaurants satisfy several of the characteristics listed in Chapter 3. Still concerned with pilferage in this industry, but not in the fast food sector, we now consider the essay by Richard Hawkins (Chapter 15) on deviance in expensive 'prime rib' restaurants. He too used anonymous self-report questionnaires to examine: 'the variety of part-time theft techniques used by waiters' (p. 287), the variations between them as manifest in pecuniary and non-pecuniary theft, the nature and functions of 'theft talk' and the role of institutionalized theft as sources of staff morale and prestige.

In Chapter 16, O'Brien, an economist, demonstrates why the stubborn presence of rip-offs in garage servicing is extremely difficult to eradicate. The flourishing scams repetitively recorded in consumer reports, journalists' exposures, government accounts and scholarly enquiries are predicated on the relative ignorance of customers relative to practitioners. (See Riis and Patric's classic (1942) observations of this activity in every state of the Union, and see every annual report in *Motoring Which?* over the past 30 years). Such customer ignorance, of course, applies also to the customers of many professionals and tradespeople (especially domestic appliance repair staffs), whose incomes are similarly liable to benefit from imbalances in knowledge, vulnerability, and therefore power. The customer with a broken-down car or the housewife with a defective heating stove is further vulnerable and disadvantaged because of the typical urgency of their need.

But garage servicing is special. As O'Brien shows, it operates under a system of 'perverse incentives': the less effective the work, the greater the earnings. Doing less than is required on a service offers a saving to the garage on materials and time while being able to charge more than is merited. But this common practice also means earlier and more frequent, rather than later and more infrequent, breakdowns and, therefore, even higher earnings from repairs. Thus a variant of Gresham's law operates by which bad garages drive out good since the returns to bad garages are higher than to good ones. Real competition does not exist because the typical customer's ignorance and his usual state of urgency prevent him from making effective judgements. And this is compounded because of the tie of particular makes of car to particular garages.

We have seen how moralities are situationally determined, not only in the context of work but also in how these can be reinforced by wider cultural elements deriving from neighbourhood and kinship. It is appropriate, therefore, to look at different political and cultural systems to see how these link symbiotically with occupational crime. Sampson, in Chapter 17, looks at what has been called 'the second economy' of the Soviet Union and Eastern Europe. They had a system where many economic activities and transactions considered perfectly legal in Western society were treated as illegal by the Soviet states but regarded as fully justified by the populace. Symbiosis of the second, informal, and the first or formal economy was particularly evident since the rigidities of the latter could only be countered by the fluidity of the former. Where chronic shortages of consumer goods were built into the system, personal contacts and the social sphere of exchange were disproportionately developed. Workplace theft was a crucial means by which materials were illicitly recycled to the private consumer.

This duality at the core of the Soviet economic system was at its most developed in Soviet Georgia where over 25 per cent of the economy was estimated to be informal. Mars and Altman, in Chapter 18 examine the cultural correlates that underlay and facilitated what was, in effect, a massive diversion of resources. They found it in the core values of Georgian society, which placed particular emphasis on the family as being at the centre of radiating personal support networks. Here, morality and social assessments were predicated on trust and loyalty within these cooperating networks (and within which sanctions for their negation were at their most savage).

## Managerial Responses

Managers face a dilemma. In being expected to manage they frequently accept an unjustified assumption – that they have greater autonomy and control than they in fact possess. Ackroyd and Thompson (1999, p. 4) pertinently point out that 'quite commonly, attempts to limit customary misbehaviour seem to have little effect'. They further note that the processes which are formative of organizational misbehaviour are, to a considerable extent, beyond managerial control. Much of the literature so far discussed supports this view. Yet, at the risk of homogenizing the whole class of 'managers', the assumption of managerial control is so pervasive and so often invalid that we have to enquire why it arises. Why should it be so tenaciously held and what are its effects?

Why the delusion of managerial control should be so entrenched and so tenaciously held has to do with the social situation and the *raison d'être* – that is inherent to the culture of many managers (Mars, 1981). The first point is that managers have knowledge of, and a degree of control and authority that is likely to be limited to the bounds of their organization. Their vision is limited since they tend to ignore the nexus of their workers outside relationships. Yet we have seen how extramural alliances and community and kinship factors can, and often do, operate together to facilitate pilferage.

A second influential aspect of managerial culture is an emphasis on individualism, managers on the whole being less appreciative of the influence of the group factors in social organization that are often commonly subscribed to by their workforces. Yet groups are vital in recruiting, training, socializing and effecting pilferage practices. They are also frequently integral in distribution.

There is a third reason for managerial myopia that has to be laid at the door of some business schools. This is evident in their failure to balance the dual dimensions of their role; they are unsure as to whether they are primarily schools or businesses. Some, though certainly not all, staffs of business schools tend to give managers what they think they want rather than what they need. As a result, we have university business schools that have markedly diverged from the traditional and primary role of the academy in its search for truth – wherever that might take it. Chapter 19 comprises Zeitlin's famous essay, together with the letter of rejection he received from his first-choice publication, the *Harvard Business Review*. His essay suggests there might be sound financial and organizational advantages in allowing a certain degree of theft in order to keep up morale. He was, in effect, arguing for controlled levels of tolerated pilferage or at least for the problem to be addressed as a potential management strategy.

Though admitting the article's originality and merit, Harvard sheltered behind its 'university status' as a justification for avoiding the need to encourage managers to grasp the implications of this most important nettle. That occurred all of 30 years ago. These attitudes, however, persist. A leading UK business school, 20 years later, would not allow me to offer short courses to managers on either occupational crime or on the implications of long-wave economic cycles because 'managers would find them disturbing'. So they might. But disturbance is hardly the primary criteria that a university should prioritize over the promulgation of research. 'Disturbance' as used here really represents the fear of causing disquiet to its customers, which might, it was thought, imperil an important source of its income. Luckily there is also evidence that some field managers may well be more ahead of such attitudes than are the managements of some business schools.

A fourth factor encouraging the delusion of managerial control is that managerial lifestyles tend to be different from those of their workers. Managers are more mobile, and have often been reared and educated in different places and in different ways to their employees. They tend to live in different neighbourhoods and enjoy different kinds of leisure. These variations tend not only to separate managers from the cultural values of their employees but also to encourage ethnocentricity and therefore make them less able to understand how their workers think.

For these reasons, then, managers are more likely to overemphasize the extent of their control, to assume they are the sole source of an organization's authority, to invariably impute pecuniary rather than, sometimes at least, a social motivation to pilferage and to ignore social and cultural pressures from workmates and communities. For the same reasons they are also likely to misinterpret the fervency of workers in defending perks or in fighting some aspects of organizational change and to ignore the need to overcome rigidities in some formal systems of reward. Senior levels, in particular, are likely to lack understanding of the collusion that has often to occur between middle and lower levels in order to get tasks completed (Bensman and Gerver, 1963). The costs of misinterpreting such behaviours and of misunderstanding motives and meanings can sometimes cost managements dear.

We can perhaps appreciate why it is, then, that the dominant approach of managements, particularly in the United States, has been to seek explanations for occupational crime not in the social organization and social milieus of their workforces, but in the individual psyches of workers. In seeking out 'rotten apples' they minimize the role of the social and embrace the psychological perspective. In so doing, they also implicitly minimize the influence of the design and social context of the jobs in their jurisdiction, over which they do have some control. Job design, we have seen, significantly underpins much workplace crime by creating the bases for its organization. We have known for many years that managers have considerable choice in the forms of organization they can adopt for any given form of technology (Trist *et al.*, 1963), yet to change social organization with the specific aim of reducing workplace crime remains an uncommon expedient.

One aspect of this orientation away from the social and into the motives of personality has led to the extensive use of integrity testing, which is particularly common in the United States. Integrity tests are 'psychological tests designed to predict job applicants' attitudes toward proneness for theft and other forms of counter productivity' (Jones and Terris, Chapter 20 of this volume). As such, of course, they ignore social context. Jones and Terris show how their use in pre-employment recruitment procedures has become a significant industry in the United States. As a part of this industry they review and compare different tests, discuss alternative types of test (such as graphology), assess validation measures and consider the commoner objections to them.

However, the users of integrity tests face significant problems other than their negation of social context. Some of these are raised by Sackett *et al.* (1989, p. 523) who note that 'as integrity tests are marketed in large part to non psychologists, [they] are marketed more aggressively than most psychological tests'. They note, too, that 'it is not uncommon to encounter questionable, if not blatantly deceptive sales tactics' and that 'research on these tests continues to be conducted primarily by test publishers' (p. 524). They note further that published comments are made about unpublished findings that are not peer-reviewed, with all the possibilities this offers for the suppression of negative findings. See also Sackett and Harris' earlier (1984) review.

Chapter 21, by Hogan and Hogan, represents an archetypal integrity test. It is concerned with aspects of deviance wider than theft – with what its authors' call 'counter productive behaviours'. They describe 'the development and validation' of a screening procedure that attempts to treat very different behaviours within a single construct, 'organizational delinquency'. These 'include substance abuse, insubordination, absenteeism, excessive grievances, bogus worker compensation claims, temper tantrums, and various forms of passive aggression' (p. 377). In furthering their aim the authors demonstrate an approach common to much of the writings on occupational deviance that can be called 'unmodified managerialism'. First, it ignores context, whether social or technical, cultural or communal: its attention is firmly fixed on the organization – but these are organizations apparently inhabited by insulated social isolates. Second, it uncritically accepts that its multiple deviant behaviours correlate to form clusters. Third, the authors accept a definition of the industrial context that is implicitly unitary – that is, as having only one source of legitimate authority. Their counterproductive behaviours appear to have only one feature in common – they are all managerial irritants.

Also concerned with forms of deviance other than theft is Hollinger's essay on employee use of alcohol and other drugs (Chapter 22). Hollinger is concerned that 'policy decisions with significant social and legal implications – such as urine testing for drug use – are being made without a clear understanding of either the epidemiology or sociology of this phenomenon' (p. 439). His essay is a vigorous counter to the approach taken in Chapter 21; in a massive numerical study he addresses age, gender, interactions with co-workers and job satisfaction.

His findings are important as policy pointers in a field that is increasingly, and narrowly, locating deviance in the individual psyche whilst ignoring its social correlates.

In Chapter 23 Bamfield and Hollinger compare modes of loss prevention in retail stores in the United States and Great Britain. Their approach does not consider cultural differences or seek other explanations for variation. Rather, they concentrate on a comparison of prevention techniques, though we lack data about comparative effectiveness. An important finding, with important implications, is the growth of non-judicial methods of crime control – identifying and banning shoplifters, in the UK and the development in the US of 'civil recovery statutes' against customer and employee thieves, the latter incidence being nearly twice that of the former.

This growing shift of responsibility for crime control from the state to private interests is one noted in other areas of social life, and its implications are profound for attempts at the control of occupational crime. Coming to be recognized by criminologists as the 'actuarial' model of social control' (Reichman, 1986), it is so called because it owes more to the risk management techniques of the insurance industry than the crime detection and punishment practices of the judicial industry. It therefore focuses on broad social categories derived from the calculation of probabilities rather than the careful individual assessments appropriate to judicial enquiry. This shift in control has been represented as foreshadowing a new kind of social order – one that depends on the classification and selection of risks and of people, on modes of loss prevention and on practices that permit the transference of risk. Together with the growth in information and security technology on which it depends, and allied to the location of deviance in individual psyches, rather than in social contexts, it points the way that private security and private responsibility in the work place seem destined to go. It appears to be a risky route 'both for the personal freedoms of workers and for managements interests in understanding and effectively influencing the incidence of occupational crime. For further implications of this 'risk society' see Beck (1992) and Mars and Weir (2000).

## References

Adams, J.S. (1965), 'Inequity in Social Exchange', in L. Berkowitz (ed.), *Advances in Experimental Social Psychology*, Vol. 2, San Diego, CA: Academic Press, pp. 267–99.

Ackroyd, Stephen and Paul Thompson (1999), *Organizational Misbehaviour*, London, Thousand Oaks and New Delhi: Sage.

Beck, U. (1992), *Risk Society: Towards a New Modernity*, London: Sage.

Bensman, J. and Gerver, I. (1963), 'Crime and Punishment in the Factory: The Function of Deviancy in Maintaining the Social System', *American Sociological Review*, **28**, pp. 588–98.

Bohannan, P.B. (1963), *Social Anthropology*, New York: Holt, Rinehart, and Winston, Inc.

Chaucer, G. (1951), 'The Manciple's Prologue', in N. Coghill (ed.), *The Canterbury Tales*, Harmondsworth: Penguin, pp. 499–502.

Cressey, Donald R. (1953), *Other People's Money; A Study in the Social Psychology of Embezzlement*, Glencoe, Ill: The Free Press.

Croall, H. (1989), 'Who is the White-Collar Criminal?', *British Journal of Criminology*, **29**, pp. 157–74.

Ditton, J. (1977), *Part-Time Crime: An Ethnography of Fiddling and Pilferage*, London: Macmillan.

Douglas, Mary (1970), *Natural Symbols; Explanations in Cosmology*, Harmondsworth: Penguin.

Douglas, Mary (1978), *Cultural Bias*, London: Royal Anthropological Institute.

Gilding, B. (1971), *The Journeyman Coopers of East London*, History Workshop Pamphlet No. 4, Oxford: Ruskin College.

Gouldner, A.W. (1957–8) 'Cosmopolitans and Locals', *Administrative Science Quarterly*, **2**, pp. 281–306 and 444–80.

Henry, S. (1985), 'Community Justice, Capitalist Society and Human Agency: The Dialectics of Collective Law in the Cooperative', *Law and Society Review*, **19**, pp. 303–27.

Hobbs, D. (1988), *Doing The Business: Entrepreneurship, Detectives and the Working Class in the East End of London*, Oxford: Clarendon Press.

Hollinger, R.D. (1991), 'Neutralising in the Workplace: An Empirical Analysis of Property Theft and Production Deviance', *Deviant Behaviour*, **12**, pp. 169–202.

Hollinger, R.D. (1997), *Crime, Deviance and the Computer*, Aldershot: Dartmouth.

Hollinger, R.D. and Clark, J.P. (1983), *Theft by Employees*, Lexington, MA: Lexington Books.

Levi, M. (1999), 'Introduction', in M. Levy (ed.), *Fraud: Organisation, Motivation and Control, the extent and causes of white-collar crime*, **1**, Aldershot: Dartmouth.

Mars, G. (1981), 'The Anthropology of Managers', London: *Royal Anthropological Institute News*, (42), February, pp. 4–6.

Mars, Gerald (1994), *Cheats at Work: An Anthropology of Workplace Crime*, Aldershot: Dartmouth.

Mars, Gerald (ed.) (2001), *Work Place Sabotage*, Aldershot: Dartmouth.

Mars, G. and Weir, D. (eds) (2000), *Risk Management*, Vols. I and II, Aldershot: Dartmouth.

Nelken, D. (1994a), 'Introduction', in D. Nelken (ed.), *White Collar Crime*, Aldershot: Dartmouth.

Nelken, D. (1994b), 'White-Collar Crime', in M. Maguire, R. Morgan and R. Reiner (eds), *Oxford Handbook of Criminology*, Oxford University Press, pp. 355–92.

Polanyi, K. (1944), *The Great Transformation*, New York: Holt Rinehart and Winston, Inc.

Reichman, N. (1986), 'Managing Crime Risks; Toward an Insurance Based Model of Social Control', *Research in Law, Deviance and Social Control*, **8**, pp. 151–72.

Riis, R.W. and Patric, J. (1942), *Repairmen Will Get You If You Don't Watch Out*, Garden City NY: Doubleday Doran.

Sackett, P.R. and Harris, M.E. (1984), 'Honesty Testing For Personnel Selection: A Review and Critique', *Personnel Psychology*, pp. 37, 221–45.

Sackett, P.R. *et al.* (1989), 'Integrity Testing for Personnel Selection: An Update', *Personnel Psychology*, **42**, pp. 491–529.

Sieh, E.W. (1993), 'Employee Theft: An Examination of Gerald Mars and an Explanation Based on Equity Theory', in F. Adler and W.S. Laufer (eds), *New Directions in Criminological Theory: Advances In Criminological Theory*, **4**, pp. 95–111.

Smigel, E.O. (1956), 'Public Attitudes Toward Stealing as Related to the Size of the Victim Organisation', *American Sociological Review*, **21** (3), June.

Sykes, G.M. and D. Matza (1957), 'Techniques of Neutralisation: A Theory of Delinquency', *American Sociological Review*, **22**, pp. 664–70.

Thompson, M., Ellis, R. and Wildavsky, A. (1990), *Cultural Theory*, Boulder, San Francisco and Oxford: Westview Press.

Trist, E.L. *et al.* (1963), *Organisational Choice*, London: Tavistock.

# Part I
# Theories, Motives and Meanings

# [1]

## PERKS, PILFERAGE, AND THE FIDDLE:

## The Historical Structure of Invisible Wages[1]

JASON DITTON

Everybody gets part of their wages in "kind." Money alone is never the sole satisfaction attached to or derived from work. Although this is obviously and institutionally so for some jobs (clergymen are not commonly held to be motivated by financial reward), and difficult to perceive for others (few dustmen feel the "call" to dispose of other people's rubbish), it is theoretically impossible to denude even the most inhospitable of work environments of some degree of satisfaction. For example, Lisl Klein mentions a researcher who once interviewed a female worker who spent all her working life in a factory picking up tiny circular pieces of cork and inserting them in toothpaste tube caps. The researcher asked her whether the work felt boring, and the girl replied: "Oh, no! They come up different every time!"[2]

While indirect and "spiritual" satisfactions of this sort are available to all who work (indeed, their existence makes work possible), temporarily ignoring the value of these delicate existential "wages," a glance at the structure of material wages forges a crucial distinction. While we all may garner a material (as well as a spiritual) rake-off on top of the official pay-packet—every job has its "perks"—the meaning of material kind wages varies essentially with the class of the recipient. When blue-collar workers get side-benefits of various kinds, these benefits act as added occupational commitment, and are proffered *instead of* exclusively direct financial reward. When white-collar workers similarly benefit, the meaningful effect of that benefit is wholly different. White-collar workers never get part of their wages in kind: instead, they may receive kind *extras*, which do not displace an appropriate amount in their salaries, and which act as unofficial rewards rather than as added commitment.

*Department of Sociology, University of Durham, Great Britain*

40

### 1. The Historical Context of Employee Theft

The appropriate interpretive context of this discrepancy in the meaning of material kind-pay is historical. Some rights to kind-pay are both universal and antiquarian, as enshrined, for example, in Leviticus:

> And when ye reap the harvest of your land, thou shalt not wholly reap the corners of thy field, neither shalt thou gather the gleaning of thy harvest. And thou shalt not glean thy vineyard, neither shalt you gather the fallen fruit of thy vineyard; thou shalt leave them for the poor and the stranger.

In early 17th century England customary rights to kind benefits were extensive, and encased within a protective body of common legislation. Whilst "common" rights are specifically those by which one or more persons have the right to take or use some portion of the profit that another's soil produces,[3] they are more generally held to refer to the batch of common, reciprocal and joint rights in which pre-industrial communities were enmeshed. This intricate web of mutual privileges and obligations provided the basis for exchange in agrarian contexts. Of the various common rights, Common of Pasture protected the grazing and manuring rights of agricultural animals upon specified land, and Common of Shack guaranteed the right of cattle to glean hay after the harvest. In rural England, the rules of Leviticus emerged as the right to herbage and gleaning for certain specified persons and strangers on half-year lands. Reciprocally, the lord of the manor had right of sheep-walk (right to feed sheep on common land), and foldage (the right to demand that tenant's flocks manure the lord's fields). Gonner adds that various universal rights also made important contributions to the rural economy.[4] Rights of pannage and mast, for example, specified the range of protected users of nuts, acorns, and even various flowers.

Common of Estover was the right of common to take wood from common or the lord's lands and forests, and specified either Plough Bote (the right to wood to repair ploughs, carts and other instruments of husbandry), Hedge Bote (wood for the repair of gates and hedges) and House Bote, which not only specified the right to wood for domestic repairs but which added, at least for freehold manor tenants, the antiquarian right to "sticks, tops and clippings for fuel."[5] Common of Tubary was the right to cut peat and turf for fuel, and the batch of common rights also included those of following and warren (fowl and rabbits), and even to dig sand, gravel and clay. Gonner comments:

> Taken together they supply the means whereby the system of cultivation was maintained, the wants of the tenants other than those met by the

41

product of the arable and the meadow were supplied, and full use made both of the waste and of the land in cultivation at such time as the crops were not in the ground.[6]

Thus, the extended package of common rights not only cemented feudalist and community ties (the lord of the manor had a special set of rights which included that of arriage from the tenant's beasts, and fencing and ditching skills from the tenants themselves), it also made a significant material contribution to the domestic and household budgets of the tenants. Domestic consumption was guaranteed either directly from cultivation, or indirectly from the exercise of right.

The Acts of Enclosure of these common rights had obvious and far-reaching effects on the material benefits which tenants had customarily come to expect.[7] The annexation of common rights (and their subsequent replacement with legal rights)[8] naturally culminated in the simultaneous creation of "property," and the propertied classes, and the ultimate criminalization of customary practices. The criminalization of custom involved both moral attempts to define "common" as bad,[9] and savage repressive measures enacted to persecute those who attempted to continue to exercise erstwhile rights.[10] Acts of Enclosure were, in the main, forced upon an unwilling populace,[11] which in some cases was physically removed from the land, as well as spiritually from the protection of ancient right.[12] In this welter of legislation, kind-benefits emerged coated in a new meaning structure—one which crucially distinguished between the propertied and the non-propertied classes. From here on, extraction of kind-benefits was to become particularly problematic for the newly created working class. The gradual translation of "rights" (held in common) into "property," or "capital" (held in particular) which the elongated processes of rural enclosure and urban industrialization effected emerged in different structural contexts (rural and urban), with noticably similar effects.

Basically, in land, we can see the gradual emergence of property *per se* from the systematic limited specification and curtailing of common rights to use land. "Rights," in a very real sense, become translated into "property" as a result of the legal process of translating universality of applicability of such rights into specificity of applicability. Enclosure of land took two forms. The gradual areal abolition of common (uncultivated) land, and the reparcelling and literal enclosure of stripcultivated land which had been previously farmed on the basis of common right.

42

Thus, the feudal picture of a village and its surrounding lands—over which the manorial lord had exclusive "rights" to a large proportion, and the villagers common "rights" to farm a small part (together with reciprocal obligations to labor for the lord on "his" land), with the rest remaining as unfarmed commonland—is replaced (through enclosure) by a scene wherein the lord's "rights" to farm exclusively have become property, the villager's common strip rights have become rented allotments, and the remaining common land has diminished considerably in size. At the same time, some villagers were wholly disenfranchised—their release from any commitments on the land collectively creating a pool of potential labor for the growing urban industrial machine.

A crucial intermediary stage in the confiscation and criminalization of rights, was their initial "engrossing": a process through which the larger units inexorably swallowed smaller ones.[13] A crucial stage in this process was the subsidiary transmutation of "rights" into graspable monetary sums. For example, vague and archaic specifications of duties and obligations of tenants to labor for the lord, became literally exchanged for direct money-rent obligations.[14] This was essentially a direct change in the legal construction of common rights, whose rather idiosyncratic and archaic nature had some severe effects on many otherwise indistinguishable beneficiaries. Gonner claims that common rights were essentially one of four possible legal varieties: *Common Appendant* (rights limited by tenancy or possession, specifically ancient and generally universal), *Common Appurtenant* (rights granted by prescription to copyholders or freeholders), *Common in Gross* (the definition of common by number or amount instead of by immediate reference to the needs or capacity of the land or its tenants) and *Common by Vicinage* (an imitation of common, generally arising out of mutual agreements to disregard trespass).[15]

The Acts of Enclosure made the hitherto relatively unknown distinction between *common appendant* and *common appurtenant* into a dividing line of crucial significance. The ability of the comparison to draw a *de facto/de jure* distinction between the actual (appendant) and legal (appurtenant) villagers refused common rights to those who sought its protection by custom, and restricted it to the smaller category of those who had legal entitlement.[16] Thus, those whose prior use of common was by proximity and sufferance failed to receive the rented allotments which villagers with appurtenant rights had exchanged for their rights.[17] Although *de facto* users had previously been able to enjoy the small rights attached to their dwellings, when an allotment was made, the landlord took the allotment, and left the cottager with nothing. The summation of all such minor losses was huge. Gonner comments:

Thus with inclosure, the number of geese owned by the poor are said to have decreased: cows were given up; the poor lost fuel, being deprived of the privilege of turf-cutting; the commonage in the stubbles which enabled them to keep pigs and geese is theirs no more; and with these went other small advantages such as gleaning, which came to be more carefully restricted.[18]

Added to this deliberate creation of a class of "poor" was some voluntary recruitment from the ranks of *bona fide* allotment holders who became disenchanted with allotment life either because of various deleterious effects of the reparcelling process,[19] or simply because of the sheer expense of fencing in the allotted land.[20] Essentially this forced a categorization of the villagers into the righteous working class, and the feckless scrounging poor.[21] So, the natural result of the intermediary process of engrossing was the translation of rights into a legally purchasable commodity, swiftly followed by the actual purchase of the allotments[22] (where they were not simply confiscated), was augmented by the percolation of industrial techniques to the fields and the subsequent reduction of the agrarian labor force. In a very real way, then, the Acts of Enclosure released a large part of the agrarian working population just at the time when labor was needed in the industrializing towns.[23] Of crucial interest here, is that this process released into urban life a working population not only used to receiving part of their "wages" in kind (an antiquarian element specifically and pointedly absent from the capitalist conception of rational production) but also one still stinging from the effects of the abrupt and cruel negation of those practices in the countryside. As one might expect, and empirical evidence supports this,[24] a major source of irritation to factory owners who took on such "idle" rural laborers was their penchant for making off with parts of the workplace or the fruits of their labor there, in addition to their wages.

To present a picture of the total negation of kind-payment would be to over-simplify. "Rights" were transmuted by two different processes into three separable categories of kind-payment. First, there was a literal specification of the *amount* which previous rights would now represent; and secondly, there was a restriction, of the previous universal *applicability* of rights. While general rights became specific financial amounts, the beneficiaries were restricted to those actively engaged in production. In fact, these two processes eventually produced three classes of recipient, which ultimately became synonymous with three categories of kind-payment: "perks" (for employers and the white-collar employed), "pilferage" (for blue-collar employees) and unequivocal "theft" (for the unemployed poor).

44

The gradual process of translating "rights" into "crimes" was, then, one of restructuring the range of applicability (and thus definition) of customary practices. The immediate effect of the Acts of Enclosure (the first stage in the process of criminalization) through the annexation of *de facto* cottagers, was the automatic relabeling of "rights" as the "privilege" of *de jure* tenants.[25] Almost simultaneously, such "privileges" were withheld from even those tenants, but immediately redistributed on the basis of "license" issued by the owners of property. When kind-benefits are distributed on the basis of license rather than of right, then they may more easily be controlled.[26] However, not all customary rights were relicensed. Those which just didn't fit into the new role into which the landlords had recast the countryside were occasionally savagely criminalized,[27] although more regularly just treated as civil of- fenses,[28] and even, on occasion, accusations to which the claim of customary practices was an acceptable defeat.[29] Importantly, the "pilferage" of wood emerged as a description of over-exuberant collection of kind-benefits by employees, a crime much more morally acceptable than the out-and-out "theft" by the non-employed.[30]

Thus, in the process of transforming reciprocal feudal labor obligations into contractual ones (and, coincidentally, the annexing of common duties such as hedging and ditching) ancient "rights" became restricted to modern employ- ees. The translation of most of the free citizenry into employees, and the erosion of rights to (withdrawable) "privilege" and "license" status, effec- tively translated customary practices from being the legitimate exercise of right, to becoming employment in kind. The very power of kind-payments lies in the fact that kind-pay generates a greater commitment to a particular employer, and in the fact that whimsical redefinition- of its receipt by the "giver" may oppress the recipient.[31] Having restricted the range of appli- cability of rights/kind-payments to those involved in work, any vestige of demands of right by the non-employed poor were unequivocably defined as "theft."[32] For the employer and landlord (and special classes of their directly employed white-collar minions) kind-benefits become perquisites, or "perks," with abstraction of kind-benefits by employees resting ambiguously between these two extremes, being simultaneously defined as a cheap way of paying part of the wages, and also vaguely immorally as "pilferage."

Accordingly, in the countryside, exercise of Common of Estover (wood- gathering) became wood-theft,[33] game-rights degenerated into poaching,[34] grazing-rights into trespass,[35] and even archaic common gleaning (if and when the gleanings could be seen by a sharp eye to be a commercially viable proposition) could become theft by finding.[36] At this stage in English history, there existed what Mantoux refers to as an "intimate connection" between the rural and urban economies.[37] In the towns, the importation of a

45

mass of dispossessed agrarian workers "set free" by enclosures, but both personally and culturally accustomed to having kind-rights, posed problems for their new employers. Additionally, those trades and types of industrial work which pre-dated capitalization had direct customary practices of their own. Welsh coal miners were accustomed to use company coal for domestic purposes,[38] coopers considered that their "samples"[39] of wines and spirits were an unalienable right, in the same way that their fellow dockers demanded their "spots" of drink from the cooper[40] and their traditional "sweepings" from the employer's cargoes.[41]

The historical context of the varieties of modern employee kind-pay emerges from this analysis. Within the structures of rural enclosure and urban capitalization, "perks," "pilferage," and "theft" may be viewed profitably as the lingering vestiges of the annexation of customary rights by the ruling class, rather than (as is usually assumed) an index of the growing amorality of the urban working class. But this context does not supply a sufficient analysis of the current situation. To specify the historical generation of conceptual difference between, for example, "pilferage" and "theft," does not adequately account for the current paradoxical interactional context of such kind-pay. Employees who are currently expected to take part of their wages in kind may simultaneously be prosecuted on some of those occasions when they do so. Workers who are involved in this contradictory form of wage-payment "can't win." The historical structure which I have described has itself been translated into a paradoxical interactional mesh through the exercise of capitalist power. The blue-collar employee is caught up in this mesh without access to legitimate interactional escape mechanisms.

The historical process of criminalization of rights is unfinished. Current employee-theft is not yet wholly drained of its original meaning as "right." The histories of individual occupations show that the subsequent development of the ambiguity of translated rights has been unequally paced. In analyzing current examples selected from the English industrial culture, three discernable stages of the development of this process emerge.[42] Taken chronologically, kind-wage-payment can either arrange itself in a young, harsh form of "wage-theft," an ambiguous middle form of "wage-pilferage," and a relatively mature, benign form of "wage-perk."

## 2. Invisible-Wage System

### 2.1 Wage-Perk Payment[43]

When "on the side" satisfaction is rigorously and extensively codified into officially institutionalized practices, we may talk of wage-perk payment.

46

Under a wage-perk system, an employee is openly and legally paid part of his wages in kind. There are no circumstances in which an employee can be prosecuted for taking advantage of this system, which is often institutionalized as such into public job advertisements. Quite often, wage-perk structures are the mature outcome of a long history of legitimizing a wage-pilferage system, especially when pilferage (as with the bus conductor's leisure time bus-pass, and the miner's coal) is particularly difficult otherwise to control. When members of management benefit (as those who have company cars and expense account lunches do), the perk is generally thought of as added incentive, if, indeed, it is not merely defined as being a necessary part of the job.[44] When the workforce are entitled to perks (such as those living in "tied" cottages) the perks themselves subtly undergo a transformation from being "extra" pay, to becoming just added commitment to the employer.[45] Those who do not nicely fit into either of these two bland categories suffer an ambiguous fate.[46]

Ultimately, wage-perk payment generally acts to the disadvantage of the workforce, especially if the latter is unorganized. As soon as it is institutionalized, the perk instantly begins to unfurl as a wage-depressant. On top of this, it systematically reduces the isolated worker's choice in the way that his wages are spent. This affects those who "live in," or "over the shop" (their wages are subsequently reduced to pay for this facility). Even more seriously, it frequently depresses the wages of those who are alleged to be motivated by higher things to absurdly cruel levels. For example, nurses and *au pairs*,[47] both have good spiritual reasons for receiving most of their material wages in kind.[48] Of course, this does not apply to consultants and archbishops who apparently need large financial compensation for taking their part in equivalently high moral worlds.

Sometimes, blue-collar employees who deal regularly and commercially with members of the public are craftily encouraged to extrude part of their wages, in gratuity form, from the customer.[49] "Wage-tip" is thus an indirect form of wage-perk. This practice costs the employer nothing (barring a disgruntled workforce, and an irritated customer constituency), but it produces a tricky conflict between server and customer. This conflict arises in the ambiguity of the word "tip," which means "wages" (and thus something routinely and regularly collected) to the employee, and "gratuity" to the customer, who clings to its original London coffee house context wherein it stood for "To Insure Promptness."[50] Of course, the only member of the public to refuse to view tips in the traditional way is Her Majesty's Inspector of Taxes. Crespi, talking of the American situation, adds: "No longer does this agency (the I.R.S.) overlook tips as casual unpredictable cash. Now every effort is being made to see tips as substantial and predictable sources of income."[51]

Attempts to aggressively "organize" tips by service workers,[52] and to "work" customers for them,[53] has spawned, as a reaction, such organizations as NOTIP (Nationwide Operation To Instill Pride) in America, the members of which, to the delight of service workers everywhere, leave little cards denouncing the practice in lieu of little coins supporting it.

Under a wage-perk regime, management/workforce distinctions are reasserted. As I have indicated, "perks" are either "extras" for management, or they are coolly defined as part of the company-supplied equipment for the job. Members of the workforce in receipt of perks face an altogether different ambiguity of definition. Perks may either be "fringe benefits" (ancient rights restricted to those members of the working class "licensed" by the fact and nature of their employment), which are generally, for example the N.C.B. coal allowance,[54] even obtainable during strikes—whereas wage-packets quite clearly are not. Or they may be *part* of wages, and thus distinctly unobtainable when employment exists but actual work is stopped. Quite frequently, in addition to this type of definitional ambiguity, some perks (for example, the bank clerk's cheap mortgage) are generally defined as part of wages (for recruitment and inducement purposes), but occasionally called fringe-benefits when they are arbitrarily reduced in a way that wages could not be.

Irrespective of this ambiguity, there are significant variations in the credibility of the costing of wage-perk kind-pay. The N.C.B., for instance, cost the coal-allowance in terms of its retail value rather than the production value (thus allowing them to make a little profit out of the fringe-benefit), but the concessionary travel allowances to which British Rail employees are entitled *are* restricted in various ways (for example, are not transferable)[55] and although "priceable" are virtually "uncostable." The principles of costing the usage of a vacant seat are arguable (should it be in terms of the full fare that might be obtained, or in terms of the actual marginal cost of adding an extra person to an otherwise unoccupied seat?) and it is also unlikely that the employee would make the journey if it were not free.

But at least such "perks" have a clear legal standing. When the "kind" payments of a wage-perk system are *un*official, then we may talk instead of a wage-pilferage system.

## 2.2 Wage-Pilferage Systems

A crucial distinction between "pilferage" and "perks" is that anybody caught pilfering is stopped, but not necessarily prosecuted. Pilferage is thus itself a

48

paradoxical state. Its immediate consequences are unpredictable, and, in historical terms, it is a transitional stage between wage-perk (which is officially institutionalized), and wage-theft (which is officially condemned). Consequently, pilferage is the name which we should logically attach to those occasions where blue-collar employees abstract value in kind from their employer under a regime where the treatment of this appropriation is unpredictable, and its *a priori* meaning thus ambiguous.

This ambiguity is not benign. It produces for the worker a theoretically and empirically strong "can't win" situation. This is not a simple mutual contradiction in demands made of the worker of the sort colloquially referred to, with increasing frequency, as a "Catch-22 situation."[56] Most importantly, the worker (enmeshed in a wage-pilferage system) is faced with incompatible demands (i.e., that he should, *and* that he should not pilfer), and on top of this, these incompatible demands are communicated in such a way as to make the contradiction "uncommentable." This is achieved by communicating incompatible demands simultaneously at different communicative levels. What happens in a wage-pilferage context is that within a single communication act, a primary negative injunction ("Don't steal"—don't take goods in kind) is expressed at the literal level, while at the more abstract, metaphoric (meta-communicative) level, a secondary and contradictory injunction ("Make up your wages"—take goods in kind) is simultaneously conveyed.

Thus, wage-pilferage systems are "Double-binds."[57] There is no theoretical or empirical escape for workers trapped in this way as there is a tertiary negative injunction prohibiting the worker-victim's pragmatic analysis of his contradictory situation, and thus obviating his escape. There are various ways that this double-bind can be thrown around the new worker. For example, an employee is told that the rate of wages is low, but this statement is accompanied by some sort of figurative or real wink.[58] Perhaps he is told that he can purchase products at "give away" (wink) prices. Or, that there are always "cheap" (wink), "spare" (wink) or "extra" (wink) goods to be had. Perhaps he is told, as I was at the Wellbread Bakery, that "they" would see that I didn't "go short" (wink), or "lose out" (wink) when I complained that the wages were low. Everybody else, I was told,[59] was able to "make a bit on the side" (wink), or, "have their little perks" (wink), or, "take the odd loaf" (wink). With the meta-communicative wink, the employer is able to craftily say something quite specific *about* the actual statements he has made. The wink eliminates the ambiguity in such "alerting phrases" as "spare," "cheap," and "extra," and settles their meaning quite definitely for those sufficiently competent or "wise" to so read the communication. Any reaction from the worker in the form of a "comment" immediately vanquishes and replaces the meta-communicative negative statement offered by the employer—*itself* a comment *on* communication. To query the meaning of the wink (in other words, any attempt to "open" up a "closed" meaning) is to effectively deny it. It is in *this* sense that the double-bind is uncommentable. A worker frankly complaining that he is being asked to pilfer part of his wages, will be told, equally frankly, that he is "imagining things," and that (here, the primary injunction is reasserted) he is *not* to take anything above his wages. Refusal of the secondary negative injunction (the wink) is simultaneously refusal of the material advantages which would accrue were the injunction not questioned.

The potential pilferer must himself qualify the possible advantages of his occupational theft with the *a priori* knowledge that what will happen to him should he be caught is, *apropos* of the employer's reaction to the theft, wholly uncertain. Of course, he may be able to solve this problem at the psychological level, and successfully define the theft *as* pilferage to himself, but this in no way guarantees a similar definition by those who stand to suffer the loss. Additionally, an equivalently ambiguous (in the sense that "pilferage" is ambiguous) legal reaction is impossible. There is no such legal offense as "Pilferage." Occupational theft is either proceeded against as "theft," or is not proceeded against because it is defined as a "perk."[60] *This* is the paradox of wage-pilferage systems. Whether or not the theft in question is defined as "theft" or as "just a perk" will depend upon quite arbitrary, extraneous and non-specifiable dictates of those in control. In other words, the "pilferer" cannot be held responsible for the meaning of his action: that meaning is decided by others, after the action has objectively occurred. For example, at Wellbreads, those employees exclusively concerned with production were accustomed to take a loaf home every day. In fact, the management catered for this contingency by making sure to bake enough bread to allow for what became collectively known as "the men's bread." However, this bread was not rationally distributed as a "perk," each man had to surreptitiously "pilfer" his loaf while the Despatch Manager (who had responsibility for baked bread) was at lunch. Despatch operatives maintained a cursory and nominal watch over the racks of stock bread from which the men took "their" bread (so as to give life to the lie that they were trying to prevent domestic pilferage) but simultaneously made sure that enough bread was freely available on the stock racks to contain unlicensed pilferage from the racks of issued bread. Presumably the general managerial policy informing this practice was that defining as "pilfering" (and, of course, processing the occasional culprit as a "thief") helped to prevent the escalation of the practice from domestic consumption. The actual zealousness of the Despatch Manager was informed by what he considered to be his "perk" of office: if he could persuade at least some of the men to buy their bread from him (the

50

official process), then he could divert some of this cash to his own pocket, and cover the loss by stealing bread from the salesmen.

There is an historical, as well as a structural sense in which pilferage is "paradoxical." At one time, pilferage was a label strictly employed only in connection with the theft of indeterminate or "ambiguous" items. Indeed, in many cases, there are still grounds for claiming that this is so.[61] Generally, however, the paradoxical nature of pilferage is currently metaphorical, whereas once it was a real issue. For example, Marx is quite right to see that the difference between "theft" and "pilferage" is a question of fact, and not one of euphemism.[62] Referring to the thefts of wood, Marx isolates three categories of theft-object: the theft of live timber (an offense against forest regulations); the theft of hewn and felled wood (*prima facie* theft of material which has been converted into property); and an intermediate, ambiguous category: the picking up and consequent "pilferage" of fallen, "dead" wood. This latter, indeterminate category lies ambiguously between live and felled wood, and is, thus, a symbolically dangerous and marginal object.[63] It was precisely at this indeterminate level that the rights of the poor were located. Marx points out:

> All customary rights of the poor were based on the fact that certain forms of property were indeterminate in character, for they were not definitely private property, but neither were they definitely common property, being a mixture of private and public right . . . It will be found that the customs which are customs of the entire poor class are based with a sure instinct on the *indeterminate* aspect of property.[64]

Some vestige of this archaic indeterminancy remains in modern formulations. Whether or not employee theft is defined as "pilferage" or "theft" varies for different industries, on different days,[65] and even, crucially, between different individuals.[66] Now, while for some practical intents and purposes, the broad empirical outlines of the criteria of everyday current distinction are clear, the situation is specifically and indefinitely ambiguous. Martin, in an extensive study of the criteria used to distinguish between pilferage and stealing by various firms, emerges with the following summary:

> *"Pilfering"* (when "legitimate") involves one or more of the following features — the items taken are of "small" value, they are taken for the worker's own use, the quantities involved are small, and the act is unpremeditated. *"Stealing"* is any taking of cash (the only definition with which no one disagreed), or one or more of the following — taking of stamps, items from "stock" goods in large quantities (by the box, sack of crate),

items over a given value, small items taken repeatedly, taking for resale, taking with premeditation and unauthorised taking when it is known that the items would be given away on request.[67]

This is a summary of all possible criteria. It does not represent a set of criteria used by any one firm in Martin's sample. It is a summary of the possible "reasons" for labeling a theft as either "pilferage" or "stealing." Interestingly, the necessity for tabulating the possibilities testifies to the very absence of a universal distinction between the two labels. Taken together, the separate criteria provide an ostensive and weak definition: it settles upon no particular criteria as crucial (except the theft of cash) and while dressed to look specific, actually contains several elastic "weasel" words like "small."[68]

Employee thefts remain ambiguous at the time of the theft. We cannot specify *a priori* whether or not they will be defined as "pilferage" or as "theft."[69] Nevertheless, this ambiguity has a systematic rather than a random effect: it disadvantages the workforce and advantages the management. This systematic distinction is traceable to the workings of a crucial hidden dimension of double-binds: power. In any double-bind, it is axiomatic that the bound has *less* interactional power than the binder. But this specific situation may or may not be compatible with the power discrepancy existing generally between the two actors. This incompatibility may be of three types. The specific situation may mirror the general, and thus be symmetrically "orthodox." This is the case when members of management pilfer. There is a power symmetry between management (the enforcers) and management (the thieves), and thus the meaning of the pilferage becomes distinctly that, as Dalton suggests,[70] of relatively unstable and individualistic "supplementary (salary) rewards." Power incompatibility between the binder and the bound may either be asymmetrically contradictory ("paradoxical"), such as when archaic custom lingers to constrain management to allow worker pilferage, or it may be exaggeratedly asymmetrical ("heterodoxical"), such as when the specific pilferage situation merely parodies the general power discrepancy between management and worker. These two latter types of incompatibility produce the second main meaning of pilferage. For members of the workforce, pilferage means collective and relatively stable "customary (wage) pilferage."

"Customary pilferage" traps the worker in a double-bind. His wages are geared down to an invisible pilferage value of his job, but his attempt to secure this invisible value could well lose him his job, and land him in court. This double-bind is heterodoxical (since there is an obvious power difference between management and worker), but is in practice weakened by the

52

simultaneous presence of various workplace "customs" which, paradoxically, bind management to allow some pilferage.[71]

It seems that pilferage for workers may become "customary" (although not yet officially a "perk") under various structurally recognizable conditions. Management often turn a blind eye to pilferage when the pilfered goods do not really constitute a loss to the firm (as Martin rather nicely asks, what is the waiter *supposed* to do with the half-empty bottles of wine?). As Mars and Hutter note, the management is especially lenient if worthless items are consumed on the premises.[72] The management may be similarly genial even if goods with some real value are pilfered as long as the loss may be euphemistically and alternatively categorized at inventory time (i.e., the pilferage must be of "kind," as inventories do not contain categories for "broken," "damaged" or "reject" money). Pilferage may also be allowed to degenerate into custom when the loss may be systematically organized into production (such as the extra 40 loaves which are baked at Wellbreads everyday to provide the "men's bread"), or when the loss is of repeatable or disposable goods.

Management may be actually keen to institute and encourage customary pilferage if they feel the act of theft will generate a hedonistic surplus (in addition to the actual value of the goods taken) and as long as they are able to simultaneously retain the right to define it as "stealing" should the need arise. In this spirit, Zeitlin considers that a "system of controlled larceny" may well be actually cheaper than paying higher wages,[73] and Aufhauser notes how slave-owners shrewdly allowed the expression of their rebelliousness through minor thefts.[74] Aside from such imaginary emotional extra "wages" accruing from the pilferage of items rather than the purchase of them on the market, there is a real sense in which (because pilfered wages are untaxed wages), illicit kind-payment is actually cheaper for both management and worker.

However, when pilferage is institutionalized and common among members of management, it is a gross mistake to similarly label it "institutionalized theft," as Dalton so accurately and eloquently argues.[75] Managerial "organised pilfering rights" are explicitly, albeit unspokenly, "unofficial rewards" for the minutiae of individual managerial achievement.[76] As Dalton shows, formal ranking is too rigid and too slow to accurately recompense managerial effort, and informal rewards supplement wages and simultaneously support the *status quo*. The unofficial reward system functions as what Dalton calls an "elastic incentive." Effort can be recognized without disrupting the more cumbersome and symbolic procedures of promotion. In

53

addition to this, "dirty work," which it would be unwise to reward directly, can be obtained. Dalton's managers obtained these rewards in kind rather than in cash, often either in the form of "foreigners" (using the company's time and resources to produce items for domestic use), or as "extras" like free petrol.

These managerial "supplementary reward systems" *are* double-binds, but their orthodox power structure makes them weak. While there is little chance of managers being prosecuted for accepting these informal rewards (at least under normal circumstances), the system *is* subterranean.[77] If formalized, it would conflict with the official reward system, and so it is generally shrouded in what Dalton refers to as "double-talk."[78] Each manager who takes advantage of the system cannot simultaneously benefit from it *and* refuse to accept personal responsibility for managing the ambiguity which is inevitably involved. Dalton cites two cases of female managers unable to thus benefit:

> Some female heads regularly, but discretely, gave certain items a "damaged" appearance. Division heads unofficially knew of this, and set no limit to the markdown that could be made, other things being equal. However, those department heads who shrank from the ambiguities of exercising their authority and asked a division manager the limit for a markdown were usually told, "30 percent" . . . (another female department head) "worried the life out of" her division heads because only rarely could she "make decisions on her own." She, too, desired "shopworn" items, including jewelry with chipped stones, but she called upon the merchandising chief for judgements on the markdown she should make, and was repeatedly given the official "30 percent." Knowing that others more than doubled this figure, she caused trouble by her gossip and insinuations.[79]

Thus, in Dalton's cases, the reward for personally accepting the management of unofficial-reward-ambiguity was an extra thirty percent on top of the standard markdown. As Martin points out, the nearest real equivalent to these unofficial managerial rewards for the workforce are the cut-price concessions for purchasing company-produced goods, and *not* items customarily pilfered.[80]

Although wage-pilferage has its advantages for management, the pilfered items may well constitute a real loss to the company. In addition, it may be, in some employment situations, difficult to meta-specify the ceiling (or, the grounds of applicability) of the secondary injunction to pilfer. A classic solution to these problems is for the management to recommend that their workers indulge in a little indirect wage-pilferage from customers.[81] Here, the firm's financial worries about amounts pilfered may be ignored safely, and

54

yet high wages do not become necessary to maintain a stable workforce. An example of such a wage-fiddle context is reported at length in my "The Fiddler."[82] At the Wellbread Bakery, the salesmen were unequivocally incarcerated in an occupational trap which specified that they be paid low wages, which could be made up either by wage-theft from the firm (which would be treated as actionable), or by indirect wage-pilferage from customers (fiddling), which only *might* lead to trouble.[83]

This occupational trap arises as a managerial decision to shift an awkward organizational dilemma onto the shoulders of the workforce. The irreconcilable demands of profit and error,[84] when coupled with the prospective difficulties of an unstable workforce,[85] have convinced the Wellbreads management to operate a recruitment policy based upon the induction of men of sufficiently worldly character to be appropriately impressed by the eventually displayed organizational rationale for fiddling customers. Once the newcomer has been committed to the firm through subtle deployment of organizational side-bets such as the (honesty) insurance-bond (which the management threaten to revoke for quitters), and the non-legal but otherwise impressive employment "contract," to which the men sign their agreement to pay shortages; and also, once he has discovered that profits are essential and mistakes inevitable, *then* he is ripe for interpreting the sly wink that accompanies supervisors' suggestions that he overcharge customers. The normal justification that it is quite safe is only too just.[86] For most of the salesmen, the relief at finding a solution dilutes any remaining moral qualms, and many salesmen go on from overcharging a bit and paying it in to the firm to cover mistakes, to making an additional bit for themselves. But fiddling, once begun, produces an income which is swiftly transformed from being "extra," to being "instead of" (wages). Although making a bit extra for themselves was "unofficial," the salesmens' salaries would have been ridiculously puny without their invisible fiddled component.[87]

We may characterize this situation as being an example of the way that strategically managed "disengaged involvement" by the powerful (power overrides the apparent contradiction in that phrase by *fiat*) produces the effect of an "illusory partnership"[88] in crime, which, when the chips are down, becomes wholly one-sided collusion. The Wellbread's managers implicitly encourage the fiddling activities of their men, but they do so with the crucial meta-communicative wink: a secondary injunction ("fiddle") actually contradicting the primary injunction ("don't fiddle"), making it simultaneously clear that the second part of the communication will be denied in any dangerous situations. Those among the men perceptive enough to read accurately the accompanying meta-message, find no solace in the hidden rider which prevents them from successfully exposing the contradictory nature of their employment: ultimately, in any enforcement situation, the management is more likely to be believed than the men.

Generally speaking then, wage-pilferage and wage-fiddle systems (inasmuch as they function as what Zeitlin refers to as a "system of controlled larceny")[89] can actually benefit those who *lose* the goods in question more than they benefit those who stand to gain them. The advantage of these systems is the power which accrues to those who control them. It does *not* lie in the possession of the material goods and services in question. This is especially so when workers (rather than members of management) pilfer or fiddle as they often have to deduct the cost of "sweeteners" from their invisible earnings in order to secure services from fellow workers who have no access to pilferage, or to customers.[90] In the "spiritual" rather than "material" sense of kind-benefits, the invisibility of invisible wages means that, for prestige and status purposes, workers may only claim that they are worth the visible portion.[91]

Crucially, in all unofficial wage-pilferage agreements, there is the "of course" clause. This rider specifies that: "Of course, this may turn out to be theft." In other words, the primary injunction *not* to pilfer may be emphasized, and the secondary negative injunction to pilfer may be denied. It is this ambiguity of outcome which is the ultimate message of wage-pilferage. The will of the pilferer is mortgaged to the manager to whom he is "technically" (as they say) a "thief." Unfortunate disobedience of concealed, ambiguous, non-specific and relatively *ad hoc* meta-rules (such as "too much" theft, of "large" items, or the "wrong" sort, "open," and so on) can transform pilferage or fiddling into outright "theft." When this happens, the wage-pilferage system becomes a wage-theft structure.

## 2.3 Wage-Theft Structure

In a wage-theft structure, harsh consequentiality replaces uncertainty.[92] The structure is wholly unambiguous, but on the other hand, there is no chance of this ambiguity being resolved positively for the thief as there is for the pilferer whose misapplications may later be redefined as a "perk."[93] On *all* occasions of unauthorized taking of kind-benefit in a wage-theft structure, the offender will be defined as a thief. *This* is the category of "pure theft" which Dalton tries to distinguish from "supplementary rewards."[94]

How does wage-theft compare with wage-pilferage? Two crucial differences are that first, contradictory imperatives are given on the same communicative level, and second, the contradiction is not uncommentable. Wage-

56

theft constitutes an empirical example of what we may refer to as Merton's Contradiction. Rather than a "can't win" situation for the actor, Merton's Contradiction proposes a "probably lose" situation for him.[95] For the working class employee, the general cultural availability of goals is in disjunctive coupling with a class-based relative unavailability of means for legitimately securing them. In action terms, the specification that the means should be legitimate ones is weaker than the specification that the goals should be attained. In some occupational situations,[96] for example, low wages are in harness with either direct (occupational) or indirect (societal) imperatives to maintain a certain standard of living which the visible component of the wage cannot support. In other occupational situations, managerial situations, managerial policy can arbitrarily create a harsh wage-theft structure. Martin offers a nice example:

> There would be trouble here if an employee took anything. He would be dismissed. I don't think there is any distinction. If he had only pinched something worth a shilling, we would dismiss him.[97]

So, compared with wage-pilferage, where the employer is in wage-supplement collusion with the employee, in a wage-theft structure, the worker has to steal part of his own wages. Leibow provides an excellent example of this. "Tonk," one of Leibow's subjects, was paid $35 per week and expected by the store owner to steal an additional $35 to make up his wages. Leibow continues:

> The employer is not in wage-theft collusion with the employee . . . Were he to have caught Tonk in the act of stealing, he would, of course, have fired him from the job and perhaps called the police as well . . . The employer knowingly provides the conditions which entice (force) the employee to steal the unpaid value of his labor, but at the same time, he punishes him for theft if he catches him doing it.[98]

There is not really a palpably separate form of indirect wage-theft. This, of course, does not mean that employees in the service industries do not "steal" from the customer, but rather that "thefts" from customers are chiefly fiddle-occasions which have misfired, and to which a rather severe control reaction has occurred.

## Conclusion

History lives on. The perpetual and perpetuating myth of the present is to believe that we are liberated from the anguish of the past. On the contrary, the greatest source of history is impregnated in the mundane and everyday

57

world of the present. The meaning of the world of work, for example, is revealed in its relationship to its past. Workers are not only, on the whole, paid as a *class*,[99] those situated at structurally disadvantaged parts receive large segments of their wages "invisibly" — as tips or fiddles from customers, or pilferage and perks from employers. The crucial common factor in these forms of "invisible wages" is the added *power* which accrues to employers through their establishment. They are meaningfully located, however, not simply as archaic relics in the gradual rational liberation of the present from the feudal bond, but as forms of domination crucial to the persistence and growth of modern capitalism because of their solution to those disciplinary problems not soluble in money alone.

## NOTES

1. The research for this article was financed by S. R. C. Grant No. HR 3603. The analysis suggested here will theoretically inform the continuing research. Richard Brown and Philip Corrigan (both of the University of Durham) have been particularly helpful in clarifying some of the ideas presented here.
2. Lisl Klein, "The Meaning of Work," *Fabian Tract 349* (1964), p.l.
3. E. C. K. Gonner, *Common Land and Inclosure* (London, 1912), p. 7.
4. *Ibid.*, p. 14.
5. *Ibid.*, p. 15.
6. *Ibid.*, p. 16.
7. Examination of particular cases has led Thompson to suggest that law: "is clearly an instrument of the *de facto* ruling class: it both defines and defends these rulers' claims upon resources and labour-power — it says what shall be property and what shall be crime — and it mediates class relations with a set of appropriate rules and sanctions, all of which, ultimately, confirm and consolidate existing class power. Hence the rule of law is only another mask for the rule of a class ... But this is not the same thing as to say that the rulers had need of law, in order to oppress the ruled, while those who were ruled had need of none. What was often at issue was not property, supported by law, against no-property; it was alternative definitions of propertyrights: for the landowner, enclosure — for the cottager, common rights; for the forest officialdom, 'preserved grounds' for the deer; for the foresters the right to take turfs." *Cf.* E. P. Thompson, *Whigs and Hunters* (London, 1975) pp. 259—261.
8. Marx (MEW, Vol. 1, pp. 231—232) himself suggests: "The customary rights of the aristocracy conflict by their *content* with the form of universal law ... The fact that their content is contrary to the form of law—universality and necessity— proves that they are *customary wrongs* ... At a time when universal laws prevail, rational customary right is nothing but the *custom of legal right*, for right has not ceased to be custom because it has been embodied in law, although it has ceased to be *merely* custom ... Customary right as a *separate domain* alongside legal right is therefore rational only where it exists *alongside* and *in addition to law*, where custom is the *anticipation* of a legal right ... But whereas these customary rights of the aristocracy are customs which are contrary to the conception of rational right, the customary rights of the poor are rights which are contrary to the customs of positive law."
9. George (*England in Transition*, p. 90) notes how enclosures were retrospectively seen as a way of dealing with crime and idleness, and Gonner (*op.cit.*, p. 360) recalls the common feeling that there was: "a disproportionate amount of crime

58

originated among those living near commons or in unenclosed parishes. Of still more gravity was the contention that, so far as these latter were concerned, commons, and to a lesser degree common right, increased idleness, proved an obstacle to industry, and led to greater poverty and wretchedness."

10.  Those who *did* attempt to continue to secure ex-rights were successfully (even as far as many commentators were concerned) branded as criminal. Thompson, however, successfully shows that "blacking" was not of ordinary criminals, but of the general agrarian populace: "These Blacks are not quite (in E. J. Hobsbawm's sense) social bandits, and they are not quite agrarian rebels; but they share something of both characters. They are armed foresters, enforcing the definition of rights to which the "country people" had become habituated, and also (as we shall see) resisting the private emparkments which encroached upon their tillage, their firing and their grazing . . . The lamentable thing about this account (an account of the hanging of some Blacks which cited them as part of a criminal subculture) . . . is that they are nothing of the sort; they are simply accounts of the commonplace, mundane culture of plebian England—notes on the lives of unremarkable people, distinguished from their fellows by little else except the fact that by bad luck or worse judgement they got caught up in the toils of the law." In Thompson's analysis of the occupations of the Windson Blacks, he found that far from being a notorious gang, the offenders were made up of approximately 50 percent laborers; 21.5 percent urban and rural craftsmen; 15.5 percent farmers; 8 percent tradesmen; and 4.5 percent gentry.

11.  Mantoux claims: "Once enrolled in Chancery, the agreements could be enforced without any further formality . . . If the consent of some small landowner was indispensable, he was asked for it in such a manner that he could scarcely refuse . . . The unlimited authority of the commissioners was no other than their own. It is not very surprising that they should have used it to their own advantage." *Cf.* Paul Mantoux, *The Industrial Revolution in the Eighteenth Century* (London, 1928) pp. 165–168. Gonner (*op.cit.,* 182) adds: "Unwilling commoners are threatened with the risks of long and expensive lawsuits; in other cases they are subject to persecution by the great proprietors, who ditch in their own demense and force them to go a long way round to their own land, or maliciously breed rabbits or keep geese on adjoining ground, to the detriment of their crops."

12.  Marx (*Capital* Vol. I) noted: "The last process of wholesale expropriation of the agricultural population from the soil is, finally, the so-called clearing of estates, i.e., the sweeping men off them. All the English methods hitherto considered culminated in 'clearing' . . . (the Duchess of Sutherland resolved) to effect a radical cure, and to turn the whole country, whose population had already been, by earlier processes of the like kind, reduced to 15,000, into a sheepwalk. From 1814 to 1820 these 15,000 inhabitants, about 3,000 families, were systematically hunted and rooted out . . . Thus this fine lady appropriated 794,000 acres of land that had from time immemorial belonged to the clan. She assigned to the expelled inhabitants about 6,000 acres on the sea-shore."

13.  Mantoux (*op.cit.* p. 172) offers the following examples: "Almost everywhere the enclosing of open fields and the division of common land were followed by the sale of a great many properties . . . the total number of farms had become much smaller in the latter half of the (18th) century. One village in Dorsetshire where, in 1780, as many as thirty farms could be found, fifteen years later had the whole of its land divided between two holdings; in one parish in Hertfordshire three landowners had together engrossed no less than twenty-four farms, with acerages averaging between 50 and 150 acres." Mantoux estimates that the number of small farms absorbed into smaller ones between 1740 and 1688 to be about four or five in each parish. This suggests a total of between 40,000 and 50,000 for the

whole of the United Kingdon, Crucially, these sales were carried out by private deed, and suffered no intervention by Parliament or from local authorities.

14.  Thompson views these unintended consequences of engrossing as a phase in yet another transition: that simultaneous translation of existing "servants" into "employees." He says: "First was the loss of non-monetary usages or perquisites, or their translation into money payments. Such usages were still extraordinarily pervasive in the early eighteenth century. They favored paternal social control because they appeared simultaneously as economic and as social relations . . . In such ways economic rationalisation nibbled (and had long been nibbling) through the bonds of paternalism." *Cf.* E. P. Thompson, "Patrician Society, Plebeian Culture," *Journal of Social History,* 4 (1974), pp. 384–385. E. P. Thompson is by far the most sophisticated and subtle commentator in this area. I have profited a great deal from his writings. However, I think he does tend to assume that the gradual exchange of perks for money is an historical process, the rational conclusion to which is faithfully reflected in the modern structure of wage-payment. This paper challenges that implied assumption, and as such, attempts to go beyond Thompson, and view the historical setting as the interpretative context for modern life.

15.  Gonner, *op.cit.,* pp. 96–100.

16.  Custom was a broader category than right. Simon suggests that for a customary practice to be accepted an such, it has to be: "uniform, certain, of reasonable antiquity and so notorious that persons would contract on the basis of its existence."

17.  Gonner (*op.cit.,* pp. 367–8) states: "Allotments, when made, vested in the owners, to whom they were a more tangible property than the small common right, the use of which in many cases was allowed by grace to the tenants. As the owner usually possessed several of these tenements, the compensation in land added materially to his property; and he was under the disadvantage besetting the poor owner who dwelt in his own cottage."
Mantoux (*op.cit.,* p. 170) adds: "As for the cottager who was traditionally allowed to live on the common, to gather his firewood there and perhaps keep a milch-cow, all that he considered as his possession was taken away from him at a blow. Nor had he any right to complain, for after all the common was the right of other men. The possessing classes were unanimous in thinking that the 'argument of robbing the poor was fallacious. *They had no legal title to the common land.'* This was so, no doubt, but they had until then enjoyed the advantages of a *de facto* situation, sanctioned by long tradition."

18.  Gonner, *op.cit.,* p. 364.

19.  Gonner (*op.cit.,* pp. 362–366) lists the various drawbacks of the allotments:
"In some cases the allotments were too small to be of any value, even when they came to the inhabitant of the cottage. In others the expense of fencing proved too great, while in other instances the very inclosure might occasion a change in the actual as distinct from the legal ownership . . . and when common allotments were made to mitigate the hardships of a class, they were unfortunately made in a form which partook in some measure of the old wils attaching to uncertain charity, and did little to foster the habits of industry or to provide a means of a self-reliant life."

20.  Mantoux (*op.cit.,* p. 170): "Once in possession of his new land the yeoman had to fence it round, and this cost him both labor and money. He had to pay his share of the expenses incurred in carrying out the Act—and those expenses were often very heavy. He could not fail to be left poorer than before, if not actually burdened with debt."

21.  George feels that Enclosure produced the "squatters, the victim of the resentment of those with common rights."

60

22.  Mantoux (*op.cit.*, p. 175) puts it even more strongly:
     "The enclosures resulted in the buying up of the land by the wealthier class; they
     lay at the root of all evils of the period — the high cost of necessaries, the
     demoralisation of the lower classes and the aggravation of poverty. 'It is no
     uncommon thing for four of five wealthy graziers to engross a large enclosed
     lordship, which was before in the hands of twenty or thirty farmers, and as many
     smaller tenants and proprietors. All these are thereby thrown out of their livings,
     and many other families, who were chiefly employed and supported by them,
     such as blacksmiths, carpenters, wheelwrights and artificiers and tradesmen,
     besides their own labourers and servants.' "

23.  Marx (*Capital* Vol. I) claims:
     "the law itself becomes now the instrument of the theft of the people's land,
     although the large farmers make use of their little independent methods as well.
     The parliamentary form of the robbery is that of Acts for enclosures of Com-
     mons, in other words, decrees by which the landlords grant themselves the
     people's land as private property, decrees of expropriation of the people ... the
     systematic robbery of the Communal lands helped especially ... to swell those
     large farms, that were called in the 18th century capital farms or merchant farms,
     and to 'set free' the agricultural population as proletarians for manufacturing
     industry. ... 'Working men are driven from their cottages and forced into the
     towns to seek for employment, but then a larger surplus is obtained, and thus
     capital is augmented.' "

24.  Tobias noted that in Birmingham in the early part of the 19th century, "the most
     prevalent crime was larceny from their masters or from shops and so forth
     committed by youngsters who had an honest job ... The large number of small
     workshops meant that many opportunities for theft existed." In addition, in the
     first decades of the century, "domestic servants were often involved in criminal
     enterprises against their masters" *Cf.* J. J. Tobias, *Crime and Industrial Society in
     the Nineteenth Century* (Harmondsworth, 1967).

25.  Mantoux (*op.cit.*, p. 171) notes how this was achieved by retrospective reinterpre-
     tation:
     "The poor inhabitants of open-field parishes frequently enjoy the privileges of
     cutting furze, turves, and the like, on the common land for which they have rarely
     any compensation made to them upon enclosure. The selfish proprietor insists
     that they had no right to such privileges, but were only permitted to enjoy them
     by indulgence or connivance."

26   Thompson (*op.cit.*, 1975 pp. 130–1, 134–5) offers a nice example in the "moral
     career" of aged timber rights in Hamsphire:
     The other critical issue was that of timber rights. ... A case was tried at Surrey
     Assizes, and decided against the tenants: they could not cut timber (unless for
     necessary repairs on their own lands) without license. But ambiguities remained
     (as well as illfeelings); what was 'timber'? What constituted 'repairs'? There was
     also the question of the license, which was to be granted not by the lord's
     Steward but by Kerby, the Woodward. Upon each license, the Woodward too a
     fee in bark and 'lops and tops' ... but Heron claimed ... the loss sustained by the
     Bishop through the waste of his tenants was nothing to the loss sustained through
     the perquisites of the Woodward ...."
     A new Steward introduced several "improvements," which, Thompson continues,
     successfully extinguished what remained of common rights.
     "The common rights in dispute here probably included grazing, and access to
     clay, marl, chalk, earth, stones, peat, turf and heath ... (but) If the tenants' right
     to cut timber on their own farms remained ambiguous (limited to wood for
     repairs) and bought them under menace of forfeit, and if in any case this timber
     was scarce, it was inevitable that they should assert more stubbornly customary
     rights (or claims) over the common land and chases."

27. For example, the notorious 1723 Black Act instantaneously transformed game-rights (which had become felonies) into capital offenses.

28. Marx (MEW, pp. 225, 235) notes how wood-theft (the instant transformation of Common of Estover) was processed as a civil, rather than as a criminal offence. He continues:
   "In short, if popular customary rights are suppressed, the attempt to exercise them can only be treated as the simple *contravention of a police regulation*, but never punished as a crime."

29. Jones shows that as late as 1849 in Wales, miners accused of coal-stealing could successfully use the defense that the mineowner was attempting to deprive them of traditional rights to free coal.

30. Marx noticed this crucial distinction between "pilferage" and "theft," (although at that stage, the distinction was based still upon the different types of regulation upon which each depended—forest regulations, and the criminal code respectively), and argued against the common suggestion that "pilferage" was *really* "theft," and that resistance to that uniformity is merely grammatical purism. While it was still common in England in the 19th century to use "pilferage" as distinct from "theft," any legal distinction is certainly missing from the 1968 Theft Act.

31. This is not to say that "employee" was a freely given status. The "masters" preferred the term "servant." Thompson (*op.cit.*, 1974, pp. 383—4) continues: "They clung to the image of the laborer as an *un*free man, a "servant": a servant in husbandry, in the workshop, in the house. (They clung simultaneously to the image of the free or masterless man as a vagabond, to be disciplined, whipped and compelled to work.) But crops could not be harvested, cloth could not be manufactured, goods could not be transported, houses could not be built and parks enlarged, without labor readily available and mobile, for whom it would be inconvenient or impossible to accept the reciprocities of the master-servant relationship. The masters disclaimed their paternal responsibilities."

32. Thompson (*op.cit.*, 1975, pp. 240—1) gives the example of the Windson foresters: "The unrestricted grazing rights they enjoyed were exceptional . . . in these great forests, concepts of property remained archaic . . . The foresters clung still to the lowest rungs of a hierarchy of use-rights . . . Little money passed among foresters; they did not go to a butcher for their meat. It was because they pursued not a luxury but a livelihood that encounters between them and the keepers were so grim . . . the law abhorred the messy complexities of coincident use-right. And capitalist modes transmuted offices, rights and perquisites into round monetary sums, which could be bought and sold like any other property. Or, rather, the offices and rights of the great were transmuted in this way—those of the Rangers, bishops, manorial lords. The rights and claims of the poor, if inquired into at all, received more perfunctory compensation, smeared over with condescension and poisoned with charity. Very often they were simply redefined as crimes: poaching, wood-theft, trespass."

33. Marx (MEW, p. 227) tries, on behalf of the wood-gatherer, to force a distinction between "live" and "dead" wood, and attempts to show the irony behind the forest-owner's treatment of gathering dead wood in the same way as he would treat somebody apprehended tearing a tree down: "In order to appropriate growing timber, it has to be forcibly separated from its organic association. Since this is an obvious outrage against the tree, it is therefore an obvious outrage against the owner of the tree. Further, if felled wood is stolen from a third person, this felled wood is material that has been produced by the owner. Felled wood is wood that has been worked on. The natural connection with property has been replaced by an artificial one. Therefore, anyone who takes away felled wood takes away property. In the case of fallen wood, on the contrary, nothing has

62

been separated from property. It is only what has already been separated from property that is being separated from it . . . The gathering of fallen wood and the theft of wood are therefore essentially different things."

In England, Thompson notes that in 1717, New Forest wood thieves faced a standard £5 fine (no mean sum for a poor man), but that by the latter half of the 18th century, the new perquisites of the ruling classes began to garner more significant legal protection. Thompson (*op. cit.*, 1975, pp. 244–5) continues:

"In 1741 the 'pretended right' of the poor was tried at Winchester Assizes, and they lost their case. But they asserted it again and again . . . Nevertheless, in 1788 at the next fall: 'The offal wood, after having been made into faggots, and a day appointed for the sale of it, was openly carried off by the people of Frensham, to the number of 6,365 faggots in one day and night.' The value of these perquisites, pretended or allowed, was unequal. In 1777 the stack wood taken by all the poor villagers was valued at £80, whereas the Ranger claimed for himself £250 (or one fifth of the fall). But the decisive inequality lay in a class society, wherein non-monetary use-rights were being reified into capitalist property rights, by the mediation of the courts of law. When the people of Frensham claimed their 'rights,' openly, and with a solidarity so complete that in 1788 no tithingman could be found to execute a warrant, they were subject to prosecution . . . It is astonishing the wealth that can be extracted from territories of the poor, during the phase of capital accumulation, provided that the predatory elite are limited in number, and provided that the state and the law smooth the way of exploitation."

34.  Jones notes how, in rural Wales, the withdrawal of fishing rights produced many "crimes" of poaching, and from an examination of 60 cases of poaching, suggests that firstly, most of the incidents had occurred on land that had been recently enclosed; secondly, most cases were prosecuted by absentee landlords (chiefly members of the "English Shooting Gentry"); and thirdly, almost half of the defendants didn't turn up for the trial. Jones suggests that it seems that:

"For certain landowners poaching was a crime worthy of social excommunication. On several occasions farm labourers were sacked as soon as their children were arrested for catching rabbits, even though the subsequent court case was sometimes dismissed." *Cf.* David J. V. Jones, "Crime, Protest, and Community in 19th Century Wales, *Llafur*, 1,3 (1974), pp. 5–15.

35.  Jones adds:

"It has been customary for local inhabitants to graze sheep and ponies on the mountain slopes during the summer, and they were clearly determined to protect their 'rights.' When the landowners tried to carry out the award (an Enclosure Act of 1858) by building walls around their allotments, they were repeatedly torn down by gangs of men."

36.  Marx (MEW, p. 234, 235) refers to the fruits of gleaning as the "alms of nature," and adds: "By its act of *gathering*, the elemental class of human society appoints itself to introduce order among the products of the elemental power of nature. The position is similar in regard to those products which, because of their wild growth, are a wholly accidental appendage of property and, if only because of their unimportance, are not an object for the activity of the actual owner. The same thing holds good also in regard to gleaning after the harvest and similar customary rights . . . the gathering of bilberries and cranberries is also (now) treated as theft."

Marx goes on to say that the bilberry and cranberry pickers have now become thieves chiefly because it is now possible to extract some commercial value from them. He continues:

"In *one locality*, therefore, things have actually gone so far that a customary right of the poor has been turned into a *monopoly* of the rich."

In other words, the acts of theft create capital for the owner of the property concerned. Taking wood-thefts as an example, the value of the wood is only turned into substance by its theft. Marx adds: "For the wood thief has become a capital for the forest owner . . . By reform of the criminal is understood *improvement of the percentage of profit* which it is the criminal's noble function to provide for the forest owner."

Outworkers were in a similar situation. Simon reports that under the Acts of 1843, outworkers were liable to prosecution if they failed to finish all their work on time, or failed to return all the materials given out. This amazing liability managed to blur the normal line between "idleness" and "pilferage," but criminalize both.

37. Mantoux, *op.cit.*, pp. 184–185. He reports:
   "The village artisan, when deprived of his field and of his rights of common, could not continue to work at home. He was forced to give up whatever independence he still seemed to have retained, and had to accept the wages offered to him in the employer's workshop . . . There is, then, an intimate connection between the movement by which English agriculture was transformed and the rise of the factory system."

38. See Jones, *op.cit.*, p. 6, 10.

39. Gilding claims that coopers have plenty of opportunity to "sample" the contents of the casks and barrells which they repair and maintain. For example, a "waxer" is a cooper's term for "his unofficial drink, gleaned or siphoned from a wine tub," and "bull" was the name of a drink unofficially created by pouring boiling water into a cask which had held liquor, and leaving it to stand for a couple of days, until the alcohol was satisfactorily gleaned from the woodwork of the tub. It was then drained into a drip-tub and kept for occasional use.

40. Most coopers share their "waxer" with gangs of dockers. *Cf.* Bob Gilding, "The Journeymen Coopers of East London," *History Workshop Pamphlet* No. 4 (1971).

41. Gilding refers to the coopers' traditional allowance system as "sweepings," and cites the attempts by the dock authorities to redefine these practices as "wholesale plunder," and thus eradicate them. Gilding then quotes George Pattison ("The Coopers' Strike at the West India Dock 1821," *Mariner's Mirror*, 12.9.1850):
   "When rum was plundered it was drunk on the quay, but sugar was an easier object to conceal and to convey through the dock gates, while the fact that sugar casks were frequently found on arrival to be broken to pieces gave sugar coopers special opportunities for plunder."

42. This typification of development is somewhat optimistic. It would be a little more realistic, perhaps, to set these types of everyday, current contradiction in the grander historical context of interminable criminalization, and subsequently new "wage-theft" as a considerably more mature form than "wage theft." To do so would be to meekly deny the bitter counter struggles of working men in attempts to halt, and turn back the processes of history, inasmuch as the latter are seen purely as oppressive. Current occasions of (weak) "wage-perk" material kind-payment are derived from workforce *re*-definition of more severe forms of contradiction, and not merely unattended contextual throwbacks waiting in the wings of history.

43. Webster defines a "perk" as "a gain or profit incidentally made from employment in addition to regular salary or wages . . . especially one made by custom expected or claimed." A "perk" may here be defined as "Preferential or concessionary access to goods or services conventionally supplied non-preferentially to the public."

64

44.  Of course, sometimes, if the "perks" come from the wrong people, or if the Law's claim to universality needs a little direct bolstering, then "perks" become "bribes." Blue-collar workers rarely achieve occupational or professional positions where bribes are possible, and so bribes become almost exclusively the scourge of the working middle classes. Nevertheless, is has recently been estimated (CUTTING 211, 30.1.76) that a $4\frac{1}{2}$ litre company car is worth a 2–4% salary increase to a managing director on £16,000 a year. (I shall bolster the arguments presented here with examples clipped from the British national daily press. These are either quoted as CASES—court reports where the offender matches a definition of an individual occupational thief—or as CUTTINGS, reports of varying status not quite or not even remotely satisfying that definition, but of vague general interest.)

45.  A nice recent example being the $2\frac{1}{2}\%$ mortgage interest rates traditionally the perk of bank employees. When Lloyds Bank recently announced that these were to be increased to 5% and NUBE complained (CUTTING 164: 24.12.75), the bank retorted that the rate was not a "negotiable" item (i.e., not part of wages).

46.  For example, a council official (CASE 12: 16.5.73) who was found with 80 tins of food (destined for a council pulverisation plant) in the boot of his car, was unsuccessfully prosecuted. He had claimed that "this practice of taking things home is accepted by many local authorities as a perk of the job." Although he was cleared, the council suspended him. In another case (CASE 155: 11.11.75) a British Rail chef was accused of 12 charges of theft of items of British Rail cutlery (including cutlery from the Royal train) worth £2,472. He claimed in his defence to have had written permission to use the cutlery for private functions, but had lost the note. He was cleared, and the judge commented (that, presumably only for British Rail employees) "it is not an offense to borrow your employer's property—even the Royal crockery—to use for a private function." In both cases, the defendant occupied an ambiguous occupational position, half-way between manager and worker.

47.  In CASE 10 (12.5.73) a French *Au pair* was conditionally discharged for stealing 3 dresses from her employers who paid her £7.50 per week—and took £5 of that back in rent. In CASE 20 (28.8.73), a cleaning lady was put on probation for stealing £16 from offices which she cleaned professionally. She was given a small room, free electricity, and £1.50 as a week's wages.

48.  Unscrupulous employers use this opportunity to make profit not only out of the goods that their employees are allowed as perks, but also by overcharging them. In "The Political Economy of Nursing Homes," (*Annals A.A.S.P.S.* Vol. 415, Sept. 1974) Mary Mendelson and David Hapgood note how nursing home proprietors have been known to charge the government $14 per day to feed their inmates whom they subsequently manage just to keep alive on $0.78 per day. Hutter similarly adds: "Free meals and lodgings are, of course, included in calculating an employee's salary. The . . . owner prefers to deduct the cost of the employee's meal and lodgings—the cost according to his own calculations—rather than pay the employee's actual value. If the employee requests cash instead of meals or the lodgings, his request is denied." *Cf.* Mark Hutter, "Summertime Servants: The 'Schlockhaus' Waiter," in Glenn Jacobs, ed., *The Participant Observer: Encounters with Social Reality* (New York, 1970).

49.  As I have already suggested, white-collar employees cannot receive tips, they can only get "bribes." Davis suggests that some "tip-sensitive" blue-collar employees get as much as 40% of their real wages from tips. *Cf.* Fred Davis, "The Cabdriver and his Fare: Facets of a Fleeting Relationship," *American Journal of Sociology;* 65 (1959), pp. 158–165.

50.  Leo P. Crespi, "The Implications of Tipping in America," *Public Opinion Quarterly,* 11 (1947), pp. 424–435. In Crespi's study, only 13% of a tipper-public

sample of 300 tip because they feel that the recipient gets a "poor salary," although over 69% agree that tipping could be eliminated if service workers got a "fair wage."

51. Crespi, *op.cit.*

52. To "organize" means to remove picturesque ambiguity and uncertainty from the practice. Davis (op.cit., p. 267) comments: "No regular scheme of work can easily tolerate so high a degree of ambiguity and uncertainty in a key contingency. Invariably, attempts are made to fashion ways and means of greater predictability and control; or failing that, of devising formulas and imagery to bring order and reason into otherwise inscrutable and capricious events."

53. To "work" a customer means to manipulate her in order to increase the probability of a tip. This may be done, for example, by "making change," i.e., to give change in small denominations so as to encourage and facilitate tips.

54. The N.C.B. (N.C.B. Statistical Tables, 1973–74) give £2.56 per week (6.4% of average weekly earnings of all workers at £40.09 per week) as the actual retail value of all allowances in kind. Interestingly, there have been no moves either from the N.C.B., or from the N.U.M. to exchange these legitimate perks for a fixed weekly sum in cash. This is not altogether surprising when it is realized that the office staff and management are *also* entitled to the same coal-allowance (albeit on a slightly reduced basis). The coal-allowance constitutes most of the N.C.B. employee's allowances in kind, although, for some, there is also a small rent allowance in lieu of a colliery tenancy. Those in non-coal-fired houses may instead have a financial allowance (for example, in North Durham, of £175 p.a.). It should be noted that in an inflationary situation, when prices rise faster than wages (as the outcome of a wages policy), wages-in-kind are better value than "real" money. It is possible that the N.C.B. employee's entitlement to his coal allowance, and the B.R. employee's entitlement to free and concessionary travel during strikes reflects the nationalized status of those industries, rather than the "fringe benefit" status of the perk.

55. Permanent British Rail salary, and wage-earning employees have preferential access to travel. Staff (who have an identity card) may purchease tickets at privileged rates—usually one quarter of the public fare—except for travel to and from work, where the first 12 miles of daily travel is free, but the remainder payable at the standard rate. On top of this, full-time staff are entitled to a variety of free tickets: none of those with less than 6 months service, 4 for those with up to 10 years, and 7 for those with over. One free ticket may even take an employee across Europe. These concessions are considered to be part of the wages of the employee inasmuch as they are his *right*, but they are fringe benefits to the extent that they are supposed to act as an inducement (or commitment).

56. A "Catch-22" situation is a theoretically strong "can't win" one. It crucially differs from the double-bind in that the contradiction involved occurs *at* one communicative level, rather than between two levels. It is theoretically strong and generates a structural impossibility for the trapped actor, whereas weaker "catches" (for example, Merton's Contradiction) merely offer structural difficulties. Catch-22 is derived from Heller's novel of the same name, wherein it functioned as a clause preventing hasty escape from the armed forces. Heller: "There was only one catch and that was Catch-22, which specified that a concern for one's own safety in the face of dangers that were real and immediate was the process of a rational mind. Orr was crazy and could be grounded. All he had to do was ask; and as soon as he did, he would no longer be crazy to fly more missions and sane if he didn't, but if he was sane he had to fly them. If he flew them he was crazy and didn't have to; but if he didn't want to he was sane and had to." To summarize, Catch-22 was a set of three, mutually contradictory rules: (1) Crazy people may be grounded, (2) One can only apply for grounding oneself,

66

and (3) To apply for grounding indicates sanity. In terms of a means-end schema:
inevitably built into the legitimate means of goal-achievement is a logically
inevitable disqualification. A particularly nice everyday mundane example of the
Catch-22 in operation is given by Birdwhistell where a typical domestic scene is
described and minutely analysed to show that a mother putting on a baby's nappy
can accustom the child to raise or lower its arm by applying two different sorts of
bodily pressure. At one instant, pressure is simultaneously applied at both points
thus sending two contradictory messages in one frame. *Cf.* Ray L. Birdwhistell,
*Kinesics and Context: Essays on Body-Motion Communication* (Harmondsworth,
1970), pp. 11–23.

57.   In terms of the means-end imagery, the "double-bind" is a situation wherein
      attempts to reach the goal by deliberately specified means are stymied by a
      meta-qualification which prevents the use of those means. The resulting contra-
      diction (which amounts to a theoretically strong structural impossibility) may be
      held to occur *between* two communicative levels. For example, Brooks (1969;
      213 *et seq*) reports that the conspirators in the General Electrice/Westinghouse
      price-rigging conspiracy had all previously received a memo warning them not to
      form cartels with the competition. Amazingly, some of the subordinates felt that
      it was not "serious," or that it was "window dressing," they assumed: "that often
      when a ranking executive ordered a subordinate executive to comply with 20.5
      (the memo on cartels), he was actually ordering him to violate it. Illogical as it
      might seem, this last assumption becomes comprehensible in the light of the fact
      that, for a time, when some executives orally conveyed, or reconveyed the order,
      they were apparently in the habit of accompanying it with an unmistakable
      wink." *Cf.* John Brooks, *Business Adventures* (Harmondsworth, 1969), p. 213 ff.
      Although the double-bind has become over-associated with analyses of schizo-
      phrenia through Laing's work, both the original formulation and the episte-
      mological basis of its applicability demand that it possibly be a feature of normal
      situations. A particularly clear statement of the logical structure of the double-
      bind is given in Batenson (*Steps to an Ecology of Mind,* 1972, pp. 177–188). The
      irony of the situation has been adopted both by Merton (*Social Theory and Social
      Structure*, p. 486) with his "circle of paradox," and by Goffman (*Frame Analysis*,
      pp. 480–486) in his discussion of the "frame trap." A particularly clear statement
      of a relatively ordinary example is given in Sprand, Ney and Mann (*The Cocktail
      Waitress: Woman's Work in a Man's World*, 1975, pp. 139–141). Here, it was
      noted that in some American bars customers occasionally ask for the "wrong"
      drink. In other words, they ask for one drink, receive another, but do not
      complain. This is considered funny in America. The customer jovially asks
      publicly for a rudely named drink, but manages to convince the waitress using
      various meta-channels of communication, that this drink *isn't* required, and that
      he wants the "usual." But how comical is this for the waitress?? She can either
      underread the situation and supply the drink that is verbally and literally asked
      for, or she can overread the situation, avoid supplying the rudely-named drink and
      pour that metaphorically requested. But either of these courses of action *can* be
      wrong. There is no theoretical exit from the double-bind, although experience (as
      in the waitresses' case) can convert actual loss into a low probability.

58.   Goffman (*op.cit.*, p. 84) notes that the wink is a collusive one with a long social
      history, and that the many meanings which it once could convey are now
      telescoped into the usual negative meta-statement.

59.   Jason Ditton, "The Fiddler: A Sociological Analysis of Forms of Blue-Collar
      Employee Theft amongst Bread Salesmen," Unpublished Ph. D. Thesis (Durham,
      1976), p. 12.

60.   At least, this must be the outcome of the official disposition. Unofficially, many
      shades of treatment are possible. Some cases are treated as neither "theft" nor

"perks," and are called (petty) "pilferage." In other words, the ambiguity need not be resolved at the reaction stage. It is even possible for the ambiguity to be officially sanctioned, and for the action to be defined (in actuality) as "theft," but not proceeded against because this verdict is qualified by its "pettiness." For example (CUTTING 0.1: 29.1.73) Cadbury-Schweppes and Rowntree-Mackintosh (quite legally) set up their own courts to try employee offenders, and have been doing so, with the blessing of the local Birmingham constabulary, since 1920.

61.  This is at least the case in terms of the meanings attached to the world by the "pilferers." Horning found that a crucial definition which rendered objects available for pilferage by the workers in his study was their definition of those objects as being "property of uncertain ownership." Some of these objects *are* of questionable ownership (for example, broken parts in the scrap barrel) but most are clearly legitimately owned, although for various reasons, have slipped into the limbo of uncertainty in the worker's eyes. In a very similar way I found that bread salesmen found it psychologically "easier" to steal bread while it was labeled "stock": a category of intermediate factory responsibility for bread. As "stock," bread was neither clearly the responsibility of despatch workers, nor yet obviously issued to the salesmen.

62.  Marx (MEW, p. 225) further claims that to claim that pilfering *"is"* theft: "mistakes the conversion of a citizen into a thief for a mere negligence in formulation and rejects all opposition to it as grammatical purism."

63.  Douglas claims that marginality is untidy experience, and that it is precisely this untidiness which is dangerous. She suggests:
"Danger lies in transitional states; simply because transition is neither one state nor the next, it is undefinable." *Cf.* Mary Douglas, *Purity and Danger* (Harmondworth, 1966) p. 116.

64.  Marx, MEW, p. 232–233.

65.  I once asked one of the Wellbreads managers what sort of overall daily shortage figure would be acceptable for the production department. He replied: "Anything up to £100, but it's very hard to say, because on some occasions, we've been £30 or £40 short, and they've not said a word, and sometimes, we're £35 or £45 short, and they'll say: 'You're short' ... you see, you can't really pin this down to a specific amount."

66.  One employer told Martin that deciding whether to label an action "pilferage" or "theft": "depends on the person, if you know a chap is a bit of a rogue, it is different from an honest man." It is also possible that "ambiguous" employees, for example gamekeepers who combine manorality with servility, have a sort of portfolio of kind-benefits comprising half of perks (representing their white-collar status) and half of pilferage (showing their blue-collar status). For example, Thompson (*op.cit.,* 1975, p. 34) notices: "These posts (gamekeepers) carried small salaries—for underkeepers £20 per annum—and if not supplemented from other sources would scarcely have constituted a livelihood. But the best posts were in fact lavishly supplemented by perquisites. Some of these were expressed, such as the use of their own sub-lodges, a hay allowance for the deer, a scale of payment for each stag, buck or hind officially killed, the use of old fence posts for firing, etc; others were unexpressed but perfectly well understood and sanctioned by usage, such as the culling for their own use of the occasional ('wounded') deer, a fairly free hand with timber, small game and herbage; still others were the wages of customary corruption (the covert sale of venison on their own account, or the acceptance of bribes from poachers as a payment for silence."
[*Footnote here:* "It is impossible to set an exact value of the perquisites of keepers; the best attempt was made later in the century in the New Forest (*Commons Journals,* XLIV, 1789: 558). A keeper who started off with a salary of

68

£20 p.a. would be unlucky, when he added to this fees for driving the walks, fuel wood (or allowance in lieu), allowance for repair of lodges, use of lodge, fees for killing deer, profit from the sale of browse wood, sale of rabbits, use of his own grazing in the forest, etc., to emerge with less than £100 p.a., and this on his own confession, before undeclared advantages are considered. Many gained very much more."]

67.   Martin, *op.cit.,* pp. 125–126.

68.   A "weasel" word is one cunningly inserted into advertising copy in order to evade the spirit, but not the letter of the law. It is difficult to sustain common-sense definitions of what "small" means when we examine the offenses for which several meat-inspectors from Boston were indicted in 1971. Among other things, the inspectors were indicted for the theft of a "handful of screws," a "spiritual bouquet" (?), a "light bulb," "half a can of shoe polish," and a "photograph." Contrarily, what does "large" mean? In CASE 37 (7.7.74) an absolute discharge was given to a man who had taken a worthless box from his employers. The judge accepted that the defendant did not know that there was a sextant inside the box.

69.   On one occasion, even Thompson's under-keepers were produced against (*op.cit.,* 1975 p. 97):
"In the case of the under-keepers, known perquisites included the use of lodges, often with orchards, gardens, grazings, fees for the unwarranted killing of deer; important timber perquisites." [*Footnote Here:* "the keepers of Cranbourne Chase (in Windsor forest) had 'all profits arising by the herbage and browse-wood windfall tree and dead branchles mastage and chimage, as well as fuel and wood for repairs.'"] "the sale of browse-wood; and the exploitation of the influence that went with office. In the aftermath of the tragedy of the Blacks, the normally compliant regarders of the forest court showed, at the last two swanimotes to be held for Windsor Forest, a flurry of guarded independence. They presented the under-keepers as a group for taking down dead trees without view (i.e., without licence or notice to a Regarder) and lopping too many branches from the trees under the pretence of browse-wood. In addition the taking for their own use of deer found wounded or accidentally killed 'is grown to be a pernitious custome.'"

70.   M. Dalton, *Men Who Manage* (New York, 1964), p. 212.

71.   For example, in the building industry, "custom" weakens the law to such an extent that (Martin, *op.cit.,* p. 117):
"The building industry always accepts that no man ever pays for nails, screws, or firewood, but if he took something bigger, it would be theft."
It is similarly traditional that meat-inspectors (who have to temper bureaucratic regulations with commercial "good sense") are entitled to extra rewards called "cumshaw" (meat for their domestic use) for thus oiling the wheels of commerce. Zurcher notes that "cumshaw" was originally a Chinese word for tip. The meat inspectors are employed by the government, but "tipped" by the companies they are allegedly checking.

72.   *Cf.* Gerald Mars, "Chance Punters and the Fiddle: Institutional Pilferage in a Hotal Dining Room," in M. Warner, ed., *The Sociology of the Workplace* (London, 1973), p. 202.; Mark Hutter, *op.cit.,* p. 206.

73.   Lawrence R. Zeitlin, "A Little Larceny Can Do a Lot for Employee Morale," *Psychology Today,* V, (June 1971), p. 26.

74.   R. Keith Aufhauser, "Slavery and Scientific Management," *Journal of Economic History,* 33 (1973), p. 819.

75.   Dalton, *op.cit.,* p. 212, 215.

76.   *Ibid.,* pp. 198–199.

77.   There is a nice historical basis for this processing distinction between management and worker. Simon reports that: "Whereas the master who broke his contract was

69

only liable in a civil action for damages or wages owing, the servant who broke his contract was punished as a criminal with imprisonment and hard labor up to three months." (in 1875). *Cf.* Daphne Simon, "Master and Servant," in J. Saville, ed., *Democracy and the Labour Movement* (London, 1954), p. 160.

78. Dalton, *op.cit.*, p. 195.

79. *Ibid.*, p. 208, 211.

80. Martin, *op.cit.*, p. 23, 126.

81. I am not here concerned with the other side of the fiddler's coin—either "dodgers" (customers who do not pay their dues, T.V. license dodgers and so on) or, "flankers"—members of the public who defraud corporations or state institutions. An interesting possibility arises, however, when members of the public depend for their means of subsistence upon financial negotiations with state institutions. This gives us, on occasion, two sorts of flankers—"scroungers" (those who defraud the D.H.S.S.), and "evaders" (those who defraud H.M. Tax Inspectors). Sometimes, those of the Right can see no distinction between "scroungers" and claimants; and those of the Left no difference between "evaders" and avoiders. A nice financial note is possible however. The D.H.S.S. estimate fraudulent benefit claims at £3.7 millions in 1974 (0.4% of the benefit total of £843 millions), and Anthony Christopher of the Inland Revenue Staff Association claims that tax-owed but written-off in 1970 amounted to between £235 and £535 millions (CUTTING, 206: 26.1.76). Taylor, Walton and Young estimate that in 1972 there were only 17 prosecutions for false income tax returns (as against 80,000 cases settled without prosecution), although there were 12,000 prosecutions for fraudulent claims from the D.H.S.S. The amounts reclaimed in these 12,000 cases was only 15% of that recovered in the 17 tax cases. Titmuss adds that of 7,937 cases of tax-evasion investigated between 1948 and 1951, £4 millions was recovered in imposed penalties, but there was not a single prosecution. While we may suggest that Social Security fraud is the prerogative of the "working" classes, the community and the country stands to lose far more through the rascally peculations of the white-collar, diligent but evasive employer.

82. Ditton, *op.cit.*

83. "Fiddling" is an ambiguous category like "pilferage." The bakery management tolerate the practice as long as irate customers do not complain. Interestingly, the salesmen at the bakery do *not* have the same pilfering rights as the production workers. It is assumed that the production staff have no outlet other than domestic consumption, and that this empirical feature of the practice will *de facto* limit the amount of bread that they will take. Salesmen, on the other hand, are assumed to have guaranteed occupational access to facilities (a round of customers) with which they could easily violate the meta-injunction of domestic usage.

84. On the one hand (profit) the sales department is strictly accountable for all the goods which its salesmen are debited with, but on the other (mistake), the process of transforming bread into money is fraught with inevitable and unintentional mistakes which will, on balance, disadvantage the firm.

85. Recruitment is expensive, so recruits must be both brought to peak efficiency quickly, and encouraged to stay there. "Fiddling" will simultaneously remove worries about being short in accounting losses, and increase wage-packets, thus decreasing labor turnover.

86. Court prosecutions (which transform the fiddle into theft) are rare, as customers only infrequently officially complain. In my current collection of over 200 CASES of employee theft taken from U.K. national newspapers over the last 4 years, only two (CASE 165: 25.11.75, taxidriver overcharging; and CASE 174: 2.12.75, London dustmen demanding tips with menaces for emptying extra dustbins) involved prosecutions for workers stealing from customers.

70

87.  In the research summer of 1973, salesmen were paid an average wage of £32.50 p.w. I asked one of the salesmen if he felt guilty about fiddling, and he replied: "I don't bother about it at all . . . I just think of it as subsidising my wages, that's all." A hotel waiter in a similar position (Mars, *op.cit.*, p. 202) said: "Who'd work for £12. 10s a week for the hours I put in? No one but a bloody fool, I can tell you. Fiddles are part of wages. The whole issue runs on fiddles, it couldn't work otherwise."

88.  The Wellbreads situation is an *active* "illusory partnership." In other words, the managers are personally involved in, and then disengaged from each recruit, and do not *passively* rely upon historical precedent and workforce custom to produce the rewards that they gain from workforce fiddling.

89.  Zeitlin, *op.cit.*, p. 64.

90.  *Cf.* Hutter, *op.cit.*, p. 213; Davis, *op.cit.*, p. 27.

91.  *Cf.* Elliot Leibow, *Tally's Corner* (Boston, 1967), p. 40.

92.  For example, CASE 3 (31.1.73) a railway porter convicted of stealing newspapers worth 57p from a train was fined £20 and asked to pay £20 costs; CASE 6 (17.2.73) a barman convicted of stealing from the till was given a £500 fine and an 18-month suspended prison sentence; in CASE 194 (23.12.75) a sheet metal worker was successfully prosecuted and fined £25 for the theft of 10p's worth of scrap metal which he had taken 15 years before.

93.  For example, CASE 29 (25.1.74). A store employee who stole store goods was fined. He claimed that he took the goods because he was underpaid. In CASE 34 (19.6.74), a coal-board official who took some envelopes worth £1.25 was discharged—but he lost his job.

94.  Dalton, *op.cit.*, p. 201.

95.  Merton's Contradiction is derived from Merton. Briefly, the same body of success-goals is held to apply to all, but social organization is such that there exist class differentials of goal accessibility. The "open-class ideology" is never sufficient to wholly mask this disjunction.

96.  Salesmen and bank clerks, for example, are particularly prone to being paid as blue-collar employees, but asked to appear at work as whitecollar ones. Abramson notes that this is often referred to as being asked to "put on the dog." Inevitably, there are those who will read the secondary injunction (to appear well) as more important than the primary injunction not to steal. Many complain of the difficulty of balancing reality with the impressions of it that are occupationally essential. An ex-bank president complained:
"A person who works in a bank is generally regarded as wealthy, no matter how small his salary. He is expected to subscribe to everything . . . live on a fairly high standard. He is compelled to look prosperous for the sake of the bank. He has to 'live up to his position.' " *Cf.* Donald Cressey, *Other People's Money* (London, 1953), pp. 56–57.
However, in banks it is not so much that there is not theft (as is commonly supposed) it is rather than all theft is unambiguously defined as stealing. This has always been so, and accordingly, there is no culture of pilferage as an employee-transmitted workplace tradition. A bank contacted by Martin commented: "In a bank there is no line (between pilferage and stealing) you just don't do it. One thing leads to another and we do ask for a high standard and maintain it." Since banks only handle money, and since there would be no way to, for example, define what "domestic consumption," or a "small" amount of money might be, allowing clerks to dip into the till on their own account would inevitably lead to a situation where, as was suggested, "one thing leads to another." On top of this, there is no inventory euphemism (such as "damaged") where "lost" money might be alternatively located. No "pilferage," then, by definition, but a considerable amount of "theft." Robin notes how banks as a whole tend to prosecute up to

71

87% of their embezzling employees, whereas department stores only bother to take about 17% to court. *Cf.* Gerald D. Robin, "The Corporate and Judicial Disposition of Employee Thieves, " *Wisconsin Law Review,* 642 (1967), pp. 685–702.

97.   Martin, *op.cit.* p. 117.
98.   Leibow, *op.cit.,* pp. 38–39. Judicial disposition of employee thieves is likely to be light although employee theft presents good opportunities for activating victim compensation. Recently (CUTTING 204: 24.1.76) a petrol pump attendant, convicted of false accounting and theft in 1972 was released from an order to repay £2,852 because she was living, with one daughter, on £8 p.w. from Social Security benefits.
99.   *Cf.* Jason Ditton, "Moral Horror vs. Folk Terror: Class, Output Restriction and the Social Organization of Exploitation," *Sociological Review* 24 (August, 1976).

*Theory and Society.* 4 (1977) 39–71
© Elsevier  Scientific Publishing Company, Amsterdam – Printed in the Netherlands

# [2]

# CRIME AT WORK:
# THE SOCIAL CONSTRUCTION OF
# AMATEUR PROPERTY THEFT[1]

STUART HENRY AND GERALD MARS

*Abstract* We argue that the theft of goods from work and their subsequent resale might usefully be considered in a social anthropological frame: as the transferring of goods from our economy's dominant market exchange sphere to what we call the illegal amateur trading sphere.

We show that pecuniary reward is alien to the amateur sphere and that a wide range of social features which belie normal market principles characterize the transactions. These features 'personalize' relationships and 'dematerialize' transactions which become part of a flow in the relationships involved.

Exchange relationships in non-individual societies, are easier to understand because they have several clear spheres of exchange each with institutional forms, moral values and vocabularies. But understanding these relationships in our society is obscured because of the apparent dominance of the market exchange sphere. The natural insulation between different spheres is breached by general purpose currency—money—and market terms pervade all forms of transaction. This fails to emphasize the social dimension and as a result explanations of non-market exchange in our society are described as motivated for economic benefit.

When legal authority, police, security or courts—all extraneous to the amateur sphere—become involved, they 'rematerialize' transactions and 'depersonalize' relationships completing a *reconversion* from the amateur sphere back to the market exchange sphere. This process is possible because 1) the social availability of a *general* language of retrospective description only acknowledges economically rational interpretations 2) the linguistic reconstruction of events occurs in contexts alien to the interaction.

Serious problems arise in both criminal processing and control when these are framed in market exchange terms and applied to the an ateur trading sphere. To avoid these problems we propose building on the normative controls typically found at work which limit categories and amounts and institutionalizing these through workplace courts.

Assessments vary about the amount of G.N.P. which is redistributed 'off the backs of lorries', through pilfering from factories and offices, via under the counter sales from shops and warehouses and by way of inflated bills and expense claims.[2] In 1976, one researcher bravely computed the grand total lost in the U.K. via pilfering and fiddling to be £1,305 millions.[3] The wheeling and dealing involved in acquiring and distributing this sum is not, in our view, part of 'normal' crime. Rather, it is a product of the activities of ordinary people who earn a basic income in full-time legitimate employment but who also take part in various kinds of on-the-side amateur property crime.

*Illegal amateur trading*

In our research on amateur property crime and particularly on the pilfering and fiddling of goods from work and their subsequent resale,[4] we have been impressed by a number of features that appear to typify these kinds of transaction. These strongly suggest that we are dealing neither with 'normal' crime nor 'normal' trade: that we are dealing, indeed, with a different kind of activity with its own rules and norms. This is not to argue that there is one distinct activity separate from other kinds of trading. Instead, we maintain that trading exchanges can be seen as a continuum ranging from commercial dealings in which the exchange is impersonal and contractual, to social transactions where the exchange is highly personalized, context dependent and more fully bound up with relationships. Examples of the latter end of the continuum can be found in the typical market exchange transactions of non-industrial societies such as barter in village or rural communities and in neighbourhood exchange among urban ghetto groups. Neither are we suggesting that any particular people are more inclined to transactions at one or other end of the continuum, but that depending upon the social context, people can and frequently do, engage in transactions at different parts of the continuum. Thus in those exchanges where a person's basic income derives from legitimate sources and where goods are obtained at little apparent personal economic cost, the emphasis shifts from the contractual to the relational end of the exchange continuum. A number of features that are common to such transactions can be identified.

The following two examples are typical of amateur trade exchange. The first is the case of a dealer selling stolen goods as a favour to a receiver; the second of a dealer selling goods as a favour to a middle man:

I was in the pub and saying, 'So many coal mines round here, where can I buy coal?' and someone says, 'Oh, we'll send George around.' So George appeared with two or three hundredweight of coal, and there was I, money in hand, about to pay him, and he says, 'Oh, you owe me a pint', something like this. So I said, 'Well where does the service end?' this type of thing. He says, 'If you need anything, let me know and I'll see what I can do.'
This mate of mine as he was at the time offers me a colour T.V. set for sixty pounds. O.K. right, but I didn't know anything on about how many's coming round. When this guy knocked the door and said to me, 'I've got it.' I expected to see a small Ford Transit; outside was a fifteen ton lorry and when he pulled the back up it was just crammed full of them. So I said 'What am I supposed to do with 'em?' and he said, 'Can you get rid of any?' So you think to yourself, alright well I'll do this guy a favour. He's got a load of 'em and he can't move 'em. So I spent all afternoon and evening and got rid of every one. You know, somebody else knew somebody else.

When we go deeper into this kind of exchange we can abstract certain characteristics which contrast with the features considered appropriate to the more common, commercial market exchange. The distinctiveness of amateur trading then becomes apparent.

There is, firstly in these exchanges, a general negation of the firmness found in commercial dealings. In particular the price, rather than being fixed in advance, is deliberately blurred, and there is no certainty that the transaction will go ahead.

CRIME AT WORK                                               247

This can be seen in the first example above, when George was later asked for 'cheap' bricks:

I said the nearest thing to coal, 'I'll have some bricks'. So he says, 'How many do you want and what colour?' So I looked at a few, and I met him in the pub and said, 'I think I need about a hundred and fifty of such and such', and he said, 'I can't promise anything but I'll keep my eyes open'.

Second, there is virtual insistence on payment for such goods being made either wholly or at least partly in kind rather than money. The phrase 'you owe me a pint' or the typical giving and receiving of gifts as part of the transaction enhances the distinction between market exchange and illegal amateur exchange, making it more difficult in the latter to accurately represent the material value of the goods involved.

Oh it was about three weeks later he turned up in his coal lorry and they were on the back. He took them off, so he says, 'Now you owe me a brandy' or something like this. When I went in the pub I put a quid or two behind the bar for him. They chalk it up on his board. See when he goes in there to buy a drink, it's paid for. It's a way of you know . . . it's like saying, 'You buy me a drink', but it's a more positive thing than that. It's a good system. It's quite nice, quite pleasant.[5]

Third, despite answering questions about why they deal in stolen goods in terms of economic rationality—they say they do it to make money—a typical feature of these exchanges is that little money is made.[6] Statements like, 'I charged the same price as I paid' or 'you can't make money out of friends' are the rule rather than the exception. Even between dealers where the quantity of goods exchanged can be large, those concerned appear to make very little profit out of their activities; indeed in terms of the time and effort they expend, it can be argued that they often make a loss. This was so in the case of the television deal quoted earlier:

So this guy went round in this big lorry all night, 'cause he had to get the lorry back, and I had to go round and collect all the money in. And when it came to it everyone got everything. I even paid for my set. I think the guy gave me a stereo for nothing, but I never made anything. I charged 'em the same price, sixty pounds, and never made a penny, not a dime, and I'd shifted the lot. I was out in the back garden burning all the cases they came in. The thing was they didn't know anybody who could set them up, and I had to go round all their houses tuning 'em in. I managed to move the whole lorry-load, cash, that night . . . He had thousands in his hand. See I had a bit of money with me and I backed people. If you wanted to pay by cheque, I'll say, 'O.K. Stu you pay the cheque to me, and I'll pay the cash for you. But even he didn't make anything on it, because it had to go back to the goods inwards, the boys in the admin. staff.

The example also illustrates a fourth feature of illegal amateur exchange; the provision of extra services such as giving credit, free delivery of goods and in this case, tuning the televisions. Such extra services further undermine the possibility of profit being made and blurs the price, but it also emphasizes the relational aspect of the transaction in that it demonstrates the goodwill and preparedness on the part of the seller to 'put himself out' for the buyer.

A fifth significant feature seen in both the brick and television examples, is the provision of credit as a matter of course. This serves continually to defer the

equalization of accounts so that there is always a need to continue the relationship.
The desirable state is never to meet the others' price exactly, so that the relationship
is never concluded. The situation is managed so as to retain an element of imbalance;
a credit surplus with one party and a debt with the other.[7]

A sixth and fundamental difference between illegal amateur and market exchange
lies in terms of their different attention to time. Market exchange places emphasis
on the completion of a transaction in the minimum possible period with a normal
expectation of the immediate availability of commodities and money. Where
deferred payments are part of the contract, the terms of payment are of course very
narrowly defined. Illegal amateur dealings, in contrast, are classically permeated
with delays, lapses, lags and pauses in time. There is time between the expressed
need for the goods and the setting up of a deal; between the sealing of an arrangement and delivery of the goods, and importantly between the receipt of goods and
'payment'.

Finally, and related to these last two distinctions, there is a difference between the
two types of exchange which lies in the concept of flow: transactions are only one
event in a series. And, though we have emphasized the distinction between illegal
amateur exchange and normal commercial exchange, we have only so far focussed
upon the exchange point of the deal. But the deal itself is set in a wider network of
related events: it possesses an essential set of preliminaries and consequences which
would be redundant in typical exchange transactions within Western market
economies, though common in those of barter economics of non-industrial society.

*Preliminaries and consequences*

While we have emphasized that amateur trade transactions offer little in the way
of personal economic gain for particular individuals, they nevertheless give an
overall benefit to the network of people within which they typically take place and
they are essentially exclusive. In such circumstances, it is not unusual for groups to
limit membership and we are likely to find that 'rites de passage' mark entry to
them: the illegal amateur trade is not dissimilar in this respect.[8]

The preliminaries begin with attempts to establish a relationship which allows
both parties to judge whether the other will make a suitable trading acquaintance.
This involves (a) an assessment of formal role play, i.e. how a person performs in
legitimate role situations; (b) a series of apparently informal 'chats' in which his
suitability as a trading acquaintance is considered; and (c) the provisional typing of
him as a prospect. If, during the course of this threefold assessment certain assumptions are not met or expectancies not satisfied, then a deal may never get underway
and the relationship never becomes established. The following examples taken from
different contexts show how a person is assessed and either rejected or accepted:

To start with I think you've got to live locally. See you go over the pub for a jar . . . and you sit there
and listen to the blokes talking and have a chat with them, because they're really sociable. If you'll sit and
listen, they'll talk all night and buy you drinks and you're "in" very quickly in that sense . . . After a

time, you know bush telegraph and all that, they know a fair bit about you. They know from the post-man where you get your letters from, and how much milk you have and who comes to see you. They know the lot. And if there's any sort of doubts about you as a person or they don't like you, then nothing you can say or do will induce them to do anything. Although they're friendly people, they'll talk to you and you can play dominoes and this sort of thing, bring you in on their darts game and so on. *It takes a long time before they'll really accept you. Not until you've been accepted will they ever offer you anything.*
There was one character who they wouldn't even dream of approaching. He was a very upright little man, a foreman, not earning particularly good money. If anything dodgy was going on, they would not let that bloke in on it. They said that through various sorts of probings, that the character was deadly honest and that you don't trust someone who is honest. See there are various sorts of attitudes and beliefs and the character that doesn't share these stands out like a sore thumb, though he's never actually tested. So somewhere his ideas just don't fit.

However, the whole of this vetting process is not something that can be hurried along. It takes time to build up a relationship, and time to accept someone as 'alright'.

It doesn't happen over just one casual meeting. It happens over say three or four times. You know something kind of sparks something off and you strike up a relationship and then they come out with it. But it's a slow progression. It's not something that happens instantly. It only happens over three or four meetings. They get to know you. He won't just kind of offer it to you there and then. It happens that you see him in the road and say, 'hello', or he'll be at a set of traffic lights and the next time he comes in you say 'Oh, I saw you last week at a set of traffic lights', and there we are . . . we're getting a relationship between two people. Then you offer him a cigarette, for instance, and he'll say, 'Well I can get you some cigarettes cheap', See, so you strike up a relationship . . . You've got to have a relationship or else everything doesn't twig.

Having got the relationship to the appropriate pitch the new prospect will then be tested with an offer or a request for 'cheap' goods. Ditton has observed that this comprises a particularly meaning-loaded question which he describes as the 'alerting phrase'; 'Classically, between sales and bakery staffs, the "alerting phrase" for those "in the know" is the demand or offer of "extra bread".'[9] He noted that this alerting phrase appears in the form of the question. 'Is there any bread about?' Indeed, he argues that an outright offer is never made as the risks and penalties of rejection are too great. Our own research confirms this to be the case. The dealing stage is opened with what members described variously as a 'test-line' or a 'probe-line' concerning the offer or request for 'cheap gear or cheap stuff':

'In our works there's a standard line that they try people out with. They say, "Would *you* like to sell me this? Not the firm but *you*?" If the bloke doesn't twig he's a berk. If he doesn't see it, it's forgotten and they don't push it any further. It's there in every situation. You can probe and if the bloke's with you you're away.'

'People don't come right out with it. They say, "I've got something a bit cheap here". They never say, 'I've got a stolen bit of gear here." All people say is . . . most people say, 'I've got a cheap bit of stuff here. Want to have a go at it?' And then there's a conversation and one might say, 'It's a bit the other way'. And the other says, 'Who's fuckin' worried?'

Despite a provisional typing of the prospect as favourable, failure to acknowledge the test-line or a rejection of the offer has a dramatic effect on the original judge-ment:

'There's an unspoken understanding that everyone is willing to buy stuff cheap and the bloke who won't buy it cheap becomes an outsider and dodgy for a start. The bloke who turns down cheap stuff and the bloke that never buys anything gets a reputation and there must be something odd about him. Don't mention it to him. Keep it quiet from him'.

Of course, like the absence of money, the strict regulation and vetting of new-comers, might have more to do with protecting members of the trade from both the awareness and consequences of the illegal nature of their enterprise, than with any desire for social homogeneity. But this begs the question of the meaning context of the enterprise, which is a matter of interpretation. Our experience suggests that although the illegality of the activity may have been the original reason for organi-zing trade in a particular way—to protect against being caught—once in operation such matters become of secondary importance.

Finally, when a prospect has been 'sounded out' and a deal concluded, there is a consequence—the conclusion of the deal will be celebrated. This is very often accomplished through drink and, as shown in the above examples follows from 'putting something behind the bar'. Drink is an ideal and very common medium for celebration. It is offered and taken in a location that is demonstrably social and which therefore makes it distinct from locations typically associated with market exchange.[10] And the 'ten bob behind the bar' is never expected to stay behind the bar or to be consumed by the recipient, but to be distributed as drink throughout the group. This kind of drinking therefore extends social contact beyond the principal parties to the transaction since it grants the donee a 'bank of social credit' he can dispense at his discretion. In doing this he is enabled to pay back obligations or to create new ones and thus can rise in prestige and esteem. Drinking thus widens the social effects of a transaction to affirm and disseminate common values through a group. At the same time the morality of each transaction is reaffirmed in terms of the groups own norm and values.

The regular conversion of resources derived from this type of trade thus binds together the members of a trading group. But in converting material resources to social ones through communal drinking it also reduces the possibility of visible capital accumulation. This in its turn reduces the possibility of differences arising within the group that can be attributed to the trade. The overall social effect of such drinking therefore, is essentially egalitarian.[11]

In short, then, illegal amateur trade has considerable claim to be regarded as existing at the social rather than the market exchange end of the transactional continuum. While like the institutions of market exchange, it is concerned with the transmission of goods, unlike market exchange it is surrounded by important social features which emphasize a different order of activity. Moreover, it is also different from conventional crime in so far as this is seen as dishonest activity carried on primarily for the pursuit of economic gain. However, a dilemma remains. Not only does the law and all its agents treat the two sets of activites as one, as indeed do other people not involved, but so apparently do the participants who are engaged in illegal amateur trade. When asked why they practice this type of trade they invariably reply in terms of market exchange: they do it 'for bargains, why else?'

Thus, in looking at amateur trading activity we find a marked distinction between description and actions that is analogous to the 'money veil' in economics: the 'real' activity is obscured by linguistic usage. How, then, can we broaden our analysis to further understand not only the behaviour of the participants but also that of 'outsiders' who so frequently come into contact with members of the trade as security officers, law enforcers and other representatives of criminal processing?

*Stripping the linguistic veil: an approach from social anthropology*

We have seen that illegal amateur exchange comprises a range of activities governed by rules very different from those normal to market exchange relationships. It might be useful therefore, to examine comparative material on systems of exchange in societies other than our own and particularly in those without money, in an attempt to gain clearer understanding of how this particular institution operates in our own society.

In offering this approach we draw on material derived from anthropological fieldwork and in so doing are able to exploit that discipline's well-established tradition of comparative methodology. A starting point is Sahlins' observation:

'A great proportion of primitive exchange, much more than our own traffic, has as its decisive function this . . . instrumental one: (that) the material flow underwrites or initiates social relations'.[12]

One of the greatest sources of insight into exchange activity comes, however, not from an anthropologist but an economic historian, Karl Polanyi, whose work has had a profound influence on anthropologists. Polanyi has shown[13] that most societies possess what he calls 'multi-centric economies'—that is they have *several* systems of exchange for different classes of goods. He was concerned to show that the market exchange sphere—though dominant in our money based economy—was only one of a number of exchange systems and that most non-industrial societies possess at least one and often two non-market spheres; these he called the redistributive and the reciprocal.

Redistribution involves the movement of goods towards a centre that administers its dispersal in ways and to people defined by the centre. It is essentially dependent on hierarchically recognized authority. A good example of a society dominated by this principle is provided by the Swat Pathans of Pakistan[14] whose rice crop, when gathered, is centrally redistributed. It accordingly forms the economic basis to political power among this people and, though other spheres than the redistributive exist, they are less significant. In our own society the redistributive sphere is represented by taxation and through social welfare payments.[15]

Reciprocal exchange on the other hand, is based on the movement of goods between people bound together in non-hierarchical and non-market ways— the transfer of goods is secondary to the relationship of the people involved—as found for instance among kin groups and in our own society through present giving.[16] Perhaps the most celebrated example derives from Malinowski's work in Melanesia among the Trobriand Islanders where much of their produce and ceremonial objects are exchanged through reciprocal arrangements of various kinds.[17]

For our purposes there are two important points to note. The first is that in such multi-centric economies as have been studied each sphere of exchange is thought of as distinct and self-contained: it has its own rules, its own morality and its own language in the form of terms appropriate only to exchanges in that sphere. The second point is that spheres are always ranked in prestige.[18] The spheres are therefore relatively insulated from each other, particularly in the absence of a common denominator currency—that is, money—which necessarily crosses all spheres. But insulation is always incomplete and even without such a currency, conversions are possible between the spheres. As we shall see, it is through this important process of conversion, the accepted ways of 'bending' rules of exchange, that we come to understand not only the economy and much of the social system of these different societies but also more of what is involved in the illegal amateur trade within our own society.

If we look first at an African society researched by the social anthropologist, Paul Bohannon who lived with the Tiv of Northern Nigeria in the days before money was widely introduced, we can see how these spheres operated and inter-acted in practice and how conversions between them were effected. Bohannon found that the Tiv operated a multi-centric economy with three spheres. The lowest prestige sphere dealt in subsistence goods, mostly food, household require-ments and clothing and exchange was effected mostly by barter or through gift giving. It was through shrewdness in operations within this sphere that a Tiv could achieve affluence but not prestige or influence. The second sphere and rated higher in prestige, was concerned with goods and those services that granted prestige. These included cattle, brass rods, knowledge of the rites and ceremonies that gave membership in exclusive 'acombo' groupings and which granted special magical powers, medicines, slaves and a special white cloth called 'tugudu'. Brass rods were used as a store of value within this sphere and all the other commodities could be measured in terms of them. Brass rods since they are acceptable for a variety of goods, are of homogeneous quality and are durable, could therefore be con-sidered as a form of money—but this use was limited to the prestige sphere.

The third and most exclusive sphere was concerned with the exchange of people who were not slaves—particularly women as wives who were essential to provide offspring for the patrilineages which could thus ensure their continuity.

Obtaining a wife among the Tiv could be achieved in two ways. The much preferred way was to exchange a women, over whom a man had control—a daughter or a ward—into the patrilineage from whom he took his wife. The greater the number of properly exchanged wives and resultant progeny, the greater a man's prestige. The second method involved making no exchange of an equivalent woman from a man's own patrilineage which meant that such a non-exchange wife had an inferior position which penalized the prospects for their children. This kind of marriage did not add to a man's prestige.

The problem that faced a young man with no woman to exchange was how to obtain a fully legitimated marriage to an exchange wife when the only 'currency' for a wife was another woman in exchange. It was here that the process of conversion operated through the practice of 'trading up'. By hard effort a young man first acquired a reputation and a surplus of subsistence goods. This gave him affluence but not influence. He would then wait until a man of influence had need for subsistence goods—as for instance when he had to provide food for a ceremonial dance or party.

But conversions across spheres are always difficult to arrange: the ranking of spheres in terms of prestige means that trading up for one partner necessitates trading down for the other and the morality of trading down is always suspect. There are always ways of accommodating to this problem however, and though among the Tiv brass rods, tugudu or magical knowledge might be exchanged for food, they would always be accompanied by a general explanation that the customer was doing a favour to the food seller: that he was acting as a sort of patron and offering him a helping hand.

Once equipped with prestige items however, an upwardly mobile young man was well on the way to deal into the top prestige sphere—to obtain an exchange wife. But an exchange wife it will be recalled could not be exchanged for prestige goods: the only equivalent for a woman was another woman in exchange.

What happened was that the young man then sought out the guardian or father of a marriageable girl. In return for her domestic and sexual service he offered prestige goods as a token of his intention to fully complete the exchange at a later date. In the interim he lacked control or guardianship over her children and she was not regarded as fully incorporated into his family. Such a wife was known as a 'Kem' wife, a wife not exchanged for another female. She was however able to become a fully exchanged wife when her husband transferred a nubile female in exchange. This usually had to take a generation—until a daughter was of sufficient age to be given to her guardian. When this happened the exchange was then complete; the 'Kem' wife became an exchange wife, the husband and his sons were eligible to become influential and the male's family continuance was assured.

Other anthropological studies have shown the validity of such an analysis in other non-industrial societies[20] and they have confirmed their possession of multi-centric economies with different degrees of insulation between spheres and with spheres possessing their own moralities, language and relative prestige rating.

It is our contention that this operation of different spheres applies as much to our own type of society as it does to non-industrial ones. Our argument is that much of the pilfering and distribution of goods from work, actually marks the transfer or conversion of goods from the market exchange sphere of our economy, where emphasis is on the material value of the goods, to a sphere where value is placed instead on the relationship between participants to an exchange. Pilferage from work then, starts a process of amateur trading which de-materializes the goods and personalizes the transaction. We suggest that these activities might be termed the illegal amateur trading sphere and we contend that it has been neglected because our use of money and a money-based language has 'blurred' its distinctive features.

Davis has already suggested that our society comprises spheres other than the evident one of market exchange. He posits the existence of four 'sub-economies' operating in the United Kingdom each identified by the rules which govern transactions within them.[21] But it is our view that there are other spheres of exchange operating within what *appears* to be the market sphere and that the social dimensions of these exchanges are often actually more important to the members than the market transactions they masquerade as. Many studies have shown for instance that workers often form spontaneous social relationships in work and develop their own norms which are used to exercise control on production and innovation.[22] These controls are then justified on economic criteria. But on examination many restrictive practices are found not to be necessarily economically motivated but intended primarily to maintain worker unity and to develop social relationships in the workplace. Of particular interest here is Roy's now classic study of quota achievement by machine shop workers and Klein's work at 'Multi-products'.[23]

Roy found that striving for and achieving the goal of quota production in a piecework system carried its own non-economic reward: that despite workers' continual references to economic benefits no one really believed he had been making money by 'goldbricking'. Klein believes that the primary purpose of fiddling is economic but she acknowledges the strong non-economic implications of its presence.

The crucial issue is not just that there exist other spheres of exchange, but to explain how it is that only one of these, market exchange, *appears* to dominate all exchanges in our society. It is our concern to show that these other exchanges are described in the language of market exchange, and that it is such description which gives the appearance of market sphere dominance. In short, it is not that different spheres are absent, rather that we fail to recognize the difference in language. And where the distinctinctions between spheres of exchange are linguistically confused, we find that serious misunderstandings can exist which have considerable implications in areas as diverse as industrial relations, social policy formation and the operation of the law.

### The linguistic construction of amateur property crime

Talk and description are integrally bound with action and social context.[24] As we have seen, in Tiv society there is no general language for talking about exchange worlds. Rather, the Tiv have different vocabularies appropriate to, and generated in, different social contexts. When talking about exchange they have three complete sets of exchange vocabulary each corresponding to their three spheres of exchange. And bases of comparison between items in different spheres are not easily made, since there is an absence of that common denominator—general purpose money. But in our society language does not essentially depend on, nor is it necessarily tied to, the social context of its generation. Yet in illegal amateur trading, which in practice negates features of market exchange, the language that is used nonetheless reflects the market very strongly. People use words such as 'perks' and 'bargains' which serve to blur the distinction between spheres. Why should this be so? Perhaps the greatest contribution to this process of blurring comes from our society's use of money—a common currency which unlike the Tiv's brass rods offers all its functions throughout all the spheres of exchange and which in turn gives rise to a general purpose language or nexus of words that govern conventional transactions such as 'rewards', productivity', 'bonus', 'incentives', 'perks' and 'bargains'.

Money allows, at least implicitly, an underlying comparative valuation—a material rating of all items or services in all spheres on the basis that it is itself a common denominator. Once money enters a society, it possesses a tendency to pervade all institutions and activities. Once the concept enters our heads it produces a momentum that leads toward the common pricing of everything. But it also does more than this. As the use of words like 'perk' and 'bargain' suggests, the extra function served by money is the provision of a general purpose vocabulary. Such a vocabulary, indeed such a language, enables us to talk *about* events in contexts *other* than those comprising their action. At the same time *talking about action* is itself a meaningful action having its own motives through which the original action is able to be reconstructed.[25]

When illegal amateur exchange is talked about between its practitioners, reconstruction is necessarily minimal and much use is made of the implicit meaning of the action. This is because members take for granted their shared assumptions. However, when talked about by practitioners to others, or by others between themselves, the implicit meaning of the action is absent and the only recourse is to a general purpose language which is framed in terms of the particular language of market exchange. Indeed, the language of the market exchange sphere has emerged as, and constitutes, *the* general purpose language governing all spheres of exchange.

We are saying that the socially accepted and thereby available way of talking about and describing exchange events in our culture, particularly the way of allocating motive to an individual's action is one in which motive must be thought of as being economically rational. This is especially so where the action talked about is being questioned and judged.[26] However, the language of economic behaviour has its own clearly defined sets of rules which allow some constructions of explanation and not others. These rules relate economic implications of certain kinds of action to the notion of individual property ownership rights. Thus, taking the economic motive in a transaction to be the sole or at least the most important, they prohibit other motives such as social relational ones. These are represented as being 'uncool', 'weak', 'superficial', 'devious rationalizations', or 'communism' and definitely not the *'real'* or 'underlying' motive. In short, when talking about this kind of behaviour people are forced to rely upon the socially available verbal resource of a general purpose language that is economically rational.

It is for this reason then, that members of the amateur trade explain their action in terms of economic rationality. When asked 'Why do you do it?', they reply in general terms that everyone can understand. They say things like, 'I've always made a few bob on the stuff I've had', 'I'm doing it for the money every time', 'All I did it for was to get a few things for myself', 'Bloody hell, I get all this gear cheap don't I? Look around me. I've got all this stuff that I'd probably have to pay through the nose for, that I probably wouldn't even have'.[27] But a closer examination of the practitioner's activity, as we have seen, shows that the *meaning* of the action to those involved is often different from that expressed. As we saw, illegal amateur traders rarely make money in the way their descriptions suggest and their activity is usually organized on socially co-operative, rather than on market principles.[28]

One implication of the use of an economically rational mode of explanation is that members may talk about certain categories of events as being criminal or undesirable, while at the same time they engage in them. This contradiction is then made to appear consistent by incorporating a mode of description in the action which removes that behaviour from the criminal category without admitting or expressing the social meaning, through relying on the accepted mode of economic explanation such as 'borrowing', 'buying cheap', 'perks', 'bargains' and in some occupational cases, considering the action as justifiable earnings.[29] Classically, one practitioner said:

'If somebody came along and said to me, "This is stolen goods. Do you want it?" I wouldn't want to know. No thanks. I wouldn't take it. But if they said "It's off the back of a lorry", I wouldn't mind. I don't think I'd like to know if they were stolen. I'd like to kid myself it was alright. I wouldn't like to know it was pinched. I wouldn't like it right out. It might enter the back of my mind but provided they didn't tell me straight to my face I would try and avoid the issue there. I'd say, "I'd like it very much".'

However, there are more serious implications of the dominance of the language of market exchange.

### General language, legal processing and social control

We have said that in most societies it is usual for exchanges to occur within single spheres and they appear as a result to excite little attention. But in all societies some exchanges occur *between* spheres. And we have noted that it is these 'intra' sphere exchanges termed 'conversions', which always excite moral judgements since in all multi-centric economies the spheres tend to be hierarchically ranked on the basis of moral and status valuations. But two factors must be considered before this analysis can usefully be extended and applied to our own type of society. The first involves the consideration of variation in our society: of acknowledging that significant numbers of people might well attach different ratings to the same activity. Some people rank the market exchange sphere as morally higher than the redistributive sphere; others rank it lower. It is arguable that such moral ratings vary very widely depending on the social context or situation in which judgements are made. The second factor comes from the presence of our general purpose language derived from market exchange. This, as we have argued, is supported on a basis of money which is by definition a general purpose commodity.

These two factors taken together provide our problem. They supply on the one hand, a set of inarticulate context dependent motives—a rationale for conversion which cannot be communicated in terms of the general language and which inverts the perhaps more conventional rating of spheres; it degrades the conventional rating granted to the market exchange sphere and elevates the amateur trade sphere. On the other hand we find that general purpose language offers a highly articulate vehicle to use in criminal processing where the primacy of market exchange is universally assumed. Indeed, on the basis of the abstract general language a specific language is developed which is peculiar to the court context, but which bears little relation to the specific context of the talked-about action. It should hardly be surprising that the coincidence of contact between the two should be negligible and that neither side should feel they are communicating with the other.

Because legal processing is accomplished in terms of the 'general' language which is a very specific form of its own highly abstract legal jargon, it depends heavily on the reconstruction of events from members' accounts and from descriptions uttered in court which are divorced from the sources of the action's generation. Legal processing also occurs in a context of formal highly ritualized account giving. The exchange which, in the event in question, constitutes the action being judged, and which occurred in its own sphere, with its own rules, meanings and language, is thus transformed in the court and becomes mystified as part of the drama of that context.[30] It is worth noting that in all the ways of talking about events that comprise the everyday activities of amateur trading, the practitioner never uses legal terms like 'handling stolen goods', 'receiving stolen goods', 'theft by an employee' or 'false accounting', which are the legal glosses applied to these activities. And since in the courts, events are reconstructed in ways which negate non-economic or social meanings, we find the value of goods assessed not in terms of qualitative values or the meaning this value has to the members of the trade but in terms of an economic statement of their price. Moreover, the actual exchange price is not seen as the significant part of the exchange. Rather, the amount of recrimination is more likely to be based in terms of the *original* price of the item. In short, the reconstruction of events in courts *depersonalizes* the amateur trading interaction and *rematerializes* the goods just as the original actions dematerialized the goods and personalized the transactions.

Fundamentally, such reconstruction by the courts is only possible because of the use of an abstract *general* language which allows a bridging to be made between the two contexts of amateur trading sphere and courtroom ritual. The actions of the amateur sphere are translated to the general language and then further translated down to the courts language. The general language is, in other words, 'filled-in' with commonsense knowledge about the context of the trade which would not be recognized by its practitioners. However, only *one* way of filling-in is given legitimacy in official or court contexts: the way which relies upon the assumptions of market exchange. Even where a non-economic motive is given credence by the questioning authorities, it is implicit that if the practitioner does not confirm their commonsense view of his crime then he will be given harsher treatment than might otherwise be the case.[31] Such an approach necessarily reduces further the possibility of communication between the parties. If these approaches are typical, then ironically the court's objectivity is reduced. Nor can it be otherwise: the two stage translation process must mask communication and indeed encourage bias when a practitioner's activity is being interpreted.

But there is a more serious indictment of the failure to give legitimacy to other ways of talking and one that affects relationships outside the courts. We have suggested that a general language couched in market terms serves to emphasize a dominance of the profit motive in transactions and serves too to limit alternate understandings. One implication of this is that those responsible for controlling behaviour may well adopt policies without adequate understanding of the social context of resultant action. Thus people responsible for controlling occupational pilferage whether police, security or management—may invoke increasing enforcement without understanding the changes that might result.

Increases in enforcement are especially likely in times of general economic stringency when pressures mount to reduce 'shrinkage', 'wastage', pilferage' and 'fiddling'. But enforcement, even if unsuccessful in economic terms is still likely to be resisted if workers see it as eroding their social benefits. Resistance can take a variety of forms depending on factors such as how collectivized is the workforce, the nature of its technology and the state of markets—both of the labour involved and of the goods handled. It can range from an increase in labour turnover to go-slows or outright strikes and can be manifest over friction points that are apparently quite removed from issues to do with pilferage or enforcement.[32]

These are obviously effects to be avoided if at all possible. But any effects are likely to be exacerbated if such extra enforcement comes from outside the organization—as for instance through the form of specialist security agencies. These people, by the nature of their roles are isolated from the normal social relationships in a work place and they are trained to see losses in pure legal and economic terms.[33] In this sense they are even further removed from 'normal' work place relationships than are managers who usually act as 'internal' controllers.

The common ground between these positions is likely to be small indeed and the ways of controlling pilferage that result are therefore likely to be mutually incomprehensible. But the problems that can arise from pilferage as well as from inappropriate enforcement are avoidable without the abnegation of control if more attention were given to natural normative controls existing in the amateur trading sphere.

### Normative control and context representatives

If, instead of increasing specialist policing and enforcement, some way could be found to harness the local sources of control that are exercised naturally by amateur trading practitioners, then both more just and also more effective controls might result. Essentially what would be involved here is for some degree of policing, enforcement and juridicial activity in the amateur trading sphere to be undertaken by the very people who practice trading.

To a certain extent, moral limits and social control in terms understandable to its members, have always been applied in the context of amateur trading. Those who fiddle and pilfer from work and trade the proceeds apply their own definitions and rules as to what constitutes theft, how their activity is defined, whom one should take from and how much one should take. Any breaking of these definitions and rules is seen as theft by the members and regarded in the same way as it is in law: it is the dishonest taking of goods for material gain and it invites local sanctions:

'Like I say there are two different sorts of stealing. I wouldn't go out and break into somewhere and nick something. That's stealing. That's bad. You know like the bloke who actually goes out and does it for a living, like breaking into somewhere and nicking a lorry-load of stuff. See the people who steal in the way I know are stealing from their works, their factories or garages. They are pilfering the odd box of this or box of that. They don't consider that wrong really. That's perks to them'.
'You know you can talk a lot about what is legal and what isn't. To my mind this is probably technically illegal. Morally it isn't because nobody is making money out of it . . . not real money. Well alright the person who's receiving the goods is saving money if you like, but he's not actually making anything. He's not going out stealing the stuff . . .not hawking it around, making a profit on it, not in actual cash terms. And the bloke who is actually selling it, he's not making much out of it. He's getting favours more than anything'.

In addition, the rules of the amateur trade place limitations on the *amount* of material that may be taken and these limits are backed by peer-set sanctions. Longshoremen (dockers) as only one example, have been found to limit their pilfering of cargoes: an economically 'rational' limit is set, which is linked through management collusion to an accepted maximum. Up to this level pilferage is legitimate; beyond it is assessed as deviant. The limit to pilferage is thus morally rated, through being tied to a sense of what is appropriate. Their formula 'working the value of the boat', relates pilferage levels to legitimate earnings and ensures that:

'If a man takes more than the value of the boat, he is taking more than his moral entitlement. This alters the nature of his action . . . Up to an agreed level, pilfered cargo is seen as a moral entitlement; beyond this it is seen as theft'.[34]

In other words, it is the quantitative aspect of their activity that is of prime importance to longshoremen in contrast to the qualitative aspect that is judged in courts: after a certain quantity has been exceeded, this changes the quality of the act.

Of course statements by participants which make distinctions between what is right and wrong in their terms cannot be taken at face value. In certain circumstances they may also serve as rationalizations, excuses and justifications which mask any sense of immorality in a wider societal sense.[35] However, no matter what functions they serve in this broader structure of events they are nevertheless rules of action which are adhered to in the context of the activity. Thus when such excesses occur, social control, usually in the effective form of social ostracism, is operated by other workers. In the dock study, one longshoreman took too much cargo: he went above the value of the boat. His fellow longshoremen then broke into his car, and the goods were redistributed. These limits and the sanctions which operate if they are broken, have also been observed in taxying, hotels, shops and among deliverymen. It is perhaps not surprising therefore, that such self administered, group, or communal controls are effective:

'At this level it doesn't seem to multiply at all. You know it doesn't get any worse or any more rampant. It works well . . . very well, and it helps the people a lot. You know from that point of view it is just not immoral . . . I think in fact it's very, very moral. I think it's a good thing'.

Indeed, at a more general level, it is gradually being realized that a just and effective form of social control for a whole range of social deviancy is that exercised by the deviants themselves. The vast mushrooming of self-help groups in the broad 'health' field, which has occurred over the last decade is testimony to a growing awareness of this principle. Various forms of deviancy ranging from alcoholism, gambling, smoking, obesity and anorexia to sex exposing, child abuse and wife battering are now found best controlled, handled and managed, not by professional controlling agencies such as doctors, psychiatrists or social workers, but by groups of deviants themselves; groups like Alcoholics Anonymous, Gamblers Anonymous, Smokers Anonymous, Weight Watchers, Anorexic Aid, Cui Bono, Parents Anonymous and Women's Aid.[36]

We suggest therefore that the same kind of controls could be achieved in the area of amateur property crime by facilitating the setting up of some form of court, situated in the workplace and composed of locally elected workers. By workers we do not mean *any* workers as in the present magistrate system. Rather we mean people from the same social context in which the activities' norms were breached.

Obviously such an idea as the self-regulation of criminal deviance will raise fears about whether the system would get out of hand; whether for instance, mini mafia-like protection rackets might emerge. Our experience suggests this is not very likely. Despite the mythology, Alcoholics Anonymous is not a drinking club; the Paedophile Information Exchange does not seek out children with whom to have sexual relations and Gamblers Anonymous does not run a syndicate. All these groups are composed of people who enjoy their deviant activity even if to a greater or lesser extent it gives them problems. To resolve their problems they curtail the activity. There is no reason to suppose that the same system would operate differently for the kind of criminal deviance we have been discussing. At present, while we know that these kinds of self regulation systems have been in operation in the U.K. sweet manufacturing industry for years, no systematic research has been undertaken on the processes at work and no assessments made of their effectiveness or perceived fairness. We are now looking into this area and we hope that our suggestions will stimulate other research.[37]

*Notes*

1. Accepted 10.3.77. We wish to thank Stan Cohen, Keith England, Raymond Firth, Chris Harris, Leonard Mars, Paul Rock and Nigel Walker for their valuable criticisms of earlier drafts of this paper. Stuart Henry wishes to thank the Social Science Research Council and the University of Kent at Canterbury for their research support, Gerald Mars is pleased to acknowledge his debt to the Nuffield Foundation who supported his thinking in this area through the award of a Research Fellowship and to Prof. Nigel Walker and the staff of the Cambridge Institute of Criminology who offered him support and hospitality during its tenure.

2. Carter estimates that 2% of G.N.P. is stolen but concentrates on 'formal' theft that appears on inventory and insurance records. See Carter, R. L. *Theft in the Market*. Hobart Papers No. 60. Institute of Economic Affairs, London, 1974.

3. Ditton, J. 'Perks, Pilferage and the Fiddle: Invisible Wages and the Hidden Economy' *Mimeo*, University of Durham, 1976.

4. Henry, S. 'Stolen Goods: The Amateur Trade', *Uupublished Ph.D. thesis*, University of Kent, 1975; Mars, G. 'Chance Punters and the Fiddle: Institutionalized Pilferage in a Hotel Dining Room' In: Warner, M. (ed.) *The Sociology of the Workplace*, London: Allen & Unwin, 1973; Mars, G. 'Dock Pilferage' in: Rock and McIntosh (eds.) *Deviance and Social Control*, London: Tavistock, 1974. Mars, G. and Mitchell, P. *Room for Reform: A Case Study on Industrial Relations in the Hotel Industry*. Open University Press, 1976.

5. This avoidance of money may also be an effective way of avoiding the illegal implications of stolen goods which would accur if they had a fixed price.

6. Henry, S. 'The Other Side of the Fence', *Sociological Review* 24 (1976), pp. 793–806.

7. Davis, J. 'Forms and Norms: The Economy of Social Relations' *Man*, 8, (1973), pp. 159–176.

8. Van Gennep, A., *The Rites of Passage* (English Translation) London, 1960.

9. Ditton, J. 'The Fiddler: A Sociological Analysis of Forms of Blue-Collar Employee Theft Amongst Bread Salesmen'. *Unpublished Ph.D. Thesis*, University of Durham, 1975, p. 277.

10. Ditton, J. *op cit.* has noted that payment for goods, which he calls the 'pay-off', occurs at a different time and place from the purchase. He accounts for this in terms of the protection it gives participants from its illegal interpretation by those not involved. However, as we have said, our interpretation is that these lags in time and place, between exchange of goods and the payment for them confirm reciprocal trust between the parties.

11. See Mars, G. 'An Anthropological Study of Longshoremen and of Industrial Relations in the Port of St. John's, Newfoundland, Canada'. *Unpublished Ph.D. Thesis*, University of

262                STUART HENRY AND GERALD MARS

London, 1972, Ch. 7, for a discussion of drink as a medium of social credit and relationship ranking. Mary Douglas has discussed spending and saving habits and the different nature of 'strong group' and 'strong grid' societies. See *New Society*, 32 (1975) p. 189 and *Natural Symbols: Explorations in Cosmology*. Barrie and Jenkins, London, 1970·

12. Sahlins, M. *Stone Age Economics*. London: Tavistock, 1974.
13. Polanyi, K. *The Great Transformation*. Boston, Beacon Press, 1960.
14. Barth, F. *Political Leadership Among Swat Pathans*. L.S.E. Monographs on Social Anthropology No. 19 Athlone Press, University of London, 1959.
15. See Davis, J. 'Gifts and the U.K. Economy'. *Man*, 7, (1972), pp. 408–429.
16. Shurmer, P. 'The Gift Game'. *New Society*, 18, (1972), pp. 1,242–1,245.
17. Malinowski, B. *Argonauts of the Western Pacific*. London, Routledge, 1922.
18. Dalton, M. *Men Who Manage*. New York: Wiley & Sons, 1964.
19. Bohannon, P. 'Some Principles of Exchange and Investment Among The Tiv'. *American Anthropologist*, 57, (1955), pp. 60–70.
20. See Firth, R. *Primitive Polynesian Economy*, 2nd Ed. London: Routledge and Kegan Paul, 1965, whose work on spheres of exchange considerably predated Polanyi.
21. Davis, J. 'Gifts and the U.K. Economy', *Man*, 7, (1972), pp. 408–429.
22. Lupton, T. *On the Shop Floor*. London: Pergamon Press, 1963.
23. Roy, D. 'Work Satisfaction and Social Rewards in Quota Achievement: An Analysis of Piecework Incentive'. *American Sociological Review*, 18, (1953), pp. 507–514. and Klein, L. *Multiproducts Ltd*. London, H.M.S.O. 1964.
24. Mills, C. W. 'Situated Actions and Vocabularies of Motive'. *American Sociological Review*, 5, (1940), pp. 904–913.
25. *Ibid.*
26. *Ibid.* Blumstein, *et al.* 'The Honouring of Accounts'. *American Sociological Review*, 39, (1964), pp. 551–566; Taylor, L. 'The Significance and Interpretation of Motivational Questions: The Case of Sex Offenders'. *Sociology*, 6, (1972), pp. 23–29.
27. Henry, S., op cit., (1976).
28. *Ibid.*
29. Henry, S. 'Fencing with Accounts: The Language of Moral Bridging'. *British Journal of Law and Society*, 3, (1976), pp. 91–100.
30. Carlen, P. 'The Staging of Magistrates Justice', *British Journal of Criminology*, 16, (1976), pp. 48–55.
31. See Taylor, op cit.
32. Goulder, A. W. *Wildcat Strike*. Harper, New York, 1965.
33. Oliver, E. and Wilson, J. *Security Manual*, 2nd Edition, Gower Press, 1974. This does not, of course, preclude them from sometimes becoming a part of the trading activity. For a discussion of how police and security co-operate with fences, see Henry, S. 'On the Fence'. *British Journal Law and Society* 4, (1977) pp. 124–34.
34. Mars, G. op cit. (1974) p. 266.
35. Henry, S. op cit. (1976) at note 29.
36. Robinson, D. and Henry, S. *Self-Help and Health*. London, Martin Robertson Ltd., 1977.
37. We are currently carrying out work on self-regulation and policing in the 'Hidden Economy' group of the Outer Circle Policy Unit. See Henry S, *The Hidden Economy*. London, Martin Robertson, 1978.

*Biographical notes:* STUART HENRY, B.A. (Kent) (Sociology) Ph.D. (Kent) (Sociology of Deviance). Currently Research Sociologist in Medical Sociology at the Addiction Research Unit, Institute of Psychiatry, University of London and a member of The Outer Circle Policy Unit working party on 'The Hidden Economy'.

## CRIME AT WORK 263

GERALD MARS, B.A. (Cambridge) (Economics and Social Anthropology) Ph.D. (LSE) (Anthropological Research on Dock Labour in Newfoundland, Canada). Presently Principal Lecturer in Industrial Sociology and Industrial Relations at the Middlesex Polytechnic; Consultant to the CDIC Unit at the Tavistock Institute of Human Relations and member of The Outer Circle Policy Unit working party on 'The Hidden Economy'.

# [3]

# Employee deviance

GERALD MARS

1 Deviancy-prone factors
2 Ways of classifying crime and deviance at work
3 Conclusion

## Overview

Deviance, as a term, comes from criminology, but in practice covers a wider range of behaviours than crime, which only refers to actions that break the law. When used in management, it normally covers illicit workplace behaviours, not all of which are illegal. Employee deviance focuses on pilferage and cheating by employees at all levels, with benefits taken from employers, customers and clients, or both. It is frequently extended to thefts of time, tax evasion/avoidance, payroll and expenses padding, restrictive 'customs and practice' and sabotage; in short, all behaviours formally disapproved of by managements that involve illicit movement of resources to employees and to managers. Called 'fiddling' in the UK, 'skimming' and 'scamming' in the USA, self-report studies have consistently shown its widespread extent, while recorded examples of employee deviance have a long history from Pharaonic Egypt through Classical Greece to the present.

Psychological explanations for deviance attempt to identify propensities associated with particular personality types. This 'rotten apple in the barrel' approach, whereby one deviant personality allegedly contaminates others, has led to extensive commercial screening programmes, especially in the USA. Situational explanations that examine how the social context of the workplace contributes to deviance and often creates it have, however, been more fruitful both for understanding and control.

Various attempts have been made to classify employee deviance, although some commentators have argued that since deviance is a feature of all occupations it is therefore not worth classifying. Most attempts, however, have been based on type of victim or type of occupation. These approaches are useful to criminologists, but do not address the wider issues of deviance of concern to managers. Other works have identified archetypes based on how jobs are designed and structured. In addition, a number of factors have been shown to facilitate deviance irrespective of how jobs are organized. Some factors derive from an imbalance of power between deviant and victim, others from the nature of goods involved and the structures mediating between them and those handling them.

Many attempts to check deviance have been, and will continue to be, problematic since deviance satisfies undeclared and covert interests, often including those of management, and because new variants and opportunities are continually offered by changing markets, forms of organization and technology. Endeavours to change work systems that ignore deviance or aim to eradicate it without understanding its social context and functions are likely to involve serious and often unanticipated effects.

## 1 Deviancy-prone factors

However jobs are classified, deviants need opportunities to exploit the differential powers they possess relative to those they exploit. Deviancy-prone factors include opportunities to make collaborative links, to operate in receptive markets and to be able to exploit various kinds of ambiguity. Several factors often operate together.

*Passing trade* is found where two sides to a transaction typically meet only once, thus precluding the build up of goodwill. Large cities are a typical milieu. Trades that deal with tourists, especially foreign tourists, offer good examples; others can be found in the hotel and restaurant trades.

*Exploiting expertise* is found where real or suggested expertise is involved in a transaction. Mechanical servicing and repairs,

## Employee deviance

particularly garage servicing, are archetypal. O'Brien (1977) specifically discusses garage 'scams', but his observations also apply more widely. As he observes, since garage customers typically demonstrate ignorance, cannot judge the service they receive and are frequently unable to move from a specific manufacturer's agent, they are particularly vulnerable. Garages can perform incomplete services but charge for complete ones, install used or cheap pirated parts but charge for premium ones and replace parts unnecessarily. Accordingly, cars break down more frequently than they otherwise would, involving further costs. Specialists exploiting expertise in these ways benefit from 'perverse incentives'. This explains why garages that perform poorly are likely to be more successful than ones that perform well. Thus, bad garages drive out good and faulty service becomes the norm. These techniques and implications extend to most repair and service trades, such as plumbing and computer repairs and to professional and quasi-professional groups; that is, whenever there is a marked imbalance in expertise and power and where normal market assessments cannot be made by customers. Incidence increases where customer needs are urgent.

*Gatekeepers* exist where imbalance exists between supply and demand and where institutional constraints inhibit competition whether it be of goods or information. Gatekeepers typically process applications for scarce permits ahead of queues, allow access to important decision makers and leak commercially sensitive information. Gatekeepers thus specialize in clearing bottlenecks for a consideration. They are particularly rife in command economies and the Third World, as discussed by Sampson (1987) in the wider context of 'informal economies' and by Altman (1989) with reference to the USSR.

*Triadic occupations* are a feature of the personal service industries, where there are customers or clients as well as employers and employees. These triadic occupations offer opportunity for collusion between any two of the triad at the expense of the third. They are very common among driver deliverers,

waiters, cashiers and throughout the retail trades, all of which feature in Mars (1994).

*Control systems* are responsible for occupational crime by their absence; that is, when they are too expensive or complicated to install relative to possible savings, or where costs of installation fall to the employer but cost of losses is borne by customers. For example, it is not considered financially viable to control the issue of trading stamps or free gifts in stores or garage forecourts. Cheap electronic controls are eroding this area.

*Ambiguity* exists where ambiguity over the quantity of a good, its quality or its exact category is inherent in its nature. This may cloak theft and be specially developed to do so. It is not easy, for example, to compute the quantity of drink consumed at a wedding; or, in the building trade, the number of bricks delivered to a site, the thickness of concrete on a path, the exact amount of copper in a building, or the gauge of zinc on a roof. Gilding (1971) gives an excellent example of constructed ambiguity in the theft of alcohol from distilleries which use traditional wooden barrels, a practice which lasted for hundreds of years until the introduction of metal barrels. Whenever market conditions move against buyers, especially at busy times, ambiguity is often deliberately increased. Price lists go missing and cash register windows become covered over or obscured when ice cream is sold on hot days, when customers surge about at New Year sales or when drinks are ordered at theatre bars during crowded intervals.

*The conversion and smuggling of goods* is relatively common. In Royal Air Forces stores watches and micrometers are categorized as 'V & A' ('valuable and attractive items'), well known as more prone to 'consumer conversion' than, say, the side of a fuselage. Storemen who guard such convertible items often operate with little supervision. They can, therefore, juggle records over time to match them to physical stocks during checks (but these rarely match between checks). Such goods, if stored in warehouses and storerooms, need to be smuggled out. Thus, V & A items which are small or can easily pass as the property of the pilferer, and items in or awaiting transit, are particularly at risk.

·Employee deviance

*Anonymity and scale.* The most common deviancy-prone factor is scale, involving the impersonality of large organizations. Henry (1988) discusses the range of justifications used by deviants and discusses how theft from a corporation is often not regarded as immoral, unlike theft from a known individual.

## 2 Ways of classifying crime and deviance at work

In some jobs deviance involves the collusion of management; in others, deviants are ruthlessly and swiftly punished. In others, deviance is organized and carried out by individuals in isolation; others require group cooperation. While deviance is seen by some employers as an incentive, almost a part of wages, and is therefore tacitly welcomed and even encouraged, some deviance undoubtedly occurs because of resentment, as a way of hitting out at the boss, the company, the system or the State.

In attempting to classify different types, the difficulty lies in imposing some form of order on such wide variations, which is probably why few attempts have been made to offer them. Green (1990) is a laudable exception, and he divides occupational crime into four categories: (1) crimes for the benefit of an employing organization; (2) crimes by officials through exercise of their state-based authority; (3) crimes by professionals in their capacity as professionals; and (4) crimes by individuals. However, this classification is restricted to crime rather than also covering the illicit but non-criminal deviant behaviours which are of interest to managers, and its categories are insufficiently exclusive; in particular, there is overlap between the third and fourth categories. A further difficulty is that classifications based on what is illegal are essentially limited: what is illegal in one country might not be so in another, and what is illegal at one time is not necessarily so at another. An approach that makes the classification of deviance follow from the classification of jobs avoids these problems.

The most effective classification, based on the exclusivity of its categories and clustering of distinct characteristics, involves a division of jobs into sub-types and follows a model

derived from social anthropology called 'cultural theory'. Cultural theory, as demonstrated by Thompson *et al.* (1990), shows that the values and attitudes of people and their behaviours are directly related to the way that their social relationships are organized. Applied to the workplace, it is dependent upon analysing the organization of work. This division of work into types based on its organization involves studying work from two standpoints. The first is whether work is group-based or carried out by individuals in isolation; the second, whether it allows a degree of autonomy or imposes strong rules and classifications on its incumbents (see GROUPS AND TEAMS).

These two dimensions of group strength and rules, when graded as strong or weak, can be placed on a 2 x 2 matrix to give four rough and ready cultural archetypes, as shown in Figure 1. This is the approach taken by Mars (1994) who divides occupations into four categories: 'hawks', 'donkeys', 'wolfpacks' and 'vultures'. Jobs in each category not only possess structural characteristics in common but also distinct arrangements to rob, cheat, short-change and pilfer customers, employers, subordinates and the State. These categories also reflect clusterings of different kinds of illicit training and career as well as distinct and different values, attitudes and justifications. Each elicits a different managerial response.

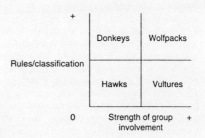

*Figure 1* The four archetypal work cultures

Employee deviance

### Hawks (weak rules/classification; weak group involvement)

Hawks, like their feathered counterparts, are competitive individualists. They perch unhappily in organizations and tend to make the rules or bend them to suit themselves. These are autonomous entrepreneurs and fixers, innovative professionals and small businesspersons. Their aim is to 'make it'. To do so they work to preserve and enhance their autonomy.

The hawks' greatest capital is knowledge and flair followed by extra-organizational networks of contacts. Their method involves insulating one set of activities from others. One senior medical hawk had buying rights to a million dollars' worth of specialized equipment. Three US companies competed for his orders so he travelled from London and visited all three:

> You can buy an 'all over' ticket that gives you unlimited travel in the States for two weeks. . . but you've got to buy it in Europe. So one company pays for me to go and see them in New York. Then I go to another company in Los Angeles and the third in Las Vegas, and I use my 'all over' ticket. But I charge the regular charge from New York to Los Angeles. . . and from New York to Las Vegas. . . . They don't mind paying at all, it's peanuts to them for a big order, but it means quite a bit to me. If I was really unscrupulous, mind, I could charge all three from London return!

The point is not that this hawk carries out unremarkable cheating but that he exploits several groups who neither know nor care that he claims similar expenses from all. They are prepared, indeed keen, to pay expenses, and each transaction is insulated. Hawk justifications are that benefits reward merit and position, no one is cheated and a scarce resource is maximally used. Attempts to control hawk deviance without building in alternative reward systems can lead to the loss of key staff. Their talents tend to be highly marketable, and because their networks are well developed, they are prone to move to rivals and take resources with them, including company clients. Hawks are not noted for loyalty or long-term strategic planning. Controls and limits to deviance are independently set, and are based on perceived market values. Managerial collusion is frequently implicit and even on exposure, sanctions are often minimal.

### Donkeys (strong rules/classification; weak group involvement)

Donkey jobs are dominated by rules, lack autonomy, are often of low status and are relatively isolated from each other. Many transport jobs are donkeys. They tend to be constrained by timetables and rules governing safety and often involve isolation. Supermarket cashiers and machine-minders are similarly constrained. Responses involve increasing their autonomy and interest by breaking rules, resentfully sabotaging systems, products and, especially in personal service occupations, relationships, or cheating. Such effects can be highly disruptive and sometimes dangerous in these jobs, especially since isolation from group influence necessarily results in an absence of group restraints. Unlike classic wolfpacks, such as traditional dockworkers, who typically work in teams, their excesses are not regulated by group controls. As a result the press periodically reports cases of donkey-job shop assistants whose houses, when raided, are often described as an 'Aladdin's cave'.

One shop cashier, each day for six months, abstracted five times her daily salary by ringing up less than the proper charge on the till and taking the difference. This was in addition to letting friends and relatives pass the checkout at minimal charge. She was never caught. Her response derived from frustration at the constraints of the job, its low status and resentment of managerial controls. As she said:

> Of course, it's a lousy firm, a really lousy firm; girls are always leaving and so are managers. A friend of mine was once ten pounds down on her till. She never fiddled a penny but the manager said she must have taken it. She was so upset she said she couldn't work there if they thought she'd

taken the ten pounds, so she left. Afterwards when they'd checked it all they discovered the error but they never wrote to her, just asked me if I saw her to tell her that it was OK. That's typical, they treat you like dirt, as if you have no intelligence at all. It's the little things like that, things you can't often remember, that makes them a horrible firm. It's horrible too because the pay is so low, even compared to similar jobs in other shops.

A lack of social solidarity is always a strong factor in donkey jobs:

It's also a lousy firm in other ways. The girls are always backbiting and bitchy; there's a lot of gossip all the time. Nobody ever accuses anyone of stealing from the tills, though. That's never ever mentioned by anyone. Nothing is ever said, even by management, even when you first start. It's just not done to mention it. New girls just have to find out for themselves.

The more managements control donkey jobs by their typical tactic of tightening constraints and strengthening rules, the more likely they are to be counterproductive. Schemes to increase autonomy and interest through job enlargement, job enrichment and job rotation are better alternatives, especially if linked to development of promotion prospects and measures to increase job security.

### Wolfpacks (strong rules/classification; strong group involvement)

Wolfpacks practise team theft; they work and steal in well-defined and stratified packs. Traditional dockwork gangs are archetypal examples, with hierarchy, order and internal controls based upon group work involving different but coordinated tasks. Many maintenance and construction crews are wolfpacks. When they pilfer or indulge in other deviance they act according to agreed rules, within agreed limits and through well-defined divisions of labour. Unlike the isolated donkeys, they therefore have to be taught the techniques and practice of deviance. Like real-life wolves, they know who is their leader and who are the

led. They use their internal organization to penalize and reward their own deviants, particularly those who exceed group set limits. They often command strong group loyalties.

Wolfpacks invariably invoke sanctions over members from jesting, through ridicule, to expulsion, the latter being effected by making it difficult to work with them. They also frequently aim to control recruitment. This is particularly effective when workers live and work in the same vicinity, as is often the case in mining, shipbuilding and dock work. Here, they merge leisure and work lives by, for instance, drinking together after work and recruiting relatives. They are able to adopt a vigorous and united role in negotiations with management and often sustain a body of what management define as 'restrictive practices', including tolerated access to activities considered deviant. Whereas hawks are impressive innovators and donkeys tend towards fatalism, wolfpacks are inherently conservative and work to long-term strategies in deviance and other concerns. They are the most stable of the work groupings. When linked to industrial strength, this frequently allows them to exchange industrial peace for managerially tolerated levels of deviance. They often resist change and innovation.

### Vultures (weak rules/classification; strong group involvement)

Vultures are also team-based but their teams, unlike wolfpacks, are minimally differentiated by rank or function. Travelling salesmen are vultures, as are waiters when linked and supported from a common base such as working for a common supervisor. Cab drivers, particularly those working from a single depot, are vultures, as are train and ship stewards. They depend upon information and support from colleagues and need the support of a group but are competitive in their own interests. The lack of established leadership roles that derives from weak classification and their paradoxical combination of competition and need for cooperation cause vultures difficulty in resolving their disputes and makes them particularly subject to rumour and to scapegoat selection. Vulture groupings tend to

### Employee deviance

be unstable, both in their constituent parts and in industrial relations behaviour, which is inclined to be turbulent. The introduction of functional ranking as, for instance, is applied to waiters in top level restaurants, however, causes them to operate more as wolfpacks.

In vulture jobs, behaviour is not reactive (as in donkey jobs) or creative (like individualist hawks) but responsive to the changing opportunities presented by management. Acceleration of pace, increases in scale, alterations in price or incentives tend not to be opposed, as they would be by wolfpacks. Instead, changes offer employees their chances. They 'ride' an unstable system which constantly bucks and threatens to throw them off.

A group of waiters at a north of England seaside resort, was convicted of overcharging for drinks. The hotel manager was cast as group ringleader. His defence was that he had 'to make a profit and ensure that stocks were right'. He said he allowed overcharging and maintained:

> The directors' attitude was the same as mine, and on occasions directors have said, in a jocular manner, 'Are these visitors' prices or ours?' I told them they should be satisfied as we were getting our share, meaning that the company was benefiting, through good stocks.

Explicit collusion of this sort between workers and first-line management is common among vultures, particularly when the victims are outside the firm. Collusive toleration to deviance by higher managements is often implicit until subject to visibility, which further enhances the inherent instability of vultures.

## 3  Conclusion

Managers face five difficulties when assessing deviance, aside from the fact that being covert it is very difficult to identify. One is a difficulty in suspending their own morality so as to make calm, rational assessments. A second is accepting that deviance is rarely 'wild' or normless but operates within culturally set moral codes, rules and limits. Although managers may not share such standards, they do need to understand them. A third difficulty lies in personalizing employee deviance ('rotten apple' theories) instead of concentrating on understanding the contexts that facilitate it. This can of course create difficulties when the context is one for which they may be formally responsible. A fourth is to accept that deviance often produces benefits, not only to deviants but also to their employers. It can bond members of teams, offer informal incentives for merit or effort when formal systems are too rigid; make boring jobs more interesting, buy off labour dissatisfaction and permit differential favouritism.

The fifth factor, linked to all of these, is that attempts to change work systems are much more likely to succeed if the jobs' culture is first identified.

Otherwise, particularly where deviance is integral to the rewards of workers, attempts at controlling it are likely to produce unanticipated consequences, especially resistance to innovation that might seem 'mindless'. The current widespread introduction of electronic controls that attempt to limit deviancy-prone factors must be considered in this context.

GERALD MARS
UNIVERSITY OF BRADFORD

## Further reading

(References cited in the text marked *)

* Altman, Y. (1989) 'Second economy activity in the USSR', in P. Ward (ed.), *Corruption, Development and Inequality*, London: Routledge. (This article looks at behaviour in the USSR, and describes the role and activity of 'gatekeepers'.)

Dalton, M. (1959) *Men Who Manage*, New York: Wiley. (The classic forerunner of much subsequent work which concentrates on the inevitable deviance involved in managing managerial careers.)

Ditton, J. (1977) *Part-time Crime: An Ethnography of Fiddling and Pilferage*, London: Macmillan. (Superb account of the deviant training of baker's roundsmen as they learn and incorporate illegal 'vulture-type' work practices.)

Gabor, T. (1994) *Everybody Does It: Crime by the Public*, Toronto, Ont.: University of Toronto

Press. (Sets occupation crime, but not deviance, in the context of crimes by 'ordinary' citizens. Interesting case studies.)

* Gilding, B. (1971) *The Journeymen Coopers of East London*, History Workshop pamphlet no. 4, Oxford: Ruskin College. (This historical trade study contains details of the example of theft mentioned in the text.)

* Green, G. S. (1990) *Occupational Crime*, Chicago, IL: Nelson-Hall. (Presents an overview and attempts a classification of occupational crime. Limited to activities against the law rather than incorporating deviance. Good account of self-report studies and references to computer crime.)

* Henry, S. (1988) *The Hidden Economy: The Context and Control of Borderline Crime*, Port Townsend, WA: Loompanics Unlimited. (A highly readable classic, originally published in 1978. Concentrates on the context in which occupational crimes occur and particularly on the nature of social relationships between the people who take part and the sub-economy they form.)

Hollinger, R. and Clark, J. (1983) *Theft by Employees*, Lexington, MA: Lexington Books. (An account of a survey of 9,000 employees and their deviance at work.)

* Mars, G. (1994) *Cheats At Work: An Anthropology of Workplace Crime*, 2nd edn, Aldershot: Dartmouth Press. (A comprehensive situational analysis which classifies occupations as cultures and assesses resulting deviance, values, motivations, moralities and techniques. Covers history, categories, proneness factors plus implications of deviance and its control for practical industrial relations.)

* O'Brien, D.P. (1977) 'Why you may be dissatisfied with garage servicing', *Motor*, 10 September. (Neatly outlines the economic bases of perverse incentives.)

* Sampson, S.L. (1987) 'The second economy of the Soviet Union and eastern Europe', *The Annals of the American Academy of Political and Social Science*, special issue on the informal economy (L.S. Ferman, S. Henry and M. Hoyman (eds)): 120–36. (A seminal collection of articles that examines the wider economic implications of all non-formalized economic activity, including occupational deviance.)

Stevenson, C.H. (1990) *Auto Repair Shams and Scams: How to Avoid Getting Ripped Off*, Los Angeles, CA: Price, Stern, Sloan Inc. (Written very effectively for the consumer by a former mechanic; useful in conjuction with O'Brien (1977).)

* Thompson, M., Ellis, R. and Wildavsky, A. (1990) *Cultural Theory*, Boulder, CO: Westview Press. (A comprehensive development of cultural theory which expands on the work of Mary Douglas, its originator.)

Zeitlin, L.R. (1971) 'Stimulus/response: a little larceny can do a lot for employee morale', *Psychology Today* 14 (June): 22, 24–6, 64. (Demonstrates how managements can avoid reorganizing jobs and raising wages by permitting a controlled amount of theft.)

**See also:** BUSINESS ETHICS; GROUPS AND TEAMS; MOTIVATION AND SATISFACTION; ORGANIZATION BEHAVIOUR; WORK ETHIC

# [4]

## EMPLOYEE THEFT AS SOCIAL CONTROL*

*JAMES TUCKER*
*University of Virginia, Springfield*

Employee theft is generally regarded as a serious offense not only by those responsible for assuring organizations operate as efficiently as possible, but by social scientists studying this phenomenon. Futhermore, in most modern settings, it is defined as criminal and subject to punishment. Although usually classified as deviant, theft is in many instances also a reaction to what employees consider is deviant behavior on the part of their employer. Consequently, a theory of social control, rather than a theory of crime, is more appropriate in explaining such theft by employees. This paper suggests that theft, as a mode of social control, is most likely among employees who occupy marginal positions in organizations, including those at the bottom of the organizational hierachy, those with little tenure, and those with few social lies. Ways of reducing employee theft consistent with this hypothesis are explored. It is concluded, however, that theft by employed members of organizations is in many cases inevitable and given the nature of modern social life likely to increase in the future.

Individuals throughout history have stolen money and property from their superiors and organizations. Aristotle, for example, complained that road commissioners and other officials often embezzled funds (Hall, 1952:36). In nineteenth century England, workers in cotton mills confiscated material on a regular basis (Tobias, 1972:165, cited in Henry, 1978:10). Likewise, an account of the Nazi occupation of Poland showed that many workplaces experienced high rates of internal theft (Gross, 1979:414, cited in Baumgartner, 1984a:310). In modern America, employee theft is quite common in business organizations. Exact figures are not known as to the extent of involvement, but loss from theft by employees may run as high as $40 billion annually (Walls, 1985).

Employee theft is generally regarded as a serious offense not only by those responsible for assuring business organizations operate as efficiently as possible, but by social scientists studying this phenomenon. Furthermore, in most modern settings, theft by employees is defined as criminal and subject to punishment. Although usually classified as deviant, employee theft is in many instances also a *reaction* to deviant behavior. Taking property is one

---

* A version of this paper was presented at the 1988 Southern Sociological Society annual meeting in Nashville, Tennessee. The following people made comments on earlier drafts: Donald Black, Theodore Caplow, Mark Cooney, Thomas Cushman, Joseph Michalski, Calvin Morrill, and Gresham Sykes.

way employees express grievances against their employers (see Baumgartner 1984a: 309- 310). It often follows the same logic as much criminal activity in that it is a form of "self-help" involving the pursuit of justice (see Black, 1984a). As such, a theory of social control, rather than a theory of crime, may be appropriate in explaining much theft by employees.

This paper adds to the understanding of this phenomenon by adhering to a theoretical strategy designed to explain variation in social control of all types (see Black, 1976; 1984b).[1] This strategy is based on considerable evidence that the way in which grievances are handled depends on the social setting in which they occur, including the relationship between the aggrieved and the alleged offender. The present analysis suggests that employee theft, as a mode of social control, is most likely among those who occupy marginal positions in work organizations. Accordingly, we may hypothesize that employee theft is inversely related to one's position in an organizational hierarchy, length of tenure, and degree of social integration. After presenting support for this hypothesis, remedies consistent with it are presented. First, however, existing explanations of employee theft are briefly reviewed and their limitations identified.

## Explaining Employee Theft

One popular explanation of employee theft is promulgated mainly by those in the industrial security profession: The propensity to engage in workplace theft is traced to deviant individual backgrounds. The theory is rarely explicit; its promoters put little effort in demonstrating the processes involved in the development of employee thieves. Instead, they focus on devices designed to discover employees who have such proclivities. A survey of the security management literature shows the efforts designed to detect theft-prone individuals to be quite elaborate. Pre-employment "paper-and-pencil" honesty tests, for example, have been claimed to be effective at discovering potential thieves (Walls, 1985), as have checks on previous employers, credit bureaus, and police agencies (Owens, 1976; Willis, 1986). Polygraph tests are advocated for similar purposes (Terris and Jones, 1982).

Another explanation, also favored by security professionals, traces employee theft to the physical opportunity available. The theory is that anyone will steal if given the chance (Lipman, 1973; McCullough, 1981). Supporters of this view advocate a number of mechanisms to keep opportunity to a minimum or to provide constant surveillance over employee activity. Complex systems of inventory control serve this purpose (Blank, 1986) as do well staffed security departments (Carson, 1977:45-79), hidden cameras (Rosenbaum and Baumer, 1983) and even anti-theft messages in "piped-in" music systems (Lander, 1981).

---

[1]"Social control" refers to the means by which people define and respond to deviant behavior, or similarly, how people handle grievances. The term "conflict management" has been used to denote the same conduct (Black, 1987).

A third explanation points to financial strains that force employees to take company funds or property (Cressey, 1953; Merriam, 1977). Theft is considered an attractive way for employees to resolve financial problems that have no conventional solutions and cannot be shared with others.[2]  A number of preventive strategies consistent with this explanatory logic have been proposed including thorough reviews of personnel policies to assure employees are adequately compensated, confidential counseling services, and policies to prevent adverse financial situations from influencing job security or advancement (Wells, 1985).

The little evidence that has been collected on employee theft does not lend much support for the explanations just described. Studies of employees who have admitted stealing show that most do not have criminal pasts or otherwise extraordinary backgrounds (Robin, 1969). Also, hiring practices established to detect theft-prone employees are often limited in their effectiveness (Hollinger and Clark, 1983:94-95). Access to company property does not necessarily lead to greater occurrences of theft. Many employees in various occupations have access to money or merchandise, but not all steal (Hollinger and Clark, 1983:69-78). Finally, a recent study also casts doubt on the importance of economic need: Neither household income, perceived adequacy of income, nor concern with personal finances were significant predictors of an individual's likelihood to steal company property (Hollinger and Clark, 1983:53-62).

Focusing less on deviant individual, physical opportunity, and financial stress explanations, social scientists concerned with workplace theft are increasingly directing attention to a relationship that appears to exist between employee dissatisfaction and deviance in the workplace. In particular, conduct that hurts employer productivity, including theft of company property, is seen as a response to perceived inequities in the workplace (Mangione and Quinn, 1975; Ditton, 1977b; Hollinger and Clark, 1982, Hollinger, 1986). The theoretical approach taken in this paper is consistent with this view, although it will be argued that the presence of dissatisfaction alone is inadequate in accounting for theft by employees.

## Employee Theft as Justice

The approach taken here does not consider the "deviant" nature of theft to be important in predicting when it will occur. Instead, taking company property is treated as one of the ways in which employees respond to deviant behavior by their employers.[3] Employees, after all, do not sit idly by when

---

[2]Cressey (1953), in a study of embezzlers, contends that identification of an opportunity and the ability to rationalize one's conduct are also necessary conditions for theft to occur. A financial need that cannot be shared, however, is considered the initial condition that must be present.

[3] The focus here does not rule out that theft may occur for other reasons. It may, for example, be recreational, where the focus is on adventure or excitement. In other instances, it may have an economic character. Such is the case when employees confiscate property

they have a grievance with their employing organization. Although law is rarely used as a remedy, they do pursue justice through other means. Employees often take matters into their own hands: They use "self-help" (see Baumgartner, 1984 and Black, 1987b).

As a mode of social control, self-help entails the expression of a grievance by unilateral aggression (Black, 1987). It can involve simple verbal criticism or harassment, but can also entail destruction of property or human life. Appropriation of property is also used as self-help. In ancient Rome, for instance, slaves were known to steal their masters property as a form of revenge (Hopkins, 1978:121, cited in Baumgartner, 1984a:309). Many animal thefts in an agricultural village in Lebanon "were either the result of personal arguments and political rivalries between individual women or extensions of rivalries between families as a result of factional tension" (Witty, 1978:301). Tribal warfare, in general, often seems to involve the confiscation of property, whether it be land, goods, or people (see Bohannon, 1967). Theft often has a normative character in modern America as well. For example, quarrels between separated spouses can involve the theft of each others belongings (see Black, 1984a:9) or, as is becoming increasingly common, their children.

Theft can also express an employee grievance. Cressey (1953), for example, notes the comments of an accountant convicted of embezzling funds from his employer: "The individual who is head of the company where I worked is extremely repulsive. He is arrogant, filthy rich, old-school type of master and servant and everything that went with it. The rebelliousness in me just cropped (up) and asserted itself without any prompting of any kind" (quoted on p. 58; also quoted in Baumgartner, 1984a:310). A hotel night clerk related a similar story: "I had this fancy grievance against the company, and the owner was not straightening it out fast enough. . .You might say it was in the spirit of retaliation" (quoted on p. 59). Comments of an employee dismissed for stealing from a clothing store in the midwestern United States reflected the same sentiment "I felt I deserved to get something additional for my work since I was not getting paid enough" (Zeitlin, 1971, quoted on p. 26).[4]

Based on an extensive study of dockworkers in Great Britain, Mars (1974) discovered that theft was viewed "as a morally justified addition to wages... as an entitlement due from exploiting employers" (p.244). Pilferage may occur "because of resentment. . .it is a way of hitting at the boss, the company" (Mars, 1982:23). Hollinger and Clark (1983), who have conducted

and sell it in "black market" (see Henry, 1978). Other theories of deviance may therefore be appropriate in explaining employee theft of these kind. "Subcultural" theory (*i.e.*, Sutherland and Cressey, 1960), for example, might best explain recreational theft, while "strain" theory (*i.e.*, Merton, 1938) could be most relevant for understanding economic theft.

[4] Some would point to such comments as examples of "techniques of neutralization" (Sykes and Matza, 1957), designed to help the employee rationalize his behavior. The approach taken here considers theft as conflict management to be a normal response to what is regarded as deviant conduct on the part of an employer. Several studies are supportive: Employee theft is often not considered criminal and thus employees do not need to rationalize their behavior (Horning, 1970:60; Altheide, 1978; Hawkins, 1984:61-64)

the most comprehensive study to date (using self- reports of almost 5,000 employees in retailing, hospital, and manufacturing industries), concluded that "when employees felt exploited by the company or by their superiors (who represent the company in the eyes of the employee), we were not surprised to find these workers more involved in acts against the organization as a mechanism to correct perceptions of insecurity or injustice" (p. 142).

Interestingly, even those in the industrial security profession, who stress the importance of other factors, suggest that employers' behavior may be partially responsible. Willis (1986), for example, argues that "Employees who feel frustrated or cheated by large, seemingly faceless bureaucracies often will commit crimes against them. A disgruntled employee may have been passed over for a promotion, given additional responsibilities with no pay increase, or denied adequate resources to do the job" (p. 26). Arnold (1985) makes a similar claim: "Employees often comment that they feel justified in stealing because employers had done something to them. . .They may have worked overtime or they may have been reprimanded for something that was not their fault" (p.28). Another security professional notes that some theft results from "revenge against an employer, or neglect on the employer's part (poor pay, unjust policies, or shady management practices)" (Sosnowski, 1985:111).

Employees do, however, express grievances in ways other than theft. The labor strike is one the more organized forms and in many cases the most violent (Brecher, 1972). Sabotage, the deliberate destruction of company property, is rarely as organized, but does represent another type of response to alleged injustices (Taylor and Walton, 1971). Grievances are expressed in less dramatic fashion as well. Gouldner (1954), for example, discovered in a study of a mining company in the midwestern United States that "miner's solidarity provided them with an effective agency for defeating innovations they disliked" (p. 150). Disgruntled workers in large corporations often express discontent by forming "counter-systems" which stress peer solidarity and reject the corporate hierarchy (Kanter, 1977): "Their rebelliousness is more likely to take the form of passive resistance. . . Or it could be gossip, joking, or ridicule" (p.150). Employees sometimes handle their conflicts using "exit" (see Hirschman, 1970), meaning they simply end their relationship with their employer. Not surprisingly, turnover is more common among dissatisfied employees (Price, 1977; Smith, 1977). Absenteeism has also been shown to be higher among employees who believe they have been treated unjustly by their employers (Adams, 1965; Green, 1980), suggesting that temporary avoidance (see Baumgartner, 1984b) is used as social control as well.

Employees, thus, pursue justice in a number of ways. Indeed, an entire "justice system" can be envisioned where strikes, sabotage, work slowdowns, absenteeism, turnover, etc. are possible penalties awaiting employers "convicted" of deviant conduct. Theft is one possible sentence. What follows is an attempt to identify conditions that seem to be associated with this remedy.

The Social Organization Of Employee Theft

As noted earlier, a growing literature shows how social control varies with its social setting. In particular, the relationship between parties involved in a disagreement strongly conditions the way in which grievances are handled (see Black, 1976; Baumgartner, 1984b; Cooney, 1987; Morrill, 1987). Employee theft also varies depending on the nature of social relations between the parties in the relationship; in this case, the employee and employer. *Employees who are marginal members of an enterprise tend to be more likely to steal employer's property as a way of handling grievances.*

Several features of an employee's position determine marginality. First is location in the organizational hierarchy: Low status employees are more marginal. The most obvious effect is lower wages, although being at the bottom has other consequences as well. In modern corporations, employees in the lower ranks are treated considerably different from those in higher positions (Kanter,1977). Clerical workers, for example, are often excluded from pension plans, educational reimbursement programs, and other fringe benefits given to managers and other professionals. Contrasts between high and low status employees are also evident if we consider the American workforce as composed of distinct "labor markets" (Piore, 1974; Edwards, 1979). Employees in the "secondary sector" have little job training or education and are confined for the most part to low skill jobs in service occupations in either the retail or wholesale trade (*i.e.*, janitors, waiters, check-out clerks). Besides relatively low pay, workers in this labor market rarely have opportunity for advancement. In addition, they are considered expendable and have little job security. Perhaps most important for its implications regarding employee theft, workers in the secondary sector generally do not belong to labor unions and have few legitimate channels to express grievances.

Theft has been reported to be common among individuals in a number of low status occupations. Waiters, for example, are known to engage quite frequently in workplace theft (Mars, 1973; Hawkins, 1984) as are other low paid employees including department store personnel (Robin, 1969) and those who work in "convenience" stores (Terris and Jones, 1982). Hollinger and Clark's research (1983:74-75) also provides evidence that low status employees are more theft prone, although the finding is conditioned by length of service. Low level workers in retail occupations (food service employees, delivery persons, stock clerks) are more likely to steal from their employers than high status persons in the same industry (managers, accountants, pharmacists). Yet the pattern for manufacturing occupations does not hold. Low status employees (assemblers, maintenance workers, solderers) in this industry are not more involved in theft than those in upper level positions (managers, engineers). This seemingly contradictory pattern can be explained with the inclusion of tenure, a second dimension of marginality.

Apart from status, tenure has its own consequences for the peripheral status of an employee and the likelihood of engaging in employee theft. Those in short-term positions tend to be more marginal to an organization. New employees have little time to develop much of a relationship with their employer, while the organization itself contributes to a gradual process of integration by delaying benefits (*i.e.*, vacation time, sick leave, profit-sharing plans). Available evidence is supportive. A study of retail stores in the midwestern United States found that one-third of employees caught stealing were employed less that six months and almost two-thirds were with the company less than two years, while less than one-fifth of those apprehended had been working five years or longer (Robin, 1969:20). Likewise, Hollinger and Clark's research (p.66) showed that newer employees as well as those looking for a new job were more involved in theft.

The apparent relationship between length of employment and theft helps explain the finding above that low status is associated with theft among retail workers, but not among those in manufacturing occupations. Turnover is notably high among low level employees in retail, while their counterparts in manufacturing firms have relatively long job tenures. The degree of job security for the latter is often augmented by more benefits and in some cases union representation. Retail employees in lower status jobs rarely have such protection. Hence, low status manufacturing workers tend to be less marginal and often have access to legitimate means to handle grievances. This tendency may account for their lower theft rates.

Hollinger and Clark (1983:69-78) reported another finding that can be explained with length of tenure. Engineers and computer specialists employed in manufacturing firms were significantly more theft prone than other high status employees in the manufacturing and other industries (including managers and administrators). Compared to the latter, whose careers typically depend on moving up a company hierarchy, technical specialists are committed more to their trade than to a particular company and often switch jobs for higher pay or more challenging work (see Miller, 1967). Consequently, engineers and computers specialists are more likely to engage in theft.

Social isolation is a third dimension of marginality that conditions how people respond to deviant behavior. The effect of atomization in other settings is well documented. In a study of a contemporary middle-class suburb, for example, neighbors were found rarely to have support to assist in the handling of conflicts (Baumgartner, 1984b). Consequently, direct confrontations between suburban disputants are rare. Instead, grievances tend to be expressed in a more covert and nonconfrontational fashion, although conflicting suburbanites more often use avoidance rather than seek compensation by confiscating property. This pattern is apparently more general (Baumgartner, 1984b:99). For instance, tribal societies without "fraternal interest groups" tend to have less episodes of violent retaliation (Thoden van Velzen and van Wetering, 1960). Likewise, negotiation, a nonviolent yet confrontational form of social control, is most likely when aggrieved parties have access to an "action-set" of supporters (Gulliver, 1969). The use of law, another direct way of handling conflicts, also tends to be greater where victims have organized group support (Black, 1976: Chapter 5).

In the workplace, social isolation is most common in firms organized by the principles of "bureaucratic control" (Edwards, 1979). This type of organizational structure differentiates employees by salary and function and creates competition for positions in a hierarchy. As a result, united opposition to employers is unlikely. Instead, employees generally handle conflicts without the assistance of others. Theft is one way in which grievances can be pursued individually and covertly.

Several studies show that much theft at the workplace is a solitary event. In a study of over 1,500 admitted employee thieves from three large department stores in the United States, 86 percent stole without involving others (Robin, 1969:23-24). Based on interviews of employees in an electronic assembly plant, Horning (1970:64) concluded that "workers who pilfer company property. . .do so without protection of the work group" A recent study of waiters showed a similar pattern: Most restaurant theft did not entail collusion (Hawkins, 1984:57).[5]     Finally, among convenience store employees in the southwest who engage in theft, most do so alone (Terris and Jones, 1982).

To summarize, employee theft appears to vary directly with the degree of marginality. The low status, temporary, socially isolated employee should be most likely to engage in this activity. Likewise, the greater the number of marginal occupations a company has, the more employee theft it should experience.

The marginality proposition can explain the well established relationship between theft and age. A common finding shows younger people are more likely to steal from their employer (Robin, 1969; Ruggiero, Greenberger, and Steinberg, 1982; Hollinger and Clark, 1983). Several explanations for this pattern have been posited, many of which point to the "moral laxity" associated with today's youth (see Merriam, 1977). Yet from the hypotheses presented here, the higher incidence of theft among younger employees can be explained by their greater presence in marginal occupations. The young are concentrated in low paying, short-term positions in industries that rely heavily on such positions. Retailing and food service occupations, for example, are popular employers of the young and tend to have higher levels of theft by employees (Ruggiero, Greenberger, and Steinberg, 1982; Hawkins, 1984). Based on the hypothesis presented here, it is not the nature of young people that accounts for their higher participation in theft, it is their disproportionate presence in marginal occupations.

## Reducing Employee Theft

The preceding analysis also has implications for efforts to reduce employee theft. As discussed above, most of the existing solutions are based on the assumption that theft is a consequence of hiring inherently dishonest employees, allowing too many opportunities for employees to steal company property, or ignoring financial difficulties that employees may face. These

---

[5] Mars (1974) noted that cooperation was common among pilfering dock workers, while Ditton (1977a) found the same pattern among bread salesmen in Great Britain. It may be best to consider collective theft as an altogether different phenomenon. Mars (1982) makes a distinction: "hawks", "donkeys", and "vultures" generally steal alone, while "wolves" steal in groups

solutions do not address the fact that much theft is social control and therefore depends on the social organization of the workplace. To make substantial progress in reducing its occurrence, then, the relationship between organizations and theft-prone occupations would need to be modified. Most importantly, *strengthening ties between employees and employers in high theft potential settings should have a considerable effect on how grievances are handled.* Evidence shows that close ties between parties is associated with more conciliatory forms of social control, where the aim is restoration of harmony to the relationship rather than imposition of sanctions by the victim (Gluckman, 1967; Nader, 1969; Black, 1976:47). More conciliatory responses would be expected as well when individuals have grievances with organizations in which they are integrated members.

Management theorists have been heavily concerned with enhancing the level of integration between employees and organizations. Many strategies have been developed with the hope that individual goals will correspond with organizational ones, making compliance with organizational demands less troublesome (see, *e.g.*, Argyris, 1964; Hertzberg, 1966). Much of this theory addresses individual characteristics while ignoring the unique structural position of marginal employees. Ouchi (1981), however, describes how some Japanese and American corporations are successful in reducing marginality. A number of practices were found to be effective including lifetime employment, job rotation, and collective decision making. Other strategies also work to strengthen ties between employees and employers and potentially alter the way in which grievances are expressed. Employee ownership is one such strategy which is currently growing in popularity in the United States. Approximately seven percent of the workforce own some stock in their company. The literature on employee ownership shows fairly substantial increases in commitment and loyalty to employer among employees who are owners (Rosen, Klein, and Young, 1986; Tucker, Nock, and Toscano, 1989). Yet, employee-owned companies, even the most egalitarian ones, have difficulty surviving without a contingent of peripheral employees, hired on a temporary basis and owning no company stock (Russell, 1985).

For many companies, then, eliminating marginal occupations may not be possible. In such cases, employers could introduce measures to change marginal employees perceptions of integration. Employee discounts, company picnics, and holiday bonuses are examples of practices designed to make workers feel more attached to their organization and undoubtedly have some effect. Yet we would expect such efforts to be limited in their effectiveness since they do not change the structural position of the marginal employee.

Theft, therefore, might have to be the cost of doing business. Given its widespread occurrence, many companies have evidently accepted theft as part of the work situation (see Zeitlan, 1971). Moreover, changes in American social life may result in more and more companies having to live with employee theft. Most significantly, Americans are more transient than they have ever been. Job switching and multiple careers are becoming commonplace. Less certain is whether the labor force will experience an increase in lower status occupations. Some argue that the Untied States economy is undergoing a "deindustrialization", which will result in an increase in demand for low-skilled workers in the upcoming years (see Bluestone and Harrison, 1982). We do know that businesses are continuing to relocate their manufacturing facilities in developing countries (see Dixon, Jonas, and McCaughan, 1983), where unionization is rare and relationships between employee and employers are further weakened by cultural differences. Finally, as a result of computer technology, many occupations are becoming more socially isolated (Zuboff, 1982), making employees more likely to use individual modes of social control, such as theft.

## Conclusions

Whatever the trends, many questions remain concerning employee theft that can only be answered with the assistance of further research. The analysis presented here is only a start. Do, for example, groups disproportionately represented in marginal occupations, such as blacks and women, engage in theft at higher rates ? Do characteristics of the organization like its size and structure affect the degree of theft ? How do employees come to define certain conduct by their employer as deviant ? Do individuals "convict" employers based on evidence ? If so, how is it collected ? Perhaps employees have different "sentences" for different deviant actions on the part of employers. What is stolen might reflect the severity of the deviant behavior. What if the opportunity for theft is not available ? What modes of conflict management are used instead ? These questions demand attention as the effort progresses to develop a better understanding of employee theft. Perhaps research of this kind will ultimately contribute to a more general theory of social control as well.

## References

Adams, J. Stacy
    1965            "Inequity in social exchange"Advances in Experimental
                    Social Psychology 2:267-299.

Altheide, D.L. Adler, P. Adler, and D.A. Altheide
    1978            "The social meanings of employee theft"Pages 90-124 in
                    Crime at the Top, edited by John M. Johnson and Jack D.
                    Douglas. Philadelphia: Lippincot.

Argyris, Chris
    1964            Integrating the Individual and the Organization. New
                    York: John Wiley.

Arnold, Gregory
    1985            "Employee theft: A $40-billion crime"Management World

Baumgartner, M.P.
    1984a           "Social control from below"Pages 303-345 in Toward a
                    General Theory of Social Control, Volume 2: Selected

Problems, edited by Donald Black. Orlando, Florida: Academic Press.

Baumgartner, M.P.
1984b      "Social control in suburbia"Pages 79-103 in Toward a
General Theory of Social Control, Volume 2: Selected
Problems, edited by Donald Black. Orlando, Florida: Academic Press.

Black, Donald
1976      The Behavior of Law. New York: Academic Press.

Black, Donald
1984a      "Crime as social control"Pages 1-27 in Toward a General
Theory of Social Control Volume 2: Selected Problems, edited by Donald Black, Orlando, Florida: Academic Press.

Black, Donald
1984      "Social control as a dependent variable"Pages 1-36 in Toward a General Theory of Social Control, Volume 1:  Fundamentals, edited by Donald Black. Orlando, Florida:
Academic Press.

Black, Donald
1987      "The elementary forms of conflict management" Unpublished paper prepared for the distinguished Lecturer Series,
School of Justice Studies, Arizona State University, Tempe,
Arizona.

Blank, Sally
1986      "Fighting employee theft: Guidelines"Management Review,
5:22-32.

Bluestone, Barry and Bennett Harrison
1982      The Deindustrialization of America: Plant Closing, Community Abandonment, and the Dismantling of Basic Industry. New York: Basic Books.

Bohannan, Paul (editor)
1967      Law and Warfare: Studies in the Anthropology of Conflict.
Austin, Texas: University of Texas Press.

Breecher, Jeremy
1972      Strike! San Francisco: Straight Arrow Books.

Carson, Charles R.
1977      Managing Employee Honesty. Los Angeles: Security World
Publishing.

Cooney, Mark
   1988          The Social Control of Homicide: A Cross-Cultural Study.
                 S.J.D. Dissertation, Harvard Law School.

Cressey, Donald R.
   1953           Other People's Money: A Study in the Social Psychology
                 of Embezzlement. Glencoe, Ill.: The Free Press.

Ditton, Jason
   1977a         Part-Time Crime: An Ethnology of Fiddling and Pilferage.
                 London: Macmillan.

Ditton, Jason
   1977b         "Perks, pilferage, and the fiddle: The historical structure of
                 invisible wages"Theory and Society 4:39-71.

Dixon, Marlen, Susanne Jonas, and Ed McCaughan
   1983          "Changes in the international division of labor", pages
                 173-192 in Crisis in the World-System, edited by Albert
                 Bergesen.  Beverly Hills, California: Sage Publications.

Edwards, Richard
   1979          Contested Terrain: The Transformation of the Workplace
                 in the Twentieth Century. New York: Basic Books.

Gluckman, Max
   1955          The Judicial Process Among the Bartose of Northern
                 Rhodesia. Manchester: Manchester University Press. (Sec-
                 ond edition, 1967)

Gouldner, Alvin
   1953          Patterns of Industrial Bureaucracy. New York: The Free
                 Press.

Green, James R.
   1980          The World of the Worker: Labor in Twentieth-Century
                 America. New York: Hill and Wang.

Gross, Jan Tomaz
   1979           Polish Society Under German Occupation: The General
                 Government, 1939-1944. Princeton, N.J.: Princeton Uni-
                 versity Press.

Gulliver, P.H.
   1969          'Dispute settlement without the courts: The Ndendeuli of
                 southern Tanzania'Pages 24-68 in Law and Culture in So-
                 ciety, edited by Laura Nader.

Hall, Jerome
    1952        Theft, Law, and Society. Indianapolis, Ind.: Bobbs-Merrill.

Hawkins, Richard
    1984        'Employee theft in the restaurant trade: Forms of ripping off waiters at work'Deviant Behavior, 5:47-69.

Henry, Stuart
    1978        The Hidden Economy: The Context and Control of Borderline Crime. Oxford: Martin Robertson.

Hertzberg, Frederick
    1966        Work and the Nature of Man. New York: World Publishing Co.

Hirschman, Albert O.
    1970        Exit, Voice, and Loyalty: Responses to Declines in Firms, Organizations, and States. Cambridge, Mass.: Harvard University Press.

Hollinger, Richard C.
    1986        'Acts against the workplace: Social bonding and employee deviance'Deviant Behavior 7,1:53-75.

Hollinger, Richard C. and John P. Clark
    1982        'Employee deviance: A response to the perceived quality of the work experience'Sociological Quarterly 23:333-343.

Hollinger, Richard C. and John P. Clark
    1983        Theft By Employees. Lexington, Mass.: D.C. Heath and Company.

Hopkins, Keith
    1978        Conquerors and Slaves: Sociological Studies in Roman History. Volume 1. Cambridge, Cambridge University Press.

Horning, Donald N. M.
    1970        'Blue-collar theft: Conceptions of property, attitudes toward pilfering, and work group norms in a modern industrial plant'Pages 46-64 in Crimes Against Bureaucracy, edited by Erwin O. Smigel and H. Laurence Ross. New York: Van Nostrand Reinhold Company.

Kanter, Rosabeth Moss
    1977        Men and Women of the Corporation. New York: Basic Books.

Lander, Eric
    1981        'In through the out door', Omni Feb.:48-107.

Lipman, Mark
     1973              Stealing: How America's Employees Are Stealing Their
                       Companies Blind. New York: Harper's Magazine Press.

Magione, T.W. and R.P. Quinn
     1975              'Job Satisfaction, counter-productive behavior and drug use
                       at work', Journal of Applied Psychology 60:114-116.

Mars, Gerald
     1973              'Chance, punters, and the fiddle: Institutionalized pilferage
                       in a hotel dining room'Pages 200-210 in The Sociology of
                       the Workplace, edited by Malcolm Warner. New    York:
                       Haldsted Press.

Mars, Gerald
     1974              'Dock pilferage'Pages 209-228 in Deviance and Social
                       Control, edited by Paul Rock and Mary McIntosh.
                       London: Tavistock.

Mars, Gerald
     1982              Cheats at Work: An Anthropology of Workplace Crime.
                       London: George Allen and Unwin.

McCullough, William W.
     1981              Sticky Fingers: A Close Look at America's Fastest Grow-
                       ing Crime. New York: American Management Association.

Merriam, Dwight H.
     1977              'Employee theft'Criminal Justice Abstracts 9:380-386.

Merton, Robert K.
     1938              'Social structure and anomie'American Sociological Review
                       3:672-682.

Miller, George A.
     1967              'Professionals in bureaucracy: Alienation among industrial
                       scientists and engineers'American Sociological Review
                       72:755-767.

Morrill, Calvin Keith
     1986              Conflict Management Among Corporate Executives:  A
                       Comparative Study. Unpublished doctoral dissertation,
                       Department of Sociology, Harvard University.

Nader, Laura
     1969              'Styles of court procedure: To make the balance'Pages
                       69-91 in Law and Culture in Society, edited by Laura
                       Nader. Chicago: Aldine Press.

Ouchi, William G.
1981          Theory Z. Reading, Mass.: Addison Wesley.

Owens, W.A.
1976          'Background data'In Handbook of Industrial and Organ-
              ization Psychology, edited by M.D. Dunnette. Chicago:
              Rand McNally.

Piore, Michael J.
1974          'Upward mobility, job monotony, and labor market struc-
              ture'Pages 73-86 in Work and the Quality of Life, edited
              by James O'Toole. Cambridge, Mass.: MIT Press.

Price, James L.
1977          A Study of Turnover. Ames, Iowa: Iowa State University
              Press.

Robin, Gerald D.
1969          'Employees as offenders'Journal of Research on Crime and
              Delinquency 6:17-33.

Rosen, Corey, Katherine J. Klein and Karen M. Young
1986          Employee Ownership in America. Lexington: Lexington
              Books.

Rosenbaum, Dennis P. and Terry L. Baumer
1983          'Measuring and controlling employee theft: A national as-
              sessment of the state-of-the-art'Journal of Security Admin-
              istration 5,2:67-80.

Ruggiero, Mary, Ellen Greenberger, and Laurence D. Steinberg
1982          'Occupational deviance among adolescent workers'Youth
              and Society 13,4:423-448.

Russell, Raymond
1985          Sharing Ownership in the Workplace. Albany: State Uni-
              versity of New York Press.

Smith, F.J.
1977          'Work attitudes as predictors of attendance on a specific
              day'Journal of Applied Psychology 62;16-19.

Sosnowski, Daniel
1985          'Curbing employee theft: How firms do it'Security Man-
              agement 29:109-112.

Sutherland, Edwin H. and Donald R. Cressey
1960          Criminology. Philadelphia: J.P. Lippincott.

Sykes, Gresham M. and David Matza
    1957            'Techniques of neutralization: A theory of delinquency'
                    American Sociological Review 22:664-670.

Taylor, Laurie and Paul Walton
    1971            'Industrial sabotage: Motives and meanings'Pages 219- 245
                    in Images of Deviance, edited by Stanley Cohen. London:
                    Penguin.

Terris, William and John Jones
    1982            'Psychological factors related to employees' theft in the
                    convenience    store    industry'Psychological    Reports
                    51:1219-1238.

Thoden van Velzen, H.U.E. and W. van Wetering
    1960            'Residence, power groups and intra-societal aggression: An
                    enquiry into the conditions leading to peacefulness within
                    non-stratified     societies'International    Archives    of
                    Ethnography 49(part 2);169-200.

Tobias, J.J.
    1972             Crime in Industrial Society in the Nineteenth Century.
                    Harmondsworth, U.K.: Penguin.

Tucker, James, Steven L. Nock, and David J. Toscano
    1989            'Employee ownership and perceptions of work: The effect
                    of an Employee Stock Ownership Plan'Work and Occupa-
                    tions 16,1:26-42. Walls, James
    1985            'Preventing employee theft'Management Review 74:45- 50.
                    Quarterly 25:72-88.

Willis, Rod
    1986            'White-collar crime: The threat from within'Management
                    Review 75:22-32.

Witty, Cathie
    1978            'Disputing issues in Sheeman, a multireligious village in
                    Lebanon'Pages 281-314 in The Disputing Process: Law in
                    Ten Societies, edited by Laura Nader and Richard F.
                    Todd, Jr., New York: Columbia University Press.

Zeitlin, Lawrence R.
    1971            'A little larceny can do alot for employee morale' Psychol-
                    ogy Today 5:22,24,26,64.

Zuboff, Shoshana
    1982            'New worlds of computer-mediated work'Harvard Business
                    Review Sept.-Oct.:142-152.

Received November 9, 1988
Accepted September 11, 1989

*Request reprints from Prof. James Tucker, 9003,*
*Barb Anne Court, Springfield, VA 22152.*

# [5]

BRIT. J. CRIMINOL. Vol. 27 No. 2 SPRING 1987

# GARMENT WORKERS: PERCEPTIONS OF INEQUITY AND EMPLOYEE THEFT

EDWARD W. SIEH *(New Jersey)* *

*This paper is concerned with the question of what garment workers did when they felt they were treated inequitably or unfairly at work. Did unfair treatment lead to employee theft? By conducting 16 semi-structured interviews with retired garment workers and employing a qualitative analysis, it was learned that neither employee theft nor other forms of deviance were often selected when responding to matters involving inequity. In only a few cases was there any indication that theft occurred as a result of the worker feeling he or she did not receive what was owed to him or her. This can be explained by the influence of the work group and the institutional mechanisms developed by the union.*

> Lumber and hardware chains, one in Pennsylvania and one in Tennessee, were surprised to discover from loss-control managers that drivers had built two entire homes from material looted from the employer. (Bottom and Kostanoski, 1983, p.20)

ESTIMATES of the cost of employee theft are astronomical. The National Council on Crime and Delinquency (N.C.C.D.) has put the amount at 15 per cent. of the United States gross national product (1978, p.5). The hidden costs include: small business failures (U.S. Chamber of Commerce, 1974), lost jobs, lost health care, lost capital investments, defaulted loans, and inflated prices (*Canadian Business,* Editors, 1976). In one midwestern company, a majority of its arbitrated employee complaints concerned issues relating to employee theft (N.C.C.D., 1978).

What is needed is an explanation for this type of behaviour that permits us to understand employee theft within the context of the work setting, and thus take some action to reduce it.

## Concept Definition

One must make the proper distinctions between employee deviance, employee crime, and employee theft. Employee deviance is a violation of any formal or informal work place norm. Employee crime refers to any illegal activity taking place at work. Included under employee crime is employee theft, which is defined as the unlawful and unauthorised intentional taking of an employer's property, with the purpose of benefiting the worker or someone who is not entitled to the property.

## The Problem

Of central importance for this study was the concern for equity, or what

* Ph.D. Stockton State College, Pomona, New Jersey.

174

GARMENT WORKERS: PERCEPTIONS OF INEQUITY AND EMPLOYEE THEFT

has been operationally defined as fairness at work, and its relationship to employee theft. Adams (1963), Blauner (1964), Dalton (1959), Jaspan and Black (1960), Berscheid, *et al.* (1968), Zinn (1974), and Gruneberg (1979) have pointed to the importance of unfairness at work and the problems associated with it. "For the younger worker, the retail employment setting provides exactly the type of inequitable work situation which may precipitate deviance against the formal organisation" (Hollinger, 1978, p.90). We need to know more about employees' deviant behaviour and the social system in which it operates.

Focussing on equity avoids the problems of attempting to extrapolate a theory of adult occupational crime from a delinquency theory which is principally concerned with unemployed juveniles. A consideration of fairness at work also attends to a central value expounded at work, particulary by the union. Most of the important theories of crime ignore equity even though it is central to the work environment. Examining fairness may help to explain why an employee who has access to many of life's valued objects risks so much by stealing. Fairness can be seen as just another form of a neutralisation technique (Sykes and Matza, 1957). It may also indicate a pre-existing philosophy that exonerates the worker.

In an argument parallelling Marxist political philosophy, which holds the capitalistic system responsible for people feeling and being cheated, the worker may feel that, since everyone is victimising him, he has a right to strike back through pilfering and fiddling. This philosophy "would exonerate those individuals whose feelings of being wronged justifies their 'getting their own back'" (Henry, 1978, p.53).

*Review of the Literature*

Employee theft has a considerable history. From the mediaeval period to the industrial revolution, wages-in-kind took the form of various rights to common land, *e.g.* the right to cut lumber or graze livestock (Gilboy, 1934; Rowe, 1968; Hay, 1975; and Linebaugh, 1981). The amount was carefully regulated by custom. With enclosure, the rights to common took on monetary connotations which meant they could now be bought and sold like other property (Thompson, 1975, p.241). This arrangement under-compensated the worker (Hay, 1975). The system of wages-in-kind was destroyed through force and fraud. The peasant, who felt he was unfairly denied what was his by tradition, supplemented his income by poaching and other forms of occupationally related crime. A wide variety of practices engaged in by the rural poor were punishable by law but were considered legitimate by them (Hay, 1975).

Present day wages-in-kind are troublesome for the worker. Wage-perquisites can depress real wages, limit spending and savings options, and be arbitrarily withdrawn. With wage-pilferage, the worker is unofficially given a wage-perquisite:

> A crucial distinction between "pilferage" and "perks" is that anybody caught pilfering is stopped, but not necessarily prosecuted. Pilferage is thus a

EDWARD W. SIEH

paradoxical state. Its immediate consequences are unpredictable, and, in historical terms, it is a transitional stage between wage-perk (which is officially institutionalised), and wage-theft (which is officially condemned). (Ditton, 1977b, pp.47–48)

## *Work group theft*

The work group is an important feature of the environment. Altheide, *et al.* (1978) argued that the discussion of wages-in-kind and other fringe benefits were a part of early job socialisation. Horning (1970) developed the concept of "property of uncertain ownership": property found at work which lacked clear ownership identification and fell into the grey area between company and personal property. This included junk, scraps, lost money, clothing, and the like. The work group permitted the taking of property of uncertain ownership, but not personal or company property.

The influence of the work group was particularly important in Mars' (1982) discussion of the "Wolves," *i.e.* miners and longshoremen who had strong work group attachments. Those who supported these norms were protected by the work group and provided with access and support. Thieves were not reported and no-one testified against them. The enforcement of official rules led to slow-downs and the eventual acceptance of a certain level of deviance. Access and support provided the worker with items he could not get otherwise. Support took either the form of assisting when a load was heavy, acting as a look-out or ignoring what was taking place.

## *Job satisfaction*

Behind any authoritative discussion of inequity at work is the over-arching problem of job satisfaction. From 1975 to 1981, the Social Science Index listed 286 different titles dealing with the subject. Industrial sabotage has been tied to job satisfaction (Taylor and Walton, 1971). Workers responded to either their powerlessness, their desire to ease the work process, or their wish to assert control over the work place. Zeitlin (1971) concluded that a certain level of employee theft should be permitted as compensation for low pay and boring work. Mangione and Quinn (1975) found a relationship between counterproductive behaviour and drug usage. Of particular note is the negative correlation found between job dissatisfaction and counterproductive behaviour for men over the age of 30. Clark and Hollinger (1981) also concluded that individuals treated unfairly at work were more likely to be involved in deviant acts against the work place.

### *Central Theoretical Concepts*

[The] norms and practices through which workers are disciplined and laid off, assigned wage rates relative to the earnings of others, and awarded

176

GARMENT WORKERS: PERCEPTIONS OF INEQUITY AND EMPLOYEE THEFT

promotions are especially critical. These matters affect the worker's sense of equity with respect to the allocation of rewards and the standards of distributive justice and therefore often determine his sense of alienation from, or integration in the industrial enterprise. (Blauner, 1964, p.25)

"Whether one wishes to promote social justice or merely to reduce economically disadvantageous industrial unrest, an understanding of inequity is important" (Adams, 1963, p.422). The concern for equity on the job and its connection to employee theft is often understated. Jaspan (1974) argued that, given a fair wage, the worker will have no reason to steal. Altheide, *et al.* (1978) believe some forms of wages-in-kind are expressions of a desire to get back at the boss or supervisors. Clark and Hollinger found that an unsatisfactory employment experience was more likely to lead an employee to "seek unauthorised redress for perceived inequities from the organisation" in the form of taking property or time (1981, p.133).

Fairness is a central value in the work place and in the home. It stems from our desire for distributive justice. Lerner (1975, 1977a, and 1977b) and Lerner and Whitehead (1980) argue that fairness is a positive motive for behaviour. This concern for fairness comes early in life. We are either born with a concern for equity (Jaques, 1970) or it is learned early on in childhood (Damon, 1981). Children quite often appeal to their parents on the basis of fairness.

When experiencing injustice, workers respond by slowing down, striking, or filing grievances. They also engage in deviant and criminal behaviour. "Men do not simply become dissatisfied with conditions they perceive to be unjust. They usually do something about them" (Adams, 1965, p.276). "Considerations of fairness and justice seem to be extremely important in determining how people respond in a potentially aggressive setting" (Donnerstein and Hatfield, 1982, p.309).

The frustration-aggression proposition theorises that workers are apt to take action calculated to restore distributive justice, and also to take aggressive action against its producer and/or beneficiary (Homans, 1982, p.xvii). Inequity produces stress (Adams, 1965; Walster *et al.*, 1973). This stress is proportionate to the level of experienced inequity (Adams, 1965). Employees learn to expect that if they work hard, they will be rewarded. Stress results when unfair treatment affects the workers' income and benefits. This tension becomes a motive for action. Actions are taken to reduce the strength of the drive. In this sense, equity theory is a drive reduction theory (Greenberg, 1982). "Accordingly, we are led to the general assertion of the reactive position that inequity motivates behaviour" (Greenberg, 1982, p.391).

Initially, a substitute response intended to lessen the strength of the stress drive is sought (such as working harder, union activities, getting drunk, or talking it over with one's spouse). Frustration sets in when it is realised that the strength of the drive (the desire for benefits and fair treatment) cannot be reduced through legitimate channels. The worker may choose to act aggressively: the greater the stress, the greater the

EDWARD W. SIEH

aggression. Thus considered, aggression, the harming or injuring of another (Baron, 1977), manifests itself when the employee fantasises about "getting even with his superiors" (Dollard, *et al.,* 1939, p.10). These harmful activities include sabotage, theft, or mutilation of company property.

A person is arguably never in a condition of permanent perfect equity but is in a state of high or low stress which occurs as a result of fading in and out of states of over-equity, equity and under-equity. A constant effort, involving checking and readjustment, is made to obtain a state of balance. Due to previous experiences, the worker knows that possibilities for inequity exist in the future. The worker therefore makes an effort to compensate for this, during periods of equity or over-equity, by engaging in behaviour characteristic of periods of under-equity. By banking a nest egg of benefits, which can be credited to his or her unofficial personal account, so to speak, the worker feels that he can restore the balance during a time when the benefits are not forthcoming. This helps to explain why a worker who appears to "have it good" will still take things that belong to the company.

Inequity is one of the central factors helping to explain employee deviance or theft. When the treatment is unfair, the income is affected, the employee feels stress which leads him to take action. The employee steals because he wants to do something about the perceived injustice at work, to get what he feels is owed to him. Equity at work may be seen as comprised of four essential elements: obligation, balance, perception and relative deprivation. Moore (1978) argues that there exists a (conscious) psychological contract between the employer and employee calling for a balance between effort and reward. This sense of balance is a matter of individual perception. Adams (1965) believes that there is a comparative process inherent in the development of expectations and perceptions of injustice. One compares what one has with what others have. This is done in relative terms.

The four dimensions of equity, obligation, balance, perception, and relative deprivation suggest that the employee would "take only what was owed" to him or her. The "taking only" connotes a concern for balance and a return to equilibrium, while the "owed to the employee" phrase identifies the concern for the obligation inherent in the agreement between the employer and the employee calling for a given amount of reward for a given amount of work, a fair day's pay for a fair day's work. This process is furthered by the work group and its influence over the worker.

*Work group influence*

Most employees do not work in isolation but are strongly influenced by the people they work with. The work group reinforces any notion of balance between reward and effort. The formation of the work group and its norms is virtually inevitable where people interact regularly. The work group offers the worker companionship, a sense of belonging, an

GARMENT WORKERS: PERCEPTIONS OF INEQUITY AND EMPLOYEE THEFT

understanding of job troubles, guides for acceptable behaviour, solutions for work-related problems, and protection for the membership (Strauss and Sayles, 1972). It also reduces conflict, provides assistance, and assures an equal distribution of the pilfered objects.

The work group's norms regulate under-producing; over-producing; telling secrets to the employer (squealing); wearing the right clothes; using tools; limitations on the amount, timing and manner of stealing; and, the appropriate targets for theft (Collins, *et al.*, 1946; Roethlisberger and Dickson, 1941; Roy, 1952; Bradford, 1976; Stoddard, 1968; Snizek, 1974; Altheide, *et al.*, 1978; Horning, 1970; and Mars, 1973, 1974, 1982).

Adherence to these norms stems from recognising the benefits of belonging to the group and respecting the power of its sanctions. Work group punishments include sabotaging the employee's work, physical injury, sarcasm, "binging" (hitting someone on the upper arm), and "vindictives" (Homans, 1950); informing management when a mistake is made in order to make the employee look bad (Strauss and Sayles, 1972); and ostracising the worker from certain social activities which means the person is not taught the secrets of the trade (Collins, *et al.*, 1946).

The work group and notions of equity come together in a number of ways. The work group reinforces the employee's perception of unfair treatment and the need to react. The work group, because of its history with the company, builds up a reservoir of knowledge and experience. A new employee who is singled out for special treatment may not know he or she is being treated unfairly, until someone in the group steps forward and tells the employee "things aren't done that way around here." They may tell the employee that the treatment they are receiving is unfair. The work group reinforces this notion of balance through its system of norms and sanctions. The employee is encouraged to take only what is owed to him or her because to take more would jeopardise the group's activities, and violate the group's norms, on what and how much can be taken.

*Opportunity*

The individual, as part of a group, will steal not only acccording to the work group's norms, but also in relation to the opportunities. When no direct contact with the targetted item exists, the thief must rely on colleagues to steal it for him. It becomes a matter of access and support. Support is found in helping to lift heavy or bulky items, or in the guise of providing lookouts (Mars, 1973, 1974).

Knowledge is also important (Clark and Hollinger, 1981). One needs to know what use an object can have or who will buy it. Risk is another variable: risk of apprehension and prosecution varies with the setting. It can be lessened with the help of other employees. Barring this help, one is left to decide on one's own whether the risk is worth it.

*Hypotheses*

Employees make a variety of responses to inequity. Some get drunk, use

179

EDWARD W. SIEH

drugs, call on the union for help, or talk over their problems with their spouse. The employee can choose to make an active or a passive response, as well as a deviant or a nondeviant response, to inequity. The choice of response will in part depend on the available opportunities. Not everyone can choose to get high on drugs, because not everyone has access to them. Not everyone can steal, because they may not have access or the necessary support, or they cannot think of how to use or dispose of what they steal.

The choice of behaviour will depend on the employee's perception that certain opportunities exist, that an acceptable level of risk is involved, and that one response is preferable to another in achieving an equitable balance with what the employee believes is owed to him. A deviant approach will be taken when the employee feels the opportunities exist, that such an approach is preferable, and that the risk is low. The choice of the active over the passive response to the perceived inequity is dependent on the level of perceived inequity. It is assumed that the greater the sense of perceived inequity, the more active the response. A behavioural typology of this argument follows:

*Behavioural Responses to Inequity*

|  | *Active response* | *Passive response* |
|---|---|---|
| Deviant behaviour | Theft | Drugs |
|  | Sabotage | Drinking |
|  |  | Sleeping on job |
| Nondeviant behaviour | Strike | Go home |
|  | File a grievance | Talk to spouse |
|  | Quit | Keep problem to self |

This model leads to the development of the following questions (a) Do employees respond to perceived unfairnes by engaging in behaviour that will restore the balance between what is given in return for what is gained? (b) Does the employee have to experience a high sense of inequity before adopting a deviant response? (c) Does the work group exert a strong influence over the worker in terms of the direction and quantity of such responses? And, (d) are perceptions of risk and opportunity indeed variables influencing employee theft?

*Methodology*

The methodology employed in this study was qualitative. It employed an "interpretive technique which seeks to describe, decode, translate, and otherwise come to terms with the meaning, not the frequency, of certain more or less naturally occurring phenomena in the social world" (Van Maanen, 1983, p.9).

Qualitative studies of employee deviance have been used by Gouldner (1954), Dalton (1959), Taylor and Walton (1971), Mars (1973 and 1974), Hay (1975), and Ditton (1977a). They conducted research based on various forms of case studies, participant observation, content analysis,

GARMENT WORKERS: PERCEPTIONS OF INEQUITY AND EMPLOYEE THEFT

interviews, and archival research. Harré and Secord (1972) argue that any effort to incorporate the same causal analysis as the physical sciences must include some understanding of the meaning assigned to items in the human environment. This is accomplished through the use of the ethogenic approach. Ethogeny is the study of social interactions and the search for causal mechanisms that are analogous to the field of the physical sciences. They argued that the meaning to be found in social interaction can be analysed with a precision that corresponds to the accuracy of measurement of physical sciences (Harré and Secord, 1972, p.126). The implementation of the ethogenic approach begins by analysing accounts of episodes which are composed of overt behaviour, thoughts, feelings, intentions and plans. This study examined the episodes involving the employee's perception that he or she was treated unfairly at work. Social behaviour is explained through the collection and analysis of participants' accounts. The goal was to discover the rules, plans, conventions, images and so forth that people use to guide their behaviour.

The informants in this study were garment workers. This industry was chosen because access was provided, because of the opportunities available for work-related deviance, because work groups could be identified, and because some measure of anonymity could be assured due to the size of the work place. Entry into the garment industry was made by progressing through the union hierarchy. Eventually, I was able to attend numerous meetings of garment workers where I contacted participants. Retired garment workers were sought out because it was believed they would be forthright and would have little reason to hide something. 16 garment workers were interviewed. The sample size limits the generalisability of the findings and no attempt is made to explain theft as found in other work settings. The research plan involved conducting semi-structured interviews with self-selected informants. Each informant was fully informed about the project, assured of its confidentiality, and asked to sign an informed consent statement.

## Analysis

The garment workers had problems with all aspects of the job. While personnel practices, work rules and informal work practices were sources of some problems, the area that caused the most difficulty was the system of rewards. Garment workers had problems with being paid not to work, underpayment of overtime, denial of wages, lost severance pay, home work, subcontracting, "making it," short bundles, sample making, missing description sheets, and miscounting garments. In response, the garment workers often did nothing, but in many cases, they went to, or threatened to go to, the union. In one particular case, when a problem arose over making the proper wages, the worker indicated that the "stealer" was used, a garment made without the required number of stitches or seams.

These problems with the system of rewards can be attributed to such factors as: concerns with "making it"; the competitiveness of the industry;

EDWARD W. SIEH

the problems with getting one's share of the rewards; and the complicated system of payment. "Making it" means reaching a level of income considered fair by the workers. By working at near maximum speed, the worker hopes to produce enough to earn the base pay plus the production bonus. This happens most often with a "repeat" garment. Familiarity breeds the speed which is needed to make a "fair" income.

The price of the garment is set by the description sheet, a device intended to promote fair wages. It describes and lays out what each seam and stitch on the garment will pay. If there is a problem with the price, the garment is sent to the price adjuster who determines, at a settlement conference, what the garment should pay. If the shop owner refuses to go along with the settled price then the workers can walk out, but not before.

With any piece rate system, complications occur when different lots of garments quickly come and go. The diversity of problems in this area indicates its complexity. These concerns are very real because the industry has a history of not paying some workers.

*Responses*

The most common response was nondeviant, and among these, the most frequent was the active response. The nondeviant-active respondent either went to the union or talked to the boss directly. The nondeviant-passive response meant the worker did nothing. Quite often the worker did what he or she could considering the opportunities. The deviant-active response was triggered by the worker's concern with "making it," *i.e.* using the "stealer" or getting an extra garment. The deviant-passive response was made as a matter of protest, or reflected the garment worker's own complicity in the matter.

Summarised data suggest that garment workers rarely resorted to deviant activity when experiencing a high sense of inequity. A small proportion of those experiencing high inequity reacted in a deviant manner. There appears to be little support for the notion that high inequity will lead to deviant responses. Both active and passive responses were adopted towards conditions of high inequity. When the level of inequity is controlled for, we continue to see the nondeviant-active response as the main approach to problem solving. It is useful to note that the garment workers were slightly more likely to take the active-deviant response under high inequity than they were under low inequity.

The deviant response to perceptions of inequity occurred in only six cases. Two cases involved what might be considered employee theft: exaggerating production records, thereby collecting more wages than deserved; and collecting wages for work done when the work rightly belonged to another person. This could be called theft of another's wages. One could also say that the use of the "stealer," when it was not encouraged by the boss, was employee theft. The stealer was used in order to increase production and thus make more money. Trying to use the stealer was one way of making an extra buck when the lot was a "stinker"

GARMENT WORKERS: PERCEPTIONS OF INEQUITY AND EMPLOYEE THEFT

(one that did not pay very well). The amount of work that went into the stinker was not balanced by the benefits attached to doing it.

There are other considerations relative to the wide use of active-nondeviant responses. These include opportunity, risk, safety, and knowlege of benefits. Opportunities existed for everyone. People were known to steal material, garment sections, and even sewing machines. Stolen items of lesser importance included needles, thread, linings, zippers, patterns, pins, etc. The most common item was the section or whole garment. An item of lesser value was not frequently stolen because one simply had to ask for it.

Although the majority of garment workers thought little theft was taking place, almost everyone could relate some instance involving employee theft. One garment worker said that it went on in almost all the places in which he had worked (Informant #13). Reports involved bosses, cutters, operators, pressers, inspectors, shop helpers, and mechanics. Bosses had cutters make extra sections from the material and then sold the extra garments "under-the-table" (Informant #5). In another case, the boss and the floorlady collaborated to collect insurance money on damaged goods (Informat #6). The boss, the floorlady and the cutter had access to the goods and the necessary support. The garment workers have collected unreported bonuses, filed false tax returns, used the "stealer," and made side deals. In some situations the collusion came from the boss and not the workers.

Four different strategies were employed when taking things out of the shop. These were the "short counter," the "purse stuffer," the "fat lady," and the "open window" routine. The "short counter" was someone who misrepresented the amount of work completed and so was paid for work that was not done. In one case, a woman, with the help of her husband, had tickets falsified at home (Informant #4). In another case, a worker who was not having her work checked handed in more tickets than completed work (Informant #5).

With the help of the sorter, a garment worker can get extra garments at the expense of another operator. This type of "short counter" shows the flexibility of the technique, for unlike the previously identified examples, the employee did not victimise the boss but the other workers. Other operators resented the faster operator getting the better deal, but they could not do much about it unless they complained to the union. Moreover, this type of "short counter" was supported by the boss not only because the boss was not victimised, but because it provided him with a chance to reward the better operators and still maintain the reward structure. Those operators who benefited from this practice do not feel it was a serious violation (Informant #21).

"Purse stuffing," the most widely identified method, involved concealing the garment in a handbag or in a bundle of old clothes. If the bag was big enough, a whole garment could be taken. "One garment worker took three garments. She would bring the pieces and complete the garment at home" (Informant #8). Any support for this technique involved looking the other

EDWARD W. SIEH

way, or arranging with another worker to borrow a section for the night, just long enough to make a copy of the pattern at home (Informant #4).

The "fat lady" routine amounted to stuffing the entire garment under the clothes the worker was wearing. Access was plentiful and support took the form of looking the other way, particularly when someone walked out of the shop with a garment hanging down below the hemline. The "open window" routine involved throwing the garment out of a window and picking it up after work.

When the workers were asked why they or someone else would take things, they often found it difficult to express a reason for it. Only a few of the workers admitted to taking anything, and when they did, it was usually within the context of taking something trivial or taking property of uncertain ownership. Many said that if they wanted something, all they had to do was to ask for it.

Their explanations can be grouped into three categories. "It is getting to be a selfish world" (Infomant #8). There is a lack of money available to them, "they like the dresses and they have no money and they have not enough intelligence" (Informant #17). "Many times, the employee does not think that they are cheating. [They] felt they were entitled to it because they worked hard" (Informant #3).

> "Well, there are girls that sometimes will take a piece of ribbon or a piece of something or you know. I think that goes on all over . . . Some say, 'Oh hell, I didn't make anything today, he owes it to me.' You know they will have that feeling that they should, or in other words, that there is no harm done to it . . . But when it is a full garment or it is two dresses of the same style [that is going too far]." (Informant #8).

These findings need to be analysed in terms of the large number of responses that were nondeviant. These responses can be attributed to the influence of the union as well as to four other factors: job perquisites, the risk involved, the work group's informal norms, and knowledge as to what could be done with a stolen piece of material.

The use of description sheets and the presence of the price adjuster suggest the strong influence of the union. Many of the garment workers had strong allegiances to the union, having worked on average 27 years in the industry. Joining was mandatory, and many of the informants held positions of union responsibility. The union expended a great deal of time, money and energy providing different services like medical assistance, educational programmes, jobs, improved working hours, and protection from the arbitrary and exploitative actions of the boss. It was also a place to get problems solved. "The times that I have gone to the union, they have given me support. They have tried to make things better. Definitely, they have given me the help that I wanted" (Informant #8).

Perception of the union is dependent on the performance of the chairlady. The protection provided by the union was personified through her role and that of the business agent. The chairlady dealt with small problems—she was the shop steward. Larger problems were dealt with by

GARMENT WORKERS: PERCEPTIONS OF INEQUITY AND EMPLOYEE THEFT

the business agent. A good business agent kept the boss on his toes and kept the lines of communication open. The settlement conference and other devices, such as the price adjuster, were intended to keep problems at a minimum.

The major focus was on the work getting out on time. If a problem could be dealt with by not filing a formal complaint, every effort was made to do so. Lots came in and went out within a few days, and any complaint about a particular lot had to be settled within a very short time if the next batch of work was not to be delayed. Other jobbers who had lots waiting were losing money, so they exerted pressure on the contractor to make a settlement, or they would have their work done in another shop. Nothing could be allowed to bog down production. The major axiom in the industry was "the more work you did the more work you got back."

Effective leaders learned the give-and-take of the industry, but also promoted the general education of the union members (Informant #20). "The union teaches us not to do bad things. The union doesn't want us and doesn't teach us to kill ourselves. The union teaches us to do a fair day's work." (Informant #17). "The union also taught us to fight until we got the deal we wanted" (Informant #20). For the most part, there was strong positive sentiment, and only a few indications of negative feelings towards the union.

Job perquisites were important too. It was quite common for the boss to permit the workers to take small pieces of material, property of uncertain ownership and old patterns. One could use a machine for personal reasons or take such items as pins, thread, and zippers. "You just had to ask. The stuff was going to be thrown out anyway" (Informant #9). Some operators used company time, equipment and material to make garments they sold to small shops. The union and the industry both frowned on this practice.

Drinking, sleeping on the job and drug usage were not much of a problem, because any of these practices meant one jeopardised the actions of other workers. The job required too much skill and co-ordination for such carelessness to be countenanced.

Another major reason for the low levels of theft and deviance was the risk attached to taking anything. A well run shop kept careful records. Employees were carefully scrutinised when suspicions arose. Operators reported on each other. If caught, one lost his or her job and sometimes got in trouble with the law. For many of these workers, their jobs meant the survival of their families (Informant #15). The workers were afraid of the boss too. "Many a boss was rough and gruff. The girls were very afraid of him" (Informant #13).

Those who took advantage of the opportunities found that assistance and support were needed. One could not steal a section unless the worker who was expecting it further down the line did not complain. Careful records were kept of the amount of material received and the number of garments made and shipped. This factor, the concern with getting the garment out on time, and the belief that the lot was a "stinker," helps in understanding the use of the "stealer" on the job.

EDWARD W. SIEH

The work group's powerful influence stemmed from the benefits it provided. These included companionship, support and protection. The workers talked things over. If someone had a problem, it was possible to find a hand (Informant #4). The work group had a number of important norms that reinforced worker solidarity. The workers could work as fast as they wanted but should not jeopardise someone's job. They should return borrowed tools, not tell secrets to the boss, not wear ostentatious clothing, or flaunt particular norms concerning an unwillingness to take the bad lot with the good:

> There are people at work in the dress shops that are hated. These employees come in strutting and everybody is naturally fuming because the style is bad and the lot is big and if an employee leaves, there is no end to it. You see if they were to stay and work, the lot would go faster. It is hard because there are people that have to work and they need the money. These people stay on the job. Then there are people that do not have to work but come in for the extra money. Some seem to care less than others and they don't give a damn. If the style is bad or difficult or time-consuming, they don't come in . . . They come in after a difficult lot is done and someone has called them up and they come in strutting like queens and sit down with a nice bundle of the next lot or repeat of the best styles. (Informant #8)

The "strutter" violates the essence of solidarity in the work group. They are treated to a diet of sarcasm, ostracism, slashed clothing, removal from the job, embarrassment, denial of access, warnings, mimicking, and heated discussions.

The garment workers had norms regulating what could be taken: you only take what you need; you should not take a full garment or two dresses of the same size; don't get another worker in trouble when you take something; don't take personal property; don't squeal on another worker unless one of these rules is violated; if you get an extra garment one time, then the next time you should be short; and finally, one method of theft should not be used too often.

A final directive concerned knowledge. The intelligent thief only took something that matched or went with something else. Some workers knew which shops would buy a dress they had made and others did not. Moreover, the worker should be smart enough not to wear a garment at a social function where someone might notice it as being stolen.

## Conclusions

There appears to be some qualified support for the hypotheses. Fairness played a large role at work. The level of inequity did not determine the type of response, but those who experienced high levels of unfairness usually confronted the problem. Most of the workers did not engage in deviant actions but instead went to the union. The union was the most important element in the selection of responses. It did a great deal to insure that fair procedures existed at work and the workers knew and appreciated this.

GARMENT WORKERS: PERCEPTIONS OF INEQUITY AND EMPLOYEE THEFT

Many of them had gone through very difficult times prior to joining the union and felt a strong loyalty because of what the union had done for them.

Besides the union, the work group played a key role in shaping the actions of the worker. The work group influenced the perception of risk and the available opportunities. Opportunity played a major part in the responses. Risk was high because careful records were kept at most shops, and the workers also policed themselves, which was necessary because of the organisation and payment of work.

Employees responded to perceived unfairness in a number of ways. Theft was rarely among them. This underscores the importance of looking at the question in depth so as to present the full picture. However, when considering the stealing and some forms of the short counter, we found the workers rationalising their actions by saying they were somehow owed what they took. They were not "making it." It was okay to take something of negligible worth but it was not appropriate to take something of value. The work group strongly supported this norm. This further supported the notion that the "workers took only what was owed to them".

The influence of the union underscores the importance of institutionally developed conflict-resolving mechanisms. Total rejection of the major hypothesis would be indicated if the union was strong and the level of theft among informants was high. This was not the case. It leads me to conclude that where the union was strong and fair, it was an important tool for resolving issues of equity at work.

The union must be strong if it is to exert a positive influence over the workers. The leadership must convince the workers that the officers are working for the worker's interest. Rhetoric must be balanced by results. Today, this is not the case. The decline in union membership and the re-examination of the role of the leadership in unions in general has created a new level of tension within the union movement. The workers are questioning the motives of the leadership and the leadership's indifference towards taking a new direction in the face of dramatic changes in the work environment. It must develop concerns for the worker that are broader than those that relate to today's job. The union cannot be arbitrary and unwilling to listen to the workers; it must recognise the importance of the give and take of negotiations and compromise. This union made an effort to do this.

If the union is not providing the means for resolving conflict at work, alternative methods will develop. The work group or an association of workers sometimes becomes the major source of influence. Management (as well as non-members of these groups) must recognise this group as representing the workers, otherwise failure and bitterness follow. Management may assign a particularly effective staff member to deal with employee relations. Whether the mechanism is formal or informal, it is important that procedures are developed for dealing with matters involving fairness at work.

This exploratory study should be recognised as forming the basis for

EDWARD W. SIEH

other research in this area. Attention should be given to a work-setting that is not union-dominated and where the workers are not desperately holding onto their jobs because they have no other alternatives. A white-collar or professional work-setting would possibly prove more fruitful in providing further tests of the hypotheses.

REFERENCES

ADAMS, J. S. (1963). "Toward an understanding of inequity". *J. of Abnorm. and Soc. Psych.*, **67,** 422–436.

ADAMS, J. S. (1965). "Inequity in social exchange". In Berkowitz, L. (eds.). *Advances in Experimental Psychology.* New York: Academic Press.

ALTHEIDE, D. L. *et al.* (1978). "The social meaning of employee theft". In Johnson, J. M. and Douglas, J. D. (eds.). *Crime At the Top.* Philadelphia: Lippincott.

BARON, R. A. (1977). *Human Aggression.* New York: Plenum Press.

BERSCHEID, E. *et al.* (1968). "Retaliation as a means of restoring equity". *J. of Pers. and Soc. Psych.*, **10,** 370–376.

BLAUNER, R. (1964). *Alienation and Freedom.* Chicago: University of Chicago Press.

BOTTOM, N. R. and KOSTANOSKI, J. (1983). *Security and Loss Control.* New York: Macmillan.

BRADFORD, J. A. (1976). "A General Perspective on Job Satisfaction: The relationship between job satisfaction, and sociological, psychological and cultural variables". (Doctoral dissertation, University of California, San Diego) Ann Arbor: *Dissertation Abstracts International.* 37/07A, DCJ77–00505, 4628.

CANADIAN BUSINESS, EDITORS (1976). "Stop employee theft: it's money down the drain". *Canadian Business,* **49,** 12–14–16.

CLARK, J. P. and HOLLINGER, R. C. (1981). *Theft by Employees in Work Organizations.* Minneapolis: University of Minnesota, Department of Sociology.

COLLINS, O. *et al.* (1946). "Restriction of output and social cleavage in industry" *App. Anthro.*, **5,** 1–14.

DALTON, M. (1959). *Men Who Manage.* New York: John Wiley.

DAMON, W. (1981). "The development of justice and self-interest during childhood". In Lerner, M. J. and Lerner, S. C. (eds.). *The Justice Motive in Social Behaviour: Adapting to Times of Scarcity and Change.* New York: Plenum Press.

DITTON, J. (1977a). *Part-time Crime.* London: Macmillan.

DITTON, J. (1977b). "Perks, pilferage and the fiddle: the historical structure of invisible wages". *Theo. and Soc.*, **4,** 39–69.

DOLLARD, *et al.* (1939). *Frustration and Aggression.* Westport: Greenwood.

DONNERSTEIN, E. and HATFIELD, E. (1982). "Aggression and inequity". In Greenberg, J. and Cohen, R. (eds.). *Equity and Justice in Social Behaviour.* New York: Academic Press.

GILBOY, E. W. (1934). *Wages in Eighteenth Century England.* Cambridge: Harvard Press.

GARMENT WORKERS: PERCEPTIONS OF INEQUITY AND EMPLOYEE THEFT

GOULDNER, A. (1954). *Patterns of Industrial Bureaucracy*. New York: Free Press.

GREENBERG, J. (1982). "Approaching equity and avoiding inequity in groups and organizations". In Greenberg, J. and Cohen, R. (eds.). *Equity and Justice in Social Behavior*. New York: Academic Press.

GRUNEBERG, M. M. (1979). *Understanding Job Satisfaction*. London: Macmillan Press.

HARRÉ, R. and SECORD, P. F. (1972). *The Explanation of Social Behavior*. Oxford: Basil Blackwell.

HAY, D. (1975). "Poaching and the Game Laws on Cannock Chase". In D. Hay *et al.* (eds.) *Albion's Fatal Tree*. New York: Pantheon.

HENRY, S. (1978). *The Hidden Economy*. Oxford: Martin Robertson.

HOLLINGER, R. C. (1978). *Employee Deviance Against the Formal Work Organization* (Doctoral dissertation, University of Minnesota). Ann Arbor: University Microfilms International: 79–18345.

HOMANS, G. C. (1950). *The Human Group*. New York: Harcourt Brace Jovanovich.

HOMANS, G. C. (1982). "Foreword". In Greenberg, J. and Cohen, R. (eds.). *Equity and Justice in Social Behavior*. New York: Academic Press.

HORNING, D. N. M. (1970). "Blue collar theft: conceptions of property attitudes toward pilfering and work group norms in a modern industrial plant". In Smigel, E. O. and Ross, H. L. (eds.). *Crime Against Bureaucracy*. New York: Van Nostrand Reingold.

JASPAN, N. (1974). *Mind Your Own Business*. Englewood Cliffs, NJ: Prentice-Hall.

JASPAN, N. and BLACK, H. (1960). *The Thief in the White-Collar*. Philadelphia: Lippincott.

JAQUES, E. (1970). *Work, Creativity and Social Justice*. New York: International University Press.

LERNER, M. J. (1975). "The justice motive in social behavior: an introduction". *J. of Soc. Iss.* **31**, 1–20.

LERNER, M. J. (1977a). "The justice motive: some hypotheses as to its origins and forms". *J. of Pers.* **45**, 1–52.

LERNER, M. J. (1977b). *The Justice Motive in Social Behavior: Hypotheses as to its Origins and Forms, II.* Research grant proposal to the Canada Council.

LERNER, M. J. and WHITEHEAD, L. A. (1980). "Procedural justice viewed in the context of justice motive theory". In Mikula, G. (ed.). *Justice and Social Interaction*. New York: Springer-Verlag.

LINEBAUGH, P. (1981). "Karl Marx, the theft of wood, and working class composition". In Greenberg, D. (ed.). *Crime and Capitalism*. Palo Alto: Mayfield.

MANGIONE, T. W. and QUINN, R. P. (1975). "Job satisfaction, counter-productive behaviour, and drug use at work". *J of App. Psych.,* **60**, 114–116.

MARS, G. (1973). "Hotel pilferage: a case study in occupational theft." In Warner, M. (ed.). *Sociology of Work*. New York: Halsted Press.

MARS, G. (1974). "Dock pilferage". In Rock, P. and McIntosh, M. (eds). *Deviance and Social Control*. London: Tavistock.

MARS, G. (1982). *Cheats At Work*. London: Allen and Unwin.

MOORE, B. (1978). *Injustice: The Social Basis of Obedience and Revolt*. White Plains, NY: M. E. Sharpe.

EDWARD W. SIEH

NATIONAL COUNCIL ON CRIME AND DELINQUENCY (1978). *Stealing From The Company: A Fact Booklet on Workplace Crime.* Hackensack, NJ: N.C.C.D.

ROETHLISBERGER, F. J. and DICKSON, W. J. (1941). *Management and the Worker.* Cambridge: Harvard University Press.

ROWE, J. W. F. (1968). *Wages in Practice and Theory.* New York: Augustus M. Kelley.

ROY, D. (1952). "Quota restriction and goldbricking in a machine shop". *Amer. J. of Soc.,* **57,** 427–442.

SNIZEK, W. E. (1974). "Deviant behavior among blue-collar workers-employees: work-norm violations in the factory". In Bryant, C. D. (ed.). *Deviant Behavior.* Chicago: Rand McNally.

*Social Science Index* (1975–1981). New York: H. W. Wilson Company.

STODDARD, E. R. (1968). "The informal code of police deviance: a group approach to 'blue-coat crime'," *J. of Crim. Law. and Pol. Sci.,* **59,** 201–213.

STRAUSS, G. and SAYLES, L. R. (1972). *Personnel.* Englewood Cliffs, NJ: Prentice-Hall.

SYKES, G. M. and MATZA, D. (1957). "Techniques of neutralization: a theory of delinquency". *Amer. Soc. Rev.,* **22,** 664–670.

TAYLOR, L. and WALTON, P. (1971). "Industrial sabotage: motives and meanings". In Cohen, S. (ed.). *Images of Deviance.* New York: Penguin Books.

THOMPSON, E. P. (1975). *Whigs and Hunters.* London: Allen Lane.

U.S. CHAMBER OF COMMERCE (1974). *White-Collar Crime.* Washington: Chamber of Commerce.

VAN MAANEN, J. (1983). "Reclaiming qualitative methods for organizational research: a preface". In Van Maanen, J. (ed.). *Qualitative Methodology.* Beverly Hills: Sage.

WALSTER, E. *et al.* (1973). "New directions in equity research". *J. of Pers. and Soc. Psych.,* **25,** 151–156.

ZEITLIN, L. R. (1971). "A little larceny can do a lot for employee morale". *Psychology Today,* **5,** 23–24; 26; 64.

ZINN, H. (1974). *Justice? Eyewitness Accounts.* Boston: Beacon Press.

# [6]

Journal of Applied Psychology
1990, Vol. 75, No. 5, 561-568

# Employee Theft as a Reaction to Underpayment Inequity: The Hidden Cost of Pay Cuts

Jerald Greenberg
Faculty of Management and Human Resources
Ohio State University

Employee theft rates were measured in manufacturing plants during a period in which pay was temporarily reduced by 15%. Compared with pre- or postreduction pay periods (or with control groups whose pay was unchanged), groups whose pay was reduced had significantly higher theft rates. When the basis for the pay cuts was thoroughly and sensitively explained to employees, feelings of inequity were lessened, and the theft rate was reduced as well. The data support equity theory's predictions regarding likely responses to underpayment and extend recently accumulated evidence demonstrating the mitigating effects of adequate explanations on feelings of inequity.

Employee theft constitutes one of the most pervasive and serious problems in the field of human resource management. Although exact figures are difficult to come by, the American Management Association (1977) has estimated that employee theft cost American businesses from $5 billion to $10 billion in 1975, representing the single most expensive form of nonviolent crime against businesses.

Traditionally, social scientists have considered several plausible explanations for employee theft. Among the most popular are theories postulating that theft is the result of attempts to ease financial pressure (Merton, 1938), moral laxity among a younger workforce (Merriam, 1977), available opportunities (Astor, 1972), expressions of job dissatisfaction (Mangione & Quinn, 1975), and the existence of norms tolerating theft (Horning, 1970). More recently, Hollinger and Clark (1983) conducted a large-scale survey and interview study designed to explore these and other explanations of employee theft. Interestingly, they found that the best predictor was employee attitudes: "When employees felt exploited by the company . . . these workers were more involved in acts against the organizations as a mechanism to correct perceptions of inequity or injustice" (Hollinger & Clark, 1983, p. 142).

Hollinger and Clark's (1983) suggestion that employee theft is related to feelings of injustice is consistent with several schools of sociological and anthropological thought. For example, in studies of hotel dining room employees (Mars, 1973) and maritime dock workers (Mars, 1974), Mars found that employees viewed theft *not* as inappropriate but "as a morally justified addition to wages; indeed, as an entitlement due from exploiting employers" (Mars, 1974, p. 224). Similarly, Kemper (1966)

argued that employee theft may be the result of "reciprocal deviance," that is, employees' perceptions that their employers defaulted on their obligations to them, thereby encouraging them to respond with similar acts of deviance. Fisher and Baron (1982) made a similar argument in presenting their equity-control model of vandalism. They claimed that vandalism is a form of inequity reduction in that an individual vandal's breaking the rules regarding property rights follows from his or her feelings of mistreatment by authorities. Recent evidence in support of this idea is found in a study by DeMore, Fisher, and Baron (1988). In that study, university students claimed to engage in more vandalism the less fairly they felt they had been treated by their university and the less control they believed they had over such treatment.

Such conceptualizations are in keeping with current theoretical positions in the field of organizational justice (Greenberg, 1987). These formulations allow more precise hypotheses to be developed regarding when employee theft is likely to occur. For example, consider equity theory's (Adams, 1965) claim that workers who feel inequitably underpaid (i.e., those who believe that the rewards they are receiving relative to the contributions they are making are less than they should be) may respond by attempting to raise their outcomes (i.e., raise the level of rewards received). Although research has supported this claim (for a review, see Greenberg, 1982), studies have been limited to situations in which persons paid on a piece-work basis produce more goods of poorer quality to raise their outcomes without effectively raising their inputs. Given earlier conceptual claims and supporting evidence associating student vandalism with inequitable treatment (DeMore et al., 1988), it may be reasoned analogously that employee theft is a specific reaction to underpayment inequity and constitutes an attempt to bring outcomes into line with prevailing standards of fair pay.

Recent research in the area of procedural justice (Lind & Tyler, 1988) has shown that perceptions of fair treatment and outcomes depend not only on the relative level of one's outcomes but also on the explanations given for those outcomes (for a review, see Folger & Bies, 1989). For example, researchers have found that decision outcomes and procedures were better

A preliminary report of the research reported in this article was presented at the annual meeting of the Academy of Management, San Francisco, August 1990.

I gratefully acknowledge the helpful comments of Robert J. Bies and three anonymous reviewers on an earlier draft of this article.

Correspondence concerning this article should be addressed to Jerald Greenberg, Faculty of Management and Human Resources, Ohio State University, 1775 College Road, Columbus, Ohio 43210-1399.

562                                   JERALD GREENBERG

accepted when (a) people were assured that higher authorities
were sensitive to their viewpoints (Tyler, 1988), (b) the decision
was made without bias (Lind & Lissak, 1985), (c) the decision
was applied consistently (Greenberg, 1986), (d) the decision was
carefully justified on the basis of adequate information (Shapiro & Buttner, 1988), (e) the decisionmakers communicated
their ideas honestly (Bies, 1986), and (f) persons influenced by
the decision were treated in a courteous and civil manner (Bies
& Moag, 1986). Such findings suggest that interpersonal treatment is an important determinant of reactions to potentially
unfair situations (Tyler & Bies, 1990).

It is an interesting idea that perceptions of inequity (and
corresponding attempts to redress inequities) may be reduced
when explanations meeting the criteria presented in the preceding paragraph are offered to account for inequitable states. This
notion was tested in the present study by capitalizing on a
naturalistic manipulation—a temporary pay reduction for employees of selected manufacturing plants. Data were available
for 30 consecutive weeks: 10 weeks before a pay reduction occurred, 10 weeks during the pay-reduction period, and 10 weeks
after normal pay was reinstated. Following from equity theory,
it was hypothesized that ratings of payment fairness would be
lower during the pay-reduction period than during periods of
normal payment (i.e., before and after the pay reduction). It was
similarly hypothesized that rates of employee theft would be
higher during the reduced-pay period than during periods of
normal payment. Such actions would be consistent with equity
theory's claim that one likely way of responding to underpayment inequity is by attempting to raise the level of rewards
received. Although not previously studied in this connection,
employee theft is a plausible mechanism for redressing states of
inequity (Hollinger & Clark, 1983).

Additional hypotheses were derived from recent research
(e.g., Cropanzano & Folger, 1989; Folger & Martin, 1986; Shapiro & Buttner, 1988; Weiner, Amirkham, Folkes, & Varette,
1987) showing that explanations for negative outcomes mitigate
people's reactions to those outcomes (for a review, see Folger &
Bies, 1989; Tyler & Bies, 1990). Generally speaking, in these
studies the use of adequate explanations (i.e., ones that relied on
complete, accurate information presented in a socially sensitive
manner) tended to reduce the negative reactions that resulted
from such outcomes and facilitated acceptance of the outcomes. From the perspective of Folger's (1986) referent cognitions theory, adequate explanations help victimized parties
place their undercompensation in perspective by getting them
to understand that things could have been worse. As such, adequate explanations were expected in the present study to lessen
the feelings of inequity that accompanied the pay cut. Thus, it
was reasoned that employees' feelings of payment inequity, and
attempts to reduce that inequity (such as by pilfering), would be
reduced when adequate explanations were given to account for
the pay reduction. Specifically, it was hypothesized that the
magnitude of the expressed inequity—and the rate of employee
theft—would be lower when pay reductions were adequately
explained than when they were inadequately explained.

## Method

### Participants

Participants in the study were nonunion employees working for 30
consecutive weeks in three manufacturing plants owned by the same

Table I
*Distribution of Attrition and Turnover Across Conditions*

| Condition | Starting *n* | Missing data | Resignations | | | Final *n* |
|---|---|---|---|---|---|---|
| | | | Before pay cut | During pay cut | After pay cut | |
| Adequate explanation (Plant A) | 64 | 6 | 1 | 1 | 1 | 55 |
| Inadeaute explanation (Plant B) | 53 | 8 | 1 | 12 | 2 | 30 |
| Control (Plant C) | 66 | 5 | 1 | 0 | 2 | 58 |

parent company. The plants were located in different sections of the
midwestern United States and manufactured small mechanical parts
mostly for the aerospace and automotive industries. The employees'
average age (*M* = 28.5 years), level of education (*M* = 11.2 years), and
tenure with the company (*M* = 3.2 years) did not significantly differ
among the three plants, *F* < 1.00, in all cases. The local unemployment
rates in the communities surrounding the three plants were not significantly different from each other (overall *M* = 6.4%), *F* < 1.00. It is
important to establish this equivalence of characteristics across research sites because the assignment of individuals to conditions was
not random across sites, thereby precluding the assumption of equivalence afforded by random assignment (Cook & Campbell, 1976).

As the study began, Plant A employed 64 workers in the following
jobs: 5 salaried low-level managerial employees (4 men, 1 woman); 47
hourly-wage semiskilled and unskilled production workers (38 men, 9
women); and 12 hourly-wage clerical workers (all women). Almost
identical proportions with respect to job type (and sex of employees
within job type) existed in Plant B (*n* = 53) and Plant C (*n* = 66).
Because some employees failed to complete questionnaires during
some weeks, and because some employees voluntarily left their jobs
during the study period, complete sets of questionnaires were available
from 55 employees of Plant A, 30 employees of Plant B, and 58 employees of Plant C. This constituted a total sample of 143 employees, distributed to conditions as summarized in Table 1. The demographic characteristics of the 40 workers who were not included in the study did not
differ significantly from the characteristics of the 143 who remained in
the study (in all cases, *F* < 2.00), minimizing the possibility that those
who remained in the study were a select group.

### Procedure

Because of the loss of two large manufacturing contracts, the host
company was forced to reduce its payroll by temporarily cutting wages
by 15% across the board in two of its manufacturing plants (Plants A
and B). This was done in lieu of laying off any employees. After this
decision was made, I was asked to help assess the impact of the wage
cuts in several key areas, including employee theft. Each of the payment-group manipulations was carried out in a separate plant. The
assignment of Plant A to one experimental condition and Plant B to
another experimental condition was determined at random. Assignment to the control group was determined by the host company's decision that pay cuts were not necessary in Plant C.[1]

---

[1] Admittedly, conducting the study in this manner meant that the
two randomly assigned groups may have been nonequivalent with respect to some unknown variables that might have otherwise affected
the results (Cook & Campbell, 1976). However, some reassurance of

The *adequate explanation* condition was created in Plant A. To effect this, a meeting (lasting approximately 90 min) was called at the end of a work week. At that meeting, all employees were told by the company president that their pay was going to be reduced by 15%, effective the following week, for a period expected to last 10 weeks. During this meeting several types of explanations were provided. On the basis of recent research (Folger & Bies, 1989; Tyler & Bies, 1990), I hypothesized that these explanations would mitigate reactions to the pay cut. The workers were told that company management seriously regretted having to reduce their pay but that doing so would preclude the need for any layoffs. They were further assured that all plant employees would share in the pay cuts and that no favoritism would be shown.[2] A relevant verbatim passage follows:

> Something we hate to do here at [company name] is lay off any of our employees. But, as you probably know, we've lost our key contracts with [company names], which will make things pretty lean around here for a little while. As a result, we need to cut somewhere, and we've come up with a plan that will get us through these tough times. I've been working on it with [name of person] in accounting, and we're sure it will work. The plan is simple: Starting Monday, we will each get a 15% cut in pay. This applies to you, to me, to everyone who works here at [name of plant]. If we do it this way, there'll be no cut in benefits and no layoffs—just a 15% pay reduction. So, either your hourly wages or your salary will be reduced by 15%. Will it hurt? Of course! But, it will hurt us all alike. We're all in it together. Let me just add that it really hurts me to do this, and the decision didn't come easily. We considered all possible avenues, but nothing was feasible. I think of you all as family, and it hurts me to take away what you've worked so hard for. But, for the next 10 weeks, we'll just have to tough it out.

In addition to these remarks, the basis for the decision was clearly explained and justified by presenting charts and graphs detailing the temporary effects of the lost contracts on cash-flow revenues. Projections verified that the cash-flow problem dictating the need for the pay cuts was only temporary, and this was clearly explained. All employees were assured that the pay cut was designed to last only 10 weeks.[3] Specifically, the employees were told the following:

> The reason I'm sharing all this information with you is that I want you to understand what is happening here. It's just a temporary problem we're facing, and one that I hope will never happen again. At least the best course of action from our accounting department is clear: The pay cuts will work, and they will not have to last longer than 10 weeks. The new jobs we'll be picking up from [name of company] will really help get us back on our feet. Hopefully, by then we'll be stronger than ever. Of course, I know we're no stronger than our people, and I personally thank each and every one of you for your strength.

The tone of the presentation was such that a great deal of respect was shown for the workers, and all questions were answered with sensitivity. Approximately 1 hr was spent answering all questions. Each response brought an expression of remorse at having to take such action (e.g., "Again, I really wish this weren't necessary."). The good intent of

this message was reinforced by the fact that the president issued the message in person.

Plant B was the site of the *inadequate explanation* condition. Here, a meeting lasting approximately 15 min was called at the end of a work week. All employees were told by a company vice president that their pay was going to be reduced by 15%, effective the following week, for a period expected to last 10 weeks. The only additional information that was provided indicated that the lost contracts dictated the need for the pay cut. No expressions of apology or remorse were shared, and the basis for the decision was not clearly described. The following verbatim remarks characterize this condition:

> It is inevitable in a business like ours that cost-cutting measures are often necessary to make ends meet. Unfortunately, the time has come for us to take such measures here at [company name]. I know it won't be easy on anyone, but [name of company president] has decided that a 15% across-the-board pay cut will be instituted effective Monday. This is largely the result of the fact that we've lost our contracts with [name of companies]. However, soon we'll be picking up jobs with [name of company], so we're sure the pay cuts will last only 10 weeks. I realize this isn't easy, but such reductions are an unfortunate fact of life in the manufacturing business. On behalf of [company president's name] and myself, we thank you for bearing with us over these rough times. I'll answer one or two questions, but then I have to catch a plane for another meeting.

Finally, because the parts manufactured at Plant C were unaffected by the lost contracts, no pay cuts were mandated there. Plant C constituted the *control* condition for the study.

## Measures

Two categories of dependent measures were used: actuarial data on employee theft, and self-report measures tapping some of the processes assumed to be underlying the theft behavior.

---

between-group similarity is provided by the demonstrated equivalence between worker characteristics, economic conditions, and job duties for both plants. Moreover, the deliberate assignment of Plant C to the control condition raises the possibility that something besides the lack of manipulation may have been responsible for the results (Cook & Campbell, 1976). However, informal postexperiment interviews with plant officials and employees confirmed that no unusual "local history" events occurred during the study period. Further assurance that this was not a problem comes from the fact that, before and after the pay cut, the control group's responses were identical to the other groups' responses for all measures used in the study.

---

[2] Before the meetings scheduled in each plant, the individuals involved (i.e., company president in Plant A and a vice president in Plant B) met with me to develop outlines of their presentations. Several carefully crafted sentences conveying salient aspects of the manipulation were prepared for inclusion in the speaker's notes. Because local company norms dictated using informal meetings instead of formal presentations, complete scripts for the entire sessions could not be prepared in advance. As a result, it was necessary to establish that key differences in the manipulated variables were actually communicated in the meetings. With this in mind, each session was videotaped, and the videotapes were played back to a group of 112 undergraduate students after all identifying information was deleted. The students were asked to indicate in which of the two tapes (Tape A for Plant A; Tape B for Plant B) the speaker (a) presented more information about the pay cuts and (b) expressed greater remorse about the pay cuts. The order of presentation of the tapes was randomized. Virtually all of the students agreed that the speaker on Tape A presented more information and expressed greater remorse. Taken together with my in-person confirmation that the manipulations were conducted as desired, these findings suggest that differentially adequate explanations were given to the two groups. Unfortunately, it was not possible to conduct further analyses on these tapes because the host company insisted that they be destroyed to prevent the unwanted dissemination of sensitive company information.

[3] Because of the sensitive and privileged nature of the internal accounting information, I was not permitted to divulge these data. Indeed, although I helped company officials present this information in understandable form, these charts and graphs were never made part of my file.

*Employee theft rates.* The measure of employee theft used for this study was the company accounting department's standard formula for computing "shrinkage." The formula yielded the percentage of inventory (e.g., tools, supplies, etc.) unaccounted for by known waste, sales, use in the conduct of business, or normal depreciation. (For a discussion of the difficulties attendant to deriving such measures, see Hollinger & Clark, 1983.) These measures were obtained unobtrusively (during nonwork hours) by representatives of the company's headquarters on a weekly basis during the study period. The persons taking inventory were aware of any legitimate factors that contributed to accounted-for changes in inventory levels (such as shipments received, supplies used during projects, etc.) but were blind to the experimental hypotheses.[4]

Because no single standard for computing shrinkage is uniformly used (Hollinger & Clark, 1983), it was not possible to compare the base rates of employee theft in the present sample to any industry-wide average. However, evidence that the employee theft rate studied here was not atypical was provided by showing that the mean theft rate for the 10-week period before the pay cut was not significantly different from the overall theft rate for all three plants for the prior year, $F < 1.00$. These data are important in that they provide some assurance that the changes in theft rates observed were not simply deviations from unusual patterns that later merely regressed to the mean.[5]

*Questionnaire measures.* Two types of questionnaire measures were needed to establish the validity of the study and to facilitate interpretation of the theft data—one group of questions to verify differences in familiarity with the basis for establishing pay (the manipulation check), and another group of questions to establish differences in perceived payment equity. The questionnaires were administered biweekly (during odd-numbered weeks in the study period) at the plant sites during nonworking hours. Because a larger, unrelated study had been going on for several months, the workers were used to completing questionnaires, making it unlikely that any suspicions were aroused by the questions inserted for this study. Participants were assured of the anonymity of their responses.

The "pay basis" measure was designed to provide a check on the validity of the payment-group variable. Participants answered four items on a 5-point scale ranging from *not at all* (1), to *slightly* (2), to *moderately* (3), to *highly* (4) to *extremely* (5). The questions were (a) "How adequate was your employer's explanation regarding the basis of your current pay?" (b) "How familiar are you with the way your employer determines your pay?" (c) "How thoroughly did your employer communicate the basis for your current pay to you?" and (d) "How much concern did your employer show about your feelings when communicating your pay?" A high degree of internal consistency was found for these items (coefficient alpha = .89).

The "pay equity" measure consisted of four items, three of which were anchored with the same scale points as the pay basis items. Specifically, participants responded to the following items: (a) "To what extent do you believe your current pay reflects your actual contributions to the job?" (b) "How fairly paid do you feel you currently are on your job?" and (c) "How satisfied are you with your current overall pay level?" The fourth item asked, "Relative to what you feel you should be paid, do you believe your current pay is: ___ much too low, ___ a little too low, ___ about right, ___ a little too high, ___ much too high?" Because only the first 3 points of this bidirectional scale were actually used, responses to this 3-point scale were combined with the 5-point unidirectional scales for the other items. Coefficient alpha was high (.84), justifying combining the individual items. The option of using existing standardized scales tapping reactions to pay (e.g., the Pay Satisfaction Questionnaire; Heneman & Schwab, 1985) was rejected in favor of ad hoc measures because these were judged to be much more sensitive to the measurement objectives of the present study (cf. Heneman, 1985).

## Results

### Preliminary Analyses

Prior to the principal data analyses, preliminary analyses were conducted to determine whether to separate the 15 biweekly questionnaire responses into three equal groups, reflecting responses before, during, and after the pay cut. The five 2-week response periods were treated as a repeated measure in mixed-design analyses of variance (ANOVAs) in which the payment group was the between-subjects factor (adequate explanation, inadequate explanation, no pay cut). Separate analyses were conducted for each of the three groups. Because no significant main effects or interactions involving the response periods were obtained in analyses for either questionnaire measure (all $Fs < 1.00$), the decision was made to combine the observations into three groups composed of more reliable observations (before, during, or after the pay cut).

Because only one employee-theft-rate figure was reported for each week (the figure was aggregate, as opposed to individual, data), it was not possible to conduct a parallel set of ANOVAs for this measure. However, separate tests were performed within each payment group to compare each week's theft rate to the mean for all 10 weeks. This process was repeated separately for each of the three response periods (i.e., before, during, and after the pay cut). Because no significant effects emerged in any of these analyses (all values of $t < .50$, $df = 9$), the decision was made (paralleling that for the questionnaire measures) to group the weekly scores into three 10-week response periods.

### Employee Theft Rate

Analyses of theft rates were based on a $3 \times 3$ mixed-design ANOVA in which payment group was the between-subjects variable, response period was the within-subjects variable, and the 10 weekly theft rates within each cell constituted the data. A significant Payment Period × Response Period interaction was found, $F(4, 56) = 9.66$, $p < .001$. Figure 1 summarizes the means contributing to this interaction.

For each payment group, simple effects tests were performed to determine whether the means differed significantly across response periods. Any significant effects were followed up with the Tukey honestly significant difference (HSD) procedure (with alpha set at .05). In addition, tests for quadratic trend components were performed using orthogonal polynomials (Hays, 1963). This analysis was performed to note trends in the data over time in a situation in which the number of available

---

[4] Although the theft-rate figures (i.e., percentage of inventory loss unaccounted for) were used internally to compute dollar-loss figures, data substantiating a specific dollar-loss amount caused by the thefts were not made available to me. Again, this decision was prompted by the company's desire to avoid potential embarrassment.

[5] Unfortunately, week-by-week theft-rate data were not available prior to the study period. As a result, it was impossible to compare the weekly theft rates during the study to earlier weekly theft rates. Thus, it was not possible to rule out the possibility raised by one reviewer that the results may reflect some seasonal fluctuations in theft that coincided with the manipulation period.

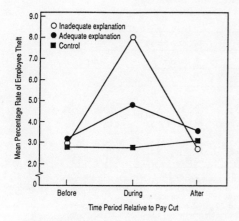

*Figure 1.* Mean percentage of employee theft as a function of time relative to pay cut.

data points was too small to use time series analyses (Zuwaylif, 1970).

A simple effects test within the inadequate-explanation condition was significant, $F(2, 27) = 9.15$, $p < .001$. Post hoc tests revealed that significantly higher levels of theft were observed during the pay reduction than before or after the pay reduction. Consistent with this configuration, the quadratic trend was highly significant, $F(1, 27) = 12.18$, $p < .001$.

Within the adequate-explanation condition, the overall simple effects test was weaker but still significant, $F(2, 52) = 3.76$, $p < .05$. This effect was the result of a similar, though less pronounced, pattern of means showing theft to be higher during the pay cut than either before or after the pay cut. Tests for a quadratic trend component failed to reach conventional levels of significance, $F(2, 52) = 2.10$, $p < .15$.

Finally, within the control group, simple effects tests revealed that the means did not differ from each other significantly across the three response periods, $F(2, 55) < 1.00$.

To establish pre- and postmanipulation equivalence, it was useful to compare means between payment groups (adequate explanation, inadequate explanation, no pay cut) within response periods. Simple effects tests showed no significant simple main effects of payment group before or after the pay cut, $F < 1.00$ in both cases. However, the effect of payment group was highly significant during the pay cut, $F(2, 27) = 10.71$, $p < .001$. Tukey HSD tests revealed that the three means were significantly different from each other. In other words, within the pay-reduction period, the theft rate in the inadequate-explanation condition ($M = 8.9$) was significantly higher than that in the adequate-explanation condition ($M = 5.7$), which was in turn higher than that in the control condition ($M = 3.7$).

## Questionnaire Responses

Responses to the pay basis and pay equity questionnaires were analyzed with ANOVA designs identical to that used for the

employee-theft measure. For these dependent variables, however, the data consisted of individual responses to the summed items constituting each questionnaire within each cell. The two questionnaire measures were not significantly correlated, $r = .07$.

For the pay basis measure, a significant Payment Group × Response Period interaction was obtained, $F(4, 280) = 256.10$, $p < .0001$. The corresponding means and standard deviations are summarized at the top of Table 2. As shown, post hoc tests revealed that employees in the adequate-explanation condition demonstrated greater understanding of the basis for pay determination than employees in the other two conditions once the explanation occurred (i.e., during and after the pay cut). The adequate-explanation manipulation successfully enhanced employees' understanding of the basis for pay determination.

A significant interaction effect also was obtained for the pay equity measure, $F(4, 280) = 29.05$, $p < .001$. The corresponding means and standard deviations are summarized at the bottom of Table 2. As shown, post hoc tests revealed that during the pay cut, employees in the inadequate-explanation condition expressed the greatest perceptions of pay inequity. Workers whose pay reductions were adequately explained to them did not express heightened payment inequity while their pay was reduced.

## Turnover

A summary of missing data and data lost because of voluntary turnover appears in Table 1. Not surprisingly, the majority of the turnover occurred among employees experiencing inadequately explained pay reductions (12 of the 52 workers, or 23.1% of those still on the job at that time). Resignations in other conditions were uniformly 5% or less. Consistent with this, the distribution of resignations over conditions during the pay-cut period was highly significant, $\chi^2(2, N = 13) = 20.48$, $p < .001$—a result of the fact that 12 of the 13 resignations occurred in the inadequate-explanation group. By contrast, the distribution of resignations across conditions was equal before the pay cut, $\chi^2(2, N = 3) < 0.5$, and after the pay cut, $\chi^2(2, N = 5) < 0.5$.

## Discussion

The data support the hypothesis derived from equity theory (Adams, 1965) that workers experiencing underpayment inequity would attempt to redress that inequity by raising their inputs—in the present case, by pilfering from their employer. Indeed, while workers experienced a 15% pay reduction, they reported feeling underpaid and stole over twice as much as they did when they felt equitably paid. Two distinct interpretations of these theft data may be offered, both of which are consistent with equity theory (Adams, 1965). First, it is possible that the pay reduction led to feelings of frustration and resentment, which motivated the aggressive acts of theft. This possibility is in keeping with recent research findings demonstrating that pay cuts are associated with negative affective reactions to organizational authorities (Greenberg, 1989) and that increases in vandalism correlate positively with perceptions of mistreatment by authorities (DeMore et al., 1988). Such an interpretation follows from a reciprocal deviance orientation to inequity

Table 2
*Data Summaries for Questionnaire Measures*

| | | Response period | | | | | |
| | | Before | | During | | After | |
| Measure/payment group | n | M | SD | M | SD | M | SD |
|---|---|---|---|---|---|---|---|
| Pay basis[a] | | | | | | | |
| Inadequate explanation | 30 | 40.70$_a$ | 4.38 | 76.10$_b$ | 6.48 | 73.73$_b$ | 5.70 |
| Adequate explanation | 55 | 43.22$_a$ | 5.58 | 42.39$_a$ | 3.40 | 43.74$_a$ | 4.93 |
| Control | 58 | 42.36$_a$ | 6.49 | 40.72$_a$ | 3.83 | 41.90$_a$ | 4.46 |
| Pay equity[b] | | | | | | | |
| Inadequate explanation | 30 | 56.87$_a$ | 5.54 | 40.20$_b$ | 7.56 | 57.43$_a$ | 6.70 |
| Adequate explanation | 55 | 61.22$_a$ | 9.57 | 59.56$_a$ | 9.52 | 56.03$_a$ | 9.37 |
| Control | 58 | 61.29$_a$ | 8.67 | 60.98$_a$ | 9.18 | 58.02$_a$ | 8.57 |

*Note.* Within each row and each column, means not sharing a common subscript are significantly different from each other beyond the .05 level on the basis of the Tukey honestly significant difference technique corrected for confounded comparisons with the Cicchetti (1972) approximation.
[a] Mean scores for the pay basis measure could range from 20 to 100. Higher scores reflect greater degrees of familiarity with the basis for establishing pay.   [b] Mean scores for the pay equity measure could range from 20 to 90. Higher scores reflect greater degrees of perceived payment equity.

reduction, which suggests that employees' acts of deviance are encouraged by their beliefs that their employers defaulted on their obligations to them by reducing their pay (Kemper, 1966). From this perspective, acts of theft may be understood as a manifestation of feelings of mistreatment.

It is also possible to interpret the thefts as direct attempts to correct underpayment inequity by adjusting the balance of valued resources between the worker and the specific source of that inequity. As such, acts of theft may be interpreted as unofficial transfers of outcomes from the employer to the employee. Because no direct evidence is available suggesting that the stolen items had any positive valence to the employees, it is impossible to claim unambiguously that the theft rates represented employees' attempts to increase their own outcomes. Although such an interpretation is consistent with a considerable amount of evidence on the distribution of rewards and resources (for reviews, see Freedman & Montanari, 1980; Leventhal, 1976), it is also possible that disgruntled employees may have been content to reduce the valued resources available to the agent of their discontent. That is, they may have been motivated to reduce the employer's worth whether or not doing so directly benefited themselves. Unfortunately, the questionnaire items that would have been necessary to provide more refined interpretations of the present data might also have aroused subjects' suspiciousness that theft was being studied, thereby creating the potential for subject reactance (Webb, Campbell, Schwartz, Sechrest, & Grove, 1981). As a result, no such self-report data were collected. Nevertheless, the results are clearly in keeping with equity theory.

The present data also reveal a critical moderator of the tendency to pilfer to restore equity with one's employer—namely, the use of an adequate explanation for the pay cut. Pay cuts that were explained in an honest and caring manner were not seen by employees as being as unfair as pay cuts that were not explained carefully. Accordingly, reactions to carefully explained underpayment also were less severe (i.e., the pilferage rates were lower). These findings add to a recently developing body of

research showing that the use of adequately reasoned explanations offered with interpersonal sensitivity tends to mitigate the negative effects associated with the information itself (for reviews, see Folger & Bies, 1989; Tyler & Bies, 1990). The explanations used in the present study were obviously quite successful in reducing costs, both to employees (in terms of inequity distress) and employers (in terms of pilferage and turnover).

An interesting and important aspect of the present study is that a sizeable portion of the participants in the inadequate-explanation condition voluntarily left their jobs during the pay-reduction period; in fact, a much larger proportion resigned than did so in any other condition (or within the same condition at other times). It is tempting to take this finding as support for the idea that quitting one's job is an extreme form of reaction to underpayment inequity (Finn & Lee, 1972) and that the voluntary turnover found here was another form of reaction to inequity. However, because of the nonrandom design of the study, it is not possible to rule out factors other than the experimental manipulation—a difficulty common to quasi-experimental studies (Cook & Campbell, 1976). Despite this problem, several facts lend support to the inequity interpretation. First, the finding that the theft rate immediately before the manipulations did not differ significantly from the previous year's theft rate suggests that nothing out of the ordinary was happening that may have been responsible for the results. Second, because the theft rate was highest precisely under the only conditions in which feelings of inequity were high (i.e., during the pay-cut period following an inadequate explanation), feelings of inequity and theft rate probably are related, both resulting from the manipulated variable exactly as predicted by equity theory (Adams, 1965) and referent cognitions theory (Folger, 1986). Because this interpretation is theoretically supported, its position is strengthened relative to alternatives that may be raised in the absence of random assignment.

Generalizing from the present findings, it appears that adequately explaining inequitable conditions may be an effective means of reducing potentially costly reactions to feelings of underpayment inequity. To be effective, however, such explanations must be perceived as honest, genuine, and not manipulative (Tyler, 1988). Still, to the extent that underpayment conditions are acknowledged and justified by employers (as opposed to ignored or minimized by them), it appears that both workers and their organizations may stand to benefit. Given the high costs of employee theft (American Management Association, 1977), it appears that explaining the basis for inequities may be a very effective (and totally free) mechanism for reducing the costs of employee theft.

Practical implications notwithstanding, the present findings raise some important questions for equity theory (Adams, 1965) about the use of various modes of inequity reduction. Whereas the focus of this study was on pilferage, turnover was another type of response that occurred. Unfortunately, the nature of the present data makes it impossible to determine the trade-offs between various modes of inequity reduction. Did some employees resign in response to underpayment while others (perhaps those with fewer options for alternative employment) stayed on and expressed their negative feelings by stealing? Or was it that the most aggrieved employees stole company property before leaving, while others simply lowered their inputs? Because the theft rates were aggregate, actuarial data and could not be traced to particular employees, and because performance data were not collected, it was not possible to determine when and how different forms of inequity-reduction behavior are likely to occur. As a result, serious questions remain regarding how different inequity-resolution tactics may be used in conjunction with each other.

Confidence in interpretations of the present findings is limited because actuarial-level dependent measures (theft and turnover) were collected in conjunction with an individual-level variable (perceived payment equity), thereby making it impossible to conduct mediational analyses of the results. Exacerbating this problem is the fact that the use of a quasi-experimental design does not allow the discounting of alternative explanations (as noted earlier). Thus, although it is plausible that inequity leads to stealing unless mitigated by an adequate explanation, it is impossible to statistically discount the alternative possibility that unknown preexisting differences between the plants constituting the payment groups (e.g., different norms against stealing or differential acceptance of management's promise that the pay cut would be temporary) may have been responsible for the results. However, in support of the present findings, it is important to note that such limitations are inherent to some degree in all quasi-experimental research designs (Cook & Campbell, 1976).

Although nonrandom assignment precludes the discounting of alternative explanations, support for the present interpretation of the data may be derived from converging sources of theoretically based data. In this case, several lines of analogous research converge with my claim that adequate explanations enhanced the acceptance of undesired outcomes. For example, Folger and his associates (e.g., Folger & Martin, 1986; Folger, Rosenfield, & Robinson, 1983) measured laboratory subjects' feelings of discontent in reaction to procedural changes that created unfavorable conditions for them. Consistent with referent cognitions theory (Folger, 1986), Folger and his colleagues found that these feelings of discontent were reduced only when

the need to make procedural changes was adequately explained. Similarly, in another line of investigation, Weiner et al. (1987) found that persons victimized by another's harmdoing expressed less anger toward the harmdoer when claims of mitigating circumstances were offered for the harmdoer's actions. Both lines of investigation show that negative affective reactions are reduced by the presentation of adequate explanatory information. As such, they provide good convergent evidence for the my claim that adequately explained pay cuts mitigated feelings of inequity and reactions to underpayment inequity.

Finally, an important question may be raised about the compound nature of the explanation manipulation used in the present study. Because the adequate-explanation condition and the inadequate-explanation condition differed along several dimensions (postulated a priori to contribute to mitigation of the effects of the inequity), it was not possible to determine the individual effects of the various contributing factors. Specifically, the explanations differed in terms of several factors. Some of these, such as the quality of the information and the interpersonal sincerity of its presentation, have been recognized as mitigating reactions to undesirable outcomes (Shapiro & Buttner, 1988). Other differences between conditions, such as possible differences in the credibility of the source (the president versus the vice president) have not yet been studied. Clearly, the unique effects of these factors are prime candidates for future research efforts.

To conclude, the results of the present study shed new light on employee theft—one of the most important problems in the field of human-resource management. The evidence confirms that employee theft is a predictable response to underpayment inequity and reveals that such reactions can be substantially reduced by the inexpensive tactic of explaining the basis for the inequity in clear, honest, and sensitive terms.

## References

Adams, J. S. (1965). Inequity in social exchange. In L. Berkowitz (Ed.), *Advances in experimental social psychology* (Vol. 2, pp. 267–299). San Diego, CA: Academic Press.

American Management Association. (1977, March). *Summary overview of the "state of the art" regarding information gathering techniques and level of knowledge in three areas concerning crimes against business: Draft report.* Washington, DC: National Institute of Law Enforcement and Criminal Justice, Law Enforcement Assistance Administration.

Astor, S. D. (1972, March). Twenty steps to preventing theft in business. *Management Review, 61*(3), 34–35.

Bies, R. J. (1986, August). *Identifying principles of interactional justice: The case of corporate recruiting.* Symposium conducted at the annual meeting of the Academy of Management, Chicago, IL.

Bies, R. J., & Moag, J. S. (1986). Interactional justice: Communication criteria of fairness. In R. J. Lewicki, B. H. Sheppard, & B. H. Bazerman (Eds.), *Research on negotiation in organizations* (Vol. 1, pp. 43–55). Greenwich, CT: JAI Press.

Cicchetti, D. V. (1972). Extension of multiple-range tests to interaction tables in the analysis of variance: A rapid approximate solution. *Psychological Bulletin, 77,* 405–408.

Cook, T. D., & Campbell, D. T. (1976). The design and conduct of quasi-experiments and true experiments in field settings. In M. D. Dunnette (Ed.), *Handbook of industrial and organizational psychology* (pp. 223–326). Chicago: Rand McNally.

568                                    JERALD GREENBERG

Cropanzano, R., & Folger, R. (1989). Referent cognitions and task decision autonomy: Beyond equity theory. *Journal of Applied Psychology,*
*74,* 293–299.

DeMore, S. W, Fisher, J. D., & Baron, R. M. (1988). The equity-control
model as a predictor of vandalism among college students. *Journal*
*of Applied Social Psychology, 18,* 80–91.

Finn, R. H., & Lee, S. M. (1972). Salary equity: Its determination,
analysis and correlates. *Journal of Applied Psychology, 56,* 283–292.

Fisher, J. D., & Baron, R. M. (1982). An equity-based model of vandalism. *Population and Environment, 5,* 182–200.

Folger, R. (1986). Rethinking equity theory: A referent cognitions
model. In H. W. Bierhoff, R. L. Cohen, & J. Greenberg (Eds.), *Justice*
*in social relations* (pp. 145–162). New York: Plenum Press.

Folger, R., & Bies, R. J. (1989). Managerial responsibilities and procedural justice. *Employee Responsibilities and Rights Journal, 2,* 79–
90.

Folger, R., & Martin, C. (1986). Relative deprivation and referent cognitions: Distributive and procedural justice effects. *Journal of Applied*
*Psychology, 22,* 531–546.

Folger, R., Rosenfield, D., & Robinson, T. (1983). Relative deprivation
and procedural justification. *Journal of Personality and Social Psy-*
*chology, 45,* 268–273.

Freedman, S. M., & Montanari, J. R. (1980). An integrative model of
managerial reward allocation. *Academy of Management Review, 5,*
381–390.

Greenberg, J. (1982). Approaching equity and avoiding inequity in
groups and organizations. In J. Greenberg & R. L. Cohen (Eds.),
*Equity and justice in social behavior* (pp. 389–435). San Diego, CA:
Academic Press.

Greenberg, J. (1986). Determinants of perceived fairness of performance evaluations. *Journal of Applied Psychology, 71,* 340–342.

Greenberg, J. (1987). A taxonomy of organizational justice theories.
*Academy of Management Review, 12,* 9–22.

Greenberg, J. (1989). Cognitive re-evaluation of outcomes in response
to underpayment inequity. *Academy of Management Journal, 32,*
174–184.

Hays, W. L. (1963). *Statistics.* New York: Holt, Rinehart, & Winston.

Heneman, H. G., III. (1985). Pay satisfaction. In K. Rowland & G.
Ferris (Eds.), *Research in personnel and human resources manage-*
*ment* (Vol. 3, pp. 115–139). Greenwich, CT: JAI Press.

Heneman, H. G., III, & Schwab, D. P. (1985). Pay satisfaction: Its multidimensional nature and measurement. *International Journal of Psy-*
*chology, 20,* 129–141.

Hollinger, R. D., & Clark, J. P. (1983). *Theft by employees.* Lexington,
MA: Lexington Books.

Horning, D. (1970). Blue collar theft: Conceptions of property, attitudes toward pilfering, and work group norms in a modern indus-

trial plant. In E. O. Smigel & H. L. Ross (Eds.), *Crimes against*
*bureaucracy* (pp. 46–64). New York: Van Nostrand Reinhold.

Kemper, T. D. (1966). Representative roles and the legitimization of
deviance. *Social Problems, 13,* 288–298.

Leventhal, G. S. (1976). The distribution of rewards and resources in
groups and organizations. In L. Berkowitz & E. Walster (Eds.), *Ad-*
*vances in experimental social psychology* (Vol. 9, pp. 91–131). San
Diego, CA: Academic Press.

Lind, E. A., & Lissak, R. (1985). Apparent impropriety and procedural
fairness judgments. *Journal of Experimental Social Psychology, 21,*
19–29.

Lind, E. A., & Tyler, T. (1988). *The social psychology of procedural*
*justice.* New York: Plenum Press.

Mangione, T. W, & Quinn, R. P. (1975). Job satisfaction, counter-productive behavior, and drug use at work. *Journal of Applied Psychol-*
*ogy, 11,* 114–116.

Mars, G. (1973). Chance, punters, and the fiddle: Institutionalized pilferage in a hotel dining room. In M. Warner (Ed.), *The sociology of*
*the workplace* (pp. 200–210). New York: Halsted Press.

Mars, G. (1974). Dock pilferage: A case study in occupational theft. In
P. Rock & M. McIntosh (Eds.), *Deviance and social control* (pp. 209–
228). London: Tavistock Institute.

Merriam, D. (1977). Employee theft. *Criminal Justice Abstracts, 9,*
380–386.

Merton, R. T. (1938). Social structure and anomie. *American Sociologi-*
*cal Review, 3,* 672–682.

Shapiro, D. L., & Buttner, E. H. (1988, August). *Adequate explanations:*
*What are they, and do they enhance procedural justice under severe*
*outcome circumstances?* Paper presented at the annual meeting of
the Academy of Management, Anaheim, CA.

Tyler, T. R. (1988). What is procedural justice? *Law and Society Review,*
*22,* 301–335.

Tyler, T. R., & Bies, R. J. (1990). Beyond formal procedures: The interpersonal context of procedural justice. In J. Carroll (Ed.), *Applied*
*social psychology and organizational settings* (pp. 77–98). Hillsdale,
NJ: Erlbaum.

Webb, E. J., Campbell, D. T., Schwartz, R. D., Sechrest, L., & Grove, J. B.
(1981). *Nonreactive measures in the social sciences* (2nd ed.). Boston:
Houghton Mifflin.

Weiner, B., Amirkhan, J., Folkes, V. S., & Varette, J. A. (1987). An attri-
butional analysis of excuse giving: Studies of a naive theory of emo-
tion. *Journal of Personality and Social Psychology, 52,* 316–324.

Zuwaylif, F. H. (1970). *General applied statistics.* Reading, MA: Addison-Wesley.

Received January 2, 1990
Revision received March 26, 1990
Accepted March 27, 1990 ∎

# [7]

## BLUE-COLLAR THEFT: CONCEPTIONS OF PROPERTY, ATTITUDES TOWARD PILFERING, AND WORK GROUP NORMS IN A MODERN INDUSTRIAL PLANT

### DONALD N. M. HORNING

Thefts by workers from their place of employment have been a source of concern to owners, managers, and labor representatives from the earliest beginnings of productive systems. More recently, they have become the onus of security officials, protection agencies, surety, bonding and insurance companies, as well as the numerous representatives of arbitration and grievance-handling agencies. This concern, however, has been largely of a pragmatic nature, focusing on the prevention, control, and regulation of theft in the plant. Thefts of this type, though constituting a significant financial loss to industry and presumably involving a significant proportion of industrial workers, have not been accorded much attention by either the students of deviant behavior or the analysts of complex bureaucracies. Even sociologists, with their empirical, analytical, and theoretical interest in normative behavior, have been conspicuously neglectful of the nonlegal activities of industrial operatives. In an attempt to bridge this hiatus, this report, which is derived from a more

46

comprehensive study of blue-collar theft,[1] focuses on the cognitive dimensions of pilfering—namely, the workers' conceptions of property in the plant, their attitudes toward pilfering, and the work groups' norms relative to pilfering.

Pilfering, peculation, filching, mulcting, poaching, embezzling, stealing, petty thievery, petty larceny and purloining are the terms used most often in describing the acts which are the focus of this inquiry. These terms, however, do not reveal the nature of the relationship between the thief and his victim: the act may be perpetrated by a person who has a viable relationship with the organization or by one who has no ostensible contact with the organization outside of its victimization. Furthermore, these terms do not reveal whether the act was committed for or against the organization—that is, whether the organization was the benefactor or the victim. Thus, a worker engaged in industrial espionage, or stealing secrets for his company, is not benefiting directly or personally by the commission of his crime. It may be noted at this point that the failure of Sutherland, and his students, to acknowledge these subtle distinctions relative to the victim has resulted in a conceptual mélange that has continued to give immeasurable difficulty. Logically, it would appear that the concept of white-collar crime should be reserved for acts committed by wage-earning employees in which the company of their employ is either the victim or the locale for the commission of an illegal act from which they personally benefit. The term corporate crime could then be applied to those crimes generally included under the white-collar crime designation, namely those committed by employees in the course of their employment and for which the company is the primary benefactor. It is in this conceptual framework that the distinction between the terms blue-collar crime and blue-collar theft is introduced.

Blue-collar crime, the more generic concept, embraces the whole array of illegal acts which are committed by nonsalaried workers and which involve the operative's place of employment either as the victim (*e.g.*, the theft of materials, the destruction of company property, the falsification of production records) or

[1] Donald N. M. Horning, *Blue-Collar Theft: A Sociological Inquiry of Pilfering by Industrial Workers* (to be published by College and University Press, New Haven, Connecticut).

as a contributory factor by providing the locus for the commission of an illegal act (*e.g.*, fighting on company property, the theft of personal property, gambling on company premises, the selling of obscene literature on company premises).

Blue-collar theft, one form of blue-collar crime, may be defined simply as the illegal or unauthorized utilization of facilities or removal and conversion to one's own use of company property or personal property located on the plant premises by nonsalaried personnel employed in the plant.

## THE METHODS AND PROCEDURES

The data on which this report is based were obtained from intensive semistructured interviews with 88 male operatives of a large Midwest electronics assembly plant. This plant was chosen because it had components, materials, and equipment that were readily pilferable and of some utility outside of the plant. The subjects represented four different job classifications: assemblers, troubleshooters, repairmen, and mule (fork-lift) drivers. These four categories were chosen for several reasons. First, it was felt that research should include all departments in the plant to prevent the workers in a given department from feeling that an accusing finger was being pointed at their department or section. Second, the research design required the selection of workers representing different levels of access to pilferable goods and materials found in the plant. Third, the research design called for workers representing a wide range of task specialization to discern the effect which different degrees of component-related knowledge had upon the incidence and pattern of employee theft. The assemblers were chosen because they had high access but low knowledge (of utility); troubleshooters, high access and high knowledge; repairmen, moderate access and moderate knowledge; mule drivers, low access and low knowledge. A total of 106 names were chosen from a list of male operatives furnished by the union; of these, fourteen refused to cooperate (a refusal rate of 13.2%). All interviews were conducted at the worker's residence. No workers were contacted at the plant, and the company was in no way involved in the planning or execution of the research.

Owing to the researcher's awareness of the workers' sensitivity to the question of pilfering in the plant and given the researcher's need to establish and maintain a climate favorable to the study, several noteworthy research techniques were employed. First, the workers were interviewed in a carefully planned sequence based upon the union leaders' perceptions of the general informal social organization of each of the departments in the work organization. Prior to interviewing the workers in the sample, all of the opinion leaders, thus identified, were interviewed and given complete information regarding the nature of the research (including copies of all research instruments). Although a few of these opinion leaders were also in the sample, most were not. The remaining subjects were then interviewed in the sequence suggested by the opinion leaders' perceptions of the status differentials extant in the informed work group. (This was accomplished by giving them the names of all of the subjects who were in their department and asking them to rank the subjects by degrees of relative influence.) This technique was employed because it was assumed that the opinion leaders and subleaders in the informal organization would become the informal emissaries of the investigator. By placing them in a position of knowledgeability, it was further assumed that the opinion leaders would seek to enhance their informal leadership role by discussing the research with the workers in their department in advance of its becoming common knowledge. This tacit acknowledgment of their leadership role, thus allowed them to play the role of the informed insider. Lacking such foreknowledge, it was felt they would most probably reject the research categorically, as their means of role affirmation. A second technique, employed in the interest of creating and maintaining a more favorable research climate, was in the realm of rumor control, or more specifically, rumor intervention. Starting with the premise that research of this type is likely to generate numerous rumors throughout the plant, several opinion leaders were asked to assist the investigator in covertly manipulating the content of the informal communication system. The opinion leaders were to inform the investigator of all rumors they heard regarding the research (*e.g.*, This is a company-sponsored project and is the precursor to a general crackdown on pilfering) and, upon instruction, they were to serve the counteractive function of introducing information (rumors) into the system which neutralized the content of the original rumor. This technique proved helpful in keeping the system of rumors

**50**    *Donald N. M. Horning*

in balance so that a particular "rumor set" didn't become "fixed" in the workers' cognitive frame of reference, thus contaminating their responses or precluding their cooperation.

## CONCEPTIONS OF PROPERTY IN THE PLANT

"Who owns the property? I ain't never thought about it much —let's see: Well, you don't mean the workers' own stuff like lunch buckets. . . . they's a lot of stuff that I don't know about —it don't seem to belong to nobody—it's just there and you can take it if you want—I suppose it's the Company's though cause you got to sneak it out—but the super he don't seem to care if you take it. There's some things you'd never take—the Company wouldn't like it—I mean like a machine or drill or completed TV set or even a Kinne tube." [2]

"If you want to look at the little parts as Company property then I guess you'd say Company property goes out of there. . . . They take tubes for their own sets . . . I don't think anybody would want any of the 'Company's property' and besides it's too big to take anyway."

"Most of it belongs to the Company—but there are some things that are furnished by the Company which ya might say we own—fur instance, I got me a little electric fan that I made from junk I found out there—I've got my name painted on it—and nobody better ever try and take it—it's mine—everybody has things like that—the Company furnishes them but they are ours —the other day they had a big fight near me cause one worker took another guy's stool—you see what I mean?"

"I bring home things that are of use to me but not to them— fur instance, the vendors will mix up the screws and you might get a few odd ones in the barrel . . . they ain't ———'s material. It came in with their material but it's not really theirs cause they didn't order it . . . It's not stealing from ——— and the vendor he don't want it, he don't know nothin about it."

"When you talk about Company property what do you mean— just everything? As far as I'm concerned there's a lot of things down there that you might say belonged to the Company cause they paid for 'em but we don't look at it that way cause they don't seem to care—we take what we want and don't worry

[2] All quotes are taken from the interview schedules.

about it—I ain't never thought about those things as Company property—It just don't seem like it is."

"I don't know about the tools—they tell us they belong to the Company but they don't seem to care about them—it's like this —a worker is on the job for several years—he's had tools and equipment checked out the whole time—he goes to check them in when he's transferred to another section and they don't even know he's got them—they've lost the sign-out card—they tell you to keep it or give it to somebody. So who do they belong to —huh?"

A careful perusal of the foregoing quotes reveals a subtle but important cognitive distinction. In responding to the questions pertaining to the theft of materials from the company, the workers continually alluded to three broad classes of property in the plant: company property, personal property, and property of uncertain ownership. The operational, if not actual, existence of three categories of property in the plant introduces a significant change in the traditional "dichotomous" conception of company property and personal property. This cognitive dissonance between the actual and the perceived forms of property may account, in part, for the failure of security forces in controlling and regulating the activities of the pilferer as well as the failure of researchers and practitioners alike to produce sound generalizations about this form of behavior.

Whether operating from a dichotomous or trichotomous conception of property in the plant, it may be noted that each category of property is perceived by the workers as consisting of a hard core of relatively distinct objects and materials about which there is little disagreement. Moving from this core centrifugally, the workers place other elements in the property complex with decreasing certainty of ownership (in the case of personal and company property) or nonownership (in the case of property of uncertain ownership). This configuration is depicted in Figure 1 with the perceived category of uncertain ownership superimposed upon the real categories of company and personal property. The personal and company property about which there is generally the least certainty (*e.g.*, scrap, broken parts, etc.) constitute the hard core of the uncertain ownership category.

52     *Donald N. M. Horning*

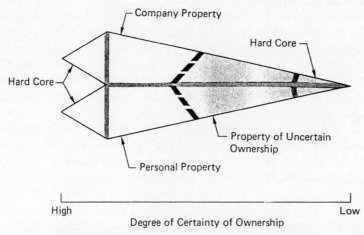

*Figure 1*    Degree of Certainty of Ownership by Type of Property

Viewed abstractly, the personal property in the plant is distinguishable from company property in that it consists of those objects which belong to specific individuals and which were purchased or produced by them at their own expense. When viewed from the workers' perspective, the boundaries are much more obscure, because personal property also includes certain forms of company property which the workers have appropriated for their own use; *e.g.* stools which have been modified for personal use; stool pads fabricated from packing material; "personal" items fabricated from junk parts; equipment on which safety devices or auxiliary devices have been attached, modified, or removed; and tools on which special grips have been added.

The hard core of personal property consists of all of the readily identifiable personal items which may be found in the plant—for example, marked or monogrammed clothing, lunch pails, inscribed jewelry, wallets, modified tools, specially adapted equipment and materials brought into the shop from the outside to be worked on for personal use. The items falling at the other end of the continuum where there is a low degree of certainty of ownership include unmarked clothing, money, jewelry, gloves and nonprescription safety goggles.

In addition to the building, fixtures, heavy machinery, and equipment, the hard core company property includes power tools, bulky and expensive components and any components, parts, materials, or tools which have a special value placed upon them by the company, such as those for which there is a checkout system or an established accounting procedure. For example, in the electronics plant under study, the components constituting the hard core of company property included: Kinne tubes (TV picture tubes), TV chassis, TV power transformers, TV masks (picture tube frames), reels of copper wire, TV tuners, pneumatic hand tools, electric drills, and portable testing equipment. The company property which had a low degree of certainty of ownership consists of the numerous materials, components, and tools which are small, plentiful, inexpensive, and expendable. This includes items such as nails, screws, sandpaper, nuts, bolts, scrap metal, wipe rags, scrap wood, electrical tape, solder, small production components (small TV tubes, resistors, capacitors, condensers, knobs, dial shafts) and small tools (ceramic adjusting tools, pliers, screwdrivers, drill bits and wrenches).

As shown in Figure 1, the category designated as property of uncertain ownership actually consists of those items of personal and company property for which legitimate proprietary claims may be made but which lie at the low degree of certainty of ownership end of the continuum. In practice, however, the workers view this as a separate category consisting of those items about which they have serious doubts concerning ownership. Thus, the items at the low degree of certainty end of the corporate ownership continuum (*e.g.*, screws, nails, nuts, bolts, scraps, waste, and certain types of tools) are viewed as not belonging to anyone. Similarly, personal items, such as lost money, a stray[3] item of clothing or equipment, are viewed as not having an owner. The hard core of the uncertain category actually consists of those items about which there is a legitimate question of ownership: scrap and waste material; nonreturnable, broken, or defective components; broken tools, etc. For example, when a screwdriver, furnished by the company, has been ground down to the point where it is too short to use and the company has the worker turn it in only to throw it away, to whom does the screwdriver belong once it has been placed in the scrap barrel? To take another example from the company under study, when one assembler received the components he was to work with, they were wrapped

[3] Not at an assigned work station or within a given worker's territory.

in a protective material which was held in place with a rubber band. The rubber bands were not salvaged; they were considered scrap by the company. To whom do they belong? Figure 1 depicts the uncertain ownership category as tapering off as one approaches the definable ownership end of the continuum. It is depicted as extending along the continuum, however, because there are occasions where the company (or individual) is viewed as having relinquished a legitimate claim of ownership through default, *e.g.*, a power tool which has been replaced by newer equipment and which has not been recalled. In every respect—legal, moral, theoretical—the object is still company property, but in the worker's view it has, by default, slipped into the limbo of property of uncertain ownership.

To complete the picture of the worker's conceptions of property in the plant, several additional observations may be noted. First, the items which fall at a particular point on the continuum do not necessarily remain fixed at that point. An item, or a class of items, may shift from the low degree of certainty end of the continuum to the high degree of certainty of ownership as conditions change. For example, in the electronics plant, solenium rectifiers were originally considered by the workers as falling within the uncertain ownership category. They were available in large quantity, were not subject to special inventory, were generally available throughout the plant and were simply discarded if defective. However, when the company introduced a loose system of control by requiring the workers to check out the quantities needed for production, the rectifiers were immediately perceived differently by the workers as they were shifted to the hard core company-property category. Second, the scope of the uncertain ownership category appears to be inversely related to the extent to which management regulates the flow of goods and materials within the plant. Thus a high degree of control, such as that which might be found in the research and development section (where there is constant danger of industrial espionage and pirating and where even the scrap may be considered classified), most probably results in a very small residual of items in the uncertain ownership category. According to several old-timers, when the electronics plant was under wartime security, the things that were regarded as of uncertain ownership "were about nil."

### WORKERS' ATTITUDES TOWARD PILFERING PROPERTY IN THE PLANT

"People have a different attitude toward the Company than they do toward each other or you. . . . They wouldn't come into your home and take thirty cents, but they will take from the Company. They figure it's got plenty of money and a few cents don't mean nothing to them . . . but for you they figure there's not so much of it."[4]

"Occasionally I'll bring something home accidentally. I'll stick it in my pocket and forget it and bring it home. I don't return those cause it's only a small part and I didn't take it intentionally."

"It's a corporation . . . It's not like taking from one person . . . the people justify it that the corporation wouldn't be hurt by it . . . they just jack the price up and screw the customer. They're not losing anything. The Company told us that last year they lost \$30,000 . . . but that was for losses of all types. It gives them a nice big tax write-off. I'll bet you a goddamm day's pay that they jack that son-of-a-bitchin' write-off way up too."

"There are several things involved . . . in the first place I work with those little bastards [tubes] all day and I have come to regard them as worthless and besides the Company gets 'em for practically nothing. But if I go out and buy them then the cost is terrible. The markup on the stuff is like drugs . . . it's very, very high. They've got plenty . . . they're not losing anything on what I take."

"Many of the workers feel that they are part of the Company and so they might not feel as guilty because they're taking from themselves."

"Never heard of anybody stealing anything from others. That's one thing. You can leave something laying around down there and no one will risk their job for taking things from others. They would be more severe on you if they caught you taking things from the workers than if you were taking from the Company. The people seem to realize most workers are rather poor and couldn't afford to lose something. A Company won't miss it like a person would. This don't make it right but it justifies it in their mind."

[4] All quotes are taken from the interview schedules.

56    *Donald N. M. Horning*

"They wouldn't think of stealing from one another: they may take tools but that's a special case because they don't consider that stealing from the worker—cause the Company gives 'em to the worker."

"I don't like the word *taken*. It's not like I was stealing those screws. They're not worth anything."

"When I look at the waste and breakage I don't feel at all guilty about it. I work with the parts all day. I have a supply right before me. I see so many broken and wasted they aren't of any value to me anymore. I have them around me all day and I don't regard them as worth much. When you are working for someone you can't see . . . I think you're more likely to not feel guilty. ———— is just a building—it doesn't mean anything to me except it's a place where I work. I don't mean nothing to them. Old man ———— doesn't know me from nobody and he doesn't care what happens to me, just so I don't foul up production."

"It's like this—if I needed a pot full of dirt for a little plant that I have and was driving along in the country and I saw this thousand-acre farm with nice dirt, I wouldn't ask the farmer for it. He'd think I was nuts. He'd probably say—'take a truckload' —sounds kind of silly don't it to ask for a pot of dirt with all that dirt there—the parts in the plant are the same. What's a little tube to————? They've got millions of them."

"Not as a rule they don't feel guilty. I know I don't—some may have guilt feelings—some may get neurotic over it but I don't. A good theoretical question is—'Is this theft?' I don't know what the answer would be though. I think that if it's for personal use it isn't but if it's for sale then it is theft."

"I heard of a guy who offered to pay someone to take some parts out for him because it was against his religion—now I think that's really low."

"I'm sure that I could go quite high in the upper supervision and get help in finding parts—they're quite helpful as long as it's for personal use. Well, you can't feel very guilty when you know even the supers approve."

The real significance of the trichotomous conception of property becomes apparent when one examines the workers' attitudes toward pilfering. Although the workers perceived three categories of property, they perceived only two victims: the company, in the case of company property and the individual, in the case of personal property. As might be expected in such a cognitive orientation, the property of uncertain ownership has no victim.

Given a tripartite conception of property and given a victim category extending from highly visible, specific individuals to nonvisible, vaguely conceptualized collectivities of stockholders, it is reasonable to expect that there is not a single attitude toward pilfering in the plant, but rather a complex configuration of attitudes specific to each property category and perceived victim. The viability of this conceptualization has already been established in Smigel's research on the shifting attitudes toward stealing as the organizational frame of reference is changed.[5] The present research suggests that these vacillating cognitive orientations also apply to pilfering in the work plant.

Insight into the workers' attitudes toward the pilfering of personal property may be obtained from an analysis of their conception of the relative frequency with which personal property is pilfered as well as their impression of the conditions under which it is likely to occur. Of the 88 subjects in the sample, only one believed that the pilfering of personal property was a frequent occurrence. The remaining 87 (99%) believed it occurred rarely or never. The workers who believed that it occurred rarely gave further insight into the workers' attitudes when they sought to explain their answers. Generally, their answers revealed that the pilfering of personal property which did occur was confined to property falling at the low degree of certainty end of the ownership continuum. When asked to explain the seemingly low incidence of pilfering of personal property, two basic responses were given. The majority of the workers responded by saying, "It just isn't done." Implied in this statement is the suggestion that a strong normative restraint, bordering on a taboo, exists in that its occurrence is unthinkable and thus does not need further explanation or rationale. The remaining workers gave replies which suggested that the visibility of the victim serves as an effective deterrent to the theft of personal property.

When asked to indicate whether they regarded the theft of personal or company property as the more serious form of theft,

[5] Erwin O. Smigel, "Public Attitudes Toward Stealing as Related to the Size of the Victim Organization," *American Sociological Review*, Vol. 21, No. 3, June 1956, pp. 320–327.

80% of the workers indicated that they regarded the theft of personal property as the more serious act. The remaining workers indicated they viewed both types of pilfering with equal gravity. None of the workers regarded theft from the company as a more serious act.

The feelings about pilfering of company property do not evoke nearly the consensus that there was on personal property. However, there is still a general pattern with almost four-fifths (78.4%), or 69, of the subjects indicating that it was wrong to take company property. Seven reported they thought it was not wrong, and twelve were uncertain. In explaining their replies, almost one-half (47.7%), or 42, of the subjects viewed the pilfering of company property as wrong because it violated the religico-moral code. They gave answers such as "It's a sin" and "God holds us accountable for all our acts" or "It's just wrong; that's all I know." Twenty-seven of those who felt it was wrong to take company property invoked a legalistic rationale with statements such as "It's against the law" or "Legally, it's wrong." The twelve workers who were uncertain generally made statements which implied the existence of a situational ethic in which the question of right or wrong could not be answered in the abstract; it depended wholly upon the circumstances attending the pilfering. Of the seven who indicated that the theft of company property was not wrong, the majority indicated that the taking of company property was not theft.

The attitudes toward the residual category of uncertain ownership was another matter. Here we begin to see a real disengagement from the traditional religious, moral, and legal restraints. Though the semantic shift was a subtle one of changing the line of questioning from the "taking of company property" to the "taking of things from the plant," the conceptual shift was very real.

Since it seems reasonable to assume that the workers' attitudes are, at least in part, a function of the perceived attitudinal milieu in the plant, the workers were asked to describe their fellow workers' feelings about the "taking of things" from the plant. Of the 88 subjects, 72 (81.8%) believed their peers do not feel guilty about their pilfering. Only fourteen workers reported their peers felt some guilt and two evaded the issue by indicating that they doubted if their peers ever took anything except on ex-

tremely rare occasions. The workers' explanations for their peers'
feelings are even more illuminating in that they provide a window through which we may view the attitudinal milieu in the
plant. These responses, which were classifiable into a number of
themes, are presented in Table 1.

Table 1

**Workers' Explanations for Their Peers' Feelings of Guilt or Failure to
Feel Guilt After Removing Goods from the Company Premises (n=86)**

|  | No. of responses | No. of subjects | % of total | % of responses in category |
|---|---|---|---|---|
| Reasons for feeling guilty |  | 14 | 16 | 100 |
| 1  conscience-centered theme[a] | 11 |  | (13) | (79) |
| 2  situation-centered theme[b] | 3 |  | ( 3) | (21) |
| Reasons for *not* feeling guilty |  | 72 | 84 | 100 |
| 1  don't regard as theft[c] | 29 | (29) | (34) | (40) |
| 2  rationalized theft | 43 | (43) | (50) | (60) |
|    a  plant lore theme[d] | (19) |  |  |  |
|    b  personal theme[e] | ( 9) |  |  |  |
|    c  managerial theme[f] | ( 8) |  |  |  |
|    d  economic theme[g] | ( 7) |  |  |  |

(Note: the numbers in paren-
theses are subtotals)

a  Conscience-centered theme: includes statements which bear some reference to the inter-
   play of conscience in determining guilt, e.g., "We're on the honor system down there so
   the only thing to prevent theft is their conscience" or "It's wrong and they know it."
b  Situation-centered theme: includes statements referring to some aspect of the situation
   which serves as the precipitant of the guilt feeling and not necessarily the act itself, e.g.,
   "feel guilty cause they don't need it" or "feel guilty cause they're taking more than they
   need."
c  Don't regard it as theft theme: includes statements which convey the notion that these
   acts do not constitute theft but are instead entirely acceptable, e.g., "They feel justified
   cause it's their company"; "it's part of the compensation for working there."
d  Plant lore theme: comprised of statements which are obviously among the sets of beliefs
   and notions that are carried along as part of the work groups' normative rationalizations,
   e.g., "The company doesn't mind if it's for personal use"; "Management doesn't mind if
   it's small parts" or "The company expects it."
e  Personal theme: comprised of statements in which reference is made to specific attributes
   of the pilferers, e.g., "They do it out of habit and so don't even think about it" and
   "It's the daredevil in us—the urge to gamble."
f  Managerial theme: made up of statements in which managerial acts and precedents are
   used as the point of departure for justifying their own acts, e.g., "We see managers doing
   it and what's good enough for them is good enough for us" or "Bosses will help us get
   stuff so how can it be wrong?"
g  Economic theme: in these, reference is made to the fact that the acts of pilfering serve
   the workers' ends as well as those of the company by saving them money, e.g., "Figure
   they're saving the company money by taking stuff they would have to throw away anyway."

60    *Donald N. M. Horning*

Of the 88 subjects in the sample, 80 (91%) reported they had pilfered goods from the plant. However, not all of these were reported as being intentional; six workers reported their pilfering had consisted of the inadvertent removal of property from the plant, *e.g.*, "I got home and found I had a pocket full of screws which I had placed there and forgot." Of the 80 subjects who had pilfered, only one-third (36%) reported that they felt guilty while two-thirds (64%) reported that they did not feel guilty. The explanation for their feelings, though classifiable under many of the same general headings as those of their peers, reveal some notable differences. Table 2 classifies the workers' own explanations for their feelings about their pilfering.

**Table 2**
**Workers' Explanations for Their Own Feelings of Guilt or Failure to Feel Guilt Arising from the Removal of Goods from the Company Premises (n=80)**

|  | No. of responses | No. of subjects | % of total | % of responses in category |
|---|---|---|---|---|
| Reasons for feeling guilty |  | 29[a] | 36 | 100 |
| 1  conscience-centered theme | 11 |  |  | 38 |
| 2  situation-centered theme | 13 |  |  | 45 |
| 3  moral-centered theme[b] | 14 |  |  | 48 |
| Reasons for *not* feeling guilty |  | 51 | 64 | 100 |
| 1  don't regard as theft | 38 | (38) |  | 75 |
| 2  rationalized theft | 13 | (13) |  | 25 |
|     a  plant lore theme | 9 |  |  |  |
|     b  personal theme | 2 |  |  |  |
|     c  managerial theme | 4 |  |  |  |
|     d  economic theme | 2 |  |  |  |

a   The subtotals are greater than the number of respondents owing to the fact that some respondents gave answers which fell into several response categories, e.g., managerial and economic.
b   Moral-centered theme: e.g., "It's a sin," and "It's against God's law."

A comparison of the data in Tables 1 and 2 reveals several interesting observations. First, in comparing the data relative to the assumptions about their peers' guilt and their own feelings, it appears that the workers are far more likely to ascribe guilt feelings to themselves (36%) than they are to others (16%). This suggests that though the normative system of the work subculture may provide the means for neutralizing acts of pilfering, thereby allowing the workers to assume their peers do not feel guilty, the workers themselves may have difficulty resolving the conflict between their work norms and the general societal norms. Secondly, it is interesting to note that of those who report they do not have feelings of guilt, the majority simply do not define their pilfering as theft. The pervasiveness of this desire to avoid labeling their acts as theft is also reflected in a number of the rationalizations which were proffered, *e.g.*, "The Company expects it" or "The Company doesn't mind."

Additional insight into the workers' attitudes toward pilfering may be obtained from their responses to the questions pertaining to the giving away and/or selling of goods and materials taken from the plant. Although about one-fourth of the 88 subjects admitted they had given goods away, only five reported they had sold pilfered goods. Almost all agreed that these acts were questionable, if not wrong. The taboo against the selling of pilfered goods appears particularly strong. Most workers indicated that the work group would not attempt to protect or cover up for the worker who was removing goods which he intended to sell.

## THE WORK GROUP NORMS GOVERNING PILFERING IN THE WORK PLANT

"There's a guy on our line who's supposed to take things all the time. They tease him a lot—he really gets it when the line goes down because of a shortage of parts. They all start saying to him 'Hey, how about bringing in some of your parts so we can work tomorrow.' I don't know if this is just bullshit or not." [6]

"I've heard of three cases where people were caught. Two who were stealing and selling were fired outright. Another was given an involuntary quit. He was asked to quit. He refused so he was fired."

"What happens if you're caught—it depends upon the item. You're fired if its large—warned if it's small. Their policy seems to point to large quantity or high value. If you take often and are caught you're fired. If you do it only occasionally, then you are just warned."

[6] All quotes are taken from the interview schedules.

"Not when the taking is on a personal use basis. It's a generally accepted practice. Everybody is doing it so why should anyone feel guilty? The workers frown on people who do it on a large scale cause they're afraid the Company will crack down on everyone. When the big operators are caught everybody feels better but they won't turn him in. That's in a way kinda funny, isn't it? If he's fired they don't feel sorry for him. He gets what he deserves."

Since attitudes do not exist in a cultural vacuum, the preceding analysis has borne the tacit assumption that the work group subculture includes a set of norms which prescribe the types of property which are pilferable, the conditions under which pilfering should occur, as well as the conditions under which the workers can expect the tacit, if not overt, support of the work group.

The workers in the sample confirmed this assumption. The mechanisms through which these norms are conveyed to the workers appear, for the most part, to be in the form of folktales about heroes and recreants. These folktales consist of a congeries of episodes about pilferers—each tale bearing its own message. For example, the description of an unacceptable *modus operandi* can be a tale describing the types of materials for which workers have been discharged or reprimanded when they attempted to remove them from the plant, or a description of the ways in which the work group will cover up for a pilferer.

As might be expected, the work group norms do not delineate specifically what constitutes a reasonable amount of pilfering (*i.e.*, when one is not exceeding the tolerable limit). However, the norms do provide two broad guidelines for the pilferer. The first sets the limit by indicating that pilfering should be confined to the "valueless" property of uncertain ownership. The second indicates that pilfering should be limited to that which is needed for personal use. To exceed these limits was viewed as a threat to the entire system. Those who exceeded the limits were no longer granted the tacit support of the work group, which includes the right to neutralize one's guilt feelings and deny oneself the definition of one's acts as theft.

## CONCLUSIONS

Within the limitations of this study, the following generalizations are suggested by the data. These may well serve as conditions with which a theory of blue-collar crime must be consistent:

A. *The Conception of Property Within the Work Plant:*

1  All property in the plant is cognitively mapped by the workers into three categories: personal property, corporate property, and property of uncertain ownership.
2  Each category of property consists of a continuum extending from a hard core of readily identifiable and nonmobile items to an outer fringe of uncertain, vacillatory items.
3  The hard-core items rarely shift from one category to another—the only category which is amenable to major shifts from the hard core is the category of "uncertain ownership."
4  Lacking a natural division between company property and property of uncertain ownership, *e.g.*, scrap *v.* nonscrap, usable *v.* nonusable, the work group will establish crude boundaries which will create such a division.
5  Property of uncertain ownership is comprised almost exclusively of company-owned goods and materials which are small, copious, and inexpensive. Given a work plant in which there is a strict company policy relative to pilfering, the uncertain ownership category would be almost exclusively made up of by-products which are thrown away or consumed in the production process.

B. *The Work Group Norms Governing Pilfering*
   *in the Work Plant:*

1  The work group subculture contains a set of norms which deal with pilfering in the plant. These norms, though necessarily vague, serve to provide the workers with a set of general guidelines relative to the acceptable *modus operandi*, the tolerable limits, the conditions of pilfering, etc.
2  Property of uncertain ownership is considered by the work

group as the only type of property that legitimately may be taken from the plant. Company and personal property, though sometimes taken, are done so without the sanction of the work group.

3  The pilfering of property of uncertain ownership is regarded as falling within the conventional morality, whereas the pilfering of other types of property is regarded as a violation of work group, work plant, and societal norms.

4  The work group norms cognitively map the taking of property of uncertain ownership in such a way as to take it out of the realm of theft. Theft has a victim; property of uncertain ownership lacks a victim.

5  Workers who pilfer company property or personal property, especially the latter, do so without the protection of the work group. The work group extends its protection only to those who operate within the folkways.

6  The pilferers of property of uncertain ownership are granted the protection of the work group only if they are pilfering within the tolerable limit. To exceed the limit is to risk losing the protection of the work group.

7  The work group norms do not clearly delineate what constitutes a reasonable amount of pilfering (*i.e.*, what constitutes a tolerable limit). There are, however, two broad guidelines: 1) what one needs for personal use and 2) that which will not jeopardize the system by focusing supervisory attention on the pilfering.

8  In plants where pilfering does not assume the form of a protest, team pilfering is taboo because it violates the definitions of the tolerable limit.

9  The work group norms of pilfering are assimilated through precept and work group folklore.

# [8]

# The Interlocking of Official
# and Unofficial Reward

Melville Dalton

## PROBLEMS OF LANGUAGE AND DEFINITION

In chapters 3 through 6 we repeatedly saw cases of unofficial favor-bartering and of one-sided rewarding. Like the ongoing action, and buried in it, these rewards are fitful and expedient. They accompany the informal phases of many settlements to smooth the way for action, to bind cliques, to cement larger groups, and to heal ruptures. We saw in the preceding chapter how official compensation in the form of salaries admits of irregular variation in the firm's effort to reward uncommon merit.* Nevertheless the obstacle of formal controls, and limits to the proportion of organizational resources that can go into salaries, often forces unofficial use of company materials and services as supplementary rewards for variable contributions from people on the same level, and from the same person at different times.

Use of materials and services for personal ends, individual or group, is, of course, officially forbidden, for in both plant theory and popular

---

\* Drucker recognizes the internal pressures for more elastic rewards in noting that "the salary system should never be so rigid as to exclude special rewards for 'performance over and above the call of duty.'" See *The Practice of Management*, Harper and Brothers, New York, 1954, p. 152.

usage this is *theft*. But our concern to pinpoint the informal phases of administration where possible requires scrutiny of this generally known but taboo subject.

Such practices are as delicate to discuss as they are to apply. For as long as rivalries can generate "reasons" there will be double talk around the concept of "reward," especially in organizations that stress "fair-dealing," "job evaluation," "merit-rated salaries," etc. The dynamics of individual and group action do not require that one agree fully with those who say that no word[1] ever has the same meaning twice, but they do demand that one recognize the difficulties of assigning absolute meanings to terms describing the kinds of situations we are dealing with.[2] What in some sense is theft, may, in the context of preserving the group and solving present problems, lose much or all of its odious overtones. We only need note the gradations of terms referring to theft to suspect this. As theft requires more ingenuity, becomes larger in amount, and is committed by more distinguished persons (whose power is often related to their importance in the operation of society), its character is correspondingly softened by such velvety terms as *misappropriation, embezzlement,* and *peculation,* which often require special libraries to define. To spare the living[3] and some of the recent dead, and to ignore differences in time and place, we can point to Cellini—and remember Pope Paul III's judgment of him that "men like Benvenuto, unique in their profession, are not bound by the laws"—Aretino, Casanova, and even Voltaire. These men were all scoundrels of a kind who, nevertheless, were esteemed for their commendable contributions to society.

Always there are genuine transitional nuances, with debatable margins, between covert internal theft and tacit inducement or reward. Immemorially the esteemed personality who also performs unique services can move closer to "theft" than others without censure.

## MANAGERIAL MOTIVATION

To talk of rewarding is to talk of motivation, and students declare, and show by their disagreement, that little is known of managerial motivation.[4] Distinguished executives and specialized students admit that the whole subject of reward is so dynamic that attempts either rigidly to define motivation,[5] or specifically to reward managers[6] are both likely to go amiss.

Our data have shown that what is a reward for one man is not for another[7] (Bingham, in Chapter 3); that the rank a manager craves at one time, he rejects at another (Evans, Revere); that the same inducements cannot be given to all on a given level because of differences in ability and demand for reward (Hardy); uses of the office of assistant-to, etc.;[8] that the organization's contact with the community may demand greater reward for some managers than for others; that "power struggles" are forbidden but do occur and must be disguised;[9] and that more than financial reward is necessary.[10]  We know that some managers are more venturesome and more inclined to "play the game" than others are.[11]  This may mean unexpected errors, losses, and gains for the organization.  In any case such managers must have greater resources and rewards than rigid planning will allow.[12]  We saw in Chapter 3 that Milo managers were concerned to maintain social as well as productive mechanisms, and that, in addition to the use of materials and services for this purpose, they juggled accounts to (a) allow full and part-time employment of the friends and relatives of plant and community associates, to (b) justify plush offices stemming from their rivalries, and to (c) keep a margin, or kind of "slush fund," in the naval sense, for emergencies—social and mechanical.

Although these practices may vary among cultures and inside a given culture,[13] and with the size, age and financial state of a firm,[14] as well as by industry,[15] they nevertheless occur widely and point to further problems for the manager who deals with other firms or other plants of his own corporation; we have but to recall Geiger's problems from having his unit compared with that of the Colloid plant.

As a result of these gaps between the inherent limitations of formal reward and the obscure complex of activities that must be rewarded, an organization's services and materials, designed for its official functioning, are repeatedly drawn on to fill the breach.  Used injudiciously, this may lead to plunder.

## THEFT: REAL AND QUESTIONABLE

Before we present cases, let us admit the probably universal existence of internal theft, individual and organized, that is more damaging than helpful to the firm and that would strain the term to be called reward for specific contributions.  Various informants report almost incredible cases of empire-building with minimum functions or contributions for many members; of favors and perquisites granted to some for no obvious important service in return; organized pilfering rights—including regular paid frolics for some of the company's members as "representatives" or "spokesmen" at some "event"; and the purely personal use of plant resources under the guise of "community relations," and sometimes not honored with a pretext.  This is reported as common in some of the large firms doing contracted work for various governmental bodies where, as we saw in Chapter 5, the pressure for economy is less.

There is, of course, widespread individual theft in which tools, clerical supplies, home fixtures, etc., are taken for personal use without the knowledge of superiors or concern for one's group or the organization, and which could not be justified in case of detection. Similar internal theft by subgroups and cliques, with lifting-license tied so closely to rank that stealing beyond one's station is punished by death, can occur even in sacred organizations.[16] Civic bodies of antiquity were similarly tapped by members.[17]

Theft may also be enforced in the group and occur systematically over a long period. For example, in a small cabinet factory in the Mobile Acres region, the employees of one department, on piece-rate pay, regularly turned in more pieces than they actually completed, and coerced newcomers to do the same to protect old hands.

Between theft and informal reward is the gray-green practice of expense-accounting, which is also related to rank. "Theft" is softened to "abuse of privilege," but the feeling of some companies is clear in their demands for explanations. Others, however, including those sensitive to the tax factor, see large accounts as "part of the man's compensation," or as necessary to "attract and hold top men," or as a practice comparable to the "employee medical program."[18]

One organization reflects this attitude in its contract with a well-known top executive. After defining his duties and authority, the company says that:

> During the continuance of the employment of [the executive] hereunder he shall be paid a weekly salary of Twenty-five Hundred ($2500) Dollars, and in addition a weekly general expense allowance of Five Hundred ($500) Dollars which shall not include travelling expenses or other items generally related thereto, which shall also be paid by the Company. There shall be no abatement or diminution of the compensation or expense allowance of [the executive] during such time, if any, as he may fail to perform the services required to be performed by him hereunder solely because of illness or physical incapacity even though such illness or incapacity may prevent the performance by him of any duties whatsoever for a period up to six consecutive months. . . . [If the executive shall be required to change headquarters around the Company operating areas he shall receive] such suitable office accommodations and such clerical and other assistance as shall, from time to time, be reasonably required by him, and of such type, character and extent as shall be consistent with the position of Chief Executive Officer of the Company. . . . [He] shall receive fair and reasonable vacations with pay, commensurate with the position and duties undertaken by him hereunder.[19]

Coercion in expense-accounting can function as in the cabinet factory cited above.  An informant from an optical company reports that lower-ranking, and obviously less imaginative, employees who rarely used expense accounts were not permitted by higher-ranking members to list their costs exactly.  Rather they were forced to inflate the report, sometimes very much, so as not to "show-up the fat accounts" of the habitual users.  Internal coercion to protect one's own masquerade might at times be justified, but apparently was not in this case.

Though parallel cases only at times, feather-bedding by labor, and the various professional and managerial practices embracing pay-backs, split-fees and rebates,[20] also lie in this twilight area.

## UNOFFICIAL INCENTIVES

In crossing the middle ground between understood theft of materials and their controlled use as inducements and rewards, one must always fight the sheep-or-goat concept of truth.  Responsible persons who succeed in this apparently broaden the system of rewards and are able to stimulate those not lured by standard appeals, or who also require other[21] incentives for greater effort.

### Individual

Because of the tacit stress on flexibility and supplementation of the more common inducements, unofficial reward is naturally directed more toward specific contributions and situations than toward rank as such. But obviously if such reward is not confidential, or if it is known and not justified in the minds of others, it is likely to follow formal rank and become systematic theft of the kind we noted above.

Although informal reward ideally is given for effort and contribution beyond what is expected of a specific rank, it is also granted for many other purposes, often unexpected and formally taboo yet important for maintaining the organization and winning its ends.  For example, it may be given (1) in lieu of a promotion or salary increase that could not be effected; (2) as a bonus for doing necessary but unpleasant or low-prestige things; (3) as an opiate to forget defeats in policy battles or status tiffs; (4) as a price for conciliating an irate colleague or making, in effect, a treaty with another department; (5) as a perquisite to key persons in clerical or staff groups to prevent slowdowns, and to bolster alertness against errors during critical periods; (6) as a frank supplement to a low but maximum salary; (7) for understanding and aid in the operation, and the defense, of the unofficial incentive system; (8) for great personal sacrifices.  There are, of course, more subtle supports which may not be articulated but are intuitively recognized and rewarded

## OFFICIAL AND UNOFFICIAL REWARD                              199

where possible.   These include: ability to maintain morale in the group
or department; skill in picking and holding good subordinates; habitual
tacit understanding of what superiors and colleagues expect but would
not in some cases want to phrase, even unofficially; and expertness in
saving the face of superiors and maintaining the dignity of the organization under adverse conditions.   This last may be aptness in masking
and supporting the fictions essential for regulation of error, and in
perpetuating symbols considered necessary by the dominant group.[22]

These performances are not exhaustive and may overlap in the same
person.   There is no fixed tie either, of course, between services rendered
and the kind of material reward or privilege granted.   Though we are
confining our discussion to positive rewards, there are also negative ones,
such as exemptions from rules binding on others, which, as we noted
in Chapter 5, was but one in the first-line foreman's repertory of inducements for production workers.

Though his general contributions were great, the Milo foreman,
Kustis (Chapter 5), illustrates the privileges given for personal sacrifice.
Kustis dropped his Catholicism, from choice but with suffering, to
become a Mason and thus demonstrate his fealty and fitness.   His
freedom to "feed gravy jobs" to his brother was outlined in Chapter 5.
But with the knowledge of his superiors, he built a machine shop in
his home, largely from Milo materials.   He equipped his drill press,
shaper, and lathe with cutters and drills from Milo.   He supplemented
these with bench equipment, such as taps, reamers, dies, bolts and
screws.   Finally, piece by piece and day by day he removed a retired
grinder from his shop.   Normally such tools were sent to another department or unit of the corporation.

Ted Berger, officially foreman of Milo's carpenter shop, was *sub rosa*
a custodian and defender of the supplementary reward system.   Loyal
beyond question, he was allowed great freedom from formal duties
and expected, at least through the level of department heads, to function
as a clearinghouse for the system.   His own reward was both social and
material, but his handling of the system unintentionally produced a
social glue that bound together people from various levels and departments.   Not required to operate machines, Berger spent a minimum of
six hours daily making such things as baby beds, storm windows, garage
windows, doll buggies, rocking horses, tables, meat boards, and rolling
pins.   These objects were custom built for various managers.   European-
born,* Berger was a craftsman and eager to display his skills.   However,

---

* In a study of production workers on piece rate in a plant of Mobile Acres,
I earlier indicated some of the differences in feeling for craftsmanship between
European-apprenticed and American-born workers.   See "Worker Response and
Social Background," *Journal of Political Economy,* 55: 323–332, August, 1947.

his American-born associates with their folklore of "one good turn deserves another," often gave him a "fee" for his work. Since everyone knew his thirst, these gifts* were usually wines, ranging from homemade "Dago Red" to choice imported varieties. But he also accepted dressed fowl, preferably duck and turkey. In some cases he made nothing, but used his influence to aid with a problem. In other cases he found a place in his department for the summer employment of someone's son, and again usually he received some unspoken favor. The transfer effect of these exchanges needs no elaboration.

Jim Speier, one of Peters' (formal chart) foremen, gave Peters great support in the latter's conflicts with Taylor. An understanding foreman and bulwark of the unofficial directorate, he made great use of both the structural and carpenter shops with Blanke's approval. He had a wood and steel archway for his rose garden prefabricated in the plant, and removed it piecemeal. Incentive-appliers estimated that exclusive of materials† the time spent on this object would have made its cost at least $400, in terms of the hourly charging rate. Also in Berger's shop, Speier had fourteen storm windows made, and a set of wooden lawn sprinklers cut in the form of dancing girls and brightly painted. For use on his farm, Speier had a stainless steel churn made that cost over a hundred and fifty dollars by the charging rate. In the same shop Speier had several cold-pack lifting pans made, also of stainless steel. According to self-styled experts on such matters, the design and workmanship of these pans was superior to anything obtainable on the market. Incentive-appliers declared that the welding, brazing, grinding, and polishing costs made the pans "worth their weight in gold."

Pete Merza, a general foreman in Springer's division, was given enough freedom in the use of building materials that his reward was seen by some—ignorant of his unofficial contributions—as approaching theft. Like Kustis, he had withdrawn from the Church to become a

---

* A colleague suggests that this "looks like bribery." It is hardly that. Rather these gifts were gestures of good will, and in some cases substitutes for favors due that could not be exchanged in the course of carrying out regular duties. One can argue that people were being persuaded to violate their official duties. With no more casuistry one can also argue that "bribes" of this kind contribute to the carrying out of official duties, and that, inside varying and debatable limits, they are a legitimate cost for the maintenance of solidarity. This is not to deny that bribery occurs in industry, as elsewhere (Flynn, *Graft in Business*, The Vanguard Press, New York, 1931, pp. 55–76), or that bestowal of gifts cannot be bribery. See "Should Companies Give?" *Newsweek*, December 24, 1956, pp. 59–60.

† No estimate was made of the cost of materials, since many of these came from the scrap pile and would have been discarded anyway.

## OFFICIAL AND UNOFFICIAL REWARD                              201

Mason, but this was more a gesture than a personal sacrifice for him. An inimitably warm and helpful person acceptable to all factions, he was really rewarded as Milo's peacemaker in the clashes between Operation and Maintenance. Informants stated that he "carried out several hundred dollars worth" of bricks and cement and used Milo bricklayers on company time to build much, or most, of his house.

In another Milo case, reorganization dropped two general foremen to the first-line level. At that time, salary decreases followed automatically. Since the two men did not wish to continue at Milo as first-line foremen, they were put in charge of warehouses as positions there opened. They understood that discreet use of nails, paint, brushes, plumbing and electric fixtures, safety shoes, etc., was acceptable as long as inventories balanced.

Unofficial rewards are of course given for uncovering *pure* theft and misuse of materials. But this calls for internal espionage, which is a harrowing and impossible role for some people. This informal role of theft intelligencer is essential in many organizations. House detectives, various guards, and company police are the conventional guardians in business and industry. But this official role advertises itself. Everyone knows who to watch, and many resent the implications of being watched. Those who play the formal role of guard and investigator are not only likely to be compromised in various ways (see below), but they cannot function at the expected level of efficiency. For as they begin to accomplish official purposes they become the focus of informal attack and are made aware that they can be put in a bad light, as Bingham was (Chapter 3) from the outset. The theft intelligencer compensates for this defect. Simultaneously filling a formal role,* he must be one who has the tact and address to conceal his role of developing intimacies to discover misuse of materials.

At Milo, such investigations were usually carried on by selected persons in both staff and line. However as rule-makers and refiners who had to justify their existence, staff groups were especially eager to avoid blots on their professional escutcheons. Meeting this inherent perspective of the staff role limited the means of unofficially rewarding staff people. Materials and services would usually be inconsistent as a reward. Hence the staff agent who successfully carried out "intelligence" assignments was usually given his next promotion six months early, which admirably fitted *his* needs, and job logic.

---

* In diplomacy, the old role of papal *legatus a latere* was similar in the sense that a formal role, usually that of cardinal, embraced a confidential unofficial function.

Some inducements were both rewards and rights, but for different people. For example, what was at first a reward to some younger officer grew with his rank and seniority into a right which he in turn doled out judiciously as a reward to demanding subordinates.* Services and materials from the company garage, and long distance telephone calls were among the items spread along this axis of reward-rights. Line officers in good standing above the level of general foreman, and certain anointed staff figures including Rees at Milo and Reynolds at Attica, frequently, if not regularly, filled their gas tanks from company stock and received car servicing including washing and waxing. Rank was exercised, with the understanding for all that interference with garage personnel and use of materials culminating in defective operation or tie-up of company trucks and tractors, or accidents of any kind attributable to such interference, would threaten or even cut off reward-rights. As the balance of rewards and rights became too heavy with rights, inevitable crackdowns cut the rights and led higher executives to call on skilled machinists from the shops, instead of garage personnel, to give tune-ups, minor repairs, etc. Machinists in a sense shared these rewards and rights by (a) escape from repetitive work; (b) association with superiors whom they never met socially and seldom officially; (c) the privilege of taking Lincolns and Cadillacs out of the plant for "trial-spins" after tune-ups, and driving home "on company time" to take their wives shopping and "be seen." All time of machinists in such activity was of course charged to their regular jobs.

The axis of reward-right has another common phase: some executives ambiguously feel a "right" to use materials and services whether granted or not, and if questioned would defend their practice as a due reward. These are the managers who put in much overtime (emergencies, meetings, etc.) without extra compensation, and who resent the time-and-a-half overtime pay of hourly-paid workers, and who assist in compiling and circulating lists of these workers whose annual incomes exceed, say, six thousand dollars. Frequently these are also the officers who angrily agree that the organization owns them and in turn, quite within the range of normal madness, protest a counter ownership of its resources. These

* Naturally, friendship was sometimes a consideration in meeting pressure from below. But where demands were made without significant contribution—and in the tone of "a right to share"—the "reward" given was sometimes a disguised penalty. At Attica one such aggressive person demanded a "share" of the house paint he knew others had received. He was given all the usual bulk-purchased and unmixed ingredients—except the drying fluid. Elated, he mixed and applied the paint. When it did not dry, the accumulations of dust and insects ruined his work. He became a laughing-stock without recourse.

## OFFICIAL AND UNOFFICIAL REWARD                    203

managers would say, sociologically, that unofficial demands call for unofficial rewards. Where people have been "oversold" by higher management's attempt to win their identification, they may of course expect greater reward than they receive and resort to supplementation.

Use of materials to supplement low salary is apparently rather common in some of the smaller firms that are less formalized and less able to pay incomes comparable to those of larger companies. In the Argo Transit Company, a firm of two hundred employees, several of the office force were variously rewarded to keep them from moving elsewhere. One individual who had reached the top pay bracket, was given an extra day off each week with pay. Another person, considered as an indispensable secretary, was each week given any half-day off she desired with pay. Since she sewed much for her family and was the only secretary in that office, she did most of her handwork there in connection with sewing. She also did all her letter writing on the job and used company materials and stamps. Use of stamps at Christmas time amounted to a bonus. As she was expected to conceal her unofficial pay and to guard the box from other employees, she evidently also received a certain psychic reward. As a practice this is of course not new. Saintly Charles Lamb, known to have hated his job at the East India Company, used his employer's time and materials and franked letters to his friends, whom he requested to write collect to him. This was probably understood and acceptable, and was not a positive reward as in the case above.

An X-ray technician—of unknown quality—in a general hospital reported that his salary was so low he was "expected to steal hams and canned food" from the hospital supplies to supplement it. Though not in the same hospital, this may be related to the Midwestern hospital thefts nationally reported in October, 1953. There many additional items were taken, but the thefts may have started as an internal reward system and then have grown to a pilfering right extending to outside persons. The typical internal use of materials is suggested by the defense of one of the hospital attendants who allegedly said she had "never seen a hospital where they didn't take things," and the hospital administrator's apparent knowledge of the thefts and reluctance to intervene.

Evidently leaks of information at the technician's hospital transformed the plan of salary supplementation into a problem of theft. For one person rewarded by the informal plan was also unofficially paid for his suggestion for keeping the system in bounds. Despite its obvious complications, his proposal that nurses leave the hospital by the rear exit was accepted. As they passed through this door their clothing and bundles were inspected.  But professional indignation and the rights of rank ended the inspection when one nurse objected that she had worked there "twenty years only to be reduced to sharing the scrub woman's entrance!"

## Unofficial Incentives for the Group

Berger's remarks above indicated the private use of work groups by some Milo managers.  As one of those referred to, Hardy's worth to the firm was unquestioned.  Presumably Stevens knew of his more overt use of materials and services, which included the necessary labor and supplies for building a fireplace in his home under construction. Through Milo offices he also ordered a plate glass for his picture window and removed the glass from Milo on Sunday.  He may have paid part of the cost of the glass since one reward-right in many firms is to allow elect members to buy through the company at wholesale prices, and less.

A recently retired Milo executive, who was a bird lover, had an eleven unit aviary built in Milo shops and installed on his large rear lawn.  Each spring he sent carpenters from the plant—and continues to receive this service possibly as a phase of his pension—to remove, recondition, renovate, and re-install the bird houses.  This person, who started the emphasis on Masonry as an unannounced requirement, frequently used the same carpenters for redecorating his home.  Lack of comparable maintenance skills apparently checked this practice at Attica, but it occurred at Fruhling though documentary support is inadequate for that plant.  As with the use of materials alone, this double employment of facilities and stores obviously may become abused "rights" that blur the line between theft and reward.  However, managers in both firms raised defenses that fluctuated between double talk and sound argument.  My bantering of intimates raised certain questions. For example, when unavoidable emergencies, errors in planning, and market changes made work shortages, was it better to let "idle" men be seen by those who were busy, to reduce the work force, or to take the idle men out of the plant to do something else, something that was usually a lark for them?  Management argued that unrest is promoted by "task inequities," and that men with nothing to do are pleased with a break in the monotony.  Inquiries to Beemer, Brady, Spencer, and various maintenance workers usually elicited strong approval of this last alternative.  For example, it was pointed out that "you get to sit down for twenty to forty minutes both ways" in traveling to and from an executive's home.  Beemer saw this as equivalent to "several coffee breaks."  Furthermore, the executive's wife "always gives us a lot of good eats." The president of the Milo union local supported the practice and held that it prevented layoffs. Management said essentially the same thing in noting that training costs and turnover were reduced, and at the same time there was no surplus of employees, for many of those "used on odd jobs" had to put in overtime at other periods. As with the machinists called on to service executive cars, those employees sporadically retained for out-plant work with some executive, derived both imponderable and concrete satisfactions. However, some first-line foremen and some workers saw the practice as "dirty," "unfair," and "taking advantage of your authority." And some people will call the practice high-level rationalization or collusion, but as in Chapter 4, it is more likely to be expediency periodically reclothed with new protective fictions.

Theft overlaps with reward-right where lower groups, foremen or workers, draw on plant resources, and higher management knows but dares not interfere, as in the hospital scandal. A European informant tells me of maintenance workers in railroad shops who drive their cars into the plant, rather than park outside as in our cases, and repair each other's cars on company time with company supplies. The cars are few and old and serve as busses as well as private vehicles. The practice is known to all, but since there is no fixed lunch hour, workers give the pretext if questioned that they work on the cars only during their lunch periods. Sometimes five to eight workers will be around one car for two or three hours at a stretch. With a short labor supply, and the practice apparently universal, management may officially protest, but usually looks the other way for fear the workers will seek jobs elsewhere.

The force of materials and services as unofficial incentives—internally for the company and externally for its ties with the community—was clearly visible in the activities of Magnesia's Yacht Club. As we saw in the preceding chapter, at least one hundred and fourteen members of Milo, and an unknown number from Fruhling, were active participants in the Club, at an individual annual fee of $50. Building additions to the Club and maintenance of its plant, as well as of privately owned boats, drew on the stores and services of Milo and Fruhling. Repair work was charged to various orders, which as we saw in Chapter 3 was done with some regular work. Propeller shafts, bushings, fin keels, counterweights, pistons, hand railings, and the like, were made and/or repaired for boat owners among the managers as well as their friends in the community.

All of this was tied in with the prevailing practice here, and throughout industry, of doing "government jobs." These include original, as well as repair, work of many kinds usually done by maintenance forces—with plant materials and equipment on job time—as a "favor" for employees at all levels.  At Milo, workers were singled out to aid the Club by doing miscellaneous government jobs.  This was a compliment to their skills and a gesture of acceptance by higherups that appealed to the impulse to serve others, however weak this urge is according to cynics, or overpowering according to some theorists.  Praise and minor perquisites were accepted as abundant rewards.  And for some, inside and across all job divisions, old rifts born in the heat of past emergencies were often healed by shared work on these unofficial assignments.  The opportunities offered by such work for exchange of obligations, for establishing warm understandings, and for blurring differences in official reward, need no comment.  Bureaucratic rationality is progressively, if unwittingly, reduced through these invasions by community recreational life.  It can be argued that government jobs aid the survival of Maintenance, which is normally at conflict with Operation in their official functions.

We need more study on the ramifications of government jobs* and unofficial services, apart from understood rewards.

### The Auditor's Dilemma

Together, theft and socially consumed materials cut into a firm's substance sufficiently to alarm auditors and staffs, committed as they are to compiling the statistics for detection, analysis, and control of all departures from the ideal, and to warrant their own pay.†

Above Milo's divisional level, concern was always shown when inventories turned up losses.  The usual reaction was to state that non-supervisory employees were to blame, and to order plant police to be more vigilant in their inspection of lunch buckets, bags, and bulging coats of outgoing personnel at the four gates.

The volume of materials "lost" was not known exactly.  But cost analysts totaled and classified all incoming materials, then removed from the compilations all items, about eighty-five per cent of the total,

---

* At least one large company outside this study sees government jobs as a problem unless limited to certain employees and done by specific people during given hours.  In this case, only salaried people may take such work to a shop set up for that purpose which operates between 6 P.M. and 10 P.M., Monday through Friday.

† Probably all organizational groups demand the stimulus of extra reward whether it be more of what they are already receiving or a greater share of those things having prestige value. The perquisite of staffs is usually the less material one of late arrival, early departure, and more socializing on the job, though additionally they, too, may participate in small government jobs.

## OFFICIAL AND UNOFFICIAL REWARD                                    207

that "could not possibly" be taken from the plant by persons on foot
without detection.  According to one analyst:

> It's not right on the nose, but about $15,000 of every $100,000 worth
> of material that *could* be taken out disappear—and never can be
> accounted for.  Books can be juggled on some things but not much on
> this.  Besides it's too damn constant.  There's no question that it's
> carried out.  If it's not, where the hell does it go to?

Some of the Milo managers and police suspected each other of carrying out materials or of collusively working with others to that end.
Voicing his suspicions, the police chief was notified that his distrust
was unfounded and insulting.  On its side, management pointed to
"statistical evidence" of police laxity.  In delivering materials and removing the product, outside truckers had somehow sandwiched in
forty-seven of some six hundred motors stored in an empty bay before
the theft was discovered by the police.  Management suspected some
of the guards of bribed collaboration.  Hardy set up a plan for un-
systematic rotation of police around the circuit of gates.  He believed
this would prevent collusion between them and outsiders.  Rotations
were made monthly, but instead of moving all the men from one gate
to the next nearest gate, only one man moved at a time and not in any
sequence of gates or period of the month.  This theory was not based
on what had happened, and it was faulty in assuming that the major
"nonproductive" consumption of materials was pure theft and was
confined to production workers.  Both in underestimating the ingenuity
of lower ranking employees and in not seeing the nature of human
association, the scheme did not prevent production workers from carrying
out materials.

First, the theft of motors was accomplished by collusion of a few
laborers with the truckers, but was concealed to protect a night supervisor.  The suspected laborers were officially laid off for other reasons.
The police were not participants.  Second, we have seen that the major
unofficial consumption of materials was by management itself, and in
many cases was not pure theft.  Finally, the theory ignored both the
backgrounds of the police and the significance of government jobs.  The
police were not overpaid, and as company watchdogs they were, of
course, persons for production workers to stand in well with.  But as
exworkers, in most cases, the police also knew plant life and had need
of government jobs for which they, too, were prepared to exchange
favors.  For example, when one of the gate guards knew that a friend
wished to carry something from the plant, he told the friend which gate
he was tending.  At the gate, with a guard on each side, the friend

making his exit approached his confidant who simulated an inspection and sent him through with a clap on the back.

### In Department Stores

The use of internal materials and services as spurs and requitals of course is not confined to factories. Department stores, with their range of commodities, are a rich field for research in the use of implicit rewards.[23] The Rambeau Mart, member of a state chain, was one of the most flourishing department stores in the Mobile Acres area, and probably owed much of its solidarity to its flexible unofficial incentives.

Rambeau had a total of three hundred and seventy employees including the clerical force and three levels of management: the store chief and his assistants, the division heads, and the department heads. The store had the usual official structure—an auditing department with appropriate specialists, a quadruplicate reporting system, explicit rules against personal use of materials and services, and a budget allowance of ten per cent to cover shoplifting. Two store detectives supplemented the controls. They were gatetenders of a kind in seeing that only employees entered the store before opening time, and in checking the parcels of outgoing employees, at quitting time only, to see that they bore sales slips and the signature of a department head. Yet the managers of Rambeau tacitly adapted its resources to individual orientations, and in a showdown clearly approved the practice.

The unofficial incentive system took various forms. When conditions allowed, and within limits, some department heads privately altered the price of merchandise to fit the local market and to satisfy their own needs. Also, department heads aided each other, but in all cases they worked inside the dual requirement of having to show a profit and to pass the scrutiny of an annual audit. The latitude that ingenuity could establish inside these limitations showed that a brand of individual enterprise still exists and is rewarded in organizations that, at least unofficially, accent individual as well as group effort.

A common practice by department heads was to take items they wanted that were "shopworn" or "damaged" and mark them down "reasonably" for their own purchase. Some female heads regularly, but discreetly, gave certain items a "damaged" appearance. Division chiefs unofficially knew of this, and set no limit to the markdown that could be made, other things equal. However, those department heads who shrank from the ambiguities of exercising their authority and asked a division manager the limit for a markdown were usually told "30 per cent."

Heads of the various men's departments usually clothed themselves from each other's stocks at little or no cost. This might be accomplished, for example, by selling a bargain stock of two thousand pairs of socks not at the agreed 59 cents per pair, but at 69 cents, which accumulated to a fund of $200 above profit requirements. A given head could draw from this to cover the suits, shoes, shirts, etc., essential for his proper grooming. The markup, like the kind and volume of stock, might vary.

Normally, merchandise control demanded that each item, even when the stock and price were uniform, have its individual stock number and price tag. But as in the case of the socks, some commodities might be thrown on a table, without their separate labels, under one posted price. This of course allowed inclusion of some lower-priced items of similar quality which, as with the socks, contributed to the private trading fund. Detailed records of what he removed for himself or others in the inter-departmental trading, and careful balancing of the dollar value of total merchandise withdrawn against the dollar value of unofficial markups enabled the department chief to meet the inventory. If emergencies prevented this, he reported his stock as larger than it was at the time of inventory; for instance, he might report thirty suits on hand, when he had only twenty-seven. Help from assistants in the inventory allowed this, but no help could postpone judgment day beyond the next inventory when this particular stock would be double-checked. To prevent abuse of this elastic incentive, there was always the threat that auditors from another unit would be present to assist at some inventory.

Department heads reciprocated in their markdown of items sold to each other. When the transaction had to be written up, the heads sometimes used a fictitious name, or the names of their new employees as customers. This utilized the fact that the employees themselves were as yet still naive, and their names were still strange in the auditing and shipping departments. Obviously intended in part to forestall such practices, the quadruplicate form requiring a name and address meant little in these cases until the employee became widely known. Where the women in these interchanges usually got only clothing, the men fully utilized the system. For example, Joe, in plumbing, wanted furniture, so he talked with Bill, head of furniture, to see what Bill wanted in plumbing of about the same value that could be exchanged. The total of their trades and adjusted records, however, did not prevent them from showing a profit in the annual audit. Where such persons work together for years this becomes simple and so unofficially acceptable that it seems natural.* Like the skeletons in every family closet, these prac-

---

* Favor-trading and adaptation of official procedures are likely to rise above any control. Even the outside organizations called in to assist in guaranteeing a certain conduct among given employees are similarly used by cliques to protect the group and to maintain the informal status of its individual members. For example, Rambeau subscribed to the service of "Willmark," an organization that

tices are not for public consumption but serve to unify the firm, as the skeletons do the family.

However, two department heads were dropped from this unit of Rambeau because of their use of company resources. Officially, one was released because of theft; the other, L. Nevers, because he wanted to transfer to another unit of the firm. The first head flagrantly took money from the tills of his salesmen, so that the following morning their cash and sales tallies did not match. This person was fired outright before he had taken a hundred dollars. But in Nevers' case light is thrown on what the internal use of materials and services meant in the context of incentives.

Nevers followed the procedures we have sketched and added his own refinements. In his accounting he was aided by one of his saleswomen whom he regularly befriended by ringing his sales on her cash drawer. However, her friendly relations with a saleswoman in another department led her to report Nevers' accounting methods and use of merchandise to the store manager and to name it as theft and malfeasance. Nevers' saleswoman, a "rate-buster," had worked with the other woman for years at Rambeau and elsewhere. Her friend's husband, shortly to return from the armed forces, had been head of a Rambeau department before being drafted. However there was uncertainty about his getting his old position back. So his wife, seeing the interpretation that could be made of Nevers' bookkeeping, and the consequences, hoped to have him fired and have her husband succeed him. She persuaded Nevers' saleswoman to report him in as bad a light as possible. The officially ignorant general manager knew roughly of Nevers' techniques and regarded him as "too good a man for the organization to lose." Forced to defend procedural dignity, he simulated a release but gave Nevers his choice of workplace among the statewide units, vigorously recommended him, and aided him in the successful transfer.

Two common merchandising policies encourage the use of goods as a supplementary incentive. First, the department head, as in other organizations, is expected to interpret policy. Second, all items are age-coded and regarded as having an approximate life expectancy. Some

---

checks on the selling behavior of clerks. This is done by confidentially sending representatives to make purchases from employees and then formally scoring and reporting each person's sales behavior to the store office. However, at Rambeau—and doubtless elsewhere—when the "shoppers" registered in the manager's office, an upper member of the grapevine heard of it and whispered the phrase "shoppers today" to an intimate on the selling floor who passed the word. But only insiders were alerted; they in effect commanded deference and aid from new and fringe members of the sales force by tacit threat of not notifying them.

items of women's clothing may be "old" in less than four months, whereas some merchandise in hardware has an indefinite life. The age-code, or purchase date of items, is recorded at inventory. If too old, this advertises both the department head's poor judgment in making the original purchase, and his failure to "move" the goods. Hence in part to escape discredit he marks down older items for disposal among employees. Of course, he simultaneously sets up counter claims. In the phraseology of Rambeau department heads these items were "odds and ends of merchandise lying around in the way that can't be sold anyhow." One of these heads declared that the "paper and handling costs" of storing or returning some items for disposal elsewhere exceeded the worth of the merchandise many times over and were, therefore, a drain on the firm.

The conditions attending demotion of a female department head support the existence of these policies. This person originally gained the post through her brother's office at state headquarters. She "worried the life out of" the division heads because only rarely could she "make decisions on her own." She, too, desired "shopworn" items, including jewelry with chipped stones, but she called on the merchandising chief for judgments on the markdown she should make and was repeatedly given the official "30 per cent." Knowing that others more than doubled this figure, she caused trouble by her gossip and insinuations. She was eventually demoted on the pretext that "store policy" demanded placement of a returning veteran—actually from another unit of Rambeau—and that hers was the logical post. Aware that the conditions of her original employment were contrary to Rambeau's merit system, she offered no resistance and was even "glad to get away from all that crazy paper work."

Thus inside the same unit, officially bureaucratic Rambeau could adjust its incentives to satisfy both its enterprising and its less ambitious managers. But in environments of this kind, the person who fits the ideal of believing that his pay matches or exceeds his worth to the firm becomes a potential isolate and requires special attention, though his contribution is valued and utilized. Higher managers naturally wish to reward this attitude, but since the employee may misinterpret any concrete informal reward as unacceptable "favoritism," the question is how? Rambeau had a female department head of this type. Of all the departments, her inventory came nearest to the expected dollar value. It would have been perfect except for the small surplus from single sales of three-for-a-price items. (The surplus also indicated departmental alertness against shoplifting.) Since she was a known devotee of bureaucratic procedure, her department in effect selected personnel like herself, and acquired a reputation for this.  When new heads for the candy counter were required they were drawn from this woman's department because of the likelihood that they would not be "free-loaders," nor tolerant of such people among other employees.  The only informal reward that Rambeau chiefs could give this person and her kind was deference, and praise before others.

Rambeau's rule-devotee had a counterpart in one unit of a drugstore chain near Mobile Acres.  She managed the drugstore's soda fountain. A problem arose from her consistently having the highest percentage of profits among the chain's soda fountain managers.  The matter was an issue among fountain heads in neighboring units of the chain, who were in personal rivalry with her.  Her success was officially honored, for the situation was competitive and fountain supervisors received a percentage of profits above a given level.  But a typical condition—which some students may mistakenly call "institutionalized theft"—existed among all the other units and worked to adversely interpret her achievement. Volume of business on the fountains was comparable in cities near the same size as was the seating capacity, facilities, and the margin of profits among all but the one fountain.  The chief difference between practices in this fountain and the others—covertly charged by the woman and admitted by some of the store managers and pharmacists—was that the other fountain heads gave food and confections free to relatives and close friends, drinks to fountain employees, and variously bartered with nonfountain employees in much the manner of department heads at Rambeau.  Unofficial reward, in the form of meals, to fountain employees was, of course, encouraged by the chain's wage rate which, while comparable to that of the local stores, was no higher than the minimum industrial rates.  Most of the fountain heads covertly rewarded their "good workers" in this way to hold them.

The practices were engaged in up to the point of maintaining at least a narrow margin of profit for the store if not for the fountain heads. The latter were apparently guided more by concern to show a small profit for the fountain—which they did not share—than by a wish to achieve the higher departmental margin that would allow them a percentage of money profits from the fountain.  Prices to the public, set by the chain's state-wide committee, were uniform throughout the system.  Excepting the one, all fountain managers discreetly helped themselves to canned foods, dairy products, and meats from the departmental stock, with the knowledge of the store manager who received free meals, and coffee at any time.  The one fountain chief allowed no gratis consumption to employees, friends, relatives, or herself.  She kept the refrigerators locked and closely supervised the handling of stock.  When emergencies prevented her from shopping for her family and she took

OFFICIAL AND UNOFFICIAL REWARD                                    213

a loaf of bread from the fountain stock, she deposited the price in the cash register. Married to a farmer-factory worker, she stressed loyalty to the store chief, customer service, and money profits for herself. Her superior could not condemn this, but he was disturbed by her boasting of her standing in the chain, and by the innuendoes from other store managers about her "pencil work." To minimize the woman's behavior, he backed his half-hearted praise of her with the logic that fountains are only a supplement to drug and cosmetic services, and that in total store profits his unit was sometimes second or lower in state rankings. But the resentment of other fountain managers—and of his own non-fountain employees against the woman's opposition to the perquisites usually allowed such personnel—forced him openly to check her records, to imply that she was making errors, and to withhold the praise she obviously craved. Higher chain officials also asked her to explain her unique performance and hinted that she could not be that much superior to other fountain managers. After two years of mounting resentments, she quit the firm. The store manager regarded her as a failure because she did not understand what he could not tell her—that her margin of profits was too high and that some social use of materials, not theft, was expected. In his mind, she was too little concerned with the system's internal harmony, and too devoted to formalities.

These practices at Rambeau and in the drugstore chain are doubtless common in many stores, but they are not made obvious to the students responsible for theory about organizational roles, job structure, resources, and pay. And they mean different things to the people involved.

## SUMMARY AND COMMENT

The diversity and range of contributions required of an administrative or functional group cannot be exactly reflected in the official system of rewards. This is an inherent, not a diabolical, shortcoming. It springs largely from (1) the assumption that the total duties and essential skills for a given job are boxed in and paid for, and from (2) the impossibility of officially recognizing some of the extraordinary contributions made by various members—often out of role—during crises.

On the first point, not only must compensation be planned to maintain minimum harmony among personnel, but the limited resources of every firm require it. On the second point, open recognition of some essential contributions would advertise conditions that should not exist, promote rivalries,* hurt official dignity, and encourage disrespect for regulations.

---

* We earlier noted Barnard's analysis of democratic rivalries, and the need in decision making to anticipate and avoid their consequences. In the 1830's an acute French visitor commented on the always smoldering envy among Americans.

Hence recourse is had to semiconfidential use of materials and services as a supplement. This can be both inducement and requital to those who must receive great recognition to do their best, and to those who would move elsewhere without the increment.

Supplementation may be accompanied by abuse to the extent (1) that the reward becomes habitual and is unrelated to contribution; (2) that it is shared by those who make no unusual contribution; or (3) that it expands and becomes coerced theft. The changing line between reward and abuse may be difficult to find and hold, but nothing can be done until the problem is faced. Evading it disposes nonparticipating personnel and the public to label all use of materials and services in this sense as theft. This cynicism cannot be eliminated by allocating ten to fifteen per cent of the budget to cover "shoplifting" by non-supervisory employees and the public. Such allocation may of course enable some managers and subordinates to hide their own theft up to this limit. But it fails to distinguish theft from essential maintenance of the social mechanism. The problem is pervaded by our tradition of political spoils,[24] and our logic that service to the organization must have a one-to-one relation to rank and explicit compensation. We must note that absence of this neat balance induces supplementation, and inflicts moral suffering among members inversely to their capacity for automatic hypocrisy.

It is unlikely that a universally applicable system of informal rewards can be set up, but it is certain that where abuse of the practice develops it will not be eliminated by moral exhortations, elaborate paper forms, or rigid policing. These restraints all help, but as we all know, those who make and apply controls may be like Cellini. If so, their close associates are likely to share their privileges* and echo the general lament of abuse by "others."

---

Here officially to study our prison system, he remarked that "the hatred which men bear to privileges increases in proportion as privileges become more scarce . . . so that democratic passions . . . seem to burn most fiercely . . . when they have least fuel." Americans, then as now, "dread all violent disturbance . . . and love public tranquillity." But in their mania for equality they attribute the success of an *equal* "mainly to some one of his defects" rather than "to his talents or virtues." For to do otherwise "is tacitly to acknowledge that they are themselves less virtuous and talented." See Alexis de Tocqueville, *Democracy in America* (trans. by Henry Reeve), 2 vols., The Cooperative Publication Society (The Colonial Press), New York, 1900, Vol. 1, p. 229; Vol. 2, pp. 307–308.

* Again speaking timelessly, but referring to earlier Americans, de Tocqueville declared that, "Whatever may be the general endeavor of a community to render its members equal and alike, the personal pride of individuals will always seek to rise above the line, and to form somewhere an inequality to their own advantage." *Op. cit.,* Vol. 2, p. 226.

Admitting the potential disruptiveness of implicit rewards, can we assure the full commitment of all abler members without them? And since we dare not preach what we practice, how do we know that we would have less disturbance and as much or more contribution without supplementation and some abuse? Can we show that the cost of, say 15 per cent, to cover theft and unofficial reward is excessive in lieu of other inducements which also cost? This is not to say that what exists is good, but to say that we do not know how bad it is until we can see it more closely.

Abuse is indefensible, but for the sake of a sharper focus on the issue let us say that as varieties of supplementation and limited abuse sap one brand of company resources, they protect other assets. For example, do they not in many cases also reduce disruptive conflict, break the monotony of routine, allow more personal expression, ease the craving for spontaneity, and to some extent catch up all levels of personnel in a system of mutual claims so that aid can be requested and hardly denied?

However, even with revision of the sheep-or-goat outlook, the problem must mark time until serious students are able in many contexts to at least look at (1) the elusive nature of organization that requires unofficial performances; (2) the relation of reward to informal services given; and (3) the relation of all reward to organizational resources, material and social.

Those who regard this chapter as merely a series of episodes on theft have missed the point. Our study of unofficial rewards is not an attempt to justify internal plunder or to say that theft by membership is inevitable. Both "theft" and "reward" derive their meaning from the social context. To insist that this context is constant—so that we can preserve the admitted convenience of fixed definitions—is to pervert meaning, block the issue, and deny that there are ethics in reward.

To repeat, the aim has been to show that however well defined official tasks may be, and however neatly we think we have fitted our personnel to these roles, the inescapably fluid daily situation distorts expected working conditions. Circumstances require various out-of-role and unplanned actions. Regardless of formal rankings, which are often only nominally based on potential for such action, some personnel more aptly do what is essential than do others. Tacitly or not, both they and their rewarders are aware of who solves problems and sustains the organization. Through time they are compensated as resources and situations allow. The process may seem to overlap with theft, or it may escape control and become theft, but able executives both utilize and contain unofficial rewards.

## DOCUMENTARY NOTES

1. S. I. Hayakawa, *Language and Thought in Action,* Harcourt, Brace and Co., New York, 1949, pp. 60–62.

2. Even in the physical sciences there are disputes about the definition, perception, and nature of matter. See the comments of two *physicists:* Martin Johnson, *Art and Scientific Thought,* Columbia University Press, New York, 1949; and J. Bronowski, "Science and Human Values," *The Nation,* 183: 550–566, December 29, 1956, and *The Common Sense of Science,* Wm. Heinemann, Ltd., London, 1951, especially chaps. 6–8. Disputes increase in the biological sciences. For example, because they combine both plant and animal characteristics, we find such organisms as *Euglena viridis* and the slime-fungi studied by both zoologists and botanists. Books from satirical to scientific levels debate the nature of *truth, fact,* and *meaning.* In the opening pages of his *Ethics,* Aristotle notes the difficulty of expecting a mathematician to see facts as *probable,* or a politician to see them as *precise.* For himself he believed that different subject matters admit of different degrees of precision in handling. See also the two works of T. V. Smith, "In Accentuation of the Negative," *The Scientific Monthly,* 63: 463–469, December, 1946 and *The Ethics of Compromise,* Starr King Press, Boston, 1956; and the numerous articles in L. Bryson et al., *Symbols and Values,* Harper and Brothers, New York, 1954, *Symbols and Society,* Harper and Brothers, New York, 1955; Anthony Standen, *Science Is a Sacred Cow,* E. P. Dutton and Co., New York, 1950; S. I. Hayakawa, ed., *Language, Meaning and Maturity,* Harper and Brothers, New York, 1954; H. Hoijer, ed., *Language in Culture,* University of Chicago Press, 1954; E. A. Burtt, *The Metaphysical Foundations of Modern Science,* Doubleday and Co., Garden City, N.Y., 1955; Howard Becker, *Through Values to Social Interpretation,* Duke University Press, Durham, N.C., 1950; Boris B. Bogoslovsky, *The Technique of Controversy,* Harcourt, Brace and Co., New York, 1928, especially chaps. 4–9; Kenneth Burke, *Attitudes Toward History,* 2 vols., The New Republic, New York, 1937, especially Vol. 2, pp. 52–256.

3. See Edwin H. Sutherland, *White Collar Crime,* The Dryden Press, New York, 1949; *The Autobiography of Lincoln Steffens,* Harcourt, Brace and Co., New York, 1931; John T. Flynn, *Graft in Business,* The Vanguard Press, New York, 1931, pp. 103–106.

4. Sumner Slichter, "Report on Current Research: Economics," *Saturday Review,* 36: 24, April 4, 1953; Arthur H. Cole, "An Approach to the Study of Entrepreneurship," *Journal of Economic History* 6, Supplement 1–15 (1946); Robert A. Gordon, *Business Leadership in the Large Organization,* Brookings Institution, Washington, D.C., 1945; Clare E. Griffin, *Enterprise in a Free Society,* R. D. Irwin, Chicago, 1949, chap. 5; John K. Galbraith, *American Capitalism,* Houghton Mifflin, Boston, 1952; Albert Lauterbach, *Man, Motives and Money,* Cornell University Press, Ithaca, New York, 1954; George Katona, *Psychological Analysis of Economic Behavior,* McGraw-Hill Book Co., New York, 1951; *Business Week,* "A Tempo Shapes a Type," April 25, 1953, pp. 56, 58, 60; C. C. Abbott, J. D. Forbes, L. A. Thompson, *The Executive Function and Its Compensation,* Graduate School of Business Administration, The University of Virginia, Charlottesville, 1957.

5. C. I. Barnard, *Functions of the Executive,* Harvard University Press, Cambridge, 1938, pp. 138–160.

## OFFICIAL AND UNOFFICIAL REWARD                    217

6. P. F. Drucker, *The Practice of Management,* Harper and Brothers, New York, 1954, p. 152; Abbott, Forbes, and Thompson, *op. cit.,* pp. 46–55.

7. See also Morris S. Viteles, *Motivation and Morale in Industry,* Norton, New York, 1953; Kornhauser, in Kornhauser, Dubin, and Ross, *op. cit.,* pp. 59–85; W. F. Whyte et al., *Money and Motivation,* Harper and Brothers, New York, 1955.

8. Also see C. I. Barnard, "Functions and Pathology of Status Systems in Formal Organizations" in W. F. Whyte, ed., *Industry and Society,* McGraw-Hill Book Co., New York, 1946, pp. 207–243.

9. The various struggles of Milo and Fruhling with their Offices. Also see Galbraith, *American Capitalism,* Houghton Mifflin, Boston, 1952, p. 28.

10. Barnard, *Functions of the Executive,* pp. 139–160.

11. Griffin, *op. cit.,* chap. 5; Gordon, *op. cit.,* pp. 305–312. Geiger's "freewheeling" bent is suggested by his remark that "The engineers aren't practical. They want everything to be exact. They can't see that in operation you've got to lie and steal and cheat a little." See also W. H. Knowles, *Personnel Management: A Human Relations Approach,* American Book Co., New York, 1955, p. 130; Robert B. Fetter and Donald C. Johnson, *Compensation and Incentives for Industrial Executives,* Indiana University, Bloomington, 1952, p. 57.

12. Abbott, Forbes, and Thompson, *op. cit.,* p. 41.

13. Lauterbach, *op. cit.,* chap. 1.

14. Katona, *op. cit.,* chap. 9.

15. *Business Week,* April 25, 1953, pp. 56, 58, 60.

16. Will Durant, *The Renaissance,* Simon and Schuster, New York, 1953, p. 401.

17. Article "Aqueducts," *Encyclopaedia Britannica,* Vol. 2, 14th edition, 1932, p. 161.

18. *Newsweek,* "Those Big-Figure Expense Accounts," Vol. 41, No. 20, pp. 87, 90–92, May 20, 1957; Seymour Mintz, "Executive Expense Accounts and Fringe Benefits: A Problem in Management, Morality and Revenue," *Journal of Taxation,* 1: 2–9, June, 1954; Abbott, Forbes, and Thompson, *op. cit.,* p. 41.

19. See various responses (public documents) to form 10-K of the Securities and Exchange Commission, Washington, D.C., for the Fiscal Year ended August 21, 1956.

20. Fred H. Colvin, *The Industrial Triangle,* Columbia Graphs, Columbia, Connecticut, 1955, pp. 95–96; Benjamin Aaron, "Governmental Restraints on Featherbedding," *Stanford Law Review,* 5: 680–721, 1953.

21. See the theory of Abbott, Forbes, and Thompson, *op. cit.,* pp. 34–38.

22. See Havelock Ellis, *The Dance of Life,* The Modern Library, New York, 1923, pp. 89–98, and Robert Dubin, *Human Relations in Administration,* Prentice-Hall, New York, 1951, pp. 336–345.

23. For an intensive study of twenty salesgirls in the setting of a large department store, see George F. F. Lombard, *Behavior in a Selling Group,* Harvard University, Graduate School of Business Administration, Boston, 1955.

24. Walter Lippmann, *A Preface to Politics,* The Macmillan Company, New York, 1913, chap. 1; Charles A. and Mary Beard, *The Rise of American Civilization,* 2 vols. in one, The Macmillan Co., New York, 1937, Vol. 1, pp. 547–557; V. O. Key, Jr., *Politics, Parties, and Pressure Groups,* 2nd edition, Thomas Y. Crowell Co., New York, 1947, pp. 316–339.

# [9]

ANNALS, *AAPSS*, **493**, September 1987

# The Political Economy of Informal Economies

## *By* STUART HENRY

ABSTRACT: This article considers the mutual interrelationship between informal economies and the wider political economy of capitalism. Four dimensions are discussed: (1) the generation of informal economies as a paradoxical outcome of distinguishing them from capitalism; (2) the support given by capitalism and reciprocated by informal economies that enables each to gain strength from their similarities; (3) the opposition to informal economies that is reflected back on the wider economy; and (4) the destruction capitalism inflicts as it attempts to colonize and co-opt informal economies and the simultaneous transformation of capitalism that occurs with their absorption into the wider structure. The article argues that as a result of these complex interrelations, the development of, and intervention in, informal economies is neither simple nor linear. Failure to take these relations into account can lead to policy and its implementation that produce many unforeseen outcomes.

---

*Stuart Henry received his doctorate in sociology from the University of Kent in Canterbury in 1976. He is currently visiting associate professor of sociology at Eastern Michigan University, where he teaches criminological theory and white-collar crime. He has taught at polytechnics and universities in England and the United States and has written numerous articles for journals and magazines. His books include* Self-Help and Health, *which he coauthored with D. Robinson;* The Hidden Economy; Informal Institutions, *which he edited; and* Private Justice.

ANY consideration of informal economic activity, however much that is concealed from the management of the state, will be incomplete if account is not taken of the wider structural context in which the activity is set. Just as it was a mistake for the study of political economy to become divorced from the study of households,[1] so the relatively recent study of the underground, irregular, and hidden economies would be seriously flawed if it ignored their interconnectedness to the wider society. The political economy of informal economies conceives of the face-to-face informal economic activities that go on in households and in informal social networks in relation to the broad macro-features of the political and economic system of capitalism.

It is important to recognize, however, that this interconnectedness between informal economies and the wider capitalist structure is not one-way. In this article I shall attempt to demonstrate that not only do informal economies emerge from the contradictions of capitalism, but they are simultaneously supportive and undermining of capitalism, as that system is of them. Put simply, informal economies both are shaped by and shape the wider political economy in which they are set. Moreover, this is also true for global capitalism's relationship with Third World informal sector employment[2] and for socialist second economies in their relationship with the state planned economy.[3]

## CAPITALISM AND ITS COMPONENT INFORMAL ECONOMIES

I take the view that the political economy of Western capitalism, rather than being a unified whole dominated by a capitalist free market economy and a facilitative state, is much more fragmentary and contradictory. As I have argued elsewhere,[4] Western industrial societies are multiplex economies containing a range of qualitatively different, conflicting, and coalescing subeconomies under the overarching domination of capitalism. These constituent economies of capitalism are not discrete or separate entities but are overlapping and interrelated, each with its own discernible identity, each also sharing features in common with the wider structure of which it is a part. For these reasons it is very difficult to be precise about where the boundaries of one subeconomy end and those of another begin.

I take the term "informal economies" to be the generic term for the range of

1. Siegwart Lindenberg, "An Assessment of tne New Political Economy: Its Potential for the Social Sciences and for Sociology in Particular," *Sociological Theory*, 3:99-114 (1985).

2. Chris Gerry, "Developing Economies and the Informal Sector in Historical Perspective," this issue of *The Annals* of the American Academy of Political and Social Science. See also Ray Bromley and Chris Gerry, eds., *Casual Work and Poverty in Third World Cities* (New York: John Wiley, 1979); Priscilla Connolly, "The Politics of the Informal Sector: A Critique," in *Beyond Employment*, ed. Nanneke Redclift and Enzo Mingione (New York: Basil Blackwell, 1985).

3. Steven L. Sampson, "The Second Economy of the Soviet Union and Eastern Europe," this issue of *The Annals* of the American Academy of Political and Social Science.

4. Stuart Henry, ed., *Informal Institutions* (New York: St. Martin's Press, 1981); idem, "The Working Unemployed: Perspectives on the Informal Economy and Unemployment," *Sociological Review*, 30:460-77 (1982); idem, "Can the Hidden Economy Be Revolutionary? Towards a Dialectical Analysis of the Relations between Formal and Informal Economics," mimeographed (Norfolk, VA: Old Dominion University, Department of Sociology and Criminal Justice, 1986); John Davis, "Gifts and the UK Economy," *Man*, 7:408-29 (1972).

POLITICAL ECONOMY OF INFORMAL ECONOMIES 139

overlapping subeconomies that are not taken into account by formal measures of economic activity. Although this term is a relatively arbitrary choice, it seems to be the least emotive or value laden of those available. It should not, however, be taken to mean that the regular economy of capitalism is wholly formal, but that informality is the predominant characteristic of the economies that we are considering here.[5]

Defining and classifying what counts as informal economies is further complicated because those who define and construct taxonomies are themselves selecting criteria based on their own structural position and interests. Indeed, this problem is reflected in the profusion of names that informal economies have attracted. As Carol Carson has observed, in addition to the catchy titles of "underground," "unobserved," and "hidden," these activities have been described as

cash, black, unofficial, informal, irregular, unrecorded, moonlight, twilight, gray, shadow, subterranean, marginal, dual, second, parallel and illegal. The choice of names sometimes reflects an author's point of view: for employment, moonlight; for tax administration, unreported; for law enforcement, illegal. Some authors have drawn distinctions among the names according to the activities they intend to cover. Others, although they have used different names, do not appear to have different coverage. In summary, a generally accepted taxonomy has not yet emerged.[6]

Accepting this position could be grounds for dodging the issue of definition and classification. However, to do so would be unhelpful, if only because the default position is likely to be one of assuming market economic assumptions and motives that, as Gaughan and Ferman point out,[7] and as I have demonstrated elsewhere,[8] are often a highly inappropriate description of much of the activity with which we are dealing.

Any all-encompassing description of the activity is bound to fail to convince. In part, this is because it will clash with ethnographic and participant accounts steeped in their own unique experience. In part it is because it will challenge observers' carefully constructed abstract categories, and in part it is because the very diversity of these subeconomies defies generalization. In commenting on the conceptual confusion resulting from lumping together a diverse range of informal activity including domestic do-it-yourself work, consumption and leisure-time activities, black labor, tax evasion, smuggling, alternative communal projects, self-help, and mutual aid, it is little wonder that Joseph Huber is moved to exclaim that "the result is conceptual 'tuttifruitti' which leads to political hodgepodge, if it leads anywhere at all."[9]

What these diverse activities have in common is certainly difficult to describe

7. Joseph P. Gaughan and Louis A. Ferman, "Toward an Understanding of the Informal Economy," this issue of *The Annals* of the American Academy of Political and Social Science. See also Louis A. Ferman and Louise E. Berndt, "The Irregular Economy," in *Informal Institutions*, ed. Henry.

8. See Stuart Henry, *The Hidden Economy* (Oxford: Martin Robertson, 1978).

9. Joseph Huber, "Conceptions of the Dual Economy," *Technological Forecasting and Social Change,* 27:65 (1985).

5. Also it is important to recognize that although it is often referred to in the singular, we are clearly talking about a number of interrelated subeconomies; hence I prefer the term in the plural.

6. Carol S. Carson, "The Underground Economy: An Introduction," *Survey of Current Business*, p. 21 (May 1984).

without first specifying the total societal context. Under socialist states, for example, informal economies often have more in common with capitalist free market activities than with the communal forms that these activities sometimes take under capitalism.[10] For advanced Western capitalist societies in times of relatively full employment, informal economies seem to share the following characteristics. They are (1) concealed from the state accounting system and are largely unregistered by its economic and criminal measurement techniques; (2) small scale; (3) labor intensive, requiring little capital; and (4) locally based, with trading taking place through face-to-face relationships between friends, relatives, or acquaintances in a limited geographical area. Beyond this, characteristics such as whether altruistic or avaricious, autonomous or parasitic, legal or illegal, using cash or using kind as a medium of exchange are generally less applicable. These are, in fact, criteria used by commentators to distinguish different constituent subeconomies.

Of the variety of classification schemes available in the literature[11] I shall adapt that used by Gaughan and Ferman in this volume and based on Sahlins's seminal work in economic anthropology.[12] Sahlins's analytical framework distinguishes exchange in any society on

the basis of the extent to which reciprocity is a central organizing principle. This produces three basic kinds of exchange: (1) intimate, which is governed by the principles of generalized altruistic reciprocity and takes place among close friends, relatives, and socially recognized kin; (2) associational, which is governed by the principle of balanced reciprocity and takes place among friends and neighbors who are members of a loose-knit social network; and (3) entrepreneurial, which is governed by the principle of negative reciprocity, self-interest, or avarice and takes place largely among strangers.[13]

Each of these kinds of exchange can be considered on a vertical plane as differing depths or levels overlapping with each other as one moves from altruistic reciprocity among intimates to negative reciprocity among strangers. At the same time each basic kind of exchange is more or less present in the variety of informal economies that we can consider on a horizontal plane.[14] For example, the social or communal economy is mainly characterized by the intimate type of exchange.[15] The do-

---

10. Sampson, "Second Economy of the Soviet Union"; Istvan R. Gabor, "The Major Domains of the Second Economy in Hungary" (Paper delivered at "The Informal Economy: Social Conflicts and the Future of Industrial Societies," First World Conference on the Informal Economy, Rome, Nov. 1982).

11. For a discussion of these, see Henry, "Working Unemployed"; Huber, "Conceptions of the Dual Economy."

12. Marshall Sahlins, *Stone Age Economics* (Chicago: Aldine-Atherton, 1972).

13. These terms are derived from the work of Sahlins and Thompson; for discussion, see Gaughan and Ferman, "Toward an Understanding"; see also Robin Cantor, Stuart Henry, and Steve Rayner, *Markets, Distribution and Exchange after Societal Cataclysm* (Oak Ridge, TN: Oak Ridge National Laboratory, 1987).

14. A similar analytical framework was developed by Georges Gurvitch for analyzing the varieties of law, each of which could exist at different levels of formality or informality. See Georges Gurvitch, *The Sociology of Law* (Boston: Routledge & Kegan Paul, 1947).

15. Carol B. Stack, *All Our Kin: Strategies for Survival in a Black Community* (New York: Harper & Row, 1974); Martin Lowenthal, "The Social Economy in Urban Working Class Communities," in *The Social Economy of Cities*, ed. G. Gappert and H. Ross (Newbury Park, CA: Sage, 1975).

POLITICAL ECONOMY OF INFORMAL ECONOMIES 141

mestic or household economy, while characterized by intimate exchange, also has elements both associational and, as many critics of patriarchy have argued, entrepreneurial.[16] The irregular economy is more typically found to be associational and entrepreneurial in character, although it too has aspects of intimate exchange.[17] The hidden economy is also largely associational with elements both intimate and entrepreneurial,[18] but it can operate with a high level of entrepreneurial exchange[19] such that it approximates the extreme end of avariciousness found to be typical of criminal economies of trade in stolen goods, prostitution, drugs, and gambling.[20]

While it is possible to break these informal economies down into their own constituent subeconomies, to do so becomes cumbersome and needlessly complex. Moreover, it forces us to choose between observer-based and participant-based criteria with insufficient data on which to base a decision. For the

16. This is why the feminist writers often opt for the phrase "domestic labor" or "hidden labor." See, for example, Jane Taylor, "Hidden Labour and the National Health Service," in *Prospects for the National Health*, ed. Paul Atkinson et al. (London: Croom Helm, 1979).

17. Ferman and Berndt, "Irregular Economy"; Leslie M. Dow, "High Weeds in Detroit," *Urban Anthropology*, 6:111-28 (1977).

18. Henry, *Hidden Economy*; Gerald Mars, *Cheats at Work: An Anthropology of Workplace Crime* (London: George Allen & Unwin, 1982).

19. Jason Ditton, *Part-time Crime: An Ethnography of Fiddling and Pilferage* (New York: Macmillan, 1977).

20. It is worth mentioning here that even regular economy market exchange can be interspersed with intimate exchange—see, for example, Harvey A. Faberman and Eugene A. Weinstein, "Personalization in Lower Class Consumer Interaction," *Social Problems*, 17:499-57 (1970)—and under imperfect competition, or monopoly, is characterized as much by avaricious exchange as are criminal economies.

purpose of the following discussion, therefore, I shall simply describe the activity and indicate the term that has typically been applied to it as this becomes relevant to the discussion of the interrelationship between constituent subeconomies and the wider social structure.

The first two dimensions of the interrelationship between these informal economies and the wider societal structure I shall consider are those of mutual support. I shall show that support occurs either (1) because of the strain toward separation that emerges as the regular economy of capitalism is growing and being established as the primary economy; or (2) because the wider capitalist economy coalesces with informal economies, exploiting, co-opting, and colonizing them as it transforms them into its own likeness. I will then go on to consider the mutual relations of opposition between informal economies and the wider structure.

### THE PARADOX OF SUPPORT THROUGH OPPOSITION

Support through opposition means that in distinguishing the overarching structure of capitalism from that which it is not, proponents inadvertently create counter structures. These take the form of subeconomies that are based on exchange structures that have been excluded from the capitalist system. Simultaneously, proponents of the subeconomies, in elaborating their own activities' differences from the wider system, help support its clarification.

As early capitalism emerged from feudalism, definitions and boundaries were created to establish bourgeois legality. The newly emerging capitalist society changed what had previously been acceptable practices, such as payments in kind, into illegal activity, parasitic on the development of capitalism. Jason Ditton, for example, has argued that the extended package of common rights enjoyed by feudal tenants had made a major contribution to household budgets but that these were stripped away by the eighteenth-century Acts of Enclosure.[21] Wood gathering, game rights, and grazing rights became the crimes of wood theft, poaching, and trespassing.[22] This was not a sudden event but one that took place at different rates and to differing degrees in different parts of the country. John Styles has shown that workers in the newly founded manufacturing industries of late-seventeenth- and eighteenth-century England constantly borrowed, bartered, and sold small quantities of materials among themselves and that "the boundaries between legitimate dealing of this kind, receiving embezzled goods and even receiving goods stolen by outsiders from workshops and warehouses were not always well defined and were disregarded by many."[23] Criminalization of the consumption of a part of one's daily labor was redefined in conjunction with capitalist development of the factory to become employee theft and embezzlement; the trading of embezzled goods came to constitute a hidden economy.

Again, it must be pointed out that although the right to enjoy the direct products of labor was denied and the activities of those who continued this practice were seen as parasitic on the wider host economy, this was not a total transformation but one of emphasis and definition. Styles reasons that workers were prepared to argue for their right to previously recognized perquisites against campaigns by employers to redefine them as frauds through the creation of laws. But, he says,

it would be wrong to imagine that such attacks [by employers] always brought about a once-and-for-all transformation of this component of a worker's income, or were intended to do so.... Indeed, most *employers* appear to have been decidedly unwilling to eradicate perquisites permanently, despite the insistence by some modern historians that this was one of the "main tasks" of capitalist development.[24]

As will be seen when I examine the supportive relations between capitalism and informal economies, there are good reasons why employers wish to retain an element of the hidden economy.

It is important to recognize, then, that informal economies can be transformed by redefinition from activity that was previously no more than innocent trading into a criminal enterprise. Although some of the original substance of the activity may remain—in the case of the hidden economy the original substance is that of an intimate and associational network of exchange—this interpretation is publicly suppressed, and the illegality and corresponding avaricious motives are drawn out as the significant dimension. As Ditton defines it, the hidden economy is seen as "the sub-commercial movement

21. Jason Ditton, "Perks, Pilferage and the Fiddle: The Historical Structure of Invisible Wages," *Theory and Society*, 4:39-71 (1977).

22. Douglas Hay et al., *Albion's Fatal Tree: Crime and Society in Eighteenth Century England* (Harmondsworth: Allen Lane, 1975); E. P. Thompson, *Whigs and Hunters* (Harmondsworth: Allen Lane, 1975).

23. John Styles, "Embezzlement, Industry and the Law in England, 500-1800," in *Manufacture in Town and Country before the Factory*, ed. Maxine Berg et al. (New York: Cambridge University Press, 1983), p. 179.

24. Ibid., pp. 204-5.

of materials and finance, together with the systematic concealment of that process for illegal gain . . . a microscopic wry reflection on the visible economic structure upon which it parasitically feeds."[25]

However, in its very drawing of boundaries, capitalism is signifying areas that may be more attractive to those dissatisfied with the existing system and it is also providing the grounds justifying participation in the hidden economy. As David Matza has observed, "The criminal law, more so than any comparable system of norms, acknowledges and states the principled grounds under which an actor may claim exemption. The law contains the seeds of its own neutralization."[26]

In addition, the banning of behaviors provides the conditions of what first Wilkins and then Young describe as "deviancy amplification."[27] Amplification occurs when those who publicly condemn and react to behavior that is deemed unacceptable exaggerate its negative aspects. Distorted presentation, such as negatively labeling informal economies as black, underground, hidden, secret, nether, and so on, creates a new situation for participants, who are then forced to respond by concealing other related information and practices. This secrecy brings new deviant solutions, increased contact with other excluded groups, and further reaction by control agents as the whole cycle is repeated in a seemingly endless spiral of negative signification.

Another sense in which the separation or distinction between informal economies and the wider system of capitalism enables both realms to grow in opposition to one another is through ongoing pronouncements that are part of the politics of oppositional discourse. These, paradoxically, generate mutual support for that which is opposed.[28] For example, when advocates of the regular capitalist economy publicly discredit irregular economy work as dangerous for employees because of the absence of protective legislation, insurance, and benefits, they simultaneously imply that regular work is safe and responsible. When they denounce the products of irregular work as unreliable and without guarantee, they are, by implication, simultaneously promoting the formal economy as accountable, predictable, and efficient. But such pronouncements also, paradoxically, invite comparisons on price, personal relations, spontaneity, flexibility, and uniqueness that may inform many regular economy participants that there are alternatives of which they might otherwise have been unaware; the pronouncements may encourage them to participate in informal economies, which they might not otherwise have done.

A further way in which the politics of defining the boundaries of capitalism can simultaneously generate informal activity is in the role played by the state. The growth of the state as a facilitator of the growth of capitalist enterprise requires that it accrue revenue from those

25. Jason Ditton, "The Fiddler: A Sociological Analysis of Blue Collar Theft among Bread Salesmen" (Ph.D. diss., University of Durham, 1976), p. 275.

26. David Matza, *Delinquency and Drift* (New York: John Wiley, 1964), p. 60.

27. Leslie Wilkins, *Social Deviance: Social Policy, Action and Research* (London: Tavistock, 1964); Jock Young, "The Role of the Police as Amplifiers of Deviancy," in *Images of Deviance*, ed. Stanley Cohen (New York: Penguin, 1971).

28. See Michel Foucault, *The History of Sexuality: An Introduction* (New York: Penguin, 1978); Elizabeth R. Morrissey, "Power and Control through Discourse: The Case of Drinking and Drinking Problems among Women," *Contemporary Crisis,* 10:157-79 (1986).

on whose behalf it acts. Taxation laws, however, not only define who and what is taxable; they also specify who and what is nontaxable. As Gutmann, an advocate of a more laissez-faire capitalism, says, "The subterranean economy ... is a creature of income tax, of other taxes, of limitations on the legal employment of certain groups and of prohibitions on certain activities."[29] He argues that the redistributive economy and the welfare state, growing employment protection legislation and sex and racial equality legislation are actually creating the grounds for capitalist employers to go outside the system, employ workers off-the-books, and so facilitate participation in the irregular economy. The problem of high levels of government involvement is particularly acute in times of high inflation. "Inflation redistributes income from income earners to government as taxpayers are pushed into higher tax brackets; squeezed taxpayers in turn try to push part of the cost of inflation onto the government by getting off-the-books income."[30]

But we need not imagine that informal economies would weaken with the withering of the welfare state. The very structure of capitalism is such that it generates its own historically specific types of informal economies, as Ferman and Ferman were first to demonstrate.[31] In their seminal article they claim that the very origins of irregular economies "lie

in structural conditions and processes in the larger society, and cannot be divorced from them."[32] They argue that modern capitalist industrial society encourages such economies by creating structural inequalities based on class, ethnic, and cultural segregation. In addition, economic specialization, protectionist trade unions, and professional associations coalesce so that some goods and services are not widely available or are too expensive for those with low or nonexistent incomes. The direct result is that a market is created outside of the formal regular economy for cheap goods and services, and, say Ferman and Ferman, "once regular patterns are established they provide training and opportunity for those members of the community who choose to earn their livelihood this way and [the patterns] are supported by a population that has few viable alternatives for the purchase of goods and services."[33]

We can see, therefore, that in its political attempt to develop, define, and protect itself from that which it is not, capitalist economic structure simultaneously creates and generates the contradictory possibilities of internal subeconomies. As these counter and parallel economies themselves gain strength from the wider structure, they also give it strength by allowing its boundaries to be defined and by providing a safety net for those who are unable to survive its competition of interests. Nowhere is this mutuality of support more apparent than when we consider the second major dimension of the interrelationship between informal economies and the wider capitalist structure, that of convergence or coalescence.

29. Peter M. Gutmann, "The Subterranean Economy," *Financial Analysts Journal*, 34:26 (1977).

30. Peter Gutmann, "Latest Notes from the Subterranean Economy," *Business and Society Review*, p. 29 (Summer 1980).

31. Patricia R. Ferman and Louis A. Ferman, "The Structural Underpinning of the Irregular Economy," *Poverty and Human Resources Abstracts*, 8:3-17 (1973).

32. Ibid., p. 5.
33. Ibid., p. 17.

COLONIZATION THROUGH
COALESCENCE

We saw in the previous section how developing capitalism did not completely remove informal economies, though it did transform their definition. The reason why employers retain that to which they are ostensibly opposed becomes clearer when the functions of informal economies are examined. Scraton and South have captured the nub of this dialectical relationship:

Essentially workers' involvement in the hidden economy represents a dynamic form of opposition to the interests of capital by the daily enactment of processes which inhibit the exploitative relations of capital over labor. . . . It constitutes an attack on the hegemony of class discipline from what "autonomous space" is available, both mental and material, to workers. It is precisely for this reason that attempts are made to incorporate pilfering and fiddling into the wage relation. Thus these activities cannot be considered outside the historical dynamic of class relations.[34]

The existence of a system of payments in kind that are not part of a formal wage or salary structure, and that can be redefined as theft or perquisites depending upon the state of the business cycle, gives employers a hidden arm of control. It allows them to reward employees for service "beyond the call of duty,"[35] but it also allows them to establish individual reward systems for the control of their overall wage bill. Gerald Mars and his colleagues have shown, for example, how in the restaurant industry

certain core workers are granted the right to pilfered food and access to the best tips in return for loyalty in policing peripheral workers who may wish to form unions and push for higher wages.[36]

Jason Ditton has similarly shown that service workers are often placed in low-wage situations by their employers who "connive at corruption" by turning a "blind eye" to employees who cheat customers. This serves as a means of deflecting employees from making losses for the company. However, once such pilfering and fiddling has been learned by novice employees as a method to cover their potential losses from mistakes, these activities are extended, often against the company and in connivance with the customer, to make a little extra side money.[37] Here we see supportive relations begin to turn into negative relations of coalescence, as I shall discuss later.

It has been argued that allowing a degree of employee theft is healthy for worker morale and helps relieve the boredom of monotonous work routines and so facilitates the wider production process.[38] More cynically, Ditton, like Scraton and South, has observed that embezzlement and other related hidden economy activities, where they are seen

34. Phil Scraton and Nigel South, "The Ideological Construction of the Hidden Economy: Private Justice and Work Related Crime," *Contemporary Crisis*, 8:11 (1984).

35. Melville Dalton, *Men Who Manage* (New York: John Wiley, 1964).

36. Gerald Mars and Peter Mitchell, "Catering for the Low Paid: Invisible Earnings," *Bulletin*, no. 15 (London: Low Pay Unit, 1977); Gerald Mars, Don Bryant, and Peter Mitchell, *Manpower Problems in the Hotel and Catering Industry* (Farnborough: Saxon House, 1979); Gerald Mars and Michael Nicod, "Hidden Rewards at Work: The Implications from a Study of British Hotels," in *Informal Institutions*, ed. Henry; idem. *The World of Waiters* (London: George Allen & Unwin, 1983).

37. Ditton, *Part-time Crime*.

38. Lawrence R. Zeitlin, "Stimulus/Response: A Little Larceny Can Do a Lot for Employee Morale," *Psychology Today*, 5:22, 23, 26, 64 (1971).

as "beating the boss" or "defeating the system," are cheap symbolic concessions for a device that actually entrenches the dependency of employees since the concession can be granted or withdrawn at will, to suit market conditions.[39]

If further evidence were needed of the functionally supportive relations between capitalism and the range of informal economies, one would only have to look at what, in the literature on the Third World, has been described as "informal income opportunities."[40] Although some argue that the informal sector is a residual form of petty commodity production operating independently of capitalism,[41] others recognize that it is relied upon in times of crisis as a means of labor absorption for the wider capitalist society, serving to disguise unemployment and stimulate new employment. Informal sector workers are disguised wage laborers since their production is subject to control by industrial capital, which sets the volume, type, and quality of the goods produced and fixes the prices below their true value.[42] Bromley

and Gerry, for example, argue that where the employees are subcontracted out-workers, or where they are self-employed, they are harnessed to the needs of large capitalist enterprises; they are dependent upon the enterprises' credit, rental of space or equipment, and supply of raw materials; or the larger enterprise is the sole buyer of the employees' product.[43]

But there is a sense, too, in which informal economies in capitalism are more than an appendage and its participants more than a marginal surplus population. Informal economies are valued as contributing to economic growth by providing low-cost consumer goods, being a test bed for innovations in business, and for oiling the wheels of industry, enabling bureaucratic restrictions to be overcome.[44]

Indeed, it is in this vein that some futurists have celebrated the usefulness of informal economies to advanced industrial capitalism. Shankland, for example, notes that "in a healthy society" formal and informal economies "sustain each other and their relationship should be a symbiotic one of mutual support." He says,

The formal sector effectively controls the commanding heights of the economy and the political system, but the informal sector is essential, not parasitic or residual . . . it operates rather at the interstices of the formal institutions of modern urban society; it cannot offer an alternative society but a complementary economic activity to the

39. Jason Ditton and Richard Brown, "Why Don't They Revolt? Invisible Income as a Neglected Dimension of Runciman's Relative Deprivation Thesis," *British Journal of Sociology*, 32:521-30 (1981).

40. Keith Hart, "Informal Income Opportunities and Urban Employment in Ghana," *Journal of Modern African Studies*, 11:61-89 (1973).

41. J. Bremen, "A Dualistic Labour System: A Critique of the Informal Sector Concept," *Economic and Political Weekly*, 11:1870-76 (1976); R. Davies, "Informal Sector or Subordinate Mode of Production? A Model," in *Casual Work and Poverty*, ed. Bromley and Gerry.

42. D. Mazumdar, "The Urban Informal Sector," *World Development*, 4:655-79 (1976); John Bryant, "An Introductory Bibliography to Work on the Informal Economy in Third World Literature," in *Bibliographies on Local Labour Markets and the Informal Economy*, ed. Ray Pahl and Julian Laite (London: Social Science Research Council, 1982).

43. Bromley and Gerry, ed., *Casual Work and Poverty*.

44. Michael Carter, "Issues in the Hidden Economy—A Survey," *Economic Record*, 60:209-21 (1984). This functional role for informal economies is particularly well documented for second economies under socialism. See Sampson, "Second Economy of the Soviet Union."

POLITICAL ECONOMY OF INFORMAL ECONOMIES 147

formal with a different, informal and more personal life style.[45]

Shankland argues that the benefits of encouraging the informal economy are enormous and are particularly useful as a way of getting new business started on a trial basis.[46] Indeed, some early capitalists founded their enterprises on materials acquired from the hidden economy. The use of materials thus acquired, as Styles says, "was widely believed to be a very common route of entry into manufacturing for men with little capital."[47]

Gershuny, in his early writings on postindustrial society, has been most credited with the benign futurist position toward the informal economy.[48] He predicts a growth of labor productivity resulting from a declining manufacturing sector and spurred on by the microtechnological revolution. This growth will continue to reduce employment opportunities in the formal sector. Fiscal and legitimacy crises will halt the traditional Keynesian public-spending solution to unemployment and will encourage the ideological shift from public provision to privatization. Rather than continuing the expansion of the service sector, argues Gershuny, we are more likely to

see an expansion of the "self-service" economy. Unable to afford formal economy services because of higher unemployment and lower income in the formal economy, people will turn to the household, the community, and the irregular economy.

Leading government officials in Western capitalist societies have claimed that the irregular economy of work off-the-books is actually indicative of the spirit of capitalism. In Britain, both Prince Charles and Prime Minister Thatcher have claimed that the irregular economy "proves that the British are not work shy." Similarly, Ronald Reagan has said that the cut-price, irregular work done by wetbacks employed off-the-books may contribute more to the U.S. economy than they take out in benefits. Their unregistered status does not allow them to draw state benefits for fear of being caught. More recently he has suggested that the necessary cut in welfare services demanded by the budget deficit creates the opportunity for local self-help and mutual-aid initiatives, from psychological support groups to neighborhood housing construction and project management, and from parent-run day care to self-help for the elderly.

There are numerous examples of the ways in which benign symbiotic relationships exist between regular capitalist enterprise and informal economies. Every time do-it-yourself tools are sold to consumers by hardware stores or when department stores sell food mixers and other household appliances, they are clearly contributing to capitalist production. They are simultaneously contributing to the household, communal, and irregular economies since these goods enable self-servicing and self-provisioning in ways that the sale of finished consumer goods do not. The phenomenal growth in industries pro-

45. Graeme Shankland, "Towards Dual Economy," *Guardian*, 23 Dec. 1977, p. 18.

46. Graeme Shankland, *Our Secret Economy* (London: Anglo-German Foundation, 1980).

47. Styles, "Embezzlement, Industry and the Law," p. 179.

48. J. I. Gershuny, "Post-Industrial Society: The Myth of the Service Economy," *Futures*, 9:103-14 (1977); idem, *After Industrial Society?* (New York: Macmillan, 1978), idem, "The Informal Economy: Its Role in Post-Industrial Society," *Futures*, 11:3-15 (1979); Jonathan Gershuny, *Social Innovation and the Division of Labour* (New York: Oxford University Press, 1983); Jonathan Gershuny and Ian D. Miles, *The New Service Economy: The Transformation of Employment in Industrial Societies* (London: Francis Pinter, 1983).

ducing home-improvement materials and tools, such as paint, paper, laminates, wood, power tools, step ladders, work-benches, screws, and nails, is not only indicative of the adaptability of capitalism to profit from new demand but also reflects the emerging contradictions that informal economies represent. People are no longer content with finished products but are increasingly demanding those that require participatory production and control, if not in the factory, then in the home, the community, and on the street: dinner sets to Tupperware parties, dining room suites to do-it-yourself. Each of these rely on domestic production or social networking or both to complete consumption.

Heinze and Olk have argued against such stabilizing strategies for capitalism based on the colonization of people's desire for participatory control. However, their preference for a "complementary network" strategy involving a deliberate policy of state encouragement and support for the informal sector seems politically naive.[49] Suggestions that laws could be amended to provide flexibility of working hours, financial support for decentralized community decision making, and legal status for alternative concerns seem to ignore the experience of other decentralized alternative projects, such as neighborhood courts and community justice.[50]

Ironically, decentralization and privatization are, as we shall see in the next section, not always benign for capitalism. The growth of informal economies can undermine some aspects of the capitalist system that spawned them, although these economies are themselves very vulnerable to being undermined.

### MUTUAL DESTRUCTION THROUGH OPPOSITION

It has been well documented that capitalist employers considerably influence the legislative content of capitalist industrial democracies.[51] In this way capitalist interests can control, undermine, or destroy informal economies, especially where these are found to be obstructive or threatening. People engaged in irregular work can be prosecuted and sanctioned under federal tax laws as can those who employ them. Similarly, those who trade in pilfered goods are subject to theft laws. Even communal economy exchanges of services can be policed through licensing laws. Clearly, direct control is cruder than co-optation, but, as Pashukanis reminded us long ago, "the judicial element in the regulation of human conduct enters where the isolation and opposition of interests begins" and where legitimation breaks down.[52]

49. See Rolf G. Heinze and Thomas Olk, "Development of the Informal Economy: A Strategy for Resolving the Crisis of the Welfare State," *Futures*, pp. 189-204 (June 1982).

50. Richard L. Abel, "Conservative Conflict and the Reproduction of Capitalism: The Role of Informal Justice," *International Journal of the Sociology of Law*, 9:245-67 (1981); James P. Brady, "Sorting out the Exile's Confusion: Or a Dialogue on Popular Justice," *Contemporary Crisis*, 5:31-38 (1981); Christine B. Harrington,

*Shadow Justice: The Ideology and Institutionalization of Alternatives to Court* (Westport, CT: Greenwood Press, 1985).

51. Richard Quinney, *Class, State and Crime* (New York: Longman, 1980); David F. Greenberg, *Crime and Capitalism* (Palo Alto, CA: Mayfield, 1981); William J. Chambliss and Robert Seidman, *Law, Order and Power* (Reading, MA: Addison-Wesley, 1982).

52. E. B. Pashukanis, *Law and Marxism: A General Theory*, ed. Christopher J. Arthur (London: Ink Links, 1978).

A less direct way of undermining informal economies is through the politics of labeling. Many of the labels such as "black," "hidden," "underground," and "subterranean" carry negative connotations. Much of the popular media accounts of these activities portray participants in the informal economy as twilight operators who are out to make a fast buck and cannot be trusted.[53] However, as with support through opposition, discussed earlier, the influence is mutual rather than one-way. When agents of capitalism attempt to control informal economies through the politics of public condemnation, the effect can be counterproductive; it can bring contempt for the established institutions of capitalism.

One very good illustration of the generation of contempt for capitalist institutions is in the growth of self-help groups to fill the gaps in care that professional care services were forced to leave owing to fiscal crises and technical limitations to growth. The success of self-help support networks in the health and social services has made self-help activities respectable in spite of much hostile criticism of their benefits from professional interest groups, such as doctors, psychiatrists, and some social workers. In so far as criticism continues, it only serves to undermine the credibility of those uttering it, not least because of their economic interests. The result is that people are now more prepared to try alternatives to professional services.[54]

An excellent illustration of the way public condemnation of informal economies undermines capitalism can be seen from the way the news media responded to the hidden economy of pilfering and fiddling at work in Britain in the mid-1970s. Until this time hidden economies had remained undiscovered and ignored by journalists. When it was found that, rather than being the practice of a few bad apples, hidden economy activity was widespread, engaged in by all sections of society and all occupations,[55] it became both newsworthy and grounds for moral outrage. On its front page the most widely circulated British newspaper, the *Sun*, reprimanded the nation with the banner headline: "STOP THIEF!" Its editorial blazed, "The truth is we are all at it. Which doesn't make it any more acceptable morally. And it doesn't make much sense either. For in the end someone has to pay. And who is that? Us!"[56] However, such categorical condemnation disregards the reality of people's experiences in informal economies. It also forces journalists to discuss difficult issues for a capitalist society such as why even its moral standard-bearers in the professions are found cheating. When doctors are found to be siphoning off clients from their practices into private care or defrauding Medicare with fictitious claims for nonexistent patients, then, as one journalist observed, the hidden economy starts to "eat away at the moral fabric of society. Very soon the line between fiddling and outright theft becomes blurred. . . . A nation on the fiddle is usually a nation in financial and moral trouble. After all when everyone else is fiddling you tend to go along."[57]

53. Stuart Henry, "Fiddling as a Media Issue," *Media Reporter*, 6:41-43 (1982).

54. Alfred H. Katz and Eugene I. Bender, *The Strength in Us: Self-Help Groups in the Modern World* (New York: Franklin Watts, 1976); David Robinson and Stuart Henry, *Self-Help and Health: Mutual Aid for Modern Problems* (Oxford: Martin Robertson, 1977).

55. Gerald Mars, *Cheats at Work*.

56. *Sun*, 9 Aug. 1976.

57. Jane Walmsley, "London on the Fiddle: Part 2," *Evening Standard*, 18 Mar. 1980, pp. 20-21.

The undermining of the wider capitalist system by informal economies is a fear that has been recognized and expressed by governments. As Walmsley has shown, in Britain, the Public Accounts Committee of the House of Commons has said, "There is a real danger of tax evasion spreading beyond the limits of the present black economy." Its chairperson said, "If people see others breaking the law without any chance of being caught it could affect tax payers who might say, 'If it's good for them, lets see if we can break the law in some other way.' " As a former chairperson of the revenue service said, "It is eroding what you might call the integrity of tax paying generally."[58]

Paradoxically, the very public condemnation of informal economic activity alerts others to its existence and serves to attract new participants who might have either remained outside or remained ignorant of its existence. These people may feel cheated by a society that claims to control such activity and especially when they find that some of its very figureheads are secretly engaged in activity from which they have been refraining.

### MUTUAL DESTRUCTION THROUGH COALESCENCE

In the course of what appear to be supportive gestures, informal economies are transformed by their relations with capitalism. The principle of co-optation operates such that underground, unofficial, and informal activities are absorbed by the larger and more profuse capitalist organizations, which take what they need and leave the rest. The most extreme version of this position has been well captured by what has become known as Geiger's Law: "When the counter culture

58. Ibid.

develops something of value the establishment rips it off and sells it back."[59] Geiger was talking about the professionalization of the intimate communal economy of self-help groups and mutual aid. What often start out as informal support groups for those who have found formal professional services unable to serve their needs may become professionalized, taken over, managed, advised, and funded by private corporate or government agencies. It is for this reason that the more successful and longest-established self-help networks have found it necessary to decline all outside support; however, many more have ambivalent relations with professionals.[60]

While, as we have seen, the domestic economy facilitates capitalism, the household's domestic system of production has also traditionally been a prime candidate for undermining from the wider matrix of capitalism. That it is a primary focus for intimacy and informal networks should not blind us to the fact that much of what we take to be the household's economy has been based on the unpaid domestic labor of women in such activities as gardening, food preparation, cleaning, child care, social support, nursing of the elderly and dependents, and medical care of sick family members.[61] Indeed, in this context, some

59. Cited as Geiger's Law by S. F. Jencks, "Problems in Participatory Health Care," in *Self-Help and Health: A Report* (New York: New Human Services Institute, 1976).

60. O. H. Mowrer, "The 'Self-Help' or Mutual-Aid Movement: Do Professionals Help or Hinder?" in *Self-Help and Health*; T. Dewar, "Professionalized Clients as Self-Helpers," in ibid.

61. Michele Hoyman, "Female Participation in the Informal Economy: A Neglected Issue," this issue of *The Annals* of the American Academy of Political and Social Science. See also Scott Burns, *The Household Economy* (Boston: Beacon Press, 1977); Ivan Illich, "Vernacular Gender," *CoEvolu-*

POLITICAL ECONOMY OF INFORMAL ECONOMIES 151

have argued, women's labor is marginalized and now serves as a reserve army of labor.[62] In some industrial societies motherhood and women's shadow domestic labor are being emphasized by a conservative social policy that "tends toward the marginalization and pauperization of those sections of the population who have lost the battle for the remaining jobs" rather than a policy that extends employment opportunities for women.[63]

Perhaps the most dramatic illustration of the way the wider structure of capitalism undermines intimate informal economies by coalescing with them is the use of social networks as a marketing device to sell capitalist consumer goods for profit. This has obviously been done in the commercialization of gift exchange, but it is at its most blatant in Tupperware parties or in the Amway perfume pyramid selling or in home-agent mail-order catalogs.[64]

We can gain considerable insight into how capitalism undermines informal economies from what members of intimate networks and communal economies say about their experiences in attempting to retain a separate identity. For example, one member of a community theater cooperative whom I interviewed during a study on co-ops[65] told me,

No more do I believe we operate perfectly as a collective could operate. Obviously it's contradicted by lots of things in the outside world. We are on one level a cooperative experimenting with new ways of doing things and on another we are a small company developing plays. One thing beyond anything else that makes that possible is economic survival. If you want to eat and do community theatre it's necessary to earn money and that means endless concessions.

Concessions to capitalism mean that capitalist principles and solutions to problems are drawn on to solve informal economy problems. For example, when a self-help housing cooperative abandons its informal social-control policy for collecting rent arrears and starts issuing court-ordered eviction notices, it is not an autonomous alternative economy. One member of a short-life self-help housing co-op echoed the inevitability of such dependence:

If you send them a notice to quit, they say, "Oh that's a bit heavy, isn't it . . . getting the law involved?" But if the law wasn't involved, people wouldn't be secure in their short-life housing. . . . So the law is already involved. I think it's a drag giving credibility to the law because the law doesn't particularly like co-ops or the people who are in them. . . . We are allowing the police to harass our members, which is very heavy but . . . if there isn't another way, then you've got to do it.[66]

By resorting to landlord-tenant law, the cooperative helps validate both capitalist society's view of credit and debt and the value of impersonal, rational, and predictable procedures. At the same time, use of capitalist remedies enables the cooperative to survive in a capitalist environment, but in a form different from and less intimate than what its members intended. It is in just such a way, then, that informal economies are undermined.

*tion,* pp. 4-23 (Spring 1982); idem, *Shadow Work* (London: Marion Boyars, 1981); Ray Pahl, *Divisions of Labour* (New York: Basil Blackwell, 1984).

62. Enzo Mingione, "Social Reproduction of the Surplus Labour Force: The Case of 'Southern Italy,' " in *Beyond Employment,* ed. Redclift and Mingione.

63. Heinze and Olk, "Development of the Informal Economy," p. 197.

64. John Davis, "Forms and Norms: The Economy of Social Relations," *Man,* 8:159-76 (1973).

65. Stuart Henry, *Private Justice: Towards Integrated Theorizing in the Sociology of Law* (Boston: Routledge & Kegan Paul, 1983), p. 218.

66. Ibid., p. 206.

It is clear that, as islands of intimacy in a sea of capitalism, informal economies are more likely to erode than are the numerous institutions of the wider social structure. However, to say this is not to deny that the reverse process occurs. Ironically, informal economies and institutions are likely to do more to modify the shape of capitalist structure than the ostensibly oppositional structures such as cooperatives and communes, since these latter are generally marginal and rarely encountered in capitalist society. Capitalism may be very successful in undercutting such opposing orders, but it cannot destroy its own institutions and therefore must continually contend with the opposing internal tendencies that informal economies sometimes represent.[67]

As I have already said, it would be an inaccurate representation to suggest that informal economies are wholly opposed to the capitalist system in which they occur, even if they often emerge from its contradictions. Indeed, as Ditton points out, the hidden economy of pilfering and fiddling, for example,

shares many structural and substantive features with business. . . . Fiddling is not in opposition to these values; salesmen [who fiddle] do not believe that fiddling will eventually overthrow the capitalist economy . . . they fully believe themselves to be part of the same commercial army. . . . Fiddling, like selling, epitomizes the capitalist "spirit." The subculture of fiddling reflects a sort of dutiful anti-hedonism . . . which provides the normative bedrock of capitalism.[68]

But here Ditton is picking up only the avaricious dimensions of the hidden economy. The hidden economy, like all informal economies, also contains communal, social, and intimate strains.[69] It is founded in part on a network of altruistic and balanced reciprocity where status may be achieved and prestige gained based more on how much is given away than on how much is made; where members of trading networks are prepared to give as much as they can and where goods and services can be traded because they are needed by others; where commodities become valued because of their special history and origins, because of who obtained them and how; and where little money is made from friends and trading partners because the rewards are more social than monetary. Insofar as the hidden economy is founded as much on altruism as on avarice, on love as on money, then this meaning is available to penetrate the wider structure of capitalism. The more that people engage in the communal dimensions of informal economies, the more they carry that experience into their relations in capitalism and the more that capitalism is changed. Such change is not major. Rather, it is a rounding of the corners of impersonal market exchange.

### CONCLUSION

The foregoing analysis demonstrates that simple statements about informal economies being caused by this or that factor or this or that system, by tax laws, capitalist inequalities, opportunism, altruism, and the like capture only some aspects of what is a dynamic and complex set of relations. At best these statements are partial accounts that leave much unsaid. At worst they are part of the politics of informal economies that seeks to impose a particular view of the world,

67. Stuart Henry, "Community Justice, Capitalist Society and Human Agency: The Dialectics of Collective Law in the Cooperative," *Law and Society Review*, 19:303-27 (1985).

68. Ditton, *Part-time Crime*, pp. 173-74.

69. Henry, *Hidden Economy*.

POLITICAL ECONOMY OF INFORMAL ECONOMIES 153

to control, manipulate, or influence it in order to serve a particular interest.

Informal economies in capitalism exist in contradictory relations with the wider structure. We have seen how they emerge from and are constantly being transformed by the wider capitalist industrial matrix; they are sometimes in opposition to and sometimes in support of capitalist institutions. We have also seen how capitalism is sometimes in opposition to them and sometimes in support of them. This interrelationship is both positive and negative, mutually supportive and mutually destructive. And, importantly, these contradictory aspects can and often do operate simultaneously. Part of the explanation for this comes from the very duality of the existence of informal economies within capitalist society. Informal economies have a degree of autonomy but are also considerably dependent. They might best be described as semi-autonomous parts of the capitalist whole.[70]

70. For a treatment of law as a semi-autonomous field, see Sally Falk Moore, *Law as Process*

These circumstances suggest that any policy that attempts to intervene to shape informal economies is going to have many more effects than the direct effects that are intended. Simple interventionist policies will have numerous unintended consequences some of which may be constructive, others of which will be less so. Any policymaking that seeks to address informal economies, such as those directed at curbing off-the-books employment or those designed to provide welfare services or to crack down on employee theft, will need to be aware of the full range of possible interrelated effects of its action. This will necessitate an appreciation of the complexity of the dialectical interconnectedness of informal economies and the wider structure in which they are set, the multifarious dimensions of which have only been sketched in this article.

(Boston: Routledge & Kegan Paul, 1978). For an elaboration of this dialectical approach, which Peter Fitzpatrick calls "integral plurality," see Peter Fitzpatrick, "Law and Societies," *Osgood Hall Law Journal*, 22:115-38 (1984).

# Part II
# Cases and Comparative Contexts

# [10]

## QUOTA RESTRICTION AND GOLDBRICKING IN A MACHINE SHOP

DONALD ROY

### ABSTRACT

When the production behavior of industrial workers is examined by participant observation, it is seen that loafing on the job may not be the simple line of inactivity that some students of the subject have thought it. Close scrutiny of the particulars of "soldiering" in one piecework machine shop revealed that group adherence to a "bogey" was but one of several kinds of output restriction in the repertoire of machine operatives and that the work group was restricting production day in and day out.

Even those sociologists who nurse a distaste for studies of industrial administration, either because the problems involved are "practical" or because they fear managerial bias, will recognize that study of restriction of industrial output may yield knowledge free of both taints.[1] Systematic "soldiering" is group activity. One may learn about the "human group" by studying behavior on a production line as well as in an interracial discussion group. And, if someone should find the knowledge useful, even for making a little money, perhaps its scientific value will not be completely vitiated.

I here report and analyze observations of restriction made during eleven months of work as a radial-drill operator in the machine shop of a steel-processing plant in 1944 and 1945. For ten months I kept a daily record of my feelings, thoughts, experiences, and observations and of conversations with my fellow-workers. I noted down the data from memory at the end of each workday, only occasionally making surreptitious notes on the job. I recorded my own production openly in the shop. I did not reveal my research interests to either management or workers. I remained "one of the boys on the line," sharing the practices and confidences of my fellows and joining them in their ceaseless war with management, rather indifferently at first, but later wholeheartedly.

As a member of the work group, I had access to inside talk and activity. As a machine operator, I could put various operations under the microscope. These were great advantages, for *restrictus vulgaris* is a wary little thing. He does not like to be studied. Where groups are so sensitive and so skilled in eluding observation, participation observation can be a sensitive detector of relevant facts and relations (although the participant observer can spoil it all by overworking this method or by claiming that it is the sole means of scientific observation). I will limit this paper to the presentation of a few discriminations which break up the blanket term "restriction" into several kinds and to a rough measuring of these restrictions in the shop where I worked.

From November 9, 1944, to August 30, 1945, I worked 1,850.5 hours. 1,350.9 (73 per cent) were "production-piecework" hours.[2] The remaining 499.6 hours were taken up with time study, rework, and set-up. In 669.4 (49.6 per cent) of the production-piecework hours, I "made out." That is, I produced enough pieces of work to "earn," at the piece rates for the kinds of work done, the 85-cent-per-hour "base rate" which we received for every hour spent on the job. I thus "earned" my 85 cents in about half the hours when there was opportunity—through completing more pieces—to earn more than

[1] In my doctoral dissertation recently accepted by the University of Chicago I analyze the literature on this problem as well as other cases which I studied in the role of known research man. Cf. also Daniel Bell, "Exploring Factory Life," *Commentary*, January, 1947; Herbert Blumer, "Sociological Theory: Industrial Relations," *American Sociological Review*, XII (June, 1947), 271–78; Wilbert Moore, "Current Issues in Industrial Sociology," *American Sociological Review*, XII (December, 1947), 651–57.

[2] I have omitted some days of work in September, 1945, because of irregularities occasioned by reorganization of the shop at that time.

that. Obversely, about half the time my "turn in" (work done and turned in) fell below the base-rate standard.

### THE BIMODAL PATTERN OF OUTPUT

My hourly earnings on production piece-work varied from $0.09 to $1.66, a range of $1.57. Table 1 shows that the spread of

TABLE 1

PRODUCTION PIECEWORK HOURS WORKED
BY TEN-CENT EARNING INTERVALS

| Earnings per Hour (In Cents) | Hours Worked | Per Cent |
|---|---|---|
| Unknown* | 103.9 | 7.7 |
| 5–14 | 3.0 | 0.2 |
| 15–24 | 51.0 | 3.8 |
| 25–34 | 49.8 | 3.7 |
| 35–44 | 150.1 | 11.1 |
| 45–54 | 144.5 | 10.7 |
| 55–64 | 57.7 | 4.3 |
| 65–74 | 63.8 | 4.7 |
| 75–84 | 57.7 | 4.3 |
| Total under 85 cents | 681.5 | 50.4 |
| 85–94 | 51.2 | 3.8 |
| 95–104 | 19.5 | 1.5 |
| 105–114 | 17.9 | 1.3 |
| 115–124 | 83.0 | 6.1 |
| 125–134 | 496.3 | 36.7 |
| 165–174 | 1.5 | 0.1 |
| Total 85 cents or more | 669.4 | 49.6 |
| Total | 1,350.9 | 100.0 |

* All "unknown" hourly earnings fell below the base-rate level of 85 cents per hour.

hourly earnings for the various jobs, or "operations" performed, was bimodal; this distribution suggests two major types of output behavior.

About one-half of my hours of piecework "earnings" fell on either side of the 85-cent-an-hour "day-rate" and "make-out" point, indicating 85 cents as an approximate median. However, this distribution by no means forms a bell-shaped curve, with 85 cents as a modal point. "Make-out" and "non-make-out"–piecework hours form two almost separate distributions, with 74.1 per cent of the 669.4 "make-out" hours concentrated in the $1.25–$1.34 interval, and

43.2 per cent of the 681.5 "non-make-out" hours clustered in two adjacent intervals, $0.35–$0.54. Concentration of "make-out" hours is even more marked. For 82.8 per cent fall within three 5-cent intervals, $1.20–$1.34, and 64.1 per cent fall within the one 5-cent interval, $1.25–$1.29.

That this bimodal pattern of hourly earnings for the ten-month period does not represent the joining of the "tails" of two temporal distributions—i.e., one for an initial learning period and the other showing completely different production behavior with the acquisition of skill—is indicated by a comparison of earning distributions for two periods of four and six months, respectively. In this comparison (Table 2) the period from November through February represents one level of skill; that from March through August, a higher level. Although the proportion of make-out hours for the second period was more than double that of the first and although concentration of make-out hours in modal earning intervals increased, the pattern was clearly bimodal in both periods. Both "levels of skill" show the same modal earning interval of $1.25–$1.34 for make-out hours. The modal earning interval for non-make-out hours advanced but one notch, from $0.35 to $0.44 to $0.45 to $0.54.

While I did not keep a complete record of the hourly earnings of my "day man" on the radial drill (I worked a "second" shift), I frequently jotted down his day's run. His figures were roughly correlative with my own. References to the diary will be made to show that I was not out of line with other operators in the shop.

The bimodal pattern was the rule of the shop. An outsider might believe that it reflects the struggle of workers with two kinds of jobs, hard and easy. He might then posit any number of reasons why the jobs fall into two piles rather than into one bell-shaped heap: some peculiarity of time-study men or some change of company policy. It would indeed be difficult so to set piece rates that it would be equally easy to "make out" on all kinds of work. But one sophisticated in shop ways and aware of all the devices of time-

QUOTA RESTRICTION AND GOLDBRICKING IN A MACHINE SHOP    429

study men would hardly credit them with either the ability or the will to turn up "tight" and "loose" piece rates in other than a single bell-shaped distribution. He would not attribute the bimodal distortion of hourly earnings to anything so improbable as bimodal distribution of hard and easy jobs. It could be that the operators, ignoring

cents an hour on Job A, he rejects that amount and drops to a level of effort that earns only 50 cents an hour and relies upon his 85-cent base-pay rate for "take home." Job B has therefore become the "gravy" job, and Job A the "stinker." Into the "stinker" bin goes A, along with 90-cent jobs, 85-cent jobs, and 60-cent jobs.

TABLE 2

PRODUCTION-PIECEWORK HOURS WORKED, BY TEN-CENT EARNING INTERVALS, PER TWO DIARY PERIODS

| EARNINGS PER HOUR (IN CENTS) | PERIOD 1 (NOVEMBER THROUGH FEBRUARY) | | PERIOD 2 (MARCH THROUGH AUGUST) | |
|---|---|---|---|---|
| | Hours Worked | Per Cent | Hours Worked | Per Cent |
| Unknown* | 66.4 | 11.4 | 37.5 | 4.9 |
| 5–14 | 3.0 | 0.5 | | |
| 15–24 | 13.5 | 2.3 | 37.5 | 4.9 |
| 25–34 | 37.8 | 6.5 | 12.0 | 1.6 |
| 35–44 | 93.0 | 16.0 | 57.1 | 7.4 |
| 45–54 | 74.0 | 12.8 | 70.5 | 9.1 |
| 55–64 | 43.1 | 7.4 | 14.6 | 1.9 |
| 65–74 | 36.8 | 6.3 | 27.0 | 3.5 |
| 75–84 | 49.0 | 8.5 | 8.7 | 1.1 |
| Total under 85 cents | 416.6 | 71.7 | 264.9 | 34.4 |
| 85–94 | 39.1 | 6.7 | 12.1 | 1.6 |
| 95–104 | 9.7 | 1.7 | 9.8 | 1.3 |
| 105–114 | 3.8 | 0.7 | 14.1 | 1.8 |
| 115–124 | 18.0 | 3.1 | 65.0 | 8.4 |
| 125–134 | 93.2 | 16.1 | 403.1 | 52.3 |
| 165–174 | | | 1.5 | 0.2 |
| Total 85 cents or over | 163.8 | 28.3 | 505.6 | 65.6 |
| Total | 580.4 | 100.0 | 770.5 | 100.0 |

* All "unknown" hourly earnings fell below the base-rate level of 85 cents per hour.

finer distinctions in job timing, sort jobs into two bins, one for "gravy" jobs, the other for "stinkers."

Let us assume that the average of worker effort will be constant from job to job. Job A might be rated as 5 cents an hour "harder" than Job B. But Job A turns out to yield 75 cents an hour less than Job B instead of the expected 5 cents an hour less. One suspects that effort has not been constant. When an operator discovers that he can earn $1.00 an hour on Job B, he will then put forth extra effort and ingenuity to make it $1.25. When, however, he finds that he can earn only 95

The pronounced dichotomy in the production behavior of the machine operator suggests that restriction might be classified into two major types, "quota restriction" and "goldbricking." The heavy concentration of hours at the $1.25–$1.34 level with no spilling-over to the next level makes "quota restriction" appear as a limitation of effort on "gravy" jobs in order not to exceed set maximums. It could also be inferred that "goldbricking" appears as a "holding-back," or failure to release effort, when a close approach to the quota seems unattainable.

QUOTA RESTRICTION

It is "quota restriction" which has received the most attention. The Mayo researchers observed that the bank-wiring group at Western Electric limited output to a "quota" or "bogey."[3] Mayo inferred that this chopping-off of production was due to lack of understanding of the economic logics of management, using the following chain of reasoning: Insistence by management on purely economic logics, plus frequent changes in such logics in adaptation to technological change, result in lack of understanding on the part of the workers. Since the latter cannot understand the situation, they are unable to develop a nonlogical social code of a type that brought social cohesion to work groups prior to the Industrial Revolution. This inability to develop a Grade-A social code brings feelings of frustration. And, finally, frustration results in the development of a "lower social code" among the workers in opposition to the economic logics of management. And one of the symptoms of this "lower social code" is restriction of output.[4]

Mayo thus joins those who consider the economic man a fallacious conception. Now the operators in my shop made noises like economic men. Their talk indicated that they were canny calculators and that the dollar sign fluttered at the masthead of every machine. Their actions were not always consistent with their words; and such inconsistency calls for further probing. But it could be precisely because they were alert to their economic interests—at least to their immediate economic interests—that the operators did not exceed their quotas. It might be inferred from their talk that they did not turn in excess earnings because they felt that to do so would result in piecework price cuts; hence the consequences would be either reduced earnings from the same amount of

[3] Fritz Roethlisberger and J. Dickson, *Management and the Worker* (Cambridge: Harvard University Press, 1939).

[4] Elton Mayo, *Human Problems of an Industrial Civilization* (New York: Macmillan Co., 1938), pp. 119–21.

effort expended or increased effort to maintain the take-home level.

When I was hired, a personnel department clerk assured me that the radial-drill operators were averaging $1.25 an hour on piecework. He was using a liberal definition of the term "averaging." Since I had had no previous machine-shop experience and since a machine would not be available for a few days, I was advised to spend some time watching Jack Starkey, a radial-drill man of high rank in seniority and skill.

One of Starkey's first questions was, "What have you been doing?" When I said I had worked in a Pacific Coast shipyard at a rate of pay over $1.00 an hour, Starkey exclaimed, "Then what are you doing in this place?" When I replied that averaging $1.25 an hour wasn't bad, he exploded:

"Averaging, you say! Averaging?"

"Yeah, on the average. I'm an average guy; so I ought to make my buck and a quarter. That is, after I get onto it."

"Don't you know," cried Starkey angrily, "that $1.25 an hour is the *most* we can make, even when we *can* make more! And most of the time we can't even make that! Have you ever worked on piecework before?"

"No."

"I can see that! Well, what do you suppose would happen if I turned in $1.25 an hour on these pump bodies?"

"Turned in? You mean if you actually did the work?"

"I mean if I actually did the work and turned it in!"

"They'd have to pay you, wouldn't they? Isn't that the agreement?"

"Yes! They'd pay me—once! Don't you know that if I turned in $1.50 an hour on these pump bodies tonight, the whole God-damned Methods Department would be down here tomorrow? And they'd retime this job so quick it would make your head swim! And when they retimed it, they'd cut the price in half! And I'd be working for 85 cents an hour instead of $1.25!"

From this initial exposition of Starkey's to my last day at the plant I was subject to warnings and predictions concerning price cuts. Pressure was the heaviest from Joe

## QUOTA RESTRICTION AND GOLDBRICKING IN A MACHINE SHOP 431

Mucha, day man on my machine, who shared my job repertoire and kept a close eye on my production. On November 14, the day after my first attained quota, Mucha advised:

"Don't let it go over $1.25 an hour, or the time-study man will be right down here! And they don't waste time, either! They watch the records like a hawk! I got ahead, so I took it easy for a couple of hours."

Joe told me that I had made $10.01 yesterday and warned me not to go over $1.25 an hour. He told me to figure the set-ups and the time on each operation very carefully so that I would not total over $10.25 in any one day.

Jack Starkey defined the quota carefully but forcefully when I turned in $10.50 for one day, or $1.31 an hour.

Jack Starkey spoke to me after Joe left. "What's the matter? Are you trying to upset the apple cart?"

Jack explained in a friendly manner that $10.50 was too much to turn in, even on an old job.

"The turret-lathe men can turn in $1.35," said Jack, "but their rate is 90 cents, and ours 85 cents."

Jack warned me that the Methods Department could lower their prices on any job, old or new, by changing the fixture slightly, or changing the size of drill. According to Jack, a couple of operators (first and second shift on the same drill) got to competing with each other to see how much they could turn in. They got up to $1.65 an hour, and the price was cut in half. And from then on they had to run that job themselves, as none of the other operators would accept the job.

According to Jack, it would be all right for us to turn in $1.28 or $1.29 an hour, when it figured out that way, but it was not all right to turn in $1.30 an hour.

Well, now I know where the maximum is—$1.29 an hour.

Starkey's beliefs concerning techniques of price-cutting were those of the shop. Leonard Bricker, an old-timer in the shop, and Willie, the stock-chaser, both affirmed that management, once bent on slashing a piecework price, would stop at nothing.

"Take these $1.25 jobs. One guy will turn in $1.30 an hour one day. Then another fellow will turn in, say, $1.31 or $1.32. Then the first fellow will go up to $1.35. First thing you know they'll be up to $1.50, and bang! They'll tear a machine to pieces to change something to cut a price!"

In the washroom, before I started work, Willie commented on my gravy job, the pedestals.

"The Methods Department is going to lower the price," he said. "There was some talk today about it."

"I hope they don't cut it too much," I said. "I suppose they'll make some change in the jigs?"

"They'll change the tooling in some way. Don't worry, when they make up their minds to lower a price, they'll find a way to do it!"[5]

The association of quota behavior with such expressions about price-cutting does not prove a causal connection. Such a connection could be determined only by instituting changes in the work situation that would effect a substantial reduction of "price-cut fear" and by observing the results of such changes.

Even if it should be thus indicated that there is a causal relationship, testing of alternative hypotheses would still be necessary. It may be, but it is not yet known, that "economic determinism" may account for quota restriction in the shop investigated. It may also be, but it is not known, that factors such as Mayo's "failure to un-

[5] John Mills, onetime research engineer in telephony and for five years engaged in personnel work for the Bell Telephone Company, has recently indicated the possibility that there were factors in the bank-wiring room situation that the Mayo group failed to detect: "Reward is supposed to be in direct proportion to production. Well, I remember the first time I ever got behind that fiction. I was visiting the Western Electric Company, which had a reputation of never cutting a piece rate. It never did; if some manufacturing process was found to pay more than seemed right for the class of labor employed on it—if, in other words, the rate-setters had misjudged—that particular part was referred to the engineers for redesign, and then a new rate was set on the new part. Workers, in other words, were paid as a class, supposed to make about so much a week with their best efforts and, of course, less for less competent efforts" (*The Engineer in Society* [New York: D. Van Nostrand & Co., 1946], p. 93).

derstand the economic logics of management" are influential.

## "WASTE TIME" ON QUOTA RESTRICTION

Whatever its causes, such restriction resulted in appreciable losses of time in the
shop. I have evidence of it from observation
of the work behavior and talk of fellow-
operators and from my own work behavior.
Since ability to "make out" early was related to skill and experience, it was some
time before I found enough time wasted on
quota restriction to record. But I discovered
early that other operators had time to burn.

One evening Ed Sokolsky, onetime sec-
ond-shift operator on Jack Starkey's drill,
commented on a job that Jack was running:

"That's gravy! I worked on those, and I
could turn out nine an hour. I timed myself at
six minutes."

I was surprised.

"At 35 cents apiece, that's over $3.00 an
hour!"

"And I got ten hours," said Ed. "I used to
make out in four hours and fool around the rest
of the night."

If Sokolsky reported accurately, he was
"wasting" six hours per day.

Ed claimed that he could make over $3.00 an
hour on the two machines he was running, but
he could turn in only $1.40 an hour or, occa-
sionally, $1.45 or $1.50 for the two machines
together. Ed said that he always makes out for
ten hours by eleven o'clock, that he has nothing
to do from 11:00 to 3:00, and has even left
early, getting someone to punch his timecard for
him.

"That's the advantage of working nights,"
said Ed. "You can make out in a hurry and sit
around, and nobody says anything. But you
can't get away with it on day shift with all the
big shots around. Jack has to take it easy on
these housings to make them last eight hours,
and that must be tough.

"Old Pete," another "old-timer" con-
fided in me:

"Another time when they timed me on some
connecting rods, I could have made $20.00 a
day, easy. I had to run them at the lowest speed
on the machine to keep from making too much.

I had a lot of trouble once when I was being
timed, and they gave me $35.00 a hundred.
Later they cut it to $19.50 a hundred, and I still
made $9.50 a day."

If Old Pete could have made $20.00 a day,
he was "wasting" four hours a day.

My own first "spare time" came on November 18.

Today I made out with such ease on the
pedestals that I had an hour to spare. To cover
the hour I had to poke along on the last operation, taking twice as much time to do 43 pieces
as I ordinarily would.

But it wasn't until March, when I experienced a sudden increase in skill, that I
was capable of making out early on any job
but the pedestals. With this increase in skill
I found the pedestals quickly fading as the
supreme distributors of "gravy." One and
one-half hours of loafing recorded on March
22 was a portent of things to come.

I stalled along tonight, turning out only 89
pieces, adding in my kitty of 40 pieces for a
turn-in of 129. Joe had a kitty of 13, and I figured that the 116 pieces left would just do him
tomorrow. I finished my last piece about 9:30
and started cleaning up the machine about ten
o'clock. I noticed that Tony was also through
early, standing around his machine.

"This is the earliest you've made out, isn't
it?" he asked.

Dick Smith remarked to me, "That's the
kind of a job I like. Then I can go at it and enjoy
it."

On April 7 I was able to enjoy four hours of
"free time."

I turned out 43 pieces in the four hours from
three to seven, averaging nearly 11 an hour (or
$2.085 per hour). At seven o'clock there were
only 23 pieces left in the lot, and I knew there
would be no point in building up a kitty for
Monday if Joe punched off the job before I got
to work. I could not go ahead with the next
order (also a load of connecting rods) because
the new ruling made presentation of a work
order to the stock-chaser necessary before material could be brought up. So I was stymied
and could do nothing the rest of the day. I had
43 pieces plus 11 from yesterday's kitty to turn
in for a total 54.

QUOTA RESTRICTION AND GOLDBRICKING IN A MACHINE SHOP     433

I sat around the rest of the evening, and none of the bosses seemed to mind.

By August I was more sophisticated in the art of loafing, and complaints of being "stymied" were not recorded.

I had good luck with the reamers and had my needed 26 pieces by six o'clock. I did 10 more for a kitty for Monday and wound up the evening's work at seven o'clock. The last four hours I sat around and talked to various operators.

I reached my peak in quota restriction on June 27, with but three and a half hours of productive work out of the eight.

## AN ESTIMATE OF THE DEGREE OF QUOTA RESTRICTION PRACTICED

The amount of quota restriction practiced by operators on the drill line may be estimated from my own production behavior.

During the ten-month diary period I received approximately 75 different piecework jobs, some of which were assigned from two to six times, but the majority of which were assigned only once. On only 31 of the jobs did I ever make out.

Of the 31 make-out jobs, only 20 afforded quota earnings of $1.25 an hour or more; 5 afforded maximum earnings of from $1.20 to $1.24 an hour; 1, maximum earnings of $1.09 an hour; and 5 of the 31 yielded maximums of less than $1.00 an hour (85-99 cents). Total quota hours were 497.8, or slightly over a third of the total piecework hours.

By extending effort past quota limits to find the earning possibilities of the jobs, I discovered that on 16 of the 20 quota jobs I could have earned more than $1.30 an hour; on 4 of the 20 I was unable to exceed $1.30 per hour.

For example, on the "NT bases," I turned out pieces at the rate of $2.55 for a test hour, and I turned them out at the rate of $2.04 for a full eight-hour shift. On the "G sockets," I was able to earn $2.53 an hour; this job was touted by experienced operators to yield $3.00 an hour.

I ran 4 other jobs at a rate in excess of $2.00 an hour. Maximums on another 4 jobs came to $1.96 or better. All but 3 of the 16 "excess-quota" jobs yielded possible earnings of over $1.75 an hour.

Besides the 16 excess-quota jobs, I found 4 "nonquota-make-out" jobs (maximum earnings less than $1.25) that showed potentialities in excess of quota limits. That I did not actually achieve quota on these 4 jobs was due to slow starts; since the 4 were not assigned to me again, I could not cash in on my discoveries. If these 4 are included, the number of jobs with excess-quota potentials total 20.

Given a quota of $1.25 an hour, or $10.00 an eight-hour day, and a job that will yield $1.25 an hour but not appreciably over that rate, the operator will have to expend a full eight hours of effort to achieve the quota. But, if the job will yield earnings at the rate of $2.50 an hour, it will take the operator only four hours to earn his $10.00. A $2.50-an-hour job is thus a four-hour job, and the remaining four hours of the workday may be considered wasted time. If the operator were to extend himself for the full eight hours on a $2.50-an-hour job and were permitted to turn in the results of his effort, his earnings would be $20.00 instead of his quota of $10.00. Thus there is incurred a financial loss to the operator as well as a loss of production time to the company when the quota is observed.

Table 3 lists the twenty jobs which showed potentialities of yielding hourly earnings in excess of $1.30. Waste time and loss in earnings is computed for each job according to maximum earnings indicated in each case by actual test and according to the number of hours devoted to each job. For instance, operation "pawls," which leads the list with 157.9 total hours worked, showed, by test, possibilities of earnings of $1.96 per hour. At potentialities of $1.96 per hour, over 36 per cent of each hour is wasted when the operator holds his turn-in to $1.25 an hour. Total waste time in the 157.9 hours expended on the pawls could then be computed at 57.2 hours, or over a third of the time actually put in. Earnings might have been, at $1.96 per hour, $309.48; whereas, at the quota level of $1.25, they would have been but $197.38—a loss of $112.10.

Total waste time for the 20 jobs is seen to be 286 hours, or 36.4 per cent of a total 786.5 hours actually put in on them. This represents a wastage of 2.9 hours on each 8-hour day put in, or a total loss of 35.75 days out of 98.3 actually worked. With potential earnings of $1,584.43 for the 98 days and

wastage of considerable magnitude—an over-all hourly income loss for 1,850.5 hours of 32½ cents an hour!

In order to generalize for the drill line from observation of my own behavior, I would have to establish (1) that I was an "average" performer and (2) that my job repertoire was representative of those of other operators.

Of the men on the same shift doing my

TABLE 3

TIME AND EARNINGS LOSSES ON OPERATIONS WITH POTENTIALITIES OF YIELDING
HOURLY EARNINGS IN EXCESS OF $1.30 PER HOUR

| Operation Tested | Total Hours Worked | Maximum (Per Hour) | Waste Time (Per Hour) | Total Waste Time (In Hours) | Potential Earnings | Earnings at $1.25 | Loss in Earnings |
|---|---|---|---|---|---|---|---|
| Pawls......... | 157.9 | $1.96 | 0.3625 | 57.2 | $309.48 | $197.38 | $112.10 |
| Pedestals...... | 120.5 | 1.71 | 0.2625 | 31.6 | 206.08 | 150.63 | 55.43 |
| NT bases...... | 111.0 | 2.55 | 0.5125 | 56.9 | 283.05 | 138.75 | 144.30 |
| Con rods...... | 94.4 | 2.33 | 0.4625 | 43.7 | 219.95 | 118.00 | 101.95 |
| Sockets....... | 75.8 | 1.76 | 0.2875 | 21.8 | 133.41 | 94.75 | 38.66 |
| B. housings.... | 46.0 | 1.96 | 0.3625 | 16.7 | 90.16 | 57.50 | 32.66 |
| Pinholes...... | 37.7 | 1.87 | 0.3250 | 12.3 | 70.50 | 47.13 | 23.37 |
| Casings....... | 28.5 | 2.03 | 0.3750 | 10.7 | 57.86 | 35.63 | 22.23 |
| Gear parts.... | 24.0 | 1.83 | 0.3000 | 7.2 | 43.92 | 30.00 | 13.92 |
| Replacers..... | 19.3 | 2.20 | 0.4375 | 8.4 | 42.46 | 24.13 | 18.33 |
| Spyglasses..... | 18.0 | 1.57 | 0.1875 | 3.4 | 28.26 | 22.50 | 5.76 |
| R. sockets..... | 14.9 | 1.48 | 0.1375 | 2.0 | 22.05 | 18.63 | 3.42 |
| Move. jaw..... | 9.6 | 1.99 | 0.3625 | 3.5 | 19.10 | 12.00 | 7.10 |
| Ped. $8.90.... | 7.0 | 2.12 | 0.4000 | 2.8 | 14.84 | 8.75 | 6.09 |
| Spot J1728.... | 6.7 | 1.91 | 0.3375 | 2.3 | 12.80 | 8.38 | 4.42 |
| G. sockets..... | 4.5 | 2.53 | 0.5000 | 2.3 | 11.39 | 5.63 | 5.76 |
| Ped. $5........ | 4.3 | 1.85 | 0.3250 | 1.4 | 7.96 | 5.38 | 2.58 |
| CB hubs...... | 4.1 | 1.65 | 0.2375 | 1.0 | 6.77 | 5.13 | 1.64 |
| SD cups...... | 1.5 | 1.89 | 0.3250 | 0.5 | 2.84 | 1.88 | 0.96 |
| Bolts........ | 0.8 | 1.96 | 0.3625 | 0.3 | 1.57 | 1.00 | 0.57 |
| Total....... | 786.5 (98.3 days) | | | 286.0 (35.75 days) | $1,584.43 | $983.18 | $601.25 |

with quota earnings at $983.18, the wage loss to the worker would be $601.25, or $6.12 per day, or 76½ cents per hour.

By this logic, if the worker could "cut loose" on the 20 jobs listed, he would average $2.01 an hour instead of $1.25. And since the 786.5 hours actually put in on the 20 jobs represented 58.2 per cent of the 1,350.9 total piecework hours for the period, and 42.5 per cent of a grand total of 1,850.5 hours that included all nonpiecework activity as well, it is evident that losses resulting from quota restriction alone could represent

kind of work, four (McCann, Starkey, Koszyk, and Sokolsky) could turn out greater volume than I and were my betters in all-around skills. Seven were below me in these respects, of them only three (Smith, Rinky, and Dooley) worked long enough to be in the core of the group. I was about average in skill and in the work assigned me.

The maximums on which the losses are figured represent only potentialities discovered in tests of relatively short duration. Yet it is likely that had I remained in the shop long enough to allow the 20 jobs an-

## QUOTA RESTRICTION AND GOLDBRICKING IN A MACHINE SHOP 435

other time around, I could have routinized many of the maximums and could have raised some of them. It is also likely that if organizational changes were instituted to induce operators to abolish quota limits and "open up" production, the writer's discovered maximums would be quickly raised to higher levels by the efforts of the group. Under adequate motivation the better operators would employ their superior skills and the results of their application would be disseminated to others. In my opinion, the production potentialities are underestimates of the output possibilities inherent in the situa-

$12.08. I therefore lost $2.08 per day, or 26 cents per hour on quota piecework. Since quota piecework represented 41.8 per cent of total hours worked, the over-all loss per day due to quota restriction alone would be $0.87, approximately 11 cents an hour.

During the last two-month period, July and August, I was "wasting" on the average over 2 hours a day while on "quota piecework." If my production during August may be considered indicative of my developed skill, and portentous of things to come had I stayed, then estimates of future wastages become greater. With 2.06 hours per quota-

TABLE 4

QUOTA HOURS LOAFED, BY PERCENTAGES OF TOTAL QUOTA HOURS
AND AVERAGE HOURS PER QUOTA DAY OF LOAFING
(By Months, March through August, 1945)

| Month | Total Quota Hours | Quota Hours Loafed | Per Cent Hours Loafed | Hours Loafed per Quota Day |
|-------|------|------|------|------|
| March........ | 69.3 | 7.6 | 11.0 | 0.88 |
| April......... | 76.3 | 10.35 | 13.6 | 1.09 |
| May......... | 69.8 | 5.15 | 7.4 | 0.59 |
| June......... | 83.5 | 15.2 | 18.2 | 1.46 |
| July.......... | 84.8 | 21.4 | 25.2 | 2.02 |
| August....... | 85.9 | 22.2 | 25.8 | 2.06 |
| Total...... | 469.6 | 81.9 | 17.4 | 1.39 |

tion. This hypothesis can be tested, of course, only through observation of experimental changes.

As a check on the foregoing appraisals, an estimate of the *actual* amount of time wasted by the writer through quota restriction may be made by reference to Table 4.

The 469.6 quota hours represented 60.9 per cent of 770.5 total piecework hours for the period, and 41.8 per cent of 1,123.2 total hours worked.

With an average of 1.39 hours "wasted" per day of "quota piecework," the average hours worked were 6.61; so, at quota limits of $1.25 an hour, or $10.00 per day, earnings while I was actually working on "quota piecework" would be $1.51 per hour for the six-month period. If I had turned in 8 hours' production per day at $1.51, my daily earnings on "quota piecework" would have been

piecework day loafed, the length of the "actual" average quota workday becomes 5.94 hours and the average earnings for "actual" work time put in becomes $1.68 per hour. At $1.68 per hour for a full 8-hour day, the writer would earn $13.44; the daily loss would then be $3.44 and the hourly loss 43 cents. And since quota piecework for August represented 71.5 per cent of total piecework for the month, the loss per day on piecework was $2.46. And, since quota piecework represented 46 per cent of total hours worked, the over-all loss per day was $1.58 and the over-all hourly loss nearly 20 cents.

This daily loss for August would be slightly reduced if the actual quota turn-in is considered in place of the assumed $1.25 per hour. The writer actually averaged $1.27 per hour on quota piecework, raising the assumed average by 2 cents per hour, or 16 cents per day. The computed average daily and hourly losses on quota piecework would then be $3.28 and $0.41, and the over-all losses would be $1.51 and $0.19.

### PIECEWORK GOLDBRICKING

On "gravy jobs" the operators earned a quota, then knocked off. On "stinkers" they put forth only minimal effort; either they did not try to achieve a turn-in equal to the base wage rate or they deliberately slowed down. Jobs were defined as "good" and "bad" jobs, not in terms of the effort or skill necessary to making out at a bare base-rate level, but of the felt attainability of a substantial premium, i.e., 15 cents an hour or more. Earnings of $1.00 an hour in relation to a $1.25 quota and an 85-cent base rate were considered worth the effort, while earnings of 95 cents an hour were not.

The attitude basic to the goldbricking type of restriction was expressed succinctly thus: "They're not going to get much work out of me for this pay!"

Complaints about low piecework prices were chronic and universal in the shop.

The turret lathe men discussed the matter of making out, one man stating that only half the time could a man make 84 cents day rate on a machine. It was agreed: "What's the use of pushing when it's hard even to make day rate?"

His 50-50 estimate was almost equal to my own experience of 49.6–50.4. Pessimistic though it was, it was less so than usual statements on the subject:

I asked Jackson if he was making out, and he gave me the usual answer, "No!"

"They ask me how I'm making out, and I always say, 'O.K.' As far as I'm concerned, I'm making out O.K. If they start asking me further, I'll tell them that this place stinks."

"The day man isn't making out either. We get a lot of little jobs, small lots. It's impossible to make out when you're getting small jobs all the time."

Joe was working on a new job, time study on some small pieces tonight. I asked him, "Something good?" and he replied, "Nothing is good any more!"

There seemed to be no relation between a man's ability to earn and his behavior on a "stinker." That the men who most frequently earned the quota goldbricked like the rest on poor jobs appears in the following extracts:

Al McCann (the man who made quota most often) said that he gives a job a trial, and if it is no good he takes his time. He didn't try to make out on the chucks tonight.

Joe Mucha, my day man, said of a certain job: "I did just one more than you did. If they don't like it they can do them themselves. To hell with them. I'm not going to bust my ass on stuff like this."

Old Peter, the multiple drill man, said "I ran some pieces for 25 minutes to see how many I could turn out. I turned out 20 at 1½ cents apiece (72 cents an hour). So I smoke and take it easy. I can't make out; so ——— it."

I notice that when Ed Sokolsky, one of the better operators on the line, is working on an operation he cannot make out on, he does not go at his task with vigor. He either pokes around or leaves his machine for long periods of time; and Paul (set-up man) seems always to be looking for him. Steve (supt.) is always bellowing, "Where in hell is Ed?" or "Come on, Ed, let's have some production around here!" Tonight I heard him admonishing Ed again, "Now I want you to work at that machine 'til three o'clock, do you understand?"

Mike Koszyk, regarded as a crack operator: The price was a poor one (a few cents a hundred) and the job tough. Mike had turned out only 9 pieces in 3 hours. When Mike takes his time, he really takes his time!

According to Al, Jack Starkey turned in 40 cents an hour today on his chuck parts. Al laughed, saying, "I guess Jack didn't like this job."

Gus Schmidt, regarded as the best speed-drill operator on the second shift, was timed early in the evening on a job, and given a price of $1.00 per 100 for reaming one hole, chamfering both sides of three holes, and filing burrs on one end of one hole. All that for one cent!

"To hell with them," said Gus.

He did not try to make out.

The possibility of covering "day rate" was ordinarily no spur to the machine operator to bestir himself on a job. A remark of Mucha's was characteristic: "I could have

QUOTA RESTRICTION AND GOLDBRICKING IN A MACHINE SHOP    437

made out," he said, "but why kill yourself for day rate?"

Average hourly earnings of less or even a little more than $1.00 an hour were usually thrown into the "day-rate" category.

Joe Mucha drilled 36 of the bases (at $8.80 per 100) today. "The most I'll ever do until they retime this job is 40," he said. "Do you know, they expect us to do 100? Why, I wouldn't bust my ass to do 50, for $8.00, when day rate is almost that!"

McCann was put to drilling some pieces at $6.50 per 100. I noticed him working furiously and walked over to see what he was doing. He asked me to figure out how many pieces at 6½ cents he had to turn out per hour to make $1.20. When I told him 18 or 19 he said, "I give up," and immediately slowed down.

A few minutes later I met him in the washroom, and he said, "I wouldn't work that hard for eight or ten hours even if I could make out. I thought I'd try it for an hour or so and see what I could do."

He figures that he was making 95 cents an hour. At lunch time he said that he had averaged $1.00 an hour for the two hours and thought maybe he would try to make out.

### THE SLOWDOWN

Resentment against piecework prices that were considered too low to offer possibilities of quota earnings often resulted in deliberate attempts to produce at lower rates than mere "dogging it along" would bring. This kind of goldbricking was particularly noticeable on jobs that came relatively often and in large lots. Toward a short order of poor price that was assigned to his machine but once or twice a year, the operator's attitude was likely to be one of "I don't give a damn," and the result would be production below "standard." But toward a low-priced order assigned every month or two and in amounts that would take several shifts to a week to process, i.e., jobs that played a major part in the operator's repertoire, the attitude was likely to be, "Just for that, you'll get as little as I can turn out and still be operating this machine!"

The hinge-base fight is an example of deliberate restriction on a major job that was regarded as poorly priced. This fight went on for at least nine months at the machine operated by Jack Starkey. During this period three men worked second shift on Jack's machine in the following sequence: Ed Sokolsky, Dooley, and Al McCann.

*December 19.*—Ed Sokolsky and Jack Starkey have not been doing well. Ed cusses intermittently and leaves his machine for long periods of time. The foremen find the machine idle, and Steve bellows about it. Ed calls the piece he is working on a "stinker." I know it is, because Ed is free with his advertising of the "gravy" he finds.

Ed seems to have constant trouble with his jig, a revolving piece attached to the side of the table. Two disks seem to stick together, and Ed is constantly (every day or so) using the crane to dismantle the jig (a very heavy one). He sands the disks and oils them, taking several hours for the cleaning operation. Steve saw the dismantled jig again tonight and bellowed, "Again?" Steve does not like it.

Paul, the set-up man, gets concerned, too, when he finds the jig torn down and Ed away somewhere. He says, "Where the hell's Ed?" in a provoked manner.

*February.*—I noticed that Ed was poking along and asked him if he had a good job. He shook his head, saying that he was making but 46 cents an hour, turning out 2 pieces an hour that paid 23 cents each.

*February 26.*—Jack Starkey told me tonight that although his job on the hinge bases was retimed, there was no raise in price. The price is still 23 cents.

I said, "All you've got to turn out is 5 an hour to make $1.15."

"I'd just like to see anybody turn out 5 of these an hour," said Jack, "with a tolerance of 0.0005!"

Later, Ed Sokolsky said that he and Jack were turning out about 24 pieces in a ten-hour period (2.4 an hour), that the job had been retimed several times, but no raise in price had been given.

Ed and Jack asked for a price of 38 cents. Ed said that they could turn out 3 an hour, but, until they got a decent price, they were turning out 2 an hour.

Toward the end of the evening I noticed that Ed's machine was idle, and Ed was sitting on a box, doing nothing.

"What's the matter, did they stop the job on you?" I asked.

"I stopped it," said Ed. "I don't feel like running it."

*March.*—Dooley worked on the hinge bases again tonight. He admitted that he could barely make out on the job, but "Why bust my ass for day rate? We're doing 3 an hour or less until we get a better price!"

This 3-an-hour-or-less business has been going on several months. The price is 23 cents; so Dooley and Jack turn in 69 cents an hour (or less).

*May.*—McCann said that Starkey was arguing all day over the price of the hinge bases. The methods men maintain that they can't raise the price "because the jacks that the parts go on sell for $14.00 apiece." They plan to retool the job and lower the price. According to McCann, Jack told them that if he didn't get a decent price he was going to make out on the job but scrap every one of the pieces.

"Jack fights it out with them," said McCann. "He'll stay right with the machine and argue. I get disgusted and walk away.

"Jack turned out 28 today," McCann went on. "That's too many, nearly 3 an hour. He'll have to watch himself if he expects to get a raise in price."

Starkey was running the hinge bases again tonight. I remarked, "I see you're in the gravy again."

His reply was, "Yeah! 69 cents an hour!"

McCann did not seem to enjoy the hinge bases either. He looked bored, tired, and disgusted all evening. His ten hours is a long stretch at day work. He cannot make out early and rest after 11 o'clock (for four hours), but has to keep on the machine until three.

*August 14.*—Al McCann was working on the hinge bases tonight, one of the jobs that he and Jack are protesting as to price. Gil (the foreman) sat and stood behind Al for at least an hour, and I could see that Al did not like it. He worked steadily, but with deliberate slowness, and did not look at Gil or speak to him. Al and Jack have agreed to restrict production on the hinge bases until they get a better price, and Gil was probably there to see what Al could really do. I think that Al and Jack could make out on the job, but not at $1.25 an hour, and they cut production to less than 80 cents an hour.

*August 16.*—Al told me that they had won a price raise on the hinge bases, from 23 to 28 cents, and another raise to 31 cents.

"But it's still not high enough. As it is now we can make exactly 94 cents an hour. We're trying to get 35 cents. We can turn out 1 in exactly 16 minutes. That's not 4 an hour. We've been giving them 3 an hour."

## AN ATTEMPT TO ESTIMATE THE DEGREE OF PIECEWORK GOLDBRICKING

I failed to earn the base rate of 85 cents for slightly over half my piecework hours, but I cannot claim that I failed in spite of a maximum effort. There were only a few occasions when I tried to "make out," but could not, and did not let failure diminish my efforts. Normally, I behaved in the manner of my fellow-operators; I "tried out" a job for a short sampling period of an hour, more or less, and slowed my pace to a restrictive one if the job did not show "possibilities." There were numerous occasions when even "trial runs" were not attempted, when I was forewarned that the job was a "stinker." Since possible output was not determined, the amount of restriction cannot be computed.

There were times when the words of various operators indicated that they could have "covered" day rate if they had tried; the expression, "Why bust my ass for day rate?" was considered adequate explanation for failure to press on to the maximum attainable. If claims of ability to achieve the scorned "day rate" could be accepted as indicative of the true possibilities inherent in a job, it is clear that the man who turned in 42.5 cents an hour for a day's average hourly earnings, and who says that he could have made 85 cents an hour, has accomplished but 4 hours' work in 8. A man who turned in 21.25 cents an hour, instead of a possible 85 cents, has done 2 hours' work in 8, and has "wasted" 6 hours. That an operator has turned in 42.5 cents an hour, or 21 cents, or 10 cents may be determined easily enough; the difficulty lies in inability to test his claims of what he could have done.

Recorded observations do allow some ob-

## QUOTA RESTRICTION AND GOLDBRICKING IN A MACHINE SHOP 439

jective estimate of losses incurred by gold-bricking in isolated cases. For instance, the four operators assigned to Jack Starkey's machine made it a practice to restrict production on the hinge bases to from 2 to 3 pieces an hour. To this restriction were attributed two price increases, from 25 cents to 28 cents to 31 cents per piece. Thus, at the 31-cent price in effect in August, and at the output rate of 3 pieces per hour, the men were turning in 93 cents per hour, or $7.44 per 8-hour day. Since their special base rate, as experienced operators on a machine handling heavy fixtures, was $1.10 per hour, they were earning 17 cents an hour less than they were paid. One of the operators involved, Al McCann, claimed that by test they could turn out 1 piece in exactly 16 minutes. At this rate they could have turned in 3.75 pieces per hour for earnings of $1.16 per hour, or $9.28 per day. "Waste" time could be computed at 1.6 production-hours, and the loss in "earnings" at 23 cents per hour.

McCann's estimate of the job's possibilities proved to be low, however; for, a few weeks later, upon abandoning hope for a further increase in piecework price, he "made out easily in 6 hours."

Al said tonight that he was making out on the hinge bases, that he got disgusted Friday, speeded up the tools, and turned in 31 pieces for earnings of $9.60 (3⅞ pieces per hour, or $1.20 per hour earnings).

"It was easy, just as easy as the frames. Now I'm kicking myself all over for not doing it before. All I did was to change the speed from 95 to 130. I was sick of stalling around all evening, and I got mad and decided to make out and let the tools burn up. But they made it all right, for 8 hours. What's the use of turning in 93 cents an hour when you can turn in $1.25 just as easy? They'd never raise a price you could make 93 cents on anyhow. Now maybe they'll cut it back."

Tonight Al made out easily in 6 hours, though he stretched the last few pieces to carry him until 10:30.

Since McCann reported a turn-in of 31 pieces for earnings of $9.60, or $1.20 an hour on the previous workday, his first day of

"making out," it was likely that his "making out" at the 6 hours involved regular quota earnings of $1.25 an hour. A turn-in of 32 pieces would net $9.92 per day, or $1.24 an hour; accomplished in 6 hours, such output would mean that McCann earned $1.65 an hour while working and was now "wasting" 2 hours a shift on quota restriction. And the $1.65-per-hour earnings meant, when compared to previous earnings of 93 cents an hour while goldbricking, that McCann had been "wasting" 3.5 hours a day each time the hinge bases were assigned to his machine; his former earnings loss had been 72 cents an hour, or $5.76 per day. (Actually less than this if "earnings" be defined as "take-home" and not as "turn-in," for McCann's "day rate" had been raised to $1.10 an hour. His personal loss would thus have been 17 cents less per hour—55 cents an hour, or $4.40 per day.)

McCann, engaged in goldbricking, estimated that he could turn out a piece every 16 minutes; this means that he saw production possibilities to be 3.75 pieces per hour and earning possibilities to be $1.16 per hour. But under piecework incentive he actually turned out 5.33 pieces per hour and earned $1.65 per hour while working. If the difference between his estimated and his achieved production can be taken as indicative of such differences in general, then the man who claims that he could have covered his day rate of 85 cents an hour but did not try to do so could have boosted his earnings to $1.21 an hour. In other words, if an operator can see day-rate earnings in a job, he can make quota earnings. My experience would seem to bear this out. If I found that I could make out on a job at day rate, such a discovery motivated me to "wring the neck" of the particular operation for quota earnings. The bimodal pattern production would suggest this; my total quota-piecework hours were 75 per cent of my total make-out–piecework hours, and the latter included short runs of once-assigned jobs that did not receive adequate "test." Though the words of fellow-operators indicated the "pour-it-on" point to be $1.00 an hour, it is possible that energetic performance on 85-cent-an-hour jobs would yield the desired quota.

By the foregoing logic a worker who limits his output to 68 cents an hour, when he thinks he can make 85 cents an hour, is "potentially" limiting output by 44 per cent instead of by the assumed 20 per cent.

## DAYWORK GOLDBRICKING

Operators on "nonpiecework," or "day-work" jobs, followed almost uniformly a pattern of restriction of the goldbricking type. They kept in mind rough estimates of output that they felt would fall appreciably below "day-rate" standards if and when the "nonpiecework" jobs were timed and priced.

Nonpiecework jobs in the shop were of two kinds: "time study" and "rework." "Time-study" operations were those that either were so newly established that they were not yet timed and priced or were jobs whose price had been "removed." In either case, timing procedures and a piecework price were expected in the immediate future.

"Rework" was the reprocessing of defective pieces that were considered salvageable. Rework carried no premium pay and no expectations of it, but rough standards of output limitation were applied.

I worked 300 hours at time study and 53 hours at rework, 16 per cent and 3 per cent of total hours put in. Thus, roughly, one-fifth of my time was employed at nonpiecework production, and for this one-fifth the operator could be counted upon, without fail, to be goldbricking. A concise bit of advice, offered by McCann, then set-up man and wise in the ways of production lines, stated the common attitude:

It was a time-study operation, drilling and tapping a set-screw hole in some sprockets. "Take it easy," advised McCann.

This advice I, already of five months' shop experience, considered unnecessary. By no stretch of the imagination could my accustomed pace on time study be regarded as other than "easy." But, under McCann's expert tutelage, I discovered that there were degrees of goldbricking, and that for time

study, a mere "punking along" exceeded worker standards.

McCann started me out at 95 speed on the drill and spot-facer, and 70 on chamfer and taps.

"Isn't that too slow for the drill?" I asked.

"It's fast enough on this tough stuff for time study. Run it that way 'til they speed you up. If you go too fast today, you won't get a good price when it's timed."

Even this slow pace looked too fast for Gus Schmidt, who watched from the next machine.

Later in the evening Schmidt said to me, "Aren't you going too fast with that time study?"

I did not think I was going very fast and told him so.

"Well, maybe it just looks fast because you're going so steady at it. You've got to slow down on time study or you won't get a good price. They look at the record of what you do today and compare it with the timing speed when it's timed. Those time-study men are sharp!"

Toward the end of the evening I raised the speeds of the taps and chamfer to 95. It was going too slow for me and actually tired me out standing around waiting for the taps to go through. My legs were tired at the end of the day; yet I had not worked hard.

Goldbricking on time study may be indistinguishable, even to a fellow-operator, from "quota restriction." On one occasion I noticed that Tony, the speed-drill man, was "fooling around," and asked him if he had made out already. Only through information supplied by Tony did I become aware that my neighbor was goldbricking on a time-study job and not relaxing his efforts after achieving quota. In order to classify operator behavior when an operator is "doing nothing," one must have access to additional facts not provided by casual observation. There are times when an operator may be mistaken in classification of his own restriction of output. He may think he is loafing on time study when he is in reality loafing on piecework.

I discovered, when I came to work, that yesterday's job on the pedestals had been timed.

## QUOTA RESTRICTION AND GOLDBRICKING IN A MACHINE SHOP 441

Joe said, "I see you didn't make out yesterday."

I had turned in 60 pieces, priced $4.90, for a day's earnings of less than $3.00. I was glad I didn't know the job was timed, with a price like that.

### REWORK RESTRICTION

I received advice on "rework" that led to the same productive results on time-study operation.

Joe finished the gears, and I spent a slow evening on time study and rework. The first job was 15 gear brackets, a time-study job. The next was the reworking of 1 jack shell.

Said Al, when I told him I was on rework, "Well, you've got all night to turn it out. When they give you a rework job, that's a sign they've got nothing for you to do."

"You mean they expect me to take all night at it?"

McCann was hesitant. "No, I don't mean that. But you can take your time."

About ten o'clock Paul (set-up man) suggested that we "take it easy."

"We're doing too much as it is, on this rework," he said.

When Ed Sokolsky heard that we had done 4, he was surprised. "I wouldn't have done that many," he said.

### AN ATTEMPT TO ESTIMATE THE DEGREE OF NONPIECEWORK RESTRICTION

An indication of the amount of restriction practiced on nonpiecework operations can be obtained in a comparison of the writer's output on a job before it was timed and priced, and his output on the same job after a piecework price was set.

One day some gear parts were assigned as time study. I accepted the advice to take it easy proffered by the set-up man, McCann, and by a fellow-operator, Schmidt, and turned in a total of 64 pieces for the day's work. The next day I came to work to discover that the job had been timed at $7.95 a hundred. Joe Mucha reported the job a good one, but I was dubious.

"It's a good job," he said. "They timed me for $1.20 an hour, and it worked out just that. You can do 16 an hour. But watch yourself, now, and don't turn in too many!"

"Don't worry, I probably won't get 100," I assured him.

Yesterday's 64 had given me the feeling that I would have to push very hard to turn out 100 ($1.00 per hour).

I had underestimated the job. My effort reached a peak of $1.83 per hour, or 23 pieces per hour, and I completed 150 pieces in 7.5 hours for average earnings of $1.59 an hour for the time worked.

After lunch I decided to try to see how many I could turn out. I did manage to complete 12 in half an hour but never got higher than 23 for the whole hour. The speeds were set at 225 for drilling and 95 for the other tools, just as I finished yesterday. At 10:30 I had completed 150 pieces.

At a price of $7.95 per 100, the 64 pieces turned out on time study would have represented average earnings of about 64 cents an hour. Since I expected to turn out no more than 100 pieces with full effort on piecework, my assumed restriction on time study was 36 per cent, with a "loss" of 36 cents an hour, or $2.86 a day, and with a time "waste" of 2.9 hours.

But with an actual subsequent output of 20 per hour for 7.5 hours, a rate of 160 per day, restriction the first day turned out to be 60 per cent, with a loss of 95 cents an hour, or $7.63 per day, and a time "waste" of 4.8 hours a day. And with a "potential" output of 23 per hour, a rate of 184 per day, restriction the first day turned out to be 65 per cent, with a "loss" of $9.55 a day, or $1.19 an hour, and a time "waste" of 5.2 hours a day.

### SUMMARY AND CONCLUSION

These appraisals of output limitation can be accepted only as suggestive of the amount of time wasted by operatives in piecework machine shops. Certainly, the "waste" is great.

I have indicated that the time "wasted" on my own quota restriction for a six-month period was 1.39 hours out of every 8. I was 83 per cent "efficient" for the 469.6 quota piecework-hours put in, by my own standards of performance, and thus could have increased production by 21 per cent by abandoning quota limitations. If my wastage of 2 hours a day on quota restriction during the last two months of employment is accepted as characteristic of the behavior of more seasoned operators, efficiency would be 75 per cent, with immediate possibilities for a 33.3 per cent increase in production on quota jobs.

Also, by experimenting with twenty jobs which represented 58 per cent of the total piecework hours put in during a ten-month period, and which offered earning possibilities beyond quota limits, I derived an estimate of "potential quota restriction" of 2.9 hours a day. This restriction represented an efficiency of 64 per cent, with possibilities for a 57 per cent increase in production.

Furthermore, from observations of the work behavior of fellow-operators, I was able to speculate with some objective evidence on the degree of slowdown goldbricking practiced on non-make-out piecework. It was pointed out that four drill operators had been restricting production at a rate of 3.5 "waste" hours out of 8, as indicated by the output achieved by one of the four men when he ceased goldbricking. Efficiency had been 56 per cent, with immediate possibilities for a 78 per cent production increase. Renunciation of goldbricking did not, in this particular case, mean fulfilment of possibilities, however; for the conversion was to quota restriction with stabilization at 75 per cent efficiency.

In addition, I essayed an estimate on daywork goldbricking, first cousin to piecework goldbricking and easily mistaken for the latter. This estimate was obtained by comparing output on a job before and after it was timed. The "before" efficiency was determined to be at least as low as 40 per cent, possibly 35 per cent, with 150 per cent

improvement in production a "cinch" and 186 per cent improvement an immediate possibility. But like the case of piecework goldbricking just cited, the switch was to quota restriction; so possibilities were never realized.

Since these appraisals were confined to the behavior of machine operators, the loss of time accountable to the sometimes remarkable restraint exercised by the "service" employees, such as stock-chasers, tool-crib attendants, and inspectors, was not considered. Likewise unmentioned were the various defections of shop supervisors. A more complete record might also include the "work" of members of management at higher levels, whose series of new rules, regulations, orders, and pronunciamentos designed for purposes of expediting production processes actually operated to reduce the effectiveness of the work force.

Confining scrutiny to the behavior of machine operators, the observer sees output restriction of such magnitude that the "phenomenal" results of the organizational innovations tried in the steel industry under the guiding genius of Joe Scanlon[6] do not seem at all surprising. The concept of "cultural drag" might be more descriptive than "cultural lag" in depicting the trailing of some of our industrial practices behind technological advance. Our organization of people for work is in general so primitive that anthropologists need not attempt to justify their interest in the "modern" industrial scene.

*Duke University*

[6] John Chamberlain, "Every Man a Capitalist," *Life Magazine*, December 23, 1946; Russell W. Davenport, "Enterprise for Everyman," *Fortune*, June, 1950.

# [11]

GERALD MARS

# Dock pilferage

## A case study in occupational theft

This paper presents part of a wider study of longshoremen[1] undertaken as an anthropologist in St Johns, Newfoundland, and more
fully reported elsewhere (Mars 1972). It is also one of a number of
case studies in occupational pilferage on which I am currently working, most collected through participant observation.[2]

Participant observation in this case was necessarily limited. I spent
eighteen months in field work as an anthropologist, living, drinking,
and spending my leisure with the longshoremen concerned. But since
the amount of work in this port was limited – Newfoundland has a
winter unemployment rate over 40 per cent and a summer one over
12 per cent – I was unable to work on the dock. Instead, I spent much
time in the Union Hall, wandering round the wharfs and sheds and
on and in vessels observing and chatting to men as they worked and
drinking with them in the evenings. My interest in pilferage as a
specific area of inquiry was peripheral to other interests and arose
relatively late in fieldwork.

In this paper I am primarily concerned to examine how 'normal'
work roles are adapted to serve the needs of institutionalized pilferage,
how this influences relationships on the dock – particularly within the
dock work gang and how the men involved perceive their actions in
terms of a prevailing morality. Suggestions are then offered for
extensions of the analysis.

### BACKGROUND TO THE PORT AND ITS OPERATIONS

St Johns hires the labour it needs on a casual basis by a procedure
known as 'the shape-up.'[3] When a ship docks, a hiring foreman
stands on deck, men form a horseshoe beneath him and the foreman
then picks from this 'shape' the twenty-six men for the gang he will

later supervise. The picking of men is carried out in the same way as schoolboys pick their football teams. Men are hired only for a particular boat which may give as little as two or as much as twenty hours work and they are paid hourly. In 1964 the hourly rate was $2 and average annual pay of regularly chosen gang members amounted only to about $2,000. 'Outside men' – those not normally hired as regular gang members – fill in on vacancies when they occur. Their earnings are lower than those of regular men and their access to pilferage much less.

In spite of the apparently casual nature of hiring, close observation revealed that predominantly the same men were rehired at each shape-up by their regular foremen. This is because a bargain exists between members of the tightly organized work gang, who need security of selection, and the foreman, who needs an output of work satisfactory to his superiors. One strand of the bargain gained by the men is job security – another is access to pilferage. Gangs are tightly knit, inward-looking groups of friends and neighbours, who spend their leisure together and among whom there frequently exist considerable kinship connexions. The gang is, therefore, the unit of work and leisure. It is also the unit by which pilferage of cargo is organized and distributed. Foremen, excluded from social activities, have in recent years largely moved away from longshore areas of residence and take no part in obtaining or distributing pilfered cargo.

The techniques governing pilferage can be explained only in the context of normal work roles and their organization. This is because organization of both legitimate and illegitimate work is based on the same work group structure – the dock work gang. It is therefore only by understanding normal working that we can see how work roles are adapted by men to carry out illegitimate tasks under cover of legitimacy.

Working normally, when a vessel is unloading general cargo, men start the process in the bowels of the ship – the hold. Cargo has to be lifted by winch or crane and dropped alongside the vessel to the quay. Here it is loaded onto a fork truck and moved to a shed or warehouse for sorting, stacking, and checking. The total task is performed in much the same way in any port, which means that the dock work gang system is, with variations, basically universal. This discussion can be regarded, therefore, as having a wider application than its single source might suggest.[4]

Figure 1 reveals the working situation in St Johns and shows the distribution of a twenty-six man gang among its different sections. The discussion refers to a gang structure designed to unload cargo, since this is the predominant type of gang structure in the port.

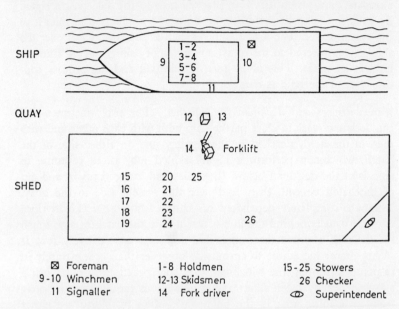

|  |  |  |
|---|---|---|
| ⊠ Foreman | 1-8 Holdmen | 15-25 Stowers |
| 9-10 Winchmen | 12-13 Skidsmen | 26 Checker |
| 11 Signaller | 14 Fork driver | ⬭ Superintendent |

FIGURE I: *Deployment of a twenty-six man gang for unloading general cargo*

## The vessel crew

*The eight holdsmen.* Men who work in the hold, often collectively called 'the hatchcrew', are organized in four pairs. Where possible, two pairs move cargo to the sling and two pairs load the sling together. Sometimes it is not feasible for all members of a hatchcrew to work together – a cargo's nature or the way it is packed might mean that two pairs of men have to stand idly by until their workmates have cleared a sufficient space.

This enforced idleness contributes to the high incidence of pilferage from ships' holds. Most pilfering of cargo takes place here rather than in the sheds. Another contributory factor is that normal work involves burrowing for cargo below the level of the hatch and therefore legitimately working for much of the time out of sight of passersby on deck.

There are two slings to each hatch. A sling is a square board, to each corner of which is fixed a hawser; these are linked to a cable and hoisted or lowered by power-operated winch. Each sling is loaded alternately and when it is fully stacked men in the hold pass a signal by hand to a signaller standing on deck who similarly transmits it to the winch driver. The loaded sling is then raised, swung out over the ship's side, lowered to the quay, and an empty sling lowered into the hold in its place. This in its turn is reloaded and the process continued until the hold is empty.

*Winch drivers and deckman (or signaller).* The two winchmen and the deckman work in close partnership both with each other and with men in the hold. Perched in the rigging, one on either side of the hatch, winchmen perform a highly skilled job, as, in response to signals of the deckman below, they raise and lower slings in and out of the hatch beneath them and over the vessel's side to the quay. They are completely dependent on signals from the deckman since they are usually behind the line of vision into the hatch: it says much for the skill of these three men that accidents are relatively few. It seems almost incredible to an outside observer that, acting purely in response to signals, the winchmen can, with practised ease, deposit a swaying, heavily laden sling exactly where it is required on the quay from its loading area in the hold while often unable to see either loading area or quayside.

To obtain such polished, almost elegant handling demands a rapport between winchmen and signaller that requires considerable time to perfect. 'You've got to be buddies to do this job,' one winchdriver remarked, 'and you've got to understand his signals – they've all got different signals.'

This rapport unites all the vessel crew and though derived from legitimate work organization is, as we shall see, indispensable to the illegitimate organization of pilferage.

### The shore crew

*Skidsmen.* Skidsmen work on the quay at the side of a ship. In this situation they are both physically and socially isolated from the gang's two main sections. Skidsmen work as a pair and handle the sling as the winchman lowers it over the ship's side. If the fork truck is waiting to load they manoeuvre the contents onto the truck's fork: if the truck is in the shed they see the sling unloaded directly to the quay.

The job is unskilled and rated low on prestige. Skidsmen have little autonomy since their rate of work is entirely set by the vessel crew. The job has a further disadvantage in that it is visible to anyone walking along the quay. This means that superintendents or managers can at any time detect an absentee or investigate a pile-up of cargo on the quayside. This visibility also of course inhibits skidsmen from pilfering and helps make the job the least desired of any in the longshore work gang.

*Fork truck drivers.* Truck drivers are regarded by longshoremen as relatively skilled men. The ability to manoeuvre not very easily controlled trucks in and out of narrow passageways is rated lower in skill than the winchdriver's job but higher than the stower's.

The job involves collecting cargo from the quay and taking it to stowers in the shed. The truck drivers can seriously affect the stowers' task; a fast moving driver, working with a fast moving vessel crew, can set a pace beyond what stowers consider reasonable. Further, a truck driver not in harmony with his stowers can make their job even more difficult by dropping cargo some distance from their sorting area, forcing them to manhandle it to their sorting area.

The social position of the fork truck driver is somewhat ambiguous. Sometimes he is regarded as a foreman's man. As one stower remarked, 'he'll work for the foreman – not the gang – he sets the pace for the stowers.' He will, however, sometimes act as a medium of communication between stowers and vessel crew when grumbles come from the shed that the vessel crew are 'hoisting' too much too quickly. This area of ambiguity about his role is thus, in part, a reflection of his physical position in the gang. Working on his own as he does, trundling his truck between shed and quay, he is – like the skidsmen – in little position to integrate with any group. Yet truck drivers do not always 'work for the foreman'. Just as his position in the gang allows him to serve the foreman by setting a pace for shed stowers, so it also allows him to perform certain services for the gang. These services include facilitating pilferage.

*The stowers.* The eleven stowers are divided into two groups: of five and six. Working under direction of the hatch checker, they sort cargo in the shed brought from the quay by the truck drivers.

The job is regarded as unskilled, not requiring specific abilities, and not very onerous. Among stowing gangs are older men who are 'carried' by the other members, men who have been injured (more often in the hold than elsewhere), men recovering from sickness, and newly inducted outside men.

It is among the stowers that most executive members of the Union are found – a result of their opportunity to communicate at work to a degree not available to other gang members. Holdsmen are isolated in groups of eight and work in pairs; winchmen and signallers relate as a group of three, while the skidsmen and truck drivers are relatively isolated. Stowers, on the other hand, in the normal course of work mix with at least four or five, more usually with ten or eleven, co-workers, and also have opportunities to contact stowers in other gangs throughout the shed. Because of this stowers are able to offer more complicated support to each other in organizing pilferage and stowers of one gang sometimes give warning of the approach of authority to stowers of adjacent gangs.

*Hatch checkers.* A hatch checker's job is two-fold: to check cargo against documents and to guide the work of stowers in allocating cargo, in piles, to await individual consignees.

A hatch checker is regarded as the foreman's unofficial deputy in the shed. He must be literate and highly skilled at 'knowing the marks'.[5] His position *vis-à-vis* the foreman is extremely secure as this knowledge is not widespread and many foremen are illiterate. He is not paid extra for his knowledge,[6] but he gains in security.

One experienced member of the Union executive described checkers as 'unpaid policemen'. By this he hastened to add he knew of no cases where a hatch checker had reported a man for theft, but rather he felt some checkers limited the amount men took. I could find no evidence of antagonism between checkers and stowers. All hatch checkers during my field work seemed well established, and relationships between them and stowers were affable. One event serves to point out the nature of this relationship.

During field work one hatch checker who had a record of sickness was off on holiday. His replacement was a shed checker whose position in the shed was regarded as none too permanent and who, it was suspected by some of the stowers, was 'after Hughie's place'. They combined to mis-sort cargo so the relief checker had no idea where any specific consignee's material would be found. By constantly mixing up different cargo they made the checker's job intolerable.

There is some measure of ambiguity in the relationship of a hatch checker to his stowers. The case above demonstrated dependence of the checker upon stowers. In pilferage, however, as we shall see, stowers necessarily depend upon the checker. In this connexion it is noteworthy that most checkers and stowers enjoy a symmetrical joking relationship (Radcliffe-Brown 1952). One checker, for instance, was constantly ribbed at the vast amount he was alleged to have pilfered. 'Clears 'em out Hughie does, don't you Hughie?' Hughie's reply was always jocular!

With this account of 'normal working' by a twenty-six man gang engaged in unloading general cargo, we can see how they perform an interrelated series of tasks. We must now consider how these work roles are adapted and how they interrelate for the performance of covert and illegitimate tasks.

### FOUR CASES OF THEFT

It must first be made clear that I was not able to observe actual examples of theft taking place in the dock. Details of instances were obtained initially from management or from traders who suffered loss in their consignments. Later in field work, material was obtained from longshoremen themselves but again without direct observation. With such information, however, it was possible to go back to several informants and to cross-check material received.

### Case 1: Men's suits

I first heard from a manager of one wharf that a cargo of men's suits had been broken into and some pilfered. In checking with the trader, I found thirteen out of a consignment of a hundred suits had disappeared between despatch in Montreal and arrival in St Johns. With this background of information I then went to informants who worked on the wharf concerned.

The sequence of events was fairly clear and cross-checking with several informants confirmed what had happened. The hatch checker had been alerted by details on his bills of lading concerning the contents of the crates: messages had passed from shed to vessel crew to warn them of 'good pickings' to be expected. The crates were then loaded by the hold crew so that two would fall when the winch was jerked. At the appropriate moment, as the sling was poised over the quay, the signaller gave an all-clear sign to the winchman, the winchman adjusted his levers, the winch jerked and the crates fell. They were only slightly damaged but this was enough to permit entry.

Following normal procedure, the crates were then moved by fork truck to the shed for attention of the stowers. The shed is hardly a safe place for pilferage as the wharf superintendent or even the company manager may appear. Superintendents, in particular, frequently walk round the sheds to make sure that work is proceeding, and, presumably, also to restrict pilferage. In this shed (as in several others) the situation of the superintendent's office is a further hazard to stowers. This is commonly set high in the shed's roof and typically has large glass windows, so the superintendent, sitting at his desk, has an overview of operations throughout the shed. First then, it is necessary to block off this view of what was going on in the sorting and unloading area.

In this instance, much other cargo unloaded with the suits was bulky and packed in large cases. The fork truck driver stacked this cargo to block off the superintendent's line of vision so he could not see the sorting area from his office. At the same time the driver also built up some other of the packing cases to form a hollow square. This enclosure then served as a changing room. Thus equipped, men were able to choose their suits at leisure, trying on different ones for size and being secure from the prying eyes of the superintendent in the roof.

Throughout the day, holdsmen, signaller, and winchmen left the vessel and made their way individually to 'the changing room'. Stowers, as they went about their normal job, kept a wary eye open for authority, but the procedure went unobserved. This cargo was removed from the dock in the usual way, secreted in the clothing of men who took the goods home at the end of the day. Men are extremely skilful in this matter. (I once walked with a man half a mile through busy streets to his home. Once inside he pulled out bottle after bottle of whisky until there were six bottles on the kitchen table.)

The following day the hatch checker reported that two crates had arrived damaged. By this time the missing suits had already been moved and were almost impossible to trace. Neither was it possible to localize the pilferage to St Johns: there was no evidence to prove the crates could not have been opened in Montreal, while the vessel was at sea, or at other ports on its route. In this connexion it must be pointed out that cargo often arrives in the port that has been interfered with prior to arrival, and longshoremen in the port are often blamed for pilferage they know has been accomplished elsewhere.

In this case, though cooperation of vessel crew, stowers, and fork truck driver were all necessary for a successful operation, actual pilferage was effected in the shed. Both management and men, however, are of the view that most pilferage occurs whilst cargo is still in the hold.

### Case 2: Transistor radios

I heard about this case, involving a cargo of radios from Germany, when discussing the general question of pilferage with one of the superintendents. 'Oh yes – they'll steal anything. They're the worst thieves in the world – only last week a crate of radios *en route* to Montreal was completely cleared out.' I asked how he was so sure they'd been taken in St Johns but he was hesitant to say. The account obtained from informants was as follows:

With stereotyped Teutonic efficiency the forwarders had marked on the outside of their crate the name of the radios, a full description (which pointed out that they were portable!), and the quantity.

The holdsmen had noticed this crate lying behind other cargo they were unloading. In a situation like this, however, one cannot just break into a crate; a member of the ship's crew will frequently be pacing the deck and occasionally peering into the hold. He is there specifically to restrict pilferage. Usually, this lookout is a ship's officer – the mate or one of his deputies. Sometimes, if cargo is not particularly valuable or not easily pilfered, the job of lookout may be delegated to a more junior officer. In this case, the man keeping an eye on men in the hold was the ship's mate.

The threat to security posed by the ship's officer is a serious one, though holdsmen can stay out of his line of vision if they know where he is positioned. On this occasion, as in other cases where holdsmen are involved, their insecurity was reduced by the signaller. His 'normal' job, discussed above, involves passing signals to the winchmen. By quick and deft movements of his hands, he tells the winchman by how much to raise, lower, and move the slings. To do this he must stand on the ship's deck on the vessel's shore-side. He is thus in perfect position not only to carry out his normal signalling but also to keep an eye on the ship's officer who, in his turn, is keeping observation on the hold crew. His arm movements, however, are not used only to coordinate the work of winch, hold, and skidsmen. In contribution to pilferage, they serve also to warn men in the hold below of the activities of the ship's officer above. So rapid and well understood can these signals be that I was never able to recognize or locate them.

Though the crate was opened by holdsmen, its allocation was divided among all gang sections though I neglected to find out if this included the normally isolated skidsmen. My main informant, a stower, had two radios – one of which he sold. Not all the gang participated, and there were some disputed exchanges since several men were scared to steal such valuable items (these radios retailed for over $150 each). They were removed from the dock under men's coats.

Except for the high value of items involved, the procedures in this case would appear to be more typical than those in the previous case in that activity was largely restricted to the vessel crew. The vessel crew's 'leavings' were then made available to stowers and, as this was a cargo in transit, there would presumably have been no need for co-operation from the hatch checker.

I neglected to find how packaging had been disposed of in this case, as it was since 'the cargo had been completely cleared out'. The usual methods are for it to be broken up, find its way into the harbour, be carried out of the docks, stuffed into other cargo – cardboard for instance, being flat, is likely to be slipped into other cargo (particularly mattresses) or to end up minus identifying marking among the normal and considerable rubbish of the shed.[7]

## Case 3: Whisky

One British ship's captain recounted what happened on a previous trip while observing the unloading of whisky. As stated previously, overseeing men in the hold is normally the mate's duty. However, in situations where cargo is particularly likely to be pilfered, especially where high-value consumption items such as whisky, for which there is an almost insatiable demand, are involved, a captain might himself take on the task. On this occasion, as he was leaning over the hatch he saw that crates were not placed quite securely on the sling. As they were hoisted the sling wobbled and one crate fell back in the hold, landing on a corner. This was sufficient to break a couple of bottles which started to leak their precious liquid. 'Almost before the damned crate was down they were there with cups and cans and what-have-you,' he stated. 'I was ready for it, you see. I knew what was going to happen. As soon as it fell, I shouted to them to stand back and made them wait till it had run away. They were pretty angry at that and wanted to know why I'd wasted the stuff – so I told them "because I don't want any more cases falling – alright?" They all laughed at that. Yes – you have a hard job with thieving. Mind you, it's not even safe to do this – they can be bloodyminded. Pilferage is found in any port, but it is worse here in my experience than anywhere else in North America. It's petty though – not organized on a large scale.'

Such an operation's apparent casualness, as the captain was aware, requires practised cooperation of winchmen, hold crew, and signaller. First, the hold pair must load a crate on the sling with great care so it falls neither too early nor too late. Second, the signaller must be well aware of what has been arranged so he can pass signals to the winchman to treat this sling load rather differently from usual. Finally, the winchman, on whose particular expertise this operation largely depends, must know exactly when to shift his gears so that, with sound science and some elegance, he can cause the crate's demise.

The captain told me that a friend of his, also a captain employed by the same company, had some years previously caught a man in the port red-handed and had called the police. The men 'for devilment' stole a lot more. 'Never again,' he swore, 'let the insurance pay up.' The captain said his company 'had largely stopped shipping general cargo to the port' and now mainly confined its operations to coal – 'directly because of this type of pilferage'.

## Case 4: Foodstuffs

Having looked at some specific examples I now turn to consider pilferage of a general category of goods taken regularly in relatively small amounts. These are often foodstuffs, particularly those considered luxuries. Those actually stolen vary, therefore, with the tastes of each individual and of his family. Access to foodstuffs is particularly easy since their packaging is minimal – they usually arrive in single-thickness cardboard containers – and often these become damaged in the normal course of a cargo's discharge.

Quite a lot of the men like sprouts, which are imported from the mainland and, being expensive, are considered something of a delicacy. When a cargo of sprouts arrives, it is usual for several men to fill a pocket or two. Holdsmen might also 'take care' of the interests of winchmen or signaller, and stowers similarly 'take care' of a truck driver.

Some men have more esoteric tastes. One had a taste for anchovies, also considered luxury goods, a middle class treat. When this man, a stower, handled cargo including anchovies he pocketed two or three tins. He had a friend with similar tastes, a stower in another gang on the same wharf. When either gang handled anchovies each stower made sure his friend was also catered for. Men similarly take special foods for their wives. They will make an especial attempt to do so on occasions when liquor is also taken from the dock. Longshore women are generally against liquor; and anchovies, sprouts, or similar delicacies are used on these occasions to reconcile them to the heavy drinking that is likely to follow 'good liquor pickings'. Stolen liquor offends the more moralistic women on two grounds: that it is liquor and that it is stolen. The implication of wives as receivers serves therefore, to undermine wifely opposition on at least one of these grounds.

## A SYSTEM OF PILFERAGE

It is apparent that a system for the operation of pilferage exists, if by system we mean a set of inter-connected parts organized together to perform a particular job with the boundary to the system being largely congruent with the work gang. To state that pilferage operates within a system is not at all the same thing, however, as suggesting that pilferage in the port of St Johns is facilitated as an aspect of organized crime in the city. For one thing, pilferage appears to be random – advance planning has little place in its organization; secondly, its distribution does not usually involve financial profit; and thirdly, it provides a secondary source of resources restricted to men whose primary source of income is legitimate longshoring.[8]

To understand the social relationships involved in this system of pilferage, we must recognize two complementary facilities that need to be exploited for theft to occur. These are (with one exception to be discussed below) not found together in the same work role. The key to understanding the system lies in observing not only that these facilities are complementary but also in perceiving how they work in alliance. They may be termed facilities of access and support. (See Table I.)

When we examine workroles of men in the longshore gang we find the technical system imposing a twofold specialization which has

*Table 1*

The division of labour in the system of pilferage as organized in St Johns. Two clear groups emerge which correspond to the technical organization of the work gang. Extreme cases within the system are the skidsmen ($--$) and the hatch checker ($++$). Foremen are excluded from the system.

| Work role | Pilferage function | |  |
|---|---|---|---|
|  | Access | Support | |
| Holdsmen | + | − | Vessel |
| Winchdrivers | − | + | crew |
| Signaller | − | + | |
| Skidsmen | − | − | Special case |
| Fork lift driver | − | + | Shed |
| Stowers | + | − | crew |
| Hatch checker | + | + | Special case |

crucial effects on the way pilferage is organized. Some men spend their day actually handling cargo: these men who have *access* to cargo are holdsmen, stowers, and checkers. Other men, though involved in the process of moving cargo from ship to shed, do not actually handle goods but instead provide *support* for men who do in fact handle and have access to cargo. Thus the winchmen, signaller, and fork truck drivers perform services with or without machinery such that each may pass long periods without ever touching a crate.

If men with access to cargo had direct and untrammelled opportunities to procure goods, then dependencies within the gang would be very different from what it is in fact. Access, as we have seen, however, is limited. Cargoes often arrive in cases that are difficult to open; men in the shed are subject to prying eyes of superiors; men in the hold must beware of ship's officers; documents have to be squared and evidence of packaging disposed of if 'access men' are to be successful pilferers. All these hazards to effective theft can only be overcome by use of the second facility-support.

It was shown that for holdsmen to gain access to the contents of crates involves support of winchman and signaller. It is a dangerous operation for a winchman simply to drop a crate from a sling, whether this is done onto the deck or back into the hold. There are many people milling around when cargo is being unloaded, and without the sure guide of the signaller serious accidents would almost certainly occur. The signaller, therefore, minimizes this risk and at the same time grants support to the holdsmen by being in a position where he warns them of the presence of ship's officers.

Within the shed, the facility of support for access men, the stowers, is provided by the fork truck drivers and the hatch checker. The truck driver's support, as we saw, is necessary to stower's access because he can move cargo to where it can (a) be more readily interfered with, and (b) provide a screen against outsider's eyes.

Hatch checkers, as the table shows, occupy a distinctive place in this pilferage system: theirs is the only work role to combine both facilities of access and support $(+ +)$. A hatch checker's normal work involves direct physical handling of cargo which grants him access while his support is necessary to others on two grounds. First, his support is necessary to square documents; secondly, 'knowing the marks' (i.e. recognizing contents of a box from its markings), and receiving bills of lading, he is in a strong position to point out the most fruitful crates or packages to open.

Two workers are excluded from this system of dependencies: these are the skidsmen who lack access to cargo and who cannot gain support $(- -)$. Their access is extremely limited because they work in the open on the quayside and, therefore, within sight of any passing member of the hierarchy. Further, their handling of any package is only transitory as they unload it from sling to fork truck; it usually needs time to delve into a box or wrench off a lid in order to get at its contents. Not only is their access thus limited, but skidsmen are also in no position to supply support to other gang members.[9] The implications of the skidsmen's lack of function in this total system of dependencies overflows the work situation and affects non-work relationships. Skidsmen usually have no close kinship affiliations with the gang. They tend to have closer connexions with the foremen, and are likely also to be excluded from drinking cliques which stem from the work organization.

We see from the table, therefore, that nearly all gang members are enmeshed in a system of mutual dependencies made necessary by the technical, safety, and security limitations which act against open access to cargo. It is because access and support are differentially allocated within the gang, however, that no one individual can exert a monopoly over either facility. This means that no one man is able, in pilferage or in other matters, to maximize his own benefits without incurring effective group sanctions. On one occasion a longshoreman, known to have a car off the dock stacked with cargo, returned to find it broken into, its contents completely cleared. It was well understood this had been accomplished by his workmates. This story was told and retold with some hilarity throughout the waterfront; the general view was that it served the victim right; he was known to be greedy and his behaviour was likely to prove a danger to all longshoremen involved in handling the same cargo.

Convictions for pilferage in St Johns are extremely rare: there were no cases during the period of field work or in the immediate past. Managers, in discussion, always insist that the lack of convictions is due to the fact that 'longshoremen always stick together. You can never get one longshoreman to testify against another.' Managers and superintendents also realize they are in a poor position to institute proceedings. Even if they caught a man red-handed, testimony would involve retaliatory action which would make work relations even more difficult than usual. Men have walked off a boat because management once placed 'watchers' in the hold to supervise the unloading of whisky. Convictions, where they have occurred, have usually been instituted by men largely outside the waterfront system of relationships; they have usually been due to alert ships' officers rather than any measures taken by management.

When longshoremen talk of relationships within their work gangs and indeed within the Union generally, they frequently emphasize the mutual trust that exists between members. Where cooperative illegal activity occurs, necessity for absolute confidence in dependability of colleagues is of crucial importance. When talking of the induction of new gang members one informant recounted the case of a Salvationist who moved into his gang before the war. Because he refused to take cargo men were suspicious and reluctant to confirm him to membership. At this time police inquiries started into the theft of a valuable cargo of wrist-watches, and they 'grilled' the new member over a period of three months. 'All that time he didn't give anything away' said my informant. 'He was really firm in the gang after that.'

Pilferage, as a cooperatively organized illegal activity reinforces technical solidarity and serves therefore to bind members of gangs further into tight exclusive groups. But the institutionalization of pilferage also affects relationships beyond the gang and extends links beyond wharf boundaries. This extension of links derives from management who, when they have exceptionally secured a successful conviction, also suspend the culprit for six months from all work on the wharf concerned.

One of my informants, a stower, had a conviction for being in possession of stolen groceries taken from the dock. He had been fined in the magistrates' court and the company then suspended him for six months from all hirings on their wharf. This extra-legal penalty could have reduced him to a position worse than that of any outside man, who at least could attend all the shape-ups on each wharf. Instead of this, however, his earnings actually increased. 'In those six months, Gerry, I was never out of a job. The men on Y's wharf saw I was always in. You see it could happen to anyone. Who knows when one of them might get caught and need a job on X's (his home) wharf?'

## 'WORKING THE VALUE OF THE BOAT': THE MORALITY AND REGULATION OF PILFERAGE

When examination is made of different cargoes and attitudes taken to them, we find most longshoremen make a sharp distinction between cargo it is permissible to steal and that which should remain untouched. Normally all consumer goods are suitable for pilferage, but taking personal baggage is considered despicable. This distinction is seen and expressed in terms of, on the one hand, cargo addressed to impersonal firms and covered by insurance, and on the other hand personal property belonging to individuals. This distinction is well demonstrated in the following quotations: one longshoreman, justifying his dislike of another remarked: 'He'd take anything – he's even taken baggage – he's nothing more than a thief.' Another, discussing pilferage of general cargo, commented: 'I can't understand what they make all the fuss about, it's all insured and nobody's heard of an insurance company going broke. In any case, they've made millions out of this port and it's us who do the work.'

When the first speaker used the word 'thief' he limited the definition to cover a narrower range of behaviour than is usual. Pilferage of cargo other than baggage is by the implication of this view not regarded as theft. The second quotation makes this explicit: pilferage is here seen as a morally justified addition to wages; indeed, as an entitlement due from exploiting employers.

Longshoremen have a phrase to describe the process of obtaining this entitlement – they call it 'working the value of the boat'. Thus, if a boat is expected to provide ten hours' work at $2 an hour then the boat is 'good for' $20 in wages. 'Working the value of a boat' in this case would mean obtaining cargo up to but not more than an estimated value of $20.

The application of this concept can be seen to fulfil a number of functions. First, it tends to institutionalize pilferage – to grant it the status of a recognized and regularly occurring activity, and a normal part of life.

Secondly, the concept expresses a level of achievement men should aspire to. To say of a man, 'he always works the value of a boat' is a compliment; a confirmation of his independence and ability to outwit employers. Not all longshoremen, however, engage in pilferage. Some members of the smaller religious sects are uncompromising in this respect. A few Salvationists and Seventh Day Adventists are known never to steal and are respected for their views. But the respect accorded them does not regard abstinence as an ideal to be emulated, indeed their behaviour is seen as crankish. One informant expressed the common view, in response to my suggestion that weren't these 'good people', when he said he thought they were 'good – but stunned' – meaning stupid. The men respect their self-sacrifice in the same way many people respect the strength of character of vegetarians, without feeling they should join them. In neither case does respect imply the regard for ideal behaviour felt by men who are only able to maintain a lower-level norm.

A third function served by the idea of 'working the value of a boat' is the provision of a formula which attempts to fix an unequivocal limit beyond which pilferage, no longer thought laudable, is instead perceived as a danger to workmates. If men go above the value of a boat it is thought they are likely to attract official intervention. Persistently doing so involves a man in sanctions applied by his co-workers.

Such a formula though readily applicable to the generality of cargo which normally arrives on regular runs is not so readily applied to exceptional items with high unit value such as the transistor radios discussed in Case II. When items such as these are taken a division of involvement and interests occurs between those who participate and those who do not and this is seen by men as a likely source of disruption to gang relationships. These occasions are, however, justified in terms of being exceptional occurrences – each occasion being regarded as a one-off event that does not disturb the validity of the general rule applicable to 'normal' cargo.

This upper limit also serves to retain pilferage within the sphere of the moral and thus the justified. If a man takes more than the value of the boat, he is taking more than his moral entitlement and this alters the nature of his action. Though to an outsider the difference might well appear only one of degree, to a longshoreman the difference is essentially *qualitative*. Up to an agreed level pilfered cargo is seen as a moral entitlement; beyond this, additional pilferage is theft. Thus, when a gang sets levels of aspiration and operates controls to limit pilferage, it is acting *not only* from a standpoint of economic rationality but also, and this is a paradox not readily appreciated off the waterfront, from one set firmly in the prevailing morality.[10]

This fixing of an upper limit can be understood as allowing men to operate within limits of certainty: men know and can forecast not only the reactions of their workmates but also managerial reactions to pilferage only when it is kept to known and specific limits. This strongly suggests that managements are also, in a very real sense, conspirators with the men; that they in effect collude in accepting a specific level of pilferage as part of an understood indulgence pattern. More work needs to be done to determine the parameters of such collusion in a variety of industries and to assess factors permitting variable levels of pilferage in different *milieux*. Where pilferage is the norm it may well have implications for analysis of industrial unrest. It appears here that pilferage, in the actor's definition of his position, is perceived as a legitimate means of redressing an exploitive contractual situation. Considered in this light, pilferage can then be appreciated as having possible implications for working class consciousness. It is perhaps a device which, in part at least, expresses alienation in an alternative manner to more open industrial and political action. This may well be one reason why managements have been reluctant to take action to eradicate it – preferring instead, despite the cries of moralists, to devise limits to its growth.

At local levels consideration should be given to the effects of technology and work organization, as these influence control over access and support facilities. In some work situations, such as the St Johns docks, technology, in determining how work is organized, has meant that these are distributed within the work group – a fact which has important effects on solidarity and the emergence of a group morality. In other situations technology or managerial direction could mean one or both facilities may well be held by persons outside the work group, or not distributed at all but monopolized by one individual. In some cases control over access and support may well be used to buttress or detract from formal authority. In others absence of control can perhaps distort planned hierarchies and relativities while similar results can follow encapsulation of both facilities within individual roles.

It appears likely, therefore, that besides questions concerning morality and rule-making – processes upon which this inquiry has focused – questions concerning prestige, authority, and power at work might also better be understood if further detailed anthropological studies were made of the incidence and distribution of covert and illegitimate activities at work.

## *Notes*

1  I carried out fieldwork as Research Fellow of the Newfoundland Institute of Social and Economic Research whose support I gratefully acknowledge. The fieldwork was carried on between 1962 and 1964. I briefly returned in 1966 when the situation was much the same. By 1972, when I last returned, technical and other changes had changed the earlier situation. A wide variety of longshore informants read the draft of this article during the last visit and there were no objections to publication.

2  These include studies of restaurant and hotel workers (see Mars 1973). Fairground staff, seaside deck chair attendants, health service consultants, ice cream sellers, public corporation executives, driver salesmen, storemen, barmen, and supermarket cashiers.

3  For the classic description of shape-up hiring see Larrowe (1955).

4  This discussion does not apply to the new wave of cargo handling technology in docks – containers, lighters aboard ship (LASH), or side- and end-loading vessels.

5  Being able to recognize contents of a package by code marks on its outside. 'Each parcel, known as a bill of lading from the covering document of title, bears a separate mark; this is shown as a rule, on each case, bag or carton. This identifying mark is known as the main mark; often there are sub-marks that denote the shipper or the quality and size of the contents' (Oram 1965).

6  Due to the Union policy of 'not splitting the membership'.

7  As a general rule men try to take the whole of a case and to dispose of both contents and packaging, since an absent case is less likely to be noticed than one which has been tampered with. Sometimes though it is not possible to dispose of a whole case and inconspicuous entry is therefore necessary. In these cases nails are removed from wooden

228                        *Gerald Mars*

crates with sharp knives and are later carefully replaced. Razors are
used to slice imperceptible U shapes in cardboard containers.

8 A very different situation is found in Bell (1959) reporting on the then
situation in New York.

9 It was not always the case that skidsmen and truck drivers were not
integrated into the gang, or that they had relatively little part to play
in pilferage. In the forties and fifties when work was much more
plentiful in St John's than in the sixties and seventies, night work was
common. At night time 'good pickings' in one hold were occasionally
loaded from the dockside not into the warehouse but into an adjacent
hold. This operation required the coordination of skidsmen and truck
drivers from both gangs. In return for their help they would often be
allowed on board and into the hold.

10 See Gluckman's classic discussion of 'reasonable' role playing (Gluckman 1955).

## References

BELL, D. 1959. 'The Racket Ridden Longshoremen.' *Dissent* **VI** (Autumn):
417–29.

GLUCKMAN, M. 1955. *The Judicial Process Among the Barotse of Northern
Rhodesia.* Manchester: Manchester University Press.

LARROWE, C. P. 1955. *Shape Up and Hiring Hall.* Berkeley, Calif.:
University of California Press.

MARS, G. 1972. An Anthropological Study of Longshoremen and of
Industrial Relations in the Port of St John's, Newfoundland, Canada.
Ph.D. Thesis: London University.

—— 1973. Hotel Pilferage: A Case Study in Occupational Theft. In
M. Warner (ed.) *Sociology of the Workplace.* London: Allen & Unwin.

ORAM, R. B. 1965. *Cargo Handling and the Modern Port.* Oxford: Pergamon.

RADCLIFFE-BROWNE, A. R. 1952. *Structure and Function in Primitive
Society.* Chapters IV and V. London: Cohen & West.

# [12]

P. Colquhoun

## CHAP. VIII.

*The magnitude of the Plunder of Merchandize and Naval Stores on the River Thames.—The wonderful extent and value of the Floating Property, laden and unladen in the Port of London in the course of a year. —Reasons assigned for the rise and progress of the excessive Pillage which had so long afflicted the Trade of the River Thames.—The modes pursued in committing Depredations as the result of a regular System, which had been established through the medium of various classes of Criminal Delinquents, denominated—River Pirates—Night Plunderers— Light Horsemen—Heavy Horsemen—Game Watermen—Game Lightermen—Mudlarks—Game Officers of the Revenue—And Copemen, or Receivers of Stolen Property.—The devices practised by each Class in carrying on their criminal designs.—General Observations on the extent of the Plunder and number of Individuals implicated in this species of Criminality.—The effects of the Marine Police in checking these Depredations.—The advantages which have resulted to Trade and Revenue from the partial experiment which has been made.—The further benefits to be expected when, by apposite Legislative Regulations, the System of Protection is extended to the whole Trade of the River.—General Reflections arising from the Subject.*

THE

THE immense depredations committed on every species of Commercial Property in the River Thames, but particularly on West India produce, had long been felt as a grievance of the greatest magnitude; exceedingly hurtful to the Commerce and Revenue of the port of London, and deeply affecting the interest of the Colonial Planters, as well as every description of Merchants and Ship-Owners concerned in the Trade of the River Thames.

The subject of this Chapter will therefore be chiefly confined to a detail of the causes, which produced these extraordinary and extensive depredations, and the various means by which they were perpetrated; and also to the remedies which have been successfully applied since the publication of the preceding editions of this Work, for the purpose of reducing within bounds, and keeping in check, this enormous and growing evil; for certain it is, that previous to the establishment of the Marine Police System, in the Month of July 1798, the increase had been regular and progressive, while the easy manner in which this species of property was obtained, generated an accession of plunderers every year.

To those whose habits of life afford no opportunities of attending to subjects of this nature, the details which are now to be given will appear no less novel than extraordinary; and with respect to the extent of the mischief in some instances perhaps incredible.

credible. The West India Planters alone have esti-mated their losses by depredations upon the River and in the Warehouses at the enormous sum of 250,000*l.* a year. It cannot be unreasonable then to suppose, that the extent of the plunder on the other branches of Commerce, which form nearly 5-6th parts of the whole value of Imports and Ex-ports, could not be less than 250,000*l.* more, mak-ing an aggregate upon the whole of Half a Million sterling* !

Surprising as this may appear at first view, yet when, by a cool investigation of the subject, it comes to be measured by the scale of the astonishing Com-merce which centers in the port of London, (accord-ing to the annexed Abstract) and the vast extent of Floating Property moving constantly upon the River Thames, and the adjacent Wharfs and Quays sub-ject to depredations; when by calculation it is also found, that the whole amount of the aggregate plun-der, great and extensive as it appears to be, does not much exceed *three quarters per cent.* on the value of the whole property exposed to danger : the Reader will be reconciled to an estimate; which from the elucidations contained in this chapter, will ultimately appear by no means to be exaggerated.

* For a specific Estimate of the plunder on all branches of trade carried on to and from the port of London, see " A Trea-tise on the Commerce and Police of the River Thames, with a summary View of the Laws of Shipping and Navigation:" by the Author of this Work.

P 4 RECAPITULATION.

# A B S T R A C T

## OF THE *IMPORTS* INTO, AND THE *EXPORTS* FROM, THE *PORT OF LONDON.*

Made up from the Public Accounts for one year, ending the 5th day of January, 1798; but differing with regard to the value, from those accounts; in which the price is estimated on data established many years ago, when the articles of commerce imported and exported were not rated at above half the sum they now fetch, *exclusive* of duty.

It is therefore to be understood, that the following Estimate of Foreign Articles is made up according to the *present value*, as nearly as it has been possible to ascertain it, by the payment of the Convoy-duties, under the Act 38 Geo. 3, cap. 76.—It exhibits a very astonishing picture of the immense opulence and extent of the commerce of the Metropolis; and accounts in a very satisfactory manner for the vast resources of the Country, which have been manifested in so eminent a degree in the course of the present and former wars.

| From whence arrived. | Number of vessels including repeated voyages | Average Tonnage. | Value of Goods Imported. £ s. d. | Value of Goods Exported. £ s. d. | Total Value of Goods imported and exported. £ s. d. |
|---|---|---|---|---|---|
| East Indies | 53 | 41,456 | 6,544,402 10 2 | 3,957,905 5 1 | 10,502,307 15 3 |
| West Indies | 346 | 101,484 | 7,118,623 12 8 | 3,895,313 18 7 | 11,013,937 11 3 |
| British Continental Colonies | 68 | 13,936 | 290,894 4 10 | 1,347,250 1 7 | 1,638,144 6 5 |
| Africa and Cape of Good Hope | 17 | 4,336 | 82,370 15 0 | 449,077 19 3 | 531,446 15 1 |
| Southern Fishery | 29 | 7,461 | 230,689 3 2 | 54 16 4 | 250,743 19 6 |
| Greenland Fishery | 16 | 4,769 | 64,142 0 0 | 0 | 64,142 0 0 |
| United States of America | 140 | 32,213 | 1,517,386 2 8 | 3,893,864 12 9 | 5,416,250 15 5 |
| Mediterranean and Turkey | 72 | 14,757 | 390,794 19 10 | 118,914 3 7 | 509,709 3 5 |
| Spain | 121 | 16,509 | 776,686 12 2 | 171,073 4 6 | 947,759 17 8 |
| Portugal | 180 | 27,670 | 414,359 7 2 | 435,877 16 2 | 855,237 3 4 |
| France | 56 | 5,573 | 15,951 17 8 | 859,974 16 0 | 875,926 13 8 |
| Austrian Flanders | 66 | 5,104 | 21,027 8 2 | 118,064 2 2 | 139,091 5 4 |
| Holland | 329 | 19,166 | 673,241 17 4 | 1,538,120 3 6 | 2,211,362 0 10 |
| Germany | 235 | 37,647 | 2,658,011 8 2 | 8,014,260 3 0 | 10,672,271 11 2 |
| Prussia | 608 | 56,955 | 220,827 14 0 | 211,662 12 0 | 432,490 6 0 |
| Poland | 69 | 17,210 | 207,477 0 0 | 35,468 18 3 | 242,945 18 3 |
| Sweden | 109 | 14,252 | 152,707 0 0 | 169,293 18 4 | 322,001 5 2 |
| Denmark and Norway | 202 | 48,469 | 94,821 3 6 | 711,082 10 8 | 805,903 14 2 |
| Russia | 230 | 56,131 | 1,565,118 7 6 | 452,106 16 7 | 2,017,225 4 1 |
| Foreign Coasting { Guernsey, Jersey and Alderney (Including repeated Voyages) | 46 | 5,344 | 218,916 12 8 | 83,291 12 1 | 302,198 4 9 |
| Ireland | 276 | 32,824 | 1,878,971 7 | 659,922 14 1 | 2,538,894 1 3 |
| British Coasting* { Coal Trade | 3676 | 650,000 | 1,700,000 0 0 | 10,000 0 0 | 1,710,000 0 0 |
| English Coasting including Wales | 5316 | 500,000 | 3,900,000 0 0 | 2,200,000 0 0 | 6,100,000 0 0 |
| Scotch Coasting | 634 | 60,000 | 200,000 0 0 | 300,000 0 0 | 500,000 0 0 |
| | 12,444 | 1,779,326 | 30,957,421 8 2 | 20,640,568 4 6 | 60,597,989 12 8 |

\* No rule being established, whereby the British Coasting trade can be valued, the estimate here given is grounded on the supposition, that the value of each cargo must amount to a certain moderate sum.—The aggregate of the whole is believed to exceed the estimate considerably.

216 ON RIVER PLUNDER.

## RECAPITULATION.

|  | Ships and Vessels. | Tonnage |
|---|---|---|
| Foreign and Coasting Trade as stated in the foregoing Table - - - | 13,268 | 1,773,326 |
| Value of Merchandize imported - - | 30,957,421 8 2 | |
| Value of Merchandize exported - - | 29,640,568 4 6 | |

| | | |
|---|---|---|
| Total imported and exported | 60,597,989 12 8 | |
| To which add the Local Trade within the limits of the Port, in the Upper and Lower Thames, and the River Lea | 235,000 0 0 | |

*With a view to give the mind of the Reader a competent idea of the whole of the property upon the River Thames, which is exposed to hazard, the following estimate is added, viz.—*

1. Value of the Hull, Tackle, Apparel and Stores of 2144 British, and Coasting vessels, trading to the port of London, without including, as above, the repeated voyages - - - - - — 8,825,000 0 0

2. Value of the Hull, Tackle, and Stores of 3507 Lighters, Barges, Punts, Hoys, Sloops, &c. employed in the Trade of the Thames, River Lea, &c. — 350,000 0 0

3. Value of 3349 Wherries, Bumboats, and Police Boats employed on the River, &c. - - - - - - - - — 25,000 0 0

70,032,989 12 8

4. Value of Goods, including Coals, exposed in Craft and upon the Quays, to the risque of pillage on an average each day in the year: (Exclusive of the Public Arsenals, Ships of War, Gunboats, Transports, and Hoys, for conveying Navy, Victualling, and Ordnance Stores, nearly equal to five Millions more) — 235,000 0 0

General Total 70,267,989 12 8

Let

Let the mind only contemplate this proud view of the Commerce of a Single River, unparalleled in point of extent and magnitude in the whole world; where 13,444 ships and vessels discharge and receive in the course of a year above three *Millions of Packages*, many of which contain very valuable articles of merchandize, greatly exposed to depredations, not only from the criminal habits of many of the aquatic labourers and others who are employed, but from the temptations to plunder, arising from the confusion unavoidable in a crowded port, and the facilities afforded in the disposal of stolen property.—It will then be easily conceived, that the plunder must have been excessive, especially where from its analogy to smuggling, at least in the conceptions of those who are implicated; and from its gradual increase, the culprits seldom were restrained by a sense of the moral turpitude of the offence; and where for want of a *Marine Police* applicable to the object, no means existed whereby offenders could be detected on the River.*

The

* While every thing connected with the present state of Europe, and the whole Commercial world, appears favourable for the accomplishment of the aggrandisement of the port of London, by the establishment of Docks (already in part adopted by the Legislature) and by a general Warehousing System, there is no opinion more erroneous and delusive than that which supposes that arrangements of this kind will supercede the necessity of a Police for the protection of the trade, and for the preservation of the public peace within these extensive repositories.

In what manner are from two to three thousand labourers, who must be frequently employed at the same time within these Docks,

(and

The fact is, that the system of River depredations grew, and ramified as the Commerce of the Port of London advanced, until at length it assumed the different forms, and was conducted by the various classes of delinquents, whose nefarious practices are now to be explained under their respective heads.

1st. *River Pirates.*—This class was generally composed of the most desperate and depraved characters,

(and those too of a class that have been accustomed to plunder, and are not restrained by any sense of the turpitude of the action) to be over-awed and controlled, if no Police shall be conceived necessary?

The risk would be immense to commercial property and pillage, in spite of the gates, and every precaution which could be taken, would probably be as extensive as it has been from the Warehouses, or from his Majesty's Dock Yards, where the want of an appropriate Police has been the cause of many abuses.

Police as recently exemplified, is quite a new science in political œconomy, not yet perfectly understood; it operates as a restraint of the most powerful kind upon all delinquents who would be restrained by nothing else. To the system of vigilance which pervades the criminal actions of labourers upon the River, joined to the imminent danger of detection, is to be attributed the general success of the Marine Police, in preventing depredations.

Wherever a proper Police attaches, good order and security will prevail; where it does not, confusion, irregularity, outrages, and crimes must be expected; wherever great bodies of aquatic labourers are collected together, risk of danger from turbulent behaviour, will be greater in proportion to the number of depraved characters, who, from being collected in one spot, may hatch mischief, and carry it into effect much easier in Docks than on the River. A Police only can counteract this; and to the same preventive system will the commerce of the Port be indebted for securing both the Docks and the Pool againts Conflagration. In fine, under every circumstance where Property is exposed, a preventive Police must be resorted to, in order to be secure.

who

who followed aquatic pursuits. Their attention was principally directed to ships, vessels, and craft in the night, which appeared to be unprotected; and well authenticated instances of their audacity are recounted, which strongly prove the necessity of a vigorous and energetic Police. Among many other nefarious exploits performed by these miscreants, the following may suffice to shew to what extent their daring and impudent conduct carried them.

An American vessel lying at East-lane Tier was boarded in the night, while the Captain and crew were asleep, by a gang of River Pirates, who actually weighed the ship's anchor, and hoisted it into their boat with a complete new cable, with which they got clear off.—The Captain hearing a noise, came upon deck at the moment the villains had secured their booty, with which they actually rowed away in his presence, impudently telling him, they had taken away his anchor and cable, and bidding him good morning. Their resources afforded them means of immediate concealment. No Police then existed upon the River, and his property was never recovered.

A similar instance of atrocity occurred about the same time, where the bower anchor of a vessel from Guernsey was weighed, and, with the cable, plundered and carried off in the same manner.

Although only these two instances of extraordinary audacity are specified, others equally bold and daring could be adduced if the limits of this Work would admit of it. When vessels first arrive in the

2                                               river

river, particularly those from the West Indies, they are generally very much lumbered. Ships in this situation were considered as the harvest of the River Pirates, with whom it was a general practice to cut away bags of *Cotton, Cordage, Spars, Oars,* and other articles from the quarter of the vessels, and to get clear off, even in the day time as well as in the night. Before a Police existed upon the River all classes of aquatic labourers having been themselves more or less implicated in the same species of criminality generally connived at the delinquency of each other, and hence it followed, that few or none were detected while afloat, and the evil became so extensive.

It was frequently the practice of these River Pirates to go armed, and in sufficient force to resist, and even to act offensively if they met with opposition.— Their depredations were extensive among craft whereever valuable goods were to be found; but they diminished in number after the commencement of the war; and now since the establishment of the Marine Police they have almost totally disappeared.

On the return of peace, however, if a system of watchful energy is not maintained, these miscreants must be expected (as on former occasions on the termination of wars) to renew their iniquitous depredations in great force, as numbers of depraved characters may then be expected to be discharged from the Army and Navy.

2d. *Night Plunderers.*—These were composed chiefly of the most depraved class of watermen, who

associated

associated together in gangs of four. or five in number ; for the purpose of committing depredations on the cargoes of lighters and other craft employed in conveying goods to the quays and wharfs. Their practice was to associate themselves with one or more of the watchmen who were employed to guard these lighters while cargoes were on board, and by the connivance of these faithless guardians of the night, to convey away in lug boats every portable article of merchandize, to which, through this medium, they often had too easy access.

These corrupt watchmen did not always permit the lighters under their own charge to be pillaged.— Their general practice was, to point out to the leader of the gang those lighters that were without any guard, and lay near their own, and which, on this account, might be easily plundered. An hour was fixed on for effecting the object in view. The Receiver (generally a man of some property) was applied to, to be in readiness at a certain hour before day-light to warehouse the goods. A lug boat was seized on for the purpose. The articles were removed into it out of the lighter, and conveyed to a landing place nearest the warehouse of deposit. The watchmen in the streets leading to this warehouse were bribed to connive at the villainy, often under pretence that it was a smuggling transaction, and thus the object was effected.

In this precise manner was a quantity of ashes and hemp conveyed in 1798, to the house of an opulent Receiver.

Receiver. Several other cargoes of hemp, obtained in the same manner, were conveyed up the river, and afterwards carted in the day time to the repositories of the purchaser, till by the vigilance of the Police Boats, a detection took place, and the whole scene of mischief was laid open.

This species of depredation went to a great extent, and when it was considered that the very men who were appointed to guard property in this situation were themselves associates in the criminality, and participated in the profit arising from the booty; and that matters were so arranged as to secure the connivance of all those who were appointed to situations, with a view to detect and apprehend delinquents; it ceases to be a matter of wonder, that the plunder in this particular line was excessive.

In many instances where goods could not be plundered through the connivance of watchmen, it was no uncommon thing to cut lighters adrift, and to follow them to a situation calculated to elude discovery where the pillage commenced. In this manner have whole lighter loads even of coals been discharged at obscure landing places upon the river, and carted away during the night.

Even the article of Tallow from Russia, which, from the unwieldiness of the packages, appears little liable to be an object of plunder, has not escaped the notice of these offenders; large quantities have been stolen, and an instance has been stated to the Author, where a lighter loaded with this article was cut from a ship in the

the Pool, and found next morning with six large casks of tallow stolen, and two more broken open, and the chief part plundered and carried away. In short, while the river remained unprotected nothing escaped these marauders.

3d. *Light-Horsemen,* or Nightly Plunderers of West India ships.—This class of depredators for a long period of time had carried on their nefarious practices with impunity, and to an extent in point of value, that almost exceeds credibility; by which the West India planters and merchants sustained very serious and extensive losses.

The practice seems to have originated in a connection which was formed between the Mates of West India ships * and the criminal Receivers, residing near the river, who were accustomed to assail them under the pretence of purchasing what is called *sweepings,* or in other words, the spillings or drainings of sugars, which remained in the hold and between the decks after the cargo was discharged. These sweepings were claimed as a perquisite by a certain proportion of the Mates, contrary to the repeated and express rules established by the Committee of Merchants, who early saw the evils to which such indulgences would lead, and in vain attempted to prevent it. The connivance, however, of the Revenue officers became necessary to get these sweepings on

* It is not here meant to criminate all the Mates of ships in this trade; for a large proportion are known to be men worthy of the trust reposed in them.

shore,

shore, and the quantity of spillings were gradually increased year after year by fraudulent means, for the
purpose of satisfying the rapacity of all whose assistance and collusion was found necessary to obtain
the object in view.

The connection thus formed, and the necessary
facilities obtained, from the sale of sweepings, recourse
was at length had to the disposal of as much of the
cargo as could be obtained by a licence to nightly
plunderers, composed of Receivers, Coopers, Watermen, and Aquatic Labourers, who having made a
previous agreement with the Mate and Revenue
Officers, were permitted, on paying from thirty to
fifty guineas, to come on board in the night,—to open
as many hogsheads of sugar as were accessible,—and
to plunder without controul. For this purpose, a
certain number of bags dyed black, and which went
under the appellation of *Black Strap*, were provided.
—The Receivers, Coopers, Watermen, and Lumpers,
went on board at the appointed time, for all these
classes were necessary. The hogsheads of sugar and
packages of coffee, &c. were opened ; the black bags
were filled with the utmost expedition and carried to
the Receivers, and again returned to be refilled until
daylight, or the approach of it, stopped the pillage
for a few hours. On the succeeding night the depredations were again renewed ; and thus, on many
occasions, from fifteen to twenty hogsheads of sugar
and a large quantity of coffee, and also in some instances rum (which was removed by means of a small
                                        pump

pump called a Jigger, and filled into bladders with nozzels, were plundered in a single ship, in addition to the excessive depredations which were committed in the same ships by the Lumpers or labourers who were employed during the day in the discharge of the cargo.—Instances have been adduced, and judicially proved, of various specific ships having been plundered in an excessive degree in this manner; and it has been estimated upon credible authority, that previous to the establishment of the Marine Police, above one-fifth of the whole fleet suffered by nightly plunder.—The ships subject to this species of depredation were generally known from the characters of the Mates or Revenue Officers who were on board, and were denominated *Game Ships*, where the aquatic labourers, called Lumpers, would on every occasion agree to work without wages, and even solicit their employers to be preferred on these terms, trusting to a general licence to plunder for their remuneration.

This nefarious traffic had long been reduced to a regular system. The mode of negociation necessary to obtain all the requisite advantages for carrying into execution these iniquitous designs, was not only perfectly understood, but in most cases, where new Officers were to be practised upon, a plan of seduction was resorted to which seldom failed to succeed, when one or more of the old practitioners in this species of criminality happened to be stationed in the ship.—In this particular line of aquatic depredations (which certainly was the most mischievous,) scenes

Q                                    of

of iniquity have been developed, which, from their extent and magnitude, could not have been credited had they stood on any other foundation than that of regular judicial proofs.

4th.—*Heavy Horsemen*, otherwise denominated Lumpers of the most criminal class, who generally selected ships where plunder was most accessible, either from the criminal connivance of the Mates and Revenue Officers, in permitting nightly plunder, or from the carelessness or inattention of these Officers.

This class, many of whom occasionally assisted in the depredations committed during the night, were exceedingly audacious and depraved. They generally went on board of West India ships, furnished with habiliments made on purpose to conceal sugar, coffee, cocoa, pimento, ginger, and other articles, which they conveyed on shore in great quantities, by means of an under waistcoat, containing pockets all round, denominated a *Jemie;* and also by providing long bags, pouches, and socks, which were tied to their legs and thighs under their trowsers.

It is a well-established fact, which does not admit even of the shadow of a doubt, that these miscreants during the discharge of what they called a *Game Ship*, have been accustomed to divide from three to four guineas a piece every night from the produce of their plunder, independent of the hush-money paid to Officers and others, for conniving at their nefarious practices.

Long habituated to this species of depredation,
8                                              they

they became at length so audacious, that it was found extremely difficult to controul them where a disposition existed to protect the cargo from pillage, and where no seduction had taken place.—And indeed, so adroit had this class of Lumpers become, that no ship escaped plunder in a certain degree, wherever they were employed, in spite of the greatest vigilance and attention on the part of many of the shipmasters.

5th. *Game Watermen,* so denominated from the circumstance of their having been known to hang upon West India ships under discharge for the whole of the day, in readiness to receive and instantly convey on shore *bags of sugar, coffee,* and *other articles,* pillaged by the Lumpers and others in the progress of the delivery of the cargo, by which they acquired a considerable booty ; as they generally on such occasions were employed to dispose of the stolen articles, under pretence of their being a part of the private adventures of the crew, for which service they usually pocketed one moiety of the price obtained.—It was by such assistance that Mates, Boatswains, Carpenters, Seamen, and Ship Boys, have been seduced, and even taught to become plunderers and thieves, who would otherwise have remained honest and faithful to the trust reposed in them. Many of the watermen of this class were accustomed to live in a style of expence by no means warranted, from the fair earnings of honest industry in the line of their profession.—An instance has been known of an apprentice lad in this line having kept both a mistress

and a riding horse out of the profits of his delinquency.

6th. *Game Lightermen.*—This class, which is composed of the working, or Journeymen Lightermen,
who navigate the craft which convey West India produce and other merchandize from the ships to the
quays are, with some exceptions, extremely loose in
their morals, and are ever ready to forward depredations by the purchase or concealment of articles of
considerable value, until an opportunity offers of
conveying the property on shore. Many of these
Lightermen, previous to the establishment of the
Marine Police, were in the constant habit of concealing in the lockers of their lighters, *sugar, coffee,
pimento, ginger,* &c. which they received from Mates,
and other persons on board of West India ships.—
These lockers are generally secured by a padlock;
they are calculated to hold and conceal considerable
quantities of goods, whether stolen or smuggled,
which were seldom taken out until after the discharge
of the lighter, unless in certain instances where
skiffs attended them.—When completely unladen,
the practice has been to remove to the road where
empty craft usually lies a-breast of the Custom-house
quay, and then carry away the stolen or smuggled
articles—and it has not seldom happened that many
of these Lightermen have, under pretence of watch-
ing their own lighters while laden at the quays, or
in connivance with the Watchmen selected by themselves, actually plundered the goods under their
                                            charge

charge to a very considerable amount, without detection.

Nor does it appear that the nefarious practices of
these Lightermen have been confined to West Indian
produce alone.   Their criminal designs were directed
to almost every species of merchandize placed under
their charge ; and the tricks and devices to which
they were accustomed to resort,  clearly evinced that
their plans for obtaining pillage had long been syte-
matized, and that they seldom permitted any opportunity whereby they could profit by making free
with property under their charge to escape their attention.  As a proof that this assertion is well
grounded, the following authenticated case, among
others which could be detailed, is stated as an instance of the extreme rapacity of this class of men.—
A Canada merchant, who had been accustomed to
ship quantities of oil annually to the London market, finding (as indeed almost every merchant experiences) a constant and uniform deficiency in the
quantity landed, greatly exceeding what could arise
from common leekage, which his correspondents
were quite unable to explain ; having occasion to
visit London, was resolved to see his cargo landed
with his own eyes ; so as, if possible, to develope a
mystery heretofore inexplicable, and by which he had
regularly lost a considerable sum for several years.
Determined therefore to look sharp after his property,
he was in attendance at the wharf in anxious expectation of a lighter which had been laden with his oil

Q 3                                          on

on the preceding day ; and which, for reasons that he could not comprehend, did not get up for many hours after the usual time.

On her arrival at the wharf, the propietor was confounded to find the whole of his casks stowed in the lighter with their bungs downwards. Being convinced that this was the effect of design, he began now to discover one of the causes at least, of the great losses he had sustained ; he therefore attended the discharge of the lighter until the whole of the casks were removed, when he perceived a great quantity of oil leaked out, and in the hold of the vessel, which the Lightermen had the effrontery to insist was their perquisite. The proprietor ordered casks to be brought, and filled no less than nine of them with the oil that had thus leaked out. He then ordered the ceiling of the lighter to be pulled up, and found between her timbers as much as filled five casks more; thus recovering from a single lighter load of his property, no less than fourteen casks of oil, that, but for his attendance, would have been appropriated to the use of the Lightermen ; who, after attempting to rob him of so valuable a property, complained very bitterly of his ill usage in taking it from them.

7th. *Mud-Larks,* so called from their being accustomed to prowl about, at low water, under the quarters of West India ships ; (or at least that class which were denominated *Game,* these being mostly the objects of pillage ;) under pretence of grubbing in the mud for *old ropes, iron,* and *coals,* &c. but whose chief

chief object, when in such situations, was to receive
and conceal small bags of sugar, coffee, pimento,
ginger and other articles, and sometimes bladders
containing rum, which they conveyed to such houses
as they were directed, and for which services they
generally received a share of the booty.—These
auxiliaries in this species of pillage were considered
as the lowest cast of thieves; but from a general
knowledge of the Receivers in the vicinity, they frequently afforded considerable assistance to the Lumpers, Coopers, and others, who collected plunder in
the progress of the ships' delivery.

8th. *Revenue Officers.*—Notwithstanding the laudable severity of the Commissioners of his Majesty's
Customs and Excise, in making examples of their
inferior servants by immediate dismission, on proof
made of any offence, or even neglect of duty; a
certain class of these officers, who are denominated
*Game*, have found means to promote pillage to a very
extensive degree, not only in West India ships, but
also in ships from the East Indies, and in every ship
and vessel arriving and departing from the River
Thames, of which it is to be lamented, that too many
proofs have been adduced. This class of officers
generally make a point of at least having the appearance of being punctual and regular in their attendance upon their duty, and by never being found absent by their superior officers obtain preferences,
where such can be given, with respect to those par-

Q 4                              ticular

ticular ships which afford the best harvest, either from being under the charge of Mates or others, with whom they have had criminal transactions in former voyages, or from the cargo being of a nature calculated to afford a resource for plunder. They are also generally acquainted with the *Copemen* or Receivers, with whom and the other officers, after seducing the Mate, (if not already seduced) they negociate for the purchase of whatever can be plundered.

In those seasons of the year, when the crowded state of the port renders it necessary to have recourse to *extra* and *Glut Officers*, the general distress of this class of men, and the expectations most of them have formed of advantages by being placed on board ships of a certain description, render it an easy matter to seduce them ; and by such means had every obstruction been removed to the perpetration of these excessive robberies, in all their ramifications, which had so long afflicted the port of London.*

9th. *Scuffle*

---

* In the throng season of the year at least 900 inferior Custom-house officers, and about 300 Excisemen, are stationed on board of ships in the Port of London, besides 82 Custom-house watermen and 36 superior Officers who do duty on the River Thames. The fair allowance of the established Tide officers may be from 50*l*. to 55*l*. a year. The preferable Officers having 3*s*. 6*d*. a day only when employed, are supposed to receive wages for 2-3ds of the year ; while the extra Officers, who have only 3*s*. a day, are not supposed to be employed above half the year : and the Glutmen not more than two months in the throngest part of the season.

Men in such situations having a trust committed to them of great magnitude and importance, in the protection of a Revenue amount-

ing

9th. *Scuffle-Hunters*—so denominated probably from their resorting in numbers to the quays and wharfs where goods are discharging, under pretence of finding employment as labourers upon the landing places, and in the warehouses, and from the circumstance of *disputes* and *scuffles* arising about who should secure most plunder from broken packages. This class of men, who may fairly be considered as the very scum of society, frequently prowl about with long aprons, not so much with a view to obtain employment, as for the purpose of availing themselves of the confusion which the crowded state of the quays often exhibits, and the opportunity of obtaining plunder; in which object they have too frequently been successful, particularly when admitted into the warehouses as labourers, where they have found means to pilfer and carry away considerable quantities of sugar and other articles, in which they were not a little countenanced, by similar offences committed by journeymen coopers and others, who, under the colour of

ing to more than Seven Millions, and receiving wages inferior to common labourers with pecuniary pressures upon them, arising from the wants in many instances of large families, assailed on all hands by temptations to connive at evil practices, as they relate both to the Revenue and the Individual—What can be expected from them ?—Humanity, policy, and even justice pleads for an increase of salary, as the best means of preserving their morals and increasing the Revenue. Other Regulations through the medium of the Police System might be established, whereby their purity might be secured, and the Revenue eased of a considerable expence, by reducing the number employed at present, often in promoting mischievous instead of useful purposes.

sanctioned

sanctioned perquisites, abstract considerable quantities of sugar, thereby subjecting the proprietors to an accumulated loss : for, in addition to the first cost or price of the article, the duties which have been paid form no inconsiderable part of the ultimate value. It is only necessary to resort to the Journals of the House of Commons, and the Appendix to the Report of the Dock Committee in 1796, in order to be satisfied, that the plunder in the warehouses has been excessive. And if credit is to be given to the evidence then brought forward, and also to the affidavits of persons, who have worked for many years in the sugar warehouses, the loss sustained on an importation of 140,000* casks of sugar has not fallen much short of 100,000*l.* a year.†

\* Sugar and Rum imported into the Port of London, from the 25th of March 1789 to the 25th of March 1799 :—

| Islands. | | | Ships, | Casks, Sugar. | Casks, Rum. |
|---|---|---|---|---|---|
| Jamaica | - | - | 151 | 64,108 | 17,279 |
| Antigua | - | - | 14 | 5,258 | 715 |
| St. Kitt's | - | - | 14 | 6,137 | 755 |
| Barbadoes | - | - | 17 | 7,961 | 65 |
| Granadoes | - | - | 18 | 6,806 | 443 |
| Mountserat | - | - | 6 | 2,742 | 568 |
| Nevis | - | - | 4 | 1,867 | 418 |
| Dominica | - | - | 14 | 4,152 | 400 |
| St. Vincent | - | - | 26 | 10,147 | 908 |
| Tortola | - | - | 3 | 789 | 109 |
| Sundry Places, including captured Islands, &c. | | | 106 | 32,739 | 2,271 |
| | | | 373 | 142,760 | 23,931 |

10th *Copemen*

10th. *Copemen or Receivers of Stolen Commercial Property.*—This mischievous class of men may be considered as the chief movers and supporters of the extensive scene of iniquity which has been developed and explained in the preceding pages of this Chapter. They were heretofore extremely numerous, and divided into various classes.* Those denominated *Copemen* formed the junto of wholesale dealers, who were accustomed to visit ships on their arrival, for the purpose of entering into contract with such Revenue Officers or Mates as they had formerly known, or dealt with, and such others as they could by means of friendly officers seduce to their views.

Their negociations were carried on in a language and in terms peculiar to themselves; and commenced by settling the price of

*Sand,* by which, in their cant language, was meant *Sugar.*
*Beans* - - or - - *Coffee.*
*Peas* - - — - *Pimento* or *Pepper.*
*Vinegar* - - — *Rum* and *other Liquors.*
*Malt* - - — - - *Tea.*

It was their custom to afford assistance wherever such articles were to be procured, by providing *Black*

---

† Independant of the excessive pillage by the labourers in the Warehouses, which has been rendered but too evident from the detections of offenders since the establishment of the Marine Police, the samples alone, which on an average are said to amount to 12*lb.* per hhd. (instead of 1¼*lb.* per hhd. in conformity to the Regulations of the West India Merchants of the 12th of June 1789,) make a net aggregate of 1,470,000 pounds of sugar, which at 10*d.* per pound amount to 61,250*l.* a year!

* See the "Treatise on the Commerce and Police of the River Thames," for a particular account of these classes.

*Straps,*

*Straps, (i. e.* the long black bags already mentioned) to contain sugar, and calculated to stow easily in the bottom of boats without being discovered on account of the colour. They also procured bladders with wooden nozzels for the purpose of containing rum, brandy, geneva, and other liquors, and furnished boats to convey the plunder from the ships during the night.

Some of these Receivers had acquired considerable sums of money by their nefarious traffic, and were able to tempt and seduce those who would permit them to plunder the cargo, by administering to their wants by considerable advances of money which, however, rarely amounted to a moiety of the value of the goods obtained, and frequently not 1-4th part, particularly in the article of Coffee.

Other classes of Receivers purchased from the Lumpers, Coopers, &c. after the property was landed, and being generally engaged in business as small grocers or keepers of chandlers' shops, and old iron and junk warehouses, they were accustomed to protect it in its transit, from one criminal dealer to another, by means of false bills of parcels.

It would fill a volume to recount the various ramifications of this nefarious traffic, and the devices used to defeat Justice and elude the punishment of the Law.*

It

* For the purpose of defraying the expence of prosecutions for criminal offences upon the River Thames, and to raise a fund for suborning

It extended to almost every article imported into, and exported from the port of London. But the dealings in stolen West India produce were by far the most extensive; at the same time it appears from recent investigation, that the *East India Company* and the *Russian* and *American Merchants*, as well as the Importers of *Timber*, *Ashes*, *Furs*, *Skins*, *Oil*, *Provisions*, and *Corn*, were also considerable sufferers. The

suborning evidence, and employing counsel for higher crimes, and of paying the penalties under the Act of the 2d Geo. III. cap. 28. commonly called the Bumboat Act; there existed a club composed of *River Plunderers*, and *Lumpers, Coopers, Watermen,* and *Receivers*, (denominated *Light-Horsemen, Heavy-Horsemen,* and *Copes*), from the funds of which the Law expences and the penalties incurred by members of the fraternity were paid. By these iniquitous means not a few notorious offenders escaped justice, while those who were convicted of penalties for misdemeanors escaped the punishment of imprisonment, and being thus screened from justice, the culprits (previous to the establishment of the Marine Police System) returned to their evil practices without the least apprehension of any other inconvenience than the payment of a fine of 40s. defrayed by the Club. The New System, however, affording means of detection in the ships where the offences were committed: what were formerly misdemeanors are now treated as larcenies, which has operated most powerfully in breaking up this atrocious confederacy, and in defeating all the nefarious designs of the criminal delinquents of which it was formed, some of whom, although apparently common labourers, resided in handsome houses furnished in a very superior style for the rank in life of the occupiers.

As a proof, among many others, of the enormous extent of the River Plunder, the convictions for misdemeanors under the Act of the 2d Geo. III. cap. 28. from August 1792 to August 1799, exceeded *two thousand two hundred*; of which number about 2000 culprits paid the penalty; partly from their own resources, but chiefly, it is believed, from the funds of the club, amounting in all to about 4000l. in the course of seven years.

Coal

Coal Merchants have likewise sustained losses to a great amount annually, while every species of goods imported have been more or less subject to depredations.

Nor has the Export Trade on the River Thames been in any respect secured against the rapacity of this phalanx of plunderers. Many well-authenticated cases have recently been developed, which prove that Hamburgh vessels outward bound, have been plundered to a considerable amount,* particularly those which were laden with sugar, coffee, and other West India produce. Outward-bound ships to every part of the world have also been more or less objects of plunder, to the numerous herds of delinquents who were employed upon the River, aided by their associates in iniquity, the Receivers.

To enter *into particulars*, or to detail specific instances, would far exceed the limits prescribed for this branch of the general catalogue of delinquency exhibited in this Work. Suffice it to say, that the most satisfactory evidence can be adduced, that the system of depredation which had so long prevailed, and which had advanced with the growing Commerce of the Port, had pervaded every species of Merchan-

---

* A Shipmaster in the trade a few months since was compelled to pay 40l. for deficient sugars plundered by Lumpers and others, who assisted in lading his vessel, notwithstanding his utmost personal vigilance and attention while the sugars were taking on board. A single Marine Police Officer would have prevented this. The effect of their power in overawing delinquents, from the nature of the system and the discipline peculiar to the institution, is not to be conceived,

dize

dize laden or discharged, as well as the Tackle, Apparel and Stores of almost every ship and vessel arriving in, and departing from, the River Thames.

Nor can it be a matter of wonder, that such pervading mischiefs should have prevailed when it is known, that above 5000 individuals, employed in various stationary situations upon the River, have, with a very few exceptions, been nursed from early life in acts of delinquency of this nature.

In a group so extensive there are unquestionably many different shades of turpitude ; but certain it is, that long habit, and general example, had banished from the minds of the mass of the culprits implicated in these offences, that sense of the criminality of the action, which attaches to every other species of theft.

---

SUCH was the situation of things in the Port of London, in the month of July 1798, when the MARINE POLICE INSTITUTION, a wise and salutary measure of Government, arose from the meritorious exertions of the West India Merchants.

The object of this Establishment was to counteract these mischievous proceedings, and by salutary arrangements *in the Science of Police*, to prevent in future a repetition of those crimes which had so long contaminated the morals of the people, and operated as an evil of no small weight and magnitude on the Trade of the River Thames.

How

How far this System, *planned* and adapted to the exigencies of the case, and carried into effect by the Author of these pages, assisted by a very able and indefatigable Magistrate, and by many zealous and active Officers, has been productive of the benefits which were in contemplation, must be determined by an accurate examination of the state of delinquency, among the aquatic labourers and others, employed at present in ships and vessels in the River Thames; compared with what existed previous to this Establishment, as detailed in the preceding pages of this Chapter.

Although much yet remains to be done to prevent the renewal of those criminal proceedings, which have by great exertions been happily in many instances suppressed.—Although the Marine Police * has been unquestionably crippled by the want of those apposite *Legislative* Regulations, upon which its energy and utility, as a *permanent Establishment*, must in a great measure depend, yet the proofs of the advantages which have resulted from it, not only to the West India Trade † (for the protection of which it was originally

---

* For a particular account of this Institution, see the "Treatise on the Commerce and Police of the River Thames," already alluded to.

† With respect to the advantages which have resulted in the aggregate, to the West India Planters and Merchants, from this New Institution, it is impossible to form any decided opinion; but estimating

'originally instituted) but also to the whole Commerce and Navigation of the Port of London, are so decided and irrefragable, that specific details are unnecessary, especially since Deputations of the most respectable Merchants from the whole Commercial Body, sensible of the benefits derived from the system, have solicited the sanction of Government, for the purpose of

estimating the savings, on an average, at 28lbs. of sugar per hhd. (which is only one half of what the Committee of West India Merchants, in their Report to a General Meeting in 1798, supposed the plunderage might have been formerly) it appears, upon this data, that the gain to the Planters, Merchants, and the Revenue, on a very reduced estimate as to the actual importation, may be thus stated.—

|  | Saving to the Planters. | Saving to the Revenue. | TOTAL. |
|---|---|---|---|
| On 115,000 casks of sugar, at 28lbs. per cask  -  - | £.97,012 | £.25,150 | £.122,162 |
| 15,000 casks of rum, at three gallons each  -  - | 9,000 | 15,000 | 24,000 |
| Coffee, pimento, and other articles, suppose  -  - | 5,000 | 10,000 | 15,000 |
| Totals  - | £.111,012 | £.50.150 | £.161,162 |

If credit is to be given to the general and specific proofs of the depredations which took place before the establishment of the Marine Police, and to the numerous documents which demonstrate the saving of property, which has been the effect of this system of prevention, the above estimate will not appear to be over-rated. In an importation amounting to above £.8,000,000 sterling a-year, it is not too much to say that $1\frac{1}{2}$ per cent. on this sum may have been saved under a system of such extreme vigilance, where every class of depredators were defeated in their iniquitous designs, and deprived in a great measure of the powers they formerly possessed, of doing mischief. The probability is, that it has amounted to more, though the fact never can be accurately ascertained.

R                                        passing

242        ON RIVER PLUNDER.

passing a Bill to extend the design, so as to afford the
same protection to the general Trade of the Port,
which has been experienced by the West India Planters and Merchants; * and requesting to be permitted to defray the expence by an annual assessment upon the Trade.

It may only be necessary in this place to state, that
under all the disadvantages and difficulties attending
the execution of this design, it may truly be said
to have worked wonders in reforming the shock-
ing abuses which prevailed.—*The River Pirates do
not now exist in any shape.—The Nightly Plunderers,
denominated Light Horsemen, have not dared in a single
instance to pursue their criminal designs.—The Working Lumpers, denominated Heavy Horse, are no longer
to be found loaded with Plunder.*—Watermen are

* At a meeting of the Committee of the West India Merchants
appointed to manage the general concerns of the Trade, held on
the 4th of January 1799, It was

" RESOLVED,

" That this Committee are deeply impressed with a high sense
of the singular advantages, which appear to have resulted to the
Commerce of the Port of London in general, but particularly to the
West India Planters and Merchants, in the protection afforded
to their property by the exertions of *The Marine Police Institution*, as well as by the General System established for the prevention of pillage and plunder arising out of the measures for
detection pursued by the Magistrates presiding at the Marine
Police Office, by which, in the opinion of this Committee, great
and extensive benefits have also resulted to his Majesty's Revenue."

not now as *formerly to be recognized in clusters
hanging upon the bows and quarters of West India
ships under discharge to receive plunder.*—Lightermen,
*finding nothing to be procured by attending their craft,
are accustomed to desert them until the period when they
are completely laden.*—*Journeymen Coopers do not wil-
fully demolish casks and packages as heretofore, since no
advantage is to be reaped from the spillings of sugar,
coffee, or other articles.*—*The Mud-Larks find it no
longer an object to prowl about ships at low water while
under discharge, since the resource for that species of
iniquitous employment, which they were accustomed to
solicit, is no longer in existence.*—*The criminal class of
Revenue Officers, who had long profited (in many instances to an enormous extent) by the nefarious practices which prevailed, have not been able to suppress
their rage against the New Police, by the vigilance of
which they feel themselves deprived of the means of pro-
fiting by the system of plunder, which they had so perfectly organized, and which, in collusion with the Revenue Watermen, they were so well able to cover by
availing themselves of their official situations, on many
occasions, in protecting to the houses of the Receivers
articles which were both stolen and smuggled.*

By means of a Police Guard upon the Quays,
which forms a collateral branch of the General
System, *the Scuffle-hunters and Long-apron-men, who
were accustomed to prowl about for the purpose of
pillage, have in a great measure deserted the quays and
landing-places; while the Copemen and Receivers, find-*

R 2                              *ing*

*ing from several examples which have been made, that their former infamous pursuits cannot be continued without the most imminent hazard, have, in many instances, declined business, while not a few of these mischievous members of society have quitted their former residences, and disappeared.*

Such has been the effect of the remedy which has been applied towards the cure of the enormous evil of River Plunder.

It is not, however, to be understood that this System has entirely eradicated the pillage which prevailed, a circumstance not to be expected, since the design was partial and limited in its nature, and only intended for the protection of West India property, although very extensive benefits have unquestionably arisen from its collateral influence, and its energy, in terrifying thieves of every description upon the River, and diminishing their depredations, which, but for the dread of detection by means of the Police Boats in the night, would unquestionably have been committed.

But while it is readily admitted that amidst the opposite attractions of pleasure and pain, it is impossible to reduce the tumultuous activity of such a phalanx of individuals to absolute order and purity, who have been in many instances reared up in habits of delinquency. And while it is a vain hope to expect that crimes can be totally annihilated, where temptations assail the idle and the dissolute, and religion and morality, or even in many instances, the

6                                                            fear

ON RIVER PLUNDER.                    245

fear of punishment, does not operate as a restraint ;
—yet is it, notwithstanding, clear to demonstration,
from the effects produced by the limited experiment
which has been made, that the General Police for the
River Thames which is in contemplation, aided by
the apposite Legislative regulations which experience
has suggested to be necessary,* must in its operation,
under the guidance of an able and active Magis-
tracy, so far diminish and keep down the depredations which were committed, as to prove scarce a
drop in the bucket, when compared to the extensive
and enormous evils which it has been the object of
the promoters of this new System to suppress.

   Although in this arduous pursuit, the Author of
this work has experienced infinite difficulties and
discouragements, yet is he rewarded by the consciousness that he was engaged in an undertaking in
which the best interests of Society were involved :—
that independent of the pecuniary benefits derived
by the State, and the Proprietors, of Commercial
Property (which already have unquestionably been
very extensive,) he has been instrumental in bringing
forward a great preventive System, and by administering the Laws in conjunction with a very zealous,

   * For the specific provisions of *the Marine Police Bill*, see
the " Treatise on the Commerce Navigation Police of the River
Thames."—The object of this Bill is rather to prevent crimes
than to punish ; and where punishments on conviction are to be
inflicted, they are of a nature which, it is to be hoped, will
operate sufficiently as an example to diminish the evil, without
the exercise of any great degree of severity.

                          R 3                        able,

able, and humane magistrate,* in a manner rather calculated to *restrain* than to *punish*,† a multitude of individuals, together with a numerous offspring, are likely to be rendered useful members of the Body Politic, instead of nuisances in Society.—The advantages thus gained (although his labours have been in other respects gratuitous,) will abundantly compensate the *dangers*, the *toils* and the anxieties which have been experienced. In the accomplishment of this object, both the interests of *humanity* and *morality* have been in no small degree promoted: unquestionably, there cannot be a greater act of benevolence to mankind, in a course of *criminal delinquency*, than that which tends to *civilize their manners ;—to teach them obedience to the* Laws ;—*to screen themselves and their families from the evils and distress attendant on punishment, by preventing the commission of crimes ; and to lead them into the paths of honest industry, as the only means of securing that real comfort and happiness which a life of criminality, however productive of occasional supplies of money, can never bestow.*—If it shall be considered (as it certainly is) a glorious atchievement to subdue a powerful Army or Navy, and thereby secure the tranquillity of a State—is not the triumph in some degree

* John Harriott, Esq. the Resident Magistrate.

† So powerful was the effect of the preventive System, wherever it was permitted to be applied, that no instance has occurred in the course of more than fifteen months, since the Marine Police was established, of sufficient grounds for a criminal prosecution having taken place by the commission of any Larceny or Felony in ships or craft under the immediate protection of the Institution,

analogous,

analogous, where a numerous army of delinquents, carrying on a species of warfare no less noxious, if not equally hostile, shall not only be subdued by a mild and systematic direction of the powers of the Law; but that the conquered enemy shall be converted into an useful friend, adding strength instead of weakness to the Government of the country?

Such has been, at least, the result of the partial operations of the Marine Police; and such will unquestionably be the issue of the general measures which have been planned and arranged, when the *Key-stone* shall be finally laid to the fabric, by passing into a Law the Bill which has been prepared for the extension of this design to the protection of the whole trade of the port of London *.

* As a proof of the approbation of the whole body of the West India Planters at the General Meeting, not only of the System of the Marine Police, but also of the Bill which has been prepared to extend its influence to the general Trade of the River Thames, the following extracts are inserted:

*Extract from the Minutes of a Meeting of a Committee of the West India Planters and Merchants—London, June 7, 1799.*

" Resolved,

" That this Committee is fully convinced that considerable advantages have been derived from the institution of the Marine Police in checking the depredations on West India produce on board ships in the River Thames; and consequently approves of the Bill for constituting the said *Marine Police*, with powers enlarged and more effective, and on a more extended plan, provided the Act for that purpose be in the first instance limited to the duration of three years, and that the whole expence of the Institution does not exceed Ten Thousand Pounds annually."

248                ON RIVER PLUNDER.

*Extract from the Minutes of a General Meeting of the West
India Planters, held by public Advertisement at Wright's
Coffee-house, Soho-square, London, June 13, 1799.*

The Right Honourable Lord PENRHYN in the Chair.

" Resolved,

" That this Meeting confirms the Report of its Committee,
and approves of the project of a Bill for the purposes, and
within the limitations stated in that Report.

" Resolved,

" That Lord Penrhyn be requested to present to the Chan-
cellor of the Exchequer, the Report of a Committee of this
Meeting, on the subject of the Marine Police Institution, and
the Resolution of this meeting approving the said Report,

" Resolved,

" That Lord Penrhyn be requested to communicate the
thanks of this Meeting to Mr. Colquhoun for the zeal, ability,
and perseverance with which he has endeavoured to form an
effectual check to the system of depredation which prevailed on
the River Thames."

CHAP.

# [13]

## A HISTORICAL DOCUMENT OF RAMESSIDE AGE

### By T. ERIC PEET

IT is a singular and distressing fact that a very considerable proportion of the original written sources for Egyptian history and archaeology still remain unpublished. This is due firstly to the fewness of those capable of translating them, and secondly to a very natural scruple on the part of those who are. Egyptian texts are never easy, and many of the renderings are so uncertain that the scholarly translator hesitates to give them unless accompanied by the evidence necessary either to support them or to enable others to improve upon them. This means that every translation ought to be accompanied by a copy of the original, or if the document be in hieratic by a transcription into hieroglyphs—an expensive matter in these days—, and by a mass of critical notes which are not only very costly to print but which repel the average reader, and thus actually detract from the historical value of the publication. Such scruples as these, though honourable, are probably exaggerated, for their consequence is that masses of material of priceless value for Egyptian history lie locked up in philologists' notebooks instead of being available for general use.

It is with this consideration in mind that I venture to publish the translation contained in this article. The papyrus in question is both incomplete and difficult. A hieroglyphic transcription of so long a document is out of the question in this *Journal*, though I hope eventually to publish one elsewhere. Rossi's facsimile (see later) aided by the short critical notes here added will enable scholars to control some of my readings, and the non-philologist may rest assured that every translation about which there is the least doubt has been marked with a query.

It is customary for historians of Egypt to dismiss the Twentieth Dynasty in a few pages as a period of decline ending in complete disaster. The evidence generally produced for this view is, rightly enough, the tomb-robbery papyri of about the reign of Ramesses X, the apparent cessation of the exploitation of the turquoise mines of Sinai after Ramesses VI, and the melancholy story of Wenamūn dating from the reign of Ramesses XII. There are, however, other documents which tell the tale less dramatically perhaps but no less unmistakably. Many of these are to be found among the papyri of the Reale Museo di Antichità in Turin. The particular papyrus to which I wish to call attention is not unknown to scholars. It was published in bad facsimile by Pleyte and Rossi in their *Papyrus de Turin*, Pls. LI to LX, and a partial translation and commentary was published by Spiegelberg[1] in *Zeitschr. f. äg. Spr.*, 29, 73 ff. In the summer of 1923, while working on the papyri in Turin, I made a complete collation of this document[2]. It con-

---

[1] The more one works among the business and legal papyri of the New Empire the more one realizes how much this branch of our subject, like many other branches, owes to the industry and scholarship of Spiegelberg.

[2] I owe some readings, probably more than I realize, to a collation previously lent to me by Gardiner.

## A HISTORICAL DOCUMENT OF RAMESSIDE AGE 117

stitutes such a striking picture of the times during which it was compiled that it seems worth while to publish here a translation in full.

The papyrus, which as at present mounted measures 133 cm. by 41, is written on both sides in a large slanting script. The true verso, *i.e.* that side on which the main fibres of the papyrus run vertically and which was almost always filled last by an Egyptian scribe, but which is here to be read first, and treated as recto, contains two complete pages of writing[1]. It is clear, however, that there is at least one page lost in front of these for on the right-hand edge near the top are the ends of two lines of such a page. The first is illegible and the second gives " He said, It is true." There are three pages of writing on the true recto and as the third of these is a short page ending with a blank of at least 7 cm. below its last line it is probable that the papyrus ended here[2], and that this side must be regarded as the verso.

It is not easy to say what is the precise nature of our document. It has its closest parallel in Papyrus Salt 124 of the British Museum[3]. This last contains a series of charges against a single individual, and, as is clear from its concluding lines, it either constitutes or is a digest of the indictment actually laid before the Vizier. Our papyrus is a little different from this. Even in its damaged state it contains charges against at least three separate individuals. Moreover Section A is headed " The records[4] which are in the hands of the wᶜb-priest Penanket." The papyrus would therefore seem to have been a list of documents embodying charges against various persons. Each document, however, is described in some detail and this fact distinguishes the papyrus from Papyrus Ambras[5] at Vienna, which gives the barest description of a series of documents dealing with the famous tomb-robberies[6]. Presumably the documents described here formed part of the temple archives of Khnum, since they were in the hands of a priest, though this is not definitely stated. Whether the papyrus is a mere catalogue of these for record purposes, or whether, like Papyrus Salt, it was to be part of an actual indictment before the Vizier or other official we have no means of knowing.

As it now stands the papyrus consists of three distinct sections and the lost pages undoubtedly contained at least one other separate section, for recto page 1 begins a new section. This section (A), recto 1, 1 to recto 2, 17, is a list of records (*šḥꜣw*) stated in 1, 1 to

[1] This recto is covered with *papier végétal* and heavily varnished, so that it is at times intensely difficult to read.

[2] Pleyte-Rossi's plates should be read in the following order: 57–8 (recto 1), 59–60 (recto 2), 51–2 (verso 1), 53–4 (verso 2), 55–6 (verso 3). The fragment of the lost page at the beginning of the recto is given on Pl. 57, left.

In Pl. 60 the narrow vertical fragment near the left edge of the right-hand page must be transferred to the left edge of the left-hand page, where it fits on. The wide gaps marked by Rossi both before and after this fragment are to be closed. On the left-hand page the large fragment shown really consists of two fragments meeting on a vertical line continuing the left edge of the narrow vertical gap shown by Rossi in the three bottom lines. These two fragments should be separated by about a centimetre.

In Pl. 52, which gives the back of Pl. 60, corresponding modifications must of course be made. The vertical fragment under the number I fits on to the right-hand edge of the papyrus, the great gap in the centre is to be closed, and the large fragment on the right is to be divided into two separate pieces with about a centimetre between them as before.

[3] *Cf.* too page 4 of the verso of Pap. Harris A (B.M. 10053).     [4] *nꜣ šḥꜣw. Cf.* Abbott Pap., 6, 23.

[5] Von Bergmann, *Hieratische Texte*, 6; *Zeitschr. f. äg. Spr.*, 1876, 1 ff.

[6] *Cf.* also the Paris leather roll published by Virey and referred to in Spiegelberg, *Studien und Materialien*, 53.

118 T. ERIC PEET

be in the charge of the $w^cb$-priest of Khnum, Penanḳet. Seventeen charges of the most varied type have survived, and if they were all well founded the accused man must have been a surprising specimen of the ancient Egyptian "crook." His name is unfortunately lost to criminology, for he is referred to throughout as "this $w^cb$-priest" or more fully "this $w^cb$-priest of Khnum." His name must thus have occurred in the lost page which precedes recto 1.

The second section (B) begins with verso 1, 1 and ends at 1, 6, where it is separated from what follows by a blank space. The section is clearly incomplete at the beginning and something is therefore lost between recto 2 and verso 1, or in other words our papyrus is incomplete at both ends. The criminals, for they are plural, do not in what is left to us display that versatility in wickedness which distinguishes the priest of Khnum, for all the charges are those of theft.

The third section (C), verso 1, 7 to the end, began with a date which is unfortunately lost but which cannot have been earlier than Year 4 of Ramesses V. The first charge is one of enormous peculations extending over a period of 10 years against a boat's-captain, whose name would seem from verso 1, 9 and verso 2, 7–8 to have been Khnumnakht[1]. It was this man's duty to carry in his boat certain taxes payable in barley to Khnum at Elephantine. He conspired "with the scribes, the inspectors and the farmers" to convert to his own use almost the whole of the grain. From verso 2, 12 to the end we are dealing with a series of miscellaneous charges. On verso 3 these become so fragmentary that we cannot ascertain what part Khnumnakht himself played in some of them, but, as there is no gap between verso pages 2 and 3, the 3rd Person Singular of 3, 1 can refer to no one else. Here then is another master spirit of the Egyptian criminal world.

The theatre of the misdeeds of these various persons is clearly Elephantine, and more particularly the temple of Khnum there. The records in the first section are said to be in the charge of Penanḳet, an $w^cb$-priest of the temple.

It is greatly to be regretted that not enough of the document remains to show us before what court these numerous offences were tried, for tried they must have been. There appears to be no evidence to indicate whether all offences both religious and lay were dealt with by the same courts in Egypt or whether there existed anything of the nature of an ecclesiastical court. In Pap. Mayer A various priests, guilty of participation in the tomb-robberies, are tried by the same court as their lay fellows[2], and there seems no reason for supposing that a priest who broke the law in Egypt was treated differently from other men, despite the various exceptions which later history affords. At the same time it might not unreasonably have been imagined that offences of a strictly religious nature by priests would be tried by a special court. Such a court would of course have consisted wholly or mainly of priests, probably those of the temple where the offence was committed. Yet there is no example of any such court, and the one court known to us consisting entirely of priests tried a civil action concerning rights in property[3] leased to the temple.

On the other hand priests were certainly eligible for service in criminal and civil courts (ḳnbt)[4]. In the Abbott Papyrus the thieves are tried for tomb-robbery by a court (ḳnbt ꜥꜣt nt Nwt) of 8 members including a high-priest and prophet of Amūn[5]. In the inscription of

---

[1] This is not quite certain owing to the lacunae.
[2] Pap. Mayer A, 11, 5 and 13; also 12, 15 and 16.
[3] Pap. Berlin 3047; *Zeitschr. f. äg. Spr.*, 17 (1879), 71 ff.     [4] SPIEGELBERG, *Stud. u. Mat.*, 61–2.
[5] Pap. Abbott, 8, 3.

## A HISTORICAL DOCUMENT OF RAMESSIDE AGE          119

Mes[1] a priest of the litter (or whatever *w<sup>c</sup>b n knit* may mean) is sent out to investigate a division of lands, for he is a member (*śr*) of the court (*knbt*) which dealt with the case. Dr. Blackman points out to me the interesting but damaged passage in the great decree of Horemhab[2] where the priesthood appears to take a very large part in the newly reconstituted courts (*knbt*) of the country.

The fact is that our knowledge of Egyptian legal procedure is extremely scanty. Not more than a dozen cases are known to us in all, and those incompletely. The documents at our command date from various periods, and deal with cases of the most varied nature, and many more papyri will have to come to light if we are ever to succeed in reconstructing the judicial system in anything like its entirety[3].

M. Moret has tried to make out a case for the existence of *tribunaux ecclésiastiques* in the Ramesside era, enjoying not only considerable power and popularity but capable of being appealed to against the decisions of the ordinary courts[4]. This case is based purely on the identity of the Mes or Mesmen of the famous oracle stele from Abydos[5] with the defendant in the inscription of Mes, an identity which must be regarded as quite hypothetical. If we do not feel able to accept this equation the ecclesiastical courts resolve themselves at once into mere judgements by oracle such as that contained in the stele mentioned above, in the British Museum ostracon published along with a Berlin papyrus by Erman and in the papyrus under discussion[6]. Such judgements undoubtedly enjoyed considerable popularity, especially in small disputes concerning property and theft, and particularly in the Theban necropolis, but we shall need much more evidence before we can presume to elevate them into the dignity of ecclesiastical courts[7].

The papyrus, or at least that portion of it which remains, is not actually dated, but it is clear from verso 2, 12–14 that it was written not earlier than the fourth year (probably after the end of that year) of the king there entitled Pharaoh, who, as is clear from lines 5–6 of the same page, is the successor of Ramesses IV Ḥeḳma<sup>c</sup>rē<sup>c</sup> Setepenamūn, or in other words Ramesses V Userma<sup>c</sup>rē<sup>c</sup> Sekheperenrē<sup>c</sup>. Maspero has rightly pointed out that these same lines show that Ramesses IV ruled six years, for to Year 6 of this king (line 5) succeeds in the yearly series Year 1 of Pharaoh, *i.e.* of the reigning king Ramesses V. Spiegelberg has removed the possible objection that a year might have been skipped in this list by noting that in lines 12–14 below a yearly peculation of 100 *khar* (50 plus 50) is stated to amount to 1000 *khar* from Year 1 of Ramesses IV to Year 4 of Pharaoh, from which it is clear that the whole period covered is ten years, giving six years for the reign of Ramesses IV.

A further question is raised by these dates. Gardiner[8] and Sethe[9] have lately shown that in the New Empire, contrary to the custom both of earlier and of Ptolemaic times

---

[1] GARDINER, *Inscription of Mes*, pp. 12–13, nn. 8–9.      [2] BREASTED, *Ancient Records*, III, §§ 64–5.

[3] Spiegelberg long ago emphasized this (*Stud. u. Mat.*, 63) and pointed out the danger of assuming that the *knbt* were standing courts of law, and that their duties were solely legal and not administrative.

[4] *Comptes-rendus de l'Académie des Inscr. et Belles-Lettres*, 1917, 157 ff.

[5] *Annales du Service*, XVI, 161–73.

[6] Further to this subject see ERMAN, *Zwei Aktenstücke aus der thebanischen Gräberstadt*, in *Sitzungsber. der K. P. Akad. der Wiss., phil.-hist. Classe*, 1910 (XIX), 330 ff.

[7] At the same time they must have put great power in the hands of the priests, who either caused the god's image to nod its head by some mechanical device or, what is perhaps more likely, reported that the image, invisible to the suppliant, had or had not done so.

[8] *Journal*, V, 190.          [9] *Zeitschr. f. äg. Spr.*, 58, 39–42.

T. ERIC PEET

the regnal years of a king were reckoned from the date of his accession and not from the calendrical New Year's Day. Now in the list which runs from verso 1, line 13 (in this line restore Year 1 of Ramesses IV) to line 9 of verso 2 it is clear that the amount of grain annually due to the temple of Khnum was 700 *khar*. Thus a full amount was exacted in the last year, Year 6, of Ramesses IV, and yet unless this king died on the date of his accession this year must have been an incomplete year. Similarly this year is reckoned as a full year in the arithmetic of lines 13–14. Put briefly the difficulty is as follows. The papyrus seems to show that certain taxes or offerings made to the temple of Khnum were calculated yearly on the basis of the regnal years of the kings. When a change of reign took place the last year of the first king must in the nature of things have been incomplete, sometimes less sometimes more. And yet in the case before us the full amount of the dues is reckoned for this defective year. Unless it be that in the case before us the Year 6 of Ramesses IV was so nearly complete that it might without injustice be counted as complete the Egyptian taxpayer would seem to have had a cause of complaint which would have more than satisfied the grumbling propensities of his modern fellow-sufferer. Did Khnum then exact his full year's dues when the regnal year was only a month or six weeks in length? Surely not. Common sense forces us to suppose that a tax in kind, such as grain, would only be exacted once on each harvest. And does it not follow as a corollary that a very short last regnal year, more particularly one containing no harvest, may quite conceivably be omitted in a list such as that before us? In other words, though the last year of Ramesses IV *for taxation purposes* was Year 6, is it not possible that he actually began a Year 7 which, as it contained no harvest, was for these same purposes omitted? If this idea is correct such lists are to be used with caution for purposes of dating.

TRANSLATION.

*Section A.*

Recto, page 1.

(1) The documents which are in charge of[1] the priest Penanket called Sed of the temple of Khnum. (2) Charge concerning the black cow which is in his possession: it gave birth to five calves[2] of Mnevis, and he carried them off and appropriated them in the field. He parted with[3] them and he took them away to the south and he sold[4] them to the priests.

(3) Charge concerning the great calf of Mnevis which he had. He parted with it and he sold it to certain Nubians of the fortress of Bîgah and received its price from them.

(4) Charge concerning his going to Thebes and receiving certain documents.........[5], though Rēˤ did not suffer him to flourish for ever. He brought them to the south in order to lay them before Khnum, but he (the god?) refused to acknowledge them.

(5) Charge concerning his debauching the citizeness Metnemeh, daughter of Pasekhety: she was wife to the fisherman Dhoutemhab son of Pentaure.

---

[1] *r iwd*, "in charge of." *Cf.* Pap. Bol. 1094, 6, 7; Pap. Bibl. Nat. 197, III, ro. 4 and vs. 7.

[2] *kmꜣ* Spiegelberg refers to Pap. Harris I, 30, 3.

[3] *šˤd dt m.* Cf. *šˤd dt n*, Pap. Salt 124, ro., 1, 7, in a similar but damaged context.

[4] Read *iw·f dit·w m* ⬭ 𓊃 ×; Coptic ϣⲓⲛⲉ.

[5] *nhꜣw n mdꜣwt n* 𓏞. Reading very uncertain.

## A HISTORICAL DOCUMENT OF RAMESSIDE AGE　　　121

(6) Charge concerning his debauching Tebes the daughter of Shuiu : she was the wife of Ahauty.

(7) Charge concerning the theft by Yem (?) of a sacred-eye amulet in the temple of Khnum. He (the priest) appropriated it together with the man who stole it.

(8) Charge concerning the handing over to the temple (?) by the priest Bekenkhons of a chest[1] in which were two......... : he opened it and he took a.........from it. He laid them before Khnum and he (the god) acknowledged[2] them.

(9) Charge concerning his coming into the inside of the fortress when he had only done 7 (??) days of drinking natron[3]. Now the scribe of the treasury, Menthuherkhepesh (*sic*) made (10) this prophet of Khnum take an oath by the Ruler saying, I[4] will not let him enter with the god until he accomplish (?) his days of drinking natron[5]. But he disobeyed and entered (11) with the god when he had three days of drinking natron (still to do ?).

(12) Charge concerning the election by the vizier Neferronpe of the priest Bekenkhons to be prophet of Khnum, whereupon this priest said to the priest Nebun, We will introduce (?) another......priests[6] and (13) we will cause the god to cast out[7] the son of Pashuty. He was examined and it was found that he had actually said it. He was made to take an oath by the Ruler not to enter the temple. But he gave (14) a bribe[8] to this prophet, saying, Let me enter with the god, and this prophet took his bribe and let him enter with the god.

Recto, page 2.

(1) Charge concerning Pharaoh's sending the overseer of the treasury Menemtir to examine the treasury of the temple of Khnum, and this priest had stolen 60 *dꜣiw*-garments from the treasury of the temple of Khnum. And they made a search[9] for them (2) and found 24 of them in his possession, he having disposed of the rest.

(3) Charge concerning the cutting off by this priest of the ear of Wenemtuemnefer, son of Beksetyt, without the knowledge of Pharaoh.

(4) Charge concerning the sending by the vizier Neferronpe of the servant Pekhal the younger and the servant Panefunezemenkhons (?), saying, Bring (?) to me the divine father

---

[1] Very uncertain; *wꜥ ꜥfdt r ḥꜣt-nṯr* (?) *iw ...wt 2 imś*.

[2] ⬜ 𓅃 𓏤 𓀁 (sic). Read *ḥnn* (?) "to nod."

[3] Read 𓂝𓏤 𓈖 𓏤𓏤𓏤 (sic) 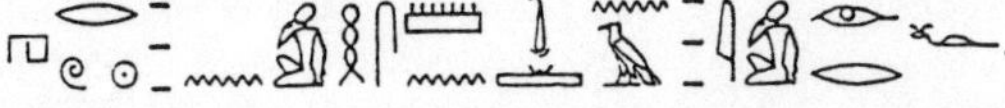 ⬜ 𓂝 �circle ... 𓈖 𓀁 𓉐 ... 𓏏 𓀘 - 𓉐 𓂋𓈖 . The *nꜣ* is most uncertain. 𓏤𓏤𓏤 is possible, but it is tempting to read an abnormal N.K. form of the numeral 7. If *iwn* is read we might supply *m nꜣi-n* after it, "while we were in our days of drinking natron," but this leaves *nꜣ* (?) *i·ir·f* unexplained.

[4] *I.e.* the prophet, whom the scribe of the treasury makes responsible.

[5] Read *i·ir·f mḥ* (?) *nꜣi·f hrw*.

[6] The text reads 𓊪𓏤𓏤 𓅓 𓈖𓏤𓏤 𓏤 𓊪𓏤 𓀘 ...... 𓉐 𓈖𓏤𓏤 𓀘𓏤𓏤 (three unintelligible vertical signs between 𓀘 and 𓉐 ). *bś* "to introduce" here seems to be III Inf. despite GARDINER, *Sinuhe*, 71. *Cf.* perhaps also SETHE, *Urk.*, IV, 82, 11.

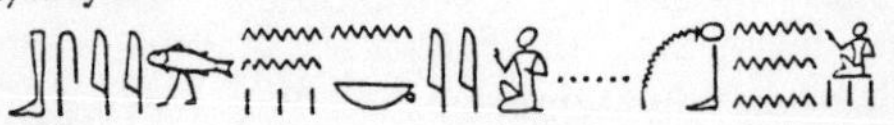

[7] *ḥꜣꜥ r bl. Cf.* Pap. Bol. 1094, 9, 9–10.

[8] *iwf dit* 𓊖 𓏤 𓂝𓏤𓈖 . Cf. *Rec. de Trav.*, 16, 60, but whether in the same sense I cannot determine.

[9] *ḥr ir iw·tw* [*ḥr*] *wḥꜣ·w*.

122                                    T. ERIC PEET

Kakhepesh. (5) Now the servants found me serving a monthly turn of the first *phyle*[1]. And so the servants left me alone, for they said, We(?)[2] will not take you during your month of service. So said they. But this priest gave them a *dʒiw*-garment of Upper Egyptian cloth and a chair and two spears(?) of copper, a tusk(?) of ivory of two cubits and a bundle of *tʼw*-vegetables[3] ......1000......fish, ......light beer, saying to them, Do not release him. [He spent?] 15 days without having............the great.........s and the chief............. (8) The ................................. (9) in the land of Egypt, for it is I who............the god(?)...... he caused them(?) to let [me?] go.............

(10) Charge concerning the leaving by Prome............of the house of Bek.........the mother...the(?)......saying to him......(11) he blinded[4] Beksetyt her daughter likewise, and they remain blind today.

(12) Charge concerning the quarrel which this priest had with the herdsman Pakamen of the temple (of Khnum?) when he answered and said to him................... (And when) (13) three months had passed Zaza died(?)[5]............he having said it[6]......

(14) Charge concerning their handing over 20 oxen to this priest in Year 1 of King Ḥekmaᶜrēᶜ Setepenamūn the great [god]. They seized(?) the oxen in his possession......... .........(15) he brought them from above(?)...he gave the oxen......he having given [them to?] the chief......also......[7].

(16) Charge concerning the giving by the priest Penanḳet of 20 *deben* of copper and three *dʒiw*-garments of Upper Egyptian cloth to this priest [in order that he might deny?] every charge[8] which was made.............

(17) Charge concerning this priest's standing up in front of this god [and saying] if he would make a good man............to thee[9]. So said he to him as he stood.......

*Section B.*

Verso, page 1.

(1) Charge concerning their stealing the large............(copper) belonging to the boat of Khnum and making away with it.

(2) [Charge concerning] their stealing 10 *rd*-garments of coloured cloth, total 15, from the temple of Anḳet Mistress of Aṣwân. The scribe of the treasury Menthuherkhepeshef who was acting as mayor of Elephantine examined them and found these in their possession, (3) they having given them to Amentekh, a workman of the Place of Truth, and having received their price. And this prince took a bribe from them and let them go.

(4) [Charge concerning] their opening a storehouse of the temple of Khnum which was under the seal of the inspectors of the granary who inspect for the temple of Khnum(?) and stealing 180(?) *khar* of barley from it.

---

[1] *iwi ᶜḥᶜ·kwi ibd n* 𓏤𓏥 (so Gardiner).

[2] *iw·w* in error for *iw·n*.          [3] *tʼw.* Cf. Pap. Harris I, 65*a*, 7–8 and 74, 5–6.

[4] *kʒmn* transitively. Cf. Pap. Tur. Judic. 5, 5.          [5] *pḥ pt* (possibly *pḥ r pt*).

[6] Rossi's facsimile (Pl. 60) is fairly accurate. *iw bn wšbt tʒi dit idd št pʒ...iw i·ir·f dd·w.* But what is the grammar of this?

[7] See Rossi's facsimile Pl. 60. The line runs: *iw·f int·w m ḥrw wnn i·ir·f dit nʒ iḥw m mšbw iw i·ir·f dit...pʒ* ⬛𓊪 𓆙𓏤 ......... | .........

[8] *wbʒt* (? for *wšbt*) *nb nti iw·tw dd·w.* For *wšbt,* a charge, *cf.* Pap. Abbott 6, 11.

[9] *ir iw·f irt wᶜ nfr n rmt...iri·w* (or *iri·f*?) *nk.*

A HISTORICAL DOCUMENT OF RAMESSIDE AGE　　　123

(5) [Charge concerning] the opening............Khnum (?)............stealing *rd*-garments of Upper Egyptian cloth. And the prophet found them in their possession and took them but did nothing to them.

(6) [Charge concerning]............a......full of the garments of the divine fathers and the priests in which they [carry] the god. They [were] found in their possession.

### Section C.

(7) [Year]......[under the majesty of the King of Upper and Lower Egypt]............life, health and prosperity, the Great God. ⟨The⟩ farmers...............the grain in order to give their 700 *khar* of barley to Khnum, Lord of Elephantine, here in the southern district. They brought them by boat (8)..................Elephantine. They were carried by boat, and they [brought?] them, and unloaded into the granary of the god and they were received for him every year. Now in Year 28 of (9) [King]...............this boat's-captain, he died. Now............, who was prophet of the temple of Khnum, brought the merchant·.....................Khnumnakht: he made him (10)............barley here in the northern district and he began to transport it by boat. Now in Year 1 of the King of Upper Egypt Ḥekmaᶜrēᶜ Setepenamūn, life, health and prosperity, the Great God, he made away with much of the barley. Now this boat's-captain (11)............nakht(??) 140 deben belonging to the treasury(?) of Khnum, ............making 7 deben of gold. The gold was not in the treasury of the temple of Khnum, and what he had appropriated of the barley was not in the granary[1] of Khnum, he having stolen (12)............Khnum. (a blank here) The six(?) rowers(?) of the crew of the boat of Khnum: they were with him in his.............

(13) [Year 1 of King Ḥekmaᶜrēᶜ Setepenamūn] received (?) at Elephantine by the hand of the boat's-captain......100 *khar*; remainder 600.

Verso, page 2.

(1) Year 2 of King Ḥ., life, prosperity and health, the Great God, 130 *khar*; remainder 570 *khar*.

(2) Year 3 of King Ḥ., life, prosperity and health, the Great God, 700 *khar*; he brought none of them into the granary.

(3) Year 4 of King Ḥ. etc. 700 *khar*: arrived in the boat of (?) the Staff, by the hand of the sailor Panekhtta 20 *khar*; remainder 680 *khar*.

(4) Year 5 of King Ḥ. etc. Received for the divine offerings of the Staff (?) of Khnum 20 *khar*; remainder 680 *khar*.

(5) Year 6 of King Ḥ. etc. 700 *khar*: he did not deliver them.

(6) Year 1 of Pharaoh, life, health and prosperity, 700 *khar*; he did not deliver them.

(7) Year 2 of Pharaoh, life, prosperity and health, arrived by the hand of the boat's-captain Khnumnakht 186 *khar*; remainder 514 *khar*.

(8) Year 3 of Pharaoh, life, prosperity and health, 700 *khar*. Arrived by the hand of this boat's-captain 120 *khar*; remainder 580.

(9) Total: barley of the temple of Khnum, Lord of Elephantine, which this boat's-captain had conspired with the scribes, the inspectors and the land-workers (11) of the temple of Khnum to purloin and appropriate to their own use, 5004 (*sic*) *khar*.

(10) (A note crowded in between ll. 9 and 11.) Now Khnumnakht(?)..................take his barley: he lives on the top of the hill: received(?) from him barley(???).

[1] *ḥr pšỉ·f wg m nš ỉt bn št m tš šnwt.*

124                                T. ERIC PEET

(12) Charge concerning the exaction by this boat's-captain of the temple of Khnum
of taxes[1]; an assessment(?) of 50 *khar* from (??) Rome, son of Penanḳet, and an assess-
ment(?) of 50 *khar* from (??) Paukhed, son of Pathewemabu, total 2, making 100 *khar* from
Year 1 of King Ḥeḳmaᶜrēᶜ Setepenamūn, life, prosperity and health, the Great God, up to
Year 4 of Pharaoh, making 1000 *khar*: he appropriated them to his own use and brought
none of them into the temple of Khnum.

(15) Charge concerning the burning by this boat's-captain of the temple of Khnum of
a boat belonging to the temple of Khnum together with its spars and its rigging. (16) But
he gave a bribe to the inspectors of the temple of Khnum and they made no report about
it. He has not (*sic*)[2] up to this day.

Verso, page 3.

(1) Charge concerning his procuring abortion for the citizeness Tarep[yt]............

(2) Charge concerning the giving by Panekhtta, a sailor of the Staffs of Khnum,......
............: he gave a bribe to the inspectors (3) and they never reported it.......

(4) Charge concerning the debauching by this sailor Panekhtta............[of X], a land-
worker of the temple of Khnum, Lord of Elephantine who is in the city of Pa..........

(6) Charge concerning the opening by the *wᶜb*-priest Payiri(?) of this............(7) and
he did it in great haste.............

(8) Charge concerning the sending by the divine father Dhouthotpe of the temple of
Month,............[3] (9) who was doing the duties of the post of divine father of the temple
of Khnum, of a (?)..............(10) letter by their hand for the scribe of the temple
Dhoutemhab. And they caused to send...............(11) caused their hides to come forth
on.............

COMMENTARY.

*Section A.*

Charges against "this *wᶜb*-priest."

The first two charges, recto 1, 1–3, deal with certain Mnevis-calves. The crime consists
in his selling these, and the simple explanation may be that they were not his to sell. But
there is another possible explanation. The Mnevis-bull, the sacred bull of Heliopolis, in
which Rēᶜ was incarnate, would seem, like the Apis, to have possessed a *ḥarīm* of cows;
and that not only in his Heliopolite home but also, to judge by our papyrus, at Elephantine, and doubtless elsewhere (see BLACKMAN, *Rock Tombs of Meir*, II, 25–7). From the
male offspring of the Mnevis and these sacred cows the new Mnevis would eventually be
chosen, and for this reason they were not to be sold or parted with.

The charge of l. 4 is obscure owing to the difficulty of the reading. Spiegelberg has
however pointed out the parallel with Pap. Rollin, ll. 2–3, and it is tempting to suppose
that the documents in question were, like those of Pap. Lee and Rollin, to be used for

---

[1] Rossi is accurate. Spiegelberg's ⟨hieroglyphs⟩ is tempting after *šdi* (to levy a tax) and perhaps
right, though the form of ⟨hieroglyph⟩ would be most abnormal. The obvious reading would be ⟨hieroglyphs⟩.

[2] *bn šw šśᶜ pȝ hrw.* Omit *bn šw* or suppose a verb lost after it.

[3] Perhaps nothing lost.

## A HISTORICAL DOCUMENT OF RAMESSIDE AGE          125

magical purposes. Or were they perhaps forged documents such as those referred to in the inscription of Mes, giving him rights which he really did not possess? In any case he laid these documents before Khnum with the evident intention of getting the god to approve either his ownership of them or his action in getting them[1]. The approval of the god was to be shown in the usual way by nodding the head (*hnn*).

Line 7 contains a charge of theft and 8 is very similar, though the exact wording is uncertain. On this occasion the god seems to have given a favourable response.

The lines that follow, 9-14, contain one of the most interesting points in the papyrus. The general sense is certain, and the priest's crime consisted in taking part in divine service and carrying the image before he had properly purified himself by washing the mouth with natron for the prescribed number of days[2]. Dr. Blackman tells me that he is aware of no evidence for fixing the number of days required for purification either by natron or by any other means[3]. If our reading of the passage is correct the period was an Egyptian "week" of ten days.

The fortress is doubtless that of Elephantine, within which the temple of Khnum lay. The interference of the scribe of the treasury Menthuherkhepeshef is explained by verso 1, 2 where we learn that this man was acting as mayor of Elephantine. It must have been in virtue of his holding this office that a purely religious question was referred to him, a layman.

Lines 12-14 are difficult owing to obscurities of reading. The vizier Neferronpe had appointed a certain Bekenkhons as a prophet, and the criminal priest in some way takes advantage of this to get rid of another *w^cb*-priest called merely the child of Pashuty, whom presumably he dislikes. The wording seems to show that this was to be done by means of an oracle. The plot is exposed and the ringleader excommunicated, but he manages to re-enter the temple service by bribing the newly appointed Bekenkhons.

The vizier Neferronpe was already known from ostraca[4] dating from the reign of Ramesses IV. For the election of *w^cb*-priests by the Vizier compare Pap. Bologna 1094, 5, 2-3[5].

The next charge, recto 2, 1, contains one point of interest, the sending of an overseer of the treasury to examine the treasury of the temple of Khnum. It is clear from this that the Pharaoh still had control of the temples in the reign to which this refers. Compare, for an earlier example, the famous Coptos decree of Nubkheperurē^c Antef where a scribe of the divine treasure of Amūn is sent to enquire into an offence, probably treason, in the temple of Min[6].

From the next charge, 2, 3, it would seem a legitimate deduction that the Pharaoh alone might order the cutting off of nose and ears.

Lines 4-9 contain an interesting charge. The vizier Neferronpe sends two messengers to summon to his presence a certain divine father Ḳakhepesh, who, judging by the use of

---

[1] To the documents quoted by ERMAN, *op. cit.*, for these oracular responses concerning the ownership of property add an important unpublished papyrus in the British Museum dealing with an oracle of Amūn.

[2] BLACKMAN, article *Purification (Egyptian)*, in *Hastings' Dictionary of Religion and Ethics*, § v, 7.

[3] He quotes, however, the difficult passage MARIETTE, *Dendera*, IV, Pl. 44c, where the mourners personifying Isis and Nephthys in the annual re-enactment of the embalmment of Osiris are purified "four times, seven days by seven days." Does this mean 28 days in all?

[4] DARESSY, *Ostraca*, 25033 etc.; WEIL, *Die Veziere des Pharaonenreiches*, § 40.

[5] For the election of priests in general see BLACKMAN, article *Priest, Priesthood (Egyptian)*, in *op. cit.*, § XII.                                              [6] PETRIE, *Koptos*, Pl. VIII.

126                          T. ERIC PEET

the first person singular in what follows, must be the writer of this papyrus, unless the
scribe has inadvertently quoted from his evidence without turning it into Oratio Obliqua.
Now the priesthood of every temple was divided into four watches (*šȝw*), each of which
served a month in turn[1], and the messengers, finding that Ḳakhepesh's watch was then in
service, decided to wait until this service should be completed. The criminal, however, who
for some reason unexplained was anxious to get rid of Ḳakhepesh, attempted to bribe the
messengers, but the result is obscured by the fragmentary state of the text at this point.
We do not know the reason of the Vizier's summons, but since the messengers of this great
official were content to wait for at least 15 days before carrying out his command we may
safely infer that a very considerable sanctity surrounded a priest during his month of
service.

The charge of ll. 10–11 is partly obscured by lacunae, and from there the difficulties
become more and more severe until we reach the end of the page.

### Section B.

#### Charges against certain unknown persons.

This section, verso 1, 1–6, is the least interesting of the three. It deals with cases of
vulgar theft, and the only matter of importance is the corruptibility of Menthuherkhepeshef, a scribe of the treasury, who was acting as prince of Elephantine.

### Section C.

This section began with a year-date in the reign of a deceased Pharaoh, of which only
the words "the Great God" remain[2]. The section describes the conditions under which the
thefts which follow were committed. If I understand the passage rightly, despite the lacunae,
the situation is as follows. The temple of Khnum at Elephantine owned some corn-land in
the "northern district," and the farmers of this land, referred to in verso 2 line 9 as
"farmers of the temple of Khnum," held their land in consideration of an annual tax to the
temple, amounting in all to 700 *khar* of barley. This barley was collected and carried by
river to Elephantine by a certain boat's-captain who died in Year 28 of Ramesses III.
Thereupon a prophet of the temple, whose name is lost, replaced him by a certain
Khnumnakht[3]. Presumably this man remained honest for the few remaining years of
Ramesses III, but in Year 1 of his successor Ramesses IV he began to purloin large
quantities of the barley with the connivance, as we see from verso 2, 9, of the "scribes,
inspectors and farmers of the temple of Khnum." If my transcription of l. 12 is correct,
other members of the boat of Khnum were also involved. Owing to the lacunae in l. 11 it
is impossible to seize the bearing of the reference to 140 *deben* of gold.

There follows a list of the defalcations in each year up to Year 3 of Pharaoh, *i.e.*
Ramesses V. The total, 5004 *khar*, is incorrect; it should be 5724. The common error of
taking a 60-sign in hieratic for an 80 may account for the 20, and the 700 is perhaps to be
explained by the fact, obvious on the original, that the scribe first missed out Year 1 of
Ramesses IV and crowded it in afterwards. As, however, totals in Egyptian account papyri
are frequently wrong, it is doubtful whether this attempt at justification is worth making.

---

[1] BLACKMAN, article *Priest, Priesthood (Egyptian)*, in *op. cit.*, § VIII, 3a.
[2] At this period the dead Pharaoh is "the Great God" and the reigning Pharaoh "the Good God."
[3] See, however, p. 118, n. 1.

## A HISTORICAL DOCUMENT OF RAMESSIDE AGE          127

The only other point of interest in this part of the papyrus is the reference to the Staff of Khnum. In verso 2, 3 we have "the boat of the Staff," in l. 4 is a reference to the "divine offerings of the Staff of Khnum," and in verso 3, 2 there is a "sailor of the Staffs of Khnum." The question of the staff of the deity has been discussed by Spiegelberg[1], who points out that we hear of the Staff of the following gods, Thoth, Hathor, Horus and Khons[2], and is inclined to think, judging from representations of such staffs on the walls of the Denderah temple, that they are to be regarded as fetishes of the deity. Each deity, he adds, could manifest himself in a staff, and thus the god became identified with the staff. The references to the Staff of Khnum in this papyrus tell us nothing more as to the nature of the conception, except that it was sometimes regarded as plural (unless this be a mere scribe's error), that it possessed its own boat on the Nile and that divine offerings were made to it.

The exact nature of the further charge in ll. 12–14 is difficult to perceive. All that is clear is that the boat's-captain diverted to his own use 100 *khar* per annum of some commodity presumably barley[3] which formed the contribution to the temple of two persons, Rome and Paukhed.

The charge of ll. 15–16 explains itself. Here the inspectors of the temple are definitely accused of venality.

The charges of verso 3 are of a varied nature and are obscured by lacunae. In l. 1 we have a charge against the boat's-captain, but the two charges which follow concern the sailor Panekhtta, unless the lacunae mislead us. Of the rest not enough remains to enable an opinion to be formed. The fact revealed in ll. 8–9 that a divine father of the temple of Month could do the duties of divine father in the temple of Khnum is not without interest.

The whole papyrus forms a vivid picture of the venality of the state officials and of the power and the corruption of the priesthood. Small wonder that when at last the priests overthrew the monarchy they proved incapable of governing the country in its place.

---

[1] *Rec. de Trav.*, 25, 184 ff.                [2] Add Amūn (Pap. Turin P. R. xxxii, 8).
[3] See, however, p. 124, n. 1.

# [14]

# deviance in the fast-food restaurant: correlates of employee theft, altruism, and counterproductivity

**Richard C. Hollinger**
*University of Florida, Gainesville*

**Karen B. Slora and William Terris**
*SRA/London House, Rosemont, IL*

Existing research suggests that employee deviance is highest in occupational settings that rely heavily on "marginal" workers—especially those who are young with little tenure—who believe that they are treated unfairly by their employers. As a test of this proposition, an anonymous survey was conducted among a two-company national sample of 341 fast-food restaurant workers. Three fifths of the respondents reported some level of personal involvement in theft of company property during the previous 6 months. In addition, more than one third were involved in "altruistic" forms of property deviance. Moreover, four fifths of the respondents reported involvement in counterproductive activities against the organization. Contrary to expectations, a slightly different explanatory solution emerged for each of the three forms of employee deviance. Personal property deviance was principally a function of age and perceived employer unfairness—both interacting with tenure. Involvement in altruistic property deviance was solely a function of age—engaged in almost exclusively by employees younger than 21 years. Production deviance,

An earlier version of this article was presented at the annual meeting of the American Society of Criminology, November 9, 1989 in Reno, Nevada. The authors recognize the efforts of Dr. Mike Boye of SRA/London House and Dr. Jane Halpert of the DePaul University Center for Industrial and Organizational Psychology for their assistance in the coordination of data-collection and analysis preparation.

alternatively, was a by-product of perceived
employer unfairness regardless of age or tenure
with the company. In sum, these findings suggest
that employee deviance may not be as much a
unidimensional phenomenon as was previously
believed.

Behavior in formal organizations is regulated by rules—both
the formal guidelines promulgated by management and the
informal norms established by the work group. Often the informally established norms observed by the workers are not
consistent with the formal rules of the bureaucracy. The resultant rule-breaking behavior has been characterized as employee deviance. Employee deviance includes both "acts by
employees against the property of the organization and the
violations of the norms regulating acceptable levels of production" (Hollinger and Clark 1983a, p. 9). Two interrelated
but largely separate bodies of scholarly research on employee
deviance have accumulated over the years: One group of
studies examined criminal acts against the property of the organization such as pilferage, theft, embezzlement, and sabotage (e.g., Altheide, Adler, Adler, and Altheide 1978; Cressey
1953; Ditton 1977a, 1977b; Franklin 1975; Henry 1978a, 1978b;
Hollinger and Clark 1982, 1983a; Horning 1970; Mars 1973,
1974, 1982; Robin 1969, 1970; Slora 1989; Taylor and Walton
1971). Another group of studies focused on other nonlarce-
nous forms of production-related deviance, such as absenteeism, sick leave abuse, tardiness, and slow and sloppy performance (e.g., Bensman and Gerver 1963; Gouldner 1964;
Harper and Emmert 1963; Roy 1952, 1959).
    These two literatures generally agree that involvement in
both forms of employee deviance is dependent on the characteristics of the worker employed, the normative integration of
their work group, and perceived levels of employer unfairness
(Hollinger 1989, p. 34). More specifically, younger employees
with little tenure in the organization who believe that their
employers treat them unfairly have been shown to be the
most highly involved in various acts of deviance against their
employers, especially property deviance and theft. In a review
of the employee theft literature, Tucker determined that the
"low status, temporary, socially isolated employee should be
most likely to engage in this activity" (1989, p. 326). According

to Tucker, the underlying cause of theft of property is the particular worker's "degree of marginality."

This conclusion is derived from a research literature that has focused on a relatively limited number of formal organizations in principally three industries: namely, manufacturing plants, retail stores, and hospitals. Although the level of employee deviance in each of these three industries seems to vary predictably in proportion to the number of employees who have "marginal" status (Hollinger and Clark 1983a, pp. 67–68; Tucker 1989) or who are not strongly "bonded" to the organization (Hollinger 1986), there should be other occupations or work settings that experience even higher levels of deviance. Specifically, Tucker hypothesized that "the greater the number of marginal occupations a company has, the more employee theft it should experience" (1989, p. 326). As such, peak levels of employee deviance should be observed in formal organizations with a disproportionately young, high-turnover, and inequitably treated work force. As a test of this marginality hypothesis, this article examines the prevalence and correlates of theft as well as other forms of employee deviance in precisely such a work setting: the fast-food restaurant.

A limited number of primarily qualitative studies have already examined various forms of employee deviance occurring within the restaurant milieu. In fact, one of the pioneering sociological analyses of the workplace normative environment focused on the "social structure of the restaurant" by Whyte (1948, 1949). More recently, occupational deviance researchers investigated pilferage in a resort hotel dining room (Mars 1973) and "ripping off" by waiters and waitresses in steak house restaurants (Hawkins 1984).

However, no one has yet examined the fast-food restaurant as a locus for employee deviance research. This empirical void is rather puzzling because these businesses constitute one of the fastest growing and largest segments of the American economy. There are approximately 160,000 fast-food restaurants in the United States, generating over $64 billion worth of sales each year ("Fast food industry" 1990).

Millions of Americans currently work or have worked in a fast-food restaurant. Moreover, many young persons receive their first exposure to the world of work in part-time jobs

waiting on customers or working in the kitchens of these eating establishments. The unique experiences and attitudes for-
mulated while at one's first job may influence an individual's
perceptions about the world of work for a lifetime. It could be
argued that the fast-food industry bears a substantial burden
of responsibility to the remainder of the business community
in shaping occupational attitudes for millions of neophyte
workers during their initial employment experience.

## METHODS

The present study is an empirical examination of self-reported
levels of employee deviance among a sample of individuals
presently working for two nationwide fast-food restaurant corporations. Most of the restaurants included in this study are
located in the midwestern and western regions of the United
States. The anonymous employee surveys were mailed during
the winter of 1987 and the spring of 1988.

### Sample

A single respondent was randomly selected from each restaurant location to receive a survey instrument. Only one employee was selected from each site to minimize negative impact of the survey on the work force and to decrease the
possibility of respondents comparing answers among themselves. Potential respondents were selected from every job
classification in the participating restaurants. For Company 1,
the total sample consisted of managers or assistant managers
(approximately 20%); the remaining 80% consisted of production employees (including shift leaders). For Company 2, the
sample was comprised of production employees (40%), shift
leaders (20%), assistant managers (20%), and store managers
(20%).

### Data Collection

Given the secretive nature of this particular phenomenon, a
self-administered, anonymous, mailed questionnaire was chosen as the principal data-collection method. The self-report
survey questionnaire has been shown to be a valid and reliable technique to gather data on less threatening forms of
deviant behavior, particularly among conventionally social-

ized individuals (see Hindelang, Hirschi, and Weis 1981). Moreover, this particular data-collection approach has been successfully used in earlier studies of employee deviance (e.g., Hollinger and Clark 1983a).

Individual questionnaires and letters were mailed out under university letterhead and returned to a university address as further assurance of the confidentiality of responses and individual identities. Although the participating companies were provided summary results of this study, no firm received individual-level responses or was able to identify which of their employees responded to the survey.

The three-page survey instrument consisted of questions designed to provide information about demographic characteristics, general employee attitudes toward the workplace, and the frequency of personal involvement in a range of deviant acts directed against the work organization.

A four-stage mailing procedure was used consisting of (a) an advance letter announcing the forthcoming questionnaire, (b) the questionnaire, including a cover letter, a $1 bill incentive and a postage-paid envelope, (c) a replacement instrument with cover letter and postage-paid envelope, and finally (d) a second replacement instrument with cover letter and postage-paid envelope.

Of the 797 questionnaires mailed to potential respondents, 384 surveys were completed and returned, yielding a final response rate of 48.2%. (Seventy-five questionnaires were returned as undeliverable.) An additional 43 respondents were not included in the analysis because they indicated they were no longer working in the fast-food industry. When we compared the personal demographics of the 341 valid respondents with nonrespondents, no significant differences were discovered that might distort our results (e.g., Goudy 1978). (Store and employee variables such as "overrings," inventory shortages, store location, tenure, age, gender, and job titles were provided to us by the participating companies and were compared by *t* tests and chi-square analyses).

## Demographic Profile of Respondents

Fifty-five percent of the survey respondents were production crew members, 19% were assistant managers, and 26% were store or district managers. Most of the respondents (more

than 70%) had been working for their present employers
longer than 1 year. About 45% of the respondents worked
more than 40 hours per week. About 67% of the respondents
reported working evenings, nights, or varied shifts.

It should also be noted that fast-food restaurants employ a
very young work force. More than half (56.3%) of our respondents were younger than 24 years; 35.2% were younger than
21 years. As is typical in the retail industry, female employees
outnumbered male 57% to 43%. Most respondents (55%) had
never been married. Approximately 43% of the respondents
had some college education, and 30% indicated that they had
two or more employers during the past year.

### Dependent Variables

Respondents were asked to report their personal involvement
in a range of different varieties of employee deviance during
the preceding 6 months. For each item, Likert-type response
choices were "never" (i.e., not even once), "seldom" (i.e.,
once in the past 6 months), "occasionally" (i.e., one to two
times in 1 month), "often" (i.e., one to two times per week),
and "very often" (i.e., three or more times a week).

The existing research on the topic of employee deviance
has generally suggested two principal categories of behavior:
namely, property deviance and production deviance (Hollinger and Clark 1982, 1983a). Unexpectedly, using factor analysis, SPSS reliability scale-creation techniques, and the face
validity of the items, *three* distinct groupings, not two,
emerged from the range of deviance items asked of these fast-
food restaurant respondents.[1] Significant employee involvement was reported in what we label as "altruistic property
deviance." A variant of personal property deviance, altruistic
property deviance is the giving away of company property
and assets to others at no charge or at substantial discount.
However, unlike personal property deviance, this variety of
property-related rule breaking does not directly enrich the

---

[1]The dependent-variable scale selection process began with orthogonal factor
analysis to identify the three main dimensions of employee deviance. Using face
validity, interitem correlations, and Cronbach's alphas scores (all ranging between .60
and .75), we finalized the selection of the specific items that made up each of our
three dependent variables.

employee involved. Rather, these are instances of employee deviance in which the company's property is used to enhance personal and social relationships with friends, family, and associates.[2]

### Personal Property Deviance

As can be seen in Table 1, the levels of self-reported personal property deviance vary greatly by item. By far, the most common form of company property taken in the fast-food restaurant is food. Almost half of the employees in the study admit-

[2]In his earlier study of employee theft in a steak house restaurant, Hawkins (1984) also distinguished between what he called "socially based" and "pecuniary" theft. In fact, the single most common form of property theft among waiters was giving "free food to friends" (1984, p. 56). We have chosen to label these forms of theft as "altruistic" rather than socially based to emphasize more clearly the benevolent, gift-giving nature of these acts.

**TABLE 1**

Self-Reported Employee Involvement in Personal Property Deviance Among a Sample of Fast-Food Restaurant Employees ($N$ = 341)

| Personal property deviance items | Involvement (%) | | | | |
|---|---|---|---|---|---|
| | Very often | Often | Occasionally | Seldom | Never |
| Have you ever: | | | | | |
| Taken merchandise or equipment from your employer without permission? | 0.6 | 2.3 | 4.7 | 13.8 | 78.6 |
| Taken company supplies or equipment for personal use? | 0.6 | 1.2 | 4.4 | 16.1 | 77.7 |
| Eaten food at work without paying for it? | 6.5 | 7.3 | 10.9 | 21.1 | 54.2 |
| Taken money from your employer without permission? | 0.6 | 0.0 | 0.9 | 4.7 | 93.8 |
| Changed company records to get paid for work not actually done? | 0.3 | 0.3 | 1.5 | 2.3 | 95.6 |

Note. Of respondents, 59.5% reported involvement in one or more of the items; 40.5% reported that they were never involved.

ted to eating food at work without paying for it; 14% admitted to doing so on a regular basis. More than one fifth of the employees also reported having taken merchandise, equipment, or supplies. Taking money or manipulating payroll records was much less frequently reported, probably because of the more serious nature of the acts and in-store control mechanisms. Overall, three fifths of the employees in the fast-food restaurants reported involvement with one or more of these personal property deviance items.

*Altruistic Property Deviance*
In Table 2, we present the four items used to represent acts of altruistic property deviance. The most common instance of this subcategory of property deviance was the unauthorized extension of employee discount privileges to one's friends. Over one fourth of the employees in the sample reported this form of rule breaking. Slightly less frequently reported was the sale of merchandise to friends at a reduced price. These unauthorized discounts were reported by almost one fifth of those responding. Abusing the refund system and actively

**TABLE 2**

Self-Reported Employee Involvement in Altruistic Property Deviance Among a Sample of Fast-Food Restaurant Employees (*N* = 341)

| | Involvement (%) | | | | |
|---|---|---|---|---|---|
| Altruistic property deviance items | Very often | Often | Occasionally | Seldom | Never |
| Have you ever: | | | | | |
| Used employee discount privileges for friends? | 0.3 | 0.9 | 10.3 | 17.3 | 71.2 |
| Sold merchandise to friends at a reduced price? | 1.2 | 0.3 | 3.8 | 11.4 | 83.3 |
| Issued or received refunds for items not actually purchased? | 0.3 | 0.6 | 0.3 | 3.8 | 95.0 |
| Actually helped another person take company property or merchandise? | 0.3 | 0.0 | 0.6 | 3.8 | 95.3 |

*Note.* Of respondents, 36.1% reported involvement in one or more of the items; 63.9% reported that they were never involved.

helping another to steal were also both reported but at substantially lower levels (about 5%). In sum, over a third of the respondents indicated that during the past 6 months they had participated in at least one act against their employer's property that directly benefited their friends or others and only indirectly profited themselves.

*Production Deviance*
In Table 3, we present respondent involvement in various types of counterproductive activities labeled production deviance. By far, the most common category of production deviance was coming to work late. Over two thirds of the respondents reported some work tardiness; most indicated that this was a "seldom" or "occasional" occurrence. The next most popular form of production deviance was faking an illness and calling in sick; almost one third of the respondents indicated that they had done so at least once in the last 6 months. The next most popular forms of counterproductive activity were coming to work hung over, working slowly or sloppily on purpose, and being absent from work without a legitimate excuse. Each of these items was reported at least once in the past 6 months by approximately one fifth of the respondents. Rarer forms of production deviance included leaving early without permission, consuming drugs or alcohol while on the job, and faking an injury to receive worker's compensation. These items were reported by fewer than 15% of the workers surveyed. Overall, four fifths of these fast-food restaurant employees reported some involvement in counterproductive activities against the organization during the past 6 months.

## Categories of Employee Deviance

Our discovery of three, not two, distinct categories of employee deviance suggests that each be examined separately. As such, our research plan includes parallel analyses of three dependent variables. We examined the five items included under personal property deviance, the four items we labeled altruistic property deviance, and the eight items making up our production deviance dependent variable.

As is the case with many forms of deviant behavior, the three employee deviance dependent variables are not "normal" statistical distributions. That is, many employees re-

**TABLE 3**
Self-Reported Employee Involvement in Production Deviance Among a
Sample of Fast-Food Restaurant Employees ($N = 341$)

| Personal property deviance items | Involvement (%) | | | | |
|---|---|---|---|---|---|
| | Very often | Often | Occasionally | Seldom | Never |
| Have you ever: | | | | | |
| Come to work late? | 2.9 | 3.8 | 18.5 | 44.0 | 30.8 |
| Left work early without permission? | 0.0 | 0.0 | 3.5 | 10.6 | 85.9 |
| Been absent from work without a legitimate excuse? | 0.3 | 0.6 | 3.8 | 15.0 | 80.3 |
| Faked an illness and called in sick? | 0.6 | 0.6 | 5.9 | 21.4 | 71.6 |
| Faked an injury to received worker's compensation? | 0.3 | 0.0 | 0.0 | 0.3 | 99.4 |
| Done slow or sloppy work on purpose? | 0.3 | 1.5 | 3.5 | 16.4 | 78.3 |
| Engaged in drug use or alcohol consumption on the job? | 0.6 | 0.0 | 0.9 | 5.6 | 93.0 |
| Come to work hung over from alcohol or drugs? | 0.6 | 0.6 | 6.5 | 14.4 | 78.0 |

*Note.* Of respondents, 82.1% reported involvement in one or more of the items; 17.9% reported they were never involved.

ported no involvement in deviant activity. Moreover, most of those who did report some deviant acts against their employers are not very actively involved. Those who are most involved in employee deviance constitute a very small proportion of the total number of respondents. This commonly observed phenomenon in the study of deviant behavior dictates a dichotomized treatment for each of the three dependent variables. The skewed distribution of our dependent variables suggests that we compare those who are not at all or minimally involved with those respondents who reported above-average levels of employee deviance.

To accomplish this dichotomization, the items in the three dependent variable scales were first standardized by computing $Z$ scores for each. This prevents a more frequently reported item (e.g., coming to work late) from dominating the remainder of items in a Likert-type scale. Next, the Z scores for each dependent variable were summed to yield three deviance scores for each respondent. All summed scores totaling less than or equal to zero were classified as "average or below" involvement. Those with sums greater than zero were classified as "above average." This procedure, which has been used in previous research on other forms of employee deviance (e.g., Hollinger and Clark 1983a), is a conservative approach forcing a comparison between those who are most involved with those who are not involved at all or who report only an occasional instance of deviant activity.

**Independent Variables**

The existing literature on employee deviance has examined an assortment of causal models purporting to explain the occurrence of this phenomenon (see Hollinger and Clark 1982, 1983a, 1983b; Merriam 1977). More recent research, however, has uniformly suggested that workers who are not personally committed to the financial success of the employing organization are more likely to engage in employee deviance. Hollinger (1986), for example, concluded that both property deviance and production deviance are more prevalent among those employees who are not well "bonded" to the organization. Tucker (1989) concluded that the marginality of many younger employees makes them more receptive to stealing from their employers. Most recently, Hollinger (1991) argued that "techniques of neutralization" are commonly used by employees, thereby minimizing in the mind of the involved employees any harm caused by their deviant acts. From this body of empirical research, three variables have been linked consistently with assorted forms of employee deviance, namely, the employee's age, their length of tenure with the firm, and perceptions of employer unfairness.

*Age*
Perhaps the single most salient variable in predicting employee deviance has been the age of the worker. In virtually every occupational setting examined, younger employees have been found to report significantly higher levels of both property and production deviance (Hollinger and Clark 1983a). For example, Ruggiero and Greenberger (1982) dis-

covered that, after only an average of 9 months on the job, more than 60% of the adolescent workers surveyed had engaged in at least one act of employee deviance; 41% committed an act of employee theft. Various explanations have been offered to account for this inordinately higher level of deviance among employees in their late teens and early 20s. One hypothesis states that younger employees are less receptive to management attempts at deterrence (Hollinger and Clark 1983b). Partially as a function of their often minimal tenure and lower occupational status, younger employees may also exhibit less commitment to their employers (Hollinger 1986; Tucker 1989). Moreover, younger employees are often less satisfied with their employment experience (Hollinger and Clark 1982). Given the age distribution of workers at typical fast-food restaurants, we predict that a very strong age–deviance relationship will be also observed among these employees. Specifically, we expect that those employees aged 20 years or younger (35.2%) will report higher levels of employee deviance than their older co-workers (64.8%) who have attained the socially significant age of 21.

## Tenure

A second variable that has consistently emerged as important in distinguishing between high and low deviance involvement is tenure of employment. As documented by Robin (1969), over one third of employees caught stealing in a retail store were with the firm fewer than 6 months; two thirds of the offenders had fewer than 2 years tenure. In their three-industry self-report study, Hollinger and Clark (1983a) confirmed that those employees who have not been with the firm long and who did not have a commitment to a career with the organization were often more highly involved in employee deviance (see also Hollinger 1986). Tucker (1989, p. 324) echoed this observation by concluding that "new employees have little time to develop much of a relationship to their employer." Given the expected importance of tenure, we compare those employees with fewer than 1 year of tenure with the firm (30%) with those with 1 year or more of experience (70%). It is expected that the short-tenured employees will report higher levels of employee deviance involvement.

## Employer Unfairness

One of the most commonly observed correlates of workplace deviance has been a prevailing sentiment among those involved that their employers have not been fair or equitable in the treatment of employees (e.g., Ditton 1977a; Hollinger and Clark 1982; Mangione and Quinn 1975; Zeitlin 1971). For example, Altheide et al. (1978) argued that employees are significantly more likely to steal from a company that is perceived of as "ripping off" its own employees. Thus, we also examined how the item—"In your opinion have your recent employers ever treated you unfairly?"—differentiates among employee deviance levels. (Response choices were "yes" and "no.") We predict that those who express that they have been treated unfairly will report above-average levels of personal property, altruistic property, as well as production deviance.

## Data Analysis

The non-normal frequency distribution in each of our three dependent variables prevents us from using an ordinary least squares (OLS) regression. As is commonly the case in deviance research, our data violate two basic assumptions of OLS regression: (a) equal variances (i.e., homoscedasticity) and (b) normal distribution of the error variances with the independent variables. Although there are several different ways to deal with this problem, we used a weighted least squares (WLS) logit regression procedure in which the dependent variable represents the odds that a given employee will report above-average deviance rather than below-average deviance involvement (Swafford 1980). This technique, modeled after that of Grizzle, Starmer, and Koch (1969), does not require the two assumptions just discussed and substitutes an appropriate chi-square significance test for the less appropriate *F* test.

Using the backward selection (i.e., exclusion) analysis as described by Swafford (1980), we separately estimated a predicted set of logits for each of the three dichotomized dependent variables from the logically possible models, including the main effects and each of the interaction terms. The principal objective of the analysis involves approximating the most parsimonious model using the common chi-square goodness-of-fit test to compare results with the saturated model (which contains all possible main effect and interaction terms—often ignored in more limited forward-regression procedures).

Our first step was to dummy code our three independent variables in the following dichotomous manner: age (1 = young [20 years and younger], 0 = old [21 years and older]); tenure (1 = low [11 months or less], 0 = high [1 year or more]); and unfair employer (1 = yes, 0 = no). These codings, in addition to the marginal frequencies, proportions, observed odds, and logits for each of our three employee deviance dependent variables, are presented in Tables 4, 5, and 6.

The regression equation underlying the saturated logit model including the variables just mentioned is as follows:

$$Ln(\Omega) = \gamma_1 + \gamma_2 A + \gamma_3 T + \gamma_4 U + \gamma_5 AT + \gamma_6 AU + \gamma_7 TU + \gamma_8 ATU$$

where $\Omega$ is the odds of reporting above-average employee deviance involvement; $\lambda_1$ is the regression constant; $\lambda_2$, $\lambda_3$, and $\lambda_4$ are the main effects; $\lambda_5$, $\lambda_6$, and $\lambda_7$ are the first-order interaction effects; $\lambda_8$ is the single second-order interaction effect; A is age; T is tenure; and U is unfair employer.

Because the log of the odds, $Ln(\Omega)$, is not an intuitively meaningful statistic, logit equations are more commonly presented by applying the exponential function (or the antilog) to both sides of the equation, after which we obtain the following:

$$\Omega = \gamma_1 * \gamma_2 A * \gamma_3 T * \gamma_4 U * \gamma_5 AT, * \gamma_6 AU * \gamma_7 TU * \gamma_8 ATU.$$

This second regression equation represents the saturated model in terms of simple odds ratios ($\Omega$), with $\gamma_1$ as the regression constant; $\gamma_2$, $\gamma_3$, and $\gamma_4$ as the odds of the main terms; $\gamma_5$, $\gamma_6$, and $\gamma_7$ as the odds of the first-order interaction terms; and $\gamma_8$ as the odds of the single second-order interaction term.

## FINDINGS

Using the previously described backward WLS logit regression procedure (see Swafford 1980), Tables 7, 8, and 9 present a parallel examination of the logically possible models explaining each of our three deviance dependent variables;

## TABLE 4

Marginal Frequencies, Proportions, Odds, and Logits for the Eight Subpopulations of the Personal Property Deviance Dependent Variable

| | Independent variables | | | | Personal property deviance | | | | |
|---|---|---|---|---|---|---|---|---|---|
| Subpopulation | Age | Tenure | Employer unfair? | Subtotal | High | Low | Proportion high | Odds high | Logits |
| 1 | Young | Low | Yes | 32 | 12 | 20 | .38 | 0.60 | −0.51 |
| 2 | Old | Low | Yes | 16 | 3 | 13 | .19 | 0.23 | −1.47 |
| 3 | Young | High | Yes | 29 | 15 | 14 | .52 | 1.07 | 0.07 |
| 4 | Old | High | Yes | 112 | 47 | 65 | .42 | 0.72 | −0.32 |
| 5 | Young | Low | No | 32 | 14 | 18 | .44 | 0.78 | −0.25 |
| 6 | Old | Low | No | 19 | 2 | 17 | .11 | 0.12 | −2.14 |
| 7 | Young | High | No | 23 | 5 | 18 | .22 | 0.28 | −1.28 |
| 8 | Old | High | No | 72 | 13 | 59 | .18 | 0.22 | −1.51 |

**TABLE 5**

Marginal Frequencies, Proportions, Odds, and Logits for the Eight Subpopulations of the Altruistic Property Deviance Dependent Variable

| Subpopulation | Independent variables | | | | Altruistic property deviance | | | | |
| | Age | Tenure | Employer unfair? | Subtotal | High | Low | Proportion high | Odds high | Logits |
|---|---|---|---|---|---|---|---|---|---|
| 1 | Young | Low | Yes | 32 | 16 | 16 | .50 | 1.00 | 0.00 |
| 2 | Old | Low | Yes | 16 | 2 | 14 | .13 | 0.14 | −1.95 |
| 3 | Young | High | Yes | 29 | 15 | 14 | .52 | 1.07 | 0.07 |
| 4 | Old | High | Yes | 112 | 28 | 84 | .25 | 0.33 | −1.10 |
| 5 | Young | Low | No | 32 | 11 | 21 | .34 | 0.52 | −0.65 |
| 6 | Old | Low | No | 19 | 3 | 16 | .16 | 0.19 | −1.67 |
| 7 | Young | High | No | 23 | 9 | 14 | .39 | 0.64 | −0.44 |
| 8 | Old | High | No | 72 | 12 | 60 | .17 | 0.20 | −1.61 |

**TABLE 6**
Marginal Frequencies, Proportions, Odds, and Logits for the Eight Subpopulations of the Production Deviance Dependent Variable

| Subpopulation | Independent variables | | | | | Production deviance | | | | |
| | Age | Tenure | Employer unfair? | Subtotal | High | Low | Proportion high | Odds high | Logits |
|---|---|---|---|---|---|---|---|---|---|
| 1 | Young | Low | Yes | 32 | 15 | 17 | .47 | 0.88 | −0.13 |
| 2 | Old | Low | Yes | 16 | 5 | 11 | .31 | 0.45 | −0.79 |
| 3 | Young | High | Yes | 29 | 13 | 16 | .45 | 0.81 | −0.21 |
| 4 | Old | High | Yes | 112 | 48 | 64 | .43 | 0.75 | −0.29 |
| 5 | Young | Low | No | 32 | 12 | 20 | .38 | 0.60 | −0.51 |
| 6 | Old | Low | No | 19 | 5 | 14 | .26 | 0.36 | −1.03 |
| 7 | Young | High | No | 23 | 9 | 14 | .39 | 0.64 | −0.44 |
| 8 | Old | High | No | 72 | 14 | 58 | .19 | 0.24 | −1.42 |

namely, personal property, altruistic property, and production deviance. Beginning with the most complex, the second-order and then each of the three first-order interaction terms are sequentially excluded from the regression equation. The equation with the remaining terms is then compared with the saturated model using the analysis goal of parsimony. That is, we want to identify the "best fit" model containing the least number of terms without differing significantly from the saturated model (containing all logically possible main effect and interaction terms).

## Personal Property Deviance

In Table 7, we present the model-selection process for the personal property dependent variable. The first step was to exclude interaction effects from the saturated model beginning with the most complex. In Model 2, we were able to

**TABLE 7**
Backward Best Fit Model-Selection Process: Personal Property Deviance

| Model | Independent variables in the model | $\chi^2$ | df | Explanation |
|-------|-----------------------------------|----------|-----|-------------|
| 1 | k, A, T, U, AT, AU, TU, ATU | 0.00 | 0 | Saturated model |
| 2 | k, A, T, U, AT, AU, TU | 0.68 | 1 | Excluded second-order interaction term |
| 3 | k, A, T, U | 9.34**** | 4 | Excluded all first-order interaction terms |
| 4 | k, A, T, U, AT, AU | 4.20** | 2 | Exclude TU interaction term |
| 5 | k, A, T, U, AT, TU | 0.76 | 2 | Exclude AU interaction main effect term (best fit model) |
| 6 | k, A, T, U, AU, TU | 3.09* | 2 | Exclude AT interaction term |
| 7 | k, A, T, U, TU | 3.28 | 3 | Excluded AT and AU interaction terms |
| 8 | k, A, T, U, AT | 6.25*** | 3 | Excluded AU and TU interaction terms |
| 9 | k, A, T, U, AU | 6.66**** | 3 | Excluded AT and TU interaction terms |

*Note.* A = age; T = tenure; U = unfair employer.
*$\chi^2$ is different from the saturated model 1 at $p \leq .25$.
**$\chi^2$ is different from the saturated model 1 at $p \leq .15$.
***$\chi^2$ is different from the saturated model 1 at $p \leq .10$.
****$\chi^2$ is different from the saturated model 1 at $p \leq .075$.

**TABLE 8**
Backward Best Fit Model-Selection Process: Altruistic Property Deviance

| Model | Independent variables in the model | $\chi^2$ | df | Explanation |
|---|---|---|---|---|
| 1 | k, A, T, U, AT, AU, TU, ATU | 0.00 | 0 | Saturated model |
| 2 | k, A, T, U, AT, AU, TU | 0.50 | 1 | Excluded second-order interaction term |
| 3 | k, A, T, U | 0.86 | 4 | Excluded all first-order interaction terms |
| 4 | k, A, T | 4.57 | 5 | Excluded U main effect term |
| 5 | k, A, U | 1.38 | 5 | Excluded T main effect term |
| 6 | k, T, U | 19.67* | 5 | Excluded A main effect term |
| 7 | k, A | 5.44 | 6 | Excluded T and U main effects (best fit model) |

*Note.* A = age; T = tenure; U = unfair employer.
*$\chi^2$ is different from the saturated model 1 at $p \leq .01$.

exclude the second-order interaction effect with no deterioration in the model. Next, in Model 3, we dropped all three first-order interaction effects. However, this time the chi-square did deteriorate, indicating that at least one of the first-order interactions was crucial to the final solution.

In Models 4, 5, and 6, we individually excluded each of the first-order interactions to determine the magnitude of their separate effect. When both the age–tenure and tenure–unfair employer interactions were omitted (see Models 4 and 6), the resultant chi-square increased substantially, indicating the importance of these two interaction terms to the model. We then dropped the first-order interaction terms in pairs (Models 7, 8, and 9) to confirm that both the age–tenure and tenure–unfair employer interaction terms should be included in the best fit solution. Because each of the three main effects is represented in at least one of the significant interaction terms, we are able to conclude that age, tenure, and unfair employer also must be included in the best fit model (which turns out to have been Model 5).

The odds coefficients for the personal property deviance best fit solution are as follows:

$$\Omega = k * A * T * U * AT * TU$$

$$\Omega = .21 * 1.40 * .84 * 3.416 * 2.80 * 28.$$

Because the two significant interaction terms include all three of the main effects, none of the odds coefficients is directly interpretable in this equation. Demonstrating the "partial" contributions of age, tenure, and unfair employer (given the interaction between them) will necessitate a graphic representation as shown in Figure 1. Using this logit regression equation and the observed odds, in Figure 1 we have calculated and then plotted the expected odds coefficients of high personal property deviance for each of the 8 subpopulations.

First note from Figure 1 that the odds of above-average deviance are generally higher for younger employees than for older employees. However, each of the eight subpopulations exhibits a slightly different level of personal property deviance because of the varying effects of tenure and perceived employer unfairness on both young and older employees alike. Specifically, Figure 1 indicates the following:

1. The lowest levels of personal property deviance is exhibited by older, low-tenured employees. Moreover, the property theft levels of this group are unaffected by perceived employer unfairness. In other words, regardless of the perceptions of their employer's treatment of them, employees aged 21 and older who have been with the firm less than a year just do not steal from their employers.

2. Alternatively, regardless of their perceptions of employer unfairness, younger employees with low tenure are the most highly involved in personal property deviance. In other words, younger, low-tenured employees will exhibit high levels of stealing—again, unaffected by the perceptions of their employer's fairness.

3. Perception of employer unfairness does have an effect but not on the newly hired. The attitude that employees hold toward their employer has its greatest effect on longer tenured employees. In fact, the highest levels of personal property deviance were observed for those employees (both young and old) who have been with the company for a year or more. When the company is perceived of as fair, these em-

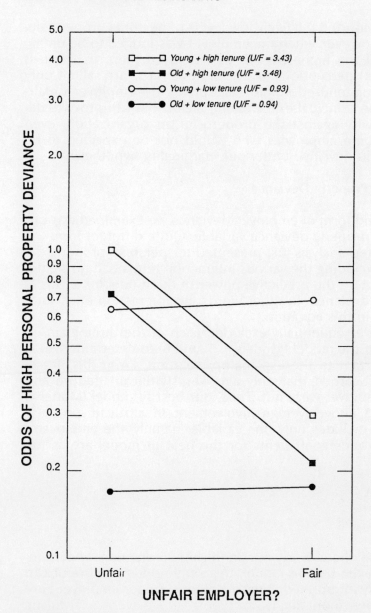

**UNFAIR EMPLOYER?**

**FIGURE 1**
Plotted expected odds of high personal property deviance involvement by unfair employer controlling for age and tenure. (U = unfair; F = fair.)

ployees reported relatively low levels of personal property deviance. However, when the employer was judged to be unfair, we found the highest levels of employee theft. In short, it seems that perceptions of corporate fairness are salient only to the long-tenured employee. Apparently, employer unfairness is the principal exacerbating factor that can provoke deviant activity against the property of an organization, even among some employees who would not be expected to be involved in deviance under our marginality hypothesis.

## Altruistic Property Deviance

The second form of employee deviance we examined was our altruistic property deviance variable. Quite different from the complicated analysis just presented for personal property deviance, excluding the various interaction terms had no significant effect on the predictive power of the model for altruistic property deviance. In other words, no interaction effects are required in this equation.

Next, we sequentially excluded each of the three main effects from the model (Models 4, 5, and 6) to determine which are important to the explanatory solution. From this procedure, we learned that only age was significant; tenure and unfair employer were not. Thus, our best fit model (Model 7) to predict above-average involvement in altruistic property deviance includes only one variable: namely, the employee's age. The odds coefficients for the best fit model are as follows:

$$\Omega = k * A$$

$$\Omega = .26 * 2.98$$

Because there were no significant interaction effects included in the best fit model, this single odds coefficient can be directly interpreted. Simply stated, younger employees are three times more likely to report above-average altruistic property deviance involvement than their older co-workers. In short, altruistic deviance is almost exclusively the result of employees under the age of 21 giving unauthorized gifts and discounts of food, services, and merchandise to their friends.

## Production Deviance

The final form of employee deviance we examined was the production deviance dependent variable. In Table 9, we present a model-selection process similar to that presented previously, although we now focused on various forms of counterproductive employee activity. As before, the backward-selection process first excluded the single second-order interaction followed by dropping all three of the first-order interactions. In Models 2 and 3, one can see that the exclusion of the interaction terms did not have a deleterious effect on the chi-square levels.

Next, in Models 4, 5, and 6, we again sequentially excluded each three of the main effects from the model. Only the exclusion of the unfair employer variable caused the chi-square value to exceed expected probability levels. Thus, for production deviance, the best fit model (Model 7) contains only the employee's perception of the employer's fairness. The odds coefficients for this final employee deviance dependent variable are as follows:

$$\Omega = k * U$$

$$\Omega = .39 * 1.91$$

**TABLE 9**
Backward Best Fit Model-Selection Process: Production Deviance

| Model | Independent variables in the model | $\chi^2$ | df | Explanation |
|---|---|---|---|---|
| 1 | k, A, T, U, AT, AU, TU, ATU | 0.00 | 0 | Saturated model |
| 2 | k, A, T, U, AT, AU, TU | 0.86 | 1 | Excluded second-order interaction term |
| 3 | k, A, T, U | 3.03 | 4 | Excluded all first-order interaction terms |
| 4 | k, A, T | 11.40* | 5 | Excluded U main effect term |
| 5 | k, A, U | 3.05 | 5 | Excluded T main effect term |
| 6 | k, T, U | 6.14* | 5 | Excluded A main effect term |
| 7 | k, U | 6.50 | 6 | Excluded A and T main effects (best fit model) |

*Note.* A = age; T = tenure; U = unfair employer.
*$\chi^2$ is different from the saturated model 1 at $p \leq .05$.

In sum, among both younger and older alike, those employees who believed that their employers were unfair to them were twice as likely to be involved in above-average levels of production deviance.

## DISCUSSION

Based both on our working hypothesis and anecdotal reports from those employed in fast-food restaurants, it is not surprising to discover that these establishments experience substantial levels of employee deviance. We predicted that these relatively higher prevalence levels are likely related to the marginal status of significant numbers of fast-food restaurant employees (Tucker 1989). For example, most fast-food restaurant workers are paid minimum wages. In addition, these employees commonly are afforded little or no promotional opportunity, often do not view this job as a career, and as such do not remain on the job for lengthy periods of time ("Fast-food industry" 1990). In other words, from what we already know about the correlates of workplace deviance, we expected the fast-food restaurant to be an ideal climate for employee theft and various forms of counterproductive activity.

On the basis of previous research, we expected that the various manifestations of property and production deviance would be explained by the same set of factors. The particular form that the deviance takes was assumed to be determined largely by the opportunities present in that particular work milieu.

We did not expect, however, that each of the three types of employee deviance examined—personal property, altruistic property, and production deviance—would be explained by a slightly different regression model. This suggests that these three types of deviance may not be the product of exactly the same causal factors interacting with opportunity. Instead, each type seems to be a relatively distinct category of deviance with a rather unique constituency of employees involved and distinctive causal determinants.

Personal property deviance, or the taking of company property for personal benefit, seems to be primarily engaged in by workers younger than 21 years with little tenure with the firm.

This finding was expected.[3] However, we have also discovered (much to our surprise) that longer tenured employees (both young and old) can be also enticed to take company property when they believe their employer to be unfair. This previously undocumented interaction effect may explain the long-observed inconsistencies noted between quantitative and qualitative employee theft study results. Whereas quantitative studies have typically suggested that younger employees are customarily involved in theft, qualitative studies have often recognized the longer tenured, disenchanted worker (Hollinger and Clark 1983a). Now we realize that both conclusions may be accurate.

Younger employees, because of their marginal status (Tucker 1989), lesser commitment to the organization (Hollinger 1986), and lower deterrability (Hollinger and Clark 1983b), perhaps will always be more likely to take from their employers. However, when longer tenured employees become disillusioned with inequitable treatment, they too can be tempted to engage in theft.

Of substantial interest to researchers and managers alike is our discovery of a distinct variation of property deviance in which there is no pecuniary benefit to the employee involved. Altruistic property deviance, or the giving of company property and assets to others, seems to be almost exclusively the deviance preference of younger employees. One plausible hypothesis suggests that, by allowing their friends and acquaintances to benefit from these charitable gifts, the involved employee accumulates interpersonal "credits," which can be "cashed in" at a later date. This is, in fact, based on a social exchange model; in many communities we may find extensive informal bartering arrangements among younger employees in which "freebies" are later reciprocated at their friends' place of work. Given the importance to insecure young people of acquiring and maintaining social relationships among

[3]To determine whether our tenure variable was masking the effect of differential occupational status, the data were reanalyzed by dichotomizing the sample between managerial and crew employees. Unlike for tenure, we discovered no interaction effects with either age or employer unfairness. This confirms that the observed effect of tenure is not a spurious artifact of the employee's occupational status. Thus, the observed effect of tenure seems to hold for both managerial and nonmanagerial personnel alike.

one's peers, the strength of the age relationship to this hybrid form of property deviance is quite easily understood.

Finally, the more pervasive production deviance seems to be exclusively linked to perceived employer unfairness among all categories of employees—young and old, long and short tenured alike. In short, these deviant activities seem to be solely a function of personal attitudes toward one's employer. If the employer is perceived to be unfair in the treatment of its workers, then coming to work late, leaving early, sloppy performance, sick leave abuse, along with alcohol and drug use on the job are twice as likely to occur (Kemper 1966).

Empirical evidence that property and production deviance is often viewed by the employee, especially among those with longer tenure, as a struggle to achieve social "equity" with one's employer (Austin and Walster 1975). According to the equity model, if rewards do not match inputs, employees who perceive unfairness in a relationship with their employer have essentially four options available to resolve the inequity (Adams 1963). First, they can "leave the field" or quit their jobs.[4] Second, they can acquiesce to the inequity. These two options obviously decrease in attractiveness the longer the employees work for their present employer. For those who cannot risk quitting their jobs and can no longer simply ignore the inequities, only two options remain. They can illicitly increase their rewards by taking company money or property— property deviance—or they can decrease their inputs by working less—production deviance (Hollinger 1979, p. 90). The results of this survey indicate that the fast-food restaurant provides exactly the type of milieu in which we should expect to find high levels of property and production deviance when perceptions of workplace inequity are high (Bersheid, Boye, and Walster 1968).

From these findings, it appears that the demographic characteristics of the work force, exacerbated by employee perceptions of employer unfairness, will largely determine both

[4]Because feelings of unfairness may prompt some employees to quit their job (and perhaps avoid the fast-food industry altogether), the observed continuum of perceived employer unfairness is more abbreviated in our sample than if quitters (and nonrespondents for similar reasons) were also represented. Hence, the finding of a significant relationship between theft and employer unfairness is even more impressive.

the prevalence and type of deviance most commonly observed. Although we recognize that employees of all ages will engage in property deviance, those organizations heavily reliant on workers younger than age 21 should expect disproportionate numbers of employees personally taking company property as well as altruistically "giving" their friends unauthorized gifts and discounts.[5] Moreover, personal property theft will occur among longer tenured employees in direct proportion to the degree in which their employers are judged to be unfair in the treatment of employees. Finally, the organization in which disproportionate numbers of all categories of employees express unhappiness with company fairness also will be victimized by an assortment of counterproductive activities.

Until now, workplace deviance has been viewed (by these researchers and others) as a collection of rule-breaking acts, all of which were presumed to be caused by the same factors.[6] The particular manifestation of employee deviance observed was assumed to be primarily the product of differential opportunity. These findings raise serious questions about this unidimensional model. Continuing to lump personal property pilferage, counterproductive activities, and altruistically motivated "gifts" together into a single generic category called employee deviance is—at least in the fast-food restaurant—not empirically justified. Future explanatory and theoretical rationales for a multidimensional typology of employee deviance depend on whether these three distinct forms of deviance are observed in other work settings as well.

## REFERENCES

Adams, J. Stacy. 1963. "Toward an Understanding of Inequity." *Journal of Abnormal and Social Psychology* 26:422–36.

Altheide, D. L., P. A. Adler, P. Adler, and D. A. Altheide. 1978. "The Social Meanings of Employee Theft." Pp. 90–124 in *Crime at the*

[5]Perhaps this is why some fast-food chains like McDonalds are now hiring senior citizens in larger proportions of their total work force.

[6]It should be noted, however, that we recognize the causal ordering may actually be reversed. That is, perceptions of company unfairness may also serve as a rationalizing technique to justify existing patterns of deviant behavior.

*top,* edited by J. M. Johnson & J. D. Douglas. Philadelphia: Lippincott.

Austin, William, and Elaine Walster. 1975. "Equity with the World: The Trans-Relational Effects of Equity and Inequity." *Sociometry* 38:474–96.

Bensman, J., and I. Gerver. 1963. "Crime and Punishment in the Factory: The Function of Deviancy in Maintaining the Social System." *American Sociological Review* 28:588–98.

Bersheid, E., D. Boye, and E. Walster. 1968. "Retaliation as a Means of Restoring Equity." *Journal of Personality and Social Psychology* 10:370–76.

Cressey, Donald. 1953. *Other People's Money: A Study in the Social Psychology of Embezzlement.* Belmont, CA: Wadsworth.

Ditton, Jason. 1977a. "Perks, Pilferage and the Fiddle: The Historical Structure of Invisible Wages." *Theory and Society* 4:39–71.

———. 1977b. *Part-Time Crime: An Ethnography of Fiddling and Pilferage.* London: Macmillan.

Fast food industry forecast. 1990. *Restaurants and Institutions* 100:22, 30–31.

Franklin, Alice Pickett. 1975. *Internal Theft in a Retail Organization: A Case Study.* Ph.D. dissertation, The Ohio State University. Ann Arbor, MI: University Microfilms.

Goudy, Willis. 1978. "Interim Response to a Mail Questionnaire: Impacts on Variable Relationships." *The Sociological Quarterly* 19:253–65.

Gouldner, Alvin W. 1954. *Wildcat Strike: A Study in Worker–Management Relationships.* New York: Harper & Row.

Grizzle, J. E., C. F. Starmer, and G. G. Koch. 1969. "Analysis of Categorical Data by Linear Models." *Biometrics* 25:489–504.

Harper, Dean, and Frederick Emmert. 1963. "Work Behavior in the Service Industry." *Social Forces* 42:216–25.

Hawkins, Richard. 1984. "Employee Theft in the Restaurant Trade: Forms of Ripping Off by Waiters at Work." *Deviant Behavior* 5:47–69.

Henry, Stuart. 1978a. *The Hidden Economy: The Context and Control of Borderline Crime.* London: Martin Robertson.

———. 1978b. "Crime at Work: The Social Construction of Amateur Property Theft." *Sociology* 12:245–63.

Hindelang, Michael, Travis Hirschi, and Joseph Weis. 1981. *Measuring Delinquency.* Beverly Hills, CA: Sage.

Hollinger, Richard C. 1979. *Employee Deviance: Acts Against the Formal Work Organization.* Ph.D. dissertation, University of Minnesota. Ann Arbor, MI: University Microfilms.

————. 1986. "Acts Against the Workplace: Social Bonding and Employee Deviance." *Deviant Behavior* 7:53–75.

————. 1989. *Dishonesty in the workplace: A manager's guide to preventing employee theft.* Park Ridge, IL: London House Press.

————. 1991. "Neutralizing in the Workplace: An Empirical Analysis of Property Theft and Production Deviance." *Deviant Behavior* 12:169–202.

Hollinger, Richard C., and John P. Clark. 1982. "Employee Deviance: A Response to the Perceived Quality of the Work Experience." *Work and Occupations* 9:97–114.

————. 1983a. *Theft By Employees.* Lexington, MA: Lexington Books.

————. 1983b. "Deterrence in the Workplace: Perceived Certainty, Perceived Severity, and Employee Theft." *Social Forces* 62:398–418.

Horning, Donald N. M. 1970. "Blue Collar Theft: Conceptions of Property, Attitudes Toward Pilfering, and Work Group Norms in a Modern Industrial Plant." Pp. 46–64 in *Crimes against bureaucracy,* edited by E. O. Smigel and H. L. Ross. New York: Van Nostrand Reinhold.

Kemper, Theodore D. 1966. "Representative Roles and the Legitimation of Deviance." *Social Problems* 13:288–298.

Mangione, Thomas W., and Robert P. Quinn. 1975. "Job Satisfaction, Counter-Productive Behavior and Drug Use at Work." *Journal of Applied Psychology* 60:114–16.

Mars, Gerald. 1973. "Chance, Punters, and the Fiddle: Institutionalized Pilferage in a Hotel Dining Room." Pp. 200–210 in *The Sociology of the Workplace,* edited by M. Warner. New York: Halsted Press.

————. 1974. "Dock Pilferage: A Case Study in Occupational Theft." Pp. 209–228 in *Deviance and Social Control,* edited by P. Rock and M. McIntosh. London: Tavistock.

————. 1982. *Cheats at Work: An Anthropology of Workplace Crime.* Boston: Allen and Unwin.

Merriam, Dwight. 1977. "Employee Theft." *Criminal Justice Abstracts* 9:380–86.

Robin, Gerald D. 1969. "Employees as Offenders." *Journal of Research in Crime and Delinquency* 6:17–33.

————. 1970. "The Corporate and Judicial Disposition of Employee Thieves." Pp. 119–142 in *Crimes against bureaucracy,* edited by E. O. Smigel and H. L. Ross. New York: Van Nostrand Reinhold.

Roy, Donald. 1952. "Quota Restrictions and Goldbricking in a Machine Shop." *American Journal of Sociology* 57:427–42.

————. 1959. "Banana Time: Job Satisfaction and Informal Interaction." *Human Organization* 18:158–68.

Ruggerio, Mary, Ellen Greenberger, and Laurence D. Steinberg. 1982.

"Occupational Deviance Among Adolescent Workers." *Youth & Society* 13:423–48.

Slora, Karen B. 1989. "An Empirical Approach to Determining Employee Deviance Base Rates." *Journal of Business and Psychology* 4:199–219.

Swafford, Michael. 1980. "Three Parametric Techniques for Contingency Table Analysis: A Nontechnical Commentary." *American Sociological Review* 45:664–90.

Taylor, Laurie, and Paul Walton. 1971. "Industrial Sabotage: Motives and Meanings." Pp. 219–45 in *Images of Deviance*, edited by S. Cohen. London: Penguin.

Tucker, James. 1989. "Employee Theft as Social Control." *Deviant Behavior* 10:319–34.

Whyte, William F. 1948. *Human Relations and the Restaurant Industry.* New York: McGraw-Hill.

———. 1949. "The Social Structure of the Restaurant." *American Journal of Sociology* 54:302–10.

Zeitlin, Lawrence. 1971. "A Little Larceny Can Do a Lot for Employee Morale." *Psychology Today* 5(June):22, 24, 26, 64.

# [15]

EMPLOYEE THEFT IN THE RESTAURANT TRADE:
FORMS OF RIPPING OFF BY WAITERS AT WORK

*RICHARD HAWKINS*
*Southern Methodist University*

The variety of part-time theft techniques used by waiters in
the restaurant trade is examined using a self-report methodology.  Using twelve hypothetical cases of ripping off in
restaurants, three potential theft targets are assessed:  the
restaurant, customers of the restaurant, and co-workers.
Predictions about the frequency of involvement of these theft
activities are tested using a sample of waiters in four
"prime rib" restaurants.  Hypotheses dealing with working
conditions and the ability to neutralize moral controls
against theft are presented to explain which waiters will be
involved in employee theft.  The theoretical implications of
"amateur trading" and pecuniary-based theft are developed in
order to show the critical role that theft activities play in
the work setting of the restaurant.  The findings have implications for the "controlled larceny" solution to the problem
of employee theft suggested by some observers.

## INTRODUCTION

The work setting in recent years has provided a fertile site for
studies of deviant behavior.  Bryant (1974:4) suggests that the
workplace be examined (a) as a source of problems which result in
deviance that carries beyond the job, e.g., work stress and its
effect on alcoholism, mental and physical illness, drug abuse, etc.,
and (b) as a setting where deviant activity can be carried on--often
with little fear of formal sanctions.  This study of theft activities
by service employees, specifically waiters working in restaurants,

---

This research was funded by a faculty development grant from
Southern Methodist University.  The following people played an
important role in the project:  Elena Argomaniz, Walter Chapin,
Fran Hawkins, Dan Lowry and Sean Quinn.  My thanks to J. Greg Getz
for his critical reading of an earlier draft of the paper.

is an example of this latter approach.  This is not an investigation
into all forms of employee deviance, which would include both
violations of criminal law and activities detrimental to the work
organization but not technically illegal, i.e., "those behaviors
committed by workers which adversely affect the economic interest
of the formal work organization" (Hollinger, 1978:1).  Such a broad
definition would include theft and inventory shrinkage, but also
work slowdowns (rate-setting), shoddy workmanship, and even sabotage of company equipment which exact an economic loss.  Robin
(1974:262) uses the narrower term, "occupational crime," to refer
to work-based law violations by "normal" persons, a perspective
closer to the one taken here.

One reason restaurant theft is of theoretical interest is the possibility of various targets or objects for larceny.  Theft in the work
setting may be directed against the restaurant, its customers, or
fellow restaurant employees.  The recognition of different theft
areas raises numerous questions.  Are customers more likely to be
victimized than restaurant management?  Do larcenous waiters choose
between targets?  Are there specialists who use one technique against
one target, or are most waiters generalists?  In addition to differences by theft target, employee theft can be divided into pecuniary
theft and "amateur trading" theft (Henry and Mars, 1978).  In the
former, the intent and outcome of theft is to make money, i.e.,
private gain.  Amateur trading tends to be dictated by social considerations of exchange:  a theft may benefit another, which sets
up an obligation to return the favor.  These reciprocal arrangements mean that illegal "transactions are only one event in a
series" (Henry and Mars, 1978:248).  We would expect to find
pecuniary theft and amateur trading, here called social theft, to
be present in the restaurant trade.

Most of the research on employee theft has focused on retail sales
personnel (Dalton, 1959; Ditton, 1977c; Hollinger, 1978; Martin,
1962; Robin, 1969; Zeitlin, 1971), blue collar workers (Clark and
Hollinger, 1981; Horning, 1970; Mars, 1974) and hospital employees
(Clark and Hollinger, 1981).  While there have been numerous studies
of restaurant employees, there has been little systematic investigation of theft by workers in what has been termed "the epitome of
a service occupation" (Butler and Snizek, 1976:209).  William F.
Whyte's classic work (1948, 1949) on restaurant workers ignores
employee theft.  Two studies of cocktail waitresses (Spradley and
Mann, 1975; Hearn and Stoll, 1975) suggest that women in this
occupation have a common work argot, share a sense of stigma about
the job (sexual connotations about the occupation), and often
develop a dislike for customers, but the authors do not link theft
to any of these job conditions.  While some restaurant research
hints at employee theft (e.g., Butler and Skipper, 1980, 1981), the
topic has not received any systematic attention.  If not for a study
in England by Gerald Mars (1973), the literature would lead us to
believe there was no problem of employee theft in the restaurant
industry.

The research by Mars using "retrospective participant observation"
is based on one hotel dining room.  While he does detail the forms

of fiddles commonly used by waiters,[1] he does not develop hypotheses
to account for various theft targets,.nor does he try to predict
which restaurant employees will be involved.  The goal of this
exploratory study of theft in American restaurants is to assess the
forms and frequency of theft involvement by waiters and to test
three hypotheses using data obtained by a self-report method.

Hypotheses on Restaurant Theft

Three hypotheses are presented in this section.  The first makes a
prediction about the theft target of waiters who steal and the
frequency of each form of employee theft.  The other two hypotheses
address the issue of which waiters will engage in employee theft
and under what types of conditions.

Donald Horning (1970), in his study of theft by employees in an
electronics assembly plant, found a differentiation was made in
theft targets.  Factory goods of uncertain ownership (e.g., scrap
metal, discarded assembly parts) were most likely to be the object
of theft, followed by company property (e.g., tools, usable
materials), with the theft of co-workers' property being a distant
third.  The last category was clearly defined as theft by plant
workers and was seldom engaged in by employees.  Following Horning,
it is proposed that a hierarchy of theft objects will be found in
restaurants.[2]  It is hypothesized that a larger proportion of waiters
will be involved in thefts from the company.  Customer-directed
rip-offs should be next in terms of the proportion of waiters involved, and theft from fellow workers should be rare.

This hierarchy of theft target involvement is predicted on the
basis of an underlying "affective proximity" of the victim dimension.  Victimization of fellow workers should have the lowest·

---

[1]The terms used by employees for their theft activities may be
important in understanding why theft occurs.  English waiters
used the term "fiddle" to refer to theft from the customers or
the restaurant, while "knock off" was reserved for activities
such as taking things from the restaurant, e.g., linen or silverware.  Our informants, described in the methodology section below,
stated that "ripping off" was a general term applied to all theft
activities.  Hence, the use of the term by waiters in this study
is analogous to both "fiddle" and "knock off" in England, (cf.
Ditton, 1977b).

[2]It is not claimed that restaurant theft has a direct analog to
theft activities in a television assembly plant, the setting of
Horning's research.  There are no customers or tips, and cash is
not readily available as a theft target.  However, it is hypothesized that a hierarchy of targets exists in both settings, representing an underlying dimension available in both retail and
manufacturing sectors.

proportion of worker involvement. There should be a greater
personal identification with the victim and a more direct sense of
theft loss. Horning found a strong taboo against stealing from co-
workers, and the same result is expected among restaurant workers.
The most frequent theft target, on the other hand, should be the
restaurant. The work situation of the waiter is important in
understanding why the restaurant is a more likely target than the
customer. Waiters are largely independent workers who use the
restaurant as a place to ply their trade. The fact that very low
hourly wages are paid in most restaurants (usually half the minimum
hourly wage rate) combined with the expectation that income is
derived from tips (Butler and Skipper, 1981) means that waiters may
have little identification or commitment to the host restaurant.
To the extent a restaurant has a corporate image, ownership of
property is less identifiable (cf. Dillon, 1973). Add to this the
fact that management-worker friction is likely to occur and that
restaurant security arrangements are likely to be perceived by
waiters as onerous and bothersome--indicating a basic lack of trust
in the employee (Butler and Skipper, 1981:26)--then it follows that
most theft should be directed against the restaurant.

Customer-directed theft should fall between co-worker and restaurant.
In this service occupation, waiters and waitresses are in a subordinate relationship to customers, relying upon the tip as a reward
for being subservient.

> The tip is traditionally a reward for good and effi-
> cient service, but many waiters and waitresses feel
> that some customers use their tipping power to demand
> a subservient attitude and special favors . . . .
> Many blamed the tipping system for their inferior
> position in relation to customers. . . . In America,
> high-status people do not receive tips for their
> services, and tipping therefore tends to lower the
> status of the recipient. (Whyte, 1948:98-99)

The problem is very salient to the waiter or waitress because tips
remain their major source of income (cf. Butler and Skipper, 1980).
Butler and Snizek (1976) report that the quality of service does
little to increase the amount of tip received for service. About
the only way the restaurant worker can increase the size of tips is
to "push" food and drink to maximize the total bill, thereby en-
larging the amount of the tip.

The basic asymmetry in the waiter-diner relationship may produce
resentment towards customers, fostering a cynical attitude toward
the clientele of restaurants (Butler and Snizek, 1976; Butler and
Skipper, 1980; Hearns and Stoll, 1975). However customers, while
usually strangers, are physically present and hence identifiable
to some extent. The fact that many waiters try to develop "call
customers" (persons who will return and ask for a specific waiter)
further increases the identification factor. Therefore it is
predicted that few waiters will be involved in customer-targeted
theft compared to restaurant-directed theft.

Turning now to the question of which waiters will be involved in theft, one set of determinants resides in the actual working conditions and the subjective judgments made about those working conditions. The second hypothesis is that the greater the dissatisfaction with one's job, the more likely that employee theft will occur (e.g., Hollinger and Clark, 1982; Mangione and Quinn, 1975). In restaurant work, the objective conditions conducive to theft might be low pay, low volume of customers, poor tips, poor schedules, or unpopular stations (subsections of restaurant assigned to work). Negative attitudes towards one's work may follow these conditions. Low volume of business and poor tips may produce boredom. Dissatisfaction over working conditions may generate cynical attitudes toward the restaurant management and may reduce commitment to the task of customer service (Hearns and Stoll, 1975). Subjective conditions such as boredom, task dissatisfaction, and poor working conditions have been shown to be associated with theft involvement (Dalton, 1959; Zeitlin, 1971).

Another area of interest is the role of management in the production of employee theft. There are two major ways in which management indirectly contributes to theft by waiters. First, the formal socialization of a new waiter makes the novice aware of the phenomenon of restaurant rip-offs. Training involves showing the worker how to ring appropriate keys on the cash register, to check register tapes, to keep track of and be responsible for dinner and bar tabs. (These tickets or tabs are checked out in serial blocks at the beginning of each shift; used and unused tickets are turned into managers during checkout at the end of each shift). The novice also receives general instructions on restaurant procedures for checking on sales, e.g., counting steaks and comparing to the number of orders written for steaks. Through this job training, the worker is made cognizant of the restaurant's security system and inadvertantly learns that some ripping off must be going on given the elaborate safeguards. In what Gary Marx (1981) describes as a major irony of social control, attempts at controlling or preventing deviance may precipitate rule violations.

A second way that management contributes to theft is by supporting informal norms which permit certain rule violations and engender a tolerance for certain types of ripping-off activities. For example, a waiter may be told that drinking on the job is not allowed, but he is given a free drink by the bartender toward the end of the shift with the advice: "If you're doing a good job, the manager won't say anything." In these subtle ways, the new worker learns that the manager expects and accepts certain rule violations. The tolerance of some rule violations contributes to the control effectiveness of the manager, whose rule enforcement, like all controllers, depends in part on the good will of subordinates. The manager who enforces petty rules will soon alienate his work staff (Butler and Skipper, 1981:22). Certain rule violations--although not necessarily in the area of ripping off--may be necessary for the worker's efficient task performance; it is then in the best

interests of the manager to look the other way.[3]  Knowledge that
managers are flexible on company rules may allow workers to generalize to theft situations, which makes it more likely that certain
forms of ripping off become legitimated.

Some managers may feel that some ripping off is justified by low
pay and may be overlooked in good waiters--what Dalton (1959) terms
"unofficial rewards."  Management may come to realize that control
is impossible and basically inefficient:  "That is, the cost of an
effective security system, plus the cost of achieving equivalent
employee stability [lack of turnover]  by increasing pay or job
quality, is greater than the loss of merchandise due to employee
theft" (Zeitlin, 1971:26).

The tolerance by management facilitates expectations of entitlement by workers:  certain forms of theft may come to be seen as a
legitimate form of remuneration:  "It's a part of my wage" (Mars,
1973:202).  To the extent these conditions are perceived by workers,
they may contribute to a system of neutralizations which justify
involvement in employee theft.

Our third hypothesis is that workers who agree with various
neutralization statements will be more likely to engage in employee
theft than will workers who do not support such neutralizations.
Following the logic of social control theory (e.g., Hirschi, 1969),
it is predicted that workers would have to neutralize the bind of
the law, the prohibitions against theft.  Those able to neutralize
such controls prior to engaging in theft should be more free to
steal, other things being equal (Cressey, 1953).


METHOD

Four major approaches have been used to study employee theft.
Participant observational studies (e.g., Ditton, 1977c; Henry, 1978;
Mars, 1973, 1974) have produced rich details of the process of
theft, but findings are limited to one work setting.  A second
method has been the analysis of official records of action taken
against employees who get caught (Martin, 1962; Robin, 1969).  Such
research is better seen as reflecting societal reaction variables
rather than determinants of theft behavior.  Low rates of official
reactions to employee deviance severely limit this approach.  A
third method can be seen in Horning's (1970) non-directive interviews of factory workers to get estimates of theft involvement.
Dalton (1959) interviewed managers to get their estimates of theft
by their employees.  The unstructured nature of the questioning of
informants limits the generalizability of this approach.  A fourth

---

[3] See as a parallel example the use of the tap by airline assembly
workers (Bensman and Gerver, 1963).  At times the company may
directly encourage certain customer-based rip-offs to facilitate
getting the job done (Ditton, 1977c).

procedure is to use anonymous self-reports of theft involvement
(e.g., Clark and Hollinger, 1981; Hollinger, 1978). Self-reports
have the following advantages: more than one work setting can be
studied; hidden deviance can be recorded; the bias of officially
reported deviance is avoided; and a standard set of questions permit
a comparable measure of theft involvement across work settings. For
these reasons, this research used an anonymous self-report format to
study employee theft.

A questionnaire was constructed by using ten veteran waiters and
waitresses as informants. These people were interviewed at length,
first alone and later in a group setting. Without being informed
of the hypotheses or concepts of the study, they were asked to
describe types of ripping-off activities encountered in their trade.
Based on their descriptions, twelve short vignettes were created to
illustrate the range of theft activity (see Appendix). The three
theft targets are represented in the twelve examples used in the
questionnaire. After the vignettes were completed, the researcher
made a judgment about which of the hypothetical rip-off situations
fit the amateur trading criteria of theft as opposed to pecuniary
theft. The waiter informants supported these judgments.

Four dinner restaurants in a large Southwestern city were selected
as the setting for research. These four "prime rib" restaurants
were similar in these ways (1) each had a separate dining and bar/
lounge area within the restaurant; (2) menu items were similar
(expensive meat and fish dishes) and were comparable in prices;
(3) waiters could take drink and food orders, although cocktail
waitresses worked in the bar area; (4) each restaurant was well
known in the city and had been in operation for a number of years;
and (5) each was incorporated, with restaurants in other cities.
A major difference purposely selected as a criterion for inclusion
in the study was the tipping system. Two restaurants utilized a
straight tip system and two used a tip pool system. These two
tipping systems present different opportunities for ripping off
fellow workers.

The names and addresses of all waiters working in each of the four
restaurants were obtained from a waiter known to the author in each
establishment. (Lists of waiters' addresses and phone numbers are
posted in each restaurant and given to each employee to facilitate
covering shifts when someone is unable to work. These semi-public
lists meant that workers could be contacted without going through
the management.) This procedure generated a sample total of eighty-
one waiters who were sent a cover letter introducing the study and
the questionnaire. Respondents were asked to estimate the number
of fellow employees who engaged in each form of ripping off given
in the hypothetical vignettes. They were also asked to report
their own involvement in each type of theft activity during the
past year.

In the cover letter, respondents were given these assurances of
anonymity. First, they were told that all waiters in four city
restaurants were included in the cover letter in case respondents
wanted to check this reassurance with friends working in the other

establishments in the sample.  Second, the waiters were told that
the restaurant management and owners were not involved in the study
and that they did not know the study was going on.  Furthermore,
they were informed that their name and address had been given to
the researcher by a waiter in their restaurant.  Third, they were
told that the results would appear only in statistical summaries
and would not be computed for each specific restaurant.  This was
done to guarantee the anonymity of information for each restaurant.[4]
Another assurance was that names and addresses did not appear on
the questionnaire, nor did the name of the restaurant.  Finally,
questionnaires were sent to the waiters' home addresses to enhance
the confidential nature of the research

As a means of trying to improve the response rate, respondents were
mailed a dollar as token payment for their participation.  This was
done on the assumption that the cognitive dissonance over the
request would help to increase the rate of response (Hackler and
Bourgette, 1973).  (This may have backfired in that some waiters
returned the money, seeing it as inappropriate.)  Respondents were
also promised a summary of the results as another incentive to
cooperate in the study.


## Ethical Issues

There is a considerable problem with any self-report form of assessing rates of involvement in deviant behavior.  To present an
inventory of theft activities to our sample of workers is, in fact,
to suggest strategies and even specific tactics of engaging in part-
time theft at work.  The ethical dilemma is that the method of
gathering data--sending specific, detailed vignettes to currently
employed waiters--is tantamount to providing them with a manual for
ripping off.  Respondents unaware of a particular technique might
use this knowledge to produce an increase in the absolute theft in
the restaurants studied.

This ethical problem was addressed in the following ways:  First,
the ten restaurant workers used as informants (not included in the
final sample) gave assurances that the activities in the vignettes

------

[4]There are two forms of risk to respondents in the study. First,
they may be specifically identified as thieves by management (who
might gain access to questionnaires) and be fired or prosecuted.
Second, if rates of theft were computed by restaurant, owners who
might acquire the data could fire everyone if theft rates were seen
as intolerably high for their establishment.  Masking the identity
of the restaurant prevents this and also protects the researcher.
For example, the owner of one restaurant in the study found out
about the questionnaire from one of his waiters and contacted me
asking for the results of the research for his restaurant.  I told
him that because specific restaurants were not identified, these
data were not available.

were standard knowledge among most restaurant workers. Even if waiters were not using a particular theft technique, they were likely to know of its existence. The questionnaire would not, therefore, provide workers with any information that they did not already possess. There was still the problem of the newly hired waiter, not yet fully socialized into the ways of ripping off, who might benefit from reading the questionnaire. To avoid this problem, a second protection was built-in to the sampling design. After lists of all waiters currently employed in the four restaurants were obtained, a two-month delay in mailing the questionnaires was imposed. It was assumed that two months would be more than enough time for a new worker to become aware of most forms of restaurant rip-offs. Ditton (1977c) in his research on fiddling by English bread salesman found that the process there took about three weeks. The informants used to generate the vignettes also agreed that a two-month delay was sufficient.

This concession to the ethical problem was achieved at some cost. The delay reduced our final response rate in two ways. As persons were sent the questionnaire to their home addresses, those who had moved during this time period may not have received the questionnaire. Of the eighty-one questionnaires, sent, ten were returned as undeliverable. Another problem with the delay is that waiters may have resigned from the restaurant and consequently did not feel obligated to respond. High turnover rates are a feature of most restaurant work (e.g., Mars, 1973:201).[5] Of the seventy-one waiters who were contacted by mail, forty-one returned the questionnaires for a response rate of 58 percent.

While a higher response rate is desirable, there is no reason to suspect that non-response was correlated with our dependent variable, theft involvement. The reputed openness of rip-off practices in area restaurants implies that fear or reticence to admit theft was not a major factor in non-response. This openness was suggested by the informants who helped construct the questionnaire. The findings reported below bear out their contention; as we shall see, the sharing of knowledge of ripping-off techniques is a salient feature of employee theft in restaurants.

The small sample size (N=41) does limit the scope of our analysis, and caution must be used in generalizing these results to other restaurant employees. While desirable for analysis purposes, large samples of theft in restaurants would require a greater diversity in work settings. In this study, there was an attempt to use only comparable restaurants, given the criteria listed earlier in this section. The use of four restaurants was designed to avoid idiosyncratic results likely to obtain if only one work place is used.

---

[5] On this issue of employee turnover, waiters in our sample were asked how long they expected to continue working at their present restaurant. Thirty-two percent indicated that they planned to quit within three months.

(This is a problem with participant observational studies such as
the research by Gerald Mars (1973:202) which used one English
dining room with a total staff of twenty waiters.)  However our
attempt to achieve homogeneous work settings reduced the potential
pool of waiters in the sample.

One reviewer raised the question of the appropriateness of using
self-reports when sample size is under one hundred.  Rather than
specifying an arbitrary sample size for a research technique, it
is better to ask how the technique is used.  For example, a common
criticism of self report inventories--more often used on juveniles
than adults--is that detail is lacking on the deviant acts set down
for respondent reaction (Sheley, 1980:57).  The use of detailed
vignettes should provide a more accurate assessment of theft involvement than would larger sample surveys without specific vignettes.


FINDINGS

Types of Theft Activity

    The forms of theft by waiters are as varied as individual
ingenuity and restaurant security systems.  As it was not possible
to assess all forms of theft, certain activities (see Table 1)

TABLE 1.  Percentage of Waiters Who Knew Fellow Workers to Have
Engaged in Theft Activity, and Those Who Reported Involvement in
Theft Activity in the Past Twelve Months (N=41)

| Theft target and type of theft | Percent knowing others involved | Percent engaging in theft activity |
|---|---|---|
| Restaurant theft (social): | | |
|     Free food to friends | 76 | 56 |
|     Take home restaurant items | 68 | 44 |
| Restaurant theft (pecuniary): | | |
|     Fail to ring food items | 61 | 30 |
|     Selling restaurant items | 44 | 15 |
| Customer theft (pecuniary): | | |
|     Bill padding | 66 | 28 |
|     Short change customer | 71 | 23 |
|     Add tip to credit card | 73 | 15 |
| Other waiters as victim: | | |
|     Take other waiter's tips | 15 | 5 |
|     Hold out on tip pool | 75* | 44* |
| Infrequent theft: | | |
|     No ring, split with cook | 15 | 5 |
|     Bring in own wine to sell | 0 | 0 |
|     Take money from register | 0 | 0 |

*N is 16, those employees who worked under a tip pool system.

representing customer, restaurant and fellow workers as victims were presented to respondents. Twelve vignettes (see Appendix) were used to assess the relative rates of theft involvement. Two items need to be defined. Bill padding is one form of customer-directed theft as illustrated in this vignette:

> Art is waiting on a large party of twelve men, all of whom have been ordering drinks from the bar during dinner. The check is to be presented to the gentleman in charge and he will pay with a credit card. After looking through all the drink tickets, Art decides to inflate the figure of the bar bill, figuring that an extra four or five dollars will not be noticed. Art presents the bill and the man pays it.

Bill padding along with short changing customers and adding tips to credit cards represent customer-directed theft.

The second item, failure to ring, is a basic technique for ripping off the restaurant. It involves delivering food items to customers without ringing up the sale on the register. In most cases the customer pays for the items, but the money is diverted to the waiter. Gerald Mars notes that "fail to ring" is the major fiddle in English restaurants, and he provides a detailed description of how waiters engineer this form of theft (Mars, 1973:202-4). This technique is included in three theft activities in Table 1: fail to ring; no ring, split with cook (where there is actual collusion between workers to pull off the theft);[6] and free food to friends. This vignette illustrates the failure to ring up food for friends, the most frequent form of theft engaged in by the waiters:

> A couple of Greg's friends come in to dinner one night and have Greg wait on them. Greg must ring up the meat order on the register, but he gives them baked potatoes, corn on the cob, and dessert free of charge [items are not rung up]. They pay the meat bill and leave Greg a large tip.

The proportion of waiters who knew co-workers who engaged in the twelve theft activities is given in Table 1. The data show that employee theft is widely known about among waiters. While it is not possible to assess the source of this knowledge (seeing other waiters steal or hearing them talk about past theft activities), the importance of the fact is that it shows theft activity is not secret, but a commonly known-about phenomenon. The significance of this finding is developed in the discussion below.

---

[6] Cooperation between workers is required for employee theft in some occupations, e.g., dockworkers (Mars, 1974), bread salesman (Ditton, 1977c). In this sample, there did not appear to be a collusion requirement for most restaurant rip-offs; splitting with others was relatively rare (see Table 1).

The percentage of waiters in the sample who reported committing
each type of rip-off activity themselves during the past year shows
that our first hypothesis on directness of victimization is supported.  The largest proportion of waiters were involved in
restaurant-based theft (indirect victim).  The proportion who rip-
off customers is lower, and very little theft occurred against
fellow workers.  Blatant theft--stealing money directly from the
cash register--was not found in the sample.[7] This is consistent
with Hornings' (1970) research which also found that direct theft
seldom occurs in the workplace.

There was one exception to the directness of victim dimension:  a
form of co-worker victimization, holding out on tip pools, was a
frequent occurrence in the restaurants which had a tip pool system
of compensation.  Waiters dislike this form of remuneration because
it penalizes good waiters (those who consistently receive good tips)
and carries poor, less effective waiters.  Here there is not a
specific direct victim in that the loss is spread out among all
waiters.  This makes holding out part of one's tip money an action
devoid of connotations of stealing directly from fellow workers
(such as taking another waiter's tip money from his table--a rare
activity in the sample).  There is also a sense of entitlement
which prevents a waiter from seeing holding out as direct theft.
He has, after all, earned it.

The distinction between pecuniary theft and socially-based theft
is also shown in Table 1.  Two examples of social theft were used.
The theft labeled "free food to friends" involves treating one's
associates to a fringe benefit of one's own work.  As many of the
friends who are treated to free food are restaurant workers in other
eating establishments, the opportunity for reciprocity is present.
Theft of restaurant items is also termed social in that sets of
glasses or silverware are often given as gifts to friends rather
than used directly by the waiter.  These two examples of socially-
based theft do have pecuniary aspects.  For example, giving free
food to friends usually means the waiter profits from a large tip
left by the grateful recipients.  Restaurant items used as gifts
remove the necessity of purchasing such gifts for cash in the
legitimate marketplace.  However, these two acts are not classified
as pecuniary because "the rewards are more social than economic"
(Henry, 1978:112).

Since the only target for socially-based theft is the restaurant,
and given the high involvement of some waiters in pecuniary theft
against the restaurant, employee theft represents a sizable source
of "inventory shrinkage" for restaurant organizations.  One reason
for the high proportion of waiters involved in restaurant-directed

---

[7] Three forms of theft given at the bottom of Table 1 were very
infrequent in this sample of waiters.  These three items, all
examples of pecuniary theft directed at the restaurant, are omitted
from further analysis.

theft is that these two motives, social and pecuniary, operate side
by side.  What is disheartening from a management perspective is
the fact that these two forms of theft are largely independent (see
Table 2).[8]  For example, very few waiters who gave "free food to
friends" also engaged in "fail to ring" as a pecuniary act, i.e.,
of the twenty-three waiters who engaged in "free foods to friends,"
only one-third also used "fail to ring," even though the method of
ripping off is identical in both cases.  There appear to be two
independent reasons for waiters biting the hand that feeds them,
illustrating the complexity of the problem of trying to reduce
restaurant-directed theft.

When only pecuniary forms of theft are examined, we find that the
rates are about the same for restaurant as target and customers as
target.  One reason that the proportion of waiters involved in
customer rip-offs is not lower is that management generally has
fewer security measures directed at preventing customer rip-offs.[9]
In other words, the opportunities for ripping off customers may be
greater than opportunities to steal from the restaurant.  Given the
greater security against restaurant theft, even more importance
should be attached to the finding that more waiters were involved
in restaurant-directed theft compared to the other two possible
targets.

The pattern of theft in the four restaurants studied reveals that
a majority of waiters were involved in exchange-based, social theft
activities, and that a minority (about one-third) were heavily involved in pecuniary theft.[10] Table 2 shows an association between

----

[8]Table 2 shows that theft activities are not highly correlated.
This implies there are multiple reasons for theft involvement.  As
this is an exploratory study, the intention was to see if certain
variables could explain different categories of theft targets and
various types of theft, e.g., pecuniary theft versus social theft.
For this reason, dependent variables are created in the next section
to see if the same hypotheses can predict different types of theft
involvement.  The fact that the hypotheses have varying success in
the endeavor suggests that all possible causal variables have not
been uncovered here, i.e., more research needs to be done.

[9]Because four different restaurants were used in the sample, it was
not possible to gather information on the direct influence of security system effectiveness and theft.  As an indirect means of
assessing security system effectiveness, waiters were asked to rate
their restaurant as to ease with which ripping off could be done.
Respondents' perceptions of ease of ripping off did not correlate
with socially-based restaurant theft, but was correlated with
pecuniary theft (Gamma = .42 for restaurant theft and .32 for customer theft--as defined in the next section).

[10]Nine waiters (22% of the sample) did not engage in any of the
twelve theft activities given as vignettes, although they knew of
others who did engage in some of the rip-off methods.

TABLE 2.  Correlation Matrix of Employee Theft Activities Using
Pearson's Phi Coefficient as a Measure of Association (N=41)

| Theft activities | 1 | 2 | 3 | 4 | 5 | 6 | 7 |
|---|---|---|---|---|---|---|---|
| 1. Free food to friends | 1.00 | .18 | .13 | .03 | .00 | .13 | .22 |
| 2. Take restaurant items | | 1.00 | .40* | .08 | .15 | .38* | .18 |
| 3. Fail to ring | | | 1.00 | .40* | .62* | .47* | .18 |
| 4. Sell restaurant items | | | | 1.00 | .40* | .31 | .41 |
| 5. Bill padding | | | | | 1.00 | .20 | .21 |
| 6. Short change customers | | | | | | 1.00 | .10 |
| 7. Add tip to credit card | | | | | | | 1.00 |

*Significant at or below the .05 level of significance based on
corrected chi square.

different pecuniary rip-offs, regardless of theft targets.  For
example, those who "fail to ring" were also more likely to pad a
customer's bill or short change a patron--all financially advanta-
geous activities.


Reasons for Employee Theft

In an attempt to test our second and third hypotheses, three dependent variables were generated from the first seven vignettes in
Table 1:  (1) social restaurant theft--respondents were classified
as having engaged in none, one, or both of these activities; (2)
pecuniary restaurant theft--involved summing "fail to ring" and
"selling restaurant items" (none, one, both); and (3) pecuniary
customer rip-offs--these three items were divided into none, one,
two or more of these forms of theft.  The last five theft items in
Table 1 were excluded from the following analysis due to their
infrequent occurrence.  Our goal in the remainder of the article is
to examine some of the possible determinants of restaurant and
customer theft.

In this sample, background variables such as education, marital
status, and degree of religious involvement did not affect rates
of ripping-off participation.  Age, found to be correlated with
employee theft by Clark et al. (1979)--with younger workers more
involved in theft--could not be assessed here.  Eighty-eight percent
of the waiters in the sample were between 18 and 25 years old.  Time
on the job, shown by Hearn and Stoll (1975) to be related to cynical
attitudes toward restaurant work and customers, did not predict
theft involvement.  We now turn to work-based factors thought to
affect restaurant and customer directed theft.

We predicted in hypothesis 2 that those workers perceiving negative
aspects in their work would be more likely to engage in employee
theft than those satisfied with their jobs.  Features of the work

setting were broken down into two major categories: objective job conditions and subjective judgments about one's work. Objective conditions included responses to ordinal items assessing each waiter's perception of volume of business (very good to very poor), level of pay at work (very adequate to very inadequate), and amount of tips at the restaurant (good tips to poor tips). None of the three objective job conditions were associated with any of the three forms of restaurant theft. (Gammas were all below .20 for these nine comparisons).

Likert-type items were used to assess attitudes toward the job, e.g., degree of boredom, attitudes toward one's supervisor, toward the owner, and questions designed to measure injustice, e.g., feelings of being treated unfairly by management, and saying management takes advantage of waiters. These subjective attitudes about one's work did not predict theft involvement when the restaurant was the target. Two factors, negative attitude toward supervisor and feelings of being unfairly treated by management, were associated with ripping off the customer (Gammas of .43 and .51 respectively). This displacement effect, or what Butler and Skipper (1981:25-26) term a "spill-over" phenomenon, means that workers unhappy with management are more likely to victimize the customer than the restaurant. This could be because there are more opportunities to rip-off customers. As noted above, restaurants are likely to have more security safeguards to protect the firm from theft than its customers.

We conclude that job-related conditions and attitudes were not associated with restaurant-directed theft and only two factors were strongly correlated with customer rip-offs. This failure to find support for hypothesis 2 suggests that job conditions do not directly affect theft behavior. However, dissatisfaction with one's work may operate through the development of neutralization which in turn could affect employee theft.

Our third hypothesis predicted that failure to develop or support neutralizing statements would prevent theft involvement by waiters. Three types of neutralizing techniques were assessed. One was the use of justification, defined as occurring when "one accepts responsibility for the act in question, but denies the pejorative quality associated with it" (Scott and Lyman, 1968:47). Second, denial of injury, i.e., no one is hurt, and third, the belief in a deserving victim, i.e., a person who brings on their own victimization (Sykes and Matza, 1957). These six statements were used to assess a weakening of beliefs (responses to Likert-type questions where "agree" and "strongly agree" were combined):

1. Justification: The management expects some ripping off by its employees (31% agreed).
2. Justification: Most waiters see ripping off as an appropriate method of getting a fair wage (17% agreed).
3. Justification: Ripping off is an acceptable way for me to supplement my low pay (12% agreed).
4. Denial of injury: The management can financially afford to be ripped off by its employees (17% agreed).

5.  Deserving victim: Drunk customers deserve to be
    ripped off (5% agreed).
6.  Deserving victim: Persons who frequent this
    restaurant deserve to be ripped off (5% agreed).

It is apparent from the low percentages of agreement that neutralization and justification are rather rare among the waiters.  This
is surprising given the high exposure to theft activities of other
waiters as well as the heavy self-involvement seen in Table 1.

There is a potential causal order problem here, as with most research
on neutralization techniques (e.g., Cressey, 1953; Hirschi, 1969;
Sheley, 1980).  Reports of past deviant acts are compared to current
statements which represent neutralizations.  While we cannot resolve
this causal order question, it is of less importance because of the
low frequency of these attitudes in the sample.  However, it could
be argued that neutralizing attitudes were important in the past,
setting up a pattern of theft which has now become accepted (see
Sheley, 1980:55).  If such a process were occurring, we would expect
new waiters to use neutralization techniques, while waiters on the
job a longer time might not.  When time on the job was used as a
control, the original non-significant relationship of neutralization
agreement and theft involvement did not change for new waiters (one
year or less) and experienced waiters (over one year as a waiter).

In conclusion, hypothesis 3 was not supported.  Agreement with neutralization statements was not related to involvement in restaurant
theft.  It remains to be explained why theft activity can be so
high without widespread agreement with neutralizations and justifications.


DISCUSSION

The failure of the neutralization hypothesis raises questions about
the role of such beliefs in producing employee theft, questions also
raised for other forms of deviance (cf. Minor, 1980; Sheley, 1980).
The fact that theft is such an open activity in restaurants may mean
that "neutralizations and rationalizations are simply unnecessary"
(Minor, 1980:115).  As Sheley (1980:51) notes, "neutralization designed to rid an individual of a moral dilemma prior to deviance
hardly seems necessary when society or subculture has already accomplished the task."  The work subculture of waiters seems to remove
the need for neutralizations.  There is some evidence that neutralizations are more likely for solitary, secretive acts of deviance
such as embezzlement (Cressey, 1953).  For example, Hindelang (1970)
notes that among youth techniques of neutralization are more likely
to account for solitary delinquent offenses where group support is
absent.  But restaurant theft is not a solitary offense in that most
waiters know it is going on and it is openly discussed.  This openness of theft activity is seen in these findings:  (a) seventy-seven
percent of the waiters said they had discussed rip-off methods with
co-workers; (b) sixty percent stated they discussed which customers

deserved to be ripped off;[11] and (c) eighty percent knew at least one other waiter who had been caught ripping off.[12] This exposure to ripping off was correlated with personal involvement in different types of theft activity (see Table 3).

There are two ways of arguing that techniques of neutralization are irrelevant to socially-based restaurant theft. If the motivation for social theft is seen as residing in making and maintaining friendships, or in the carrying out of reciprocal exchange, then it might be argued that there is a built-in neutralization of "appeal to higher loyalties" (Sykes and Matza, 1957). But neutralization

---

[11]One respondent noted that waiters will try to anticipate which customers will stiff them (leave no tip): "There's a habbit [sic] among waiters at my restaurant to 'size up' customers as they come in as to whether they are 'red-necks' or not. (A red-neck doesn't tip, or if he does, only very little. He also eats a lot of bread, has his steaks well-done, and puts ketsup on them.)"

[12]Respondents indicated that in almost every case the person was fired when caught, but not referred to the police. Five respondents reported they had been caught ripping off in the past. Four of the five reported continuing theft involvement at their current place of employment.

TABLE 3. Exposure to Theft Activities and Amount of Self-involvement in Theft Talk for Three Types of Employee Theft Using Gamma (N=41)

| Items | Restaurant (social) | (pecuniary) | Customers (pecuniary) |
|---|---|---|---|
| Number of other waiters known by respondents to have been caught: none one-five over five (N=8 17 16) | .12 | .55 | .38 |
| Discuss rip-off methods with co-workers in the restaurant: never occasionally often (N*=9 24 6) | .48 | .69 | .63 |
| Discuss which customers deserve to be ripped off: never occasionally often (N*=16 21 3) | .52 | .76 | .56 |

*N does not total 41 due to non-response.

must be considered an active process, one consciously engaged in prior to the act to free the actor of any moral qualms (Cressy, 1953). If it is so embedded in socially-based theft that it is not verbalized, its active nature seems to be absent. Consequently, the concept of neutralization from social control theory does little to explain social restaurant theft.

There is a second reason why techniques of neutralization are irrelevant to social theft: the linguistic issue of defining the act. Henry and Mars (1978) suggest that the non-economic basis of some part-time theft prevents perpetrators from viewing their behavior as stealing. As long as the motivation is exchange, not profit; reciprocity, not gain; altruism, not advantage; "theft" connotations can be avoided. Stealing has a linguistic base in the market-economy and legal systems, but not in the vocabulary of the illegal amateur trader. When the traditional "language of market exchange" (Henry and Mars, 1978:256) is denied, the techniques of neutralizations may be literally uncalled for or inappropriate.

This argument would not explain involvement in more pecuniary theft, activity less open to such linguistic manipulation. Here another sense in which restaurant theft is social must be recognized to account for the failure of the neutralization hypothesis. Theft at work is a source of talk and a ground for communication among workers. It becomes part of the work culture and attendant folk-lore of the occupation (cf. Horning, 1970). Theft-talk as shop-talk permits the achievement of status in the eyes of co-workers, a form of work-based identity. Discussions of ripping-off techniques result in attributions of experience, competence, and craftiness to waiters. Seen in this way, theft talk becomes a valued activity, increasing group solidarity among waiters (cf. Zeitlin, 1971). In the words of one of Henry's (1978:97) informants: "There's no point in doing it if you can't tell people about it."

In this sense, all theft activities in restaurants have a social dimension in that group solidarity is achieved. However this does not mean that all theft is social theft. Following the usage of Henry, social theft refers to "amateur trading" activities engaged in primarily without concern for financial gain, i.e., where the intention is purely to do someone a favor. Henry found that the recipient of the favor is often not in the work group, but someone outside it (cf. Henry and Mars, 1978; Henry, 1978).

Theft-talk serves many of the same functions which atrocity stories do in work settings. Atrocity stories are "dramatic events staged between groups of friends and acquaintances that draw on shared understandings about the way of the world. The teller is cast as hero . . . [and through such stories] social structures and parties to them are rendered rational and comprehensible" (Dingwell, 1977: 375). Here such talk informs the newcomer of the work culture and folklore, serving to socialize the novice into the flow of the job. It contributes to a sense of comradery as well as worker morale, viz., theft-talk enriches an otherwise routinized task performance. Worker discussions of ripping off, like theft itself, allows the waiter to "take matters into his own hands, assume responsibility, make decisions and face challenges" (Zeitlin, 1971:24).

Talk about restaurant rip-offs is also a controlling mechanism whereby workers set the boundaries of appropriate targets and amounts of theft, what English dockworkers call the "working value of the boat" (Mars, 1974). Within these worker discussions of theft reside both legitimating motives as well as built-in controls to limit theft activity (e.g., Ditton, 1977a:248). In this vein, Stuart Henry (1978) presents a proposal to control worker theft by relying upon workers and their subcultural expectations.

A recognition of the function of workers' talk and its relation to developing status on the job gives new meaning to Zeitlin's (1971: 22) assertion that "a little larceny can do a lot for employee morale." Those seeking to limit employee theft must realize that the subservient nature of service work creates problems of status and that alternative sources of building status on the job would need to be devised to replace the centrality of employee theft and its resultant talk.[13] Only then will an alternative to Zeitlin's (1971) admittedly risky solution of "let them steal" be possible.

---

[13]If theft talk is a critical aspect of work identity, future research might focus on the extent to which this talk is accurate. It is possible that workers could make up rip-off stories to satisfy co-workers. Here as elsewhere talk rather than action may be a more frequent occurrence.

REFERENCES

Bensman, Joseph and Israel Gerver
     1963    "Crime and punishment in the factory: the function
             of deviancy in maintaining the social system."
             American Sociological Review 28:588-98.
Bryant, Clifton D.
     1974    Deviant Behavior: Occupational and Organizational
             Bases. Chicago: Rand McNally.
Butler, Suellen and James K. Skipper, Jr.
     1980    "Waitressing, vulnerability, and job autonomy."
             Sociology of Work and Occupations 7:487-502.
     1981    "Working for tips: an examination of trust and
             reciprocity in a secondary relationship of the
             restaurant organization." Sociological Quarterly
             22:15-27.
Butler, Suellen and William E. Snizek
     1976    "The waiter-diner relationship." Sociology of
             Work and Occupations 3:209-222.

Clark, John P., Richard C. Hollinger, and Leonard F. Smith
     1979    Theft by Employees in Work Organizations: A
             Preliminary Final Report. University of
             Minnesota: unpublished.

Clark, John P. and Richard C. Hollinger
     1981     Theft by Employees in Work Organizations.
              University of Minnesota:  unpublished.
Cressey, Donald R.
     1953     Other People's Money.  New York:  Free Press.
Dalton, Melville
     1959     Men Who Manage.  New York:  Wiley.
Dillon, M.C.
     1973     "Why should anyone refrain from stealing?"
              Ethics 83:338-40.
Dingwall, Robert
     1977     "'Atrocity stories' and professional relationships."
              Sociology of Work and Occupations 4:371-396.
Ditton, Jason
     1977a    "Alibis and aliases:  some notes on the 'motives'
              of fiddling bread salesmen."  Sociology 11:233-55.
     1977b    "Learning to 'fiddle' customers."  Sociology of
              Work and Occupations 4:427-50.
     1977c    Part-time Crime:  An Ethnography of Fiddling and
              Pilferage.  London:  Macmillian.
Hackler, James C. and Patricia Bourgette
     1973     "Dollars, dissonance, and survey returns."
              Public Opinion Quarterly 37:276-81.
Hearn, H. L. and Patricia Stoll
     1975     "Continuance commitment in low-status occupations:
              the cocktail waitress."  Sociological Quarterly
              16:105-14.
Henry, Stuart
     1978     The Hidden Economy:  The Context and Control of
              Borderline Crime.  London:  Martin Robertson.
Henry, Stuart and Gerald Mars.
     1978     "Crime at work:  the social construction of
              amateur property theft."  Sociology 12:246-63.
Hindelang, Michael
     1970     "The commitment of delinquents to their misdeeds:
              do delinquents drift?"  Social Problems 17:502-509.
Hirschi, Travis
     1969     Causes of Delinquency.  Berkeley:  University of
              California Press.
Hollinger, Richard C.
     1978     "Employee deviance against the formal work
              organization."  Paper presented at the annual
              meetings of American Society of Criminology.
Hollinger, Richard and John Clark
     1982     "Employee deviance:  a response to the perceived
              quality of the work experience."  Work and
              Occupations 9 (February):97-114.
Horning, Donald N.M.
     1970     "Blue-collar theft:  conceptions of property,
              attitudes toward pilfering, and work group norms
              in a modern industrial plant."  In Erwin O. Smigel
              and H. Laurence Ross (eds.), Crimes Against
              Bureaucracy.  New York:  Van Nostrand.

EMPLOYEE THEFT IN THE RESTAURANT TRADE                         *67*

Mangione, Thomas W. and Robert P. Quinn
    1975    "Job satisfaction, counterproductive behavior, and drug
            use at work." Journal of Applied Psychology 60:114-116.
Mars, Gerald
    1973    "Hotel pilferage:  a case study in occupational theft."
            In Malcolm Warner (ed.), The Sociology of the Workplace.
            New York:  Halsted.
    1974    "Dock pilferage."  In Paul Rock and Mary McIntosh (eds.),
            Deviance and Social Control.  London:  Tavistock.
Martin, J.P.
    1963    Offenders as Employees.  New York:  St. Martin's Press.
Marx, Gary T.
    1981    "Ironies of social control:  authorities as contributors
            to deviance through escalation, nonenforcement and
            covert facilitation."  Social Problems 28:221-246.
Minor, W. William
    1980    "The neutralization of criminal offense."  Criminology
            18:103-120.
Robin, Gerald D.
    1969    "Employees as offenders."  Journal of Research in Crime
            and Delinquency 6:17-33.
    1974    "White-collar crime and employee theft."  Crime and
            Delinquency 20:251-262.
Scott, Marvin B. and Stanford M. Lyman
    1968    "Accounts."  American Sociological Review 33:46-62.
Sheley, Joseph F.
    1980    "Is neutralization necessary for criminal behavior?"
            Deviant Behavior 2:49-72.
Spradley, James P. and Brenda J. Mann
    1975    The Cocktail Waitress.  New York:  Wiley.
Sykes, Gresham M., and David Matza
    1957    "Techniques of neutralization:  a theory of delinquency."
            American Sociological Review 22:6640.
Whyte, William F.
    1948    Human Relations in the Restaurant Industry.  New York:
            McGraw-Hill.
    1949    "The social structure of the restaurant."  American
            Journal of Sociology 54:302-308.
Zeitlin, Lawrence R.
    1971    "A little larceny can do a lot for employee morale."
            Psychology Today 5:22,24,26,64.

APPENDIX

The following hypothetical situations were created to assess various
forms of ripping off which might occur in restaurant work.

Free Food to Friends

A couple of Greg's friends come in to dinner one night and have
Greg wait on them.  Greg must ring up the meat order on the register, but he gives them baked potatoes, corn on the cob, and dessert
free of charge.  They pay the meat bill and leave Greg a large tip.

## Take Home Restaurant Items

Lennie, after doing his check out and getting ready to go home,
will occasionally pick up a restaurant glass and put it in his coat.
He has just about finished a service for twelve of glasses from the
restaurant.  Next, he plans to collect a twelve-place setting of
restaurant silverware.

## Fail to Ring Food Items

Four customers are seated at one of Ben's tables, two elderly men
and their wives.  The two men each order the cheapest main course
item on the menu and the women order salads.  Ben rings up the
main course items on the register, but does not ring up the salads.
After the meal is finished, Ben presents the bill with the two
main course items rung up and the two salads written in by hand and
totaled.  The two men pay the full amount, plus a tip, and Ben
pockets the price of the salads.

## Selling Restaurant Items

Three conventioneers are asking Carl about the restaurant.  They
especially like the decor and particularly the drink glasses with
the restaurant's inscription on them.  They ask Carl if they could
buy two glasses and he obliges them for two dollars a glass.  Carl
keeps the money.

## Bill Padding

Art is waiting on a large party of twelve men, all of whom have
been ordering drinks from the bar during dinner.  The check is to
be presented to the gentleman in charge and he will pay with a
credit card.  After looking through all the drink tickets, Art
decides to inflate the figure of the bar bill, figuring that an
extra four or five dollars will not be noticed.  Art presents the
bill and the man pays it.

## Short Change Customer

After a particularly difficult time with a group of highly demanding and rude customers, Ian presents the bill expecting little or
no tip.  After several minutes, one of the customers lays several
ten dollar bills on top of the tab.  Ian picks it up and brings it
back to the register area to count the money.  He finds that the
tens are all new and on a bill of $37.50 there are five new ten
dollar bills.  He figures that the customer was not aware of the
fact that the bills stuck together.  Ian, feeling that they unknow-
ingly left him ten dollars too much, does not inform them of the
mistake.  He returns change of $2.50, keeping the ten.

## Add Tip to Credit Card

John goes to a table to pick up the customer's Master Charge receipt after they have left the table and finds that they have left him no tip. He looks at the charge and realizes that the customer has only signed it, leaving his copy with the rest and not totaling out the amount. John adds a 15% tip and totals it out, throwing away the customer's copy of the Master Charge form.

## Take Other Waiter's Tip Money

Matt's station has been very slow, while the waiter in the next section of tables has been quite busy. There is a tip tray on one of the busy waiter's tables which has been there for some time after a large party departed. Matt is sure the other waiter has not noticed the size of the tip; in passing the table, Matt quickly takes a five off the bottom of the stack of bills on the tip tray, figuring the other waiter will never miss it.

## Hold Out on Tip Pool

Ned works in a restaurant which utilizes a tip pool procedure. At the end of the night all the waiters pool their tips and, after the restaurant takes out a certain percentage, the waiters split the remainder between them. Ned receives a $20 tip on a $35 bill. At the end of the night he only turns in $5 of the $20 tip.

## No Ring, Split with Cook

Don, a waiter, has gotten to know the head cook quite well. They work out a system whereby Don writes up some of his dinner orders and turns them into the cook without ringing them up on the register. At the end of the night, Don will split the money collected in this way with the cook.

## Bring in Own Wine to Sell

Frank has been selling quite a few bottles of Mateús Rose to his customers. He decides to bring in several bottles of his own (which he obtained on sale) and to sell them to the customer at the inflated restaurant price and pocket the difference between what he paid for it and what the restaurant charges.

## Take Money from Cash Register

Ken, during a slow point in the evening, notices that one of the cash registers has been left unattended as the cashier was called away to the phone. Looking around and seeing no one, Ken quickly opens the register and takes a few twenties off the stack, pretending to make change.

*Request reprints from Richard Hawkins, Southern Methodist University, Dallas, TX 75275.*

BU

# Why you may be dissatisfied with garage servicing

**Professor O'Brien, lecturer in economics, believes that there are perverse incentives working in the motor trade which ensure that the garage which performs poorly is likely to do well. What's more, he reckons that the motor industry could remedy the situation, if only it cared.**

THE widespread dissatisfaction with the standards of garage servicing isn't because there is something morally different about people who work in the car trade but simply the result of perverse economic incentives which the motor industry could remedy if it cared for us motorists.

Around half the economic activity in this country takes place through the price system. People are allowed to choose what they spend money on, and their choice determines not only what is produced — bread or ballbearings, television sets or loo seats — but who should thrive in producing it. If Fagg End and Co. produce meat pies with cigarette ends in, people will stick to Sainsbury's pies. Sainsbury flourish and Fagg End go bankrupt. Simple.

But for this system to work it is vital that two conditions be met: that the consumer should have speedy knowledge of defects in any goods or service which he purchases — he should realise that Fagg End pies are contaminated and not munch through the butts — and that he should have some alternative so that he is not forced through circumstances to consume Fagg End pies because there is no substitute.

For most of the competitive price system these conditions are fulfilled. Either there are expert buyers (for ballbearings) or the defects are readily ascertainable. The incentives which the system throws up are, then, those which benefit the consumer. A firm which produce only left shoes would speedily go out of business. But a garage which services cars and only does *half the work* prescribed by the manufacturer, is likely to flourish. There are *perverse incentives* which ensure that the garage which performs poorly is likely to do well.

The incentives are perverse because both of the conditions for efficient operation of the system — knowledge, and the existence of competitive alternatives — are absent. First, the consumer of garage services has no knowledge of whether a service has been performed properly, and it is difficult for him to check this up. This means

that a garage can, with impunity, charge for a full service which has only been half done. The evidence (from the detailed and well supported reports on garage servicing carried on several occasions by *Which?* magazine) would seem to suggest, as the economist's profit maximising "model" of the firm would predict, that this is the norm.

For if a garage habitually does half the service its costs are very much lower than if it had done the full service; and since it can charge the full price, because of the ignorance of the consumer, its profits are maximised when it does as little of the service as it can get away with.

There is probably some lower limit below which the garage will not go in skimping the service, because the risks of detection then become too high. Casual observation would suggest that, for most garages, this minimum involves an oil change, together with two other operations which are themselves the

result of perverse incentives — the unnecessary replacement of plugs and points. It now seems to be normal to replace both of these items when they are only half worn out. The consumer of garage services generally does not know enough about the manufacturer's recommendations to argue about this; he lacks knowledge and he has no alternative as he is presented with a *fait accompli* when he goes to collect his car and he either pays the bill or does not get his car back. The garage makes a profit on the supply of these unnecessary items; while their inclusion in the minimal service performance makes the customer think that the rest of the job has been done.

If he suspects otherwise, he will find it hard to establish the truth; and harder still to persuade the garage to take the car back and do the job properly. Not only is it certain that they will only do some of the jobs, but by causing hostility through complaining he may well risk, at the very least, having his car handled roughly.

Immediate mechanical failure as a result of deficient service is extremely unlikely. It will occur only after a lag; and the garage, far from being held responsible, is likely to profit through rectifying the fault.

Even if the consumer has perfect knowledge of what hadn't been done to his car he has very little alternative but to keep on patronising an unsatisfactory garage. For one thing he is limited by the franchising system for the first year of his car's life; and if the car is at all unusual he is limited to the manufacturer's agent thereafter. This can be an acute problem in the case of some imported cars which are handled through few agents and their spares are very specialised. Secondly, and very importantly, the scope for home maintenace is extremely limited — again this applies particularly to some of the more complex imported vehicles — so that the

unfortunate owner is always going to have to use the garage trade and probably one particular part of it.

The car owner is therefore virtually locked in to the present unsatisfactory system which ensures maximum profits for minimum performance. The results of the *Which?* surveys are then exactly what the economist would predict in these circumstances. What can be done about this situation?

There are a number of ways in which the situation could be improved. Firstly, and most importantly, manufacturers have got to start thinking again in terms of home maintenance. This means that handbooks should be comprehensive and easily understood and, above all, that vehicles should be accessible and not require large quantities of special tools. They should be prepared to provide decent tool kits or at least to list a minimum tool kit which would be required to do routine work.

Secondly, (although I dislike recommending this, I think that it is justified in this peculiar economic situation) the dissatisfied customer should be able to seek the help of the Weights and Measures Inspectorate in conjunction with the local DoE testing station. For a small fee it should be possible to have a vehicle inspected after service to see whether the work has been done properly; and the customer should have the assistance of the Inspectorate if it has not. The motoring organisations are extremely reluctant to get involved in disputes between customers and garages; they could help more than they do.

Thirdly, the education of car users, which the technical colleges already do on a small scale, could be extended. In some areas it is a very dedicated motorist who manages to find a car maintenance course which he can attend. Finally, house purchasers should start asking builders to install inspection pits in their garages, as was the practice pre-war. This would greatly assist the hapless motorist both in checking that a service has been completed and also in performing a service himself. Like the full tool kits, the accessible motor cars and handbooks which gave instructions about all the details of servicing and routine maintenance, these have largely disappeared from the scene and this has helped to bring about the present situation.

If the result of these changes were to be, in part, a reduction in the size of the servicing industry, this would be to the benefit of the consumer. He will always need the elite — the true mechanic — for overhaul and rebuilding work. But the relative balance of demand would have been shifted in favour of the elite of the trade, thus helping to raise the overall standard of garage work.

The present situation is a sorry one (as anyone who checks their car thoroughly after service will find out) and some sort of improvement is very necessary.

But I'm sure I'd get nobody in the garage trade to agree with me.

*If you're in the garage trade and don't agree with Professor O'Brien, then write in. Space will be made available for you in Forum — Ed.*

HONEYSETT

# [17]

ANNALS, *AAPSS*, **493**, September 1987

## The Second Economy of the
## Soviet Union and Eastern Europe

*By* STEVEN L. SAMPSON

ABSTRACT: The second economies of the Soviet Union and other East European countries derive from structural inadequacies in the socialist planning system and from the cultural and historical evolution of each East European society. This article combines the structural and cultural approaches to the second economy and focuses on four of its most prevalent forms: peasant household production, the shadow economy within socialist enterprises, the underground factories of Soviet Georgia, and the hidden economy within the retail and service sectors. In all cases, social linkages and cultural values provide frameworks for economic activities. The second economy helps to alleviate consumer shortages and bureaucratic bottlenecks in all these societies. It also acts as a social mollifier, channeling dangerous political frustrations into consumerism, swindling, or petty corruption. Yet the overall effect of the second economy is a corrosive one: as a surrogate reform, a second economy tolerated by the authorities only reproduces the fundamental flaws of the formal economy. Moreover, it exacerbates the gap between society and the state, between "us" and "them."

---

*Steven L. Sampson, a cultural anthropologist, received his Ph.D. in 1980 from the University of Massachusetts, Amherst. He has carried out ethnographic fieldwork on town planning and local politics in Romania and is the author of* National Integration through Socialist Planning: An Anthropological Study of a Romanian New Town *and articles on various aspects of informal systems in Eastern Europe. He has recently coauthored a book on the anthropology of Denmark's second economy, entitled* Uden Regning *[Without receipt] and is preparing an extended anthropological study of the informal sector in Eastern Europe.*

WERE an international commission of experts asked to design a society where the second economy would thrive best, they would probably design the Soviet Union.[1] Press reports and scholarly analyses have shown that the second economy is an integral part of everyday life in all the socialist societies. Ironically, the second economy in these countries is often the equivalent of the market or primary economy in capitalist countries.

Some of these activities are simply what we would term capitalist entrepreneurship: the peasant who cultivates her private plot and sells the produce on the free market, speculative trading, middleman fees, renting property, money lending, and operating a private firm.

Other forms of the second economy found in Eastern Europe are common to all advanced economies, socialist or capitalist. These include producing or selling illegal goods such as narcotics or providing illegal services such as prostitution; pilfering from the workplace; skimming cash receipts; conducting unregistered or untaxed trade; and paying off police or inspectors to ignore such activities.

Finally, there are second economy activities that are neither typically capitalist nor universally illegal: the informal or illegal activities that enterprises use to fulfill their plan; underground factories; paying bribes or tips in order to buy something in a store or to induce planners and controllers to revise plans; buying and reselling goods obtained from shops for foreigners; and selling

scarce or rationed goods taken from the state.

Popular accounts have tended to term the second economy of Eastern Europe—hereafter "Eastern Europe" is meant to encompass the USSR and other countries of the Eastern bloc—"islands of capitalism" in which the spirit of free initiative thrives in spite of stifling bureaucracy.[2] The official East European press looks on the second economy as a "corrosive" factor, robbing the formal economy of essential goods, services, and labor time. Illegal or informal economic activity is an example of a "backward mentality" destined to disappear as the socialist system is "perfected."[3]

This only begs the question of why—after 70 years of socialism in the Soviet Union, 40 in the other East European countries—these backward mentalities

1. This sentence is paraphrased, by permission, from Gregory Grossman and Vladimir G. Treml, "Measuring Hidden Personal Incomes in the USSR," in *The Unofficial Economy*, ed. Sergio Alessandrini and Bruno Dallago (Aldershot: Gower Press, 1987).

2. For example, Yuri Brokhin, *Hustling on Gorky Street* (London: W. H. Allen, 1976); Hedrick Smith, *The Russians* (New York: Quadrangle, 1983); Robert Kaiser, *Russia: The People and the Power* (New York: Pocket Books, 1976); Konstantin Simis, *USSR: The Corrupt Society—The Secret World of Soviet Capitalism* (New York: Simon & Schuster, 1982); David Shipler, *Russia: Broken Idols, Solemn Dreams* (New York: Times Books, 1983); David Willis, *Klass: How Russians Really Live* (New York: St. Martin's Press, 1985); Lev Timofeev, *Soviet Peasants—or the Peasants' Art of Starving* (New York: Telos Books, 1985).

3. Speaking of corruption in the Soviet Republic of Georgia, Eduard Shevardnadze, who was then first secretary of the Georgian Communist Party—and is now the USSR's foreign minister—made the very un-Marxist statement that "there are people in whom the spirit of private ownership seems to be inborn." *Zarya Vostoka*, 3 Nov. 1973, quoted in David Law, "Corruption in Georgia," *Critique* (Glasgow), no. 3, p. 103, (Autumn 1974). The current Soviet campaign against persons with "unearned incomes" stresses the particular need for "improving ideological and political work and . . . molding in each person an attitude of irreconcilability toward the private-ownership mentality." "Alien to Our Morality," TASS report, 10 Aug. 1986.

not only exist, but seem to be thriving as never before. This has led some analysts, including some East Europeans, to see the second economy in terms of its "lubricating" function.[4] Some go so far as to assert that "were it not for the second economy, the entire system would collapse."[5]

In fact, the second economies of Eastern Europe are at once liberating, corrosive, and lubricating. The starting point for an analysis of Eastern Europe's second economy is to see it in the context of the total economic system. The second economy is an integral part of the official, planned economy, sometimes complementing it, sometimes hindering it directly, sometimes competing with it.

This article examines Eastern Europe's second economies as both a structural aspect of socialism and as cultural and historical products of specific East European societies. Because the second economy has been studied largely by economists, much of its noneconomic character has been overlooked. Recent studies by anthropologists show the

second economy to be an expression of deeply rooted social and cultural features of each society. These features are best revealed not by aggregate data but by micro-level everyday interactions that form the core of most anthropological field studies. Hence the combination of the political-economic and sociocultural factors can help explain both the tenacity of the second economy in Eastern Europe and the variations from one socialist society to another.

## SECOND ECONOMY RESEARCH ON EASTERN EUROPE

Within Soviet studies, the analysis of the second economy commenced a decade ago with the seminal articles by Simes, Katsenelinboigen, and especially Grossman.[6] A recent bibliography on the Soviet/East European second economy now lists over 150 items.[7] A major collection has been edited by Grossman, and the Hungarian economists have been especially productive.[8] Anthro-

---

4. Cf. Charles Schwartz, "Corruption and Political Development in the U.S.S.R.," *Comparative Politics,* 11:425-43 (July 1979); Gregory Grossman, "The Second Economy of the USSR," *Problems of Communism,* 26(5):40 (Sept.-Oct. 1977). Among East Europeans, the Hungarians have particularly emphasized a lubrication approach. Cf. Istvan Gabor, "The Second (Secondary) Economy," *Acta Oeconomica,* 22:291-311 (1979).

5. Smith calls it "an essential lubricant for the rigidities of the planned economy." Smith, *Russians,* p. 86. Meanwhile, a U.S. Select Committee on Soviet Internal Developments concluded that it "lubricates the joints of a creaking system." Quoted from Stuart Henry, "The Informal Economy: How Revolutionary Is It?" *Crime and Social Justice,* 2:8 (1987). See also Istvan Kemeny, "The Unregistered Economy in Hungary," *Soviet Studies,* 34:364 (July 1982).

6. Dimitri K. Simes, "The Soviet Parallel Market," *Survey,* 21(3):42-52 (Summer 1975); Aron Katsenelinboigen, "Coloured Markets in the Soviet Union," *Soviet Studies,* 29:62-85 (Jan. 1977); Grossman, "Second Economy of the USSR"; idem, "Notes on the Illegal Private Economy and Corruption," in *The Soviet Economy in a Time of Change,* by U.S., Congress, Joint Economic Committee (Washington, DC: Government Printing Office, 1979), pp. 834-55.

7. Gregory Grossman, "The Second Economy in the USSR and Eastern Europe: A Bibliography" (Berkeley-Duke Occasional Papers on the Second Economy in the USSR, no. 1, University of California, Berkeley, and Duke University, updated, March, 1987).

8. Gregory Grossman, ed., *Studies in the Second Economy of Communist Countries* (Berkeley: University of California Press, 1988); Janos Kenedi, *Do It Yourself: Hungary's Hidden Economy* (London: Pluto Press, 1982); Istvan Gabor, "The Second Economy in Socialism: General Lessons of the Hungarian Experience," *Papers on*

pological studies have appeared on Poland, Soviet Georgia, and Central Asia, and Grossman and Treml's survey of 1900 Soviet émigrés promises to give valuable information on the second economy in the USSR.[9]

Nevertheless, our knowledge remains limited by the geographic areas studied and by political restrictions placed on the research, both of which skew or bias the research. Many studies of the Soviet second economy focus on the non-Russian republics, while our information on the East European states aside from Hungary and Poland is confined to descriptive studies or press reports of corruption.[10] Research is also hampered

by a lack of empirical data, due to deliberate concealment by the authorities, simple ignorance, or conceptual confusion.[11] Consequently, as in other areas of Soviet studies, second economy

---

*Labor Economics* (Budapest: Karl Marx University of Economics, 1984); Peter Galasi, "Peculiarities and Limits of the Second Economy in Socialism (the Hungarian Case)," in *Economics of the Shadow Economy,* ed. Wulf Gaertner and Alois Wenig (New York: Springer-Verlag, 1985), pp. 353-61; Peter Galasi and Gyorgy Sziraczki, eds., *Labour Market and Second Economy in Hungary* (New York: Campus, 1985).

9. Janine Wedel, *The Private Poland: An Anthropologist's Look at Everyday Life* (New York: Facts on File, 1986); Gerald Mars and Yochanan Altman, *Private Enterprise in the USSR: The Case of Soviet Georgia* (Aldershot: Gower Press, 1987); idem, "The Cultural Bases of Soviet Georgia's Second Economy," *Soviet Studies,* 35(4):546-60 (Oct. 1983); idem, "The Cultural Bases of Soviet Central Asia's Second Economy (Uzbekistan and Tajikistan)," *Central Asian Survey* (in press); Grossman and Treml, "Measuring Hidden Personal Incomes in the USSR"; introduction to Grossman, "Second Economy: A Bibliography."

10. Examples from Simis's *USSR: The Corrupt Society* and Smith's *Russians* overwhelmingly concern Georgians, Armenians, and Azerbaijanis. Law's "Corruption in Georgia" also infers that the same is true for the Russian republic. Other studies of East European—that is, non-USSR—second economies used in this survey include the following: Horst Brezinski, "The Second Economies in Eastern Europe," in *East European Economic Trends and East-West Trade: U.S., West*

*and East European Perspectives,* ed. P. Marer and P. Van Veen (forthcoming); Steven Sampson, "The Informal Sector in Eastern Europe," *Telos,* no. 66, pp. 44-66 (Winter 1985-86); Horst Brezinski and Christoph Roos, "The Development of the Second Economy in Hungary," *Korean Journal for East-West European Studies,* 1:95-127 (Fall 1985); Andrzej Korbonski, "The 'Second Economy' in Poland," *Journal of International Affairs,* 35(1):1-15 (Spring-Summer 1981); Anders Åslund, *Private Enterprise in Eastern Europe: The Non-Agricultural Private Sector in Poland and the GDR* (New York: St. Martin's Press, 1985); idem, "Private Enterprise in Poland, the GDR and Hungary," in *Bidrag til Öststatsforskning,* 11(1):26-34 (Jan. 1983); Horst Brezinski, "The Second Economy in the GDR—Pragmatism Is Gaining Ground," *Arbeitspapiere des Fachbereichs Wirtschaftswissenschaft,* Neue Folge Nr. 7, Universität-Gesamthochschule Paderborn, BRD (Feb. 1987); Ilse Grosser, "Personliche Wirtschaften in Bulgarien—Jungere Entwicklungen," *Südosteuropa,* 33(9):491-507 (1984); Per Ronnås, "The Role of the 'Second Economy' as a Source of Supplementary Income to Rural Communities in Romania: A Case Study," *Bidrag til Öststatsforskning,* 11(1):34-43 (Jan. 1983), Steven Sampson, "Rich Families and Poor Collectives: An Anthropological Approach to Romania's Second Economy," ibid., pp. 44-77; Horst Brezinski and Paul Petrescu, "The Second Economy in Romania—A Dynamic Sector," *Arbeitspapiere des Fachbereichs Wirtschaftswissenschaft,* Neue Folge Nr. 6, Universität—Gesamthochschule Paderborn, BRD (Dec. 1986). Finally, the best sources of press reports from the Soviet Union are the *Current Digest of the Soviet Press* and *Radio Liberty Research* (Munich) and for the other East European countries *Radio Free Europe Research* (Munich).

11. These issues are elucidated in Peter Wiles, "What We Still Don't Know about the Soviet Economy," in *The CMEA Five Year Plans (1981-1985) in a New Perspective: Planned and Non-Planned Economies* (Brussels: North Atlantic Treaty Organization, Economics and Information Directorates, 1982).

analyses often rely on anecdote, media reports, and speculative estimation.[12]

In the East European context, the study of second economy activities would include those that are unplanned, unregulated, unreported, privatized, and/or illegal. This would cover a wide range of activities, and scholars differ over precisely what should be included.[13] Considering the second economy as extraplan behavior, which may or may not have beneficial consequences for the official economy, Marresse's syncretic definition is useful: "The second economy includes all of the nonregulated (legal and illegal) aspects of economic activities in state and cooperative organizations, *plus* all unreported activities, *plus* all forms of private (legal, semilegal, and illegal) economic activity."[14]

Measuring the extent of the second economy has proven difficult due to lack of data and conceptual confusion. It appears less widespread in heavy industry, banking, finance, and the military and more pervasive in sectors such as construction, food, repairs, light industry, transport, wholesale and retail trade, and personal services from doctors' services to waiters' services.[15] Because second economy activity may vary widely from one sector to another, and because definitions of the second economy may differ for different researchers, statements that estimate the second economy as being from 10 to 50 percent of a country's gross national product have little comparative value.[16]

Private agriculture, for example, is a key component of the second economy

15. Peter Wiles, using "commonsense and literary evidence," states that larger objects are harder to steal, divert, or sell; hence trains and planes are not part of the black economy. Similarly, "where audit is easy (banks) or important (weapons) there will be less corruption." At the other end of the scale, building and car repairs are such that "there seem to be few uncorrupt transactions." See Peter Wiles, "What We Still Don't Know," *CMEA Five Year Plans*, by North Atlantic Treaty Organization.

16. The figure of 10-50 percent is a summary of statements by knowledgeable Soviet émigrés. The variation most likely reflects differing perceptions of the second economy as being strictly black or illegal transactions, or including black plus legal private production, kolkhoz marketing, and trading. See Zev Katz, "Insights from Emigres and Sociological Studies on the Soviet Union," in *Soviet Economic Prospects for the Seventies* (Washington, DC: Government Printing Office, 1973), p. 90. Hungarian estimates of up to 50 percent of gross national product derive from a second economy that includes criminal theft, black theft of raw materials and labor time, all "black value added," "benign plan violation" within socialist factories in order to achieve the plan—the shadow economy—legal private and cooperative production, plus bribes and tips. Wiles makes a good case for excluding benign plan violation from the second economy, thereby bringing it down to 7-25 percent worldwide. See Peter Wiles, "Second Economy, Its Definitional Problems," p. 10. A final note of caution regarding estimates of the second economy comes from Istvan Gabor, who states that "the widely quoted estimate of 16-19 percent of the entire GNP being created in the second economy draws its credence solely from the prestige of the person who made the estimate." Gabor, "Second Economy in Socialism," p. 29.

12. Prospects for empirical research, personal fieldwork, or scientific collaboration with East European researchers remain dim, if not nonexistent. Hungary, where second economy research is officially sanctioned, remains the exception.

13. Cf. Grossman, "Second Economy of the USSR"; Dennis O'Hearn, "The Consumer Second Economy: Size and Effects," *Soviet Studies,* 32(2):218-34 (Apr. 1980); Peter Wiles, "The Second Economy, Its Definitional Problems," in *Unofficial Economy,* ed. Alessandrini and Dallago; Peter Galasi, "Peculiarities and Limits."

14. Michael Marrese, "The Evolution of Wage Regulation in Hungary," in *Hungary—A Decade of Reform,* ed. P. Hare, H. K. Radice, and N. Swain (London: Allen & Unwin, 1981), p. 51. This definition is discussed in particular by Brezinski in his "Second Economies in Eastern Europe."

in all the socialist countries. The output of collective farmers' personal plots provides from 30 to 42 percent of total agricultural output in the USSR, Hungary, Bulgaria, and Romania.[17] In Poland, where 77 percent of all agricultural land is in private hands, the legal private sector occupied almost 32 percent of the labor force in 1983.[18]

In commerce, the second economy is pervasive. O'Hearn's analysis of Soviet press reports indicates that 80-85 percent of all gasoline ends up on the black market, 25 percent of the internal fish catch is poached from state lands, and 25 percent of all distilled alcohol is produced and sold outside the state sector.[19] Soviet emigre interviews suggest that 18 percent of all consumption expenditures were given to private individuals and that 30 percent of all home food was purchased outside the public sector or via connections.[20] The Soviet Union has permitted the lowest level of

legal private commercial activity in Eastern Europe. The largest amount is in Hungary, where between 1970 and 1983 the number of private shops and restaurants doubled, to 19,293, to constitute 26 percent of all shops.[21]

The second economy service sector is similarly extensive, inasmuch as personal relations between seller and client—established via bribes, tips, or friendship—determine whether the service will be of acceptable quality. Despite the fact that second economy labor can be from two to five times more expensive than that procured by the official economy, a Moscow survey showed that 70 percent of house repairs were carried out privately, most of this by illegal or unregistered repairmen.[22] In Georgia from 97 to 99 percent of repairs to home and household items were done privately.[23] Soviet investigations routinely show that on days when state service enterprises are audited, receipts are one and one-half to two times higher than on "normal" days.[24]

Private construction brigades, agricultural harvest and forest-clearing brigades are common throughout the USSR and Eastern Europe. They often receive two to five times the official wage, even though they are hired by state enterprises.[25] In Poland, private firms con-

---

17. Brezinski and Petrescu, "Second Economy in Romania," p. 3; Horst Brezinski, "The Second Economy in the Soviet Union and Its Implications for Economic Policy," in *Economics of the Shadow Economy,* ed. Gaertner and Wenig, p. 363; Allen Kroncher, "CMEA Productive and Service Sector in the 1980's: Plan and Non-Plan," in *The CMEA Five Year Plans,* by North Atlantic Treaty Organization, p. 204.

18. Andrzej Bloch, "The Private Sector in Poland," *Telos,* no. 66, pp. 129, 131 (Winter 1985-86).

19. O'Hearn, "Consumer Second Economy," pp. 232, 227; Vladimir Treml, "Alcohol in the USSR: A Fiscal Dilemma," *Soviet Studies,* 27(2):161-77 (1972); idem, "Alcohol in the Soviet Underground Economy" (Berkeley-Duke Occasional Papers on the Second Economy in the USSR, University of California, Berkeley, and Duke University, 1986; reprinted in *Studies in the Second Economy of Communist Countries,* ed. Grossman).

20. Gur Ofer and Aaron Vinokur, *Private Sources of Income of the Soviet Urban Household* (Santa Monica, CA: Rand, 1980), pp. 70, 58.

21. Brezinski and Roos, "Second Economy in Hungary," pp. 104-5.

22. O'Hearn, "Consumer Second Economy," p. 225.

23. Ibid.

24. S. P. Artemov, "Sluzhba byta v desiatoi piatiletke," *Den'gi i Kredit* [Money and credit], no. 12, p. 23 (1976), cited in Dennis O'Hearn, "The Second Economy in Consumer Goods and Services," *Critique* (Glasgow), no. 15, p. 103 (1982).

25. Kroncher cites a ratio of nearly 11:1 in his "CMEA Productive and Service Sector," p. 200. Other descriptions of these brigades are described in Simis, *USSR: The Corrupt Society,* pp. 258-61,

structed 52 percent of urban housing and 66 percent of housing in rural areas.[26]

Income and employment figures for the second economy give additional indication of its extent. Poland's 470,000 private enterprises accounted for 24 percent of total employment and generated 20 percent of money income in 1980, the latter rising to 32 percent in 1983.[27] In Hungary about three-quarters of the population receives additional income from the second economy.[28] Incomes from the second economy often greatly exceed official wages in Georgia.[29] A Soviet emigre survey indicated that 11 percent of all households' total income derived from private sources.[30] However, among the 10 percent of Soviet families who reported income from tips, bribes, and speculation, extra income

averaged 79 rubles per month, or about 2 weeks of the average wage.[31]

The extent of second economy activity seems to be greater in the southern Soviet republics, especially in Georgia and Central Asia. Second economy activities are also more extensive in outlying regions, ethnic enclaves, and the more ruralized republics. There are several reasons for this: inadequate supplies of consumer goods and services combined with persistently high demand that force people to use private or illegal channels; more autonomous rural households able to carry out private production; higher birth rates making for larger and stronger networks of kin, friends, and connections; family-centered moral codes that view the state and its officials as enemies; poor chances of upward mobility into the Soviet establishment for non-Russian minorities; and the Soviet state's inability to enforce laws or carry out control in outlying zones or among traditionally hostile ethnic groups.[32] Czechoslovakia and the German Democratic Republic, both industrialized and urbanized, probably have more reduced second economies than other areas of Eastern Europe.[33]

An integral part of second economy activity is corruption. Although difficult

and in Grossman, "Second Economy of the USSR," p. 36. Sizable incomes for such traveling brigades of agricultural and forest workers are reported in Romania by Ronnås and Sampson, in Hungary by Kenedi, and in the German Democratic Republic by Brezinski, where such "after-work brigades can easily charge 3 to 4 times the official wages plus 'fringe benefits.' " See, respectively, Ronnås, "Role of the 'Second Economy,' " p. 38; Steven Sampson, *National Integration through Socialist Planning: An Anthropological Study of a Romanian New Town* (Boulder, CO: East European Monographs, 1984), pp. 153-56; Kenedi, *Do It Yourself,* passim; Brezinski, "Second Economy in the GDR," p. 9; *Die Welt,* 20 June 1980.

26. Wedel, *Private Poland,* p. 40.

27. Korbonski, " 'Second Economy' in Poland," p. 2; Bloch, "Private Sector in Poland," p. 157.

28. Gabor, "Second Economy in Socialism," p. 32; Kroncher, "CMEA Productive and Service Sector," p. 205, citing *Wall Street Journal,* 22 Mar. 1982.

29. Law, "Corruption in Georgia"; Wiles, "What We Still Don't Know"; Mars and Altman, *Private Enterprise in the USSR.*

30. Ofer and Vinokur, *Private Sources of Income,* p. 51.

31. Ibid., p. 33. This would also include income derived from pilferage or sale of pilfered items, but not private wages, such as from moonlighting. Grossman's "Notes on the Illegal Private Economy" provides an excellent summary of such income sources.

32. See Mars and Altman, *Private Enterprise in the USSR.* Non-Russian ethnic groups also rank high on Peter Wiles's "continuum of dishonesty." Wiles, "What We Still Don't Know," app. II.

33. Brezinski, "Second Economies in Eastern Europe," p. 9; idem, "Second Economy in the GDR." Czech data are sparse, though see Leonard Silk, "The Mystery of Czech Affluence," *New York Times,* 20 June 1986.

to quantify, the extent of corruption—bribes to planners, hush money to police, nepotism and influence peddling—is indicated by the continuing stream of reports in the official press. The importance of this is also revealed in periodic campaigns against illegal, nonlabor, or speculation incomes in Poland, the USSR, and Romania and in the spectacular corruption scandals recently revealed in Moldavia, Uzbekistan, and Kazakhstan, where millions of illicit rubles were made over several years.[34] Bribes and payoffs are a normal part of daily life in the USSR, beginning with the payoff for a good room in the obstetric ward, ending with the payoff for a quality burial plot.[35]

## THE SECOND ECONOMY IN OPERATION

A closer look at the operation of the most widespread aspects of a typical second economy will enable us to see how the second economy is integrally related to the wider structure of socialist society.

### Peasant household production

Domestic production of food has always been a source of household consumption and personal income for East Europeans. One form of this private farming, in which farmers own their own lands and livestock and grow food for personal consumption, on contract to the state, or sale on the market. Another form of household production is the combining, by collective farm families, of domestic resources with the small plots of land allocated to them by the collective.

Private farming is the principal form of peasant production in Poland, while such farms occupy less than 5 percent of peasant households in the rest of Eastern Europe. Óften these peasants resort to the illegal second economy to procure fertilizer, tractors, and transport to market. Moreover, since the free markets may have regulated price ceilings, peasants may also engage in various subterfuges to obtain desired prices for their produce.

The typical collective farmer uses the collective as a resource to be exploited, working not for the collective but on the collective for the household enterprise. Collective farm wages are low, but fodder payments and the production of the personal plot are channeled into household production. Other resources of the collective may be borrowed, purchased, or stolen.[36]

---

34. See fn. 10; Philip Hanson, " 'Nonlabor Incomes' in the USSR," *Radio Liberty Research,* 172/86, 24 Apr. 1986. As several observers have noted, campaigns against economic crime seem to concentrate disproportionately on the non-Russian republics and on non-Russian nationalities, thus appealing to Russian nationalist sentiments as well. During the early 1960s, for example, most of the black marketeers who were executed had Jewish surnames.

35. Detailed especially in Simis, *"USSR: The Corrupt Society,"* pp. 205-47. See also Wojciech Markiewicz, "A Small Hand-Book for the Bribe-Giver: Tokens of Gratitude," in *Survey,* 29(3):195-98 (Autumn 1986), translated from *Polityka* (Warsaw), 30 Aug. 1986. Romania, Bulgaria, and Poland, where the bribes are often in dollars or dollar coupons, are similar in this respect, as they suffer from extreme shortages in virtually all spheres of social, economic, and cultural life, from procuring social services and consumer goods to obtaining cultural products such as books.

36. Sampson, "Rich Families and Poor Collectives." See Joel Halpern and David Kideckel, "Anthropology of Eastern Europe," *Annual Review of Anthropology,* 12:277-310 (1983), for further references on the relation between the collective farmer and the household. On the peasant-worker

A third form of family food production is the complex household enterprise produced when peasant-worker households add wage income from nonagricultural employment plus the resources of their workplace to agricultural wages, fodder inputs, and household labor. This combination of homegrown food, wages, payments in kind and income from sale of household produce can give these suburban households a standard of living that is often higher than those in nearby towns. Extra income from this household economy is often used in extravagant status displays, such as in the building of giant three-story houses.

Urban dwellers throughout Eastern Europe frequently complain about price-gouging peasants who demand speculative prices for their goods or who in Poland refuse to accept anything but Western currency. Yet the peasants must cover additional costs such as illegal transport, living in the city, security for bad harvests, and so forth. The collective farm's personal plot system can be viewed as a form of exploitation in which the collective frees itself from the obligation of paying the peasants a decent wage.[37] The point is that private plot production is an integral part of the collective farm wages and not something carried out beyond normal work. That is, private plot production is necessary for peasant subsistence. The peasants are forced to use the second economy to earn this wage. The peasants and peasant-workers cultivate this plot on their second shift.

There is ample evidence to show that first economy production suffers as a result—both on the collective and in the factory.

## The shadow economy of the socialist factory

Managers of Soviet factories are constrained by central planning decisions, central allocations of supplies, and limitations on wages and labor discipline. Plan fulfillment is every manager's prime concern, if only because this is the only way his or her career can advance. Hence, various extra-plan strategies are used to cut through bureaucratic bottlenecks or to procure supplies, transport, repair, extra labor, and spare parts. This shadow economy involves misreporting to the authorities and bribing or making connections with other managers in what are known as family circles.[38] Most factories retain a fixer (in Russian, *tolkach*), who functions as middleman, broker, and network entrepreneur. In order to procure these scarce resources, managers resort to what Grossman calls "the Four B's: barter, black market, bribe and *blat*" (Russian for "connections" or "influence").[39] The most important application of the Four B's is with planners. Influencing them to decrease the plan norms or increase allocations of supplies is crucial for any manager who contemplates plan fulfillment.

The Four B's are not a new develop-

---

strategy, see in particular John Cole, "Family, Farm and Factory: Rural Workers in Contemporary Romania," in *Romania in the 1980's*, ed. Daniel N. Nelson (Boulder, CO: Westview Press, 1981), pp. 71-116.

37. See, in particular, Timofeev, *Soviet Peasants*, and the review symposium on this book in *Telos*, no. 68, pp. 109-27 (Summer 1986).

38. "Family circles" is a term used by Joseph Berliner in *Factory and Manager in the USSR* (Cambridge, MA: Harvard University Press, 1957), pp. 259-63. My use of "shadow economy" comes from Gregory Grossman, "The 'Shadow Economy' in the Socialist Sectors of the USSR," in *CMEA Five Year Plans*, by North Atlantic Treaty Organization, pp. 99-115.

39. Grossman, " 'Shadow Economy' in the Socialist Sectors," p. 108.

ment. Berliner's informants from the 1930s and 1940s describe similar strategies.[40] However, there is evidence that as the East European economies grow more complex, production bottlenecks are increasing.[41] This means that shadow economy behavior must be tolerated even more, even though "benign plan fulfillment" can easily be transformed into embezzlement and illicit production.[42]

### The underground factories

Underground factories in the Soviet Union tend to specialize in small, simply manufactured, easily transportable and marketable consumer items such as "ladies underwear, meat *pirozhiki,* brooches made of a couple of plastic cherries or fashionably tailored artificial leather jackets."[43] Numbering in the "tens of thousands,"[44] they comprise mostly workshops producing high-demand consumer goods in moderate quantities. Underground factories normally coexist inside a state factory, using it as a cover to conceal the illicit use of supplies, funds, labor, transport, and distribution networks. While the state enterprise operates normally and achieves its plan, the surplus capacity is unofficially used to manufacture additional goods. These may be identical or may differ slightly from the goods described in the official profile of the factory.

Profits from the underground factory can only be partially invested. These second economy entrepreneurs may spend their profits as conspicuous consumption on big houses, vacations, cars, and feasts and to help offspring or godchildren pay their bribes to get good job placements or enter medical school.

Many underground entrepreneurs are Jews, who have been denied avenues of social mobility in the universities, army, policy, or party apparatus.[45] Many factories are located in the USSR's ethnic republics, where ethnicity serves as a mobilizing network and as a shield against controls. Considerable factory production costs go for bribing planners, inspectors, police, and even party officials.[46] Bribe expenses usually average 15-20 percent of illicit earnings.[47]

Take, for instance, Mars and Altman's study of an illicit biscuit factory in Soviet Georgia. The factory was inherited by two Jewish owners from their fathers; a third owner, a Gentile, was added later. The Gentile's social network was important for keeping the factory safe. A hidden production of four times the quantity of biscuits allowed in their plan was being produced.[48] Excess capacity was created by bribing planners and functionaries in those ministries that allocated the ingredients for biscuits. Additional ingredients were purchased from outside suppliers who themselves

40. Berliner, *Factory and Manager in the USSR;* idem, "The Informal Organization of the Soviet Firm," *Quarterly Journal of Economics,* 66(3):342-63 (Aug. 1952).

41. Grossman, " 'Shadow Economy' in the Socialist Sectors," p. 115.

42. Peter Wiles discusses the difference between "benign" and "malign plan fulfillment." The terms are his. Wiles, "What We Still Don't Know."

43. Simis, *USSR: The Corrupt Society,* p. 157.

44. Ibid., p. 147.

45. Ibid., p. 153.

46. Simis writes that the "black" millionaire Laziashvili had an annual income of R10-12 million and paid out R1 million yearly to Georgian party officials, including the minister of internal affairs. Ibid., p. 166. See also "The 'Black' Millions," *Radio Liberty Research,* 179/177, 27 July 1977.

47. Simis, *USSR: The Corrupt Society,* p. 166.

48. Mars and Altman, *Private Enterprise in the USSR,* chap. 6.

may have been pilfering from their own factories. Packaging and labeling were carried out via links with a paper and printing plant. Workers were paid extra, but the full details were concealed from them. Distribution was always a key problem, since police watch all the main roads and can stop trucks to examine their bills of lading. Successful distribution thus entailed bribes to virtually the entire police department of the region. The extra production was sold to retailers at a 15 percent discount off the normal wholesale price. Retail outlets sold the biscuits at official state prices and pocketed the income.

At every stage, personal support networks were necessary to ensure production and distribution and to cope with periodic crises. Anyone in a higher position in the second economy must have large networks of kin, friends, clients, or patrons. In the biscuit factory, the three owners had complementary networks: one had kin within the factory, one had friends and kin in other factories, and the third had a social network that included particularly important police officials. Combining these network linkages and their entrepreneurial talents, the factory owners achieved a comfortable profit.

*Private and illegal
trade and services*

The second economy operates extensively both in socialist retail outlets and among legal private traders and service people. Quality goods are frequently held back by managers and warehouse attendants and allocated to friends or black marketeers. Only the remainder reach the shop, where the salesclerk may hide more desirable goods under the counter. Via bribes or tips—or by virtue

of friendship—the salesclerk sells the privilege to buy the item, which may cost more than the item itself.

Legal private traders are often discriminated against by the state in the allocation of merchandise, as well as subject to high taxes and controls. Hence they are often forced to resort to illegal strategies such as selling contraband, defrauding customers, or skimming receipts. Hungarian shopkeepers defraud their customers out of 8 billion forints each year. In Szczecin, Poland, 20 percent of all private entrepreneurs were convicted and fined for tax evasion in one year.[49] Bribes to obtain supplies and protection money to controllers are part of normal business operations. A Polish study showed artisans admitting to have paid 12 percent of their turnover in bribes and having received 18 percent of their supplies from illegal sources.[50]

For East European consumers, the key to procuring anything in the second economy is to establish some kind of private relationship with the seller. Kenedi describes three possible bases for such a relationship: the cash payment, bribe, or tip given when buyer and seller do not know each other and do not expect to have a long-term relationship; the mutual favors exchanged between friends and acquaintances in which services are exchanged reciprocally; and the wide-ranging social obligations founded on kinship and friendship in

49. Åslund, "Private Enterprise in Poland, the GDR and Hungary," p. 28.
50. J. Urban, "Prywatna Inicjatywa" [Private initiative], *Zycie Gospodarcze,* 22 Dec. 1968, cited in Åslund, "Private Enterprise in Poland, the GDR and Hungary." The difference between the Polish and East German private traders' problems is summarized by Åslund when he says that the Polish trader must pay a bribe to the supplier, whereas his East German counterpart need only give a tip—*lapowki* versus *Trinkgeld.* Ibid., p. 29.

which the exchange is permanently unbalanced.[51]

It is common for cash payments to develop into favors or favors to evolve into a more stable friendship. Friendship relations are more dependable and less risky, since no cash is passed around. In the East European situation, where so many goods and services are in short supply, there is a crucial need to establish wide-ranging social exchange networks. Hence, the second economy brings together widely disparate social categories: professors become friends with shoe salespeople, engineers court butchers, and so forth.[52] East European traditions of commensality and drinking help forge and solidify these relations, especially where certain foods and beverages are themselves difficult to obtain. In Romania, for example, offering a guest a cup of coffee is not just a sign of hospitality but an indication that one has the networks to procure coffee and may also be willing to share them.[53]

In the East European second economy, who one knows is more important than the money one has. Those who stand in line for coffee, theater tickets, or bureaucratic permits may have the requisite cash but are without the necessary social connections. Those with strategically placed kin, friends, colleagues, clients, and patrons can bypass the lines.

Such private arrangements attest to the inventiveness of many East Europeans, but these also demand time, energy, and exasperation and create obligations that cannot always be fulfilled. There are winners and losers. The losers are those who lack the money, the connections, and/or the ability to turn their official job into an unofficial source of income.

Finally, space does not permit a discussion of the hard currency shops to which most East Europeans—Poles excepted—are denied access. In some countries, payment in Western currency or goods from these shops competes with payment in local currency. In Romania, Western cigarettes, particularly Kent, function as a currency of the country's second economy. Available only in the hard currency shops, they are procured via special relations with foreign tourists or students, with diplomats, or via family visiting from abroad. Like money, Kents are anonymous, divisible, and relatively long lasting. They can even be counterfeited by stuffing empty packs with Romanian cigarettes!

## STRUCTURAL AND CULTURAL VARIATIONS

East European second economies vary from country to country. These variations are based on specific interactions between structural, cultural, and historical factors.

Taking structural factors first, it appears that second economies will tend to be more extensive in those countries where (1) there is a large private sector, as in Poland and Hungary; (2) where the

51. On the establishment and maintenance of such personal relations, see especially Kenedi, *Do It Yourself;* Wedel, *Private Poland;* Mars and Altman, *Private Enterprise in the USSR;* idem, "Cultural Bases of Soviet Georgia's"; Sampson, "Rich Families and Poor Collectives"; idem, "Informal Sector in Eastern Europe."

52. On the role of friendship in Eastern Europe, see Sampson, "Informal Sector in Eastern Europe"; Vladimir Shlapentokh, *Love, Marriage and Friendship in the Soviet Union* (New York: Praeger, 1985).

53. On food and drink symbolism in Eastern Europe, see Charlotte Chase, "Symbolism of Food Shortage in Current Polish Politics," *Anthropological Quarterly,* 56(2):76-82 (Apr. 1983); *East European Quarterly,* 18(4), *Special Issue on Alcohol in Eastern Europe* (1985).

rural populations are relatively large, as in Poland, the Balkans, and the USSR; (3) where the official economy is less effective due to the predominance of "reds" over experts, resulting in irrational planning policies, as in Albania, Romania, the USSR, and Bulgaria; (4) where the regime has not resolved basic problems of distributing food and consumer goods, as in Romania, Poland, and the USSR; (5) where foreign influences, tourism, and Western currency are more extensive, as in Poland, Hungary, the Baltic states, and the German Democratic Republic; and (6) where the control organs are less effective due either to laxity at the center, as in Poland and Hungary, or to resistance of a hostile periphery or ethnic minority. This resistance occurs in the non-Russian republics, the less urbanized Balkans, and minority areas throughout Eastern Europe, such as Kosovo and Transylvania, and among Gypsies, Jews, Armenians, Volga Germans, and so forth.[54]

These structural factors give each socialist state a different type of second economy, even though their relative sizes—as a proportion of gross national product—might be similar.

The structural variables cited operate in the cultural-historical context of each society. Cultural factors are manifest as specific cultural behaviors, value orientations, or institutions especially conducive to second economy production, exchange, or consumption or compatible with the kinds of informal social networks on which the second economy is based.

Some cultural behaviors conducive to the second economy are those that stress conspicuous display as indicators of personal prestige: skills in the ability to fast-talk bureaucrats or police; in squeezing favors or obligations out of people who are in high positions; in establishing patron-client or friendship networks with wide-ranging groups of people; and in publicly expressing one's linkages to others via gift giving, social togetherness, commensality, or alcohol use.

Cultural values compatible with an extensive second economy at least in the Soviet Union and the Eastern bloc countries are those that prioritize primary kin affiliations over allegiance to formal institutions like workplace, party, trade union, or state. Where nepotism is a moral duty and "faith in the state" is low, there will be little moral disapproval in appropriating state resources for private ends. As Kenedi says, "We must not allow the state to wither away. It's the only one we have. And if there were no such thing as the state, it would have to be invented."[55] In addition, societies that place a high value on personal honor and risk-taking behavior to prove one's honor will also be compatible with second economy behavior. Georgia and Soviet Central Asia are very much kin based, "honor and shame" societies.[56] Poland and Romania are notable for their lack of any "faith in the state."[57]

Finally, there are cultural institutions

54. A preliminary attempt to deal with the ethnic nature of the second economy in Yugoslavia has been carried out by Vjeran Katunaric, "The Socioethnic Nature of the Hidden Economy" (Manuscript, Department of Sociology, University of Zagreb, 1984).

55. Kenedi, *Do It Yourself,* p. 57.
56. Mars and Altman, *Private Enterprise in the USSR;* idem, "Cultural Bases of Soviet Georgia's"; idem, "Cultural Bases of Soviet Central Asia's."
57. Sampson, "Rich Families and Poor Collectives"; idem, "Informal Sector in Eastern Europe"; Korbonski, " 'Second Economy' in Poland"; Wedel, *Private Poland.*

such as having large families, clan systems, godparenthood, ritual friendship, and feasting that help to form social networks of deep obligations based on long-term trust. Large networks, obligations, and trust are keys to success in any second economy. They can help to procure money, whereas money cannot always procure obligations and trust. Large family traditions are obvious facilitators. An Uzbek or Kazakh—from Soviet Central Asia—with six siblings has available to him the networks of a dozen cousins and six other in-laws and their networks.

Since cultural and structural factors interact over time, historical factors also determine the nature of the second economy in each East European society. Poland's second economy seems to have achieved a head start as a result of the Nazi occupation.[58] Many anti-Nazi patterns regarding the importance of informal connections and suspicion of higher authority were continued under the Soviet occupation. In Romania, the nepotism and bribery that developed during the Ottoman occupation have continued today as patterns of deference to authority, misrepresentation, bribes, gifts to local elites, and the overt nepotism of General Secretary Ceausescu, whose wife, children, brothers, and in-laws occupy high party and state posts.

The existence of historical precedents

does not mean that East Germany, Hungary, or Czechoslovakia could not develop Georgian or Balkan cultural patterns. Political oppression and economic mismanagement could easily stimulate them. Hence a Soviet émigré sociologist has bemoaned the gradual Georgianization of Soviet society.[59]

We should not be surprised to see cultural factors achieving their own momentum such that they aggravate preexisting structural inadequacies. This has clearly been the case in the USSR, Poland, and the Balkans.

### ORIGINS, CAUSES, AND EFFECTS

While some second economy activities are intrinsic to socialist economies and can be found in the earliest accounts of Stalinist industrialization, most analysts maintain that they have blossomed in the last 10-15 years.[60] There are several reasons for this: the proletarianization of farmers and housewives and their integration into large-scale collective farms or factories; the spread of large workplaces to outlying republics and rural areas; urbanization, foreign influences, and rising consumer aspirations that have not been met by the state

58. Korbonski writes, "The fifteen-year period spanning the wartime German occupation, the postwar Communist takeover, and the Stalinist era was accompanied by the presence of a dynamic parallel market." This has meant that "Poland, most likely ahead of the other East European countries, became a good example of the coexistence of two socioeconomic systems: the *pays legal* and the *pays reel*." Korbonski, " 'Second Economy' in Poland," pp. 8-9. This same continuity argument is stressed as well in Wedel, *Private Poland.*

59. Shlapentokh, *Love, Marriage and Friendship,* p. 213.

60. Cf. Grossman, "Second Economy of the USSR," pp. 31, 36-37; idem, "Notes on the Illegal Private Economy," p. 46; idem, " 'Shadow Economy' in the Socialist Sectors," p. 113; Brezinski, "Second Economies in Eastern Europe," p. 8; idem, "Second Economy in the Soviet Union," p. 367; Kroncher, "CMEA Productive and Service Sector," p. 195; George Schöpflin, "Corruption, Informalism and Irregularity in Eastern Europe: A Political Analysis," *Südosteuropa,* 34(4):210 (1985); Dieter Cassel and E. Ulrich Cichy, "Explaining the Growing Shadow Economy in East and West: A Comparative Systems Approach," *Comparative Economic Studies,* 28(1):34 (Spring 1968).

sector; the decline of terror as a control mechanism, the population's increasing disrespect for state institutions as the institutions show themselves permanently unable to meet basic needs for housing, goods, and services; and the increasing degree of sophistication in second economy strategies, replacing simple bribes with intricate networks of friendship and exchange.[61]

Why do East Europeans use so much of their time and energy and put themselves at such great risk to pursue second economy activity? Clearly, the manifest reason is that people want to make more money and managers want to fulfill the plan. Yet these human motives have political, economic, and sociocultural foundations.

East European economies are politicized economies. A wide range of economic decisions are made by political organs. The political priorities that lie in the plan, the priority of heavy over light industry, production over consumption, industry over services, all generate political responses. Strikes, protests, and riots are one type of response. The second economy is another.

The immediate economic cause of the second economy is the shortage of desired goods and services. The underlying cause of *these* shortages is the shortage of labor. Workers hold back their labor in the first economy in order to use it for consumption—standing in line; leisure—or for moonlighting.[62]

These structural causes feed into the East Europeans' feelings of estrangement from their workplaces, institutions, and the bureaucracy. Workplaces remain institutions to be exploited—"them"—rather than collective property to be safeguarded. The pervasive attitude that "everybody is doing it" and that the elites are getting their own special fringe benefits—what might be called the third economy—creates a moral atmosphere that makes it natural to resort to second economy strategies.

The second economy clearly has a lubricating effect insofar as it helps supply goods and services that the formal economy does not. In its shadow form, it provides the "baling wire and chewing gum" that keep the socialist enterprises from breaking down completely.[63]

In adding extra incomes and raising living standards, the second economy also functions as a social mollifier.[64] Resentment at the privileges of the elite is ameliorated by the masses' petty swindling, bribes, and moonlighting. Outlying republics or ethnic groups attain living standards in the second economy that surpass those of Moscow or

61. Janos Kenedi summarizes this trend: "It's not enough to know how to read between the lines—one has to squeeze through them." Kenedi, *Do It Yourself,* p. 97.

62. This statement is supported not only by virtually all Western journalistic accounts but by East European émigrés in the West who are amazed at the intensity of labor in most Western factories. Istvan Gabor has stressed "labor withholding" as the key to understanding the second

economy. Moreover, he cites several Hungarian studies where between 75 and 98 percent of the workers stated that they could be working harder. Moreover, low work intensity also leads to "negligent and indolent work, 'notorious' absenteeism, being late, frequent changing of workplaces, arbitrary shortening of worktime," and so forth. With labor withholding as the norm, workers earn extra money either by working overtime or in the second economy. See Gabor, "Second (Secondary) Economy," p. 296.

63. O'Hearn, "Consumer Second Economy," p. 231. As Grossman, Brezinski, Gabor, and Cassel and Cichy have all stated, the second economy is itself a kind of surrogate reform, insofar as what was once illegal is now tolerated.

64. The term "social mollifier" is used by Cassel and Cichy, "Explaining the Growing of the Shadow Economy," p. 34.

Leningrad. Instead of protesting, people find individual solutions. This may explain why some of the officially low-paid groups in these societies, such as peasants and service workers, are so politically passive: their second economy incomes make up for it.[65]

Yet the lubricating and mollifying functions are offset by its corrosive function. By stealing labor time, materials, or funds from the first economy, the second economy makes the formal system even more inefficient than it is already. Labor is wasted, goods are shoddy, and no one really seems to care. Inside the enterprises, extra-plan improvisation covers up for the fundamental deficiencies of central planning.

Moreover, the constant swindling of the state perpetuates a moral gap between individuals and institutions. The "us"-"them" dichotomy or "underground society"[66] rhetoric may sound romantic, but the reality of the second economy is inequality, exploitation, and a lack of solidarity among those not part of the social networks. People are expected to defraud each other, lie to each other, falsify statistics, and misrepresent them-

selves in public encounters. People are kept off balance by the paradox of pervasive shortage and by the fact that nothing is every totally unavailable. There are always success stories of people who got hold of the seemingly unobtainable item—from an American record album to an exit visa. Hence people blame themselves if they cannot get hold of a desired commodity: they simply are not smart enough.

Due to the political, economic, and moral effects of the second economy, society degenerates into competing bands.

## CONCLUSION: CAN THE SECOND ECONOMY BE REFORMED?

Each new second economy scandal brings renewed calls for "strengthening ideological training" and "perfecting the organs of control." To this Mikhail Gorbachev has added a policy of "openness" (*glasnost*) in revealing instances of corruption and second economy activities. Yet a genuine solution to the corrosive aspects of the second economy must attack it at its political, economic, and sociocultural roots. Ideological exhortations, propaganda, threats of more control, and revelations of scandals in this or that enterprise or republic are not directed toward these roots. This is why they invariably do not work.

One step toward reducing the second economy's corrosive effects with respect to societal integration would be to legalize certain forms of second economy entrepreneurship now illegal and to give the private sector priority equal to that of the socialist sector in allocations, support, and expertise. To date, the East European regimes have largely tolerated the private sector, typically leaving it to

65. By contrast, workers in heavy industry, often in large homogeneous towns, are heavily dependent on state supplies via shops or direct deliveries to the factory. When these supplies fail—as occurred in Poland—the second economy channels are only of limited usefulness. Hence the only alternative is political action. See John Montias, "Economic Conditions and Political Instability in Communist Countries: Observations on Strikes, Riots and Other Disturbances," *Studies in Comparative Communism*, 13(3):283-301 (Fall 1980); Ole Norgaard and Steven Sampson, "Poland's Crisis and East European Socialism," *Theory and Society*, 13(4):773-99 (1984).

66. Cf. Kemeny, "Unregistered Economy in Hungary," p. 363; Kemeny speaks of "an underground country." See also Elemer Hankiss, "The Second Society" (Manuscript, Institute of Sociology, Hungarian Academy of Sciences, 1986).

fend for itself, often illegally.

A second solution must attack the problematic nature of the first economy. Since one cause of first economy inefficiency is lack of information due to the population's general lack of interest, some ways of stimulating workers' allegiance to these institutions might be sought. The easiest way would be to institute a form of genuine workers' control, a key demand in the Polish labor movement. Workers' control over both plan formulation and the profits that accrue from it might stimulate attitudes in which pilferage would be discouraged.

Of course, both these solutions touch on the sacrosanct leading role of the party in economic decision making. Just as the second economy is a political reaction, these solutions are also political ones.

As it stands today, East Europeans continue to cultivate their metaphorical private plots, squeezing every last bit of value from them whether it be legally or illegally. Peasants who sell their sacks of vegetables at the market, workers who pilfer parts from the factory, truck drivers who sell state gasoline, bureaucrats who arrange residence permits to Moscow, the Romanian kiosk woman who rents out her sole copy of *Newsweek* by the hour to the locals, all are cultivating their private plots. Anticorruption campaigns and control measures cannot eliminate "personal plot socialism."[67] They are not intended to. Rather, their scope is to reset the boundaries of how much private activity is tolerated, how much in the way of materials can be pilfered, how much state labor time can be used for personal needs.

Real efforts to eliminate the personal plot would only produce more problems for the first economy and a politically volatile populace. Here the Hungarian solution seems to offer a probable course of action for other East European regimes. Encouraged by the state to take second jobs and set up private businesses, each Hungarian citizen now has the right to work 16 hours per day. If someone cannot attain the good things in life, they now have only themselves to blame. Socialism, once a reaction to the capitalists' lengthening of the working day, has now found in it a solution to its own problems.

Legitimating the second economy in this way only covers up its political, economic, and moral roots. Such reforms bode ill for the first economy. The history of socialist Eastern Europe shows that economic difficulties produce political aftershocks. The institutionalization of personal-plot socialism will be no exception.

67. See my review of Timofeev's *Soviet Peasants* in *Telos*, no. 68, pp. 114-17 (Summer 1986), for a fuller exposition of "personal plot socialism."

# [18]

*SOVIET STUDIES*, vol. XXXV, no. 4, October 1983, pp. 546–560

## THE CULTURAL BASES OF SOVIET GEORGIA'S SECOND ECONOMY

By Gerald Mars and Yochanan Altman*

### 1. *Introduction*

THE primary purpose of this paper is to demonstrate, with the aid of illustrative cases, the link between the core values of Georgian culture and the working principles of its second economy. We aim to show that only by first understanding underlying cultural forces can we begin to grasp the reasons why Georgia, of all the Soviet Republics, should possess such a dynamic and deeply entrenched second economy (Grossman, 1977)—estimated by some scholars at over 25% of the Republic's GNP (Wiles, 1981).

The method we have adopted to obtain our data is a unique variant of anthropological fieldwork and a methodological note is therefore in order.

### 2. *A Note on the Sample and on our Method*

The method we adopted to delineate the core cultural features of Georgian society and which was also used to obtain our case material is what we term 'retrospective reconstruction'. Its mode is primarily anthropological. This is to say, it depends for its primary data upon anthropological fieldwork within a living bounded community—in this case among a community of 5,000 recently arrived immigrants from Soviet Georgia to Israel. Our method was to use this community as a data base to allow a reconstruction of institutional features as these existed—and still exist—in Soviet Georgia. It involved residence and social participation among the community for a period of over sixteen months by at least one and for some periods by both of us. This has been supplemented by a visit by one of us to Soviet Georgia, by continuous searches into the Georgian and Soviet press and by regular contact with specialists on Georgia including native Georgians in the UK.

### (i) *The sample*

We are aware that Georgian Jews are in some respects not culturally synonymous with the Georgian majority and we have been particularly concerned in checking our data to ensure the applicability and relevance of our findings to the wider Georgian scene.

It is believed that Georgian Jews have a history of settlement at least since the eighth century and that they have consistently enjoyed a freedom of residence and worship unusual in the history of the Jewish diaspora. We have found that our informants, though following Jewish food taboos and maintaining a ban on marriage outside their faith, were nonetheless more integrated into their host society than Jews in other Soviet Republics (Ben Zvi, 1963; Ben Ami, 1965). Their lingua franca was Georgian and, as Mark Plisetsky, a Soviet ethnographer, has observed:

Generally speaking Georgian Jews live the same way as their Gentile neighbours . . . have the same customs, furniture, domestic equipment and dress. Wedding ceremonies too are the same, the only differences are a few songs in Hebrew of a religious or ceremonial nature . . . Jews and Georgians have the same names. (Plisetsky, 1931, p. 36)

In their economic activities Georgian Jews did not operate in any sense as an ethnic or sub-economy. The majority of our informants, though over-represented in trading occupations, were nonetheless widely spread in the lower and middle levels of the economy and in their economic relationships predominantly worked alongside non-Jews and were involved with them in a wide range of social and leisure activities. This extensive integration into the wider Georgian society did not, however, preclude a massive exodus to Israel in the early 1970s—a phenomenon more fully explored elsewhere.

The majority of our sample are from the rural areas of Georgia which, according to the 1979 Soviet census, contain half of the total population. However, according to Dragadze (1976) there are close links between town and country while Parsons (1982) argues that 'Georgians consider rural Georgia as the repository of the nation's cultural heritage'. We feel justified, therefore, in regarding our sample of Georgian Jews as a suitable source of effective data on the wider Georgian scene.

## (ii) *The Method*

Since our method depended primarily upon the anthropological mode of participant observation we were thereby able to cross-check information received from different informants. We made intensive use of key informants, used structured interviews, and collected life histories. The principal language used in fieldwork was Ivrit—modern Hebrew. We came to recognise three fieldwork phases that are conceptually, though were not necessarily chronologically, separate.

*Phase I* involved straight anthropological fieldwork: the focus was to collect data on our migrants *in* Israel; to chart their social relations, to identify their principal social institutions and their basic cultural postulates. A further aim was to identify the differences as well as the similarities between our sample and that of the indigenous peoples of Georgia. As well as providing useful data on settlement in Israel this phase allowed the growth of trust by enquiring into relatively unworrying aspects of their social life as it unfolded at the time, *i.e.* 'How are marriages arranged *here*?' 'How are economic relationships organised *here*?'

*Phase II* then attempted to translate the understanding of observed social process retrospectively to Georgia. 'How were marriages arranged over there?' 'How were economic relationships organised over there?'

*Phase III* was directly concerned with second economy relationships in Georgia which can only really be understood when one has prior understanding of social institutions derived from Phases I and II. The questions here dealt with how people participated in or had experience of second economy activity in Georgia. The emphasis was on building up detailed cross-checkable case studies which then provided our basic resource for secondary analysis. Attention was constantly paid to the typicality of our data.

We believe that the unique contribution of anthropological fieldwork as a primary tool to an enquiry such as ours is two-fold: first, the core of its methodology depends on building rapport over time within the context of a close-knit community—which thus allows the build-up of good will and trust. At the same time it offers the opportunity to cross-check and validate the data obtained. It can therefore look in depth into questions which other methods of data collection may only hope to scratch on the surface. Second, anthropology's principal claim to academic specialism is that it concentrates on culture, that is, on the transmission of shared values and attitudes and on the characteristic ways by which people confront their everyday existential issues. In doing so it applies a conceptual approach to data that is holistic and which therefore encourages a linkage across the main institutional areas of social life. The operation of informal economies can thus more readily be considered within their social and cultural milieu.

### 3. *Georgian Society's Core Values*

#### (a) *General*

Our delineation of Georgian core values is primarily derived from our involved anthropological participation within our sample community in Israel. They conform, however, with our expectations derived from anthropologists who have made a speciality of other Mediterranean and Latin cultures. Peristiany (1966) and Davis (1977)—to mention just two—agree on the basic cultural homogeneity of this region.

While the pre-revolutionary Caucasus enjoyed considerable attention, the extent and quality of later work, however, are much more limited. The standard Soviet ethnography, *Narody Kavkaza* (Kardanov, 1962) devotes its overwhelming attention to the material culture of past generations. We attempted to monitor existing material from the West (*e.g.* Grigolia, 1939) and more recent journalistic impressions (*e.g.* Dragadze, 1976) which broadly conform with our own systematic findings.

To be accepted in Georgian society involves descent and membership in families where both sides are noted for respectability. This is a feature found not only in Georgia but also elsewhere, all along the shores of the Mediterranean (Peristiany, 1966). Georgian families are bilateral: they trace descent on both sides but stress the male line and within it an emphasis on agnates—on the solidarity and mutual obligations of brothers. When an individual's acts are evaluated this is done in the context of an assessment—and of continual reassessment—of his family and its honour. The same assessments, though less pronounced, apply also to associates and to friends.

Women are important in Georgian society as the articulation points between groups of males and the ensurers of male descent. Whereas the honour of men is achieved by assertion and dominance, the honour of women is passive and mainly associated with sexual modesty. As with manly honour, their passivity reflects also on the wider honour of their family and therefore of their menfolk, and to a lesser extent on that of their associates.

Honour, and its corollary shame, are constant preoccupations in Georgia. Within family groups spheres of action are well defined; they do not overlap and they are non-competitive—everyone knows their place. Beyond the family, however, these limitations

## GEORGIA'S SECOND ECONOMY                                    549

are reversed. Insecurity and instability in the perpetual ranking and re-ranking of personal relationships is the norm. Males have therefore constantly to prove themselves as men. They are, in this respect, perpetually 'on show'. They need constantly to demonstrate their worthiness to public opinion in general and to their peers in particular. This requires the demonstration of 'manliness' and use of goods in display and consumption.

In this kind of 'honour and shame' society where peer approval is so important hierarchical official relations are resented and resisted and are the source of perpetual conflict. The individual Georgian sees honour accruing to families and sees families linked by a common honour. In such a context there is little role for the state or for any centrally-organised hierarchy. Relationships need always to be personalised and abstraction has no place.

### (b) *Competition*

Competition involves conspicuous display and the necessary involvement of one's peers in relationships of obligation. Feasts and bouts of excessive and competitive drinking are extensive in Georgia, whilst sitting rooms, which are the essential preserve of men, are the physical base for the demonstration of display items. Dressing up is important, as is eating out with friends in cafes and restaurants. All of these activities will affect a man's standing and influence the formation of his own network (discussed later) including the ranges of choice he will have in selecting spouses for himself and later for his children. So the Georgian is pushed to obtain resources which are practically non-existent in the formal economy. It is this which provides the underlying personal motivation and the dynamic force which boosts the republic's second economy.

### (c) *Trust*

Trust is the basis of honour. A man who is not trusted has no honour: a man without honour cannot be trusted. Of course trust is a fundamental requirement in the operation of the second economy. When deals are illegal one cannot make contracts nor ask for the help of the law. Therefore a man's word has to be his bond. An illegal financier who used to give loans solely on a man's word of honour told us that a person who abused the trust given to him would be socially excommunicated. In this kind of society to be dishonoured is to face social discredit, but it is discredit that goes beyond the individual, since the whole family is contaminated; and not only the core family but the associated in-laws as well. One way to show the interchange between trust and honour is to look at the way loans are given at times of crisis. We will do this in the second part of this paper by presenting a case study.

### (d) *Networks*

If trust is important to the second economy, networks—particularly those based on the family—are its backbone. In a highly personalised society, where a person is measured on his honour—and on the honour of his closest associates—the body of people to whom he can personally relate and through whom he can extend relations with others who might latently prove significant becomes an individual's major resource. The extent and weight of a person's network are the primary determinors for the type of occupation he will be able to enter. And when he is in a post he can use his network to facilitate the gaining of honour, whilst the gaining of honour will facilitate the further growth of his network. Networks are thus crucial in the obtaining and distribution of resources and are central to understanding the second economy. While the paper focusses upon the role of family and kinship as the basis of personal support networks, what we call 'network cores', we would emphasise that such cores are supplemented by peer group membership. This is why the possession of brothers is particularly valued: they are both kin and the source of same generation peer contacts.

## (e) *Taking risks*

Reckless risk taking is a valued macho attribute in Georgia and the successful gain both in honour and in resources. Risk taking, however, is also a necessary attribute for business ventures and its high social valuation provides a necessary validation for activity that is the object of formal discrimination. This urge to gamble therefore goes some way to explain why people accept the constant pressure of daily risk taking when they engage in regular second economy work, and also why the entrepreneurial spirit should be so pronounced in Soviet Georgia despite Moscow's persistent attempts to control it. But these are entrepreneurs of a different mould from those traditionally associated with Western capitalism—with the development of thrift and with Weberian ideas of deferred gratification: these are gambling entrepreneurs concerned to spend and to display.

The taking of risks is essentially linked to the operation of networks as providing the basis of one's personal support in crises. Having a large and strong network means taking less risks, since networks are a major resource to take advantage of in times of need. The absence of an effective network, as we shall see, means either that a person is limited to less risky jobs or is involved in a greater chance of exposure and conviction.

We offer these core features of Georgian culture, not to present them as iron laws that formalise or rigidly channel conduct, but as ideals that are expected to be followed. Though the norms of ordinary life might fall short of expected behaviour the ideals nonetheless set the standard.

## 4. *Case Study: The Market Trader: How the Culture Underlies the Second Economy*

The following case is told by an informant who at the time was seventeen years old. The subject of the story is his father who was a small businessman, running a small shop in a typical Georgian small town market holding some forty shops and a few stalls. The events happened at the beginning of the 1970s. Such traders are particularly vulnerable to checks or raids because, in the nature of their occupation, they necessarily commit offences. The most common offences are overcharging, selling unlicensed items and selling lower class items as of higher quality.

On Monday the traders got warning of a possible raid sometime during the coming week. The warning arrived from a person who was not a trader but had much invested interest in the market. He was "a silent partner" to some of the shops there. This person had a link to somebody in Tbilisi who would be expected to know of such things. A check with the local officials failed to verify the warning. They did not know anything, but people in the market nonetheless took the warning seriously. After all it came from a highly regarded person. Some of them closed their shops for the whole week—most of these were the more established shopkeepers. Some said they were sick, others had family obligations. You don't need too much of an excuse. The rest, including my father, could not afford to close entirely. So they tried their luck.

A few stayed open all the week—others closed only on certain days. My dad closed on Tuesday and Wednesday and opened on the Thursday. Thursday, being market day, involved obviously a higher risk—but also a higher chance for earning, especially as some shops did not operate because of the scare. The special control committee arrived on Thursday. It was a central committee on an irregular check mission—and that is why the local officials were not told.

This is a rather common method of by-passing the local authorities. This was an *ad hoc* committee of eight persons working in two sub-groups, comprising persons from the commerce departments in some local governments and representatives from the central office of the *OBKhSS* (the economic police).

A local boy of fourteen was given some money to buy a few things at my dad's shop. The boy was probably a Komsomolnik (a member of the communist youth, who take on—among other civilian duties—help in controlling consumer prices). Three men, disguised as customers, watched him. He purchased a pair of trousers and was charged 4·4OR instead of 3·60R; a pair of socks for 3·20R instead of 1·20R and an elastic band for underwear of which he got 7m. instead of 9m. as charged. The control men identified themselves, charged my dad with speculation (which is a criminal offence) and ordered him to close his shop, which was thereafter sealed until a formal inquiry was set up. He was taken immediately to the town's police station.

The rumour spread immediately at the market place and details quickly reached our home—though we lived some two hours away by train from the market. At once all our relations and neighbours came in to share the tragedy with us. My father's brothers and my mother's cousin—who happened to be visiting the town at that time—started to plan how to get him out of the mess. First of all, all the goods we had at home were dispersed quickly to face a possible police raid on our home. They were put, for the time being, at my father's brother's place.

My uncles and my mother's cousin made contact with the head of the police station where my father was arrested. It seemed possible to release him for a considerable amount of money. My mother's cousin proved to be of crucial importance. He was much richer than our family—he ran a factory in Tbilisi and had many contacts with officials there and knew in person the man who had issued the warning to the market traders.

He asked this person to come urgently from Tbilisi and both went to see a senior policeman. Of course they took a lot of risk, since they demanded the release of my father as well as the dropping of the charges against him. The charges however could not be dropped though they were much reduced. This was arranged for 5,000R to be handed in in cash. [Comparing this account with other information and discussing this case with other informants revealed that this was not an excessive demand in the given circumstances.] How was the sum raised in a short time? 2,000R were given by my family. Part of it we held at home as a matter of regularity for emergencies. The rest was given as a loan by my relatives. 3,000R were raised by the traders in the market—both Jews and gentiles.

The loans were given under no guarantee, without any condition or specified time for their return. It was all done on the understanding that a person's honour commits him and his family to see to it that the loans are returned as soon as possible. In this particular case it took 18 months to return the lot.

On his release, father went together with a few others (including me) to empty his shop of the illegal goods he held there. [Instead of 34 items he was licensed to deal with, he stocked 240, which means simply that this state-owned shop was used to run a private business. If caught and convicted of this offence he would have been sentenced for 'sabotaging the state's economy', for which the minimum sentence is 15 years imprisonment.] Luckily, dad was clever enough to have left a window unlocked—through which we managed to get in with the help of the gatekeeper who was given 100R. We dispersed the goods among the other shops in the market—the traders had authorised the gatekeeper to open their shops to do it. But a considerable amount was loaded on a van we brought with us. On leaving, we phoned to our house from the gatekeeper's home, saying: "the birds are on their way" which was an agreed code meaning; "the goods are on the way—be ready to disperse them".

My mother's cousin was driving. He was a man in his thirties and very tough. Since it was early morning, we were easily detected by the police patrols and were ordered to stop. [Police patrols are a constant factor to consider when delivering illegally. There should be a bill of lading (*faktura*) specifying the source and destination of all goods in transit. This is why most illegal deliveries are carried out during daytime when the likelihood of raising suspicion is low.] Of course we could not stop and a chase developed. But we knew the roads very well and managed to get away. On arrival we unloaded at my mother's cousin's place, since our home could already have been under surveillance. Small traders were waiting with cash to buy the goods off us at purchase price [that is—not to take advantage of the person's difficulty]. Within 90 minutes all was gone.

In what sounds like an adventure story we can detect all the values which function both as instigators to action and as the necessary preconditions for a successful operation. Trust is an essential key factor in raising a large sum of money in a short time, as well as in exchanging goods only on word of honour. Networks are the skeleton on which this case successfully came to a (relatively) happy end. Without the help of his family, the tradesmen-colleagues and his neighbours, this trader would have been doomed. One can argue, however, that had his network been larger and stronger (to include for instance senior police) he would have been saved from troubles at the outset. But he took risks without having a strong enough backing and was lucky to escape, though at considerable monetary as well as other cost (he could not go on with his trade).

An example of such a powerful network in operation was told to us by the son of a powerful second economy financier whose brother had been arrested for an economic offence. The Attorney General of that region, who was on the monthly 'pay roll' of this person's father, was approached to help but sent a messenger to say that he could not help in this particular case. His father's reply was: 'Tell him who sent you, that if my son is not released this evening—he will have no job to return to tomorrow'. Within twenty four hours our informant's brother had been released and the charges quashed.

## 5. *The Social Correlates of Occupations*

If we look at some representative occupations in terms of their related networks and the risks involved in them, we find (see Table 1) that there is a close relationship between occupations and personal networks: a small and/or weak network enables an individual to operate only in a low-risk occupation. A strong and/or extended network allows for the taking of bigger risks and allows entry into more prestigious occupations. Earnings, as

TABLE 1

REPRESENTATIVE OCCUPATIONS AND THEIR RELATED NETWORK CORES, RISKS AND INCOME

| Occupations | Network Cores* | | Risk Involved | | | Monthly Income Formal and informal |
|---|---|---|---|---|---|---|
| | Occupational weight | Total score | Low | Medium | High | |
| **Group I** Personal services and shopfloor workers | | | | | | |
| (a) Barber | 1+1 | 2 | ✓ | | | 400–600R |
| (b) Shoemaker/ repairer | 1+1+1+2 | 5 | ✓ | | | 400–600R |
| (c) Hatter | 1+1+1+1 | 4 | ✓ | | | 300–500R |
| (d) Small snack-bar operator | 2+1+1+1+1+1 | 8 | ✓ | | | 300–400R |
| (e) Blue-collar worker | 1+2+1+1+1+1+1+2+1 | 11 | ✓ | | | 250R |
| | Average | 6·0 | | | | |
| **Group II** Middlemen and small business operators | | | | | | |
| (f) Shop assistant | 1+2+2+1+1+2+1 | 10 | ✓ | | | 300–500R |
| (g) Shoemaker: foreman and middleman | 2+1+1+1+2+1+1+2+1 | 12 | | ✓ | | 600–900R |
| (h) Taxi driver | 3+1+1+3+2+3+1+1 | 15 | | | | 800–1,000R |
| (i) Small shopkeeper | 2+1+1+1+1+1 | 8 | | ✓ | | 500–800R |
| | Average | 11·25 | | | | |

Group III
Professional and executives

| | | | | | |
|---|---|---|---|---|---|
| (j) | Supermarket manager | 3+3+3+3+3+3+1+1 | 20 | | 2,000R–2,500R |
| (k) | Small factory executive | 3+1+3+3+3+3 | 16 | ✓ | 1,000–2,000R |
| (l) | Medium factory executive | 2+2+3 | 7 | ✓ | 1,000–1,500R |
| (m) | Big factory executive | 3+3+1+3+3+3+3 | 19 | ✓ | 2,000–10,000R |
| (n) | Import warehouse executive | 3+2+1+1+1+1 | 9 | ✓ | 3,000–5,000R |
| (o) | Physician (GP) | 1+3+3+3+3 | 16 ✓ | | Starter 1,000R Specialist up to 15,000R |
| | | Average | 14·50 | | |

*Network cores are computed here from males within the nuclear families of origin and marriage. We thus include father of ego, father of wife, brothers, sisters' husbands and wife's brothers. Their 'weight' is then calculated on the basis of a rating of their occupation, classified into: personal services/shop floor labour=1 point; middlemen/small businessmen=2 points; professional/executives=3 points. Only socially active persons are considered. The deceased and young are excluded. Though network cores are kinship based their extension depends upon peer group contact.

TABLE 2

FORMAL SOVIET VALUES VS THE GEORGIAN VALUE SYSTEM

| Principle | Formal Soviet Values | Georgian Values |
|---|---|---|
| 1 | Separation and insulation of private life from work life. | There is a fusion of work life and private life. |
| 1 (a) | Since private and work lives are conceptually separate they are not rated vis-a-vis each other nor seen as competing for personal resources. | Since private and work lives are fused within one conceptual system the resources from one can be used in the service of the other. Since private concerns are dominant, work roles and resources are therefore subordinate to private concerns. |
| 2 | Recruitment on impartial universalistic merit. | Nepotism as a moral duty. |
| 3 | Hierarchical organisation: directives go down; information flows up. | Patron-client networks: directives come from where the real power is vested; information flows along network lines. |
| 3 (a) | Officials are responsible to the official above them and for the work of subordinates. | Officials are primarily responsible to the claims of obligation and reciprocity imposed by network relationships. |
| 3 (b) | Work roles and relationships are unambiguously defined. | Work roles and relationships are part of a total role set (work is not set apart from the rest of life). |
| 4 | Decisions are based on rules and analogies. | Decisions are submitted to honour commitments. |
| 5 | Every role is replaceable. | Every role holder is network-bounded. |

would be expected, are linked to risk, and risks and earnings are both linked to honour—all derive from the effectiveness of network.

A barber (Case (a)) defined the risks in his job in these words:

To start with, people have their personal barbers, and they definitely would not give me in [report to the authorities for overcharging or supplying extra services]. They amount to 85% of our clients. For the rest, we [he and the other seven in his barbers' shop] run a quota. Everyone in his turn will take on outsiders, since you cannot charge them above the basic rate. But even, say, they catch you: what would they do? It's peanuts we're talking about. The most I would get is a warning from my cooperative headquarters. But it is different with a grocer because for him to make profit would mean to charge on some items at least 200% more and then when you are caught, either you pay every penny you've earned or you spend your life in jail.

This informant knew what he was talking about. He had tried for two years to be a grocer and had had to quit. The risk was too high: with a personal network score of only 2·0 (see

Table 1) he lacked adequate support—he could rely on no effective network either to prevent troubles or to mitigate them if they arose. Persons lacking effective networks can only make an adequate living by entering personal service occupations where their second economy activities are limited to regular clients. These they can charge more for that extra touch—the personal service—which is so highly considered in a macho society.

Of course it is not only low-status jobs which involve low risks. The qualified physician benefits from both high status *and* low risks. The physician (Case (o)), like the barber, the tailor, the hatter and the small cafe operator, makes his real money through strictly face-to-face interaction: the service giver and the client are the only parties to a transaction, thus minimising the chances of detection. But such professionals and their low-risk earnings are exceptional and the market accordingly recognises and adapts to the demand for places at medical school. Entrants must therefore be highly talented or able to command massive resources. In Tbilisi University's medical school, the only one in Georgia, competition for entrance is so rigorous that we were told that there were twenty applicants for each place and that a fee of 'up to 50,000R'[1] could be charged to ensure one's admittance. Here again a strong network is required to raise such large sums.

The medium risk occupations—those in Group II, middlemen and people in small business—are also mainly in contact with a regular circle of clients. But they also have more dealings with strangers, and the nature of their interaction is not always face-to-face as it is in personal service. This necessarily makes them more prone to detection if they break the rules and hence reinforces their need for strong backing from a good, reliable network. The average total score of those in Group II occupations is 11·25 compared with 6·0 in Group I.

In high-risk occupations the need for a strong network is paramount and here the average score is 14·50. Any small-town factory or supermarket has to obtain informal authority from the head of the local economic sector or from the *ispolkom* chairman himself. Usually too the head of the local police also has to be involved—at least passively. These officials are often placed on a monthly payroll and so too are their subordinates. As one factory executive explained: 'And what if the *ispolkom* chairman or the head of police is on leave? We have to pay their deputies, just in case they are in charge when some trouble occurs'.

Surprisingly, however, some high-status, high-earning, high-risk jobs are not backed with an influential network. Indeed, to take the case of one medium factory executive (1)—the production manager in a foodstuffs factory of several hundred workers—he made a deliberate choice to be extremely cautious. He used to practice only overproduction, that is, to make use of the state's machinery—but he would obtain raw material and labour at his own expense. He was careful not to reduce the standard of his products and he produced only the items he was licensed to. He was also careful about how he organised his factors of production—what Georgians call his 'combination'—so that many of his shop floor workers would not know too much about it.

When we compare this executive's situation with that of our big factory executive (m) we get a very different picture. He was considered one of the four most powerful people in his town. As production manager in a light furniture factory with a staff of 1,400 he had to have the backing of all the powerful job holders in his enterprise which involved a much higher order of necessary coordination. On his monthly payroll were the head of the enterprise, the *ispolkom* chairman and his deputy, the head of the police plus three of his staff. They required a combined monthly 'salary' bill of 1,500R.

This person not only used state machinery for production and the formal distribution chain to dispose of it—as did executive (l)—but he also reduced the product's standard, acquired raw material from his formal supply, produced with it products which were in high demand—not necessarily those he was licensed to—and finally distributed B quality products to meet his quota while A quality products found their way to the second economy. In this way he satisfies two aims. Firstly by skimping on the quality of his formal production he is able to obtain extra scarce materials for his informal production. Second, by ensuring a higher quality for his informal production he ensures that it obtains a head start in competiton for sales against the formal products.

However, the figures in Table 1 need care in interpretation. There can be cases where either a strong network would not necessarily be of benefit to a person or where a good and risky position is held without an adequate supporting network. The first position is highlighted by the blue-collar worker (e) who had an extensive familial network, but who could not benefit from it. He had eloped with his wife rather than submit to parental choices and vetoes and his network could therefore be regarded as damaged. Neither family was happy with the match. (This, by the way, brings out the role of women in the second economy—on which we have no space to elaborate here.) Without capital, without effective family, he had to enter blue-collar shop floor work where only occasionally was he offered extra work for second economy production—thus explaining his relatively high pay for manual work.

High pay alone does not however indicate high honour. In this culture, where individual autonomy is highly valued, the closeness of earnings between Groups I and II does not point up the essential differences between a job that allows one to take risks and a job that does not. Perhaps even more striking as an example of the care necessary in interpreting Table 1, is the case of the executive of a central warehouse (n) who was in control of imported consumer goods. These are of course in high demand. We believe this person was placed in that position *because* he possessed only a weak network and would thus not have been able to take full advantage of his highly sensitive job.

## 6. Conclusions

Having presented the core values of Georgian society and looked in some detail into their operation 'on the ground', we would now like to suggest some tentative conclusions concerning their articulation within the Georgian national economy. The most obvious conclusion from our data is the deep discrepancy they suggest between the formal, bureaucratic model of the Soviet economy—the way the economy is supposed to work— and the nepotistic, highly personalised entrepreneurial nature of Georgia's economy—the way that economy *really* works. Why, for instance, the key institutionalised function of the *tolkach*—the 'fixer'—in the Soviet economic system (Berliner, 1952) has no equivalent in the Georgian economy, nor in the Georgian language. The *tolkach* as such does not exist in Georgia. This is not because the system does not need this function but because the function has no need to be formalised and concentrated in a single role. It is a function that is dispersed and is always latently active within personal networks. Every Georgian is a potential *tolkach* in his own interest or in the interest of his network.

Since the formal system is predicated upon the idea of an individual's insulated occupancy of a role it follows that defective role performance should be curable by the replacement of the performer. This approach is always subject to some modification but the extent of its limitation in Georgia is almost finite in a culture so based upon personal networks. Here replacing one person by another cannot really change anything. The Moscow and (especially since 1973) some of the Tbilisi authorities have been concerned for years to bring an end to the Georgian way of running their republic. Their most serious attempt was the replacement of Mzhavanadze as first secretary of the Georgian Communist Party in the early 1970s. However, in its essentials the system has not changed, and the reasons are clear; in a network-based culture, though a person can be replaced, networks continue to exist. Persons will use personal support networks to try to find a lead to the new appointee, or if he proves too difficult to deal with, find a way to get rid of him or make his task impossible by limiting access to the social resources he needs.

We were told by an informant who was the personal chauffeur of an *ispolkom* chairman, and who thus had free access to much delicate information, that it was normal practice when a job changed hands to pass over the job's associated networks. Thus, in a 'casual conversation' the new appointee, if an outsider, would always ask: 'Are there any people around to count on?', and his predecessor would then reply: 'If you need anything—you can trust . . .'

In a similar way networks are used to mitigate penalties and to reduce disturbances on the occasions that exposure proves inevitable: criminal charges are reduced in scale; the honour code ensures that collaborators remain unrevealed to the authorities and evidence is removed or tampered with—all through the use of personal support networks.

But networks can also operate coercively—reciprocities and obligations have to be matched—not just in the immediate or short term but essentially because they become *part of a flow* that binds network members together. In such circumstances each network member finds that the network acts as a net; each member becomes a resource to others—a link in a chain upon which many others may depend. An informant who tried to stop fixing higher education entrance found himself trapped in this way by the demands of his network. He was not given the chance to leave his position. We thus can see that a network acts like a net in two senses: for some it can act as a safety net; for others it becomes an entanglement. 'A fence is built of wire and one man builds another' says a Georgian expression that neatly encapsulates this idea of linkages and networks. A factory executive explained it this way:

> You can't be innocent. Once you occupy a certain position, people expect you to pay them and if you don't—they will either see to it that you're replaced or that you're incriminated [and thus removed forcibly]. This is not difficult to fix. Everyone assumes there can be no genuine mistakes—a mistake would immediately incriminate you.

But normally such coercion is unnecessary. People remain in networks and conform to the social expectations these require because their *total* social situation demands it.

When the significance of network affiliation is considered alongside the macho virtue of risk taking, we can see how their combination is crucial to the idea of excess. In no way can the average—not the exceptional—Georgian male conform to the model of Soviet eco-

## GEORGIA'S SECOND ECONOMY                                                559

nomic man. Formal income counts for only a proportion of total income, and it is extra income from the second economy that is vital to a full social role that requires excess in feasting and display. As our informants say 'if you are poor and the house is empty—then where is your pride?' Georgian men not only benefit economically from 'screwing the system'—their very honour as men demands that they should screw it excessively.

We believe we can now go some way in explaining why the Georgian second economy should be larger in real terms than the second economies of other Soviet-type republics. To be sure, other Soviet-type economies display the same kind of second economy practices (see for example the works of Staats, 1972; Berliner, 1957; Katzenelinboigen, 1977; 1978 (b); Simis, 1982). They too depend for much of their informal economic activity on 'friends of friends'. But it is the degree to which networks in Georgia are institutionalised as a means of linking individuals through trust-based honour commitments that form the cornerstone of Georgia's second economy. The difference may appear to be merely one of degree but it is based on a fundamental cultural distinction.

We hope we have demonstrated how a concern with the central interest of anthropology—the idea of culture, the application of the concept of personal support network and the alliance of these to the anthropological method of patient participant observation, can produce understanding of an economic system that would otherwise be unobtainable. Other Soviet-type economies based on different cultural core values may well display high levels of second economy activity. Ofer and Vinokur (1979), for instance, suggest that this is the case in the Central Asian Republics—well known to be second only to Georgia in this respect. It is not sufficient, however, to consider merely the overall outcome of second economy activity. If this phenomenon is to be understood it must be examined in the context of its cultural setting. Recourse to the methods and concepts of anthropology is we would argue, the only way that this can be achieved.

*Middlesex Polytechnic*

*This study was funded by The Nuffield Foundation (UK). An earlier version of this paper was delivered to the Western Slavic Association Conference at Honolulu, Hawaii, in March 1982.
    [1] Simis (1982) states that the standard fee at the same time to which our information refers was 15,000R. We would however expect the price to be higher for Jews than for non-Jews.

*References*

Ben-Zvi, I. *Israel's Exiled,* Ministry of Defence Publications, Tel-Aviv 1963 (Hebrew).
Ben-Ami. *Between the Hammer and the Scythe,* Am-Oved, Tel-Aviv 1965 (Hebrew).
Berliner, J. S. 'The Informal Organisation of the Soviet Firm', *Quarterly Journal of Economics,* 1952, p. 342–365.
Davis, J. *People of the Mediterranean.* Routledge & Kegan Paul, London 1977.
Dragadze, T. 'Family Life in Georgia', *New Society* 19 August 1976, p. 393–5.
Grigolia, A. *Custom and Justice in the Caucasus: the Georgian Highlanders.* University of Pennsylvania, Philadelphia 1939.
Grossman, G. 'The Second Economy of the USSR', *Problems of Communism,* September/October 1977, pp. 25–40.
Katzenlinboigen, A, 'Coloured Markets in the Soviet Union', *Soviet Studies,* Vol. XXIX, No. 1, (January 1977) pp. 62–85. *Soviet Economic Planning,* M. E. Sharpe, NY 1978.
Kardanov, B. A. et al. *Caucasian Life* (Vol. 2) Publication of the Academy of Sciences, Moscow 1962 (Russian).

560

*The Anthropology of Drinking.* Cambridge University Press, 1983.

Parsons, R. 'National Integration in Soviet Georgia', *Soviet Studies,* Vol. XXXIV No. 4, (October 1982) pp. 547–69.

Peristiany, J. G. (ed). *Honour and Shame.* Weidenfeld and Nicolson, 1966.

Plisetsky, M. *Religion and Customs of Georgian Jews.* Moscow 1931 (Russian).

Ofer, G. & Vinokur, A. 'The Private Sources of Income of the Soviet Urban Household'. Research Paper. *Kennan Institute for Advanced Russian Studies.* Washington, DC, January 1980.

Simis, K. *USSR: Secrets of a Corrupt Society,* Dent, 1982.

Staats, S. S. 'Corruption in the Soviet System', *Problems of Communism,* January/February 1972.

Wiles, P. J. D. *Die Parallelwirtschaft.* Sonderveröffentlichung des Bundesinstituts für Ostwissenschaftliche und Internationale Studien, Cologne, 1981.

# Part III
# Managerial Responses

# A Little Larceny Can Do a Lot For Employee Morale

by Lawrence R. Zeitlin, an industrial psychologist, who is 40 years old. He spent 10 years in industry before returning to academia in 1963. He took a B.A. from Harvard, an M.A. from Roosevelt University and a Ph.D. from Northwestern University in 1954. The American Board of Professional Psychology honored him as a diplomate in organizational and industrial psychology in 1969. He is a professor of industrial psychology at City College, City University of New York, and enjoys sailing and photography in his spare time.

A close friend of mine, an accountant, told me of an experience he had recently when he audited the books of a corporation. It became apparent that the office manager was dipping into petty cash to the extent of about $2,000 a year. He reported this fact to the president. The president responded, "How much are we paying him?" "Ten thousand a year," replied the accountant. "Then keep quiet about it," said the president. "He's worth at least $15,000."

Employees in American business steal between 8.5- and 10-billion dollars a year. About four billion of this total is theft in cash and merchandise from retail establishments. The remainder is lost through kickbacks, bribery, theft of time, and loss of corporate secrets.

Thefts of merchandise alone amount to approximately five per cent of the yearly sales of American retail establishments, and internal losses outweigh external losses by about three to one. That is, the stores' own employees steal three times as much as do shoplifters.

**Monitor.** Obviously, business is aware of employee dishonesty. Most retail establishments have some form of internal security system to discourage dishonest employees. Some employ guards at sensitive merchandise-handling points; others require employees to carry company-provided handbags or to leave their coats in company-monitored cloakrooms. Several companies utilize undercover investigators and plainclothes detectives, aided by electronic security measures, to detect thievery on the part of employees.

Despite the precautions taken to minimize "shrinkage," employees concoct elaborate schemes to steal, and in most cases they get away with it. The ratio of theft incidence to prosecution is lower for this kind of theft than for any other form of grand larceny. For the dishonest employee, crime pays. Or does it?

Considering the time and effort involved, the risk of detection and subsequent discharge, and the real (although small) risk of prosecution, the

Harvard
## Business Review
Soldiers Field, Boston, Massachusetts 02163


28 December 1970


Professor Lawrence R. Zeitlin
Baruch Graduate Center
Bernard M. Baruch College
257 Park Avenue South
New York, New York 10010

Dear Professor Zeitlin:

When your new article "Employee Theft as Informal Job
Enrichment" first came in, I had high hopes for its
possibilities for HBR. Your thesis is a very original
and unusual one, and personally I find it quite
intriguing and provocative. I am all the more sorry
to have to report, therefore, that the final decision
goes against your article for HBR. To be perfectly frank,
the consensus is that your conclusions—especially the
idea of a tolerable amount of theft—aren't consistent
with the ideals of HBR. This problem might not exist if
we were a commercial magazine, but the difficulty is a
very real one in view of our university status.

I am returning the manuscript with our regrets that we
cannot use it. I trust you will send it to the editors
of other magazines. I should think there would be a
good chance that another publication would want to use it.

Sincerely yours,

David W. Ewing
Senior Associate Editor


DWE:b


actual return on employee theft is poor. If we divide the total amount of merchandise lost through internal employee theft (about three billion dollars a year) by the total number of people employed in retail establishments, the amount stolen per person is approximately $300 a year, or about $1.50 each working day.

Of course, some employees steal a great deal more, others considerably less. But the evidence indicates that well over 75 per cent of all employees participate to some extent in merchandise shrinkage. This theft may range from trivial to important—from taking paper clips or typing paper home for the youngsters' homework to misappropriating substantial amounts of cash or merchandise. The fact remains that in retail establishments internal theft averages out to an unevenly distributed five per cent

to eight per cent of the typical employee's salary.

**Bread.** The dishonest employee uses considerable ingenuity. In one case reported in *The Wall Street Journal*, drivers for a retail bakery routinely turned over as many as 4,000 loaves of bread a day to supermarket managers in return for kickbacks. Because retail prices were rising, the bakery couldn't tack the cost of thievery onto the retail price of the bread. So, the company began charging drivers the full wholesale price (29¢ per loaf) for bread unaccounted for. The firm said that it made the move to "remove indifference among the drivers and create a sense of responsibility." What it created was a sense of ingenuity. Drivers countered by continuing their illicit sales and replacing the bread so disposed of with day-old

bread purchased for 10 cents a loaf from the company's day-old bread store

**Dull.** Why does the dishonest worker spend so much energy figuring out ways to steal from his employer? One answer is the nature of the job. Most retail jobs are unspeakably repetitive and boring. Advancement usually is limited. The typical retail worker has relatively little freedom of action or decision-making autonomy. If he deals with customers, he must subordinate his own desires to those of the customer. And salaries are low. It is no wonder that in such jobs, employee dissatisfaction is rife and turnover is relatively high.

In order to increase employee work motivation and to decrease turnover, management may choose one of two alternative courses. It can follow the policies described by Frederick Herzberg [*P.T.*, March 1968] and other management theorists and enrich the jobs. By providing increased variety of work, opportunity for advancement, and opportunities for individuals to assume responsibility, management can increase the quality of the work situation. Or, if management chooses not to improve low-quality jobs, it can increase worker pay and benefits to the point where, although the job is unpleasant, it is too good to leave.

**Initiative.** But management has chosen, largely by default, to reject both approaches, so workers seem to have taken matters into their own hands. When the average retail employee becomes dissatisfied with his job, if he doesn't quit, he starts stealing from his employer. He gets back at the system. In a sense, the intellectual and physical challenges provided by opportunities to steal represent a significant enrichment of the individual's job. He can take matters into his own hands, assume responsibility, make decisions and face challenges. The amount he gets away with is determined solely by his own initiative. He is in business for himself.

**Out.** In one two-year study, I found job enrichment to be the chief motive behind employee theft in a large Midwestern clothing store. The most convincing evidence came from interviews with 32 persons who had been discharged for stealing. None had been prosecuted, of course, though the personal take had, in at least one case, run to a few thousand dollars. Eight of the ex-employees admitted that they stole primarily for cash. For the most part they had been young (mean age, 24), and recently hired, working at low-paying jobs in warehousing or stockroom operations. They sold the merchandise directly to friends and associates.

A group of six employees could give no reason other than "impulse" for their theft. The store had virtually no internal security, and apparently temptation became too much. Job enrichment is an unlikely motive for this group: they were considerably older (mean age, 36) and many held trusted, responsible positions. In fact, the employee with the largest amount of recorded theft—well over $4,000 worth of men's clothing—was a department manager. (Most of the garments were recovered, untouched and unworn, from his rumpus room. Many were ludicrously out of size.) Such seemingly "pathological" thefts involved little challenge and little planning.

**Benefit.** The remaining 18 employees produced surprising responses when I interviewed them sympathetically outside the store context, several months after they had been fired, and assured them that there would be no punitive action. Each of them indicated a sense of satisfaction at "getting away with it." Although most of them knew that they were doing wrong, few of them felt any sense of guilt or remorse. A common comment was: "It's not really hurting anybody—the store can afford it." In fact, one fellow argued ingeniously that his thefts of men's clothing *benefited* the store, by his being seen around town in the New Look. They often looked upon theft as a condition of employment: "the store owed it to me," or "I felt I deserved to get something additional for my work since I wasn't getting paid enough." Many of the ex-employees blamed work conditions: boredom, long periods of inactivity, low commissions, supervisors who treated them poorly.

Only rarely did members of this group sell the merchandise. In many cases they gave it as gifts to members of their families and to friends.

Bosses of the discharged employees in all three groups rated them "good" or better on a performance-review system. They had worked for the store, on the average, considerably longer than the average "hon-

est" employee. Most were caught by security police who had been hired from the outside because management thought they were losing the merchandise to "outsiders." In most cases, the supervisors were honestly surprised—in fact they were convinced only when the security people caught several employees redhanded. It was the store management's bewilderment over the nature of its merchandise thefts that led to my being retained to study the problem.

**Pay?** While it is probable that no job-enrichment or salary increase would have prevented theft by the six persons who stole for impulsive reasons, we can make a fair case that such changes might have minimized theft among the other 26 employees. But would this have paid off for the employer? The average annual theft for all employees in the discharged group amounted to slightly less than

---

*"The dishonest worker is enriching his own job in a manner that is very satisfactory (for him). This enrichment is costing management, on the average, $1.50 per worker per day. At this rate, management gets a bargain. By permitting a controlled amount of theft, management can avoid reorganizing jobs and raising wages."*

---

$200 a man a year, which is considerably less than the national average. It is hard to see what significant modifications in salary or job responsibility could be made with this small an investment.

The dishonest worker is enriching his own job in a manner that is very satisfactory (for him). This enrichment is costing management, on the average, $1.50 per worker per day. At this rate, management gets a bargain. By permitting a controlled amount of theft, management can avoid reorganizing jobs and raising wages. Management still keeps most business decision-making functions in its own hands and retains workers without increasing salaries and benefits. (I should emphasize that a man who enriches his job by stealing does not suddenly become a "good" employee; rather, he gives the *appearance* of a good employee so as not to attract attention to his illicit activities.

But in many cases this is all that is necessary. Simply *being there* is sufficient for many jobs. It is common knowledge in financial circles that the man with his hand in the till is never absent.)

**Toolbox.** The important word is *control.* Properly utilized, controlled employee theft can be used as another implement in management's motivational toolbox. As in the case of most motivational tools, costs and conditions of utilization must be carefully studied. (Ethically, of course, it would be more desirable for management to motivate employees by means other than inviting them into lives of petty crime. It is traditionally considered better to have workers directing their energies toward furthering the course of the business rather than toward satisfying their individual larcenous desires.)

Before deciding to minimize or eliminate employee theft, management should ask itself these four practical questions:

1. How much is employee theft actually costing us?
2. What increase in employee dissatisfaction could we expect if we controlled theft?
3. What increase in employee turnover could we expect?
4. What would it cost to build employee motivation up to a desirable level by conventional means of job enrichment or through higher salaries?

**Cost.** Setting aside ethical and emotional considerations, management may decide that the monetary cost of enforcing honesty is too great. That is, the cost of an effective security system, plus the cost of achieving equivalent employee stability by increasing pay or job quality, is greater than the loss of merchandise due to employee theft. In such a case, a system of controlled larceny may be in order.

In order to set up such a system, management would first decide upon the amount of merchandise it could afford to lose. Once it has discovered the tolerable limits of employee theft, management would enforce these limits. An effective, informal signaling system would have to be developed to show awareness of employee theft, and swift action would have to be taken when the theft exceeded the established limit.

At the same time, management would have to maintain a figurehead (Continued on page 64.)

S/R *(Continued from page 26.)*
security system. After all, the major benefit of employee theft is the job enrichment provided by the individual's attempt to beat the system. If all need for precaution is eliminated, then the employee gets no satisfaction from theft. All he gets is a slight addition to his income in merchandise instead of in cash.

**Tolls.** Here is an example of implementation in real life of such an informal, controlled-theft job-enrichment approach:

The port authority of a large Eastern city had a great deal of difficulty keeping toll takers on its bridges and tunnels. Back when security was lax, there was much demand for jobs as toll takers. In fact, in the 1930s, one had to offer a bribe (about $1,000) to get even a temporary summer position. But by 1950, an elaborate security system (locked cash boxes, numbered tickets, remote indication of fares, etc.) had made a drastic reduc-

---

*"Theft serves as a safety valve for employee frustration. It permits management to avoid the responsibility and the cost of job enrichment or salary increases at a relatively low amount of money per man."*

---

tion in employee-theft opportunities. Simultaneously, the turnover of toll takers rose to an unprecedented high. As can be imagined, collecting tolls honestly is an extremely tedious job that offers relatively little opportunity for personal gratification, minimal chance for advancement, and little opportunity to make decisions.

**Limit.** The personnel manager, together with the director of the toll-collecting operation, determined between themselves that the total cost of reducing theft to a minimum was excessive. Admittedly, they saved money in tolls, but personnel turnover cost them more than the amount saved. By this time, the authority knew almost to the penny how much money should be collected per toll booth—as a function of traffic. They determined that they could tolerate toll-taker thefts of $10.00 a week a man.

Although it is no longer possible for individual toll takers to put tolls directly into their pockets, a clever toll taker can figure out ways to collect a portion of the tolls for himself. For example, he can buy a book of com-

muter tickets and when a traveler pays the full toll in cash, the collector can ring up the price of a ticket and place the difference in his pocket. Of course, this can be done only a few times a day, since a check is run on the distribution of ticket numbers per booth. In fact, the collector must exercise considerable ingenuity to get away with $10 a week.

If the toll taker exceeds the $10 theft limit more than once or twice, the toll-collection manager has an informal system to signal to the collector that he is under suspicion. A brightly painted authority police car parks right in front of the malefactor's toll booth. The toll taker gets the message. Theft drops back to a tolerable level.

**Valve.** Such a system then meets all of the requirements described previously. The managers first determined the cost of absolute enforcement and found that when the turnover costs were included, the price was simply excessive. So, they calculated the allowable amount of theft. The actual theft requires considerable ingenuity on the part of the employee because the authority has some fairly sophisticated procedures for monitoring employees. The employee can steal but it takes work. Finally, they worked out an informal signal to let the employee know when he exceeds tolerable limits. Occasionally, of course, it is necessary to discharge an employee for excessive thefts when he doesn't get the message. This serves to keep the rest "honest."

Theft serves as a safety valve for employee frustration. It permits management to avoid the responsibility and cost of job enrichment or salary increases at a relatively low amount of money per man per year. Uncontrolled theft can be disastrous for any business concern but *controlled* theft can be useful. Employee theft, used as a motivational tool, can be an economic benefit to an organization, if management finds it too costly to meet its traditional responsibility to make jobs rewarding and to pay a living wage.

I do not advocate abandonment of the traditional responsibilities of management, but I suggest that management adopt a more realistic and certainly less hypocritical attitude to business "honesty" and publicly recognize that there is benefit to be obtained by utilizing employee theft as a motivational tool.

# [20]

## INTEGRITY TESTING FOR PERSONNEL SELECTION: AN OVERVIEW

JOHN W. JONES and WILLIAM TERRIS

London House, Inc.
Park Ridge, Illinois 60068

*We review the strengths and limitations of a wide variety of personnel selection procedures designed to control employee theft, including interviews, reference checks, criminal background checks, credit checks, graphology, and paper-and-pencil integrity tests. We examine preemployment integrity tests in more depth. Also reviewed are major concerns about integrity tests, including evidence of validity, classification accuracy, adverse impact research, test takers' reactions, and privacy protection, to name a few. We discuss the role of integrity tests in controlling negligent hiring claims. Finally, we review the* Model Guidelines for Integrity Testing Programs *(Association of Personnel Test Publishers, 1990).*

Employee theft is widespread, difficult to detect, and the most costly crime against business (American Management Association, 1977). Hefter (1986) and Hollinger and Clark (1983) surveyed thousands of employees and estimated that one in three employees steal at work. Examples of employee theft includes (a) theft of cash, merchandise, and property; (b) damaging merchandise to buy it on discount; (c) unauthorized work-break extensions; (d) misuse of discount privileges; (e) getting paid for more hours than worked; (f) unauthorized use of company resources (e.g., company phones, client lists, facilities); and (g) fraud.

Meinsma's (1985) research suggests that anywhere from 10% to 30% of all business bankruptcies can be attributed in part to employee dishonesty. This is best illustrated by claims that many of the failures in the savings and loan industry are fraud related ("Crime," 1990). The most current research on the prevalence of employee theft is summarized as follows:

Portions of this article were presented at the 1990 annual spring conference of the Personnel Testing Council of Northern California, Sacramento, California.

1. Hollinger and Clark (1983) surveyed thousands of employees and found that on average, the percentage of retail, hospital, and manufacturing employees admitting to theft was 42%, 32%, and 26%, respectively.
2. Slora (1989) surveyed hundreds of fast-food and supermarket employees and found that 60% of fast-food employees and 43% of supermarket workers admitted to stealing company cash and property.
3. Carey (1989) reported an increase in internal bank fraud and embezzlement from approximately $165 million in 1981 to approximately $534 million in 1987.
4. Arthur Young, Inc. (1988) documented a 5% increase in the retail industry's shrinkage rates from 1982 to 1987, representing approximately $1.8 billion in losses attributable to the increase alone.

Parenthetically, it is worth noting that most of the base-rate research probably underestimates the amount of theft because most of it is based on either anonymous admissions or detected theft. Underestimates occur because people tend to underreport theft using a self-report strategy, and most acts of employee theft are never detected.

Businesses adopt two general approaches to reduce theft losses. The first has been to alter the work environment so as to preclude the possibility of theft. This strategy is primarily aimed at shoplifters and includes the use of undercover security officers, closed-circuit televisions, special sensor tags on each inventory article, and other methods of control. Although these systems may be effective in reducing theft by shoplifters, employee thieves often circumvent them (Terris, 1986).

A second approach has been to concentrate on the preemployment screening process to minimize the selection of job applicants most likely to engage in theft-related activities. This approach is aimed at employee theft. Preemployment screening appears to be one of the methods of choice for organizations in their efforts to control employee theft (Sackett & Harris, 1984; Sackett, Burris, & Callahan, 1989). Theft rates are typically lower, sometimes by as much as 50%, in those organizations that conduct careful and extensive preemployment screening (Baumer & Rosenbaum, 1984; Jones, 1989a).

The purpose of this article is to describe screening methods that companies use to establish an honest and dependable workforce, with special emphasis on preemployment integrity tests. The use of paper-and-pencil integrity tests spans over 40 years (Ash, 1988). These psychological inventories are relatively easy to administer and have scientific studies documenting their ability to screen out applicants most likely to engage in on-the-job theft. Advantages and limitations of different types of integrity assessment procedures are summarized in Table 1.

## Integrity Assessment Procedures

### Employment Interviews

The traditional interview is an important part of almost every company's personnel selection procedures. Unfortunately, although there have been many studies investigating the various types of validity of the employment interview (McDaniel, 1988; Schmitt, 1976), there has been no published research, to our knowledge, investigating the effectiveness of the interview as a method to predict and reduce employment theft. The typical interview does not cover theft issues. Moreover, the traditional interview yields low levels of validity. Structured interviews yield higher validity coefficients. Traditional employment interviews need to be validated against theft criteria before they can be viewed as a viable integrity screening procedure.

### Reference Checks

The major purpose of the reference check is to verify information that applicants have previously supplied to the company. Moreover, applicants expecting checks are thought to be more truthful in the information they supply to the company. Usually, reference checks are costly and time consuming when one considers the amount of information that is obtained. Perhaps this is why most companies do not perform complete reference checks on most applicants. There is little if any direct evidence that the use of reference checks actually reduces employee theft (cf. Terris, 1986).

Although reference checks are probably desirable, they do have major limitations in terms of obtaining information relevant to em-

**TABLE 1**   Preemployment Integrity Screening Methods Available to Businesses and Industry

| Screening method | Convenience issues | Main problems | Main advantages |
|---|---|---|---|
| Integrity tests | Can easily be made part of the usual screening procedure | Company representatives must be trained to appropriately use test scores<br>Not all integrity tests are thoroughly validated | Validity evidence exists<br>Generally not offensive<br>No adverse impact (meets equal opportunity guidelines)<br>May discourage dishonest applicants from applying |
| Selection interview | Usually part of hiring procedure<br>Often time consuming | No evidence of validity with theft criteria<br>Difficult to determine applicant's truthfulness in discussing theft and counterproductivity<br>Can create adverse impact | Inexpensive (already part of hiring procedures)<br>Structured interviews show more promise than traditional interviews |
| Reference checks | Often time consuming | Little evidence of validity<br>Most misconduct is undetected<br>Company reluctant to give negative information | May increase truthfulness of applicants<br>Verifies information provided on application form and résumés |

| | | | |
|---|---|---|---|
| Criminal background checks | Commonly available but lengthy turnaround required | Not all criminals are on record<br>Information obtained must be job relevant | Very complete and verifiable data can be obtained if available |
| Credit checks | Quick but somewhat costly | Relevance to theft not clear<br>May not meet equal opportunity guidelines | Obtains information relevant to financial need and fiscal responsibility |
| Graphology | Faddish<br>Complicated scoring procedures exist | No evidence of validity against theft or any criteria when controlling for content<br>Difficult to standardize | None identified |

*Note.* This table has been adapted from Jones and Terris (1989).

121

ployee theft. One problem is that employers are often reluctant to give negative information concerning past employees because of possible lawsuits. In fact, dishonest employees caught stealing sometimes make a deal with their employers in which employees agree to resign and return the money or property in return for a good or at least neutral reference from employers. A more important problem is that in most companies, the employer is not really aware of which employees are stealing. Another problem is that there is little evidence as to the validity or accuracy of data obtained from reference checks. Finally, job applicants can usually easily omit from the reference list the names of any companies where they are known to have stolen money or merchandise.

## Criminal Background Checks

Criminal background checks and investigations can vary from little more than a reference check to a complete investigation of an individual's entire life. Usually, the background check is limited to a check on a person's past criminal history. Arrest records, although probably valid, are seldom used to make a hiring decision because of possible legal ramifications. Several states ban employers outright from either asking about or using arrest information to make a hiring decision (Ash, 1989). Although federal laws apparently do not absolutely forbid using arrest information, using arrest records to make hiring decisions would probably result in an adverse impact against some protected minority groups.

Convictions, on the other hand, can be considered when making a hiring decision. However, one possible requirement is that only job-related criminal histories can be considered. For example, an applicant with a prior conviction for theft could be denied employment in a company where the opportunity for on-the-job theft is great (i.e., sales clerks in a jewelry store). It is not yet certain if a company can use irrelevant convictions. Actually, the question of relevant versus irrelevant convictions is essentially an empirical question, and research is needed to show whether a certain type of conviction is predictive of future employee theft.

There are a number of problems with criminal checks. First, legal and practical obstacles make it time consuming and difficult to obtain criminal records from a variety of federal, state, and local jurisdictions. Any information obtained is likely to be incomplete or misleading. For example, most theft is never detected (i.e., who did it). Most detected crimes never lead to actual arrest and many arrests do not lead to a conviction. Furthermore, many convictions are based on plea bargaining or some other type of reduced sentencing. It should also be remembered that employee thieves are almost never caught or convicted (Slora, 1989).

## Credit Checks

Some employers use credit checks to make a hiring decision. The rationale is that applicants with either a great need for money or a history of irresponsible financial management are thought to be greater risks for positions of trust. Although there apparently is no empirical evidence to support this belief, it appears reasonable to assume that individuals who really need a great deal of money would be more tempted to steal than those without such a need. However, credit checks would seem to have a high probability of producing an adverse impact against certain protected minorities, and there is no available research to document the proposition that credit histories are predictive of future theft.

## Graphology

No research exists showing that the results of a graphology exam, or handwriting analysis, predict theft criteria. In fact, few validation studies have even been conducted in which graphology results were compared with job performance measures. Graphology exams are also difficult to standardize. Although complicated scoring procedures exist, it is difficult to determine the qualifications of graphologists. Graphology does not appear to be a viable selection procedure for predicting employee theft.

## Psychological Assessment

Historically, attempts to predict criminal behavior with personality tests have not been successful (Schuessler & Cressey, 1950). Commonly used personality tests such as the Sixteen Personality Factor questionnaire (Cattell, Ebert, & Tatsuoka, 1970) and the Minnesota

Multiphasic Personality Inventory (MMPI; Dahlstrom & Welsh, 1960) have not been found to consistently predict employee theft. More recently, an extensive amount of research has been conducted with paper-and-pencil integrity tests (O'Bannon, Goldinger, & Appleby, 1989; Sackett & Harris, 1984; Sackett et al., 1989).

## Preemployment Integrity Tests

Integrity tests are psychological tests designed to predict job applicants' proneness for theft and other forms of counterproductivity. Most integrity tests are designed to measure job applicants' attitudes toward, perceptions of, and opinions about employee theft. These types of selection instruments are typically called *overt integrity tests*. Parenthetically, preemployment integrity tests were designed for hiring a quality workforce and were not constructed or validated to help psychologists make recommendations for parole, sentencing, or rehabilitation decisions. Further research is needed for these other types of applications.

Validation research that complies with test development guidelines of the American Psychological Association has been published by integrity test publishers (O'Bannon et al., 1989). Although integrity tests differ from one another in important ways, leading overt integrity tests measure attitudes related to one or more of the following psychological constructs: tolerance of others who steal, projection about the extent of theft by others, acceptance of rationalizations for theft, interthief loyalty, antisocial beliefs and behaviors, and admissions of theft-related activities.

Employee thieves have a fairly stable psychological profile that is statistically different from other employees. Paper-and-pencil integrity tests can accurately measure the various dimensions of this profile. Overt integrity tests were developed to be consistent with the congruence theory of attitude–behavior relationships (Ajzen & Fishbein, 1977; Jones, 1989b). This theory shows that attitudes are the best predictors of behavior when the attitudinal qualities being measured (i.e., context, target, action, time reference) are very consistent with the relevant behavior being predicted. For example, attitudes toward theft in the workplace should be better predictors of on-the-job theft criteria than attitudes toward delinquency in general.

*Integrity Test Validity*

Sackett and his associates (Sackett & Harris, 1984; Sackett et al., 1989) have been studying employee theft for over 10 years. These researchers cited over 120 studies in their reviews. Many of the studies cited were validation studies of different integrity tests. In their 1989 review of integrity testing practices, Sackett et al. (1989) concluded that professionally developed integrity tests yield useful levels of validity:

> The present review found a large number of [criterion-related validity studies with external criteria] including large-scale predictive studies in which a substantial number of employees were subsequently dismissed for theft on the job and studies using a broad range of criteria, including absence, turnover, and supervisory ratings. Thus, a more compelling case that integrity tests predict a number of outcomes of interest can be made. (p. 520)

Sackett et al. (1989) reviewed studies that incorporated a wide variety of test validation strategies, including: (a) correlation with polygraph admissions, (b) correlation with subsequent job behavior (e.g., detected theft on the job), (c) correlation with a self-report of past theft or other illegal activities, (d) monitoring storewide variables (e.g., shrinkage) before and after the introduction of an integrity testing program, and (e) contrasting the test scores of particular groups, such as convicts, with those of the general population. Although no one study or procedure was totally convincing, the convergence of a consistent and statistically significant pattern of results supports the conclusion that professionally developed integrity tests yield useful levels of validity.

In another independent review of integrity tests, O'Bannon et al. (1989) reviewed over 270 studies on over 40 different integrity tests. They also reviewed a wide variety of validation studies that used different research designs and theft criteria, including: (a) contrasted groups research, (b) background check research, (c) admissions research, (d) predictive validity research, and (e) time series research. O'Bannon et al. concluded that useful levels of validity exist with professionally developed integrity tests:

> Studies of contrasted groups indicate that average honesty test scores
> differ for groups with different levels of integrity. . . . A large body of
> research exists showing the relationship between honesty test scores and
> admissions of wrong-doing. . . . Several time series studies have shown
> that an integrity test can have a positive impact on organizational mea-
> sures such as inventory shrinkage and terminations for theft. (p. 92)

Unlike general personality testing and other types of personnel
selection procedures, there has been a great deal of validity research
showing that integrity test scores predicted theft behavior (cf. O'Bannon et al., 1989). Although over 40 integrity tests are in use today
(O'Bannon et al., 1989), much of the current research with integrity
tests has been conducted with overt integrity tests such as the Personnel Selection Inventory (PSI; cf. McDaniel & Jones, 1988; Sackett &
Harris, 1984). For example, Terris (1979a) found that an overt integrity test accurately predicted theft admissions made in preemployment polygraph examinations. Ash (1971) was able to obtain a similar pattern of results with another overt integrity test. Yet, the
validity of integrity tests is not limited to polygraph admissions.
Overt integrity tests have also been found to predict the following
theft criteria: (a) supervisors' ratings of employees' dishonesty (Jones
& Terris, 1983a), (b) applicants who are likely to get caught stealing
once hired (Jones & Terris, 1981), (c) applicants who have a criminal
history (Jones & Terris, 1985), and (d) applicants who are likely to
make theft admissions in an anonymous testing situation (Jones,
1980, 1981; Terris, 1979b).

McDaniel and Jones (1988) conducted a meta-analysis of the
PSI. Criterion-related validity data from 1,806 people across 23 samples were quantitatively summarized. All samples met predetermined
decision rules. The mean validity coefficient equaled .50. These
results are summarized in Table 2. A review of this table indicates
that the integrity test yields useful levels of validity.

Longitudinal studies have shown that a group of convenience
stores using the PSI experienced a 50% reduction in shrinkage over
a period of approximately 18 months (Terris & Jones, 1982). This
impact-on-losses study was replicated in a home improvement center
chain (Brown, Jones, Terris, & Steffy, 1987). Several other studies
(Jones & Terris, 1984; Terris & Jones, 1982) have shown that both
applicants and employees from high-theft stores scored more poorly

on integrity tests than did applicants and employees from low-theft stores. Finally, a quasi-experiment showed that employees working in supermarkets that used integrity tests reported significantly less theft by their coworkers than employees working in a matched group of supermarkets that did not screen their employees (Jones, 1989a).

Despite useful levels of validity, it is recommended that companies use honesty tests as only one part of their overall personnel selection process. Any discrepancies between procedures can then be analyzed and additional information obtained. Overreliance on honesty test results is discouraged. In addition, applicants should never be labeled *dishonest* or *counterproductive* if they score below standards on any personnel selection procedure.

## Classification Accuracy

Personnel selection procedures become necessary when the applicant pool is larger than the number of job openings. Everything else being equal, as the validity of a selection procedure increases, the number of classification errors decreases (i.e., "false positives" and "false negatives"). Nonetheless, classification errors occur with all personnel selection systems (Martin, 1990; Martin & Terris, 1990).

Some critics of honesty testing have argued that too many honest applicants are incorrectly rejected (i.e., commonly called "false positives"). Assume the following[1]: (a) 1,000 applicants apply for 500 positions; (b) a large number of applicants may steal, but only 5% will be caught stealing; and (c) a highly valid honesty test successfully identifies 80% of the dishonest applicants. This would produce the following outcome:

| Test Score | Caught stealing | | Total |
|---|---|---|---|
| | No | Yes | |
| Pass | 490 | 10 | 500 |
| Fail | 460 | 40 | 500 |
| Total | 950 | 50 | 1,000 |

[1]Although the numbers are arbitrary, they do represent common findings in this area.

TABLE 2   Meta-Analysis of the Validity of the Personnel Selection Inventory Honesty Scale

| Analysis categories | Total number of r's | Mean sample size | Sample size | Observed mean r | Observed SD | Sampling SD | % variance | Residual SD | 90% CV |
|---|---|---|---|---|---|---|---|---|---|
| *All samples (all criteria)* | | | | | | | | | |
| 1. All samples (all criteria) | 23 | 1,808 | 79 | .50 | .12 | .09 | 48 | .09 | .39 |
| *Analysis by criterion category* | | | | | | | | | |
| 2. Self-report criteria | 18 | 959 | 53 | .53 | .11 | .10 | 82 | .05 | .47 |
| 3. All other criteria | 5 | 847 | 169 | .46 | .13 | .07 | 29 | .11 | .32 |
| *Analysis by subject category* | | | | | | | | | |
| 4. Employees/applicants | 19 | 1,463 | 77 | .48 | .13 | .09 | 47 | .09 | .36 |
| 5. Students | 4 | 343 | 86 | .55 | .08 | .08 | 92 | .02 | .52 |

128

Analysis by subject category for self-report criteria

| | | | | | | | | |
|---|---|---|---|---|---|---|---|---|
| 6. Employees/applicants | 14 | 616 | 44 | .52 | .12 | .11 | 81 | .05 | .45 |
| 7. Students | 4 | 343 | 86 | .55 | .08 | .08 | 92 | .02 | .52 |

Analysis by predictor anonymity category

| | | | | | | | | |
|---|---|---|---|---|---|---|---|---|
| 8. Anonymous predictor | 17 | 855 | 50 | .54 | .11 | .10 | 82 | .05 | .48 |
| 9. Not anonymous predictor | 6 | 951 | 159 | .45 | .12 | .07 | 33 | .10 | .33 |

Analysis by knowledge of criteria category

| | | | | | | | | |
|---|---|---|---|---|---|---|---|---|
| 10. Samples where applicant knows of criterion | 19 | 1,429 | 75 | .54 | .09 | .08 | 84 | .04 | .50 |
| 11. Samples where applicant does not know of criterion | 4 | 377 | 94 | .33 | .07 | .09 | 100 | .00 | .33 |

*Note.* CV = coefficient of variation. In this meta-analysis, the observed mean is not corrected. The residual standard deviation is the square root of the variance remaining after the correction of the observed variance for sampling error. This table was adapted from McDaniel and Jones (1988).

129

One should note that although the false negative rate is low at 1%, the false positive rate is high at 46%. Also, of the 500 who fail, 92% were not caught stealing. Critics sometimes conclude that the use of honesty tests result in too many errors. This criticism is incorrect for several reasons: First and foremost, however high the false positive rate is in this example, the rate is always higher with a less valid procedure (see Martin & Terris, 1990). For example, if applicants are hired on a random or first-come, first-hired basis (i.e., validity is assumed to be zero), the following outcome is expected:

| Test Score | Caught stealing | | Total |
|---|---|---|---|
| | No | Yes | |
| Pass | 475 | 25 | 500 |
| Fail | 475 | 25 | 500 |
| Total | 950 | 50 | 1,000 |

As can be seen, the false negative rate increases to 2.5%, whereas the false positive rate under these conditions increases to 47.5%. Of the 500 who fail, 95% were not caught stealing. Apparently, some critics believe that an employer can hire everyone with the result that there are no false positives. However, in a true personnel selection situation, an employer really cannot hire everyone. In this last example, if the first 500 are hired, the remaining 500 must be rejected because there are only 500 positions.

At a more basic level, it is doubtful that getting caught is an appropriate criterion to use to estimate false positives. The problem is that of the 95% of the people who are not caught stealing, a large number did in fact steal but were not caught (cf. Jones, Ash, Soto, & Terris, 1990; Slora, 1989). This produces a tremendous increase in the apparent rate of false positives. However, if one assumes that 50% of the applicants steal significant money or merchandise and that the test correctly identifies 80% of those who steal (both caught and not caught), then the following outcome is expected:

*Integrity Testing for Personnel Selection* 131

| Test Score | Caught stealing | | Total |
|---|---|---|---|
| | No | Yes | |
| Pass | 400 | 100 | 500 |
| Fail | 100 | 400 | 500 |
| Total | 500 | 500 | 1,000 |

In this example, the overall false positive is 10%, and of those who fail, only 20% did not steal. The number of employees who steal at work should be used to estimate classification accuracy rates, not the number of employees caught stealing. Alternative strategies for estimating classification accuracy rates also exist.[2]

If a professionally developed honesty test is implemented, theft-related losses should go down or at least be lower than those of a comparable location or store that does not use honesty tests. If a company can provide evidence that an honesty testing program is effective, then it is difficult to question the business necessity of the program. Yet, even though integrity tests can predict employees' theft proneness, they must be fair to all detected minority groups, and they should be relatively inoffensive to applicants. In the next two sections, we discuss these issues.

### Adverse Impact Analysis

Personnel selection methods, including integrity tests, should not adversely discriminate against any race, sex, or age group (Equal Employment Opportunity Commission [EEOC], 1979). All of the lead-

[2]One can also use the Taylor-Russell tables (see Taylor & Russell, 1939) to estimate classification accuracy. Personnel psychologists can make the following assumptions: (a) An integrity test's validity typically ranges from .40 to .60 (cf. McDaniel & Jones, 1988), (b) usually 60%–80% of all applicants score above standards on an integrity test (cf. O'Bannon, Goldinger, & Appleby, 1989), and (c) the proportion of employees considered satisfactory (i.e., dependable with no history of theft) typically ranges from 60% to 80% depending on the type of theft or counterproductive behavior used to determine base rates (cf. Hollinger & Clark, 1983; Slora, 1989). Even with this procedure, classification accuracy estimates based on these parameters will be more accurate than estimates based on theft apprehension rates.

ing integrity tests report a lack of adverse impact against protected groups (cf. O'Bannon et al., 1989; Sackett et al., 1989). Female applicants do as well or better (i.e., more honest) than male applicants in most of the studies reviewed, and no racial or age differences have been found. Still, adverse-impact studies should routinely be conducted for any selection method that a company chooses to control employee theft.

An example of a large adverse-impact study conducted on the PSI Honesty scale is summarized in Table 3. This study, based on 42,074 job applicants, showed that the preemployment honesty test met the EEOC's 4/5ths Rule and yielded no statistically or practically significant differences between applicant groups. The pattern of results obtained in this study is fairly typical across integrity tests.

## Test Takers' Reactions

Unlike preemployment polygraphs, the majority of job applicants are typically not offended when they take a paper-and-pencil integrity test (cf. Ryan & Sackett, 1987). Jones and Joy (1991) found that 82% of the applicants who took the PSI had no objections to the test. The few applicants who did object to the test had only minor objections, and they were reliably more likely to score below standards on the test (i.e., in the dishonest direction). It appears that employment applicants with both tolerant attitudes toward theft and a history of dishonest activities are the most likely to get defensive about and object to taking preemployment integrity tests. Most job applicants seem to understand the job relevance of an integrity test (Jones & Joy, 1988).

**TABLE 3**   Adverse-Impact Analysis for an Honesty Test

| Applicants | N | Percentage | Percentage passing |
|---|---|---|---|
| Whites | 32,117 | 76.3 | 67.6 |
| Blacks | 6,777 | 16.1 | 67.8 |
| Hispanics | 2,305 | 5.5 | 67.6 |
| Other | 875 | 2.1 | 74.8 |
| Total | 42,074 | 100.0 | 68.0 |

## Privacy Issues

Jones, Ash, and Soto (1990) concluded that preemployment integrity tests do not seem to infringe on the workplace privacy rights of job applicants if professionally developed tests are selected, implemented, and interpreted. Those researchers reviewed a large number of privacy issues that must be considered when using preemployment integrity tests. For example, companies should use integrity tests only if they have an obvious business exposure to employee theft and other counterproductivity. In this situation, integrity tests are one of the most effective and reasonable approaches to a very real business problem.

Strategies exist to protect job applicants' privacy rights when they take an integrity test (Jones, Ash, Soto, & Terris, 1990). For example, the integrity test selected should meet all professional and legal standards for test development, implementation, and general use. The test should include only questions that are permissible according to federal and state laws. Applicants should sign an informed consent agreement when applicable, and all applicants should be administered the test in a quiet, comfortable, test-taking environment. Only properly trained company representatives should have access to applicants' test scores on a need-to-know basis. Public disclosure of test scores should be avoided at all costs. Finally, completed test booklets and scoring keys should always be locked up.

## Candid Responses

Some people assume that smarter job applicants may deduce the purpose of the preemployment tests and skew their answers to falsely reflect a more honest disposition. Yet Jones and Terris (1983b) found that job applicants' intelligence test scores were not related to their honesty scores. Smarter people do not score better on the integrity test (cf. Werner, Jones, & Steffy, 1989).

Also, integrity tests typically contain a separate distortion scale to determine whether job applicants are being candid in their answers. Applicants are also discouraged from trying to "fake good" or distort their answers on integrity tests because the instructions state that any attempt to provide inaccurate answers can be detected and could invalidate the test results.

### Alternate Explanations

Psychological integrity tests are primarily effective because they screen out theft-prone individuals and screen in more honest and dependable employees. However, there are additional explanations that could further explain the reduction in theft. One such explanation is that the use of a valid selection procedure creates an organizational climate that is unfavorable to theft. Employees prone to steal may be less likely to consider the possibility of theft if their fellow employees obviously disapprove of theft (cf. Hollinger & Clark, 1983).

Another possibility is that using an integrity test sends a message to all applicants and employees that the company is committed to preventing theft and will do something about it. Perhaps this serves as a warning signal to all employees. This is the deterrent effect.

A third possible explanation is that any selection system sensitizes the entire workforce to these types of issues. Using a psychological test to screen out theft-prone applicants usually generates a great deal of discussion about theft in all levels of the organization. It is possible that values and opinions may be changed somewhat in the process.

A fourth possible explanation is that the implementation of a personnel selection procedure creates system changes of one type or another within the organization. For example, interviewers may begin to do a better job interviewing, perhaps security personnel will become more vigilant, and so on.

### Negligent Hiring

Companies have a legal responsibility to provide a safe and crime-free workplace. Employers may be held liable for negligently hiring employees who prove to be dangerous or dishonest workers. An employer who negligently employs a counterproductive individual may be liable to third parties whose injury or loss is proximately caused by the employer's negligence.

The tort of negligent hiring addresses the risk created by exposing members of the public to a potentially dangerous or dishonest individual. The doctrine of respondeat superior is based on the theory that the employee is the agent of the employer. Case law has concluded that liability is predicated on the negligence of an employer in placing an applicant with known propensities that should have been discovered by reasonable investigation in an employment position in which, because of circumstances of employment, it should have been foreseeable that the hired individual posed a threat of injury to others.

Many companies use preemployment integrity tests to prevent negligent hiring claims. For example, security guard companies want to avoid hiring dishonest guards who may plan and execute a theft of cash or property at the location they are guarding. Such an activity, with or without a weapon (e.g., an armed robbery), could put the company that provided the guard services at risk for a lawsuit.

For example, a manufacturer of gold sunglass frames for the U.S. government recently recovered over $300,000 against a security firm on the theory of negligent hiring. A guard from the national security firm was involved in three thefts of gold used in the making of sunglass frames. The security firm was found liable for negligent hiring. In upholding the jury verdict, the court also stated that an employer had a continuing duty to retain in its service only those employees who are fit and competent (*Welsh Manufacturing v. Pinkerton*, 1984).

Negligent hiring cases are becoming more popular. Preemployment integrity tests can help companies better control this type of legal exposure. Companies that use valid integrity tests to carefully screen job applicants will reduce their exposure to negligent hiring claims.

### Model Guidelines for Integrity Tests

The Association of Personnel Test Publishers (APTP; 1990) published the *Model Guidelines for Preemployment Integrity Testing Programs*. These guidelines are to be used in conjunction with other professional and legal standards on the proper use of personnel tests. The APTP developed these guidelines to ensure that both test publishers and test users adhere to effective, ethical, and legal integrity testing practices in the following areas: (a) test development and selection, (b) test administration and scoring, (c) test use and accuracy, (d) test fairness and confidentiality, and (e) public statements and test-marketing practices. Companies would benefit from guidelines that help them to properly select and use preemployment integrity tests.

### Nonproprietary Versus Proprietary Tests

In the field of psychological testing, two different strategies exist for the development, research, scoring, interpretation, and dissemination of psychological tests. We now briefly discuss both strategies and their relevance to preemployment integrity testing practices.

The first strategy involves the distribution of nonproprietary tests by test publishers. The publisher sells the test, the scoring key, and a manual, which includes norms, interpretation guidelines, and reports on the test's reliability and validity. Test publishers evaluate the credentials of potential users to ensure that the purchaser has been appropriately trained, educated, and qualified to administer, score, and interpret the nonproprietary test results. Publishers abide by a three-tier credentialing system to determine who can purchase nonproprietary tests.

At the most restrictive level, nonproprietary tests are made available to individuals with specific training and experience in a relevant area of assessment. This usually includes members of professional organizations (e.g., the American Psychological Association) or professional licensees (e.g., state-licensed psychologists). Users of nonproprietary tests have full responsibility for demonstration of reliability, validity, compliance with relevant EEOC laws, and so forth. Many clinical tests (e.g., the MMPI) typically fall into this category.

The second category involves proprietary tests, which are developed, normed, scored, and researched by the test publishers, who provide continuing service and support to clients. The largest group of proprietary tests includes educational and professional credentialing tests (e.g., the Law School Admissions Test, the Scholastic Aptitude Test). Users of proprietary tests typically have an in-house testing specialist or an outside consultant available to monitor the test user's testing programs. Proprietary test publishers often have their staff (e.g., psychologists, psychometricians) serve as the testing specialists to their clients. For example, psychologists on the staff of leading integrity test publishers provide ongoing psychological expertise and consultation to their clients. This ensures that qualified professionals supervise a company's testing practices to see that effective, legal, and ethical testing procedures are followed.

Nearly all preemployment integrity tests are proprietary tests. For these test, the publisher, not the user, has the responsibility for test development, scoring, and research. This being the case, users of proprietary tests are not required to be credentialed by the publishers. Publishers of proprietary tests provide training and guidance to test users on how to properly implement and use a testing program. Both publishers and users play a vital role in ensuring the quality and fairness of preemployment integrity testing practices.

## Conclusions

There are no simple solutions to controlling employee theft and other forms of counterproductivity. However, theft reduction through personnel selection appears to be an effective strategy for protecting bottom-line profits. Research is always needed to determine the extent to which any personnel selection procedure is a valid measurement of job applicants' propensity for on-the-job counterproductivity. Companies should consider the following issues before choosing and implementing any selection strategy designed to control employee theft and counterproductivity:

1. Use only selection procedures that have been thoroughly validated. Ideally, the validation effort would include a variety of strategies because each validation approach has different strengths and weaknesses. Nearly all of the existing validation research has been conducted with psychological integrity tests.
2. Adverse-impact analyses should be conducted for any selection procedure being considered. These analyses should be performed in accordance with the EEOC guidelines.
3. The integrity test should only be used as one part of a more comprehensive assessment program. The test should be used in accordance with professional and legal standards (cf. APTP, 1990).

## References

Ajzen, I., & Fishbein, M. (1977). Attitude–behavior relations: A theoretical analysis and review of empirical research. *Psychological Bulletin, 84,* 888–918.

American Management Association. (1977). *Crimes against business project: Background and recommendations.* New York: Author.

Arthur Young, Inc. (1988). *An ounce of prevention: The Tenth Annual Survey of Security and Loss Prevention in the Retail Industry.* New York: Author.

Ash, P. (1971). Screening employment applicants for attitudes toward theft. *Journal of Applied Psychology, 55,* 161–164.

Ash, P. (1988, August). *A history of honesty testing.* Paper presented at the 96th Annual Convention of the American Psychological Association, Atlanta, GA.

Ash, P. (1989). *The legality of preemployment inquiries.* Park Ridge, IL: London House Press.

Association of Personnel Test Publishers. (1990). *Model guidelines for preemployment integrity testing programs.* Washington, DC: Author.

Baumer, T. L., & Rosenbaum, D. P. (1984). *Combatting retail theft: Programs and strategies.* Boston, MA: Butterworth.

Brown, T. S., Jones, J. W., Terris, W., & Steffy, B. D. (1987). The impact of preemployment integrity testing on employee turnover and inventory shrinkage losses. *Journal of Business and Psychology, 2,* 136–149.

Carey, J. J. (1989, March). *Fraud awareness in banking.* Paper presented at the 12th Annual Bank Auditor's Conference, Fort Lauderdale, FL.

Cattell, R. B., Ebert, H. W., & Tatsuoka, M. M. (1970). *Handbook for the Sixteen Personality Factor Questionnaire (16PF).* Champaign, IL: Institute for Personality and Ability Testing.

Crime major cause of S&L woes, FBI says. (1990, April 12). *Chicago Tribune,* p. 3-1.

Dahlstrom, W. G., & Welsh, G. S. (1960). *An MMPI handbook.* Minneapolis: University of Minnesota Press.

Equal Employment Opportunity Commission (EEOC). (1979). Adoption of questions and answers to clarify and provide a common interpretation of the Uniform Guidelines on Employee Selection Procedures. *Federal Register, 44,* 11996–12009.

Hefter, R. (1986). The crippling crime. *Security World, 23,* 36–38.

Hollinger, R., & Clark, J. (1983). *Theft by employees.* Lexington, MA: Lexington Books.

Jones, J. W. (1980). Attitudinal correlates of employees' deviance: Theft, alcohol use, and nonprescribed drug use. *Psychological Reports, 47,* 71–77.

Jones, J. W. (1981). Attitudinal correlates of employee theft of drugs and hospital supplies among nursing personnel. *Nursing Research, 30,* 351–359.

Jones, J. W. (1989a). Measure for measure: Is your testing program paying off? *Journal of Staffing and Recruitment, 1*(2), 57–62.

Jones, J. W. (1989b, June). *Attitude-behavior relations: A theoretical and empirical analy-*

sis of preemployment integrity tests. Paper presented at the First Annual Conference of the American Psychological Society, Alexandria, VA.

Jones, J. W., Ash, P., & Soto, C. (1990). Selecting honest employees while protecting job applicants' privacy rights. *Employee Relations Law Journal, 16,* 561–575.

Jones, J. W., Ash, P., Soto, C., & Terris, W. (1990). An occasion for invasion. *Security Management, 34,* 68–72.

Jones, J. W., & Joy, D. (1991). *Empirical investigation of job applicants' reactions to taking a preemployment honesty test.* Manuscript submitted for publication.

Jones, J. W., & Terris, W. (1981, July). *Predictive validation of a dishonesty test that measures theft proneness.* Paper presented at the 18th Interamerican Congress of Psychology, Santo Domingo, Dominican Republic.

Jones, J. W., & Terris, W. (1983a). Predicting employees' theft in home improvement centers. *Psychological Reports, 52,* 187–201.

Jones, J. W., & Terris, W. (1983b). Personality correlates of theft and drug abuse among job applicants. In *Proceedings of the Third International Conference on the 16PF test* (pp. 85–94). Champaign, IL: IPAT Press.

Jones, J. W., & Terris, W. (1984). *The organizational climate of honesty: Empirical investigation* (Techn. Rep. No. 27). Park Ridge, IL: London House Press.

Jones, J. W., & Terris, W. (1985). Screening employment applicants for attitudes toward theft: Three quasi-experiments. *International Journal of Management, 2,* 62–72.

Jones, J. W., & Terris, W. (1989). After the polygraph ban. *Recruitment Today,* May/June, 25–31.

Martin, S. L. (1990). Estimating the false positive rate for alternative measures of integrity. *Journal of Business and Psychology, 4,* 385–389.

Martin, S. L., & Terris, W. (1990). The four-cell classification table in personnel selection: A heuristic device gone awry. *Industrial Psychologist, 27*(3), 49–55.

McDaniel, M. A. (1988, April). *Employment interviews: Structure, validity, and unanswered questions.* Paper presented at the Third Annual Convention of the Society for Industrial and Organizational Psychology, New Orleans.

McDaniel, M. A., & Jones, J. W. (1988). Predicting employee theft: A quantitative review of a standardized measure of honesty. *Journal of Business and Psychology, 2,* 327–345.

Meinsma, G. (1985). Thou shalt not steal. *Security Management, 29,* 35–37.

Pruitt v. Pavelin, 685 P.2nd. 1347 (Ariz. App. 1984).

O'Bannon, R. M., Goldinger, L. A., & Appleby, G. S. (1989). *Honesty and integrity testing: A practical guide.* Atlanta, GA: Applied Information Resources.

Ryan, A. M., & Sackett, P. R. (1987). Preemployment honesty testing: Fakability, reactions of test takers, and company image. *Journal of Business and Psychology, 1,* 248–256.

Sackett, P. R., & Harris, M. E. (1984). Honesty testing for personnel selection: A review and critique. *Personnel Psychology, 37,* 221–246.

Sackett, P. R., Burris, L. R., & Callahan, C. (1989). Integrity testing for personnel selection: An update. *Personnel Psychology, 41,* 421–429.

Schmitt, N. (1976). Social and situational determinants of interview decisions: Implications for the employment interview. *Personnel Psychology, 29,* 79–101.

Schuessler, K., & Cressey, D. (1950). Personality characteristics of criminals. *American Journal of Sociology, 55,* 476–484.

Slora, K. (1989). An empirical approach to determining employee deviance base rates. *Journal of Business and Psychology, 4,* 199–219.

Taylor, H. C., & Russell, J. T. (1939). The relationship of validity coefficients to the practical effectiveness of tests in selection. *Journal of Applied Psychology, 23,* 565–578.

Terris, W. (1979a). Attitudinal correlates of employee integrity: Theft-related admissions made in preemployment polygraph examinations. *Journal of Security Administration, 2,* 30–39.

Terris, W. (1979b, July). *Attitudinal correlates of theft, violence and drug use.* Paper presented at the 17th Interamerican Congress of Psychology, Lima, Peru.

Terris, W. (1986). *Employee theft: Research, theory, and applications.* Park Ridge, IL: London House Press.

Terris, W., & Jones, J. W. (1982). Psychological factors related to employee theft in the convenience story industry. *Psychological Reports, 51,* 1219–1238.

Welsh Manufacturing v. Pinkerton Inc., 474 A.2d 436 (RI 1984).

Werner, S. H., Jones, J. W., & Steffy, B. D. (1989). The relationship between intelligence, honesty, and theft admissions. *Educational and Psychological Measurement, 49,* 921–927.

*Received June 11, 1990*
*Accepted October 20, 1990*

Requests for reprints should be sent to John W. Jones, London House/SRA, 1550 Northwest Highway, Park Ridge, Illinois 60068.

# [21]

Journal of Applied Psychology
1989, Vol. 74, No. 2, 273–279

# How to Measure Employee Reliability

Joyce Hogan and Robert Hogan
University of Tulsa

Employee reliability (or unreliability) is often conceptualized quite narrowly—for example, as employee theft. But theft is just one element in a larger syndrome of antisocial behavior. Consequently, employee screening procedures that focus on theft necessarily ignore a number of other indicators of unreliability; these include substance abuse, insubordination, absenteeism, excessive grievances, bogus worker compensation claims, temper tantrums, and various forms of passive aggression. In this article we describe the development and validation of a personality measure designed to assess a construct called organizational delinquency. Data from several studies show that scores on this measure are related to a wide range of indicators of both positive and negative work performance. Persons with low scores on the measure engage in a variety of counterproductive behaviors on the job; persons with high scores tend to be well liked by their supervisors and coworkers. We also discuss the economic consequences of using this measure.

Unreliable employees engage in a variety of undesirable behaviors ranging from theft and sabotage to absenteeism and insubordination; in so doing, they also generate substantial direct and indirect costs for their employers. One way to solve this problem is to screen out in advance those persons whose proclivities will tend to undermine the success of the organization.

Sackett and Harris (1985) identify several problems that limit our understanding of and ability to assess employee unreliability; three of these are particularly pertinent. First, surprisingly little is known about the nature of workplace deviancy and few investigators have studied the structure of honesty. Second, there are serious problems with the nature and quality of the criterion data used to support the validity of most honesty tests. Correlations between two tests will not establish the external validity of either; test validity depends, in part, on relationships with relevant nontest behaviors. And third, honesty has not been studied in relation to other personality constructs.

A first step toward understanding workplace deviancy is to identify the key underlying construct. In our view, counterproductive acts such as theft, drug and alcohol abuse, lying, insubordination, vandalism, sabotage, absenteeism, and assaultive actions are elements of a larger syndrome that we call organizational delinquency. To call this a syndrome suggests that employees who steal are likely to engage in other delinquent acts as well; consequently, assessments in which applicants answer a set of questions focused on their tendency to steal sample only a portion of the organizational delinquency construct.

This article has two goals. The first is to describe the development of a personality measure designed to assess employee reliability and evaluate its construct validity. The measure is a reference test for the organizational delinquency construct. A more general goal is to strengthen the case for the usefulness of personality measurement in personnel selection.

Correspondence concerning this article should be addressed to Joyce Hogan, Department of Psychology, University of Tulsa, 600 South College Avenue, Tulsa, Oklahoma 74104.

## Defining the Delinquency Construct

To study deviancy, it would be useful to have a dependable measure of delinquent tendencies. In an earlier analysis, Gough (1948, 1960) proposed that people are normally distributed along a continuum of socialization so that some are unusually scrupulous and conscientious, most are normally rule-compliant, and some are hostile to the rules and conventions of society. Past a certain point, their hostility will lead to conflicts with the law and even to incarceration. This analysis suggests that there are people who, although hostile to rules, manage to avoid becoming involved with the legal system and, therefore, are not identified as delinquent. We believe that they are the people who cause most of the problems in organizations.

Gough administered the California Psychological Inventory (CPI; Gough, 1987) to a large sample of incarcerated felons and identified 54 items that reliably discriminated between delinquents and nondelinquents. This 54-item Socialization scale is designed to assess maturity and rule compliance at one end and delinquent tendencies at the other; it has proven to be a powerful measure of pro- and antisocial behavior (cf. Hare, 1985). For example, Gough tested felons and nondelinquents ($N = 10,296$) with the measure in several different countries (e.g., Korea, India, Puerto Rico) in several different languages and found a point-biserial correlation of .73 between scale scores and the delinquency–nondelinquency criterion (Gough, 1965). Because the scale is a reliable predictor of delinquency, an evaluation of its internal structure will to some degree reveal the structure of the delinquency syndrome. Several competent studies of the structure of the CPI Socialization scale (e.g., Rosen, 1977) converge on the view that it reflects at least four themes: hostility toward rules and authority, thrill-seeking impulsiveness, social insensitivity, and alienation. Our work builds on and extends this earlier CPI-based research.

## Development of the Employee Reliability Index

Our research is based on the Hogan Personality Inventory (HPI; Hogan, 1983, 1986). The HPI has the same measurement

Table 1
*HPI–HIC Correlations With Delinquency Criterion*

| Theme & component HICs | Felons vs. working class nonfelons[a] | Felons vs. college students[b] | College students' self-reported delinquency[c] |
|---|---|---|---|
| Hostility to rules | | | |
| School success | .20* | .67* | .00 |
| Avoids trouble | .73* | .68* | 69* |
| Thrill-seeking impulsiveness | | | |
| Not experience seeking | .33* | .25* | .22* |
| Enjoys crowds | −.44* | −.30* | .01 |
| Exhibitionistic | −.37* | −.42* | .09 |
| Social insensitivity | | | |
| Easy to live with | .43* | .28* | .25* |
| Alienation | | | |
| Good sense of attachment | .36* | .36* | .44* |
| Not depressed | .43* | .37* | .10 |
| No guilt | .54* | .49* | .26* |

*Note.* HPI = Hogan Personality Inventory; HIC = homogeneous item composites.
[a] $N = 143$.  [b] $N = 185$.  [c] $N = 145$.
* $p < .01$, one-tailed.

goals as the CPI (i.e., to assess factors associated with successful adaptation to and performance in everyday life). The CPI scales measure *folk concepts:* dimensions from the natural language with broad, cross-cultural significance for everyday living; the HPI scales are based on the "big five" theory: the view that the trait vocabulary can be described in terms of three to six broad dimensions of interpersonal evaluation (cf. Digman & Inouye, 1986). The six scales of the HPI (Intellectance, Adjustment, Prudence, Ambition, Sociability, and Likeability) are composed of 43 "homogeneous item composites" (HICs; Zonderman, 1980), small and highly coherent subscales. For example, the HPI Adjustment scale contains HICs for self-esteem, sense of identity, good attachment, no somatic complaint, no anxiety, no guilt, no depression, and calmness.

We used HPI to specify more precisely the personality syndrome associated with delinquency. To do this, four groups completed the inventory: (a) 40 incarcerated delinquent persons from Arizona, arrested for drug-related offenses; (b) 103 working-class nursing aides from an inner-city hospital; (c) 38 police cadets from a suburban department; and (d) 145 college students. The delinquents were assigned a score of 0, and the nondelinquents were given a score of 1. In addition, the college students completed a questionnaire asking about their past delinquent behavior (e.g., drug use, promiscuity, arrests); the questionnaire was scored by summing the number of nondelinquent items endorsed. Nineteen of the 43 HICs were significantly associated with these delinquency criteria. We chose 9 of them for our final scale on the basis of their correlations with the delinquency criteria and their correspondence with the structure of deviancy as revealed in the earlier factor analytic studies of the CPI Socialization scale. The HICs and their correlations with the delinquency criteria are listed in Table 1. The HICs come from the scales for Intellectance (school success), Adjustment (not depressed, no guilt), Prudence (avoids trouble, good sense of attachment, not experience-seeking), Sociability

(enjoys crowds, exhibitionistic), and Likeability (easy to live with). The delinquents received low scores for school success, not depressed, no guilt, avoids trouble, good sense of attachment, not experience-seeking, and easy to live with and high scores for enjoys crowds and exhibitionistic. These HICs pick up the same themes that are reflected in the CPI Socialization scale: hostility to rules and authority (school success, avoids trouble), thrill-seeking (not experience-seeking), insensitivity (easy to live with), and alienation (not depressed, no guilt, good sense of attachment). Delinquents, once again, received low scores on these HICs.

Test–retest reliability was evaluated in two samples. A group of undergraduate students ($N = 90$) completed the HPI twice over a 4-week interval. The employee reliability scale was scored from the HPI protocols; the test–retest correlation was .76. A second sample of employed adults ($N = 36$) completed the HPI twice over a 4-week interval; the test–retest correlation was .90. The internal consistency reliability (Cronbach, 1951) was .63; this modest coefficient reflects the fact that the scale is composed of items from five relatively orthogonal HPI scales, and this procedure is guaranteed to reduce scale homogeneity.

We evaluated sex, race, and age differences in scale scores by using an archival sample of employed adults who had been tested within the last 5 years. Table 2 presents scale means and standard deviations for men ($N = 1,637$), women ($N = 590$), Whites ($N = 1,154$), Blacks ($N = 253$), under 40-year-olds ($N = 1,215$), and over 40-year-olds ($N = 207$). In a practical sense, there were no sex differences; however, Blacks tended to score higher than Whites, and older persons scored higher than younger ones.

## Scale Validation

### *Criterion Measurement*

The crucial problem in test validation concerns defining appropriate indexes of nontest performance (Dunnette, 1966; Ho-

Table 2
*Employee Reliability Scale Means and Standard Deviations by Subgroup*

| Employee reliability | Men ($N = 1,637$) | Women ($N = 590$) | Whites ($N = 1,154$) | Blacks ($N = 253$) | Age < 40 yr. ($N = 1,167$) | Age ≥ 40 yr. ($N = 207$) |
|---|---|---|---|---|---|---|
| M | 45.4 | 46.5 | 46.3 | 50.1 | 44.5 | 49.1 |
| SD | 8.0 | 8.3 | 7.5 | 7.1 | 8.6 | 6.9 |

gan, DeSoto, & Solano, 1977; Hogan & Nicholson, 1988). How is delinquency manifested in organizations? Most researchers focus on theft or self-reports of such behavior. Sackett and Harris (1985), for example, analyzed 16 studies using theft or admissions of theft as criterion data. Although theft is a major problem, it is only one facet of the larger construct of organizational delinquency. Excessive absences, tardiness, malingering, equipment damage, drug and alcohol abuse, grievances, suspensions from work, insubordination, and ordinary rule infractions are all components of the delinquency syndrome. Moreover, as Sackett and Harris point out, it is extremely difficult to obtain hard criterion data for theft or other comparably flagrant delinquent acts while individuals are actually employed. Fortunately for research purposes, delinquent tendencies have other manifestations. The following examples support the notion that delinquency is a multifaceted syndrome.

Hogan, Hogan, and Briggs (1984) collected data on 56 drivers employed by a large freight transportation company. The company maintained extensive personnel records; consequently, a variety of objective criteria reflecting performance as a driver were available for each person. Data for 13 variables were collected from personnel files for an 18-month performance period. These variables were intercorrelated and the matrix was factor-analyzed and rotated to a varimax solution. Six factors emerged that accounted for 70% of the matrix variance. Table 3 presents this solution. Factor 1 represents flagrant acts of delinquency, with chargeable (employee at fault) accidents as the most serious and expensive deviant behavior in which a truck driver can be involved. Note that warning letters and suspensions also load on this factor. Factor 2 consists of more subtle

but hostile activities; filed grievances, absences, and worker compensation claims can be interpreted as forms of passive aggression against the company. Factor 3 represents the company's response to deviant behavior, and the last three factors are less directly related to delinquency. In a second study of line-haul drivers (long distance, overnight tractor-trailer; $N = 110$) employed by the same company, Hogan, Peterson, Hogan, and Jones (1985) collected the same criterion variables identified in Table 3 and replicated the factor structure.

Data from two additional studies further support the claim that organizational delinquency is multifaceted. Hogan, Arneson, Hogan, and Jones (1986) gathered both supervisor ratings and objective criterion data on a sample of habilitation therapists ($N = 169$) employed at a state hospital for the profoundly retarded. Seven performance variables were factor-analyzed by using the same procedures from which Table 3 was generated. Three factors emerged that accounted for 61% of the variance in the matrix. The first factor consisted of supervisor ratings; the second factor was defined by injury hours, incidents of malingering, and sick leave hours. Number of times late and number of disciplinary actions loaded on the third factor. In a similar study of hospital service workers ($N = 201$), Raza, Metz, Dyer, Coan, and Hogan (1986) found two factors underlying the performance data that accounted for 59% of the variance. The first consisted of supervisor ratings and the number of times an employee had been counseled for aberrant job behavior. The second factor was defined by number of unexcused absences from work and hours of sick leave taken; these data were for a 12-month period. These last two examples imply that, in jobs where opportunities for theft are minimal, deviant behavior will

Table 3
*Factor Analysis of Criterion Data*

| Criterion variables | Factor 1: delinquency | Factor 2: absenteeism | Factor 3: negative sanctions | Factor 4: organizational visibility | Factor 5: no fault | Factor 6: supervisor's ratings |
|---|---|---|---|---|---|---|
| Chargeable accidents | .91 | | | | | |
| Warning letters | .80 | | | | | |
| Suspensions | .44 | | | | | |
| Grievances | | .62 | | | | |
| Absences | | .61 | | | | |
| Medical absences | | .55 | | | | |
| Workers compensation claims | | .44 | | | | |
| Suspension letters | | | .68 | | | |
| Discharges | | | .67 | | | |
| Commendations | | | | .48 | | |
| Nonchargeable accidents | | | | | .71 | |
| Supervisor's ratings | | | | | | .60 |
| Health history | | | | | | −.38 |

emerge in more subtle ways. Even more interesting is the fact that objective indexes of delinquency are relatively independent of supervisory evaluations of job performance; this suggests that sociopathic employees may sometimes charm their supervisors, whereas honest but grumpy employees may annoy them.

The foregoing examples show that, although flagrant acts of theft and property destruction are relatively rare, absenteeism and malingering (more subtle forms of delinquency) are more common. It is especially interesting to note that supervisors' ratings normally load on a separate factor from the delinquency clusters. Finally, these examples show that an adequate measure of employee reliability must have a broad "band width" in order to capture the inherent complexity of the criteria. Highly homogeneous scales, each targeted at a specific facet of organizational delinquency and used together in a battery, would be even better than a broad band width scale, but that is a future research project.

## Concurrent Validation Studies

Thirteen concurrent validation studies provide data for evaluating the employee reliability scale. The subjects were all working adults who completed the HPI, which was then scored for employee reliability. All objective performance data were taken from company or public files. Criterion data in the form of supervisor ratings or rankings were developed as part of the research projects.

Table 4 summarizes the measures and correlational results (uncorrected for attenuation) for each of the concurrent studies. This table makes three interesting points. First, the reliability scale predicts a wide range of performance criteria varying from commendations to claims filed for equipment failure (a situation caused by carelessness or failure to perform required inspections). Also interesting is the range of occupations sampled here. There are at least four occupational types in Table 4 as defined by the Holland (1985a) categories: Realistic (truck driver and service worker), Social (counselor and therapist), Enterprising (sales persons and managers), and Conventional (dispatcher and power plant worker). Finally, the reliability scale is correlated with both objective and subjective criteria. Supervisors' ratings were used in two studies where objective data were unavailable (Guier, 1984; Montgomery, Butler, & McPhail, 1987); in these cases, however, the incumbents were closely supervised and the raters may have been more aware of the employee's reliability. In contrast, truck drivers spend large amounts of time working without supervision. The ratings gathered by Montgomery et al. provide empirical anchors for interpreting employee reliability; persons with high scores tend to be described as accurate, punctual, and having a good attitude, whereas persons with low scores tend to be described as hostile, frequently late for work, and careless.

## Utility

With direct cost accounting we can estimate the economic consequences of using the employee reliability scale for selection (Hogan et al., 1986). Approximately 5% of the state government work force in Idaho is employed at a hospital for the profoundly retarded. These same employees accounted for about 25% of the state medical insurance claims filed in 1985. Because the jobs are physically demanding, we tested employees with both physical strength measures and the HPI; both sets of measures were associated with job performance, job injuries, and insurance claims filed. There were significant correlations between the employee reliability scale and the number of job-related injuries reported, the number of incidents compensated by the state insurance fund, and actual dollars compensated for the injuries reported over 18 months. We formed two groups of employees: those who scored at or above ($N = 88$) and those who scored below ($N = 90$) the population mean for the reliability scale ($M = 46$; Hogan & Hogan, 1986). Persons scoring below the mean reported nearly four times the number of injuries (38.5 versus 10.9) and filed nearly twice as many claims (1.41 versus .94) as those scoring above the mean. In addition, the average claim was $757 for the lower scoring group versus $203 for the higher scoring group. That is, each claim for the low scoring employee was almost 4 times as expensive as each claim for the high scorers.

## Construct Validity

Landy (1986, p. 1183) notes that there is a crucial difference between the predictive value and the meaning of test scores: For some time, . . . *validity* was considered a correlation between a predictor and a criterion. . . . Such a positivist view was (and remains) only minimally helpful in developing . . . a basic understanding of what was being measured. . . . [Consequently] the emphasis on the meaning of test scores is as important today as it was 30 years ago."

To explore the meaning of scores on the employee reliability scale, we correlated it with the scale scores of four well-validated inventories: the California Psychological Inventory (CPI; Gough, 1987); the Minnesota Multiphasic Personality Inventory (MMPI; Hathaway & McKinley, 1967); the Self-Directed Search (SDS; Holland, 1985b); and the Armed Services Vocational Aptitude Battery (ASVAB; U.S. Department of Defense, 1980). Correlations between the employee reliability scale and the scales of these inventories are presented in Table 5.

The CPI is the most carefully validated measure of normal personality among the currently available commercial inventories. A group of male and female public school principals in northeastern Oklahoma completed the reliability scale and the CPI, and correlations were then computed with the 18 standard scales of the CPI (Hogan & Zenke, 1986). The results presented in Table 5 indicate that low employee reliability scores are associated with aggressiveness, hostility, self-indulgence, and impulsivity, whereas high scores are associated with conscientiousness, attention to details, rule compliance, and social maturity (Socialization, Self-Control). Correlations with the CPI scales for Social Presence and Self-Acceptance further suggest a pattern of conformity and modesty at the high end of the reliability scale.

The MMPI is widely used in industry to determine emotional stability. It is used extensively by police departments (Butcher, 1985) and the nuclear power industry (Davis, 1986; Dunnette, Bownas, & Bosshardt, 1981) to evaluate a person's ability to work in psychologically sensitive positions. Correlations between the MMPI and employee reliability further illuminate

Table 4
*Summary of Concurrent Validation Studies Using Employee Reliability*

| Source | Sample | Criteria | |
|---|---|---|---|
| Hogan, Hogan, & Briggs (1984) | 56 truck drivers | Number of commendations received | .51** |
| | | Number of discharges from work | −.28* |
| Guier (1984) | 65 psychiatric counselors | Supervisor ratings; overall job performance | .25* |
| Hogan, Peterson, Hogan, & Jones (1985) | 110 line-haul truck drivers | Number of grievances filed | −.18* |
| | | Number of commendations received | .15* |
| | | Number of claims filed for equipment failure | −.25* |
| Raza, Metz, Dyer, Coan, & Hogan (1986) | 201 hospital service workers | Number of times counseled for aberrant behavior | −.18* |
| Hogan, Arneson, Hogan, & Jones (1986) | 178 habilitation therapists | Number of injuries sustained | −.17* |
| | | Number of incidents reported to insurance fund | −.17* |
| | | State insurance dollars spent for medical treatment | −.18* |
| Montgomery, Butler, & McPhail (1987) | 163 nuclear power plant workers | Supervisor ratings of attitude | .16* |
| | | Supervisor ratings of punctuality | .23** |
| | | Supervisor ratings of accuracy | .16* |
| | | Average supervisor rating | .21* |
| Hogan, Jacobson, Hogan, & Thompson (1987) | 76 service operations dispatchers | Number of absences above allowable | −.49** |
| Driskell, Salas, & Hogan (1987) | 135 Navy electronics technician students | Course completion time | .16* |
| Muchinsky (1987) | 105 customer service representatives | Supervisor ratings of quantity | .18* |
| | | Supervisor ratings of teamwork | .24* |
| | | Supervisor ratings of overall performance | .19* |
| Muchinsky (1987) | 145 telemarketers | Sales performance | .26* |
| | | Lead generation | .34* |
| | | Fund raising | .30* |
| Muchinsky (1987) | 44 field sales representatives | Supervisor ratings of overall job performance | .29* |
| Muchinsky (1987) | 50 office managers | Supervisor ratings of follow-through | .38* |
| | | Supervisor ratings of adaptability | .35* |
| | | Supervisor ratings of overall performance | .26* |
| Johnson (1988) | 320 adults | Rated severity of alcoholism | −.62** |

* $p < .05$, one-tailed.    ** $p < .01$, one-tailed.

the meaning of the latter measure. We asked a group of male police cadets ($N = 108$) enrolled in an urban police academy to complete the reliability scale and the MMPI; correlations with the MMPI scales appear in Table 5. The pattern of correlations with the MMPI validity scales (Lie, Validity, and K) suggests that employee reliability is associated with conscientiousness and carefulness in normal populations. The correlations with the MMPI clinical scales indicate that persons with high scores on employee reliability are modest, nonaggressive, and restrained. The negative correlations for Paranoia and Hypomania also suggest that realistic and nonimpulsive tendencies go with higher scores. Correlations with Welsh's factor scales further indicate that high scores are associated with maturity, self-confidence, and self-restraint. Finally, MacAndrews (1965) developed what is widely regarded as the MMPI criterion measure of alcoholism; in a sample of 108 police cadets, the correlation between MacAndrews's scale and the reliability measure was −.51.

To examine the relationship between employee reliability and the vocational interest scales of Holland's SDS, a sample of male and female public school teachers ($N = 109$) and a sample of bomb disposal trainees ($N = 97$) completed the SDS and the HPI, which were scored for employee reliability. Correlations in Table 5 suggest that employee reliability is most highly associated with Realistic and Social interests; thus, persons with high scores on the reliability scale prefer practical work with

people (e.g., law enforcement). In addition, the correlation with the SDS Conventional scale suggests a preference for rules, procedures, structure, and predictability. The modest correlation with the Enterprising scale further suggests that high scores on reliability predict self-confidence and rule-abiding tendencies. Persons with high scores on employee reliability tend to enjoy social working environments and tasks requiring conformity rather than creativity.

Finally, Table 5 indicates that employee reliability is unrelated to individual differences in cognitive functioning as assessed by verbal and quantitative scales of the ASVAB (it is always useful to know how a new scale is related to intelligence in a normal population).

## Discussion

We have argued that antisocial behavior is a syndrome whose components include hostility toward authority, impulsiveness, social insensitivity, and feelings of alienation. These characteristics predispose people to defy rules, ignore social expectations, and avoid commitments to other people and organizations. These tendencies are normally distributed in the general population. Persons who are unusually hostile, insensitive, and alienated quickly (and usually permanently) run afoul of public authority. Persons who are only moderately hostile, impulsive, insensitive, and alienated have careers marked by frequent job

Table 5
*Correlations Between Employee Reliability and CPI,
MMPI, SDS, and ASVAB Scores*

| Scale | |
|---|---|
| **CPI scales ($N = 190$)** | |
| Dominance | −.12* |
| Capacity for Status | −.06 |
| Sociability | −.12* |
| Social Presence | −.31** |
| Self-Acceptance | −.31** |
| Well-Being | .37** |
| Responsibility | .29** |
| Socialization | .46** |
| Self-Control | .70** |
| Tolerance | .12* |
| Good Impression | .49** |
| Communality | −.13* |
| Achievement via Conformity | .42** |
| Achievement via Independence | .14* |
| Intellectual Efficiency | .10 |
| Psychological Mindedness | .13* |
| Flexibility | −.05 |
| Femininity | .16** |
| **SDS scales ($N = 206$)** | |
| Realistic | −.35** |
| Investigative | .11 |
| Artistic | .08 |
| Social | .30** |
| Enterprising | .12* |
| Conventional | .20** |
| **MMPI scales ($N = 108$)** | |
| Lie | .62** |
| Validity | −.24** |
| K | .63** |
| Hypochrondriasis | .19* |
| Depression | .13* |
| Hysteria | .23** |
| Psychopathic Deviate | −.10 |
| Masculinity–Femininity | −.08 |
| Paranoia | −.17* |
| Psychasthenia | .02 |
| Schizophrenia | −.02 |
| Hypomania | −.36** |
| Social Introversion | .03 |
| Welsh's A | −.54** |
| Welsh's R | .42** |
| **ASVAB scales ($N = 97$)** | |
| WK | −.09 |
| AR | .07 |

*Note.* CPI = California Psychological Inventory; MMPI = Minnesota Multiphasic Personality Inventory; SDS = Self-Directed Search; ASVAB = Armed Services Vocational Aptitude Battery.
* $p < .05$, one-tailed. ** $p < .01$, one-tailed.

change, job dissatisfaction, and limited achievement (Staw, Bell, & Clausen, 1986).

We also argued that persons who are only moderately antisocial engage in a wide variety of delinquent behaviors on the job ranging from insubordination and tardiness through frequent absenteeism to theft, sabotage, and even arson. This argument suggests that it is useful to consider alternatives to theft as an index of dishonesty, in part because theft has a low base rate in normal organizations and in part because it is only one element of the larger behavioral syndrome that we call organizational delinquency.

Using a broad-gauged inventory of normal personality, we developed through empirical means a scale designed to assess tendencies toward organizational delinquency. We provide evidence that this scale is correlated with a wide variety of undesirable work behaviors at the low end and various commendable behaviors at the high end. Finally, correlations with the scales from other standard inventories show that persons with low scores for employee reliability are, as predicted, hostile, impulsive, insensitive, self-absorbed, and unhappy. Conversely, persons with high scores are mature, thoughtful, responsible, and possibly somewhat inhibited. The employee reliability scale is a valid and reliable measure of the organizational delinquency syndrome and it provides an alternative to more narrowly focused honesty measures.

## References

Butcher, J. N. (1985). Personality assessment in industry: Theoretical issues and illustrations. In H. J. Bernardin & D. A. Bownas (Eds.), *Personality assessment in organizations.* New York: Praeger.

Cronbach, L. J. (1951). Coefficient alpha and the internal structure of tests. *Psychometrica, 16,* 297–334.

Davis, S. (1986). *Individualized counseling in organizations.* Paper presented at the First Annual Conference of the Society for Industrial and Organizational Psychology, Chicago.

Digman, J. M., & Inouye, J. (1986). Further specification of the five robust factors of personality. *Journal of Personality and Social Psychology, 50,* 116–123.

Driskell, J., Salas, E., & Hogan, J. (1987). *Personality correlates of Navy electronics technicians training performance.* Orlando, FL: Naval Training Systems Center.

Dunnette, M. D. (1966). *Personnel selection and placement.* Belmont, CA: Wadsworth.

Dunnette, M. D., Bownas, D. A., & Bosshardt, M. J. (1981). *Electric power plant study: Prediction of inappropriate, unreliable, or aberrant job behavior in nuclear power plant settings.* Minneapolis, MN: Personnel Decisions Research Institute.

Gough, H. G. (1948). A sociological theory of psychopathy. *American Journal of Sociology, 53,* 359–366.

Gough, H. G. (1960). Theory and measurement of socialization. *Journal of Consulting Psychology, 24,* 23–30.

Gough, H. G. (1965). The conceptual analysis of psychological test scores and other diagnostic variations. *Journal of Abnormal Psychology, 70,* 294–302.

Gough, H. G. (1987). *California Psychological Inventory administrator's guide.* Palo Alto, CA: Consulting Psychologists Press.

Guier, L. R. (1984). *Validation of personality measures for selection of psychiatric counselors.* Tulsa, OK: University of Tulsa.

Hare, R. D. (1985). Comparison of procedures for the assessment of psychopathy. *Journal of Consulting and Clinical Psychology, 53,* 7–16.

Hathaway, S. R., & McKinley, J. C. (1967). *Manual for the Minnesota Multiphasic Personality Inventory.* New York: Psychological Corporation.

Hogan, J., Arneson, S., Hogan, R., & Jones, S. (1986). *Development and validation of personnel selection procedures for the job of habilitation therapist.* Tulsa, OK: Hogan Assessment Systems.

Hogan, J., & Hogan, R. (1986). *Hogan personnel selection series manual.* Minneapolis, MN: National Computer Systems.

Hogan, J., Hogan, R., & Briggs, S. (1984). *Development and validation of employee selection tests for combination drivers.* Tulsa, OK: University of Tulsa.

Hogan, J., Peterson, S., Hogan, R., & Jones, S. (1985). *Development and validation of a line-haul driver selection inventory.* Tulsa, OK: University of Tulsa.

Hogan, J., & Zenke, L. (1986). Dollar-value utility of alternative procedures for selecting school principals. *Educational and Psychological Measurement, 46,* 935–945.

Hogan, R. (1983). A socioanalytic theory of personality. In M. Page & R. Dienstbier (Eds.), *Nebraska Symposium on Motivation.* Lincoln: University of Nebraska Press.

Hogan, R. (1986). *Hogan Personality Inventory manual.* Minneapolis, MN: National Computer Systems.

Hogan, R., DeSoto, C. B., & Solano, C. (1977). Traits, tests, and personality research. *American Psychologist, 32,* 255–264.

Hogan, R., Jacobson, G., Hogan, J., & Thompson, B. (1987). *Development and validation of a service operations dispatcher selection inventory.* Tulsa, OK: Hogan Assessment Systems.

Hogan, R., & Nicholson, R. (1988). The meaning of personality test scores. *American Psychologist, 43,* 621–626.

Holland, J. L. (1985a). *Making vocational choices: A theory of vocational personalities and work environments* (2nd ed.). Englewood Cliffs, NJ: Prentice-Hall.

Holland, J. L. (1985b). *The Self-Directed Search: Professional manual—1985 edition.* Odessa, FL: Psychological Assessment Resources.

Johnson, J. A. (1988). *HPI correlates of alcohol abuse.* Unpublished manuscript, Pennsylvania State University, University Park.

Landy, F. J. (1986). Stamp collecting versus science: Validation as hypothesis testing. *American Psychologist, 41,* 1183–1192.

MacAndrews, C. (1965). The differentiation of male alcoholic outpatients from nonalcoholic psychiatric patients by means of the MMPI. *Quarterly Journal of Studies of Alcohol, 26,* 238–246.

Montgomery, J., Butler, S., & McPhail, S. M. (1987). *Development and validation of a selection test battery for radiation protection technicians.* Houston, TX: Jeanneret & Associates.

Muchinsky, P. (1987). *Validation documentation for the development of personnel selection test batteries for telecommunications service jobs.* Ames: Iowa State University.

Raza, S., Metz, D., Dyer, P., Coan, T., & Hogan, J. (1986). *Development and validation of personnel selection procedures for hospital service personnel.* Tulsa, OK: University of Tulsa.

Rosen, A. S. (1977). On the dimensionality of the California Psychological Inventory socialization scale. *Journal of Consulting and Clinical Psychology, 45,* 583–591.

Sackett, P. R., & Harris, M. M. (1985). Honesty testing for personnel selection: A review and critique. In H. J. Bernardin & D. A. Bownas (Eds.), *Personality assessment in organizations.* New York: Praeger.

Staw, B. M., Bell, N. E., & Clausen, J. A. (1986). Dispositional approach to job attitudes: A lifetime longitudinal test. *Administrative Science Quarterly, 31,* 56–77.

U.S. Department of Defense. (1980). *Armed Services Vocational Aptitude Battery (ASVAB) counselor's guide.* Fort Sheridan, IL: Military Enlistment Processing Command.

Zonderman, A. B. (1980). *Inventory construction by the method of homogeneous item composites.* Unpublished manuscript, Johns Hopkins University, Baltimore.

Received March 19, 1987
Revision received June 17, 1988
Accepted June 29, 1988 ■

# [22]

# Working Under the Influence (WUI): Correlates of Employees' Use of Alcohol and Other Drugs*

RICHARD C. HOLLINGER

*In response to the use of alcohol and other drugs in the work place, policy decisions with significant social and legal implications—such as urine testing for drug use—are being made without a clear understanding of either the epidemiology or etiology of this phenomenon. This article presents the major theoretical perspectives on employees' substance abuse and assesses the desirability of integrating them. Using data from an anonymous mail survey of 9,175 employees of 47 organizations in three industries, the author analyzed responses to items addressing age, gender, social interaction with coworkers, and satisfaction with one's job to determine any relationship between these variables and self-reported instances of working while intoxicated. The findings indicate that the employees most likely to work under the influence of alcohol or other drugs were men younger than 30 years, and that the likelihood of their—or other employees'—doing so increased when they felt unhappy about their jobs and socialized frequently with coworkers off the job. The author discusses the implications of these findings for both deviance theory and policies for employee assistance programs.*

The phenomenon of the abuse of alcohol and other drugs has long been recognized as an important social problem. Recently, however, societal concerns about the negative effects of such abuse have focused on the work place (e.g., Saltman, 1977). Policy makers are now formulating responses to the perceived prevalence of the problem. For example, even without much empirical evidence of cost effective-

ness (Roman, 1982), many corporations have implemented various employee assistance programs (EAPs) to help workers overcome

*The research reported in this article was supported under grants 78-NI-AX-0014 and 79-NI-AX-0090 from the National Institute of Justice. The opinions expressed are those of the author and do not necessarily represent the position of the U. S. Department of Justice. The author thanks Ronald Akers, Harrison Trice, Paul Roman, Gideon Sjoberg, Bill Sonnenstuhl, and Paul Steele for their constructive comments on earlier versions of this article.

*Richard C. Hollinger is an associate professor in the Department of Sociology and in the Center for Studies in Criminology and Law, University of Florida, Gainesville, Florida 32611.*

The Journal of Applied Behavioral Science
Volume 24, Number 4, pages 439-454.

440                    THE JOURNAL OF APPLIED BEHAVIORAL SCIENCE Vol. 24/No. 4/1988

drug or drinking problems before they become too debilitating (Sonnenstuhl & Trice, 1986; Steele, 1984). Moreover, approximately half of the *Fortune* 500 corporations are thought to use urine tests to monitor drug use by employees and job applicants (O'Keefe, 1987; Masi, 1984), despite widespread concerns about the tests' accuracy and deterrence effects (Sonnenstuhl, Trice, Staudenmeier, & Steele, 1987).

Many of these responses by work organizations stem from a particular set of assumptions about the underlying causes of drug and alcohol problems. Nearly all treatment programs are either implicitly or explicitly predicated on the assumption that substance abuse and dependence constitutes a medical disease, which employees import into the work place rather than acquire there (Archer, 1977; Trice & Beyer, 1982). This "medicalization" of the problem may be philosophically appealing to employers because it attributes drug and alcohol abuse to factors unrelated to one's job or work place. A growing number of scholars, however, have questioned the validity of this disease model (Conrad & Schneider, 1980; Archer, 1977). This alternative body of research instead hypothesizes that organizational and occupational factors are causally related to substance abuse in the work place.[1]

This article represents an exploratory attempt to integrate studies of the abuse of alcohol and other drugs in the work place. It presents an analysis of self-reported intoxication on the job, which incorporates both the personal characteristics of the workers along with the organizational and occupational factors intrinsic to the work milieu.

## THEORY

With the exception of an early study, (Straus & Bacon, 1951), scholarly inquiry into an assortment of industries and occupations has established that an inverse relationship exists between employees' social status and drinking problems in the work place (e.g., Plant, 1979; Warkov, Bacon, & Hauskins, 1965). A preponderance of evidence indicates that the worker who abuses alcohol is significantly more likely to be male, single, and from an occupation of lower socioeconomic status (Fillmore & Caetano, 1982). This literature is less definitive as to why these particular workers are overrepresented among the abusing population. Three distinct theoretical perspectives have emerged, each purporting to establish a causal explanation for substance abuse in the work place:

1. the occupational and organizational culture perspective,
2. the work-related strain perspective,
3. and the importation perspective.

### Occupational and Organizational Culture

Perhaps the most widely accepted perspective on alcohol abuse in the work place holds that the informal cultures of various occupations and work organizations offer relatively high support for on-the-job intoxication. Some argue that certain individuals select occupations in which alcohol is readily available or its abuse more easily concealed (Plant, 1977, 1978). Except for isolated studies (e.g., Hitz, 1973), the epidemiological data do reveal significantly higher levels of alcohol-related mortality among workers in specific occupations, such as bar and restaurant employees, newspaper owners, publishers, and journalists (Guralnick, 1962).

Even when an occupation does not make alcohol significantly more available to its members, the culture of a particular work organization may permit greater on-the-job consumption and intoxication. Those adopting the organizational culture perspective (e.g., Trice & Beyer, 1985) assume that drinking at work primarily results from weak formal management controls and accountability (Roman & Trice, 1970). For example, Manello and Seaman (1979) maintain that railroad employees of some organizations consume relatively high levels of alcohol because engineers are rarely constrained by their supervisors or peers from becoming intoxicated, despite the rather obvious safety implications of this.

Some have further suggested that a great deal of on-the-job drug use is anchored in workers' inability to distinguish the social boundaries between work and nonwork situations (Manello & Seaman, 1979). Active support for or passive toleration of one's intoxicated peers is thought to originate in leisure-time drinking that later leads to diminished informal social control over alcohol abuse within the work setting (Cosper, 1979). Sonnenstuhl and Trice's (1987) study of tunnel workers ("sandhogs") in New York City uncovered an excellent example of the significant effects of occupational and organizational culture on both on-the-job and after-work alcohol consumption.

## Work-Related Strain

The second most widely held perspective maintains that the strain and alienation inherent in work settings promote alcohol abuse among employees (Roman & Trice, 1970, 1976). Although Robinson (1942) argued long ago that dissatisfied workers drink more, Roman and Trice were the first to suggest that alcohol abuse directly results from job-related stress. They argue (Trice & Roman, 1972) that nine "risk factors" contribute to alcoholism among workers, particularly those in positions of higher and middle-level status. Although the causal relationship between employees' drinking problems and these risk factors has not yet been conclusively verified, the findings of several empirical studies allow one to infer that Roman and Trice may be correct. For example, Mangione and Quinn (1975)

found a correlation between dissatisfaction with one's job and drug use (as well as forms of counterproductive behavior), albeit only for men more than 30 years old. Parker (1979) has demonstrated that occupational status inconsistency affects patterns of alcohol consumption. Other researchers (e.g., Schramm, Mandell, & Archer, 1978) have found that factors such as time pressures, occupational mobility, and thwarted career ambition influence substance abuse, which further supports the work-related strain perspective.

## Importation

The importation perspective on on-the-job substance use has not yet been clearly articulated in the literature. According to this viewpoint, if intoxication at work is not a function of either a unique occupational culture or of various sources of strain within the organization, then perhaps it results from employees' "importing" drinking and drug problems into the work place. That is, intoxication at work may directly reflect the level of substance abuse occurring in society at large.

Note that those occupations with the highest levels of alcohol-related morbidity and mortality also have high concentrations of young men, who belong to the segment of the general population with the heaviest drinkers and drug users (see Cahalan & Room, 1974). Thus, one might wonder whether variations in substance abuse and its consequences might stem not from characteristics of the organization or occupation, but from the number of "high-consumption" young men employed.

Empirical investigations into the effects of the work place on alcohol abuse have thus far concentrated either on the organizational or occupational culture or on work-related strain, but not on both simultaneously. In perhaps the most significant test of multiple theories to date, Parker and Brody (1982) have used measures from both paradigms in a large survey of drinking problems within a single urban community. Although they lend some support to an integrated perspective, their results were not dramatic. When they examined organizational culture measures, the only support they obtained for this perspective was a significant relationship between increased drinking problems and leisure time spent with coworkers who drank. They also found only weak support for the work-related strain perspective, as they determined that employees with drinking problems were also more likely to have jobs with the highest levels of complexity.

Parker and Brody's findings suggest that further research into the work place correlates of on-the-job substance use would be beneficial, particularly if indicators of both work place culture and stress were included into an equation along with measures for the importation perspective. By simultaneously considering all three perspectives, we can better assess the advisability of integrating them.

## THE STUDY

### Methods

The data reported in this article were collected during a comprehensive study of theft, deviance, and other forms of counterproductive activity in the work place (Hollinger & Clark, 1983).

After receiving assurances of corporate and individual anonymity, 47 separate business corporations located in three different metropolitan areas—Minneapolis-St. Paul, Dallas-Fort Worth, and Cleveland—agreed to participate in the study. The 47 organizations were in the three most populous industry sectors in the U.S., and included 16 retail store corporations, 21 general hospitals (representing the service industry), and 10 electronic manufacturing firms. They ranged in size from 150 employees to more than 10,000 workers at multiple locations. Random samples of employees were drawn from mailing lists provided by the corporations.

The typical retail organization employee was a sales clerk working for a large department store in a suburban shopping mall. The typical hospital employee was a nurse in a large metropolitan hospital. The typical manufacturing firm employee was an assembler or engineering technician building computers or electronic equipment components. With only a few exceptions, the respondents did not belong to any labor unions.

Workers were randomly selected from all levels within each organization. These were sent an anonymous, self-administered survey questionnaire through the mail. We obtained a total of 9,175 responses, a return rate of 53.8%.[2] The questionnaire addressed various issues related to the workers' current employment circumstances, including the frequency of their personal involvement in a broad range of work place activities considered deviant, such as pilfering, theft, abuse of sick leave, and sloppy workmanship.

### The Dependent Variable: Working Under the Influence

Previous research has employed an assortment of operationalizations to measure—both directly and indirectly—the level of drug and alcohol use in the work place. For example, some studies have examined alcohol-related morbidity and mortality data for various occupations (Guralnick, 1962). Some have compared drinking problems among various groups of employees (Manley, McNichols, & Stahl, 1979; Parker & Brody, 1982). Some have surveyed labor leaders (Steele, 1981) and workers to assess their perceptions of the prevalence of substance abuse (Steele & Hubbard, 1985). Other researchers have measured the frequency with which supervisors are expected to deal with alcoholic employees (Roman, 1974; Trice & Beyer, 1982). Using even more direct methods, those conducting case studies of specific occupations and organizations have used personal interviews and self-report surveys to ascertain the actual prevalence of drinking both on and off the job (Plant, 1977, 1978; Seaman, 1981).

The dependent variable for the study discussed in this article was a self-reported, individual-level survey measure I have labeled "working under the influence" (WUI). Specifically, respondents were asked, "How often have you (during the past year) come to work under the influence of alcohol or drugs?"[3] The analytical categories[4] were the following:

1. almost daily,
2. about weekly,
3. 4–12 times per year,
4. 1–3 times per year, and
5. never.

Table 1 indicates that the proportion of respondents who reported any substance abuse at work was 6.5%, ranging from 3.2% of the

hospital employees to 7.6% of the retail employees to 12.8% of the manufacturing employees.

Comparing the reliability of these data to other epidemiological estimates is difficult because of the wide variation in prevalence noted by the few other studies of this type. The most recent research into levels of WUI demonstrates that the prevalence of on-the-job alcohol consumption varies widely by industry and culture. For example, Davies (1981, p. 48) reports that data collected for different industries in Scotland indicate that

> 64 per cent of the males interviewed in the brewery personally admitted consuming alcohol during working hours; so did 20 per cent in the shipyard, 11 per cent in the engine/propulsion unit manufacturer, and nine per cent in the vehicle factory.

Even within a single industry, substantial variation apparently occurs in the percentage of workers using alcohol on the job. Seaman (1981) found that among employees of seven major U.S. railroads, the percentage who in-

Table 1

Self-Reported Incidence of Coming to Work While Under the Influence (WUI)
of Alcohol or Other Drugs by Type of Industry

| | Type of industry | | |
| --- | --- | --- | --- |
| | Retail (N = 3,512) | Manufacturing (N = 1,474) | Hospital (N = 4,040) |
| *Frequency* | | | |
| Never | 92.4% | 87.2% | 96.7% |
| N | (3,246) | (1,286) | (3,906) |
| 1–3 times per year | 4.6% | 7.3% | 2.2% |
| N | (162) | (107) | (88) |
| 4–12 times per year | 1.6% | 3.1% | .6% |
| N | (57) | (46) | (26) |
| About weekly | .8% | 1.3% | .3% |
| N | (29) | (19) | (14) |
| Almost daily | .5% | 1.1% | .1% |
| N | (18) | (16) | (6) |
| Total reporting some instances of WUI | 7.6% | 12.8% | 3.2% |
| N | (266) | (188) | (134) |

dicated they had seen coworkers drink on duty during the year prior to the study ranged from a high of 60% for one company to a low of 12% for another (the median was 36%). Perhaps even more alarming, given the safety risks this poses, Seaman further reports that a median of 17% of the respondents knew of coworkers who were too drunk or hung over to perform their duties during the previous year. Similarly high levels of abuse were reported in a recent survey of psychologists: One-third knew of colleagues impaired by alcohol, but most said they chose not to confront their peers (Thoreson, Budd, & Krauskopf, 1986).

The extent to which drugs other than alcohol are used on the job is more difficult to document. Until epidemiological data specific to the work place become available, one can only extrapolate information from surveys of drug use by the general population. For example, Miller, Cisin, Gardner-Keaton, Harrell, Wirtz, Abelson, & Fishburne (1983) found in a national survey that 27.4% of the respondents aged 18–24 years reported using marijuana during the previous month. Another national survey found that 52% of the respondents working at least 30 hours per week admitted to using marijuana at some time in their lives. Among students and those working fewer than 30 hours per week, the figure was more than 60% (O'Donnell, Voss, Clayton, Slatin, & Room, 1976). Since drug testing prior to and during employment has become more routine, more data may emerge indicating the extent to which drug use occurs while at work. For example, random urine tests for drug use by employees and job applicants from one corporation yielded positive results for 24% of those tested, almost all indicating marijuana use (Spain, 1987). Furthermore, Kandel and Yamaguchi (1987, p. 874), in discussing their work on employment instability, state that "drug behavior appears to be a very efficient marker for identifying a group of young people who

are at especially high risk of experiencing job mobility in their work careers."

In sum, based on this sketchy empirical record generated from a handful of studies, one can only conclude that the proportion of employees who come to work intoxicated, use alcohol or other drugs on the job, or exhibit symptoms of substance abuse are largely in the minority. With respect to drinking problems, Roman and Trice (1976, p. 447) estimate that only "3 to 5 percent of the work force in any organization, with variations depending on the age, sex and ethnic composition" suffer from alcohol abuse or dependence. This type of skewed distribution is quite commonly found in studies of many types of deviant behavior. A pronounced lack of variance in the dependent variable, however, causes statistical analysis problems, for critical assumptions about normalcy with respect to frequency distributions are violated. For the study reported in this article, the extremely small number of employees who reported they had ever been intoxicated at work (6.5%), combined with the even smaller number admitting to frequent intoxication, suggests a dichotomous treatment of the dependent variable. I thus compared employees who reported coming to work intoxicated to those who claimed they had never done so.

### The Independent Variables

The goal of this article is to determine whether empirical support exists for integrating three theoretical perspectives that have been used separately to explain substance abuse among workers. The limitations of the data do not allow for an exhaustive test of all three theories. Instead, I have selected representative measures for each perspective. The effects of the occupational and organizational cultures are measured by the frequency with which respondents reported interacting with their fellow employees outside of work. Work-related strain was estimated by assessing the respondents' reported degree of satisfaction with their jobs. Finally, the respondents' age and gender, which have proven to be important predictors of alcohol abuse by members of the general population, are used as proxy measures for the importation perspective.

### Interaction Outside of Work

The occupational and organizational culture perspective is based on the assumption that workers who interact with one another away from the job site will, at a minimum, be more tolerant of any deviance by their peers. Because much of socializing outside of work commonly occurs in places such as bars and restaurants in which alcohol (and sometimes other drugs) may be consumed, I hypothesized that persons who frequently associate with their coworkers are more likely to use—and abuse—alcohol and other drugs. This hypothesis has empirical support, for Parker and Brody (1982) found that interactions among coworkers outside of work were correlated with drinking problems. Indeed, extensive socialization among employees after work usually serves as an indicator of a well-developed occupational or organizational culture supportive of leisure-time drinking (Cosper, 1979). Thus, to measure the respondents' involvement with an organizational or occupational culture, I examined their answers to an item asking how frequently one "gets together with fellow workers after work." Those who indicated they did this at least monthly were classified as "often," and those who reported they did this only a few times a year or not at all were classified as "seldom."

### Job Satisfaction

Despite its foundation in common sense, measuring the effects of work-related strain on behavior on the job has not been easy (Herold & Conlon, 1981). Indeed, researchers have had substantial difficulty demonstrating a direct causal relationship between vocational problems or general happiness with one's occupation and alcohol abuse (e.g., Hardy & Cull, 1971; Schramm et al., 1978). Nevertheless, based on the conclusions of Parker and Brody (1982) and Mangione and Quinn (1975), I hypothesized that persons who are specifically dissatisfied with their current jobs are more likely to come to work under the influence of alcohol or other drugs. Intoxication presumably serves as a means of coping with work-related strain (Roman & Trice, 1976). In a previous study, I demonstrated that a significant relationship exists between dissatisfaction with one's job and theft and other forms of counterproductive employee behavior (Hollinger & Clark, 1982). Based on items used in this earlier analysis, to measure work-related strain I examined responses to an item asking, "All in all, how satisfied are you with your present job?" The response choices were "very satisfied," "somewhat satisfied," "somewhat dissatisfied," and "very dissatisfied."

### Age and Gender

The literature on occupational substance abuse clearly indicates that the type of person most likely to use alcohol or other drugs at work is the most common user in the general population: someone who is young and male (Cahalan, 1970; Kandel, 1980, 1984). For this reason, the third and fourth independent variables for this analysis are age and gender. If the importation perspective is relevant to an explanation of WUI, then these variables should act as significant predictors of intoxication in the work place. The sample used for this study should present an excellent test of the importation perspective, for 71% of the respondents were women and the median age was 30 years.

### Data Analysis

As noted above, a skewed frequency distribution for the dependent variable violates assumptions about normalcy, thereby preventing an ordinary least-squares (OLS) regression analysis. Because the dependent variable is dichotomous, I instead employed a weighted least-squares (WLS) logit regression procedure. This offers the advantage of allowing one to conduct a straightforward analysis of a dichotomous dependent variable that otherwise might require a complicated series of contingency tables. Logit regression permits a researcher to simultaneously assess the additive effects of several independent variables. Moreover, one may easily measure the possible interaction effects of the independent variables within the same analysis. The only drawback to this technique involves the presentation of results. Logit regression yields an unorthodox "odds coefficient" instead of the more common standardized regression coefficient or nonparametric measure of association found in contingency table analyses. Specifically, the logit regression coefficient for this analysis represents the odds of a particular employee's reporting to work under the influence of alcohol or other drugs during the year prior to the study.

Using the backward selection analysis procedure Swafford (1980) describes, I estimated a predicted set of logits for the dichotomized dependent variable based on the logically possible models, including both the main effects and the various k-level interaction terms. I then derived the best-fit model by sequentially dropping terms from the saturated model, using a chi-square goodness-of-fit test until I reached the most parsimonious equation. Because of the log of odds is not an intuitively meaningful statistic, logit equations are commonly presented after one applies the exponential function (the anti-log) to both sides of the best-fit equation. The coefficients in the resulting logit regression equation are "partials" representing each variable's separate effects on the odds of a particular category of

respondents' being found in the deviant category—that is, WUI.

I dummy coded the four independent variables as the following: after-work interaction (1 = often, 0 = seldom), job satisfaction (1 = dissatisfied, 0 = satisfied), age (1 = younger than 30 years, 0 = 30 years and older), and gender (1 = male, 0 = female). Table 2 presents the marginal frequencies, proportions, observed odds, and logits for each of the 16 logically possible subpopulations.

## RESULTS

I had hypothesized that each of the four independent variables—after-work interaction with coworkers, dissatisfaction with one's job, age, and gender—would serve as predictors for the dependent variable, working under the influence (WUI) of alcohol or other drugs. Before we consider the multivariate relationships, note that that the zero-order relationships with the dependent variable provide a preliminary confirmation of my expectations. All four of the independent variables acted separately to predict substance use in the work place.

The strongest zero-order relationship was achieved by age. Respondents under the age of 30 years were almost four and one-half times more likely than their older peers to report to work under some level of intoxication, as the following shows.

$$\Omega = k * age$$

$$\Omega = .027 * 4.476$$

where $\Omega$ is the odds of coming to work under the influence of alcohol or other drugs, and k is the regression constant.

Consistent with the extant literature on drug abuse in society and the work place, the data indicate that at the zero-order level, the respondents who came to work intoxicated were

Table 2

Marginal Frequencies, Proportions, Odds, and Logits for
the 16 Subpopulations of the Sample*

| | Independent variables | | | | WUI Frequencies | | | | | |
| | Age | Gender | Get together | Job satisfaction | Subtotal | Yes | No | Proportion yes | Odds yes | Logits |
|---|---|---|---|---|---|---|---|---|---|---|
| **Subpopulation** | | | | | | | | | | |
| 1. | Y | M | O | DIS | 216 | 64 | 152 | .30 | .42 | − .87 |
| 2. | O | M | O | DIS | 113 | 9 | 104 | .08 | .09 | −2.41 |
| 3. | Y | F | O | DIS | 510 | 73 | 437 | .14 | .17 | −1.77 |
| 4. | O | F | O | DIS | 209 | 6 | 203 | .03 | .03 | −3.51 |
| 5. | Y | M | S | DIS | 111 | 16 | 95 | .14 | .17 | −1.77 |
| 6. | O | M | S | DIS | 172 | 8 | 164 | .05 | .05 | −3.00 |
| 7. | Y | F | S | DIS | 320 | 25 | 295 | .08 | .08 | −2.53 |
| 8. | O | F | S | DIS | 342 | 3 | 339 | .01 | .01 | −4.61 |
| 9. | Y | M | O | SAT | 600 | 118 | 482 | .20 | .24 | −1.43 |
| 10. | O | M | O | SAT | 533 | 41 | 492 | .08 | .08 | −2.53 |
| 11. | Y | F | O | SAT | 1,433 | 95 | 1,338 | .07 | .07 | −2.66 |
| 12. | O | F | O | SAT | 994 | 26 | 968 | .03 | .03 | −3.51 |
| 13. | Y | M | S | SAT | 240 | 23 | 237 | .01 | .01 | −4.61 |
| 14. | O | M | S | SAT | 553 | 17 | 536 | .03 | .03 | −3.51 |
| 15. | Y | F | S | SAT | 730 | 40 | 690 | .05 | .06 | −2.81 |
| 16. | O | F | S | SAT | 1,678 | 12 | 1,666 | .007 | .007 | −4.96 |

*Key: Y = younger than 30 years, O = 30 years and older, M = male, F = female, O = often, S = seldom, DIS = dissatisfied, SAT = satisfied

almost three times more likely to be male than female. This finding is particularly interesting because men were a distinct minority in this sample (i.e., 29% of the respondents).

$$\Omega = k * \text{gender}$$

$$\Omega = .046 * 2.831$$

Although the importation variables function well as predictors of WUI, the measures for organizational and occupational culture and for work-related strain also prove significant at the zero-order level. For example, the respondents who reported socializing frequently with their coworkers outside the job were almost three times more likely than the others to report coming to work intoxicated.

$$\Omega = k * \text{get together}$$

$$\Omega = .036 * 2.864$$

Empirical support also exists for the work-related strain perspective, although it has the weakest zero-order relationship to WUI. Employees who expressed dissatisfaction with their jobs were almost twice as likely to report to work while intoxicated.

$$\Omega = k * \text{job satisfaction}$$

$$\Omega = .058 * 1.958$$

As indicated, each of the independent variables predicted respondents' WUI at the zero-order level. Determining the partial effects of these factors, however, is the principal focus

*Occupational Crime*

of this analysis. The logit (WLS) regression analysis—using a backward solution—enables one to assess the separate effects of each independent variable while holding the remaining factors constant. Table 3 presents the logically possible models for the four independent variables.

The models in Table 3 result from the interaction terms' being sequentially excluded (starting with the most complex) from the saturated equation so as to determine their individual contributions. Working toward the goal of parsimony, each time I dropped a term from the model I compared the goodness of fit to the saturated model. Table 3 shows that when all the first-, second-, and third-order interaction terms were excluded, the goodness-of-fit chi-square showed no significant differences. Only when I attempted to sequentially drop the main effects from the model did I find significant deterioration in the goodness of fit. This indicates that the "best fit" model is an additive one containing all four of the main effects and none of the interaction terms. The following equation represents the solution with the best fit—model number four—for predicting the odds of an employee's coming to work under the influence of alcohol or other drugs.

$$\Omega = k * age * gender * get\ together * job\ satisfaction$$

$$\Omega = .001 * 3.703 * 2.82 * 2.049 * 1.744$$

Because none of the terms in the "best-fit" model interacts with any other, one can directly compare the strength of these partial coefficients with the zero-order odds coefficients reported above. For example, although the effect of age has become somewhat reduced (from the zero-order level), the respondents under 30 years of age were still almost four times as likely as their older peers to come to work intoxicated, even when all the other factors are held constant. In addition, the best-fit model's partial for gender is nearly

Table 3
Model Selection Process*

| | Independent variables in the model | d.f. | $\chi^2$ | Explanation |
|---|---|---|---|---|
| *Model* | | | | |
| 1. | k, age, gender, how often, satisfaction, AG, AH, AS, GH, GS, HS, AGH, AGS, AHS, GHS, AGHS | 0 | .000 | Saturated model |
| 2. | k, age, gender, how often, satisfaction, AG, AH, AS, GH, GS, HS, AGH, AGS, AHS, GHS | 1 | .034 | Exclude third-order interaction terms |
| 3. | k, age, gender, how often, satisfaction, AG, AH, AS, GH, GS, HS | 5 | 6.92 | Exclude second-order interaction terms |
| 4. | k, age, gender, how often, satisfaction | 11 | 18.28** | Exclude all interaction terms |
| 5. | k, age, gender, how often | 12 | 52.17*** | Exclude satisfaction's main effect |
| 6. | k, age, gender, satisfaction | 12 | 68.30*** | Exclude how often's main effect |
| 7. | k, age, how often, satisfaction | 12 | 150.16*** | Exclude gender's main effect |
| 8. | k, gender, how often, satisfaction | 12 | 164.79*** | Exclude age's main effect |

*Key: A = age, G = gender, H = how often, S = satisfaction
**"Best-fit model"
***$\chi^2$ is significantly different from the saturated model's (number 1), with $p \leq .01$.

identical to the zero-order odds indicating that the male respondents were almost three times as likely as the female respondents to come to work intoxicated.

The effects of getting together with one's coworkers and job satisfaction have become slightly reduced in strength from their zero-order levels, but they remain significant factors for contributing to work place substance use. Respondents who socialized outside of work with their fellow employees at least monthly were almost twice as likely to come to work under the influence of alcohol or other drugs as were their peers who reported socializing less frequently or not at all. Employees who felt dissatisfied with their current jobs were almost 75% more likely than their more contented counterparts to report to work intoxicated.

## CONCLUSION

Although more research is obviously necessary, this exploratory analysis suggests that representative measures of three different theoretical perspectives serve as significant and relatively strong predictors of employees' working under the influence (WUI) of alcohol or other drugs. These results lend tentative support to Parker and Brody's (1982) contention that the phenomenon of WUI requires a multiple-theory explanation. Not surprisingly, the younger employees (i.e., less than 30 years old) were far more likely than their older peers to come to work intoxicated. This fact, combined with the finding that the male respondents tended far more frequently than the female respondents to be involved in WUI, suggests that substance use at work directly reflects patterns of substance use in the general population. Despite the considerable strength of the variables of employees' age and gender, however, these two factors alone do not explain all the variation for the dependent variable.

Intoxication from alcohol and other drugs at work is not simply a function of personal characteristics imported into the job setting, but also results from factors related to the work place. Specifically, measures for both culture and strain remained in the best-fit equation as independent, additive effects. Regardless of their age and gender, the employees who socialized with one another outside the job were twice as likely to come to work intoxicated as their counterparts who did not socialize with coworkers, and workers who felt dissatisfied with their jobs were also significantly more likely to report WUI. That these two partial coefficients remain in the best-fit model suggests that organization and occupational culture and work-related strain may both exacerbate any propensities for deviance found among certain groups of employees.

In sum, the employees most likely to report to work intoxicated were not only young and male, but also those who socialized regularly with their coworkers and felt unhappy about their current jobs. Indeed, socializing with one's fellow employees during one's leisure time may represent an important mechanism linking imported personal characteristics with work-related strain, which may increase one's probability of working under the influence of alcohol and other drugs.

## DISCUSSION

### Theoretical Implications

The findings of this analysis have implications for both the specific explanatory perspectives on WUI and for broader theoretical models of deviance. With the exception of such recent studies as Parker and Brody's (1982), research into the occupational aspects of substance use has typically emphasized either the organizational or occupational culture perspective or the work-related strain perspective, and all but ignored the importation perspective. The data

450 THE JOURNAL OF APPLIED BEHAVIORAL SCIENCE Vol. 24/No. 4/1988

reported in this article indicate that **all three** perspectives are relevant to the phenomenon of WUI. Therefore, the most productive theories of intoxication from alcohol and other drugs should be integrated ones, reflecting the multitude of factors that combine to result in deviant behavior.

To illustrate this, let us examine how the separate effects of age, gender, coworker interaction outside of work, and dissatisfaction with one's job can additively produce higher levels of deviance. The following discussion is grounded primarily in two popular deviance paradigms, the "social learning" perspective (Akers, 1986) and "social control/bonding" theory (Hirschi, 1969).

The literature on alcohol and other drugs clearly demonstrates that younger people, especially young men, are the ones most likely to become intoxicated outside the work place. They are also likely to interact socially with other young people, including some of their coworkers. These young employees are much more likely than their older coworkers to engage in such leisure-time activities as dating, going to restaurants and bars, attending professional sports events, and participating in amateur sports and recreational activities (Cosper, 1979). Many of these activities incorporate the consumption of alcohol and other drugs. Workers who use and abuse such substances may "differentially associate" outside of work with others who do the same, thereby positively reinforcing one another's behavior (Akers, 1986). Such employees may also learn "toleration definitions" to account for their coworkers' intoxication.

If such employees also feel a pronounced dissatisfaction with—or apathy about—their jobs, such strain may encourage them not only to become personally involved in WUI, but also to accept or encourage such behavior by their coworkers. Substance use at work thus comes to serve as a means of coping with work-related strain and boredom. That is, dissatis-

faction with one's job may be the precipitating factor that brings intoxication already supported by a subculture into the work place itself. Employees who are disgruntled, younger, and male may perceive less of a distinction between their leisure-time activities and work.

Furthermore, if an intoxicated employee's coworkers tolerate or feel indifferent about WUI, the intoxication will not likely be subject to detection or constraints (Roman & Trice, 1976). This suggests that a theory of control, such as social bonding, may also prove relevant to the findings of this analysis. Younger employees exhibiting the highest levels of WUI may also have the least to lose if detected, as they generally have the shortest tenure with a firm and lowest occupational rank. In terms of Hirschi's (1969) social bonding theory, younger employees have the least "attachment" to coworkers and only minimal "commitment" to their current employers, occupations, and careers (see Hollinger, 1986). Only when employees achieve increased occupational status do formal and informal organizational controls yield the desired deterrence effect, for only then do employees feel a substantial "stake in conformity." Employees older than 30 years, even those who feel dissatisfied about their jobs, generally are constrained from participating in rule-breaking behavior—and suffering the consequences, such as possible loss of employment—by the social responsibilities and financial obligations they have usually acquired by this age.

## Policy Implications

The findings of this analysis have several implications for policy, especially with respect to employee assistance programs seeking to address WUI. The factors distinguishing the typical intoxicated employee in the work place from the remainder of a organization's personnel create at least three important dilemmas for EAP policy makers.

The first dilemma is that the employee who typically uses alcohol or other drugs at work may be one whose intoxication is the **least likely to be detected** by others at the job site. Even under the best of circumstances, substance use by employees is hard to discover (Masi, 1984). The EAP strategy of "constructive confrontation" assumes that an impaired employee's supervisor or coworker(s) will initiate a request that the troubled worker obtain assistance with the problem (Sonnenstuhl, 1986). Because of the common differences in age and social status between younger employees and their supervisors, however, detection during the early stages of substance abuse may be difficult. This is particularly the case when younger employees socialize with their peers—not with supervisory personnel—outside the work place, thus all but guaranteeing that these coworkers will tolerate or even shield their substance use at work.

The second dilemma is that the worker most in need of help from an EAP may the one **least likely to receive treatment**. Because of their short tenure and sometimes temporary status with an organization, younger employees do not always receive full health insurance benefits (Sonnenstuhl & Trice, 1986). This was especially true for the three industry groups included in the study discussed in this article. Many companies will choose the less-expensive option of firing "problem" employees rather than investing in their improvement. Management may view younger employees with lower status who feel dissatisfied with their jobs as "not worth the expense," and may pass them from one company to the next in a form of corporate musical chairs.

Finally, the data suggest that even if young male employees who abuse alcohol or other drugs are given opportunities for assistance, they may be the **least willing to participate in EAPs**. Earlier analyses of the study's findings indicated that many of the dissatisfied employees in the sample had already "terminated

themselves" psychologically from their employers and were actively seeking new jobs (Hollinger & Clark, 1982; Hollinger, 1986). If the measures for WUI used for this study indicate that workers become intoxicated as a means of coping with stressful working conditions, why should one presume that "constructive confrontation," counseling, or any other EAP technique would ameliorate the situation? Indeed, the prospect of being labeled "deviant" as a result of having one's substance abuse discovered may actually precipitate or accelerate an employee's departure from the organization.

Perhaps the major problem with "medicalizing" the use of alcohol and other drugs is reliance on the possibly erroneous assumption that the problems precipitating WUI are personal in nature and unrelated to the work place itself (Sonnenstuhl & Trice, 1986). Previous success with construction confrontation has largely resulted from its motivating employees with drinking or drug problems to obtain treatment so that they may save their jobs (Sonnenstuhl & Trice, 1986). This strategy may indeed prove effective when used for impaired employees over 30 years of age who do not wish to risk losing employment and damaging their careers (Sonnenstuhl & Trice, 1986). Younger, dissatisfied employees, however, may not share this fear and thus may not respond as positively to constructive confrontation. In sum, this article suggests that current EAP policy assumptions may have to be reconsidered if these programs are to benefit the significant group of younger employees who come to work under the influence of alcohol and other drugs.

## NOTES

1. Although the abuse of drugs other than alcohol has obvious relevance, the vast majority of research on the links between occupation and substance use has focused on employees' abuse of alcohol. Specifically, two separate bodies of re-

search on occupational alcoholism have evolved, one of which has investigated the impact of alcohol abuse on job performance, examining how intoxication affects productivity, accident rates, turnover, absenteeism, and the like (see Trice, 1962, 1980). Although the dysfunctional effects of alcohol abuse on employees' behavior presents an interesting area for inquiry, this article treats substance abuse in the work place as the dependent variable.

2. This return rate cannot be directly compared to those for other self-administered, mail questionnaires without an adjustment for errors and attrition resulting from employee turnover. That is, if one were to remove from the employee population those who had terminated their employment during the period between the preparation of the corporate mailing lists and the selection of the study's sample, the adjusted return rate would provide a better approximation of the levels at which variable relationships are not affected by lack of response. Based on an intensive re-examination of corporate personnel files from five randomly selected organizations, the "adjusted" return rates for these corporations were 74%, 69%, 66%, 75%, and 56%.

3. Because employee intoxication was not the exclusive focus of this study of deviance, the questionnaire used the same item to ask respondents about their use of alcohol and use of other drugs. Although in retrospect it may have been ideal to obtain separate data for both phenomena, this is not possible now. Because this article primarily addresses employees who come to work while intoxicated, this single, combined item should serve our present theoretical needs.

4. These analytical categories reflect some collapsing of the original response categories for statistical purposes.

## REFERENCES

Akers, R. (1986). *Deviant behavior: A social learning approach* (2nd ed.). Belmont, CA: Wadsworth.

Archer, J. (1977). Occupational alcoholism: A review of issues and a guide to the literature. In C. Schramm (Ed.), *Alcoholism and its treatment in industry* (pp. 2–28). Baltimore: Johns Hopkins University Press.

Cahalan, D. (1970). *Problem drinkers*. San Francisco: Jossey-Bass.

Cahalan, D., & Room, R. (1974). *Problem drinking among American men*. New Brunswick, NJ: Rutgers Center of Alcohol Studies.

Conrad, P., & Schneider, J. W. (1980). *Deviance and medicalization: From badness to sickness*. St. Louis: C. V. Mosby.

Cosper, R. (1979). Drinking as conformity: A critique of sociological literature on occupational differences in drinking. *Journal of Studies on Alcohol*, *40*, 868–891.

Davies, J. B. (1981). Drinking and alcohol related problems in five industries. In B. D. Hore & M. A. Plant (Eds.), *Alcohol problems in employment* (pp. 38–60). London: Croom Helm.

Fillmore, K., & Caetano, R. (1982). Epidemiology of alcohol abuse and alcoholism in occupations. In *Occupational alcoholism: A review of research issues* (pp. 21–88). Washington, DC: Government Printing Office.

Guralnick, L. (1962). *Vital statistics special reports: Vol. 53, No. 2. Mortality by occupation and industry among users 20 to 64 years of age: United States, 1950*. Washington, DC: U. S. Department of Health, Education and Welfare.

Hardy, R. E., & Cull, J. G. (1971). Vocational satisfaction among alcoholics. *Quarterly Journal of Studies on Alcohol*, *32*, 180–182.

Herold, D. M., & Conlon, E. J. (1981). Work factors as potential causal agents of alcohol abuse. *Journal of Drug Issues*, *11*, 337–356.

Hitz, D. (1973). Drunken sailors and others: Drinking problems in specific occupations. *Quarterly Journal of Studies on Alcohol*, *34*, 496–505.

Hirschi, T. (1969). *Causes of delinquency*. Berkeley: University of California Press.

Hollinger, R. C. (1986). Acts against the workplace: Social bonding and employee deviance. *Deviant Behavior*, *7*, 53–75.

Hollinger, R. C., & Clark, J. P. (1982). Employee deviance: A response to the perceived quality of the work experience. *Work and Occupations*, *9*, 97–114.

Hollinger, R. C., & Clark, J. P. (1983). *Theft by employees*. Lexington, MA: Lexington Books.

Kandel, D. B. (1980). Drug and drinking behavior among youth. *Annual Review of Sociology*, *6*, 235–285.

Kandel, D. B. (1984). Marijuana users in young adulthood. *Archives of General Psychiatry, 41,* 200–209.

Kandel, D. B., & Yamaguchi, K. (1987). Job mobility and drug use: An event history analysis. *American Journal of Sociology, 92,* 836–878.

Manello, T. A., & Seaman, F. J. (1979). *Prevalence, costs, and handling of drinking problems on seven railroads: Final report* (Report of the U. S. Department of Transportation, Federal Railroad Administration). Washington, DC: University Research.

Mangione, T. W., & Quinn, R. P. (1975). Job satisfaction, counterproductive behavior, and drug use at work. *Journal of Applied Psychology, 60,* 114–116.

Manley, T. R., McNichols, C. W., & Stahl, M. S. (1979). *Alcoholism and alcohol related problems among USAF civilian employees* (AFIT Technical Report 79–4). Wright-Patterson Air Force Base, OH: Air Force Institute of Technology, U. S. Air Force University.

Masi, D. A. (1984). *Designing employee assistance programs.* New York: American Management Association.

Miller, J. D., Cisin, I. H., Gardner-Keaton, H., Harrell, A. V., Wirtz, P. W., Abelson, H. I., & Fishburne, P. M. (1983). *National survey on drug abuse: Main findings 1982.* Rockville, MD: National Institute on Drug Abuse.

O'Donnell, J., Voss, H. L., Clayton, R. R., Slatin, G. T., & Room, R. G. (1976). *Young men and drugs—A nationwide survey* (Research Monograph No. 5). Rockville, MD: National Institute on Drug Abuse.

O'Keefe, A. M. (1987, June). The case against drug testing. *Psychology Today,* pp. 34–35, 38.

Parker, D. A. (1979). Status inconsistency and drinking behavior. *Pacific Sociological Review, 22,* 77–95.

Parker, D. A., & Brody, J. A. (1982). Risk factors for alcoholism and alcohol problems among employed women and men. In *Occupational alcoholism: A review of research issues* (pp. 99–127). Washington, DC: U. S. Government Printing Office.

Plant, M. A. (1977). Alcoholism and occupation. *British Journal of Addiction, 73,* 309–316.

Plant, M. A. (1978). Occupation and alcoholism:

Cause or effect? A control study of recruits to the drink trade. *International Journal of Addiction, 13,* 604–626.

Plant, M. A. (1979). *Drinking careers: Occupations, drinking habits, and drinking problems.* London: Tavistock.

Robinson, D. (1942). Social disorganization reflected in middle class drinking and dancing recreational patterns. *Social Forces, 20,* 455–459.

Roman, P. M. (1974). Settings for successful deviance: Drinking and deviant drinking among middle- and upper-level employees. In C. D. Bryant (Ed.), *Deviant behavior: Occupational and organizational bases* (pp. 109–128). Chicago: Rand-McNally.

Roman, P. M. (1982). Employee alcoholism programs in major corporations in 1979: Scope, change, and receptivity. In *Prevention, intervention and treatment: Concerns and models.* Rockville, MD: U. S. Department of Health and Human Services.

Roman, P. M., & Trice, H. M. (1970). The development of deviant drinking behavior. *Archives of Environmental Health, 20,* 424–435.

Roman, P. M., & Trice, H. M. (1976). Alcohol abuse and work organizations. In B. Kissin & H. Begleiter (Eds.), *The biology of alcoholism: Vol. 4. Social aspects of alcoholism* (pp. 445–517). New York: Plenum.

Saltman, J. (1977). *Drinking on the job: The $15–million hangover.* New York: Public Affairs Committee.

Seaman, F. J. (1981). Problem drinking among American railroad workers. In B. D. Hore & M. A. Plant (Eds.), *Alcohol problems in employment* (pp. 118–128). London: Croom Helm.

Schramm, C. J., Mandell, W., & Archer, J. (1978). *Workers who drink.* Lexington, MA: Lexington Books.

Sonnenstuhl, W. J. (1986). *Inside an emotional health program.* Ithaca, NY: New York State School of Industrial and Labor Relations, Cornell University.

Sonnenstuhl, W. J., & Trice, H. M. (1986). *Strategies for employee assistance programs: The crucial balance.* Ithaca, NY: New York State School of Industrial and Labor Relations, Cornell University.

Sonnenstuhl, W. J., & Trice, H. M. (1987). The

social construction of alcohol problems in a union's peer counseling program. *Journal of Drug Issues, 17,* 223–254.

Sonnenstuhl, W. J., Trice, H. M., Staudenmeier, W. J., Jr., & Steele, P. (1987). Employee assistance and drug testing: Fairness and injustice in the workplace. *Nova Law Review, 11,* 709–731.

Spain, N. M. (1987). Employee drug screening and the law: Part I. *Security Systems, 16,* 22–23.

Steele, P. D. (1981). Labor perceptions of drug use and drug problems in the workplace. *Journal of Drug Issues, 11,* 279–292.

Steele, P. D. (1984). Assessing employee assistance programs: Intra- and extra-organizational influences. *EAP Research, 1,* 36–45.

Steele, P. D., & Hubbard, R. L. (1985). Management styles, perceptions of substance abuse, and employee assistance programs in organizations. *Journal of Applied Behavioral Science, 21,* 271–286.

Straus, R., & Bacon, S. D. (1951). Alcoholism and social stability: A study of occupational integration in 2,023 male clinic patients. *Quarterly Journal of Studies on Alcohol, 12,* 231–260.

Swafford, M. (1980). Three parametric techniques for contingency table analysis: A nontechnical commentary. *American Sociological Review, 45,* 664–690.

Thoreson, R. W., Budd, F. C., & Krauskopf, C. J. (1986). Perceptions of alcohol misuse and work behavior among professionals: Identification and intervention. *Professional psychology: Research and practice, 17,* 210–216.

Trice, H. M. (1962). The job behavior of problem drinkers. In D. J. Pittman & C. R. Snyder (Eds.), *Society, culture and drinking patterns.* New York: John Wiley.

Trice, H. M. (1980). Job based alcoholism and employee assistance programs. *Alcohol Health and Research World, 4,* 4–16.

Trice, H. M., & Beyer, J. M. (1982). Social controls in worksettings: Using the constructive confrontation strategy with problem-drinking employees. *Journal of Drug Issues, 12,* 21–49.

Trice, H. M., & Beyer, J. M. (1985). Using six organizational rites to change culture. In R. H. Kilman, M. J. Saxton, R. Serpa, and Associates (Eds.), *Gaining control of the corporate culture* (pp. 370–399). San Francisco: Jossey-Bass.

Trice, H. M., & Roman, P. (1972). *Spirits and demons at work: Alcohol and other drugs on the job.* New York: Cornell University Press.

Warkov, S., Bacon, S. D., & Hauskins, A. C. (1965). Social correlates of industrial problem drinking. *Quarterly Journal of Studies on Alcohol, 26,* 58–71.

# [23]

ELSEVIER

Security Journal 7 (1996) 61-70

Security
Journal

# Managing losses in the retail store: A comparison of loss prevention activity in the United States and Great Britain

Joshua Bamfield*[a,1], Richard C. Hollinger[b,2]

[a]School of Business, Nene College, Northampton, NN27AL, UK
[b]Director, Security Research Project, Department of Sociology, University of Florida, Gainesville, FL, USA 32611-7330

## Abstract

Using data from recent surveys of loss prevention and security professionals in the United States and the United Kingdom, retail shrinkage levels, perceived sources of loss, and typical retail security countermeasures are compared. Although hard to directly compare, average retail shrinkage levels seem somewhat lower in the UK than the US. While employee (i.e., staff) theft is thought to be a larger problem in the US, in Britain shoplifting and employee theft are thought to be rather equally sized problems. Security spending seems higher in the US, but rates of increase in the UK insure that parity will occur quite soon. The use of pre-employment screening (i.e. vetting) and formal loss prevention awareness programs are used less frequently in the UK. In both countries the replacement of staff by detection technology is a growing trend, although currently more prevalent in the US. Moreover, in both the UK and the US, there is evidence that non-criminal justice sanctioning alternatives are increasing in popularity.

*Keywords:* Loss prevention; Security; Employee theft; Shoplifting; Comparative

## 1. Introduction

Perhaps one of the most significant challenges faced by contemporary society is the growing problem of crime. Survey after survey places the 'crime problem' at the top of the list of important US social problems. Great Britain is currently experiencing its own moral panic about an increase in crime, the breakdown in social cohesion, and growing lawlessness — seen, unfairly or not, as an unwanted form of 'Americanization.' The growing concern about increasing crime levels is significant for, not only the general public, but for the business community as well. When busi-

nesses are victimized by crime, society as a whole pays a 'crime tax' in terms of elevated insurance premiums and higher costs for products when they are purchased by consumers. The increasing cost of crime against business is not a recently discovered phenomenon, however. As early as 1975, non-violent crimes against business were estimated to cost American companies well over $40 billion per year (American Management Associations, 1977). Extrapolating for inflation and increasing levels of criminality, more recent estimates for the United States place the overall annual financial impact for employee theft alone at between $15 and 25 billion (Shepard and Dustin, 1988).

Achieving profitability in the retail store has always been hampered by an assortment of challenges; one of the most significant is crime. The retail industry not only encompasses a growing share of the world economy, but bears an increasing share of crime victimizations. Because of open door access to both the general public and employees alike, the increasing prevalence of crime is especially problematic. For example, crime in 1993-94 (Speed et al., 1995) cost

---

* Corresponding author.
[1]Joshua Bamfield is the Head of Business at Nene College — Northampton United Kingdom. He is the author of numerous articles on loss prevention and retail security, most recently focused on the cost/benefits of emerging EAS technologies.
[2]Richard C. Hollinger is the Director of the Security Research Project at the Department of Sociology, University of Florida, United States. The Security Research Project is a corporately supported research institute dedicated to the better understanding of loss prevention and security issues.

62                        *J. Bamfield, R.C. Hollinger / Security Journal 7 (1996) 61–70*

UK retailers $2.4 billion which was 0.4% of the GDP (based on £1 = $1.5617), while in the same period US retailers lost an estimated $27.3 billion (derived from Hollinger and Dabney, 1994). For most trade sectors, retail crime costs account for nearly 2% of total annual retail sales, equivalent in both countries to over one-quarter of all retail profits. These numbers are so large that no other form of property crime (e.g. personal robbery, household burglary, auto theft) comes close to equaling the annual economic impact of crimes against business, especially crimes against retailers (Lary, 1988). Nevertheless, the impact of crime upon retailers and their organizational response to crime has attracted little concern from either the general public or academic criminologists.

The central research questions of this paper include the following. First, how much crime is occurring in the typical US and British retail corporation? Second, what are retailers on both sides of the Atlantic doing to inhibit crime related losses? We will limit our principal focus to non-violent larceny and theft from shops by customers, staff, and vendor representatives. Although they are important, we have excluded from this discussion an assortment of conventional crimes committed against retail businesses, such as burglary, terrorism, robbery, snatch and grab, till snatches, or arson since these offense categories pose different methodological issues. While there is some evidence that some forms of conventional crime is constant or decreasing, this is not true for shoplifting, employee theft, and vendor fraud. In fact, during 1993–94 these three sources accounted for 71.4% of total UK retail crime losses (Speed et al., 1995).

## 2. Methodology

This study will be a comparison of data collected recently in both the United States and the United Kingdom. Three large retail security surveys conducted in both countries using a common methodology will be the primary source of information (See Table 1). These quantitative data will be supplemented by semi-structured interviews with 25 security

managers from large retail businesses in the UK. A brief overview of the specific security surveys that have been used in this report follow:

### 2.1. The US national retail security surveys (Hollinger and Dabney, 1994)

This was a study of conventional retail theft (by employees, shoplifters, and vendors) conducted at the University of Florida which asked respondents to provide shrinkage information (covering theft and wastage and administrative error) from which theft data are then derived. An assortment of loss prevention strategies are also tallied. Retailers with an estimated 15% share of the US market by value replied in 1994 (9% response rate).

### 2.2. The UK national survey of retail theft and security (Bamfield, 1994)

This study was run from Nene-Northampton (UK) in 1993–1994. It was intended to replicate directly the above mentioned University of Florida studies of the US retail industry, with additional questions asked to reflect the interests of UK security specialists. A 14.8% response rate gave results for retailers responsible for 24.7% of UK retailing.

### 2.3. The UK retail crime costs surveys (Speed, Burrows, and Bamfield, 1995)

These surveys are modeled after the Home Office British Crime Survey of personal crime. Rather than being asked directly about shrinkage, respondents were asked to give information on the actual and perceived amounts of known and unknown crimes. The figures are regarded as having a high level of credibility, as shown by their use by the Home Office. The surveys are financed by the British Retail Consortium (BRC). The 1995 study was a compromise between the Bamfield/University of Florida 'national survey' and the BRC Speed/Burrows 'crime costs' approach and was funded by the BRC and Nene. The response rate was 20% from retailers who accounted for 41% of UK retail sales.

Table 1
Comparison of three survey samples used in the analysis

| Survey | Sample size (response rate) | Annual retail sales (million) | Number of stores | % of market | Survey type |
|---|---|---|---|---|---|
| 1994 National Retail Security Survey Hollinger and Dabney (USA) | 327 (9%) | $210588 | 68000 | 15.0% | Shrinkage |
| National Survey of Retail Theft and Security/ Bamfield 1994 (UK) | 297 (14.8%) | £35000 | 18700 | 24.7% | Shrinkage |
| Crime Costs Survey 1993/94 Speed, Burrows, Bamfield/ BRC (UK) | 480 (20.0%) | £64000 | 30800 | 41.0% | Crime costs |

*J. Bamfield, R.C. Hollinger / Security Journal 7 (1996) 61–70* 63

Hollinger and Dabney's University of Florida study was sponsored by the US National Retail Federation and funded by the Sensormatic Electronics Corporation. The Speed et al. survey was run by British Retail Consortium as part of its Crime Initiative, and the Bamfield study was sponsored by major companies including Dixons, Tesco, and Boots. Without this support it is unlikely that a conventional study could have attracted a satisfactory response rate. All three studies have been cross-sector surveys, with data published at a market sector level. However, while the UK studies have attempted to collect data from small retailers (as small as one store) as well as large, Hollinger and Dabney's study excludes businesses with fewer than ten stores. The sample surveyed in each case has been stratified to ensure that a range of business size was included and all business sectors in retailing. Hollinger and Dabney have limited the size of the grocery sample, because they found that grocers tended to be over-represented in the final results. Subject to this, each survey used a small random sample of retailers within each stratum. Concentration levels in retailing mean that a small number of organizations are responsible for a large proportion of turnover and shrinkage. The surveys involved self-administered questionnaires posted to retail security managers. Response rates in the UK and USA have been relatively low (9% in the USA and 20% in the UK) so caution has to be exercised in interpreting the results. Further data on each of the three surveys is found in Table 1.

### 2.4. Face-to-face interviews

In addition to the above mailed surveys, face-to-face semi-structured interviews with security managers of 25 UK companies were carried out in 1993 and 1994, and a focus group was connected with the Bamfield (1994) study. The security managers were drawn from 15 large companies (whose individual 1992 turnover exceeded $390 million) and ten smaller companies: in all, nine were from food and grocery companies and 16 from non-food. Combined sales were £9250 million ($14 billion).

### 3. Shrinkage and loss prevention in the UK and USA

While a burglary or a robbery is evident soon after it occurs, however, most crime by customers and employees often goes unnoticed. In fact, only 2.15% of UK retail theft is detected at the time of the offense (Bamfield, 1994). A stock or inventory loss may not be discovered except by audit. Even with electronic point of sale (POS), the retail business does not have completely accurate information about exact

merchandise stock levels in each branch. There is no effective method of knowing whether an audit loss is caused by administrative error (e.g. the goods not delivered, incorrect prices charged, or a credit note not processed accurately), deterioration or damage to merchandise (particularly in clothing, produce or butchery), marketing adjustments (price amendments to make a sale), or to theft itself. Thus, retailers generally have no audit trail to provide a direct means of measuring their crime losses.

Instead, retail loss rates have historically been inferred by using so-called 'shrinkage' estimates which are calculated as a percent of total sales at retail. Shrinkage collectively represents the losses due to employee theft, shoplifting, vendor fraud, plus wastage and administrative error. Although all recognize that shrinkage may not be a very accurate direct measure of retail theft, nevertheless, shrinkage is universally used in both Britain and the USA to provide an insight into the levels of 'unknown' error and theft.

In the USA, Hollinger and Dabney (1994) reported a shrinkage figure of 1.95% at retail during fiscal 1993. Extrapolated at the national level for the entire retail industry ($1.4 trillion), this shrinkage rate would be equivalent to $27.3 billion. The most recent UK data (Speed et al., 1995), reports data through weighted averages (a UK average of 1.31%). When this average is recalculated on the same basis as Hollinger and Dabney's study, this produces a figure for UK shrinkage of 1.64% (which compares well with Bamfield's 1994 figure of 1.62%). This indicates that as a percentage of sales, US shrinkage for fiscal 1993 was 18.9% greater than the UK ratio.

In principle, 'shrinkage minus administrative error' is equal to losses from retail crime — shoplifting, employee, and vendor theft. UK respondents estimated that 23.0% of their shrinkage was administrative error while Hollinger and Dabney (1994) reported the US statistic as 19.2%. If accurate, this would mean that the actual 1993 US theft rate was 1.57% and the UK rate 1.26%.

The lack of regular surveys using a consistent and reliable methodology makes it difficult to assess whether the retail theft rate has increased over the past 10 years. Hollinger and Dabney (1994) state that normal statistical variation in their own surveys (possibly owing to differences in sample) may explain the variation in shrinkage rate from 1.79% of retail sales in 1991 to 1.95% in 1994, fluctuating between these extremes in the intervening years. Hollinger and Dabney's US shrinkage estimates for 1991–1994 are higher than those reported in the mid 1980s, which were based on different methodologies and sampling procedures. An Arthur Young (1984) study estimated

64 *J. Bamfield, R.C. Hollinger / Security Journal 7 (1996) 61-70*

Table 2
UK and US retail shrinkage rates

|  | Shrinkage rates (% Sales @ Retail) | |
|---|---|---|
|  | USA | UK |
| Department stores | 2.00 | 1.16 |
| N = | 23 | 22 |
| Supermarkets | 1.79 | 1.48 |
| N = | 34 | 27 |
| All stores | 1.95 | 1.65 |
| N = | 312 | 371 |

(Sources: British Crime Survey 1993/4 and 1994 National Retail Security Survey)

that US shrinkage was 1.60% in 1984. Similarly, it is difficult to compare the current UK unweighted shrinkage rate of 1.65% with the Touche Ross (1989) estimate of 1.50% of retail sales and the Home Office (1986) estimate of £1000 million (1.01% of sales), which all use different samples and methodology. UK retail crime statistics in the mid-1980s were crude. For example, only 20% of respondents were able to give a detailed breakdown of losses from theft for the Home Office survey.

Because it is possible that some of the above differences between countries has resulted from variance in the kind-of-business composition of the surveys, comparative data have been extracted for two particular kinds of retail business which vary minimally between the USA and UK, namely, department stores and grocery/supermarkets. Categorization errors are likely to be comparatively rare in these two retail market categories. Their importance in UK retailing can be measured by the fact that they were responsible for 40.6% of total retail sales (1993/4). US shrinkage exceeded UK in both department stores and supermarkets (see Table 2). US department stores' shrinkage was 2.00%, against 1.16% in the UK, while US supermarkets reported 1.79% against 1.48% in the UK.

## 4. Perceived source of losses

Shrinkage data, as we have seen, provide only a rough guide either to the incidence of retail crime or trends. The implications for how to prevent retail crime and losses are very important, as there are few known facts in retail security. Perceptions of loss and sources of loss become the main determinants guiding the deployment of security resources. Security managers create their own social construct of reality (Weick, 1979), with mental models built by experience, culture/conditioning, and enactments. One such example of this social construction of reality is loss prevention executives' estimates of the attribution of the various sources of loss which contribute to the overall shrinkage/ shortage level for the firm.

As is shown in Table 3, theft by customers in the UK, at 38.3%, was thought to be more significant than that by employees (34.8%); while in the USA, employees were thought to be a greater source of loss (42.1%) compared to customers (32.4%). However, perceptions of retail loss seemed less starkly contrasted when examined by specific market sector. For example, department stores in both countries felt that customers were the greater source of loss, while supermarkets attributed larger percentages of loss to employees (although the UK figure for employee theft is not significantly different from that for customer theft).

## 5. Retail security and loss prevention

This section details the various differences and similarities between US and UK retail loss prevention and security approaches in terms of both inputs and outcomes.

### 5.1. The loss prevention or security department

The key task of retail loss prevention is how to target resources to inhibit theft and to measure secu-

Table 3
UK and US perceived sources of loss

|  | Perceived sources of loss | | | | | | | |
|---|---|---|---|---|---|---|---|---|
|  | Staff | | Customers | | Vendors | | Admin Error | |
|  | USA | UK | USA | UK | USA | UK | USA | UK |
| Department stores | 34.2 | 24.3 | 43.0 | 49.7 | 4.4 | 6.0 | 18.4 | 20 |
| N = | 23 | 22 | 23 | 22 | 23 | 22 | 23 | 22 |
| Supermarkets | 42.0 | 39.0 | 33.4 | 37.0 | 11.0 | 2.0 | 13.5 | 22 |
| N = | 34 | 27 | 34 | 27 | 34 | 27 | 34 | 27 |
| All stores | 42.1 | 34.8 | 32.4 | 38.3 | 6.3 | 3.9 | 19.2 | 23.0 |
| N = | 312 | 371 | 312 | 371 | 312 | 371 | 312 | 371 |

(Sources: British Crime Survey 1993/4 and 1994 National Retail Security Survey)

*J. Bamfield, R.C. Hollinger / Security Journal 7 (1996) 61–70* 65

rity outcomes effectively (see Cornish and Clarke, 1986). The retail security function has the objective of combating theft and so minimizing retail crime losses. The highly specialized nature of the security task and the difficulty of designing appropriate performance criteria (e.g. there is no unambiguous measure of theft) may give security managers considerable discretion in setting objectives, expectations, and resource targeting. There are no inter-firm comparisons of security inputs or outputs which can be used by a chief executive to monitor the effectiveness of the company's security operations.

Although some forms of external crime (e.g. burglary, robbery, etc.) are not included in this analysis, we recognize that conventional crime is also a major concern for retail security management. However, the principal attention of loss prevention departments is focused on two types of theft, namely, thefts by customers and thefts by staff. Because retailers identify only a fraction of all thefts which occur in the store, it is usually impossible to know how most thefts are carried out and whether customers (and which category of customer) or employees steal more. Further difficulties for the security manager are created by the fact that in all types and sizes of retail company the prime means of inhibiting theft comes from the work of sales personnel (see Hayes (1991) and survey data in Bamfield (1992 and 1994)) rather than the security department itself. In larger stores a retailer may use dedicated security staff as guards or detectives, but these are intended to assist salespeople (or inhibit violence) rather than be the primary defense against shoplifting and employee theft. The security function usually has no direct control over sales staff, and in the UK will usually consist of ex-police or ex-military personnel with no retail background.

### 5.2. The loss prevention or security manager

In the US it is now rare for a loss prevention vice president to have a police or FBI background. Most have risen up the ladder of retailing in the loss prevention, operations, or finance departments. It is a much different situation in Britain. In the UK interviews, 93% of the retail security managers had a police, private security, or military services security background. Many security departments are now using more non-police staff, but only two out of 15 companies interviewed with security departments had more than 50% of management and administrative staff drawn from non-police/security backgrounds.

Sales staff are seen as the main defense against theft: they were responsible for the bulk of arrests — apprehending 69.9% of arrested customer thieves in the UK (Bamfield, 1994) and 55.5% in the USA (Hollinger and Dabney, 1994). Staff training in anti-theft procedures, staff awareness, and encouragement of staff honesty is seen as being important parts of the loss-prevention approach.

### 5.3. Spending in loss prevention and security departments

In 1994, UK retailers spent 0.37% of annual sales on their security departments (an increase of 39% in 1 year (Speed et al., 1995)), while US retailers spent 0.45% of annual sales — 21% more per $100 million (Hollinger and Dabney, 1994). If UK security spending continues to grow at the present rate, it will exceed pro rata US spending by the end of 1995. US department stores, whose shrinkage was a little above average, set their security expenditure at 25% below the US national average. In contrast, UK department stores, which claimed to have lower shrinkage rates, spent 32% more on security than the UK overall average.

The use of third party security staff and leased security equipment gives the central security department an extensive purchasing and contract compliance role in place of the need to do everything itself. In 1993/4 UK retailers spent £113.8 million on in-house security staff, but £165.1 million on third party staff including cash services. There was evidence of some discrimination in the choice of third-party activities; they tended to be used for specific needs such as uniformed guards, cash collection, trial (honesty) shoppers, while in-house security employees were used in more strategic roles such as 'dedicated security staff' (i.e. investigative work plus the ability to switch from role to role), store detectives, and trainers (Speed et al., 1995). These data were not collected for the US retailers.

### 5.4. Cooperation between law enforcement and retail loss prevention

In the UK, the Retail Crime Initiative is a joint approach (funded directly by large retailers) involving the Home Office and the British Retail Consortium to curb crime. Major outputs have been the all-retailer Crime Cost Surveys, local studies of crime in town centers (e.g. Redbridge), a series of advice leaflets for shops, the development of common software to provide a crime database (aimed to update the central BRC database monthly or quarterly), and the Metropolitan Police Joint Robbery Intelligence Desk which collects data on all retail robberies irrespective of which police force is involved in order to provide early warning and to help police in targeting retailers at risk. It is too early to say how effective these initiatives will prove to be. Police initiatives include the Shopwatch schemes which provide a mechanism for shops to warn other stores when sus-

66                    *J. Bamfield, R.C. Hollinger / Security Journal 7 (1996) 61–70*

pected or actual shoplifting is taking place. In the USA there are intra-city and regional store information exchanges (both electronic and manual), but nothing yet organized on a national basis. A significant achievement for US retailers has been the enactment of civil recovery statutes. These laws allow retailers to use tort law to recover civil damages and penalties outside of the already overwhelmed criminal justice system.

## 6. Comparative use of loss prevention strategies

The use of four different types of loss prevention strategies will be discussed. These are: pre-employment screening techniques, staff awareness programs, asset control policies, and the use of security systems and equipment. Overall, these findings suggest that US retailers have in place a somewhat more sophisticated range of policies, procedures, and equipment to combat theft.

### 6.1. Pre-employment screening

US retailers place considerable emphasis on vetting procedures (or employee integrity screening) for new staff (Hollinger and Dabney, 1994). More than three-quarters of US retailers claimed to verify previous employment, had multiple interviews, and asked for references. About 50% checked for a previous criminal record, 46% checked credit records, and one-third carried out honesty tests, driving history, checked schooling or college records, and screened for drugs. 17% asked for financial bonds against fraud. In substantial contrast, the UK interviews indicated that many staff, particularly part-timers, were hired without verification of any information they supplied at all, but that 40% could be expected to take up references and verify previous employment. Some of the US mea-

sures would be regarded as contrary to civil liberties in the UK. Drug screening is hardly ever used (Bamfield, 1994). The pre-employment screening use of lie detector tests has been discontinued in the USA following legislation. This more aggressive attitude of US retailers towards rigorous screening of the backgrounds of new staff is consistent with a situation where staff are believed to be responsible for the single largest proportion (42. 1%) of shrinkage.

### 6.2. Awareness programs

Staff awareness programs mostly involve training and communications about security, and include: procedures for credit cards, security emphasis in induction, the use of videos, regular presentations to staff, telephone hot lines, etc. US retailers used 4.7 staff awareness policies compared with the UK average of 3.0. An emphasis upon staff awareness may be a critical part of the loss prevention approach. As is shown in Table 4, the UK and the US ordinal rankings were similar (Spearman significant at 1% [two-tailed test]). However, only 36% of UK retailers gave regular presentations on security to staff, and the use of videos and staff security newsletters was lower, possibly (according to the security managers interviewed) because of the derisory nature of much of the material available. Other differences, which may be more cultural, concern incentives to report staff who steal: 46.9% of US retailers reward staff who report deviant co-workers (6% in the UK) and 52.1% have an anonymous 'hot line' compared to only 10% in the UK. The interviews indicated that where they were provided in the UK, 'hot lines' were little used. Many US retailers have honesty/ethics programs and pay significant rewards for information; these, plus intercountry cultural differences may make 'hot lines' more effective in the US.

Table 4
Use of loss prevention awareness programs

| | Percentage of retailers using the program | | |
|---|---|---|---|
| | UK | USA | US ranking |
| Set procedures for credit cards | 69 | n.a. | — |
| Security emphasis in induction | 49 | 81 | 1 |
| Staff notices and posters | 43 | 66 | 3 |
| Regular presentations on security to staff | 36 | 74 | 2 |
| Regular sales/security staff meetings | 33 | n.a. | — |
| Security videos | 27 | 62 | 4 |
| Security newsletters | 16 | 45 | 7 |
| Anonymous telephone 'hot line' | 10 | 52 | 5 |
| Security tape/cassette programs | 8 | 14 | 9 |
| Honesty incentives | 6 | 47 | 6 |
| Enclosures with pay slip | 6 | 28 | 8 |

(n.a. not asked)
(Sources: British Crime Survey 1993/4 and 1994 National Retail Security Survey)

*J. Bamfield, R.C. Hollinger / Security Journal 7 (1996) 61-70*                67

### 6.3. Asset control policies

Asset controls include such policies as merchandise receiving (inward) controls, controls over sales voids, price changes, waste removal, refunds, and the transfer of goods between stores. On average, each UK firm uses 4.1 asset control policies compared with 8.1 in the US. Table 5 shows the 11 different asset control policies that were assessed. Although, the national rankings between the two countries was not dramatically different, the usage levels in the UK were significantly lower. For example, among the UK respondents, only 'inward (receiving) controls' and 'merchandise transfers between stores' were used by half or more of the respondents. Alternatively, in the US none of the asset control policies was regularly used by less than half of the retailers — and most were used by 70% or better of the respondents. Only in the supermarket do we find UK retailers, who have focused on installing good systems and controls for many years, reporting comparable levels of asset controls (i.e., an average of 8.3 asset control policies against the US average of 8.5).

### 6.4. Security systems

Security systems and equipment (covering CCTV, safes, electronic article surveillance [EAS], loop alarms, etc.) are perhaps the easiest part of loss prevention to introduce, subject only to physical and budgetary constraints. The average use of security systems from a list of ten, was 4.5 (UK) to 5.1 in the USA. Although the rank ordering of security systems is virtually identical (as shown in Table 6), American retailers had five devices which were used by more than 44% of firms (namely, CCTV, mirrors, lockable

displays, cables-locks-clamps and electronic article surveillance), but there were only two devices used by 44% or more of UK retailers (CCTV and Mirrors). There were other significant differences as well. For example, there were great disparities in the use of cables and chains and EAS between US and UK retailers. Moreover, UK retailers also used fewer uniformed guards and detectives (see Table 7). Recent high CCTV investment in the UK (46% of all security investment in 1993/4) has produced higher levels of CCTV usage in UK department stores and supermarkets than in the US. However, the UK CCTV average for all retailers was only 50% compared with the US average of 56.7%. Apart from CCTV, US security systems usage exceeded UK usage, although use of guards by UK department stores was greater than the US. Based on installation, UK perceptions of the effectiveness of security equipment seemed similar to that of US retailers.

## 7. Arrests and treatment of offenders

In 1993/4 US retailers caught 27 employee thieves per $100 million sales compared with 14.0 staff thieves per $100 million sales in the UK (see Table 8). However, UK retailers apprehended more than twice as many shoplifters per $100 million sales than US retailers — 326.9 per $100 million sales compared with 154 in the USA per $100 million. UK arrests of shoplifters fell 23% between 1992/3 and 1993/4, mainly, it is thought, as a result of companies accepting a more 'deterrence-oriented' paradigm. Staff arrests rose 9%. Shoplifting apprehensions seem to have fallen in the US also: the 1993 rate per $100 million sales was 22.8% higher than the 1994 rate (Hollinger, 1992). It is difficult to tell from these

Table 5
Use of asset control policies

| | Percentage of retailers using the policy | | |
| --- | --- | --- | --- |
| | UK | USA | US ranking |
| Goods inward (receiving) controls | 53 | 77 | 4 |
| Controls of transfer of goods between stores | 50 | 73 | 5 |
| Refund controls | 49 | 90 | 1 |
| Void controls | 39 | 85 | 2 |
| Price amendment controls | 38 | 68 | 6 |
| Controlled access to cash handling areas | 38 | 77 | 3 |
| Searches of employees | 32 | n.a. | — |
| Employee package checks | 29 | 63 | 7 |
| POS bar coding and scanning | 28 | 53 | 11 |
| POS exception reports | 26 | 61 | 9 |
| Waste removal controls | 25 | 58 | 10 |
| Unobserved exit controls | n.a. | 62 | 8 |

(n.a. not asked)
(Sources: British Crime Survey 1993/4 and 1994 National Retail Security Survey)

Table 6
Use of security systems

|  | Percentage of retailers using the system | | |
|---|---|---|---|
|  | UK | USA | US ranking |
| CCTV | 50 | 57 | 1 |
| Observation mirrors | 44 | 55 | 2 |
| Lockable displays | 34 | 47 | 5 |
| Floor safes | 33 | n.a. | — |
| Cables, locks, chains, clamps | 29 | 47 | 3 |
| EAS | 24 | 47 | 4 |
| Loop alarms | 19 | 26 | 6 |
| Ink tags | 8 | 16 | 8 |
| CCTV linked EpoS | 7 | 14 | 9 |
| Observation booths | 5 | 19 | 7 |
| Subliminal messages | n.a. | 2 | 10 |

(n.a. not asked)
(sources: British Crime Survey 1993/4 and 1994 National Retail Security Survey)

figures whether retailers are putting as much emphasis upon detecting staff crime as upon customer theft, given the perceived relative importance of both causes (see Table 3).

Only a proportion of thieves are handed to the police: in the US, 54% of shoplifters and 52% of employee thieves. In the UK, the 1994 figures were 68% of shoplifters and 42% of staff thieves. The main reasons given in 1992/3 (Bamfield 1994) by UK retailers for not handing all offenders to the police were 'take up too much staff time' (24.5%), 'avoid prosecution of old people,' 'disturbed juveniles, etc.' (23.6%), 'low success in the courts' (19.7%), 'penalties not a deterrent'(18.5%), and 'low prosecution rate by Crown' (17.2%). For a staff thief, the most likely penalty (86.7%) was to be fired. Kay (1992) suggests

Table 7
Percentages of organizations reporting use of certain security systems

|  | CCTV | | Detectives | | Guards | |
|---|---|---|---|---|---|---|
|  | USA | UK | USA | UK | USA | UK |
| Department stores | 70.8 | 77.0 | 79.2 | 59 | 25.0 | 59 |
| Supermarket | 70.3 | 96.0 | 70.3 | 52 | 62.2 | 56 |
| All stores | 56.7 | 50.0 | 36.5 | 14 | 35.0 | 23 |

(Sources: British Crime Survey 1993/4 and 1994 National Retail Security Survey)

Table 8
Arrests and treatment of employee and customer offenders. Rate per $100 million annual sales (turnover)

|  | Suspected employee theft rates/$100 M | | | | | |
|---|---|---|---|---|---|---|
|  | Arrests | | Police/prosecution | | Civil demand | |
|  | USA | UK | USA | UK | USA | |
| Department stores | 38.5 | 7.5 | 22 | 4.0 | 6.1 | |
| Supermarket | 18.5 | 4.1 | 6.5 | 2.1 | 4.7 | |
| All stores | 27 | 14.0 | 13.2 | 5.9 | 6 | |
|  | Suspected customer theft rates/$100 M | | | | | |
|  | Arrests | | Police/prosecution | | Civil demand | |
|  | USA | UK | USA | UK | USA | |
| Department stores | 260.5 | 372.8 | 193.2 | 346.7 | 138.8 | |
| Supermarket | 343.7 | 389.8 | 178 | 210.5 | 171.5 | |
| All stores | 154 | 326.9 | 83.2 | 222.3 | 67.1 | |

Rate per $100 m retail sales (assuming $US1.5617 = £1)
(Sources: British Crime Survey 1993/4 and 1994 National Retail Security Survey)

that only one-half of cases of customer theft reported to the police led to a prosecution. While one-quarter of security managers interviewed had a stated policy of handing all staff thieves over to the police, investigation of their company data showed that around 40% would not have made a strong case for the police or the courts. Thus, the emphasis is upon terminating the suspects employment (and thus ending the apparent 'problem') rather than pursuing the case in court. This same line of logic is generally found in most larger US companies as well.

The perceived ineffectiveness of the police and judiciary in handling what is usually petty theft, has led to the development of non-judicial methods of dealing with thieves including banning from stores (44.5% of shoplifters in the UK (Bamfield, 1994)) and civil recovery procedures (23.6% of US shoplifters (Hollinger and Dabney, 1994)). Store banning of apprehended thieves, which involves the thief signing a legal document excluding him or her from the store or shopping center, has been an ad hoc response by British retailers to the costs and perceived limitations of the judicial system, and developed from an initiative from retailers in Birmingham (High Street).

In the USA, in response to lobbying from retailers, 43 states have passed 'civil recovery' statutes since 1973. While these statutes differ in details, the basic thrust is to make shop theft a civil tort, enabling the retailer to recover damages (most typically $200 or three times the dollar loss) from the thief or parents, if the offender is a juvenile. American retailers are learning slowly how to make best use of the legislation, which potentially could make the loss-prevention function a profit center under certain circumstances. According to Hollinger and Dabney (1994), US retailers placed civil demands on 15.3% of employee thieves and 23.6% of customer thieves. Even more significant, over a third (35.6%) of department store shoplifters and 35.1% of supermarket shoplifters were subjected to this non-criminal sanction. However, there is already anecdotal evidence from the USA that undue reliance upon civil demand in a predictable manner may be losing its deterrent effect and may actually encourage offending by some groups. Thus, retailers in the UK and the USA are spending less on apprehending and criminally processing shoplifters and instead, are looking for other innovative ways to combat theft.

## 8. Conclusions

The shrinkage rate is probably a little under one-fifth higher in the US than in the UK. There is evidence that retail theft has been increasing since the mid/late 1980s, but the data are not very robust. One of the main responses to perceived growth of crime against retailers has been resulted in a philosophical shift away from the traditional 'police/arrest' paradigm to a 'loss prevention/ deterrence' approach. Employees are thought to be the single most significant cause of theft in the USA, while both staff and customers are perceived to be of roughly equal importance in the UK. These perceptions are capable of variability from year to year (Hollinger and Dabney, 1994). Security spending is higher (as a proportion of annual sales) in the US, but the growth in UK security spending is so high that the spending rate per $100 million sales should reach US levels by the end of 1995. In security, the same process has been seen as elsewhere in retailing — the replacement of staff by high tech detection equipment. UK penetration by security equipment is lower than the USA, although UK spending on equipment (particularly CCTV surveillance) is now high. Staff awareness policies are also less well developed in the UK. Major differences are seen in asset control programs and employee integrity screening (in which US retailers more aggressively attempt to screen out new applicants who may potentially be a security risk). A key feature of loss prevention was the shift from a culture of 'criminally arresting' thieves to one based more on civil deterrence and crime avoidance. In both the UK and the US, there is evidence that retailers are reducing the apprehension of customer thieves and using non-criminal alternatives for both customer and staff thieves, particularly for minor offenders. There is some evidence that UK retailers are adopting some aspects of this 'loss prevention' approach, although UK retail security is still traditionally police-oriented in much of its personnel, culture, and attitudes.

## References

American Management Associations (1977) Summary Overview of the 'State of the Art' Regarding Information Gathering Techniques and the Level of Knowledge in Three Areas Concerning Crimes Against Business. Washington, D.C.: National Institute of Criminal Justice.

Young, A. (1984) The Arthur Young/IMRA Survey of Retail Loss Prevention Trends: Fifth Annual Survey of Loss Prevention Executives, NY: Arthur Young.

Bamfield, J. (1992) Beating the Thief: A Retailer's Guide to Electronic Article Surveillance Systems, Hove: RMDP, Ltd.

Bamfield, J. (1994). National Survey of Retail Theft and Security Northampton: Nene College.

Cornish, D. and Clarke, R. (Eds.) (1986). The Reasoning Criminal: Rational Choice Perspectives on Offending. New York: Springer-Verlag.

Hayes, R. (1991). Retail Security and Loss Prevention. Stonham, MA.: Butterworth Heinemann.

Hollinger, R.C. and Clark, J.P. (1983). Theft by Employees. Lexington, MA.: Lexington Books.

Hollinger, R.C. (1993). 1993 National Retail Security Survey, Final Report, Gainesville,Fl: Department of Sociology, University of Florida, December.

Hollinger, R.C. and Dabney, D.A. (1994). 1994 National Retail Security Survey, Final Report. Gainesville, FL: Department of Sociology, University of Florida, December.

Home Office Working Group on Shop Theft (1986). Report London: Home Office.

Kay, P. (1992). In pursuit of prosecutions. Retail Week 7 (February).

Lary, B.K. (1988). Thievery on the inside. Sec. Manage. 32, 79-84.

Shepard, I.M. and Dustin, R. (1988). Thieves at Work: An Employer's Guide to Combating Workplace Dishonesty. Washington, DC: The Bureau of National Affairs.

Speed, M., Burrows, J. and Bamfield, J. (1995) Retail Crime Costs: 1993/4 Survey. London: British Retail Consortium.

Touche Ross (1989). Retail shrinkage: the drain on profits — 1989 survey results. London: Touche Ross on Behalf of the Association for the Prevention of Theft from Shops.

Weick, K. (1979). The Social Psychology of Organizing. Reading, MA: Addison Wesley.

# Name Index